BIBLICAL THEOLOGY

BIBLICAL THEOLOGY

VOLUME 2

The Special Grace Covenants
— Old Testament —

JEFFREY J. NIEHAUS

LEXHAM PRESS

Biblical Theology: Volume 2, The Special Grace Covenants (Old Testament)
© 2017 by Jeffrey J. Niehaus

Lexham Press, 1313 Commercial St., Bellingham, WA 98225
LexhamPress.com

First edition by Weaver Book Company.

Print ISBN 9781683591467
Digital ISBN 9781683591474

Cover design: Frank Gutbrod
Interior design and layout: { In a Word }

CONTENTS

PREFACE

Although a table of contents gives an outline of this volume, it may also be helpful to present a brief overview and linkage of the topics it contains. The main organizing factors are two: (1) the special grace nature of the covenants involved, and (2) the dynamic of God's work—in every case of covenant creation—that we have called the Major Paradigm. We discuss each special grace covenant with this paradigm in mind and show how the process of God's work in producing each covenant is articulated in the steps of the paradigm. The process thus shows the dynamic of God's covenant creation grounded in God's being and played out in the world with an eschatological trajectory.

In addition to those major topics, topics especially germane to the individual covenants form part of the discussion of each covenant. So, for example, the course of Abram's calling and life preparatory to the "cutting" of the Abrahamic covenant and the events that follow that cutting—events that include life under the covenant and further covenant *torah*—occupy a few chapters. A conceptually parallel sequence characterizes the Mosaic covenant materials with additional discussion of matters that arise—the ontology of the divine name and the warfare against Rahab/Egypt, followed by life under the Sinai covenant, including—after the renewal covenant of Deuteronomy—the Conquest and its rationale, the role of deception (two items that have their eschatological counterparts), the challenge of idolatry, the spiritual life of the old covenant (with anticipation of new covenant realities), the Lord and prophetic experience (also with a look toward new covenant realities), and finally the failed missional aspect of the Mosaic covenant (again, with a forward look to life under the new covenant). The Davidic covenant is considered next (1) in terms of the Major Paradigm and (2) in terms of its relatedness to previous covenants and to the new covenant.

Danvers, Good Friday, 2017

Acknowledgements

I would like to acknowledge the help and encouragement I have gained from others as I have continued this work, and in particular to my colleague, Douglas Stuart, for encouraging the sharing of new work for critical feedback among members of our Biblical Studies Division as chair of that division—and likewise to all my colleagues in the division who have provided such feedback from time to time. I also want to express gratitude for the help of research assistants, Fiona Paisley, David Smiley, Valine Mullen, and Ruby Lee, especially in the preparation of the bibliography and Scripture reference sections. This work might not have been possible—or would at least taken much longer to compose—were it not for the trustees of Gordon-Conwell, who have supported a program of faculty sabbaticals that makes it possible for faculty to devote serious time to research and writing. I am grateful to my wife, Margaret, for her support and her prayers. Last, and first in importance, I am grateful to the head of the church who so justly said, "Without me you can do nothing."

ABBREVIATIONS

AION	*Annali dell'Instituto Orientale di Napoli*
ANETBT	*Ancient Near Eastern Themes in Biblical Theology.* Grand Rapids: Kregel, 2008.
BA	*Biblical Archaeologist*
BAR	*Biblical Archaeology Review*
BASOR	*Bulletin of the American Schools of Oriental Research*
Bib	*Biblica*
BZ	*Biblische Zeitschrift*
CBQ	*Catholic Biblical Quarterly*
CT	*CuneiformTexts from the Bablyonian Tablets of the British Museum*
EI	*Eretz-Israel*
HBT	*Horizons in Biblical Theology*
HUCA	*Hebrew Union College Annual*
IEJ	*Israel Exploration Journal*
JAOS	*Journal of the American Oriental Society*
JBL	*Journal of Biblical Literature*
JETS	*Journal of the Evangelical Theological Society*
JJS	*Journal of Jewish Studies*
JNES	*Journal of Near Eastern Studies*
JSOT	*Journal for the Study of the Old Testament*
JSOTSS	*Journal for the Study of the Old Testament: Supplement Series*
NICOT	New International Commentary on the Old Testament
NSBT	New Studies in Biblical Theology
Or	*Orientalia*
OTS	Old Testament Studies
RA	*Revue d'assyriologie et d'archeologie orientale*

RB	*Revue Biblique*
Rel	*Religion*
Sem	*Semitica*
TA	*Tel Aviv*
TB	*Tyndale Bulletin*
TDNT	*Theological Dictionary of the New Testament.* Edited by G. Kittel and G. Friedrich. Translated by G. W. Bromiley. 10 vols. Grand Rapids: Eerdmans, 1964–1976.
TR	*Theologische Rundschau*
TS	*Theological Studies*
UF	*Ugarit-Forschungen*
VT	*Vetus Testamentum*
VTSup	*Vetus Testamentum Supplements*
WO	*Die Welt des Orients*
WTJ	*Westminster Theological Journal*
ZA	*Zeitschrift für Assyriologie*
ZAW	*Zeitschrift für die alttestamentliche Wissenschaft*

INTRODUCTION

Some years ago I proposed a sequence or dynamic of ideas that outline God's work: God as king, God's kingdom, God's covenant(s), and God's covenant administration.[1] I followed that proposal with a more detailed outline, which I termed the Major Paradigm in a book that I consider something of a preface to the present work.[2] That paradigm is the following:

1. God works
2. through the Word or a prophet
3. to wage war
4. to make a covenant with a people
5. to constitute that people as his people
6. God establishes a temple presence among them because he will live among them.

The Major Paradigm has informed and continues to inform the discussions of God's different covenants in the present work. The outline shows God's consistency throughout history, and it culminates in the eschatological ("last days") reality of the new covenant and the new heavens and the new earth and the new humanity, which show the created substance of the Lord's final realization of his presence in all things—when

---

1   Jeffrey J. Niehaus, *God at Sinai: Covenant and Theophany in the Bible and Ancient Near East* (Grand Rapids: Zondervan, 1995), 83–84.

2   Jeffrey J. Niehaus, *Ancient Near Eastern Themes in Biblical Theology* (Grand Rapids: Kregel, 2008), 30–32, 172–76. Hereafter abbreviated *ANETBT*.

he himself is that all-inclusive temple. Greg Beale has recently articulated a similar body of ideas:

> The Old Testament is the story of God, who progressively reestablishes his new-creational kingdom out of chaos over a sinful people by his word and Spirit through promise, covenant, and redemption, resulting in a worldwide commission to the faithful to advance his kingdom.[3]

Such a *general* characterization no doubt occurs naturally in one form or another to anyone who thinks seriously about the pattern of divine activity in kingdom formation and advance throughout the Bible. So William Dumbrell has articulated five major themes throughout the Bible (new creation, new covenant, new temple, new Israel, and new Jerusalem), and as Beale notes, quoting Dumbrell, "The entire scheme of the Bible is structured around the movement 'from creation to new creation by means of divine redemptive interventions,' climaxing in Christ's death, resurrection, enthronement, and second coming, which concludes all things."[4] Such a summary may—and should—sound familiar because it states what Christians have understood for a long time. In that sense, biblical theologies are individual reformulations of essentials the Bible has always offered.[5] The present work is no exception.

The "divine redemptive interventions" mentioned above occupy this biblical theology, and in particular (although not exclusively) the *dynamic* of those interventions that involve covenant creation. That is so because God's covenant making activities in many ways *epitomize* those interventions, both in the mode of their realization (as the Major Paradigm seeks to illustrate) and in their goal, for they all have the same goal:

---

3   G. K. Beale, *A New Testament Biblical Theology: The Unfolding of the Old Testament in the New* (Grand Rapids: Baker, 2011), 16. Beale adds: ". . . and judgment (defeat or exile) for the unfaithful, unto his glory."

4   Ibid., 22, quoting William Dumbrell, *The End of the Beginning: Revelation 21–22 and the Old Testament* (Homebush West, NSW: Lancer, 1985), 166, 196; cf. William Dumbrell, *The Search for Order: Biblical Eschatology in Focus* (Grand Rapids: Baker, 1994).

5   Cf. more recently Walter C. Kaiser Jr., *The Promise-Plan of God: A Biblical Theology of the Old and New Testaments* (Grand Rapids: Zondervan, 2008); James H. Hamilton Jr., *God's Glory in Salvation through Judgment* (Wheaton, IL: Crossway, 2012); Peter J. Gentry and Stephen J. Wellum, *Kingdom through Covenant: A Biblical-Theological Understanding of the Covenants* (Wheaton, IL: Crossway, 2012); Thomas R. Schreiner, *The King in His Beauty: A Biblical Theology of the Old and New Testaments* (Grand Rapids: Baker, 2013).

the creation of an iteration of God's kingdom presence (i.e., God's presence in a form of his kingdom) that conduces toward the circumstances in which the new covenant becomes possible, by which covenant in turn God's transformative kingdom presence becomes an experiential reality for God's people both now and to come. The beginnings of that trajectory were mapped out in volume 1, and volume 2 continues the process.

Two things are to be noted and affirmed about the Major Paradigm if it is to be understood correctly with its implications.

First, the Major Paradigm differs in its creational form from all of its subsequent iterations. That is so because God did not have to overcome anything when he created the world, whereas he did have to overcome the opposition of sinful agents in every subsequent intrusion into history to make a covenant. By affirming this reality we differ from a tradition of scholarship that sees Genesis 1:2 as implying that God had to "overcome" chaos before he could create the world. This view was argued most extensively by Hermann Gunkel, who saw Genesis 1:2 as a sanitized borrowing from the Chaoskampf of Babylonian myth.[6] I have argued elsewhere that a better view sees the biblical account giving a true version of affairs, in which the תהו ובהו ("formless and void") of Genesis 1:2 is a description of primordial material the Lord used in the process of creation. I argue the same in the present work. Gunkel's idea has been continued in one form or another by other scholars (e.g., Bernard Batto), and even Barth may show its influence in his characterization of Genesis 1:2 as the primordial occurrence of Nothingness (*das Nichtige*) confronted and dealt with by God before the creation.[7] As is argued in volume 3 of this biblical theology (chap. 4), this view constitutes a serious mistake: it undermines God's omnipotence and seriously misunderstands Genesis 1:2—a fundamental verse in a foundational passage for a biblical theology.

Second, the Major Paradigm is eschatological in its trajectory. Another way of putting this as I have put it to my students for decades is that creation implies eschatology, or the possibility of eschatology: if one understands Genesis 1:1, then Revelation 21:1 is implied, granted only God's saving grace that is everywhere manifest in the Bible. As I affirmed in an article nearly a decade ago:

---

6   Hermann Gunkel, *Schöpfung und Chaos in Urzeit und Endzeit: Eine religionsgeschichtliche Untersuchung über Gen 1 und Ap Joh 12* (Göttingen: Vendenhoeck und Ruprecht, 1895), 114–21.

7   Cf. B. F. Batto, *Slaying the Dragon* (Louisville: Westminster John Knox, 1992). For Barth and discussion cf. volume 3 of *Biblical Theology*, chapter 4.

Moreover, if we credit God with knowing ahead of time that Adam and Eve would fall, we may add the creation covenant itself to God's overall program of covenants that lead to renewal, because redemption is implied in creation. That is, because of God's character, God as creator has an ultimate covenantal commitment to restore all that he has created, including a new heavens and earth and a new humanity. Put another way, the new heavens and earth of Revelation 21:1 are a result of God's gracious covenant commitment, which was eternally part of his being when he made the original heavens and earth (Gen. 1:1). One result is that, as the saying goes, *Endzeit* parallels *Urzeit*.[8]

Warped as Gunkel's approach to Genesis was, his very title shows a glimmer of the same understanding— *Schöpfung und Chaos in Urzeit und Endzeit*. *Endzeit* in some way restores *Urzeit*. How could, for example, Isaiah, Peter, and John speak of a new heaven and a new earth (Isa. 65:17; 66:22; 2 Peter 3:13; Rev. 21:1) if this were not so? Consequently, the first iteration of the Major Paradigm is pristine, although it sets or shows (because of the divine consistency) the pattern of all God's subsequent incursive and covenant making activity throughout the Bible:

1. God works
2. by his Spirit
3. through the *Preincarnate* Word
4. to create the original heaven and earth
5. God establishes a covenant with the first humans
6. God's covenant establishes those people as God's people
7. God establishes a temple (Eden) among those people, because he will reside among them

This Paradigm fits the facts, one of which is that God did not have to overcome anything in order to create the original heaven and earth. So there is no warfare in the first form of the Major Paradigm as there is in all the subsequent articulations of it. Because of the Fall and sinful human history, God did intervene throughout that history, waging war in order to to make covenants that were stages in his overall redemptive program.[9] The culminating and eschatological iteration of the Major Paradigm is

---

8   Jeffrey J. Niehaus, "An Argument against Theologically Constructed Covenants," *JETS* 50, no. 2 (2007): 272.

9   Cf. Niehaus, "An Argument," 271–73.

accomplished by the work of the incarnate Word in the new covenant, and this parallels or forms the corresponding "bookend" to the original creative/covenant making activity illustrated by the first occurrence of the Major Paradigm:

1. God works
2. by his Spirit
3. through the *Incarnate* Word
4. to war against and defeat his foe(s)
5. God establishes a covenant with a people
6. God's covenant establishes that people as God's people
7. God establishes a temple among his people, because he will reside among them

In this case, as has been long understood, eschatology embraces everything from the incarnate ministry of the Son onwards, culminating in his Parousia. We are, as the author of Hebrews notes, in the "last days" (1:2). Accordingly, the temple establishment portion of the Major Paradigm enjoys both an already fulfillment and a not-yet fulfillment: the church corporately (and the individuals in it) in the "already," the comprehensive eschatological temple that is the Lord in the "not yet."

Scholars who hold a traditional view of Scripture have also affirmed a unified Bible, and they have recognized that this Bible presents a history of God's activities among people with a salvific trajectory. Early in the history of the development of biblical theology, J. C. K. von Hofmann, who first coined the term *Heilsgeschichte*, made this affirmation.[10] We quote Paul House's summary:

> Hofmann stated that the Old Testament recorded God's efforts to redeem the human race. Within the text are stages of this process. Each succeeding stage describes God's redemptive methods in that era. Finally, God's people find salvation in Jesus Christ, God's perfect means of redemption.[11]

---

10   J. C. K. von Hoffmann, *Weissagung und Erfüllung im Alten und im Neuen Testamente: Ein theologischer Versuch,* 2 vols. (Nördlingen: Verlag der C. H. Beck'schen Buchhandlung, 1841–1844). The first occurrences are in volume 1, page 8.

11   Paul R. House, *Old Testament Theology* (Downers Grove, IL: InterVarsity Press, 1998), 23. I recommend House's review of the birth and development of biblical theology in his initial chapter as a first-rate, a lucidly written introduction to the subject. His book as a whole deserves similar praise.

The "stages of the process" are God's covenant making intrusions, and the Major Paradigm articulates the place of God's covenant making within the larger dynamic—the origin, the immediate and secondary agents, and the goals—of that covenant making intrusion in each historical case, from creation to new creation. In each case, the origin is God the Father, the immediate agent is the Holy Spirit through the secondary agent who is the Word/a covenant mediator prophet, and the goals are the acquisition and formation of a people into a covenantal people, and finally *mutatis mutandis* a temple presence among that covenant people.

THE ADAMIC COVENANT

Since the publication of volume 1, it has become clear that the nature and purpose of the Adamic covenant as presented in that volume have been on the one hand understood and appreciated and on the other hand misunderstood and rejected.[12] I would like to take the opportunity afforded by the presentation of this entire biblical theology to make some points that may be helpful in the Introduction to volume 2. The points under discussion are the following: (1) the understanding of genres involved in identifying the literary/legal boundaries of the Adamic covenant, (2) the fact that the Adamic covenant has not been abrogated, (3) the common grace nature of the Adamic covenant, (4) the concomitant idea that the Adamic covenant is not salvific, and (5) the abandonment of the older ideas of a "covenant of works" as a characterization of the Adamic covenant, and also the idea of a "covenant of grace."

Genres: The Literary/Legal Boundaries of the Adamic Covenant

Some years ago I published an outline of Genesis 1:1–2:3 that identified parts of the passage as parts one could find in a second millennium BC international (Hittite) suzerain-vassal treaty.[13] I believe it is hard to avoid recognizing, at a minimum, that the elements are to be found in the pericope and that they articulate the parts also found in the ancient

---

12   For an example of understanding and appreciation, cf. Jens Bruun Kofoed, Fjellhaug International University College, Copenhagen, Denmark (RBL 2015 by the Society of Biblical Literature), http://www.bookreviews.org/pdf/10029_11112.pdf; for the latter, cf. some posts at Amazon.com.

13   In the book *God at Sinai*, referred to at several points in the pages that follow.

treaties. As I wrote in volume 1 of *Biblical Theology*, it seems reasonable to admit that these elements show the covenantal nature of God, since they are also found in other divine-human covenants. One may stop short of allowing Genesis 1:1–2:3 to be a covenant, although the reasons for doing so do not seem compelling to me and I have addressed them in volume 1 and in an article.

If one allows that the treaty form defines the pericope, other conclusions inevitably follow. One conclusion is that Genesis 2:4–25 is purely a narrative (contrasted to the combination of narrative plus covenant and list genres apparent in Gen. 1:1–2:3) that gives supplemental information regarding the Adamic covenant, in particular (among other things) the Lord's placement of the man in Eden, his command regarding the trees, his creation of the woman, and the man's reception of the woman. Genesis 2 thus gives historical material and supplemental *torah* after the covenant has been presented (in Gen. 1:1–2:3), just as one finds later in the narratives of the Abrahamic covenant, the Mosaic covenant, and the new covenant, and I have outlined elsewhere this pattern of divine covenant making and supplementing activity.[14]

Another conclusion that follows the genre identifications of Genesis 1:1–2:3 and Genesis 2:4–25 has to do with Genesis 3. The record of life under the Adamic covenant properly begins in Genesis 3. The narrative of the Fall (Gen. 3:1–7) comprises the first part of that history. The next part of Genesis 3 narrates the Bible's first covenant lawsuit, when the Lord comes into Eden and the judicial process of that lawsuit takes place, with the resultant curses and, unexpectedly, the Lord's gracious restoration of Adam and his wife to their offices (Gen. 3:21). It is important at this point to be able to recognize the difference between a covenant and a covenant lawsuit. Genesis 1:1–2:3 outlines the Adamic covenant. Genesis 2:4–25 gives further details and further *torah* for that covenant, after the pattern of subsequent narratives of divine-human covenant institution that is followed by further details and *torah*. Genesis 3:1–7 begins the history of life under the Adamic covenant. Genesis 3:8–19 presents the Lord's covenant lawsuit against his rebellious vassals.

There is a long-standing error according to which some scholars have

---

14 Cf. Prolegomena in volume 1 of *Biblical Theology*, 5–6; and chapter 4 of this volume. Cf. earlier Niehaus, "God's Covenant with Abraham," *JETS* 56, no. 2 (2013): 255–71. On a broader understanding, Genesis 1–2 may be said to constitute the Adamic covenant, consisting of Genesis 1:1–2:3 (covenant institution) and Genesis 2:4–25 (further history and supplemental *torah*).

thought Genesis 1–3 constitutes the Adamic covenant. This misconception did not begin with Louis Berkhof, but he represents it well.[15] It was repeated some years ago by Meredith Kline.[16] Greg Beale has recently advocated the same.[17] The problem with this analysis is twofold. First, among other things, it fails to recognize that Genesis 1:1–2:3 contains the outline of a second millennium BC international treaty and thus within itself presents the essential covenant institution. We have documented and stated this in several places, including the display offered below.[18] Second, it also fails to recognize the covenant lawsuit nature of material in Genesis 3.

We are in a position to know the difference between a covenant and a covenant lawsuit, something modern people did not understand very well if at all before discoveries of ancient near eastern materials that show the same genres. Now that the difference can be understood, analysis of the materials found in Genesis 1–3 can be specific and *true to the genres involved*. At this point it will be illustrative to engage in further detail with the characterization of these chapters, and more broadly Genesis 1–5, given by my former mentor and colleague, Meredith Kline. Kline was,

---

15 Cf. Louis Berkhof, *Systematic Theology* (Grand Rapids: Eerdmans, 1939), 213.

16 Cf. Kline, *Kingdom Prologue: Genesis Foundations for a Covenant Worldview* (Overland Park, KS: Two Age Press, 2000), 14–15. Kline notes, "Certainly the substance of *berith* was present in the kingdom order described in Genesis 1–3. It was characterized by precisely those elements that constitute a covenant, for it was produced through divine words and acts of commitment and it was subject to the sanctions of ultimate divine blessing and curse," 15. This characterization of the early chapters of Genesis is arguably too generalized, however, and can be refined, as our analysis of Genesis 1:1–2:3 will show. It is here argued that the so-called first creation account (Gen. 1:1–2:3) contains *within itself* the essential elements of a second millennium BC treaty/covenant.

17 Beale, *New Testament Biblical Theology*, 43: "The essential elements of a covenant are found in the Genesis 1–3 narrative: (1) two parties are named; (2) a condition of obedience is set forth; (3) a curse for transgression is threatened; (4) a clear implication of a blessing is promised for obedience." This again is too generalized, and one might note that a more precise detailing of the covenant elements in Genesis 1:1–2:3 *alone* (thus identifying Genesis 1 as the sole chapter that presents the Adamic covenant institution) appeared sixteen years before Beale's analysis, in a work he cites in other respects (namely, *God at Sinai*, 1995, 143–50). For a dispensational understanding, which takes Genesis 3 as embodying a different "Adamic" covenant, cf. Charles F. Baker, *A Dispensational Theology* (Grand Rapids: Grace Bible College, 1971), 87–103; cf. discussion in Niehaus, "Covenant and Narrative, God and Time." *JETS* 53, no. 3 (2010): 535n1; 538–39.

18 Cf. Niehaus, *God at Sinai*, 144–47; "Covenant and Narrative," 540.

of course, aware of the second millennium treaty form, and his work on Deuteronomy as an embodiment of that form has been of great service. With regard to the early pages of Genesis, however, his analysis (in his first five chapters) was in one sense too general. We will consider the literary form of the creation account, and the role of Genesis 3. But first, speaking of the second millennium treaty form, he writes:

> The several standard sections of this treaty-form provide serviceable categories for the analysis of the creational covenant. The first two chapters of the following analysis include data that would be found in the preamble and historical prologue, the opening sections of the treaty form. Chapter 3 corresponds to the treaty stipulations or law; chapter 4, to the sanctions section. Finally, chapter 5 will trace the history of the creational covenant, with the tragic failure of the first man to obtain the proposed grant of the eternal kingdom. Our use of the standard sections of the ancient treaty form in this way should not be misunderstood as suggesting that the earliest chapters of Genesis have the literary form of a treaty. However, the fact that these treaty sections serve as satisfactorily as they do as an analytical framework for describing the sum and substance of these chapters does support illuminatingly the identification of the creation order as a covenantal arrangement.[19]

Kline's analysis has merit, but more detailed study can improve it. A display of the analysis of Genesis 1:1–2:3 will be helpful in this regard:

The Adamic/Creation Covenant

Element	Genesis 1:1–2:3	
Title	1:1	
Historical prologue	1:2–29	Words of the Great King
Stipulations	1:28	Be fruitful . . . fill . . . subdue . . . rule
Deposition		
Regular Reading		
Witnesses	1:31	God
Blessings	1:28, 2:3	
[Curses	2:17b][20]	

---

19   Kline, *Kingdom Prologue*, 21.

20   As I have noted, the curse material in Genesis 2:17 is relevant because, even though Genesis 2:4–25 does not present or enshrine the Adamic covenant, it is a narrative

Without discussing every detail of this form, we note the following. The first chapter of the creation narrative material includes the most important elements that one finds in a second millennium BC international suzerain-vassal treaty. It includes data that would be found in the introduction and historical prologue of such a treaty: a preamble/title identifies the Great King, and Genesis 1:1 accomplishes that God is the Creator and also thereby the Suzerain, and the linkage of these concepts was well understood in the ancient Near East. Genesis 1:2–29 in effect constitute the historical prologue, because those verses tell the good things the suzerain has done for the vassal: in this case, he has created the whole world as their "very good" environment, and he has created the vassals themselves. The remaining material in Genesis 1–2 (i.e., Gen. 1:30–2:25) includes the witness section (Gen. 1:31, which comes toward the end of the treaty), and the subsequent curse—in case the man (and/or woman) partake of the forbidden tree. (One finds, more completely, all the stipulations in Genesis 1:28 and 2:16–17). Kline's characteristic identification of Genesis 1:2 as the witness to the covenant is perhaps somewhat out of place according to a strict analysis, because the witness section of a treaty came toward the end, and not near the beginning of a treaty (although witnesses are summoned at the beginning of biblical covenant *lawsuits*).[21]

Chapter 1 of Genesis accordingly constitutes a narrative overview of God's creation work, and includes the elements of a treaty/covenant. Chapter 2 of Genesis is also narrative, and zooms in on some details of the prior historical prologue, including the creation of the man and woman. It also gives details of blessing and curse (vv. 16–17). It may thus be viewed as supplemental data to the historical prologue already given in Genesis 1:2–29, including supplemental *torah* (the same pattern we note in God's other covenant making episodes, which are also followed by supplemental narrative material and *torah*). Provision of supplemental *torah* in this fashion may perhaps be viewed as part of the Lord's pedagogy.

We note at this point that chapter 3 cannot be considered to be part of the creation covenant proper. The total stipulations given in Genesis 1:28 and Genesis 2:16–17 include a curse that becomes the issue in Genesis 3,

---

(subsequent to the covenant institution narrative of Gen. 1:1–2:3) that focuses in on the Lord's dealing with those he has created. Moreover, it provides supplemental *torah*.

21   It ought to be noted that I had published the covenant outline of Genesis 1:1–2:3 five years before Kline published the material quoted above. Cf. Niehaus, *God at Sinai*, 144–47.

when the Lord must bring *lawsuit* against Adam and his wife because they have broken the law already given in Genesis 2:17.[22]

The term "sanctions" is another way of characterizing that law. The sanctions section of a treaty tells what curse(s) will befall the vassal should he break the treaty. That role has been filled by Genesis 2:17. Chapter 4 is subsequently a narrative that tells of Cain and Abel, of the murder committed by Cain and its consequences for him and his offspring. This was not at all in view in the "sanctions" section of the covenant (Gen. 2:17). Genesis 4, then, gives us further history of life after the Fall, although still under the Adamic covenant (just as Israel's history detailed their sins after the Mosaic covenant institution).

The Adamic Covenant Has Not Been Abrogated

I agree with the first half of what Kline says of his own fifth chapter, "Finally, chapter 5 will trace the history of the creational covenant, with the tragic failure of the first man to obtain the proposed grant of the eternal kingdom." I cannot agree with all of it because Genesis does not contain any "proposed grant of the eternal kingdom." God has proposed nothing in the creation covenant. He has made a covenant in which Adam had a part, and Adam disobeyed its terms. We can agree with the first part of his statement: "Chapter 5 will trace the history of the creational covenant." Kline recognizes that the subsequent narratives of Genesis and beyond "trace the history of the creational covenant," which accordingly has not been abrogated. One might see the exclusion of Adam and Eve from the Garden as an abrogation of the Adamic covenant, but neither Kline nor I see it that way. The relevant verses only say, "So the LORD God banished him from the Garden of Eden to work the ground from which he had been taken. After he drove the man out, he placed on the east side of the Garden of Eden cherubim and a flaming sword flashing back and forth to guard the way to the tree of life" (Gen. 3:23–24). Banishment from the Garden does not constitute abrogation of the covenant, especially in view of the Lord's clothing Adam and his wife and the significance of that act. A later parallel is the Lord's exile of his people from the Promised Land for breaking the Mosaic covenant, yet when they were in exile the Mosaic covenant had not been abrogated but remained in effect until Jesus was born under it and eventually fulfilled it and replaced it with the new covenant.

---

22 Cf. discussion in volume 1 of my *Biblical Theology*, 106–10.

The Common Grace Nature of the Adamic Covenant

Some have found the characterization of the Adamic covenant as a common grace covenant to be problematic. Although I gave a brief explanation of this in volume 1, it may be that more clarification is needed. This is so especially because people traditionally think of common grace as including both the elect and the non-elect. Obviously if the Adamic covenant has continued in force (as Kline and I agree that it has), it now covers and provides for both the elect and the non-elect. So it is a common grace covenant in the way that phrase is usually understood.

Although that much is clear, I used the term common grace in a somewhat different way when I characterized the Adamic covenant as a common grace covenant *before the Fall*. I used it in this sense: had Adam not sinned, the Adamic covenant would have covered all human beings (as it did before the Fall), although they would have been without sin and would thus have been a covenant of grace commonly distributed to all— that is, a common grace covenant in that different sense. Since the Lord continued the Adamic covenant after the Fall, it has become a common grace covenant in the sense generally understood.

The Concomitant Idea That the Adamic Covenant Is Not Salvific

The Adamic covenant was given before the Fall. God was witness to the covenant when he declared *all the results* of it to be "very good" (Gen. 1:31).[23] Even if one takes the supplemental material and *torah* of Genesis 2:4–25 into account, the result is the same: God made everything good and there was nothing from which Adam and his wife needed to be saved at that point. The covenant itself was not salvific. However, if Adam or his wife ate the forbidden fruit, they would have come under the covenantal sanction—they would "surely die." The fact that a challenge came after the covenant was made does not make the covenant a salvific covenant. It was not a covenant by which anyone could be saved. After our first parents broke it, however, they needed a savior.

---

23   Or, on Kline's understanding, Genesis 1:2 which, although I think Genesis 1:31 is a better candidate for the witness portion and I discuss this in volume 1, makes no difference to the issue at hand.

THE ABANDONMENT OF TWO OLDER IDEAS: THE NOAHIC-NEW COVENANT GROUP AS A "COVENANT OF GRACE" AND THE ADAMIC COVENANT AS A "COVENANT OF WORKS"

The Westminster Confession and covenant theology since the seventeenth century have operated with concepts that served well when people knew less, but those concepts should be abandoned now in favor of more informed views that are just as faithful to the Bible as the older covenant theologians tried to be.

The grand scheme of a covenant of grace is one such concept—and for several reasons. First, it is not true to what covenants were in the ancient world. Neither Moses nor anyone else in the ancient world ever called any collection of covenants a single covenant (the one exception being a covenant and its renewal, so, e.g., the Sinai covenant and its renewal the Moab covenant constitute the final form of the Mosaic covenant, which is always referred to subsequently in the Bible in the singular as the law or the covenant the Lord made with Israel, etc.). Nothing in the Bible mandates that the Noahic covenant-new covenant collection be called one covenant.

Second, to call them one covenant obscures the fact that the Noahic covenant is a common grace covenant, and the Abrahamic-new covenant complex consists of special grace covenants.

Third, it also obscures the fact that the Noahic covenant renews the Adamic covenant and forms one legal package with it, under which all humans continue to live. A simpler characterization, and one that is more *sachgemäss*, would be, first, to recognize that the Adamic and Noahic covenants, as a covenant and its renewal, constitute one legal package under which all humans live; and second, to call the collection of special grace covenants—the Abrahamic covenant-new covenant collection designed for people elect out of all humanity—not a special grace covenant, but a special grace program.[24]

The so-called covenant of works is another concept that ought to be given up because the phrasing is unnecessary and in itself unclear. Adam was called to do works in the covenant named after him (cf. Gen. 1:28; 2:16–17). In that *one regard* he was no different from any vassal under any of the subsequent divine-human covenants. They were all called to do works. To say such is not the case is simply an act of denial. The difference between Adam and those who followed him in the other divine-human

---

24 Cf. the diagram and brief discussion in volume 1 of my *Biblical Theology*, 34.

covenants was that Adam was not in a fallen state when he was created into the Adamic covenant. As a consequence, he *could have done the work* required by the covenant. His work, however, would not have confirmed the covenant. God had already done that, as the form criticism of Genesis 1:1–2:3 shows. Rather, his obedience would have enabled him to continue under the creation covenant in an unfallen state.

The role of the forbidden tree and of Adam vis-à-vis the tree become very important at this stage of the discussion. Adam was to "keep" the Garden of Eden. How was he to keep it? One cannot reasonably fault him for not anticipating the serpent and God never faults him for this. In fact, there is no evidence God warned him in advance about the serpent. One can, however, fault Adam for not dealing with his fallen wife in an appropriate way, whatever that would have been. I have suggested it would have been to refuse the fruit from her hand and to refer her case to the Lord. Had he done those things, he would have done righteously. The whole sequence of events under discussion, however, occurred after the Adamic covenant was established. It describes events in human life under the covenant and after the covenant had come into existence.[25]

It has been proposed by analogy that, had Adam behaved righteously, he would have passed a test and so the tree of knowledge has been considered probational. It is important to be clear on what this means. First, Adam did not have to do anything under the covenant to *earn* God's approbation. Because Adam and every other entity created in the Adamic covenant were pronounced by God to be "very good," Adam already had God's approbation. The idea of probation classically in covenant theology means something different: Adam had to pass the test provided by the serpent's temptation—or by his wife's offer of the fruit—and had he done so, his probation or probationary period would have terminated successfully.[26] What then? Life without death? But Adam already had life without death, since the curse of Genesis 2:17 was precisely that he would die if he ate the fruit, which implies he would not die if he did not eat the fruit. Apotheosis into heaven? That would not seem to fit well with the mandates of Genesis 1:28. Receiving the Spirit to dwell within him, which could be called "eternal life" in a spiritual sense, such as we know under

---

25   In other words, it does not characterize the covenant itself, but behavior of vassals under the covenant.

26   In other words, Adam was in a probationary period that would eventually show whether he would or would not obey the command of Genesis 2:17. He was already approved (*probare*) by God, but he would soon also be proved (*probare*).

the new covenant? That is an attractive parallel with the result of the second Adam's obedience, but one cannot answer with certainty. Clearly probation in this special and limited sense seems to make sense—God gave Adam an opportunity to show his ability to say no to sin and to be obedient—but the data are too limited to warrant extensive conclusions.[27] One could as easily characterize the matter differently and affirm that Adam would be faced with a challenge regarding the tree, and, as in other covenants that required works, if he had obeyed the law (i.e., done that particular "work"), the life of the covenant would simply have continued unimpaired and the mandates of Genesis 1:28 would have been carried out in an unfallen world.[28]

Finally, it may be reasonable to suggest that God would have dealt summarily with the serpent/Satan once Adam had rejected/triumphed over him, just as God dealt a fatal blow to Satan later by the obedience of the second Adam. It also seems reasonable to suggest that God would have imparted his Spirit to dwell in Adam and his descendants after this triumph—again by analogy with the result of the second Adam's work—although we are not in a position to suggest when such an impartation would have occurred.

One thing is important to understand: any righteous act Adam could

---

27   Louis Berkhof, *Systematic Theology* (Grand Rapids: Eerdmans, 1941), 242 (*sub* b. *The doctrine of the covenant of works*, (b) *An element of probation*), may be taken as representative of the traditional view when he says: "While apart from this covenant Adam and his descendants would have been in a continual state of trial, with a constant danger of sinning, the covenant guaranteed that persistent perseverance for a fixed period of time would be rewarded with the establishment of man in a permanent state of holiness and bliss." There is no way to prove this, although it depends on a reasonable parallel between the first Adam and the second, since the approved work of the second Adam did win eternal life for those under his headship. There can be no doubt that Adam was the federal head of the human race ("For as in Adam all die, so in Christ all will be made alive," 1 Cor. 15:22), so that his obedience would have meant blessing to all his descendants.

28   It is worth note that the ideas of a "covenant of works" and of a "probation" have evolved in the history of theology. The term *foedus operum* ("covenant of works") was first used by Dudley Fener in 1585. The covenant of works idea had already become common in Reformed theology by 1590, though it was not adopted by everyone—some members of the Westminster Assembly in the 1640s opposed it. While John Calvin had spoken of a probationary period for Adam, a promise of life for obedience, and the federal headship of Adam, he did not speak of a covenant of works. Cf. Robert Letham, *The Westminster Assembly: Reading Its Theology in Historical Context* (Philipsburg, NJ: Presbyterian & Reformed, 2009), 227–28.

have done would have come from the Lord anyway, if the case of the second Adam can be a guide in such matters. And just as the second Adam was obedient even to death on a cross, it seems parallel that the first Adam should have been obedient with regard to the tree of knowledge. In other words, he should not have eaten of it. The failure of the first Adam with regard to his tree necessitated the work of the second Adam with regard to his tree. The first Adam in effect *ate death*, the second Adam *tasted death* for us. Nonetheless, the work of the second Adam was the obedience of faith (cf. Rev. 1:5), and so the work of the first Adam (had he done it) would have been the obedience of faith.[29] Faith leads to work as its inevitable fruit. Nonetheless, works earn us nothing; we are saved by faith alone. There should be no illusion, therefore, that refusal to call the Adamic covenant a covenant of works somehow implies a position inconsistent with the need for justification by faith alone in a fallen world.

It follows from such unavoidable facts that it is not very helpful—if it is helpful at all—to characterize the Adamic covenant as a covenant of works. It was a covenant that included works, as did all the divine-human covenants. The only unarguable difference as regards the vassal was that Adam, being without sin, could have done the work.[30] In the matter under discussion, he could have abstained from the tree of knowledge and he could have referred his wife's sin to the Lord.

What the Lord would have done had Adam behaved so we cannot know, if we are to be honest. I think it reasonable that Adam and whatever human race might have followed him (supposing a second wife, or a forgiven and restored first wife?—which latter, however, seems unlikely given the sanction of Gen. 2:17) would have carried on with the cultural mandate. Eventually perhaps, by analogy with the eschaton, an ultimate "heavenising" of earth (as Kline puts it) would have been inaugurated, and things would have ended up looking much as they will look once the new heaven and the new earth come to be.

The title "covenant of works" is not, however, necessary to any of this.

---

29 This statement will probably be meaningless or at least easily misunderstood by one who has not read the discussion of faith in the Prolegomena of volume 1 of this *Biblical Theology*; and cf. also volume 3, chapter 4, "Faith and Sin."

30 Another possible difference was the character of one of Adam's works—rejection of the fruit of the tree—which, on the classical understanding, would have earned temptation-free life for himself and the human race subsequently, because he was uniquely, among vassals, the federal head of the human race (cf. Berkhof and discussion above). But again, there can be no proof of this possibility.

The need of a sinless second Adam to do the work that would undo the failure of the first Adam does not require that one give the Adamic covenant such a title. The old characterization does have the virtue of indicating that Adam, unlike the vassals of the subsequent covenants, could have done the work God wanted because he was without sin, and that any subsequent covenant would very clearly have to be sustained by God's grace because his vassals routinely sinned and fell short, as they could not help doing in their fallen state. But again, one does not have to call the Adamic covenant a covenant of works in order to establish this distinction, which is obvious to anyone. Moreover, even the Adamic covenant before the Fall (and had there been no Fall) would also have been sustained only by God's grace because every created thing is a gift that owes its very existence to him.

SIN CANNOT ANNUL A DIVINE-HUMAN COVENANT

It has been noted that all God's covenants are both unconditional and conditional. They are unconditional in the sense that each of them continues until it has fulfilled God's purpose for it. They are conditional in the sense that each of them has conditions for the vassals under them. The unconditional nature of God's covenants also means sin cannot annul any of them.

The common grace covenants have that unconditional aspect—human sin cannot annul them. The Adamic and Noahic covenants continue in force to this day because they are the legal charter of the world and the renewal of that charter. They continue even though what Isaiah foretold is happening before our eyes: "The earth is defiled by its people; / they have disobeyed the laws, / violated the statutes / and broken the everlasting covenant" (Isa. 24:5; cf. Gen. 9:16).[31] They will continue until the end.

The special grace covenants also cannot be annulled by human sin, but that does not mean they continue until the end. The Abrahamic covenant is no longer in force—it no longer functions as a covenant. The clear sign of its cessation *qua* functioning covenant is the abrogation

---

31 However, once Isaiah's prophecy finds its fulfillment, the Lord will judge and destroy the earth and bring a new heaven and a new earth, at which time the Adamic-Noahic covenant complex will come to its end. Cf. discussion in volume 1 of *Biblical Theology*, 210–13.

of circumcision, the covenant sign.[32] Nonetheless, it continued in force until its purposes had been accomplished, no matter what the sinfulness of the people who lived under it (who like Abraham lived under its "requirements . . . commands . . . decrees and . . . instructions," Gen. 26:5). Likewise, the Davidic covenant was unconditional: It continued in force no matter how badly the kings of Israel behaved. It continued in force until it had served its purpose. It continued until God's temporary suspension of kingship in Israel prepared the way for the true David, who had always and eternally been Israel's king supernally and outside time. But the Davidic covenant no longer functions as a covenant today because its purpose has been fulfilled in Christ, the ultimate David ("the beloved").

So then these three remain: the Adamic, Noahic, and new covenants. The first two form one legal package that provides an ongoing world in which the new covenant can progress in the present form of God's kingdom on earth.

A NOTE ON RIGHTEOUSNESS

In volume 1, I devoted an excursus to what N. T. Wright had written in *What St. Paul Really Said* regarding righteousness. I argued there that God's righteousness was not to be understood simply as his covenant faithfulness. Instead, righteousness throughout the Bible means only one thing: conformity to a standard. In matters of biblical righteousness, *the standard is God's nature,* to which he is always faithful, and to which humans may be faithful in some degree with divine help. Any of God's covenants is an expression of God's nature but only a partial expression. So God's righteousness—his faithfulness/conformity to his own nature—includes but is not limited to his covenant faithfulness. A separate book could easily be devoted to this idea because, even though the understanding of righteousness as conformity to a standard seems to have been fairly obvious to people in the ancient Near East and is often recognized by scholars today, there is hardly consensus on the application of that idea to matters of divine and human righteousness. Some help with regard to Wright's misunderstanding of righteousness (which he actually shares with a long tradition of scholarship) has been provided by Charles Lee Irons.[33] Irons does not devote his book to the concept advanced here, but

---

32 Cf. discussion in chapter 4 of this volume.

33 Charles Lee Irons, *The Righteousness of God: A Lexical Examination of the*

he does interact with the view that God's righteousness is his covenant faithfulness and shows its defects in some key passages (e.g., Phil. 3:9 and Rom. 10:3), advocating the traditional view that God's righteousness is *given* to us (i.e., imputed righteousness).

As regards the present work and my own view, I repeat because I want to make it very clear that I do not rule out God's covenant faithfulness as one aspect of his righteousness, but insist that God's covenant faithfulness is only *one* expression, or illustration, of God's righteousness. God's righteousness is not limited to his faithfulness to a covenant he created. God's covenant faithfulness is, rather, one example his of faithfulness to his *nature*—and his nature is the ultimate standard—as that nature/standard is expressed in any of his covenants. Nonetheless, God's faithfulness to any or all of his covenants is not the only expression of his righteousness. Appendix E in volume 3 provides a categorization of all biblical occurrences of the words "righteous," "righteousness," "righteously," and related verbs, along with some explanatory comments. A detailed study of these occurrences requires more space than is possible now, but it is hoped the data provided in Appendix E point clearly enough to the correctness of the view advocated here.

Covenant-Faithfulness Interpretation (Tubingen: Mohr Siebeck, 2015). Cf. the review by Thomas Schreiner: https://www.thegospelcoalition.org/article/book-reviews -righteousness-of-god-lee-irons.

CHAPTER ONE

Prelude to the Abrahamic Covenant

This study now enters the realm we have called special grace, and that realm begins with the call of Abram. The Lord will soon initiate a covenant with the patriarch. Issues to be considered now include (1) general matters, for example, common grace and special grace, literary issues such as historical backgrounds and historical prologues of treaties/covenants, covenant idioms including "to cut a covenant" and how they bear on the Noahic and Abrahamic covenant narratives especially, unconditionality and conditionality of the divine-human covenants; and then (2) matters more focused on the narratival material of Genesis 12–14, namely, the call of Abram, the significance of Abram's altar in Genesis 12, the promise of land, Abram's ruse in Egypt, Lot's choice, Abram's rescue of Lot and subsequent encounter with Melchizedek, Melchizedek's blessing and Christology, and a summary analysis of the Abrahamic materials in terms of the Major Paradigm. A good part of this chapter, then, follows and deals with the narrative sequence of Genesis 12–14, although more general theological and interpretive discussions form the first and last parts.

COMMON GRACE AND SPECIAL GRACE

Like all human beings, Abram stood (and would as long as he lived on earth continue to stand) in a common grace covenantal relationship with God under the Adamic and Noahic covenants. But now God would become Abram's suzerain and redemptive Lord in a new covenant—a special grace covenant that is unprecedented and unique.

The Abrahamic covenant is unprecedented because up to this point all humans, like Abram, have stood only in a common grace covenantal relationship to God, living under the terms of the Adamic covenant and then, after the Flood, living under the terms of the legal package formed by the Adamic and Noahic (or creation and re-creation) covenants. All humans continue to live under those covenants to this day and will do so until the Lord returns. But now with Abram begins a series of special grace covenants that have to do not merely or even primarily with maintenance of the common grace order but with redemption of an elect subset of human beings within that order.[1]

The Abrahamic covenant is thus unprecedented because it is the first special grace covenant. It is also unique because it contains within itself the germ of three subsequent special grace covenants: the Mosaic, the Davidic, and the new. All of those covenants together—the Abrahamic, the Mosaic, the Davidic, and the new—are parts of and play their respective roles in God's special grace program or plan of redemption that eventuates in a new humanity and a new heavens and a new earth. In other words, the special grace program aims at restoring or recreating what was lost under the original common grace (Adamic) covenant and as such it has an eschatological trajectory.

The special grace program is apparently necessitated by the fact that not all people can be part of the needed restoration. If everyone could be saved, God's redemptive work could take place in terms of only a common grace program that, being common grace, would include everyone. Paul makes it clear that such cannot be the case (cf. Rom. 8:19–30, and especially vv. 29–30, "For those God *foreknew* he also predestined to be conformed to the image of his Son, that he might be the firstborn among many brothers. And those he predestined, he also called; those he called, he also justified; those he justified, he also glorified" [emphasis added]. The significance of God's foreknowledge and election in the Pauline context of a restored creation [Rom. 8:19–24] will form part of our discussion of the new covenant).

---

1   It should be noted that, although the Lord particularly—or *specially*—saved Noah and his family, that does not make the covenant that followed that act of salvation a special grace covenant. The Lord did not save Noah and his family *by a covenant*. The Lord saved them and then, *subsequently, made a covenant* through Noah that applies to all people—and so we call that Noahic covenant a common grace covenant. It is a common grace covenant because all people live under it.

HISTORICAL BACKGROUND

I have made the point in volume 1 of *Biblical Theology* and in an article that the special grace covenants, like the common grace covenants, are reported to us in historical narratives. This may seem an obvious point but it has implications that are not—or seem not to have been—so obvious. Some of the implications have to do with the treaty or covenant elements that are reported or not reported, or reported across a space of narrative material rather than within a compact treaty document, as has been seen already in Genesis 1 (with supplementary narrative data and *torah* in Genesis 2), and will be seen even more in the narrative material that includes the components of the Abrahamic covenant. The same is true of the other divine-human covenants, which are also given to us in spacious narratives. As we approach the Abrahamic covenant we see that the narrative form of reporting provides something the ancient treaties did not provide, namely, a historical *background*.

One could see already in the case of the Noahic covenant that the Flood narrative gave a historical background for that "treaty." That is, the narrative of Genesis 6–8 provided the sort of historical material that is alluded to in the historical prologues of second millennium BC international treaties, documenting the good things the suzerain had already done for the vassal before the treaty was created. Sometimes the ancients provided such a background as well but they provided it, not in the historical prologues of the treaties, but in their annals. In other words, an ancient suzerain might provide a narrative of his interactions with some vassal-to-be and then, afterwards, create a treaty with that lesser king that made him a vassal. That treaty would then contain a historical *prologue* that alluded to, or gave a shorter account of, the historical *background* material recorded in the annals. As noted in the Prolegomena in volume 1, such ancient annals, along with the historical prologues of treaties, were the major genres of historiography in the ancient world.

In the Noahic case the literary function of Genesis 6–8 is at least two-fold: to give the reader an account of God's judgment on humanity and the salvation of Noah and his household on the one hand, and to give the reader the salvific historical *background*, which forms a basis for God's treaty relationship with Noah in Genesis 9 on the other.[2] That material would normally be alluded to in the historical prologue portion of the

---

2   It is important to distinguish between a historical *background*—a historical narrative that comes *before* the narrative of a covenant's institution—and a historical

covenant but in Genesis 9 that is not the case. Instead, one is given only the background in the narrative of Genesis 6–8 that leads up to the covenant of Genesis 9. We can now see that the author treats God's history with Abram in somewhat the same way so that Genesis 12–14 forms the historical background to the Abrahamic covenant that is "cut," or created, in Genesis 15. In the case of the Abrahamic covenant, however, we are also given the historical prologue (Gen. 15:7) that alludes back to the historical background (Gen. 12–14 broadly speaking, Gen. 12:1–3 specifically referenced by Gen. 15:7). The following simple diagram illustrates these observations:

Covenant Mediator	Historical Background	Covenant	Historical Prologue
Noah	Genesis 6–8	Genesis 9:1–17	None
Abram	Genesis 12–14	Genesis 15:1–21	Genesis 15:7

The diagram recalls that the Lord made covenants through covenant mediator prophets, of whom Adam was the first, Noah the second, and Abram the third. Put another way: Adam mediated the Adamic, common grace covenant; Noah mediated the Noahic, common grace renewal of the Adamic covenant; and Abram mediated the first special grace covenant, the one named after him.

The Abrahamic covenant was cut, or created, in Genesis 15, and it is important to be clear on this matter. Many scholars believe the Abrahamic covenant begins in Genesis 12 but that cannot be the case. The terminology of Genesis 15:18 makes it impossible. One may draw an analogy from the ancient world (an analogy which, however, does not apply to all of the biblical covenant institution narratives as will be explained below). A covenant did not exist in the pagan ancient Near East until it was fully articulated and formally ratified or entered into, apparently by an oath, sometimes also by an animal dismemberment ritual of the sort Genesis 15 and Jeremiah 34 report. The full articulation normally took the form of a document—an inscribed treaty. As we have seen in the Bible, the full articulation of the two common grace covenants—the Adamic and the Noahic—took place in each case in the context of a historical narrative: the Genesis 1:1–2:3 creation account for the Adamic covenant (with, in Genesis 2, supplemental historical data and *torah*, especially

---

prologue—a section *within* the treaty/covenant that alludes to the earlier, historical background. Cf. discussion above (pp. 30–33) and Niehaus, "Covenant and Narrative," 542.

in Gen. 2:16–17) and, in the narrative of Genesis 9, the Genesis 9:1–17 account of God's declarations to Noah which formally articulate that covenant. The same is true for the Abrahamic covenant. Not only does it have a historical background (Genesis 12–14), which functions as a narrative preface to the covenant making episode, it also, like the Adamic and Noahic covenants, is articulated in a narrative context (Genesis 15, with supplemental *torah* in Genesis 17 and 22). The formulation of each of these covenants takes place within the flow of a narrative. There is no record of an actual document, that is, no treaty carved in stone, for any of them. They are all narratives that contain the essential elements of a second millennium BC international treaty. Their author thereby informs any cognizant reader that a covenant has just taken place even though certain formal elements (e.g., a ratifying ceremony or an oath) may not be present. Indeed, in the case of Genesis 1:1–2:3, the word "covenant" is not even used.[3]

COVENANTS UNCUT AND CUT

At this point it will be helpful to consider the terminology of covenant ratification in Genesis 15 where we are told: "On that day the LORD cut a covenant with Abram" (Gen. 15:18, author's translation). It is no accident that the idiom כרת ברית ("to cut a covenant")" occurs first in this covenant. The idiom is not used of the common grace covenants but only of the special grace covenants, beginning with the Abrahamic covenant in Genesis 15:18. We now note the reason for this distinction.

The symbolism of the cutting is just this: one who enters into a covenant that is cut may fall out of the covenant, that is, be *cut off* from covenant fellowship through disobedience (cf. Gen. 17:14 for the Abrahamic covenant, Exod. 12:15 [in an anticipatory way, with regard to the Passover institution] and Exod. 31:14 [with regard to the covenant sign, the Sabbath] for the Mosaic covenant; cf. similarly, though without the term "cut," in Ps. 132:11–12 for the Davidic covenant).[4]

---

3   The same is true of the Davidic covenant narrative (2 Sam. 7:1–17), but cf. chapter 17.

4   Cf. further discussion in Niehaus, "God's Covenant with Abraham," 268–69; cf. likewise chapter 4, 55–56. For the concept "cut off" and its significance (i.e., "cut off from his people"), cf. Jacob Milgrom, *Leviticus 1–16: A New Translation with Introduction and Commentary* (AB 3; New York: Doubleday, 1991), 457. Cf. further Douglas K. Stuart,

The same is not true, however, of the Adamic and the Noahic covenants. Human beings violate those covenants every day—polluting the earth, murdering other humans—yet they continue under those covenants (ruling over the earth, subduing it, being fruitful and multiplying) until the curse that applies in both of those covenants is fulfilled (i.e., they die naturally in fulfillment of Gen. 2:17, or else by lawless violence—or, as sometimes happens with murderers and certain others, they are put to death according to law in some countries, sometimes in fulfillment of Gen. 9:5-6). In other words, it is impossible to *be cut out of* (or *lose one's membership in*) the Adamic and Noahic covenants (except eventually through death).[5] Nonetheless, both the Adamic and Noahic covenants had conditions and obligations. The Adamic covenant conditions had to do with the cultural mandate and the trees of Eden. The Noahic covenant effectively reaffirmed the cultural mandate of the Adamic covenant and added the condition of the death penalty for murder. There may have been other conditions as well that are not recorded in Genesis 9; Isaiah 24 may allude to them:[6]

Exodus, The New American Commentary, vol. 2 (Nashville: Broadman and Holman, 2006), 283–85, who sums it up well: "The statement that a person would be cut off from Israel was not juridical guidance for those enforcing laws but a prediction from God of the fate of the unfaithful. Not to be faithful is not to belong to God's people even if living among them . . . and therefore not to enjoy their covenant blessings in the long run" (285).

5   One might argue that the Noahic death penalty equates to being "cut off" from the Noahic covenant, or from the Adamic/Noahic covenant complex, although it is not stated as a penalty for covenant breaking, but as an affront to the *imago Dei*. That may be significant. Murder under the Adamic covenant was not punishable by death, but it is under the Noahic and Mosaic covenants—as one may expect when God reveals progressively the significance and consequences of things. In the foundational passage (Gen. 9:5, the background to Lev. 24:17, 21), the ground is the *imago Dei*, and we remember that imago is an imago of the Spirit. That fact may explain the unique significance of murder in the Noahic and Mosaic covenants (as rooted in the *imago Dei*), and may also be the Old Testament parallel to, or adumbration of, the sin against the Spirit under the new covenant. The topic requires more exploration than it can receive here.

6   Dumbrell, *Creation and Covenant*, 28, avers that the phrase "my covenant" in Genesis 6:18 in and of itself implies that the Lord *alone* is obligated in the Noahic covenant. The phrase unfortunately cannot carry such weight because the Lord refers to *all* of his covenants—and to each one several times—as "my covenant." Cf. Niehaus, "Covenant: An Idea in the Mind of God," *JETS* 52, no. 2 (2009): 241n63. Nonetheless, we agree with Dumbrell that the Lord does maintain the Noahic covenant despite human failure. But the same is true of all the divine-human covenants: God maintains each covenant until

The earth is defiled by its people;
   they have disobeyed the laws,
violated the statutes
   and broken the everlasting covenant. (v. 5)

As was noted—and given the universality of judgment in Isaiah 24—
the phrase "everlasting covenant" arguably alludes to the Lord's earlier
characterization of the Noahic covenant (Gen. 9:16). It would appear,
then, that people under that common grace covenant made in Genesis 9
also had "laws" (תורת) and "statutes" (חקות), although one is only told of
them later in Isaiah 24. Similarly, the Abrahamic covenant (Genesis 15)
had "commands" (מצות), "decrees" (חקות) and "instructions" ("laws,"
תורת), although one only learns of them later in Genesis 26.[7] Nonetheless, one could break those common grace laws and statutes and yet not
be "cut out" of the covenant: one might indeed live to a ripe old age
although in sin.

By contrast, as in the passages cited above (Gen. 17:14; Exod. 12:15;
31:14), a person who breaks the Abrahamic covenant or the Mosaic covenant *can* be cut off from the covenant and *no longer be one of the people
of the covenant*. However, such a person, though he is no longer a member of the covenant, may also go on living. For example, many people
who disobeyed the Mosaic covenant, which was cut at Sinai (and later
renewed on the plains of Moab with a new generation just prior to their
entry into and conquest of the Promised Land), lost their place in the
covenant: they wandered in the wilderness for nearly forty years but
then, as Hebrews puts it, their bodies fell in the desert and they failed to
enter into God's promised covenant rest "because of their unbelief" (Heb.
3:7–19; cf. Ps. 95:7–11; faith, or amening who God is and what he is doing,
is the *sine qua non* of salvation under any divine-human covenant, as
noted at the end of the Prolegomena). Subsequently, throughout Israel's
sin-racked history, many people broke covenant unrepentantly and thus
fell out of covenant membership, yet they continued to live physically
in Israel. Indeed, Elijah's despondency in 1 Kings 19 is corrected by the

---

its purpose has been accomplished, irrespective of the covenant breaking of vassals under
any of the covenants; cf. discussion on pages 33–35 and chapter 4.

7   See further discussion in chapter 4. Cf. volume 1, page 97, the discussion of Eve's
supposed "addition" to the Lord's command not to eat of the tree of the knowledge of good
and evil, which we consider another example—the first example—of supplemental data
given later regarding the Lord's earlier instructions in a covenant (the Adamic covenant).

Lord who can only claim 7,000 Israelites who have not become apostate (1 Kings 19:18). Likewise (as will be argued below in chapter 4), one may, through unbelief and the disobedience that characterizes unbelief, fall out of, or be cut out of, the Abrahamic or the Davidic covenant—yet go on living.

To summarize, membership in the common grace covenants *cannot be forfeited* but membership in the special grace covenants *can be forfeited*. One may violate the legal package formed by the Adamic and Noahic covenants, but no matter how much or how often one violates those covenants, one cannot be excluded from membership in them while one lives. This is so because the Lord sends his rain and sunshine on the just and unjust alike (cf. Matt. 5:45) as he continues to sustain the common grace order as a context in which his special grace salvific program can continue to operate. By contrast, one who violates the Abrahamic, Mosaic, or Davidic covenants can be excluded from membership in them yet also go on living in the common grace context and under the common grace covenantal package formed by the Adamic and Noahic covenants.[8]

Although neither the Adamic nor the Noahic covenant was "cut," covenant idioms do occur in some of the material. We have commented on the nature of the Adamic or Creation covenant, and on the lack of covenantal idioms or even the term "covenant" in Genesis 1–2. The narrative material of those chapters and especially of Genesis 1 makes it clear that God created the cosmos in a relationship with himself that one may call covenantal, since the creation narrative contains all of the elements that later came to be recognized as parts of a covenant. In other words, the very acts of creation were covenantal in nature, contributing to the formation of a created order that existed and always exists in a relationship with the Creator and that has all the elements of a covenant and that is also an expression of the Creator's covenantal nature.[9]

Genesis 9 reports the Noahic covenant, which renews the Adamic covenant, and although, like the Adamic covenant material, it does not

---

8   This principle is most easily illustrated from the Mosaic covenant material as we have indicated, but is also true of the other Old Testament special grace covenants as we will show. The new covenant is obviously a more sensitive case to be discussed in its place.

9   Since God's relation to creation entails what we have come to recognize as covenantal elements (e.g., he is the Great King, he has provided good things—including existence and a context for it—and, where volition is possible, he has given certain requirements and certain consequences for obedience or disobedience), it is reasonable to say that God's nature is covenantal.

use the idiom "to cut a covenant," the Noahic chapters do use covenant idioms. Instead of כרת ברית they use the idioms נתן ברית (lit. "to give covenant," Gen. 9:12) and הקים ברית (lit. "to confirm covenant" or "to carry out covenant," Gen. 6:18; 9:9, 11, 17).[10] We have noted that it is impossible to be cut off from the Adamic or Noahic covenants. However, in order to make it clear that a covenant *is in view*, Moses uses terms in the Noahic chapters that he also uses later with regard to special grace covenants, covenants from which one *can* be cut off. The terms he uses (נתן ברית and הקים ברית) can be true both of the Noahic, common grace covenant, and of the special grace covenants. Any of them can be "confirmed," "carried out," or "given" *in an ongoing sense*. These phenomena are consistent with the idea that as we progress through the Bible certain facts or doctrines are articulated with increasing clarity and definition. The Noahic usages, then, convey the Lord's promise (e.g., Gen. 6:18) that he *will put into effect*, and continue to "give," a covenant *he will soon institute*.[11]

If we look ahead to the Abrahamic materials, however, it is of more than passing interest that the same terminology confronts us in Genesis 17

---

10   Cf. *BDB*, 879. The lexicon notes the translation "to carry out" covenant in addition to the more traditional renderings "confirm" and "establish" for הקים. We advocate such translations as "confirm," "carry out," or "put into effect" as best communicating what is going on in the passages that use the idiom. Tellingly, *BDB* advocates the translation "*carry out, give effect to . . .* oath, covenant, vow, word, plan, command," in Genesis 26:3, where the Lord says, "I will give all these lands and will *carry out* the oath [with "oath" as synecdoche for "covenant" והקימתי את־השבעה] I swore to your father Abraham." Cf. also in this sense Levitcus 26:9, Deuteronomy 8:18, 1 Samuel 1:23, 1 Kings 6:12—and Jeremiah 23:20: "The anger of the LORD will not turn back / until he fully accomplishes (i.e., has fully *carried out*, עד־הקימו) / the purposes of his heart."

11   For the view that הקים ברית in Genesis 6:18 indicates continuation of an already existing—i.e., Adamic—relationship (which, it seems to me, would imply an Adamic covenant), cf. William Dumbrell, *Covenant and Creation*, 25–26. We note here that I have agreed with Dumbrell on the theme of the idiom הקים ברית (cf. Niehaus, "Covenant and Narrative," 546—with respect to Genesis 17). I think he has correctly sensed one nuance of the Noahic uses of the idiom: the covenant the Lord will make with Noah will also *continue*, with additions, the Adamic provisions (and it will continue them with Noah and his household alone, not with the rest of humanity who will perish in judgment). It does so, however, not in a mere continuation of the Adamic arrangement, but in a distinct, *renewal* covenant which, like other renewal covenants, both repeats and further nuances data of the original covenant (for the Noahic vis-à-vis the Adamic, cf. Gen. 9:1–3 as compared with Gen. 1:28); cf. Niehaus, "An Argument against Theologically Constructed Covenants," *JETS* 50, no. 2 (2007): 266. Discussion of הקים ברית and other covenant instituting and sustaining idioms appears in chapter 5 of this volume.

that we saw in the Noahic chapters: here again the idiom "to cut a covenant" is not used but the other covenantal phrases (נתן ברית and הקים
ברית) occur. The reason is clear and is consistent with later usage of the
idioms in the Old Testament. In Genesis 17 the Lord is not cutting a new
covenant but continuing and adding *torah* to an already established covenant. The Lord already cut the Abrahamic covenant in Genesis 15. The
terminological usage in Genesis 17 *is* somewhat analogous to Genesis 9
where, however, the idiom כרת ברית was avoided for the reason noted
(namely, the covenant was not *cut* because it is not a covenant from which
one can be *cut off*) and the other idioms were used instead. Thus the *reason* for the use of the other idioms in Genesis 17 is *partly* different from
the reason for their use in Genesis 6–8 and it is important here to make
a distinction: the terms are used in the Noahic materials to indicate that
the Lord is going to "carry out" and "go on giving" or "sustain" a covenant
that he will implicitly soon make (although he will make the covenant
without using the idiom "to cut a covenant"); the terms are used in Genesis 17 to indicate that the Lord will continue to "give" and "carry out" the
Abrahamic covenant that *was* "cut" in Genesis 15. Once again, the terms
do not in and of themselves mean a covenant is being *renewed*. In fact,
as we shall see, those terms are not subsequently used of any covenant
renewal. Moreover, for clarity's sake we will henceforth in most cases
use other translations for those phrases. We will translate the phrase נתן
ברית in a way one might call more literal, namely, "to give/go on giving
covenant"; we will usually translate the phrase הקים ברית "to carry out/put
into effect/sustain covenant" and only occasionally, when it seems more
fitting, "to confirm covenant" (i.e., to reaffirm commitment to, although
not legally to renew).[12] We will see that to continue "to give" or "to carry
out" an already existing covenant does not mean ipso facto, and by the
terminology alone, to renew it. The Noahic covenant does in fact renew
the Adamic covenant but the terminology does not prove that fact.

As was noted, Genesis 17 does *not* renew the Abrahamic covenant but
only continues to "give" it and sustain it. Moreover, Genesis 17 not only
repeats material from Genesis 15 (see chap. 4) but also adds supplemental

---

12   Some weeks after writing the above I was pleased to receive a freshly published
article that understood these phrases in a similar way (although without exploring them
throughout the OT, and as a subordinate point in the context of a study with a different
area of concern); cf. David Andrew Dean, "Covenant, Conditionality, and Consequence:
New Terminology and a Case Study in the Abrahamic Covenant" *JETS* 57, no. 2 (2014):
298–301.

torah to the Abrahamic covenant cut in Genesis 15. We note once more
that the same phraseology can be used in the Noahic materials and in
Genesis 17, because in both cases the issue is one of sustaining or putting
into effect a covenant. The following display makes the terminological
parallels between the Noahic covenant material and the Abrahamic clear:

Covenant	Idiom	Occurrence
Noahic	נתן ברית	Genesis 9:12
	הקים ברית	Genesis 6:18; 9:9, 11, 17
Abrahamic	נתן ברית	Genesis 17:2
	הקים ברית	Genesis 17:7, 19, 21

The idioms seem to be used interchangeably in both narratives—that
is, they seem to carry much the same force. We might add that although
we do not think the idioms are ever used of a covenant renewal, their use
in the Noahic corpus does perhaps carry the nuance that, in the covenant
the Lord has in view with Noah, the Lord will continue to "give" (נתן)—
that is, will in some ways continue to render effective (הקים)—what was
provided in its precursor, the Adamic covenant, to which allusion was
made in Genesis 9:1–3. The way Genesis 9:1–3 echoes Genesis 1:28 points
in this direction. It should also be noted that only one of these verbs is
used in the perfect in these materials and that is הקים: "This is the sign
of the covenant which I have put into force between myself and all flesh
which is on the earth" (Gen. 9:17, author's translation). After saying he
would do so (Gen. 9:9, 11), the Lord finally says he has done so. There is
no covenant "cutting" here but the Lord has now rendered the promised
(and articulated) covenant effective—that is, "put it into force" or "set it
in motion."[13]

We find subsequently in the special grace covenants, that the Lord
first cuts a covenant and then, once that covenant has come into existence—been "cut"—as a legal entity, the Lord puts it into effect. This is
logically the case with any of the covenants just as with any treaty or
contract: The treaty or contract may have been drawn up and signed by
the participating parties, but only once that has happened can the treaty
or contract go into effect. It is only a theoretical (though in the abstract

---

13   It follows that the Lord made only one, and not two, covenants with Noah. The
Lord promises a covenant in Genesis 6:18, and puts it into force or makes it a reality in
Genesis 9.

legal) entity until someone puts it into effect—in other words begins to carry out its provisions.

Such is the case with the Abrahamic covenant. The Lord tells Abram, "My covenant is with you" (בריתי אתך, Gen. 17:4), and this is consistent with the covenant's having been cut in Genesis 15:18. The idioms noted above, then, and used in Genesis 17, have the sense that the Lord commits himself to putting into effect (Gen. 17:7, 19, 21) and sustaining (*continuing* to "give," Gen. 17:2) the covenant that is "with" Abram because it has already been cut.[14] In this regard we translate the phrase ואתנה בריתי in Genesis 17:2 as "I will *give/continue to give* my covenant between me and you" instead of the way it is usually translated, for example, "I will *make* my covenant between me and you" (emphasis added). As will be seen, this more literal translation of the verb נתן is consistent throughout the Old Testament and can help clarify matters where it occurs with regard to a covenant, as in the case just considered.

If one looks further ahead one sees that the new covenant promise in Jeremiah uses neither of the idioms noted above but rather uses the phrase כרת ברית ('to cut a covenant") throughout:

> "The days are coming," declares the LORD,
>   "when I will make a new covenant
> with the people of Israel
>   and with the people of Judah.
> It will not be like the covenant
>   I made with their ancestors
> when I took them by the hand
>   to lead them out of Egypt,
> because they broke my covenant,
>   though I was a husband to them,"
> declares the LORD.
> "This is the covenant I will make with the people of Israel
>   after that time," declares the LORD.
> "I will put my law in their minds
>   and write it on their hearts.

---

14   One might think analogously of the *continuing* "filling" with the Spirit that occurs under the new covenant; cf. Ephesians 5:18, where the "filling" with the Spirit is an ongoing aspect of believers' lives, and a repeated effecting of the blessing of the covenant as God continues dynamically to work in us.

> I will be their God,
>> and they will be my people.
> No longer will they teach their neighbor,
>> or say to one another, 'Know the LORD,'
> because they will all know me,
>> from the least of them to the greatest,"
> declares the LORD.
> "For I will forgive their wickedness
>> and will remember their sins no more." (Jer. 31:31–34)

The covenant cutting idiom (כרת ברית) is used in this passage with regard to two covenants: the Mosaic covenant (which the Lord cut with his people in the past, v. 32) and the new covenant (which he will cut with his people at some indefinite time in the future, vv. 31, 33). It would be consistent with usage of כרת ברית in the Old Testament if the new covenant promised in Jeremiah 31 were indeed a new covenant and not (as some have argued) a renewal of the Mosaic covenant. However, as our survey will show, the idiom alone is not sufficient to prove that point. The promise of Jeremiah will be discussed later when we take up adumbrations of the new covenant that emanate from the Mosaic covenant and subsequent writings of the prophets of the old covenant.

Before departing the discussion of covenant cutting, however, we note that the use of the idioms for covenant institution ("cutting") and ongoing covenant effecting ("giving," "carrying out," etc.) in the rest of the Old Testament is consistent with what has been seen thus far. A survey of the idioms under special gracewill show that the verb כרת ("to cut") is used either when a previously nonexistent covenant is created or when a previously existent covenant is being renewed—much like the situation in the ancient Near East in which a suzerain renews a treaty with the son of a departed vassal king. The Moab covenant (i.e., Deuteronomy) is such a renewal vis-à-vis the Sinai covenant (and thus Deut. 29:1 uses כרת for the creation of the renewal covenant). By contrast, the verbs נתן ("to give") and הקים ("to carry out") are used when the *ongoing giving* or *carrying out* (i.e., continuing to "realize"—make real and effective) of *an already existing covenant* is in view. A few other verbs are also used infrequently in connection with covenant institution, for example, שים ("to place," "set") and בא ("to enter into"). These matters are taken up more fully in chapter 5.

CONDITIONALITY AND UNCONDITIONALITY

Before we turn from the common grace covenants to the special grace covenantal program that starts with Abram—and as we stand at the figurative hinge of both sets of covenants—it seems opportune to take up the subject of conditionality and unconditionality with respect to all of these covenants, both common grace and special grace. We have already briefly raised the issue when discussing the Adamic covenant (vol. 1, chap. 2), and will raise it again when we discuss the Abrahamic and Davidic covenants (chap. 4 of this volume), but now we consider an overview of both types of covenant with respect to this one issue.

First Point: No Divine-Human Covenant Is without Conditions

The first point to make or rather restate is that *there is no divine-human covenant without conditions*. Positively, both the Adamic and the Noahic covenants *command* what has been called the "cultural mandate." Negatively, both have a death penalty consequent upon specified actions (the eating of the fruit, the shedding of human blood). As has been noted, however, the general "death penalty" of the Adamic covenant, though it continues until the eschaton (i.e., we all die), does not mean exclusion from the covenant for humanity, who continue to live under it. There is therefore no condition whose breaking means termination of the covenant. Adam broke the command, but the covenant continued. The same is true for all the subsequent covenants: none of them is conditional in the sense that breaking them terminates the covenant. In other words, the continuation of the covenants does not depend on the vassal's faithfulness. But under the special grace covenants, the *vassal's* continuation in the covenant *is* conditional upon his or her obedience to the covenant. In the general sense stated above, then, all the divine-human covenants are conditional.

The evidence confirms this understanding. Since all of these covenants continued for some time despite the sinful behavior of those under them, their continuance does not seem to have been conditional upon the behavior of those vassals. According to the usual understanding (with which we here take issue), they should thus be termed "unconditional." Again, the Adamic and Noahic covenants continue to this day, although people are abusing their trust under those covenants, and while people continue to be fruitful and multiply, the bloodshed of humans abounds.

Second Point: How Conditions Affect Covenant Membership

There is no question, therefore, whether or not a particular covenant contains conditions, since they all do. The point is whether or not those conditions—or rather the violation of them—affects membership in the covenant community and the answer for the common grace covenants is different from the answer for the special grace covenants. It is clear under the Adamic covenant that one can break the covenant yet go on living under its blessings, as the cases of Adam and Eve, Cain, Lamech, etc., all illustrate—they continued to rule (that is at the very least they prevailed in their fallen environment to the extent that they could survive and function) and to be fruitful and multiply. And this is not because the Lord renewed the Adamic covenant (before Noah) for he did not: God's entry into the Garden after the Fall involved neither a covenant termination nor a covenant renewal but rather a judicial inquiry and judgment process—not a covenant but a *covenant lawsuit*—with the added grace that the Lord would not summarily execute them but rather sustain them so they could continue to carry out the cultural mandate he gave them under the Adamic covenant, a covenant the Lord still kept in force, although he would also later renew it with Noah.

We reiterate the principle that one may violate a condition of one of these two covenants and yet not be excluded from membership in it. The Adamic and Noahic covenants, or as we have said the common grace legal package formed by them, will continue to the end. Although individuals violate those covenants every day, the human race is not excluded from membership—until the eschaton, when all of them are unfaithful/break the covenant (Luke 18:8), and the Lord puts an end to those covenants (Isaiah 24) because there is no point in sustaining them any longer.[15] No one can be cut off from membership in the Adamic + Noahic covenant complex or package as we have called it until that person dies. A person's death fulfills the curse ("You shall surely die") but until then the person may—all people may—continue to live under the covenant package and know the covenantal blessings just as Cain did—the first to shed human blood.

The special grace covenants however are another matter. As has been

---

15   The Lord sustains them until the eschaton so they can continue to provide a common grace context in which the last and consummate special grace covenant—the new covenant—can continue to operate. Once faith is no longer present (Luke 18:8), no one can be saved and the purpose for continuing the common grace package thus no longer exists, so the Lord terminates it and brings a new heaven and a new earth.

noted, a member of any of those covenants can be "cut off" from covenant membership, and that is the point of applying the idiom, "to cut a covenant," to those covenants only, and not to the common grace covenants.

Third Point: All of God's Covenants Are Unconditional

We have said all the Lord's covenants are conditional. However, all the Lord's covenants are also *unconditional*. Let us take the Mosaic and Davidic covenants as examples. We know the Mosaic covenant continued until the new covenant was cut, in spite of much Israelite covenant breaking and ensuing covenantal judgments. Likewise, the Davidic covenant continued until the new covenant was cut, in spite of the failure and even outright rebelliousness of some individual kings. Such data evidence a principle already noted: God will continue any covenant he has made for as long as is necessary for that covenant to fulfill God's purpose(s) for it. In that sense, every divine-human covenant is unconditional.

"Conditional" and "unconditional," therefore, are unfortunate terms for any of these covenants because the terms are not adequately descriptive and can be misleading. None of the covenants is purely conditional or purely unconditional. All contain conditions—and thus could be called conditional— and yet they all continued for some time (and the Adamic and Noahic still do) in spite of the failure of some vassals to meet the conditions—and so they could be called unconditional. With regard to the special grace covenants, although individuals may drop out of—be "cut off" from—membership in the covenant community because they failed to meet the conditions of the covenant, the covenant itself goes on and will continue until it has accomplished what the Lord purposes to accomplish with it because the Lord will sustain it.

Finally, regarding covenant terminology, we note that the idiom "to cut a covenant" has to do with individual membership in a special grace covenant and not with the conditionality or lack of conditionality of any special grace covenant, since God will keep any special grace covenant going as long as he wants—no matter who sins and is because of sinning "cut off" from membership in the covenant.

GOD ACTS: THE CALL OF ABRAM

With the principle firmly in place that the terminology "to cut a covenant" distinguishes the inception of the Old Testament special grace covenants from all prior covenantal history—the time before Genesis 15 when there were only the common grace covenants—the legal nature of God's call on Abram in Genesis 12 can be properly understood.[16] Since God is suzerain over all the earth, he has every right to call upon Abram and make of him any requirements or promise any blessings the Lord may choose. All of that is true for God and Abram under the legal arrangement that prevailed over the world in Abram's day as it does in ours: the creation and re-creation covenants that formed and form one legal package under which all humanity continue to exist, conduct their affairs, and are daily and ultimately accountable to God for everything, whether they know it or admit it or not.

So when the Lord spoke to Abram and gave him commands in Genesis 12, he had every right to do so under the already existing covenants. His commands do not for a moment imply that an Abrahamic covenant had suddenly come into existence. But God's action does institute the first step of the Major Paradigm with regard to the process that will result in the Abrahamic covenant. The Lord commands and he makes a promise: "Leave your country, your people and your father's household and go to the land I will show you" (Gen. 12:1). When the Lord says these things he begins to lay the proximate historical foundation for the covenant that he will soon create with Abram. In anticipation of Abram's obedient response, the Lord also makes some promises that are full of covenantal overtones:

> I will make you a great nation
> and I will bless you;
> I will make your name great,
> and—Be a blessing!
> I will bless those who bless you,
> and whoever curses you I will curse;
> and all peoples on earth
> will be blessed through you. (Gen. 12:2–3, author's translation)

---

16   Obviously, and as we have already seen in Jeremiah 31:32, the idiom "to cut a covenant" can also be used not only for the inception of a covenant when that inception is a new event, but also to refer back to the inception/institution of a particular covenant in Israel's past. This is true of references to the institution of the Mosaic covenant and, as will be seen, of the Davidic covenant.

The scope of these promises is global and that is appropriate in the aftermath of the Tower of Babel episode. The Lord promises to make Abram's name great and the promise is an ironic echo of the ambition of Babel, whose tower builders wanted to "make a name" for themselves (Gen. 11:4). The Lord will also make Abram's descendants a "great nation," which ironically echoes the goal of national cohesion and greatness also aimed at by the tower builders. The builders of Babel aimed for things that Christ will bring to pass—a great and unified people with a direct connection to heaven—but they aimed in a way contrary to the way of Christ. Theirs was the way of human ambition and self-exaltation, the opposite of yieldedness to God and his purposes. The Lord's way is different, and he will use Abram and his covenant with him to begin the work of special grace that will accomplish those goals. The Lord will see to it that "all peoples on earth will be blessed through" Abram. That blessing will undo the dispersion of peoples according to different languages that took place as God's judgment on the tower builders. God's judgment undid them and sent them into a dispersion that has become worldwide. But the Lord's provision through Abram will work to reunite a dispersed humanity into the Abrahamic household, the household of faith (cf. Gal. 6:10). Since the Abrahamic promise is, as Paul later identifies it, the promise of the Spirit, one sees here implicitly the promise of Pentecost.

On a related and important note, it is no small matter in this passage that the Lord not only promises to bless Abram and make his name great, he also commands Abram to be a blessing (Gen. 12:2). Translators normally render the phrase in question "and you will be a blessing." However, the Hebrew verb is in the imperative and there is no scribal error. The Lord is not simply telling Abram that he *will* be a blessing, although he does that in effect ("all peoples on earth will be blessed through you," Gen. 12:3). The Lord is commanding Abram to *be* a blessing. In other words, he is saying: "Abram, I am blessing you; therefore you go, and be a blessing to others." The command establishes henceforth a firm biblical principle for human conduct that we should bless others as we are blessed.[17]

---

17 For example, Jesus instructs his disciples as he sends them forth to do the works he has been doing, "Freely you have received, freely give" (Matt. 10:8); and Paul writes of "the God of all comfort, who comforts us in all our troubles, so that we can comfort those in any trouble with the comfort we ourselves have received from God" (2 Cor. 1:3–4).

THE PROMISE OF LAND

Abram obeys God and takes his family and possessions with him to Canaan. His obedience is an act of faith, and as such it has him doing what the Father is doing. The Lord appears to him there, and this appearance is the first theophany described as such since God approached the man and the woman in the Garden as part of his judicial or covenant lawsuit process. When the Lord appears to Abram, he makes an important declaration: "To your offspring I will give this land" (Gen. 12:7). The Lord makes this promise to Abram and his offspring and fulfills it through Moses and Joshua. At the moment, however, it is only a promise. It is one of the events that form the historical background of God's dealing with Abram, a background to which the Lord will allude when he makes his covenant with Abram in Genesis 15. It may be significant that the Lord speaks (in the Hebrew imperfect): "To your offspring I *will give* this land." It is a promise, just like all of the promises of Genesis 12:2–3 but, just like those promises, it is not yet a *blessing of the covenant*, since the Abrahamic covenant does not yet exist. Later when the Lord cuts the covenant with Abram, he says (in the Hebrew perfect), "To your descendants I *give* this land" (Gen. 15:18). The perfect can also be translated "I *have given*," which is to say, "Now that you and I are in covenant, Abram, the land is as good as yours. Even though you do not yet possess it I have now given it to you." In other words, the imperfect is used when the statement is only a promise for the future; the perfect is used once the promise is anchored in the context of an established covenant at which moment the promise becomes, not the *promise* of a blessing, but a blessing. Moreover, at that time the blessing is unconditional for a reason to be examined below.[18]

ABRAM'S ALTAR

Abram builds an altar "to the Lord, who had appeared to him" (Gen. 12:7). This is not the first altar on biblical record, since Noah built an altar to the Lord apparently as an act of thanksgiving for his deliverance through the Flood (Gen. 8:20). But Abram's altar, the second on record, follows and commemorates a theophany, and the same is true of many

---

18   We will discuss this and the role of Genesis 12:1–3 in the overall context of the Abrahamic covenant narrative in chapter 4, which takes up the unity of the Abrahamic covenant.

subsequent altars built to the Lord by, for example, Abraham on Moriah (Gen. 22:9), Isaac at Beersheba (Gen. 26:25), and Jacob at Bethel (Gen. 35:1, 3, 7). Other altars built by the patriarchs also commemorate the Lord in some way, often with the accompanying statement that he "called on the name of the Lord," for example, Abram at Bethel (Gen. 12:8) and at Hebron (Gen. 13:18), Isaac at Beersheba (Gen. 26:25), and Jacob at Shechem (Gen. 33:20). The patriarchs built these altars in memory of the Lord and/or to "call upon his name." They served as places of offering and thanksgiving at a time when there was no temple presence of the Lord. That temple presence would not come until the Mosiac covenant, at which time what we have called the Major Paradigm would find full expression in the Lord's warfare against Egypt, his liberation of and establishment of a people for himself in a new covenantal relationship, and the concomitant establishment of a tabernacle or temple so that he might dwell among his people.[19]

ABRAM'S RUSE

Abram and Sarai go to Egypt to avoid a famine in Canaan and so begins the peculiar history of relationships between Egypt and God's covenant people. The passage is famous for Abram's ruse by which he has Sarai tell the Egyptians that she is his sister, which is half true since she is his half-sister (Gen. 20:12). The half that remains untold of course is that she is also Abram's wife. Abram will later try the same ruse on Abimelech (Genesis 20), and we will have more to say on the topic, including the morality of his deceptions, when we discuss Abraham's sojourn in Gerar.[20] For now it is enough to note the deception, and note also that it had beneficial results for the patriarch: Pharaoh treats Abram well for Sarai's sake and Abram acquires cattle, maidservants and menservants, and camels (Gen. 12:16; cf.13:1).

Abram's sojourn in Egypt entails circumstances and events that foreshadow Israel's experience in Egypt. We note them here but also note that such foreshadowings are not what scholars call "types." The usual treatment of a type-antitype relationship assumes that the Old Testament provides the type (e.g., the Conquest) and the New Testament provides

---

19 Cf. discussion in chapters 6–8.

20 Cf. also Abraham's statement to Abimelech (Gen. 20:13) and the issue of historiography and laconic reporting noted in volume 1, chapter 3.

the antitype (e.g., the Lord's return in judgment, as in Revelation 19). On such an understanding of typology, any Old Testament event or circumstance that foreshadows or is paralleled by another Old Testament event or circumstance is not called a type and the event or circumstance that parallels it is not called an antitype. This convention is not as arbitrary as it may seem since it rests on the fact that the relevant terminology only occurs in the New Testament: Paul speaks of Adam as "a pattern of the one to come" (Rom. 5:14), that is, of Christ or the second Adam, and the word translated "pattern" is the Greek *tupos,* from which our word "type" derives. So New Testament parlance itself establishes the concept of typology (as an OT entity foreshadowing a NT entity) and in this case more specifically establishes the concept of Christology (which is a Christ-specific category of typology) in which Adam foreshadows Christ. Consequently, when one event or circumstance foreshadows another within the Old Testament, one rests content by convention to say that such foreshadowing does not constitute a typological relationship, and one reserves that category for Old Testament adumbrations of New Testament events or circumstances. But again, this is only a matter of convention. The wittiness of God who is outside time and who orchestrates and uses history according to his purpose is behind such parallels in one way or another whether they occur within one Testament or between two Testaments.

Geerhardus Vos rightly observed that typology (the type-antitype relationship) and Christology (the type-antitype relationship as it applies to an OT individual and Christ, e.g., Adam or Moses as a type of Christ) are forms of prophecy.[21] The same may or may not be claimed for parallel realtionships that take place short of the New Testament, that is, within the Old Testament. But even if such adumbrations are not prophetic, they indicate certain thematic recurrences within the flow of Old Testament history. This appears to be the case when one considers the parallels between Abram's experience in Egypt and Israel's later experience there. The parallels may be displayed as follows:

Abrahamic Example	Mosaic Example
Abram and family go to Egypt	Jacob and family go to Egypt
Pharaoh treats Abram well	Pharaoh treats Jacob well

---

21   Cf. Geerhardus Vos, *Biblical Theology: Old and New Testaments* (Grand Rapids: Eerdmans, 1948), 144–45.

Abrahamic Example	Mosaic Example
for Sarai's sake	for Joseph's sake
The Lord afflicts Pharaoh and	The Lord afflicts Pharaoh and
his household with diseases	Egypt with diseases/plagues
for wrong bearing toward Sarai	for wrong bearing toward Israel
Pharaoh releases Abram	Pharaoh releases Israel
and family	
(ultimately, to go to Canaan)	(ultimately, to go to Canaan)
Abram leaves Egypt wealthy	Israel leaves Egypt wealthy

Along with Vos and probably most scholars, we would not call this set of parallels typological although the individual experience of Abram and his family anticipates the corporate experience of his descendants, Israel, in noteworthy detail. Such correspondences do occur within the flow of history. A notable example from our own nation is the set of parallels between the assassinations of Presidents Lincoln and Kennedy and the circumstances surrounding both events. One is not a type or forecast of the other, yet the parallels exist and are as remarkable as those between Abram and Israel displayed above.[22] The best category for understanding such parallels is apparently the Lord's providential orchestration of history in which he does not create the parallels but allows humans to make choices that result in their creation. If this understanding is correct—and it seems to state a bare minimum on which agreement could be found—it would apparently follow that humans think and choose in ways that will tend to repeat themselves under similar conditions and circumstances. One might consider in this regard the oft-quoted saying by George Santayana that "those who cannot remember the past are condemned to repeat it."[23] After the Second World War that saying seemed (and may still seem) to contain much wisdom but it may not be as wise as it sounds since it is also true that those who *do* know their history may be forced to see it repeated. Human nature does not change, so human choices will continue to create parallels within history, and the fact that some people know what has happened in the past can be no guarantee that the same or similar things will not happen in the

---

22 For parallels, cf. http://historynewsnetwork.org/article/1109.
23 George Santayana, *Life of Reason* (New York: Scribner's, 1905), 284.

future—nor indeed that those who know the past may not *do* the same things anyway. Knowledge alone is not power—or at least, knowledge held by some individuals is not ipso facto power sufficient to prevent what they or other individuals choose to do.[24]

LOT'S CHOICE

The story of the quarrel between the herdsmen of Lot and Abram and of Lot's choice to dwell near the cities of the plain is well known. The nature of his choice is less well understood. One may call it a combination of divine providence and human free will—a combination that in its very nature is beyond the comprehension of fallen intellects. Both the human nature of his choice and God's providential presence in the background are apparent from the brief narrative of Genesis 13:5–17.

The most striking thing about the choice Lot makes may be that Abram invites him to make it. That is, Abram offers Lot a completely free choice, whether he will choose Canaan to the west or the region of Sodom and Gomorrah to the east: "Is not the whole land before you? Let's part company. If you go to the left, I'll go to the right; if you go to the right, I'll go to the left" (Gen. 13:9). How can Abram make such a generous offer? How can he resign his own preference, whatever it might be, in favor of his cousin? The answer may be found in two all-important facts: The Lord has blessed Abram, and Abram has faith—that is, he amens God. As a blessed man and also with faith in the God who is true to his word of blessing, Abram can in turn bless his cousin Lot. So we have the first report of Abram's obedience to the Lord's command "Be a blessing" (Gen. 12:2). Abram demonstrates implicitly here the truth of faith, that "faith is the assurance of things hoped for, the substance of things unseen" (Heb. 11:1). Abram trusts the Lord to fulfill the promise of land he has made to Abram's offspring (Gen. 12:7). He is thereby set free from the insecurity that shores itself up by whatever means by not grasping at the land for himself, but trusting God to dispose of it according to his providence.

That providence works itself out through Lot's choice. Lot is given complete freedom to choose what real estate he will. He chooses the land to the east, which leaves Canaan, the land to the west, open to Abram in prospect. Once the choice is made and Lot has departed, the Lord speaks to Abram and repeats his earlier promise to him:

---

24   If one wanted proof of such a fact one need look no further than Romans 7:14–20!

Lift up your eyes from where you are and look north, south, east and west. All the land that you see I will give to you and your offspring forever. I will make your offspring like the dust of the earth, so that if anyone could count the dust, then your offspring could be counted. Go, walk through the length and breadth of the land, for I am giving it to you. (Gen. 13:14–17)

The Lord not only repeats his promise to Abram, he adds to it. In Genesis 12:7 he promised to give the land to Abram's offspring; now, he promises to give it to him. The promise is not only figurative. Abram does in fact acquire some of the promised land, although only a small part and through purchase. Nonetheless, it is an earnest of what is to come. Another part of the Lord's promise is less clear. He promises to give the land to Abram and his offspring "forever." This term has been encountered and discussed before in connection with the Noahic covenant. There it was noted that the Hebrew term (עוֹלָם) did not mean "forever" in context but rather, "very long lasting," or the like. The same evaluation applies here inasmuch as here again the land in question will be replaced when the Lord establishes a "new heavens and a new earth." At that time the territory known anciently as Canaan and more recently as Palestine will no longer exist. Or if it does exist, and if the heavenly Jerusalem is located in it, it will only exist as a part of a completely new creation and thus not literally the land that Abram's descendants inherited. One may find appealing, here, Lewis's portrayal of a new "heavens and earth" that appear to be constantly renewing and become better and more pure—Platonic idea behind Platonic idea, to put it in terms of a common grace intimation—in *The Last Battle*, the final, eschatological novel of his *Narnia* series.[25] If Lewis to whom some have, understandably and pardonably, referred as "the thirteenth apostle," is anywhere near correct, one may anticipate such an "ideal" Canaan with a heavenly Jerusalem as the center of government in a new heavens and a new earth. But it will be a new heavens and a *new* earth and not the old, and certainly not the old Canaan or Palestine.[26]

The Lord also makes another promise to Abram: he will make his

25 Cf. C. S. Lewis, *The Last Battle* (New York: Macmillan, 1956), 160–74.

26 See further discussion in chapter 10 of volume 3. One may, of course, suggest that the Lord's promise of the land "forever" is an eternal promise because it represents an idea in the mind of God (the prototype) and is fulfilled in an eschatological and imperishable counterpart—a counterpart dimly prefigured by the land of Canaan itself.

offspring like "the dust of the earth" (עֲפַר הָאָרֶץ, Gen. 13:16). The word translated "dust" here is the same word (עָפָר) used when the Lord made the man out of the "dust of the ground" (עָפָר מִן־הָאֲדָמָה, Gen. 2:7) and the phrase could be meant to be evocative. This is the first time since the Fall narrative that the word has appeared in the Old Testament, and it may evoke a memory of Genesis 2, in which man is made of dust, and Genesis 3, in which the Lord tells him he will return to the dust from which he was made. If present, the allusion suggests that Abram's offspring—also made of dust—will be as numerous as the dust of the ground. This may be an example of the sort of wordplay and allusion not uncommon in the Pentateuch or later Old Testament books.[27]

ABRAM TREADS ON THE LAND

The Lord's final word to Abram after Lot parts from him is an instruction to "walk through the length and breadth of the land," for he says, "I am giving it to you" (Gen. 13:17). The statement forms part of the background to Genesis 15:18–20, in which the Lord tells Abram in greater detail just what land it is and whom he will have to dispossess in order to fulfill the promise. There are two salient features to the Lord's statement, one of them clear, the other symbolic.

The clear statement is, "I am giving it to you." The Hebrew verb is actually in the imperfect, so that the better translation reads, "I will give it to you." In any case, the theological content of the statement would have been clear to any ancient near eastern person. That is, the Lord would "give" Abram the land according to a particular mechanism: the mechanism of conquest (this remains true even though as was noted the gift of the land was stated in the perfect at Gen. 15:18 as evidence that once the covenant was established the gift of land was considered by God a *fait accompli*). When a god in the ancient world "gave" land to a king he usually "gave" it by such means: the god's gift to the king amounted to a mandate for conquest. And as Cyrus Gordon has pointed out, Abram had the status of a "king" in ancient Canaan, with an "army" of his own, which as we know was able to disrupt an allied force of easterners effectively

---

27 Cf. the term in Proverbs 8:26 and discussion by Duane Garrett, *Proverbs* (Nashville: B&H, 1993), 109.

enough to rescue Lot and his family from their clutches (Gen. 14).[28] One later learns that Abram's descendants will be the ones to carry out this conquest mandate. But it is given to him as head of the household that will conquer.

The symbolic part of the Lord's utterance has to do with Abram's walking the length and breadth of the land. The implicit symbolism would probably be obvious to a reader of any generation: the right to walk around on some land could easily be understood as a right possessed by the one who owned the land. That is the symbolism and it partakes of a larger symbolic complex, which includes such symbolic gestures as Joshua's command that his men put their feet on the necks of the five captured kings at Makkedah (Josh. 10:24), a gesture known to have been practiced by the Assyrians as well. The symbolic complex also includes the Lord's promise to David's Lord that he will "make your enemies a footstool for your feet" (Ps. 110:1). Another and closely related example is the gesture of handing over the sandal as a symbol of transferring real estate, as in Boaz's deal with the kinsman-redeemer in the book of Ruth where we read: "In earlier times in Israel, for the redemption and transfer of property to become final, one party took of his sandal and gave it to the other. This was the manner of legalizing transactions in Israel" (Ruth 4:7). The sandal in this case stood for the foot of the man who wore it and symbolized his right as owner to walk on the property. The kinsman-redeemer transfers the right and thus the property to Boaz. Consequently, when the Lord tells Abram to walk the length and breadth of the land he is calling for a symbolic action that says Abram (in the persons of his descendants) will come into ownership of that land and have the right to walk freely on it.[29] This is the first of a number of symbolic actions the Lord commands his prophets. Another is his command to Jeremiah to buy land symbolic of a future restoration in the face of a seemingly irreversible Babylonian onslaught (Jer. 32), and his commands to Ezekiel to undergo actions symbolic of the future siege of Jerusalem and the Lord's own future sin-bearing (Ezek. 4), and to shave his head with a sword and divide the hairs into three portions as a symbol of the Lord's looming threefold judgment against his people (Ezek. 5).

---

28 Cf. Cyrus Gordon, *The Common Background of Greek and Hebrew Civilizations* (New York: Norton, 1965), 288–89.

29 Cf. Niehaus, *ANETBT*, 66–68.

GOD WAGES WAR THROUGH A PROPHET:
ABRAM AND THE WORLD-CONQUERING ARMY

The next steps in the Major Paradigm are God's warfare by his Spirit through a prophet. Although Abram is not called a prophet until Genesis 20:7, the fact God has revealed himself to him and spoken with him makes it clear that he is a prophet, and Genesis 15 will make it clear that he is a covenant mediator prophet.

Abram's warfare as a prophet involves his rescue of Lot from an armed alliance that apparently included forces of Hammurapi (the "Amraphel" of Gen. 14:1, 9).[30] Amraphel was king of Shinar (i.e., Babylonia) and was allied with four other kings (Gen. 14:1, 9) in war against the kings of Sodom and Gomorrah and their allies (Gen. 14:1–12). The eastern coalition defeats the kings of the west, and seizes the goods and food of Sodom and Gomorrah and also takes Lot and his possessions (Gen. 14:11–12).

When Abram hears that Lot has been taken captive he musters "318 trained men born in his household" and goes in pursuit (Gen. 14:14). He apparently plans a nighttime attack on two flanks: "During the night Abram divided his men to attack them, and he routed them" (Gen. 14:15). We also read: "He recovered all the goods and brought back his relative Lot and his possessions, together with the women and the other people" (Gen. 14:16). The narrative introduces new data at this point—this is the first time we have read of "people" other than Lot taken captive—and this is not the first case of supplemental data provided in subsequent narrative regarding an event. It is left unclear whether "the women and the other people" are only those of Lot's household, or other people of Sodom and Gomorrah generally.

What is not ambiguous is that Abram planned and executed a successful attack against the allied forces. How large were forces he engaged? Hermann Gunkel, with his lamentable but consistent skepticism about the historicity of biblical, and especially patriarchal, narratives, remarked that a force of 318 men does not defeat "a world-conquering army."[31] One

---

30   Abram was a prophet and he was waging war. We suggest that he had the wisdom to do so by the Spirit. Cf. Melchizedek's later statement to Abram, that the Creator God "delivered your enemies into your hand" (Gen. 14:20). Cf. the discussion of the Spirit and gifting in volume 1 of *Biblical Theology*, 138–53.

31   Hermann Gunkel, *Genesis: Übersetzt und Erklärt* (Göttingen: Vandenhoeck & Ruprecht, 1901); English translation by William Herbert Carruth, *The Legends of Genesis* (Chicago: The Open Court Publishing Company, 1901), 8.

may agree that such a feat is highly unlikely, although Gideon later defeats a large allied force of "Midianites, Amalekites, and other eastern peoples" (Judg. 6:33) with only 300 men in another nocturnal attack, thus showing the military advantage that good tactics and the element of surprise can confer on a small band attacking a much larger force (Judg. 7). However, *pace* Gunkel, there is no way of actually knowing how many people Abram's force "routed." He may not have attacked the whole allied army but only a detachment that had control of some goods and captives, including Lot and his possessions. It is better not to embrace a reconstruction that favors only one interpretive possibility but has no *unambiguous* data to support it.

BY HIS SPIRIT, FEW DEFEAT MANY: ABRAM'S SUCCESSFUL WARFARE

Gunkel's idea does resonate, however. Abram was taking on a formidable force when he set out with only 318 men to liberate his captured cousin. He had no way of knowing how much of the eastern army he would have to engage. Nonetheless, he did engage them successfully, and it would not be unreasonable biblically to see the Spirit involved as the source of the military wisdom of his stratagem and its success.

The Lord has chosen at various points in history to accomplish important victories for his kingdom advance by using what is small or weak relative to the opposing force, as the following brief list illustrates:

1. Abraham rescues Lot and others, defeating some forces of the much larger eastern coalition with 318 men of his own household.
2. Moses defeats Egypt, one of the world's most powerful empires of the day, singlehandedly as the Lord works through him.
3. Joshua and Israel defeat Canaanite forces that are numerically and technologically superior.
4. Gideon defeats a superior force of Midianites with 300 men.
5. The apostles frustrate those superior in number and institutional power who would suppress the gospel, and win some 3,000 new subjects for the kingdom in one day.

Such examples—perhaps especially when viewed together—have much to teach. For now we note they all illustrate a principle later expressed by Paul, that "the foolishness of God is wiser than human

wisdom, and the weakness of God is stronger than human strength"
(1 Cor. 1:25), and again, "God chose the lowly things of this world and
the despised things—and the things that are not—to nullify the things
that are, so that no one may boast before him" (1 Cor. 1:28–29).

ADUMBRATION OF ABRAM'S WARFARE

Abram's warfare symbolically anticipates a later warfare. Abram is a
prophet who wages war against the forces of Babylon and her allies. He
rescues some people taken captive by Babylonian forces. The New Testament parallels are obvious. Christ is a prophet who wages war against
Babylon and her allies. He rescues people who had been taken captive
by her, and he uses numerically smaller forces to do so (cf. item 5 above).
The parallel is symbolically understood, since Babylon is a figure for
the world dominating enterprise of Satan, not only in Revelation 17 but
transtemporally.[32]

ABRAM AND MELCHIZEDEK

After Abram's successful foray he meets with the king of Sodom and with
Melchizedek, king of Salem. The king of Sodom's generously offers the
recaptured goods to Abram, but Abram refuses: "I have raised my hand to
the LORD, God Most High, Creator of heaven and earth, and have taken
an oath that I will accept nothing belonging to you, not even a thread or
the thong of a sandal, so that you will never be able to say, 'I have made
Abram rich'" (Gen. 14:22–23).

The first and perhaps most important part of this declaration is the
fact that Abram identifies the Lord (Hebrew, "Yahweh") to the king of
Sodom: He affirms that Yahweh is God Most High and Creator of heaven
and earth. The implication is that, by this time, people have largely forgotten the name and person of the true God so that when he is named
to a pagan he must also be identified. Abram is apparently one of the few
people on earth able to make the identification. Another is Melchizedek,
of whom we read presently. But first there are some other aspects of
Abram's oath that merit attention. One is the formality of raising one's
hand in oath, or in implication of an oath, which is recorded first here,

---

32 Cf. discussion in chapter 10 of volume 3.

but then subsequently in the Old Testament. The next is that Abram will not accept even "a thread or the thong of a sandal" from the king. These items have to do with clothing but may imply more. We are ultimately clothed with Christ and his righteousness. And, as we have seen, a sandal may imply the ownership of property, in which case Abram may be rejecting implicitly any offer of property ("the thong of a sandal") from the king. Or it may imply one's daily "walk," which must be provided for and led by the Lord and no human king. This is not to say one can argue for such symbolism in the passage. On the other hand, a reader sensitive to the symbolic or figurative value of these elements throughout the Bible may find such associations naturally and even inevitably coming to mind as he or she reads the account.

The feature of Genesis 14 that usually seems paramount to theologians is not the wars of the eastern coalition, however, nor the account of Abram's encounter with the king of Sodom, but the account of his encounter with Melchizedek. The reason for this preeminence is no doubt to be found in the high Christology given Melchizedek in Hebrews 7.

One should be grateful to the author of Hebrews not only for providing a book that explains the relationship between the priesthood of the old covenant and that of the new but also for providing a superlative—also the Bible's most extensive and lucid—example of Christological interpretation, all in what Origen called the author's "elegant Greek."[33]

The account first recalls that Melchizedek was "king of Salem" (Gen. 14:18). Salem is Jerusalem, and one finds the ancient name in Assyrian inscriptions as *uru shalimu*, that is, "city of peace." The author of Hebrews interprets Melchizedek's kingship of Jerusalem figuratively: as "king of Salem," Melchizedek is also ipso facto "king of peace" (Heb. 7:2). Now the phrase, "king of peace" may appropriately recall the promised child who will be "prince of peace" (Isa. 9:5), and the term used there for "prince" (שׂר) is cognate with the Akkadian word for "king" (Akk. *sharru*). As a Christological figure, Melchizedek implicitly points toward a future peace the world cannot give but which Melchizedek-Jesus will give his followers by the indwelling Spirit. That peace cannot be an absence of conflict, since Jesus has already said his followers will be blessed when they are persecuted for his sake (Matt. 5:11). Rather, the promised peace is the *soundness* produced by the Spirit as he works in believers to reform them

---

33   As quoted in Eusebius, *Church History*, 6.25.1114; cf. Alan C. Mitchell, *Hebrews* (Collegeville, MN: Liturgical Press, 2007), 2.

into the Lord's image and likeness—"new creations" in Christ (2 Cor. 5:17).

Melchizedek's name like names throughout history also has a meaning. An ancient Hebrew would probably have understood the name to mean "righteous king" or "legitimate king"—one who acquired throne and kingdom by a legitimate process of inheritance and who was not a usurper.[34] However, the construct nature of the name also makes possible another interpretation and the author of Hebrews uses it. He interprets the name as "king of righteousness" (Heb. 7:2). The interpretation suits the figure because, again, Melchizedek foreshadows Jesus who is "King of righteousness" as well as "King of peace."

Once the book of Hebrews identifies Melchizedek as a Christological figure, the door is open to recognizing an associated significance in another part of the narrative—one not discussed as such in the New Testament. Melchizedek brings out bread and wine, which he presumably shares with Abram (Gen. 14:18). The elements are barely mentioned. But the New Testament parallel of bread and wine used at the Last Supper is so apparent that to avoid it one must deliberately choose to ignore it, or else reject it as a coincidence rather than a true parallel. But there is no need to reject it. To recognize the parallel is only to take another step on the interpretive journey the author of Hebrews has already begun for us and with us. A similar parallel appears between the covenant ratifying meal Moses and the elders have on Sinai, on the one hand, and the Lord and the Last Supper the disciples have with Jesus, on the other.[35] The Last Supper may justly be called a covenant ratifying meal if only symbolically because it foreshadows a literal covenant ratification—Jesus' ratifying the new covenant with his blood. The crucifixion is the "cutting" of the new covenant that brings it into existence in human history.

Melchizedek blesses Abram and the significance of his blessing will be considered momentarily. It is first noted that Abram gave the king of (Jeru)Salem "a tenth of everything" (Gen. 14:20). The author of Hebrews uses this fact to advantage when he displays the superiority of the Melchizedek priesthood over the Aaronic or Levitical priesthood, arguing that Levi in effect paid tithes to Melchizedek (and thus to Christ), since Levi was in Abram's loins when Abram paid the tithe (Heb. 7:4–10). This logic plays a role in one's understanding of the old and new covenants and of the impermanence of the former and eternality of the latter.

---

34   Cf. volume 1 of *Biblical Theology*, chapter 6.
35   Cf. discussion in chapter 8 of this volume.

MELCHIZEDEK'S BLESSING

Melchizedek is "priest of God Most High" (Gen. 14:18). Melchizedek blesses Abram. The data form parts of an argument both for the Christology of Melchizedek and for the superiority of Melchizedek's priesthood over that of the Mosaic covenant: "Without doubt the lesser person is blessed by the greater" (Heb. 7:7). Melchizedek declares:

> Blessed be Abram by God Most High,
> Creator of heaven and earth.
> And blessed be God Most High,
> who delivered your enemies into your hand. (Gen. 14:19–20)

The blessing first identifies "God Most High" as "Creator of heaven and earth," and although the Hebrew word translated "Creator" comes from a different root (קנה, "to acquire, own") from that used in Genesis 1, the word pair, "heaven and earth" make a direct allusion to Genesis 1:1.[36] Melchizedek calls upon the Creator to bless Abram. But how shall he bless him? The answer is implied by the rest of the blessing. Melchizedek next blesses God Most High who, he tells Abram, "delivered your enemies into your hand." One may consider God's military assistance to Abram to have been a blessing and so it was, but further blessing is called for. That blessing is what follows in biblical divine-human relations (as the Major Paradigm illustrates) once God has waged war through a prophet-figure against his foes, namely, the blessing of a covenant that will set the relationship between God and the human on a new footing and open up further possibilities for development of that elective relationship.

The pattern of God's warfare followed by a covenant with a prophet through whom he waged war has already occurred in the case of Noah. That warfare brought judgment on all humanity and led to the making of the second great common grace covenant. The warfare waged by "God Most High" was, by contrast, against the enemies of Abram's household in the person of Lot and, apparently, those who were of his house. God worked redemptively for Lot through Abram; after that redemptive warfare, God will cut a covenant with Abram and, through him, with his offspring. The pattern foreshadows the ministry of Christ. God waged warfare through the ministry of his Son, whose works were warfare and

---

36 Cf. further study of the verbs for "create" in the discussion of election, foreknowledge, and predestination in chapter 7 of volume 3.

that warfare came before the covenant cutting (the crucifixion), which, however, was the penultimate act of war in his earthly ministry. That warfare was redemptive. The cross-work was redemptive and all of the Son's work before it was redemptive, whether it took the form of healing, deliverance, or his words which were Spirit and life (John 6:63). The pre-cross-work warfare was redemptive in a limited way because it set people free from a physical affliction (by healing or deliverance, e.g., from an epileptic demon) or from a spiritual affliction (e.g., from a demon or demons, as in the case of the Gadarene demoniac), or by introducing them to his words that were truth and prepared the way for the fuller new covenant revelation of truth. The ultimate act of war, the victory, was the resurrection. That victory in turn validated the cut covenant for those who are truly the offspring of Abraham, the household of faith, the Israel of God. The Abrahamic covenant and the new covenant are thus expressed by the Major Paradigm because each participates in a similar dynamic or pattern of divine redemptive activity. The Major Paradigm as it articulates the Abrahamic realities is as follows:[37]

The Major Paradigm and the Abrahamic Covenant

1	God works	Genesis 12–14
2	by his Spirit	[cf. Isa. 45:1]
3	through the Word/a prophet-figure [cf. Gen. 20:7]	Genesis 14:13–14
4	to war against and defeat his foe(s)	Genesis 14:8–16
5	God establishes a covenant with a people	Genesis 15
6	God's covenant establishes that people as God's people	Genesis 15, 17
7	God establishes a temple among his people, because he will reside among them	

The Major Paradigm takes an early or preliminary form in Abram's case because the Abrahamic covenant contains no temple presence. It is also true that the Holy Spirit is not mentioned. But as has been noted the Spirit is the one who confers authority on individuals. He conferred imperial authority on Cyrus (Isa. 45:1) and that included the authority

---

37 The Major Paradigm as it articulates the new covenant appears in chapter 1 of volume 3.

to conquer. So one may venture to say the Spirit was the one who gave Abram his success over the "world-conquering army" of Genesis 14 and probably also the one who inspired his strategy in a successful campaign against the coalition army.

The Lord goes on to cut a covenant (in some ways the center of the Major Paradigm) with Abram, and that covenant forms the subject of the next chapter. That covenant cutting is unique because it anticipates the two major covenants for the Lord's people that will establish forms of the Lord's kingdom: the Mosaic covenant (for the OT form of the kingdom) and the new covenant (for the NT form).[38]

In retrospect then the character of Genesis 12–14 is affirmed. Those chapters contain historical material regarding the Lord's dealings with Abram, including his calling from his homeland into *terra incognita*, the warfare he waged—against the king of Babylon and his allies (an adumbration of the Lord's eschatological warfare against "Babylon the Great")—to redeem members of his household, and his encounter with Melchizedek with all of its Christological implications. All these events have paradigmatic or symbolic value. Of equal importance, they furnish the historical background or foundation upon which the great Suzerain will found a special grace covenant with Abram. Genesis 12–14, however, *do not function as part of the Abrahamic covenant*, which first comes into existence in Genesis 15—any more than Exodus 1–19 function as part of the Mosaic covenant, which first comes into existence in Exodus 20. The chapters do provide a record of God's dealing with Abram before the Lord initiates a covenant with him. The record in several ways foreshadows Christ, initiator of the new and better covenant.

---

38   Also and consequently, the Mosaic covenant and the new covenant are both covenants with and for all the people. This distinguishes them from the Davidic covenant, which is a covenant with David for the royal line.

CHAPTER TWO

THE ABRAHAMIC COVENANT

W e explore now the institution and nature of the Abrahamic covenant. The events of Genesis 12–14 prepared the way for the Lord to
enact that covenant. He has shown himself to be a faithful protector and
provider for Abram—One who can aptly become his personal suzerain
in a special grace covenant relationship. He was always so *in potentia*
but has now shown himself to be so to his chosen creature who had not
known him in a fallen world.

COURTSHIP AND MARRIAGE

The language of courtship and marriage can help illustrate the development of the relationship between the Lord and Abram. Up to the time
of covenant institution, God has been, so to speak, the suitor—he has
wooed his beloved, blessed his beloved (Genesis 12–13) and provided
various good things for his beloved. All those generous acts *are* part of
a relationship, but it has been the relationship of a suitor to his love—to
his fiancée, to borrow a term from courtship. Now it is time to enter a
marriage, which, as Hugenberger has demonstrated, is also a covenant relationship.[1] And the relationship God initiates in Genesis 15—the special
grace covenant relationship—is as different from what has gone before
as marriage is different from courtship or being affianced. Now, in the

---

1   Gordon Hugenberger, *Marriage as a Covenant: Biblical Law and Ethics as Developed from Malachi* (Grand Rapids: Baker, 1994).

marital/covenant relationship, comes a whole new set of privileges and responsibilities.[2]

TO MAKE A COVENANT: COVENANT STRUCTURE AND SYMBOLISM OF THE NARRATIVE

The step of the Major Paradigm considered now is that of covenant making. For the third time we encounter a covenant articulated in the form of a narrative. The difference in this case is that we witness a covenant cutting (or ratifying) ceremony as the Lord in theophany passes between the cut-up pieces of the ceremonial animals (Gen. 15:17). The significance of this act is well understood but is restated here for the sake of completeness. First it is proper to document the covenantal structure of the narrative:

Genesis 15:1–21	Second Millennium BC Covenant Structure	
15:1, 7	Title	"I am Yahweh"
15:7	Historical Prologue	"who brought you out"
[26:5]	Stipulations	"because Abraham obeyed my voice and kept my charge, my commandments, my statutes, and my laws" (reaffirmation of the Abrahamic covenant with Isaac)]
15:4, 6–7b	Blessings	promises heir, land
15:18–19	Grant	"to your descendants I give this land"
15:9–11, 17	Solemn Ceremony (= Curse)	passage between cut-up animals

Some considerations are especially important in this narrative. First, we are not offered a written covenant. Abram did not carry a covenant document away from this experience. Rather, we have a narrative with the elements of a covenant and—for the first time—the record of a covenant cutting ceremony. Those data alone show that the Lord herewith

---

2   Cf. the discussion in Niehaus, "An Argument against Theologically Constructed Covenants," *JETS* 50, no. 2 (2007): 259–73.

creates a covenant with Abram, even if we had not been told, "On that day the Lord cut a covenant with Abram" (Gen. 15:18, author's translation).

Second, the covenant has the form of a second millennium BC treaty. The narrative includes, among other things, a historical prologue (v. 7) and blessings (vv. 4, 6–7b), a combination of elements found to date only in second millennium BC international treaties. The data thus form an implicit argument for a Mosaic date of composition for the passage although they fall short of proof (because, e.g., someone tomorrow might dig up a first millennium treaty cast in the older, second millennium form).[3] Nonetheless, the legal form of the covenant narrative does make it *consistent* with a Mosaic date for the passage because from a form-critical standpoint the passage is at home in the second millennium.[4]

Third, there are no stipulations. The Lord gives Abram no "laws" in Genesis 15. But we do learn, when the Lord reaffirms the covenant with Isaac, that the Lord gave Abram "commandments, statutes, and laws" (Gen. 26:5). Those were not the possession of humanity in general but came to Abraham in the context of the special grace covenant relationship created in Genesis 15 and given supplemental *torah* in Genesis 17 and (apparently) subsequently. One of those covenant stipulations was the requirement of circumcision for Abram for himself and his descendants (Gen. 17:10–14). The Lord also alludes to other requirements within the Abrahamic narratives: "For I have chosen [lit. "known"] him, *so that* he will direct [lit. "command," the word from which "commandment" is derived] his children and his household after him to keep the way of the LORD by doing what is right and just [lit. "righteousness and justice," the same things the Lord would command Israel under the Mosaic covenant and—as later covenant lawsuit showed—Israel failed to do (cf. Isa. 5:7)], *so that* the LORD will bring about for Abraham what he has promised

---

3   Cf. Noel Weeks, *Admonition and Curse: The Ancient Near Eastern Treaty/Covenant Form as a Problem in Inter-Cultural Relationships* (Edinburgh: T&T Clark, 2004), 47. Weeks discusses the case of a fragmentary treaty between Ashurbanipal and the tribe of Qedar, which includes four lines of historical material, including the misdeeds of the tribe's previous ruler, contrasted with the good Ashurbanipal has done for the tribe. The historical data are extremely brief and anomalous among discovered first millennium treaties.

4   We also affirm, however, that the report is historical and not a literary creation superimposed on history, not even by Moses. Moreover, God's covenantal way of dealing with Abram was also an expression of God's own nature, as our initial discussion of the covenant form has indicated (vol. 1, chap. 1).

him" (Gen. 18:19, emphases added). This verse alone shows us the Abrahamic covenant was not simply unconditional.

Fourth (and finally), there is a theophanic passage between the cut-up animals. Treaties could be ratified by this sort of ritual passage between dismembered animals in the ancient Near East. The vassal would walk between the cut-up pieces of certain beasts. The animals were apparently not sacrifices to the gods but rather symbols of the vassal's fate should he break the treaty. The symbolism was, "Let the same fate befall me as has befallen these animals should I break the treaty." Extrabiblical documentary evidence for this ceremony is somewhat scant.[5] Anecdotal evidence may appear in the annals of some kings where we see rebellious vassals punished in ways that would be consistent with their having participated in such a ritual. For example, the last great Assyrian suzerain, Ashurbanipal, says of one rebellious vassal, "I threw Dunanu on a skinning table and butchered him like a lamb."[6] But the Old Testament itself provides evidence that explains the ceremony. Jeremiah reports how the men of Judah and Jerusalem made a special covenant with the Lord to release their slaves, a stipulation of the law they had not been observing. The men later reneged on their promise, and Jeremiah records the Lord's word of judgment to them:

> The men who have violated my covenant and have not fulfilled the terms of the covenant they made before me, I will treat like the calf they cut in two and then walked between its pieces. The leaders of Judah and Jerusalem, the court officials, the priests and all the people of the land who walked between the pieces of the calf, I will hand over to their enemies who seek their lives. Their dead bodies will become food for the birds of the air and the beasts of the earth. (Jer. 34:18–20)

The passage between cut-up animals is clearly a symbolic covenant ratifying ceremony. It is like signing a treaty and, like signing a treaty, it means there is no treaty or covenant until the ratification process has been finished. Covenant ratification *in this form* in the ancient Near East was also, as we have seen, a self-imprecatory procedure that called the covenant curses down on the one who passed between the animals. Normally the vassal made that passage, but in Genesis 15 it is the Lord in theophany who makes the passage. According to the symbolism, then,

---

5   Cf. for a few examples, M. Weinfeld, "The Covenant of Grant in the Old Testament and in the Ancient Near East," *JAOS* 90 (1970):184–203.

6   Cf. *God at Sinai*, 176.

the Lord promises to take upon himself the covenant curse if the covenant is broken. The curse is not stated but is symbolized by the fate of the animals that have suffered death. So by taking the vassal's place in the ceremony, the Lord promises to take the punishment of death upon himself if the Abrahamic covenant is broken by Abram or his offspring. As Paul says, we are that offspring: "If you belong to Christ, then you are Abraham's seed, and heirs according to the promise" (Gal. 3:29). Consequently, the Lord's passage between the cut-up animals in Genesis 15:17 expresses or symbolizes his promise to take upon himself the penalty of death for Abraham and his offspring—a promise fulfilled on the cross.[7] It is a promise of substitutionary atonement.

As Abram prepares the animals for this ritual, he wards off carrion birds from the carcasses (Gen. 15:11). Such birds would naturally consume the animal parts as they began to decay. Abram prevents such a fate, at least symbolically for the moment. The action—if only symbolic—may prefigure what happened to Christ, who fulfilled the symbolism of the curse passage and of whom Peter says (quoting Psalm 16):

David said about him:

> "I saw the Lord always before me.
>   Because he is at my right hand,
> I will not be shaken.
> Therefore my heart is glad and my tongue rejoices;
>   my body also will rest in hope,
> because you will not abandon me to the realm of the dead,
>   *you will not let your Holy One see decay.*
> You have made known to me the paths of life;
>   you will fill me with joy in your presence."

Brothers, I can tell you confidently that the patriarch David died and was buried, and his tomb is here to this day. But he was a prophet and

---

7   Kline, *Kingdom Prologue*, 295–300, has thus characterized the circumstances of the theophanic passage between the cut-up pieces in Genesis 15:17 as a presage of the sacrificial sufferings of Christ: "The darkness, the sword's violence, the broken flesh, accursed death, abandonment. God's oath-passage was a commitment to the death-passage of Jesus in the gloom of Golgotha. It was a covenant to walk the way of the cross." One may characterize the passage figuratively as an "oath-passage," but we have more to say about this in chapter 4.

knew that God had promised him on oath that he would place one of his descendants on his throne. Seeing what was ahead, he spoke of the resurrection of the Christ, that he was not abandoned to the realm of the dead, nor did his body see decay. God has raised this Jesus to life, and we are all witnesses of it. (Acts 2:25–32, emphasis added)

Abram has the privilege of being the one who does "not let" the sacrificed animals "see decay"—figuratively because he prevents the carrion birds from ravaging the animal corpses.[8] In this role he has the honor of paralleling God who will "not let" his Messiah "see decay." This is the first but not the only time God puts Abram in a parallel position to himself: when Abraham must sacrifice his "only son whom [he] love[s]" (Gen. 22:2), he has the honor of paralleling God's act of offering "his only son" (John 3:16), "whom [he] love[s]" (Matt. 3:17).

TWO COVENANTS IMPLIED IN THE NARRATIVE

We just saw how the Lord's passage between the cut-up animals—a ritual from which the phrase "to cut a covenant" (i.e., "to ratify a covenant") apparently originated—foreshadows the new covenant. The Lord's covenant with Abram also foreshadows another covenant: the Mosaic. It does so in two ways. First, the animals used in the Lord's passage are the same animals available for sacrifices of various kinds under the Mosaic covenant (cf. Leviticus 1). (And so, the Lord's passage between those animal parts signals that his sacrifice of himself will be sufficient to satisfy all of the sacrificial requirements of the Mosaic law, and this is one of the ways the Son of Man "fulfills the law," cf. Matt. 5:17).

Second, the conclusion of the chapter gives Abram a prophecy of his descendants' future bondage in Egypt and their deliverance from that bondage (Gen. 15:13–14); in the same breath it gives him a list of nations or peoples his descendants will conquer—those who will inhabit the Promised Land in that time (Gen. 15:18–20). In this way the Abrahamic covenant narrative anticipates the bondage in Egypt, the Exodus, the law (via its implied sacrificial requirements), and the Conquest—all of which form the context in which the Mosaic covenant will arise, take form and,

---

8   A form of decay, since even decay as we understand it is a process of ravaging by microscopic organisms. And the animals would decay. The symbolism is only momentary.

via its conquest commands, lead to the inheritance of the land and geographical kingdom formation under Moses and Joshua.

Earlier in the passage the Lord made a general promise of the land to Abram: "I am the Lord who brought you out of Ur of the Chaldeans to give you this land to take possession of it" (Gen. 15:7). But what exactly is the nature of that promise? Moshe Weinfeld was the first to suggest an explanation based on an ancient near eastern parallel. He thought the gift in question was a form of ancient near eastern land grant such as those made by, for example, Ugaritic kings to worthy citizens. The king would grant some land to a citizen and invite him to go and take possession of it. The gift was typically to the citizen and to his descendants in perpetuity. Subsequently Gordon Wenham, in his Genesis commentary, followed Weinfeld's suggestion as the preferred explanation of the gift in Genesis 15. Weinfeld's characterization has become the usual way scholars talk about this gift.[9] However, a better analogy is available. Other ancient inscriptions tell that a god or gods would give a king certain lands in prospect, to "take possession." However, the king must "take possession" not simply by entering the land and settling in it—as the Ugaritic citizen was entitled to do—but rather by *conquering* it and taking it from its present inhabitants. That is what Abram's descendants will have to do. A divine grant that entails conquest is clearly a better example for our purposes because it parallels the gift of Genesis 15 in every way: it is a divine grant to an elect human who is a partner in a (in Abram's case clearly covenantal) relationship, but the gift must be possessed through a conquest that God (or the gods in the pagan scenario) will enable the vassal to accomplish; indeed, *the divinely given ability to conquer the promised land* is *no small part of the gift*. An example from the annals of Tululti-Ninurta I of Assyria (1244–1208 BC) illustrates this sort of conquest grant:

> At that time, from Tulsina the . . . mountain [the region] between the cities Sasila [and] Mashat-sarri on the opposite bank of the lower Zab, from Mount Zuqusku [and] Mount Lallar—the district of the extensive Qutu— the entire land of the Lullumu, the land of the Paphu to the land Katmuhu [and] all the land of the Subaru, the entirety of Mount Kasiliari to the border of Nairi [and] the border of the land M[akan], to the Euphrates— those regions the great gods allotted to me.[10]

---

9   Cf. further discussion in chapter 4.

10   Grayson, *Assyrian Rulers*, vol. 1, 236–37 (A. O.78.1, column iv, lines 24–35). So the last great Assyrian emperor, Ashurbanipal, says, "The lands of my enemies they counted

The Lord's gift of land to Abram—not only of land but also of peoples to conquer—has a very similar ring:

> To your descendants I give this land, from the river of Egypt to the great river, the Euphrates—the land of the Kenites, Kenizzites, Kadmonites, Hittites, Perizzites, Rephaites, Amorites, Canaanites, Girgashites, and Jebusites. (Gen. 15:18–21)

Abram, and what's more Abram's descendants, thus stand in the place of ancient royalty. They have a gift from above: a royal prerogative of conquest. In their case, the true God will give them authority to conquer the foes and displace them so they can inherit their land and inhabit it in their place.

THE PROMISE AND CONDITIONS OF THE CONQUEST AND ITS ESCHATOLOGICAL IMPLICATIONS

There will be more to say about the Conquest, but one complex of ideas must be set forth now in an anticipatory way: ancient rulers claimed divine sanction for their wars of conquest, and every such war was supposedly an act that would extend the effective rule of their gods among humans. The gods commanded the wars in order to secure more humans as obedient vassals. The same was not true of the biblical Conquest. That was, by contrast, a war of judgment that God planned to bring upon the Canaanites because of their sin. The Lord's words to Abram make this very clear: "You, however, will go to your fathers in peace and be buried at a good old age. In the fourth generation your descendants will come back here, *for the sin of the Amorites has not yet reached its full measure*" (Gen. 15:15–16, emphasis added). Abram will go to rest. Not to him falls the work of Conquest. His descendants will accomplish that work, and the reason is clearly given: "the sin of the Amorites." The Conquest will come when the sin of the inhabitants has reached its full measure. What does that mean? Their sin will make them utterly ripe for judgment. Their consciences will be seared. At that time there will be few if any in the land who would be able to turn to the Lord, no matter how convincingly he displayed his goodness and power.

---

into my hands" ("they" being the gods) (Piepkorn, *Ashurbanipal*, 28–29, column i, lines 12–13).

Rahab is a case in point—or rather, her case is the exception that proves the point. She appears on the "honor roll of faith" (Heb. 11:31), but she is the only one in Jericho who does. She is the only one to exercise faith. By that act of faith, both she and her household are saved (Josh. 2:12–13, 17–20; 6:22–25). Perhaps according to the household principle noted earlier, both she and her household were saved into eternity. Or perhaps her household was saved only for this life. Although Hebrews 11 implicitly affirms Rahab's eternal salvation, the Bible gives no hint of the same for her household. Nonetheless, Rahab stands as an example of faith. James characterizes her actions as proof of her faith: "In the same way, was not even Rahab the prostitute considered righteous for what she did when she gave lodging to the spies and sent them off in a different direction? As the body without the spirit is dead, so faith without deeds is dead" (James 2:25–26). By saying "In the same way," James compares Rahab's deeds as evidence of her faith with those of Abraham, which were evidence of his faith (cf. James 2:21–24). The exercise of faith—giving birth to deeds that prove the faith was true—justified the one who believed, and meant that person could be credited with righteousness in both cases (Gen. 15:6; James 2:23, 25). Works do not save us, but our works show that the faith by which we *are* saved is a true faith.

The uniqueness of Rahab's faith among her people proves what we affirmed on the previous page: "At that time there will be few if any in the land who would be able to turn to the Lord, no matter how convincingly he displayed his goodness and power." Rahab proves this when she tells the spies: "We have heard how the LORD dried up the water of the Red Sea for you when you came out of Egypt, and what you did to Sihon and Og, the two kings of the Amorites east of the Jordan, whom you completely destroyed" (Josh. 2:10). Everyone has heard of the Lord and his mighty deeds, yet among them all only Rahab affirms, "the LORD your God is God in heaven above and on the earth below" (Josh. 2:11). The others do not take her step of faith. Instead, their hearts melt in fear of the God of Israel (Josh. 2:9, 11). But as the apostle says, fear has to do with judgment, whereas perfect love casts out fear (1 John 4:18). Rahab moves away from fear and moves toward the saving love of God. She does so by faith. By doing so she also steps away from her past, her culture, and the religion of her culture. Her religion claimed there were many "great gods of heaven and earth," but she now affirms that *Israel's* God is "God in heaven above and on the earth below" (Josh. 2:11). Her statement does not explicitly claim that Israel's God is the only God but it does implicitly turn away from the pantheon under which she grew up. In the pagan world of the second millennium BC—and in the pagan world for centuries after—her statement was and would be a radical rejection of polytheism, a rejection articulated not with the precision of a fully formed and informed theology but with the clarity of a nascent faith.

In Jericho, and apparently in Canaan, only Rahab had such faith. Consequently, the situation was similar to what it will be when the Lord returns to judge the world: "However, when the Son of Man comes, will he find faith on the earth?" (Luke 18:8). The answer is no. The resultant scenario appears in Revelation 19 when the Lord returns with his saints to judge the earth. Just as the sinfulness of the inhabitants will have reached full measure when Abram's descendants come to inherit the land (Gen. 15:16), so the sinfulness of the earth's inhabitants will have reached full measure when the Lord comes to judge the earth (Luke 18:8; Rev. 19). When sinfulness has reached its *full* measure, faith becomes impossible. That is so because sin is fundamentally a lie—sin is that which does not amen God. It is thus by definition untruth. One who is *utterly sinful* has thus become *utterly a person of the lie*. Because faith is an act that "amens" the truth, such a person cannot exercise faith. Such a person has become ontologically untruth. When humanity comes to that state, no one will be in a condition to be saved, and the time will have arrived for the Lord to draw history to its close. That Day is prefigured in the Conquest, and the key to understanding it lies in the Lord's words to Abram.

A NOTE ON ABRAHAMIC COVENANTAL HISTORIOGRAPHY

All historiography in the Bible and in the ancient Near East arose out of covenantal contexts. So it is appropriate to say that all such history is covenantal literature. We have presented this idea and will return to it when we conclude our study of the Abrahamic covenant.[11] For now we reaffirm it and understand that Genesis 16–25 present a history of Abram and his immediate family subsequent to the Lord's covenant cutting with him. The history is subsequent to the covenant and inevitably conditioned by it: everything that now transpires for Abram and his family does so under the aegis of the covenant and may be evaluated in terms of it—that is, in terms of its promises and the nature of the covenant God and what he may subsequently require of covenant members. A good deal of historiographical material follows Genesis 15, including the attempt to build

---

11   Cf. volume 1 of *Biblical Theology,* chapter 1.

a family through Hagar (Gen. 16), the divine and angelic visitation at
Mamre (Gen. 18:1–15), Abraham's plea for Sodom and Gomorrah (Gen.
18:16–33) and God's judgment on those cities (Gen. 19:1–29), the episode
of Lot and his daughters (Gen. 19:30–38), Abraham's sojourn in Gerar
(Gen. 20), the birth of Isaac and the dismissal of Hagar and Ishmael (Gen.
21), the testing of Abraham in the mountains of Moriah (Gen. 22) and
much more, up to the narrative of Abraham's death (Gen. 25:1–11). Such
a mix of personal history (Sarai's proposal to use Hagar, the dismissal
of Hagar and Ishmael) and international history (the judgment on the
two city states, Abraham's treaty with Abimelek of Gerar) is evocative of
genres known in the ancient Near East—a personal history or story (such
as "The Tale of Sinuhe" in Egypt), and international history (records of
treaties and of judgments and conquests found in ancient near eastern
royal annals). But the author presents them in an unusual mixture. The
reason for this mixture is not because the accounts are derivative of pagan genres but because they are genuine historiography. They offer what
happened with the detail and accuracy that are necessary if a clear and
more or less sequential record is to appear.

GENESIS 17 AND THE ABRAHAMIC COVENANT

After the episode of Hagar and Ishmael in Genesis 16 (to be discussed
later), Genesis 17 provides further details of the Abrahamic covenant.
It begins with a theophany ("the Lord appeared" to Abram), in which
the Lord identifies himself as El Shaddai, that is, "God the mountain-
one" (compare Assyrian addresses to the god Ashur as šadû rabû, "the
mighty mountain"), an epithet either intended to identify God as the
one to be found on mountaintops (such as Moriah, Horeb/Sinai, the
Parable Mount, the Mount of Transfiguration and, ironically, the Mount
of Olives where he was betrayed), or as one who is like a mountain,
strong and unshakable.[12] When the Lord appears he immediately gives

---

12   One finds the identification of Shaddai with Akkadian šadû as far back as the
late nineteenth century; cf. George A. Barton, "National Israelitish Deities," in *Oriental
Studies: A Selection of the Papers Read before the Oriental Club of Philadelphia, 1888–1894*
(Boston: Ginn & Co., 1894), 101 (citing Halevy, *Recherches Bibliques*, 52), that Shaddai
may be an archaic form of šadû, "mountain," and that the form may mean "dweller on the
mountain." Cf. Knut Tallqvist, *Akkadische Götter-epitheta* (Helsinki: Societas orientalis
Fennica, 1938), 221 (documenting šadû rabû as a divine name).

two commands: "walk before me and be blameless" (Gen. 17:1).[13] He then promises to confirm his covenant with Abram and to increase his numbers greatly (v. 2). As has been noted, the Hebrew idiom used here, "to confirm covenant" [נתן ברית], is used of covenants already in existence that are now being reaffirmed/ "given" in an ongoing sense.[14] Because the Abrahamic covenant came into being in Genesis 15, that understanding makes perfect sense here.

The Lord has already given Abram two commands at the outset of his appearing and he now adds to those. He adds the command of circumcision for Abram and all males belonging to his household (Gen. 17:10–14). He also changes Abram's name to Abraham (with the implicit command that Abram accept the change and go by that name from now on [Gen. 17:5]), and Sarai's name to Sarah, and he commands Abraham to call her Sarah from then on (Gen. 17:15). Abraham obeys the commands. He institutes circumcision among all the males of his household (Gen. 17:23–27), and he henceforth refers to Sarai as Sarah (e.g., Gen. 17:17). His obedience demonstrates his faithfulness to the covenant—his faith in action—fruit of a faith the Lord credited to him as righteousness (Gen. 15:6).

A significant aspect of the circumcision the Lord commands is that it applies to those not of Abraham's blood:

> You are to undergo circumcision, and it will be the sign of the covenant between me and you. For the generations to come every male among you who is eight days old must be circumcised, including those born in your household or bought with money from a foreigner—those who are not your offspring. Whether born in your household or bought with your money, they must be circumcised. My covenant in your flesh is to be an everlasting covenant. Any uncircumcised male, who has not been circumcised in the flesh, will be cut off from his people; he has broken my covenant. (Gen. 17:11–14)

The last statement makes it clear that those born outside the family, and even those bought with money, are part of the covenant community since any member who does not undergo circumcision "will be cut off from his people; he has broken my covenant." The commandment

---

13   Or a hendiadys, "Walk/live blamelessly before me."

14   Cf. Dumbrell, *Covenant and Creation*, 26; Moshe Weinfeld, "*berît*," *TDOT*, vol. 2: 253–79, esp. 260. The covenant idioms used in Genesis 17 have been discussed in chapter 1, and will be further discussed in chapter 5.

of circumcision for all males in the Abrahamic community, foreigners included, anticipates the ultimate goal of the Abrahamic covenant: that in Abraham's seed all the nations would be blessed—a goal fulfilled by Christ and the mission of his Holy Spirit but also prefigured here.[15]

At this point we are in a position to understand how the Abrahamic covenant relates to the other covenants it anticipates. We have already seen how the new covenant is foreshadowed in the self-imprecatory passage the theophanic glory makes between the cut-up animals in Genesis 15, and by the circumcision command in Genesis 17. We understood that two covenants were anticipated in that Abrahamic covenant: the new covenant in Christ's blood, but also the Mosaic covenant with its fulfillment of the promises of land and offspring that would possess the land after a period of oppression in a land not their own. The Lord has added a further promise in Genesis 17, and it implies yet another covenant: "I will make nations of you, and kings will come from you" (Gen. 17:6). The promise of kings anticipates an Israelite monarchy, which began with Saul but was more truly and importantly grounded through David, from whom would come not only kings but also the incarnate King.[16] There is also room for a figurative meaning because God's people in the new covenant (those from many nations who are Abraham's "offspring," Gal. 3:29) are made a "royal" priesthood (1 Peter 2:9) by the work of David's royal Son.

It is important to note here that Genesis 17 does not present another covenant the Lord made with Abraham in addition to the one "cut" in Genesis 15. The Lord's appearance in Genesis 17 *does* have to do with covenant relations as he indicates when he says, "I will confirm/give in an ongoing way my covenant between me and you" (ואתנה בריתי ביני ... ּ, בינך, Gen. 17:2, author's translation).[17] The covenant he means, however, is the covenant he made with Abram in Genesis 15, and he now adds further data explicative of that covenant.[18]

---

15   Because Paul identifies circumcision as a sign of Abraham's faith (Rom. 4:11) by which Abram entered the Abramahic covenant in Genesis 15, circumcision prefigures the doctrine that one is saved only by faith, just as Abraham was.

16   Cf. further discussion in chapters 1 and 17; and in volume 3, chapter 1.

17   As I have indicated elsewhere, the Lord can use the phrase "my covenant" to refer to covenants he has already made (Niehaus, "Covenant: An Idea," 241n63).

18   The unity of the Abrahamic covenant is discussed in the context of the Abrahamic covenant narrative material in chapter 4.

GENESIS 22 AND THE ABRAHAMIC COVENANT

We noted that Genesis 17 repeats or reaffirms promises made in Genesis 15. Once those promises are made in Genesis 15, they become part of that special grace covenant the Lord "cuts" with Abram. However, those promises were also made earlier in Genesis 12:1–9, for example, the promise of offspring (v. 2) and the promise of land for that offspring (v. 7). When God made those promises, Abram related to him in the context of the Adamic/Noahic covenants—that is, the common grace covenants. Once the special grace covenant is instituted in Genesis 15, Abram does still relate to the Lord in the context of those common grace covenants, but also now in the context of the new, Abrahamic covenant. The Lord has proceeded by stating and restating promises, and it may be he does so for Abraham's instruction and encouragement. Moreover, as the Lord restated promises in Genesis 17, he also restates a promise in Genesis 22.

Without rehearsing the wonderful and familiar account of the sacrificial substitution that takes place at Moriah, we affirm the typological/Christological aspects of it in which the Lord provides a substitutionary sacrifice for the offspring of Abraham—and we in turn are that offspring (Gal. 3:29) for whom God has in the fullness of time provided the substitutionary sacrifice. We should not turn from an overview of the narrative, however, without considering what it implies for Abraham's status. For the Lord calls the patriarch into a high and rare position. He makes him parallel with God himself: Abraham is called to be the father who is prepared to sacrifice his only begotten son of promise, and chooses to do so because God commands it. Because God's commands are expressions of his nature, there is another way of putting Abraham's case: he must be willing to sacrifice his promised son if he would be faithful to the nature of God, who will sacrifice his own promised Son (cf. Isa. 9:5) to satisfy the just requirements of his nature. Such an act by Abraham would consequently be both an act of faith and an act of righteousness (conformity to God's nature).

Abraham's call was a lofty one, and it was a call fulfilled by faith. We are told in Hebrews: "By faith Abraham, when God tested him, offered Isaac as a sacrifice. He who had embraced the promises was about to sacrifice his one and only son, even though God had said to him, 'It is through Isaac that your offspring will be reckoned.' Abraham reasoned that God could even raise the dead, and so in a manner of speaking he did receive Isaac back from death" (Heb. 11:17–19). Abraham, in other words, amened what God was doing when God commanded the sacrifice of Isaac. One sees Abraham's faith in his words as well as his acts. He told his servants, "We will worship and then we will come back to you" (Gen. 22:5b), and he even told Isaac, "God himself will provide the lamb for the burnt offering, my son" (Gen. 22:8).

Nonetheless, and even though one learns from the book of Hebrews that Abraham "reasoned" he could possibly have his son back by a resurrection, faith and reason are not incompatible, and they do not necessarily rule out emotion. Abraham's call may also have been a test, and one may expect that Abraham had tumultuous feelings to battle as he proceeded to the mountain and up the mountain with his son and that he did not arrange the wood and bind his son on top of it without strong emotions. Nonetheless, in all of this one may see the hand of God the potter, who shapes his people with wisdom and out of love, however hard the shaping may feel to the person at the moment. Through Abraham's obedience, the Lord shaped the patriarch into a parallel with God himself, and one may take this as a prefiguration for the conformity to himself that God now works in all his people.[19]

We now turn our attention to two other important aspects of Genesis 22. The first is the translation of a verb in Genesis 22:14; the second is the covenant reaffirmation that takes place in Genesis 22:16–18.

Jehovah Jireh [20]

In Genesis 22:14 one reads, "So Abraham called that place The LORD Will Provide (יהוה יראה). And to this day it is said, 'On the mountain of the LORD it will be provided (יראה).'" The Niphal of the verb, translated "it will be provided," is also used often of theophanies, "He appeared/will appear," and that translation possibility should not, it seems to me, be excluded here. On the basis of that possibility an alternate translation of the verse could be: "So Abraham called that place 'One Will See the LORD.' And to this day it is said, 'On the mountain of the LORD he [the LORD] will appear (i.e., "be seen").'"[21] If this reading is correct—and

---

19   The Lord calls Hosea similarly into a situation parallel with the Lord: both the Lord and his prophet are married to faithless wives and see illegitimate children as the result. Cf. discussion in chapter 15.

20   Jehovah Jireh is commonly taken as a divine name, yet the passage makes it clear that it is a place name (Gen. 22:14). Of course the better transliteration is not "Jehovah," but "Yahweh."

21   Or, with a witty play on the meanings of the verb, "So Abraham called that place

it is entirely possible grammatically—the verse becomes prophetic or anticipatory of a later reality, when the Lord does in fact *appear* to David at the threshing floor of Arauna the Jebusite, the future site of the Solomonic temple: "Then Solomon began to build the temple of the LORD in Jerusalem on Mount Moriah, where the LORD had appeared (נִרְאָה) to his father David. It was on the threshing floor of Araunah the Jebusite, the place provided by David" (2 Chron. 3:1). It is noteworthy that here, as in Genesis 22:14, the Niphal of the verb (רָאָה) is used.

Covenant Reaffirmation of Genesis 22: Covenant Narrative Conclusion

The second matter to consider in Genesis 22 is the covenant reaffirmation that takes place in Genesis 22:16–18. Here, as in Genesis 17, the Lord re-affirms promises made earlier. He reaffirms (Gen. 22:17a) the promise of numerous offspring made in Genesis 12:2 and instituted covenantally in Genesis 15:5; he reaffirms (Gen. 22:17b) the promise of conquest both made and instituted covenantally in Genesis 15:18–20; and he reaffirms (Gen. 22:18) the promise of Genesis 12:3b that through Abraham's offspring all nations on earth will be blessed. This last promise was made when Abram still lived only in the context of the Adamic/Noahic covenants—before the Lord "cut" a new covenant with him in Genesis 15. It is now confirmed within the context of the Abrahamic covenantal narrative material.[22]

'The LORD *will see to it* (i.e., provide).' And to this day it is said, 'On the Mountain of the LORD he [the LORD] *will be seen* (i.e., appear).'" The Old Testament is no stranger to such witty use of a verb and its conjugations; cf. Jeremiah 23:2, 4: "Because you [the shepherds of the Lord's flock] have not *bestowed care on* them [פְּקַדְתֶּם], I will *bestow punishment on* [הִנְנִי פֹקֵד] you" (v. 2); "'I will place shepherds over them who will tend them, and they will no longer be afraid or terrified, *nor will any be missing* [וְלֹא יִפָּקֵדוּ],' declares the Lord" (v. 4). The Jeremiah example is *a propos* because it involves the witty use of the same verb (in this case, פָקַד) in the Qal and the Niphal, just as in Genesis 22:14 (with רָאָה).

22 That is, as additional, affirmative data imparted to Abraham as he lives under the Abrahamic covenant (cf. chap. 4). David affirms the same promise in the messianic Psalm 22:

> All the ends of the earth shall remember
>   and turn to the LORD,
> and all the families of the nations
>   shall worship before you.
> For kingship belongs to the LORD,
>   and he rules over the nations. (vv. 27–28)

The Lord did rule over the nations in David's day, and before and after, even if they did

All these reaffirmations or confirmations are made on the declared ground of Abraham's obedience to the Lord's command to sacrifice his son (Gen. 22:16,18b), and here a word is in order. It is à propos now to draw upon observations made earlier about God and time. Since God is outside time, he can foreknow exactly what may be future in a human timeline, because for him it is at once future, present, and past. So Paul can say that "those God foreknew, he also predestined to be conformed to the likeness of his Son" (Rom. 8:29). It follows that God foreknew how Abraham would be obedient even to the offering of his only son (Gen. 22:16).[23] That obedience, as James tells us, was the proof that Abraham's faith was real (James 2:20–24). Therefore, when the Lord "credited" Abraham's faith to him as righteousness (Gen. 15:6), it was on the basis of a sure knowledge that Abraham's faith was *true faith*, and that Abraham's faith would show its truth by appropriate obedience—works—later on (i.e., after Genesis 15 and, to our point, in Genesis 22). God knew all this because for him *the faith and the works that resulted from it and showed it to be a true faith* were all, and continue to be, a present reality—not to mention that God knew the workings of Abraham's soul. The faith and the works that issue from that faith are like a tree and its fruit, organically and constitutionally connected.[24]

---

not recognize his rule or even his existence. But the day will come when "all the families of the nations shall worship" the Lord, and that is penultimately fulfilled in the Great Commission, and ultimately fulfilled in the new heavens and earth.

23   Cf. further discussion of foreknowledge and of God's foreknowledge in particular in volume 3, chapter 7.

24   In a similar vein, Paul writes of Abraham's faith regarding the promise of a son: "Against all hope, Abraham in hope believed and so became the father of many nations, just as it had been said to him, 'So shall your offspring be.' Without weakening in his faith, he faced the fact that his body was as good as dead—since he was about a hundred years old—and that Sarah's womb was also dead. Yet he did not waver through unbelief regarding the promise of God, but was strengthened in his faith and gave glory to God, being fully persuaded that God had power to do what he had promised. This is why 'it was credited to him as righteousness'" (Rom 4:18–22). We accept Paul's statement regarding Abram's spiritual condition even if, when Sarai asked him to build her a family through Hagar, "Abram agreed to what Sarai said" (Gen 16:2). We are nowhere told that Abram "wavered through unbelief." We are only told that he "agreed/submitted" to do what Sarai asked (Heb. וישמע אברם לקול שרי). Interestingly, the idiom is the same one used when Adam "*paid heed to the voice* of [his] wife" and ate of the forbidden fruit (Gen. 3:17). Cf. discussion in volume 1 of *Biblical Theology*, chapter 3, and further discussion in chapters 3 of this volume.

We have to note that the Abrahamic covenant, although it contains the promise of the Mosaic, Davidic, and new covenants, is itself no longer a functioning covenant. This becomes instantly obvious if we consider that the covenant sign—circumcision—is no longer a covenant sign for God's people. One cannot be a participant of the Abrahamic covenant without taking upon oneself the covenant sign; therefore, if the covenant sign has been abrogated, participation in the covenant is no longer possible.[25] Whatever was promised and of eternal import in the Abrahamic covenant has been taken up in the new covenant, as Paul argues so eloquently.

We now present the promises made by the Lord to Abraham. Once we have surveyed them we will be in a better position to assess the relationship of the Abrahamic covenant to the three great covenants, the Mosaic, the Davidic, and the new, which follow it:

Promise to Abraham	Fulfillment
Father of nations	New covenant
Father of kings	Mosaic, Davidic, new covenant
God of Abraham's descendants	Mosaic, Davidic, new covenant
Canaan an enduring possession for Abraham and descendants	Mosaic [Davidic, new covenant]

Clearly God fulfills three of these promises under the Mosaic covenant. Yahweh is the God of Abraham's descendants through Isaac, and he does give Canaan to them as a possession. Kings do come forth from Abraham genetically and rule God's people under the Mosaic covenant. The first of these is Saul.

Moreover, the promise of kings leads eventually to the Davidic covenant, in which the Lord establishes the Davidic monarchy with its implicit promise of an ultimate messianic King (2 Sam. 7:1–17; cf. Psalm 2).

These promises may also be seen to find their ultimate fulfillment in the new covenant. There nations become God's people and they may truly be called Abraham's children according to Galatians 3:29. New covenant

---

25 It is clear that circumcision, as a practice also required by the Mosaic covenant, has been replaced by baptism as a covenant sign, and when Paul argues so strenuously against circumcision, he is arguing against that circumcision that would submit the person who undergoes it to participation in the Mosaic covenant. However, it remains true that circumcision—whether as *part* of the Mosaic covenant or as a *sign* of the Abrahamic covenant—is no longer a covenant sign or covenant practice for the true Israel, God's people in the new covenant.

believers are a royal priesthood (1 Peter 2:9). As for the promise of Canaan, it may be understood in two senses. The expression often translated as "an everlasting possession" (e.g., NIV) uses the Hebrew word עולם, which we have noted may mean either "everlasting" or "of long duration," depending on the context. With respect to the Mosaic covenant one may say that the meaning (with regard to the possession of Canaan) is "of long duration" but not "everlasting," since Israel lost possession of Canaan for nearly two thousand years after the Diaspora. On the other hand, since Canaan is arguably to be the center of world government when the heavenly Jerusalem descends among us (e.g., Rev. 21; cf. Isa. 2:1–4; Micah 4:1–4), one could view Canaan as indeed an "everlasting possession" of the *true* Israel, the Israel of faith, even if ethnic Israel's ownership of it suffered a hiatus of two millennia. We will have more to say about this in our discussion of biblical eschatology.[26]

Similarly circumcision, although it has passed away as a covenant sign with the passing away of the Abrahamic and Mosaic covenants, has been replaced by a new covenant sign, baptism, which represents what God in fact always wanted from his people: a character genuinely transformed by their covenant relationship, sometimes referred to in the Old Testament as a circumcised heart.[27]

God made promises to Abraham that would only be fulfilled in later covenants. It is important at this stage to remember a simple but important fact: a covenant and a promise are two different things. That became clear in the discussion of Genesis 12:1–3. There it was noted that God's promises, and even his command to "be a blessing," took place before God actually "cut" the covenant with Abram in Genesis 15 that would lead to fulfillment of those promises. God may promise something to someone, or even command something of someone, but the mere fact that God makes a promise or gives a command does not mean the promise and/or command create a covenant—even though it is God who makes the promise or gives the command. This was the case in Genesis 12:1–3 vis-à-vis Genesis 15 (cf. v. 18).

Moreover, a promise made in *one* covenant may be fulfilled in, or as part of, *a later covenant*. Nonetheless, the fact that two covenants share a promise does not make those two covenants one covenant. God may make a promise to Adam's wife, for example, that her offspring will bruise

---

26 Cf. in particular remarks in the Summary of volume 3, where the possibility of an archetypal, ideal and yet geographical Promised Land is raised.

27 Cf. further discussion in chapter 13.

the serpent's head. God makes that promise in the context of Adam's and his wife's covenantal relationship to God under the creation covenant that God chose mercifully to sustain despite their breaking of it. Christ fulfills that promise. But the promise that links the two bodies of covenant material—the Adamic and new covenantal narrative material—does not make the Adamic covenant and the new covenant one covenant. The case in Genesis 15 is perhaps more clear. When the Lord passes theophanically between the cut-up pieces of the animals, he symbolically promises to take upon himself the punishment for covenant breaking by Abram and his successors. But when Christ fulfills that promise by laying down his life on the cross, he does not thereby make the Abrahamic covenant and the new covenant one and the same covenant. A promise is made in one covenant— in the Abrahamic covenant—by the symbolism of its ratification. The promise is fulfilled in another covenant. But the two covenants are still two, distinct covenants, each with its own distinct and different provisions and requirements—including, as was noted, different covenant signs.

The foregoing discussion of the Abrahamic covenant enables us to conclude thus: whatever God promised in the Abrahamic covenant has been fulfilled, or accomplished, or was/is in the process of being accomplished, by God in one or more of the covenants that have succeeded it.[28] Nonetheless, the Abrahamic covenant itself, *qua* covenant, is no longer in force. That has become clear from the simplest consideration: the sign of membership in the covenant—circumcision—is no longer required to be practiced by God's people as a covenant sign. Circumcision has been replaced by baptism, the new covenant sign, just as the Abrahamic covenant itself has been replaced by the new covenant as the one extant, functioning special grace covenant for God's people.

---

28 Discussion of the Mosaic, Davidic, and new covenants will illustrates this statement more fully.

CHAPTER THREE

Hagar and Ishmael, Sodom and Gomorrah, Abraham and Abimelek

ABRAHAM: COMMON GRACE, ESCHATOLOGY, AND PROPHECY

The topics that form the title of this chapter also embrace the themes of common grace, eschatology, and prophecy. They comprise Genesis 16–21, chapters that offer a number of interrelated themes. They are organically connected because they all have to do with Abraham and his relationship to the common grace order, as well as global eschatology and finally the prophetic nature of the life of God's people in the world. The last topic, "the prophetic nature of the life of God's people in the world," involves an important matter for the church: how God's people, the true children of Abraham, can and should represent God prophetically in the world of common grace until the Lord returns to judge that world. We take the headings of this chapter seriatim, understanding they also involve the penultimate step of the Major Paradigm as regards the Abrahamic covenant: the life of God's people, *whom he has made his people*, in the world.

HAGAR AND ISHMAEL

Abram's dealings with Hagar give us an opportunity to study Abram and his relationship to a person whose offspring will not be part of the Abrahamic covenant (cf. Gen. 17:20–21). The history of that relationship does not start auspiciously. We know the *sinfonia domestica* that led to an encounter between Hagar and a divine emissary. A lack of faith started the trouble: Sarai would not wait for the Lord to fulfill his promise of offspring to Abram. She counseled her husband to take her Egyptian handmaid, Hagar, and build a family through her. To *invent* one's own way of fulfilling God's promise rather than waiting on him to fulfill it only argues a lack of faith *at that point* and not an absolute and defining absence of faith in the person. Nonetheless, it was a lack of faith in Sarai—a refusal to amen the Lord.[1] Abram does as she says and the idiom used to describe his choice is significant. It has been noted but is repeated here for fuller discussion. We are told "Abram agreed to what Sarai said" (Gen. 16:2). The Hebrew idiom says literally "Abram paid heed to the voice of Sarai" (שְׁמַע לְקוֹל: וַיִּשְׁמַע אַבְרָם לְקוֹל שָׂרָי; cf. the more accurate KNJV: "And Abram heeded the voice of Sarai"). The Hebrew idiom is the same one the Lord used to rebuke Adam in the Garden: "Because you *paid heed to the voice of your wife* and ate fruit from the tree about which I commanded you, 'You must not eat from it'" (Gen. 3:17, author's translation). It was noted the idiom suggested Adam had erroneously treated his wife as though she were his suzerain or had authority over him, and the same is now true of Abram with respect to his wife. The parallelism can be set forth as follows:

Genesis 2–3	Genesis 15–16
Yahweh commanded regarding the fruit (2:17)	Yahweh promised fruit (15:4)
Adam paid heed to his wife (3:17)	Abram paid heed to his wife (16:2)

---

1   The failure of faith is ineluctably credited to Sarai and not to Abram because she originated the idea, but not because Abram's faith also did not fail at that point. What Paul says—noted and discussed in the pervious chapter—does not contradict this understanding: "And not being weak in faith, he did not consider his own body, already dead (since he was about a hundred years old), and the deadness of Sarah's womb. He did not waver at the promise of God through unbelief, but was strengthened in faith, giving glory to God, and being fully convinced that what He had promised He was also able to perform" (Rom. 4:19–21). Paul then relates Abram's ongoing faith in the Lord's promise specifically to Genesis 15:6, "And therefore 'it was accounted to him for righteousness'" (Rom. 4:22). In other words, Abram was strengthened in faith to the point of "amening" the Lord *in Genesis 15:6*. After that, however, he did have a failure of faith when he agreed not to "amen God" but rather take the alternative course Sarai proposed. He had another such failure when he once again told her to say to Abimelek that she was Abraham's sister. Nonetheless, he showed great faith in Genesis 22. Abraham did not have the Spirit as we do, but even we who have the Spirit may falter in amening God at any point in our lives. No one lives a life of perfect faith from nanosecond to nanosecond. Therefore the love of Christ, from which we cannot be separated, is all the more precious.

Genesis 2–3	Genesis 15–16
Adam set aside Yahweh's command,	Abram set aside Yahweh's promise,
having accepted his wife's *torah*	having accepted his wife's *torah*
and took the fruit (2:6b)	and produced wrong fruit (16:4)

The use of "fruit" in a *double entendre* gives point to the parallelism. In each case the husband had a word from the Lord. In each case he chose his wife's *torah* over the Lord's *torah*. In each case his decision led to a wrong choice regarding fruit. Both cases illustrate lack of faith. We defined faith as amening God—his nature, his deeds, his *torah*. That amening means one embraces and lives in accordance with the Lord—with his nature—and hence the close nexus between faith and righteousness. In each case the husband was faced with a choice: choose his Lord's *torah*, or choose his wife's *torah*. Both chose the latter, and in both cases their choices produced exceptionally bad results.[2]

HAGAR AND THE ANGEL OF THE LORD

Now that the choice has been made and Ishmael has been the result, we turn to the events that follow soon after his birth. Once Hagar had conceived him, she began to think less of her still barren mistress (Gen. 16:4b). She was eventually forced by Sarai's jealousy to flee both master and mistress. After Hagar fled, the angel of the LORD encountered her and asked, "Servant of Sarai, where have you come from, and where are you going" (Gen. 16:8a). The most significant thing about this encounter is the identity of the angel of the LORD. Although one cannot establish that identify with certainty there is a good possibility the angel was the

---

2   It is noteworthy that, when Abraham later dismisses Hagar and the infant Ishmael at Sarah's insistence (cf. Gen. 21:9–11), the Lord encourages him with the same idiom considered above: "In all that Sarah has said to you, pay heed to her voice [שְׁמַע בְּקֹלָהּ]" (Gen. 21:12, author's translation; the idiom interchangeably uses the prepositions לְ and בְּ, cf. *BDB*, 1034). The difference appears to be that, in the cases regarding the fruit in the garden and the decision to produce a child through Hagar, the man chose *on his own* to "pay heed" to his wife's voice, thus effectively substituting her *torah* for the Lord's. In Genesis 21, however, it is the Lord who *tells* Abraham to pay heed to his wife's voice. The fact that the Lord commands it shows that, in this case, Sarah's desire was aligned with what the Lord wanted to accomplish, and the Lord affirmed this to Abraham by saying, "Pay heed to Sarah's voice."

Lord himself—the preincarnate Son. That is so because the term מַלְאָךְ (like its Greek counterpart) means "messenger," and a divine messenger need not be a *created being*. There are several passages in which the term may be used to indicate, not a created being (i.e., an angel) but rather the preincarnate Son. In all those passages the divine identification is suggested by the fact that the term angel and some other term signifying God, are used interchangeably. That happens in Genesis 16 when Hagar names the well where the angel of the LORD met her *Be'er Lahai Roi* (i.e., "well of the Living One who sees me") because, "She gave this name to the *LORD* who spoke to her" (Gen 16:13a, emphasis added).

If the angel of the LORD was the Lord and not a created being, he had no need to ask her, "Where have you come from, and where are you going," any more than the Lord had any need to ask Adam whether he had eaten of the fruit (Gen. 3:11). When the all-knowing and all-sufficient One asks a human for information, it must be for some other purpose than God's own education or edification. It may be the Lord gave Hagar an opportunity to unburden herself of her feelings—something she may have done even though her recorded statement is brief ("I am running away from my mistress Sarai," Gen. 16:8b).[3] For now we turn to explore passages in which the angel of the LORD may be understood to be not a created angel but rather the preincarnate Son.

THE LORD AS THE ANGEL OF THE LORD IN THE OLD TESTAMENT

Genesis

There are four cases in Genesis in which the angel of the LORD could be the preincarnate Son, and two others in which the Lord appears as a man but with angelic associations of some sort. We consider the angel of the LORD passages first.

1. Hagar and the Angel of the LORD

The first angel of the LORD passage we consider is the one just noted in Genesis 16:

---

3   A similar example on the purely human plane could be the encounter between the Shunammite woman and Elijah in 2 Kings 4. Cf. chapter 14.

16:7—"The angel of the LORD found Hagar near a spring in the desert."

16:9—"Then the angel of the LORD told her, 'Go back, submit to your mistress.'"

16:10—"The angel added, 'I will so increase your descendants . . .'"

16:11—"The angel of the LORD also said to her,

> 'You are now with child
> and you will have a son.
> You shall name him Ishmael,
> for the LORD has heard of your misery.'"

As was seen, the inspired author and not merely Hagar herself subsequently presents this event as an encounter with the Lord: "She gave this name to the *LORD* who spoke to her" (Gen. 16:13a, emphasis added). Because the writer calls the one who encountered Hagar both the "angel of the LORD" and "the LORD," the two seem to be identical in this case.

Germane to the birth announcement of Ishmael, because of its form, is another birth announcement from heaven, in Matthew 1:20—"an angel of the Lord [note lack of definite article, ἰδοὺ ἄγγελος κυρίου] appeared to him in a dream and said, '. . . what is conceived in her is from the Holy Spirit. She will give birth to a son, and you are to give him the name Jesus, because he will save his people from their sins'" (Matt. 1:20–21).[4]

The format in both announcements is the same:

1. Statement of pregnancy
2. Prophecy of birth of a son
3. Command to name the son
4. Etymological reason for the appointed name

The birth announcement foretells the birth of God's Son, so it seems likely the one called "an angel of the Lord," who makes the announcement to Joseph, is a created angel and not an uncreated messenger (the preincarnate Son). The same may be indicated by the lack of the definite article

---

4   The LXX in Genesis 16:8, 10, 11—"the angel of the Lord"—uses the definite article appropriate to the Hebrew construct [ὁ ἄγγελος κυρίου]; cf. the absence of the definite article in Matthew 1:20.

(contrast LXX of Gen. 16:7, 9, 11).[5] The birth announcement formula in Matthew 1 parallels formally the birth announcement to Hagar, but that does not mean the angel of the LORD in Genesis 16 might not be the Lord. The birth announcement pattern seen in both cases appears to be standard, if one can use the word "standard" for such an extraordinary event. More to the point is the claim of the text that this "angel" who spoke with her was the Lord: "She gave this name to *the LORD who spoke to her*: 'You are the God who sees me'" (Gen. 16:13, emphasis added).

2. Jacob's Dream and the Angel of God

The second case of angelic identity with God occurs when the "angel of God" appears to Jacob in a dream regarding what might be called the "fleecing" of Laban:

> The angel of God said to me in the dream, "Jacob." I answered, "Here I am." And he said, "Look up and see that all the male goats mating with the flock are streaked, speckled or spotted, for I have seen all that Laban has been doing to you. I am the God of Bethel, where you anointed a pillar and where you made a vow to me." (Gen. 31:11–13)

Here the "angel of God" who appeared to Jacob called himself "the God of Bethel." It may be that Jacob mistakenly took him for an angel (a created messenger of God), or it may be that he rightly called him a messenger not fully realizing the implications of what he said.

3. The Angel and Jacob's Blessing

The third case of angelic identification with the Lord refers not to one historical event but to Jacob's whole life as he blesses Joseph and refers to an angel as God:

> Then he blessed Joseph and said,
> "May the God before whom my fathers
> Abraham and Isaac walked,
> the God who has been my Shepherd
> all my life to this day,

---

5   Although a good translation of the Hebrew construct should include the definite article, so this point is hardly decisive for Old Testament examples.

> the Angel who has delivered me from all harm—
> may he bless these boys." (Gen. 48:15–16)

Jacob identifies God as his shepherd and as an angel, and each identification has its own importance. One may think of a shepherd as one who leads the sheep to good pasture. He also has a protective role, although that is not stated here. When Jesus identifies himself as the Good Shepherd, his first characterization has to do with the guiding and providing aspects of shepherding (John 10:2–9; for the protective aspect, cf. John 10:11–13). In Jacob's blessing on Joseph the protective role is reserved for "the Angel who has delivered me from all harm" (v. 16). Not only has he saved, he is now called upon to bless. Since both the "shepherd" and the "angel" are appositives to "God" in the poem, and since their roles of leading the sheep, providing good pasture for them, and being their deliverer or savior are all roles that Jesus later attributes to himself, it seems reasonable to infer that Jacob, led by the Spirit when he blessed Joseph, spoke of the preincarnate Son. Whether he understood the supernally filial aspect of the one he called upon does not matter. A prophet can say more than he understands, as he allows or gives way to the Spirit who works in him (cf. Jer. 20:9) and who cooperates with his background and vocabulary to articulate what God wants to say through the man.

4. The Angel of the LORD on Mount Moriah

The fourth case of angelic identification of an angel with the LORD occurs in Genesis 22, but it is more questionable than the ones considered up to this point:

> But the angel of the LORD called out to him from heaven, "Abraham! Abraham!" "Here I am," he replied. . . . So Abraham called that place "The LORD Will Provide." And to this day it is said, "On the mountain of the LORD it will be provided." The angel of the LORD called to Abraham from heaven a second time and said, "I swear by myself, declares the LORD, that because you have done this and have not withheld your son, your only son, I will surely bless you and make your descendants as numerous as the stars in the sky and as the sand on the seashore." (Gen. 22:11, 14–17a)

Here too the angel of the LORD is apparently identified with the Lord, and he may be the Lord. Nonetheless, what the angel says is ambiguous:

"I swear by myself, declares the LORD" (v. 15). The angel may just be quoting the Lord at this point, and that may be the more natural way to understand the verse.

One thing emerges from all this: the Lord is a God who conceals himself (cf. Isa. 45:15), and a God who reveals himself (cf. Isa. 45:19).[6] God therefore allows ambiguity or incompleteness in angelic/theophanic events in order to drop a hint that more is going on than one may understand at the experiential or reportorial moment. Unresolved revelation of that sort can and ought to humble one who encounters just the *report* of it, but also raise hope and expectation of future and more complete revelatory acts by God. God intends that very thing (cf. Heb. 1:1–2).

The Lord as a Man with Angelic Associations

In addition to the angelic examples noted above, there are two cases where the Lord appeared to patriarchs as a man but with angelic overtones or associations of some sort. The first is the Lord's visit to Abraham, appearing as a man before the judgment of Sodom and Gomorrah. The second is his encounter with Jacob at the Jabbok ford.

1. Three Men at Mamre

The first example of the Lord's (apparently) appearing as a man is his visit to Abraham at Mamre: "The LORD appeared to Abraham near the great trees of Mamre while he was sitting at the entrance to his tent in the heat of the day. Abraham looked up and saw three men standing nearby" (Gen. 18:1–2). The Lord is identified as one of the three men who visited Abraham. However, the other two men are angels, as the subsequent narrative makes clear. This invites the idea that the man who appeared to Abraham and who was the Lord may in fact have been the preincarnate Son: three men = three angels or messengers, one of them uncreated. He comes to judge the cities of the plain, and Abraham calls him the "Judge of all the earth" and receives no correction for doing so (Gen. 18:25). Both facts would both be consistent with the filial identity of the "man" as the Lord. The judicial aspect would be consistent with God's Sonship as Jesus later says, "The Father judges no one, but has entrusted all judgment to the Son" (John 5:22). It is the Son who will judge the world at the end of

---

6   In Isaiah 45, the Lord conceals himself (apparently) from the nations, but also in some ways from Israel (Isa. 45:15); but he also reveals himself to Jacob (Israel) (Isa. 45:19).

all things, and the judgment on Sodom and Gomorrah is as a type of that eschatological judgment (cf. Rev. 11:8).[7]

2. Jacob's Wrestling Match with God

The second case of the Lord's appearing as a man in Genesis is his famous wrestling match with Jacob (later characterized by Hosea [12:3–5]):

> So Jacob was left alone, and a man wrestled with him till daybreak. When the man saw that he could not overpower him, he touched the socket of Jacob's hip so that his hip was wrenched as he wrestled with the man. Then the man said, "Let me go, for it is daybreak." But Jacob replied, "I will not let you go unless you bless me." The man asked him, "What is your name?" "Jacob," he answered. Then the man said, "Your name will be no longer Jacob, but Israel, because you have struggled with God and with men and have overcome." Jacob said, "Please tell me your name." But he replied, "Why do you ask my name?" Then he blessed him there. So Jacob called the place Peniel, saying, "It is because I saw God face to face, and yet my life was spared." (Gen. 32:24–30)

Jacob wrestled with a man but called him God. It should be noted that the man with whom he wrestled gave Jacob a new name, just as the Lord gave Abram and Sarai new names—names that resonate in the history of the Lord's covenant people. Hosea's commentary on Jacob's contest identifies the "man" and "God" (Gen. 32:30) as "God" and an "angel":

> In the womb he grasped his brother's heel;
> as a man he struggled with God.
> He struggled with the angel and overcame him;
> he wept and begged for his favor.
> He found him at Bethel
> and talked with him there—

---

7   Cf. further discussion, chapter 8 of volume 3; biblical references to Sodom and Gomorrah include the original event (Gen. 18:20; 19:24, 28), references to Sodom and Gomorrah in the covenant lawsuit genre (Deut. 29:23; 32:32; Isa. 1:9, 10; Amos 4:11; Jer. 23:14), judgment on other nations compared to that on Sodom and Gomorrah (Isa. 13:19; Jer. 50:40 [Babylon]; Jer. 49:18 [Edom]; Zeph. 2:9 [Moab]), historical reference in a salvation context (Rom. 9:29), and comparison of eschatological judgment to that on Sodom and Gomorrah (Matt. 10:14–15; 2 Peter 2:6; Jude 7).

the LORD God Almighty,
the LORD is his name of renown! (Hosea 12:3–5)

The man of Genesis 32 is called "God" (Gen. 32:30; Hosea 12:3) an "angel" (Hosea 12:4), "the LORD" (Hosea 12:5), and "the LORD God Almighty" (Hosea 12:5). The multiple identifications show the man to be an angel and also God/the LORD. An interpretation such as God the messenger—the preincarnate Son—seems a reasonable one, and more biblically consistent and palatable than the "water demon" of an old scholarly tradition.[8]

Exodus

In addition to the examples from Genesis there are three cases in Exodus that show a comparable identification of an angel and the Lord: the burning bush encounter, the pillar of cloud and fire, and the angel the Lord says he will send ahead of his people into the Promised Land.

1. The Burning Bush

The first and most famous of these is the burning bush episode:

There the angel of the LORD appeared to him in flames of fire from within a bush. Moses saw that though the bush was on fire it did not burn up. So Moses thought, "I will go over and see this strange sight—why the bush does not burn up." When the LORD saw that he had gone over to look, God called to him from within the bush, "Moses, Moses!" And Moses said, "Here I am." "Do not come any closer," God said. "Take off your sandals, for the place where you are standing is holy ground." Then he said, "I am the God of your father, the God of Abraham, the God of Isaac, and the God of Jacob." At this, Moses hid his face, because he was afraid to look at God. (Exod. 3:2–6)

In this account Moses identifies the angel of the LORD as God. The fiery presence also conveys overtones of the Holy Spirit as becomes clear later (cf. Ezek. 1:26–28).

---

8   Cf. Hermann Gunkel, *The Legends of Genesis* (Chicago: The Open Court Publishing Company, 1901), 353; Claus Westermann, *Genesis 12–36* (Minneapolis: Augsburg, 1985), 515–19.

2. Pillar of Fire and Cloud

The second example in Exodus seems equally unambiguous:

> Then the angel of God, who had been traveling in front of Israel's army, withdrew and went behind them. The pillar of cloud also moved from in front and stood behind them, coming between the armies of Egypt and Israel. . . . During the last watch of the night the LORD looked down from the pillar of fire and cloud at the Egyptian army and threw it into confusion. (Exod. 14:19–24)

Moses apparently identifies the angel of God and the LORD. Both are associated with the pillar. Because in this case the angel of God traveled before Israel, and then came around behind them, he clearly had two functions: he was forerunner but also "rear guard" or defender/deliverer. The roles would be consistent with his identification as the preincarnate Son, who was later revealed as forerunner (Heb. 6:20) and deliverer (Rom. 11:26).

3. The "Angel" of Exodus 23

In some ways the most arresting account of an angel in the Pentateuch comes in Exodus 23. The Lord describes the angel he will send ahead of Israel into Canaan:

> See, I am sending an angel ahead of you to guard you along the way and to bring you to the place I have prepared. Pay attention to him and listen to what he says. Do not rebel against him; he will not forgive your rebellion, since my Name is in him. If you listen carefully to what he says and do all that I say, I will be an enemy to your enemies and will oppose those who oppose you. My angel will go ahead of you and bring you into the land of the Amorites, Hittites, Perizzites, Canaanites, Hivites, and Jebusites, and I will wipe them out. (Exod. 23:20–23)

The angel the Lord promises has three outstanding characteristics. First, the Lord's "Name" is in him. Second, has the prerogative to forgive sins (or not to forgive them). Third, he will go ahead of the Lord's people into the Promised Land. The Lord himself is associated with all three aspects: the Lord has prepared the place to which the angel will lead, the Lord will be an enemy to all Israel's enemies if they do what the angel says (but perhaps not forgive if they do not), and the Lord will wipe out the inhabitants of the Promised Land as the angel leads his people into it. The close association is intensified by statements such as, "If you listen carefully to what *he* says and do all that *I* say" (clearly making the two entities parallel), and "*My angel* will go ahead of you and bring you into the land . . . and *I* will wipe them out." The three characteristics of this angel bear closer examination.

The most salient quality of the angel is that the Lord's Name is in him. We know the name in the ancient Near East had to do with the essential nature of the one who bore it. When it comes to the Lord, this is so much the case that the Name can be used to represent the Lord himself. So he says of the Solomonic temple: "I have consecrated this temple, which you have built, by putting my *Name* there forever. My eyes and my heart will always be there" (1 Kings 9:3, emphasis added). The "eyes and heart" are a synecdoche (*pars pro toto*), telling us the Lord himself will be there. "Forever" here as elsewhere is not necessarily a good translation, since the word it translates means fundamentally, with respect to time, a *long time* (possibly, but not necessarily, eternal). In any case, the Lord is telling Moses and Israel that his Name is in the promised angel. This is such an unusual expression that it probably indicates something more than the sustaining presence of the Lord who undergirds his angels and all other creatures. The statement that the Name is "in" the angel suggests the angel is one in whom the Lord's Spirit or Presence resides in a remarkable manner—perhaps *fully* (cf. Col. 2:9, "For in Christ all the *fullness* of the Deity lives in bodily form," emphasis added)—because the Name denotes God entirely.[9]

Another attribute of the angel points to his being the preincarnate Son. If Israel rebels, the angel "will not forgive your rebellion, since my Name is in him." The angel will not forgive their sins. However, that implies he *could* forgive their sins, for if he *could not* forgive sins the warning that he *would not* forgive sins would be irrelevant. But as Jesus affirmed, only God can forgive sins (cf. Mark 2:1–11). So the angel's prerogative of (implicitly granting or) not granting forgiveness points to his being the preincarnate Son who later, when incarnate, claimed the same prerogative for himself (cf. Matt. 9:6 and parallels).

Finally, the Lord promises, "My angel will go ahead of you and bring you into the land of the Amorites, Hittites, Perizzites, Canaanites, Hivites,

---

9   A similar but not identical privilege is true of the children of God under the new covenant, who have the Spirit residing in them.

and Jebusites, and I will wipe them out." It may be a commonplace idea worth repeating: the Conquest anticipates in the natural realm the successful ministry of the Son in the spiritual realm, and once more at the eschaton. As Joshua led Israel to conquer the Promised Land, so Jesus our forerunner has secured our hope for us beyond the veil (Heb. 6:19–20). That is an *already* conquest. The *not yet* conquest will come when the Lord returns with his saints to defeat his enemies (cf. in much the same spirit Exod. 23:22, "I will be an enemy to your enemies and will oppose those who oppose you"), prefatory (Rev. 19) to his kingdom establishment of a new heavens and a new earth (Rev. 21). It would be consistent with all the above if the angel of Exodus 23 (an uncreated messenger, forerunner, and deliverer who will lead his saints into a battle that is a type of the eschatological conflict)—the one in whom God puts his Name—were the preincarnate Son.

4. The Angel of God's Presence

The final mention of an angel with apparently divine identity occurs in Exodus 33, although the angelic aspect is clarified only later in the Old Testament. The Lord says, '*My Presence* will go with you, and I will give you rest'" (Exod. 33:14, emphasis added). Later Isaiah reflects on the Exodus experience: "In all this their distress He too was distressed, and the *Angel of His Presence* saved them" (Isa. 63:9, author's translation, emphasis added). The "Angel of His Presence" in Isaiah 63 is apparently explanatory of God's "Presence" in Exodus 33—which is to say the angel is equivalent to God. For the angel to be equivalent to God he must be, not a created angel, but a messenger who is also God—the preincarnate Son.

In light of the data presented above the following conclusion seems warranted: repeated parallelism in the passages indicates identity of the Lord and the angel of the LORD (or God and the angel of God). This does not contradict Hebrews 1:13–14 ("To which of the angels did God ever say, 'Sit at my right hand until I make your enemies a footstool for your feet'? Are not all angels ministering spirits sent to serve those who will inherit salvation?") because the word "angel" also means "messenger"—and in these passages the messenger may be the preincarnate Son.

Special Grace Occurrences

These angel of the LORD passages—all of which have some claim to portraying the preincarnate Son in ministry or service to people—all occur in the literature of the special grace covenants, and so in some sense under their aegis. Even Hagar is a member of the Abrahamic household when the theophany becomes part of her experience, and the Lord's appearance and care for her son, Ishmael, is part of his faithfulness to promises the Lord made to Abraham when the patriarch was living under special grace covenant named after him. Moreover, the angel of the LORD passages appear only in the literature of the Abrahamic and the Mosaic covenants. The fact that the preincarnate Son did not appear in such a way to people under the common grace covenants would be consistent with the Son's eschatological salvific role in which the special grace covenants culminate.[10] He appears, then—before his incarnation— to people under the special grace covenants and to them alone, and these appearances are a foretaste of a better and future reality, a time when he appears incarnate—only a precursor to his appearance at the end of days, when he returns in a glorified body to gather his own to himself and glorify them with him.

HAGAR AND ISHMAEL COVENANTALLY CONSIDERED

Abraham's dealings with Hagar on the other hand have to do with his relationship to the common grace realm and its blessings. The Lord's answer to Abraham's prayer for Ishmael makes it clear that the boy is a creature of common grace. Nonetheless, Hagar stands out in biblical theology because Paul takes her as an emblem for the law, and Paul's distinction between Hagar's offspring and the children of the promise should help produce a proper understanding of the biblical covenants. These ideas are important for the following discussion.

From the Lord's promises to Abraham it is clear that Hagar's son and inferentially his offspring are outside the special grace covenant relationship the Lord makes with Abraham and his descendants. Abraham asks the Lord to bless Ishmael—the only son he has so far—who we should note has been circumcised and is thus *formally* part of the Abrahamic covenant community: "And Abraham said to God, 'If only Ishmael might live under your blessing!'" (Gen. 17:18). The Lord responds in a way that makes the divide between Ishmael and his future on the one hand and the future of the Abrahamic covenant line on the other very clear:

---

10   Understanding that the Lord came to minister in the "last days" (cf. Heb. 1:2, ἐπ' ἐσχάτου τῶν ἡμερῶν τούτων).

Then God said, "Yes, but your wife Sarah will bear you a son, and you will call him Isaac. *I will establish my covenant with him* as an everlasting covenant for his descendants after him. And as for Ishmael, I have heard you: I will surely bless him; I will make him fruitful and will greatly increase his numbers. He will be the father of twelve rulers, and I will make him into a great nation. *But my covenant I will establish with Isaac,* whom Sarah will bear to you by this time next year." (Gen. 17:19–21, emphases added)

God will surely bless Ishmael with a blessing that in some measure alludes to and fulfills the common grace mandate of Genesis 1:28: the Lord will "make him fruitful and will greatly increase his numbers." The Lord also blesses Ishmael with a blessing that is analogous to the promise of royal offspring to Abraham (Gen. 17:16) when he says: "He will be the father of twelve rulers, and I will make him into a great nation" (Gen. 17:20). But the blessings of *the covenant with Abraham* will be greater: Abraham's wife "will be the mother of nations; kings of peoples will come from her" (Gen. 17:16). The Abrahamic covenant provides offspring in nations and kings over them, greater blessings to which the blessings of Ishmael are a minor, though non-trivial, parallel.[11] The culminating and emphatic statement is this: "But my covenant I will establish with Isaac" and, as we have shown, the better translation is "But my covenant [i.e., with you, Abraham] I will keep/maintain in force [אקים] with Isaac."[12] The understanding of the blessings of Abraham is that the Lord will work through the Abrahamic covenant to bring people of all nations to himself and make them a royal priesthood. He will thus accomplish the cultural mandate given to the man and the woman in Genesis 1:28 but in a special grace way: to fill the world with a multitude, a royal priesthood, born not of the flesh or of a husband's will but of the Spirit of God (John 1:13).[13]

---

11   The Lord will make Ishmael into "a great nation," but Sarah will be "mother of *nations*"; twelve kings will come from Ishmael, but numberless kings will come from Sarah.

12   See discussion of covenant idioms above (pp. 24–31), and below, chapter 5.

13   Once again: The Lord's statement, "But my covenant I will establish with Isaac," does not indicate a different covenant later to be established with Isaac; rather, it is a promise that the Lord will put and *keep in force* the Abrahamic covenant with Isaac (which he does in Gen. 26:2–5).

A BRIEF LOOK AHEAD: HAGAR AND SINAI

The contrast between the Lord's treatment of Abraham and his line, and his treatment of Ishmael and his line, finds theological clarification in the New Testament. Paul distinguishes the two lines by distinguishing between their mothers:

> Tell me, you who want to be under the law, are you not aware of what the law says? For it is written that Abraham had two sons, one by the slave woman and the other by the free woman. His son by the slave woman was born in the ordinary way; but his son by the free woman was born as the result of a promise. (Gal 4:21–23)

Hagar of course is the slave woman and Sarah the free woman. Hagar's son was born, to use the language of John 1:13, "of a father's will," or as Paul puts it, "in the ordinary way" (Gal. 4:23). Sarah's son, on the other hand, was born "as the result of a promise" and was correspondingly "the son born by the power of the Spirit" (Gal. 4:29). The association of the promise and the Spirit is important because Paul understands that the universal blessing promised to Abraham ("all peoples on earth will be blessed through you," Gen. 12:3) comes when one is born of the Spirit—as Isaac analogously somehow was born by a miraculous work of the Spirit, since his parents were as good as dead when it came to childbearing, and as Jesus *par excellence* was—although his physical conception in the womb was by the Spirit, whereas our spiritual birth into a new life comes by the Spirit after our natural birth (John 3:5).[14] Accordingly, birth by the Spirit makes Isaac, Jesus, and ourselves all Abrahamic "children of promise."

But not all are children of promise. Paul develops a metaphor that parallels the mothers of the elect and non-elect lines with locales associated with the old and new covenants, respectively:

> These things may be taken figuratively, for the women represent two covenants. One covenant is from Mount Sinai and bears children who are to be slaves: This is Hagar. Now Hagar stands for Mount Sinai in Arabia and corresponds to the present city of Jerusalem, because she is in slavery

---

14 New Testament passages that use the terms "born" and "Spirit" together have to do only with Sarah's child of promise (Gal. 4:29), Jesus (Luke 1:35), and believers in Jesus (John 3:5, 8).

with her children. But the Jerusalem that is above is free, and she is our mother. (Gal. 4:24–26)

Paul associates Hagar with the old covenant and with Mount Sinai because the Lord gave the old covenant there; he also associates it with "the present city of Jerusalem" because Jerusalem is also under the old covenant—although such was apparently not Jesus' wish as he declared, "O Jerusalem, Jerusalem, you who kill the prophets and stone those sent to you, how often I have longed to gather your children together, as a hen gathers her chicks under her wings, but you were not willing" (Matt. 23:37; cf. Luke 13:34). The inhabitants of the earthly Jerusalem (or most of them) were not willing to come under Jesus' "wing," that is, under the aegis of the new covenant. Since the earthly Jerusalem rejected their Messiah, Paul associates the new covenant with the "Jerusalem that is above," which "is free, and she is our mother." The children of that "free" mother are also free. They are the ones "born by the power of the Spirit" (Gal. 4:29). The metaphorical structure of Paul's argument can be displayed as follows:

Hagar / Sinai covenant / Jerusalem / law / bondage

Sarah / new covenant / Jerusalem above / Spirit / freedom

In that schema Hagar is the old covenant and Sarah is the new covenant. The consequence of such an understanding is great because it excludes those who are under the law, once the promise of the Spirit has become available:

Now you, brothers, like Isaac, are children of promise. At that time the son born in the ordinary way persecuted the son born by the power of the Spirit. It is the same now. But what does the Scripture say? "Get rid of the slave woman and her son, for the slave woman's son will never share in the inheritance with the free woman's son." Therefore, brothers, we are not children of the slave woman, but of the free woman. (Gal. 4:28–31)

Just as Ishmael persecuted Isaac (the "one born by the power of the Spirit"), so now those born under the law persecute those born of the Spirit. Paul would know since he was once of those persecutors. But Paul now takes God's word to Abraham (Gal. 4:30) and applies it to those under the law who persecute the church: "The slave woman's son will never share in the inheritance with the free woman's son."

ISHMAEL'S CIRCUMCISION AND HIS DESTINY

It may seem strange that Ishmael is circumcised, just as Isaac is, and yet his future turns out to be so different from that of his younger half brother. The Lord (i.e., the angel of the LORD as discussed above) states the difference between them when he informs Hagar:

> You are now pregnant
> and you will give birth to a son.
> You shall name him Ishmael,
>   for the LORD has heard of your misery.
> He will be a wild donkey of a man;
>   his hand will be against everyone
> and everyone's hand against him,
> and he will live in hostility
>   toward all his brothers. (Gen. 16:11–12, author's translation)

That pronouncement is dramatically different from the Lord's promise regarding Isaac, and we repeat the relevant verses for emphasis:

> And Abraham said to God, "If only Ishmael might live under your bless-ing!" Then God said, "Yes, but your wife Sarah will bear you a son, and you will call him Isaac. I will establish my covenant with him as an ev-erlasting covenant for his descendants after him. And as for Ishmael, I have heard you: I will surely bless him; I will make him fruitful and will greatly increase his numbers. He will be the father of twelve rulers, and I will make him into a great nation. But my covenant I will establish with Isaac, whom Sarah will bear to you by this time next year." (Gen. 17:18–21)

The Lord has more blessing in store for Ishmael than one might expect from the angelic pronouncement of Genesis 16. Nonetheless—and the promise of great nationhood and twelve rulers to come from Ishmael notwithstanding—the far greater blessing comes to Isaac: "But my cov-enant I will establish with Isaac, whom Sarah will bear to you by this time next year." One would rather be found in the Lord's covenant with Abraham than possess the whole world and yet be outside that covenant. The adversative ("But my covenant I will establish with Isaac") suggests clearly enough that ultimately Ishmael—circumcision notwithstanding—will fall out of membership in the Lord's covenant with his father.

As a student of mine astutely commented, Abraham's circumcision of

Ishmael—along with all the other males in Abraham's household—speaks of Abraham, not of Ishmael. Abraham circumcised all the males in his household *as the Lord commanded him to do*. So Abraham showed his faithful obedience to the Lord's command. For Abraham, circumcision was an outward sign of an inner faith by which he entered the covenant "cut" in Genesis 15 (cf. Rom. 4:11). For the others in his household, however, circumcision was an external sign of a formal inclusion in that covenant. Their membership entailed obedience to the "commands, decrees, and instructions" (Gen. 26:5) we later learn the Lord gave Abraham in the context of the covenant. Nonetheless, any of those circumcised people would only be saved by faith. With them it was true as Paul said of Israel: "Not all who are descended from Israel are Israel" (Rom. 9:6), and again: "Nor because they are his descendants are they all Abraham's children. On the contrary, 'It is through Isaac that your offspring will be reckoned'" (Rom. 9:7). As with other special grace covenants, any member of the Abrahamic covenant—or put another way, anyone who had received the covenant sign and thereby formally entered into the covenant—could fall out of the covenant and lose actual membership in it. The lack of faith would sooner or later become manifest as disobedience.[15]

We turn now from Sarah and Isaac , Hagar and Ishmael—who are paradigmatic of the old and new covenants and those who live under them—to the judgment on Sodom and Gomorrah, which is paradigmatic of the final judgment.

SODOM AND GOMORRAH

Sodom and Gomorrah are mentioned twenty-three times in the Bible. Some of the notices occur in historical material: geographical and topographical notices (Gen. 10:19; 13:10), the account of the battle of the kings (Gen. 14:2, 8, 10, 11), and the account of the Lord's judgment on the two cities (Gen. 18:10; 19:1, 24, 28). The majority of the occurrences, however, are in covenant lawsuit material in the Old Testament—that is, against Israel (Deut. 29:23; Isa. 1:9–10; Jer. 23:24; Amos 4:11), against Babylon (Deut. 32:32; 13:19; Jer. 50:40), against Edom (Jer. 49:18), and against Moab and Ammon (Zeph. 2:9).

The use is somewhat different in the New Testament. Jesus uses the

---

15   This statement naturally implicates the new covenant, and the possibility of falling out of membership in it is discussed in chapter 3 of volume 3.

judgment on Sodom and Gomorrah in a comparison to show how severe
the judgment will be on any town that does not receive his disciples, and
that judgment will be worse than the judgment on Sodom and Gomorrah (Matt. 10:15) because those towns will have been offered more from
the Lord than Sodom and Gomorrah ever were; Paul refers to Sodom
and Gomorrah in his argument about the Jews' forfeiture of their calling
(Rom. 9:29, citing Isa. 1:9); Peter uses them in a historical review of God's
judgment ethos, which includes fallen angels, the Flood, and Sodom and
Gomorrah (2 Peter 2:6); and Jude mentions them in a similar frame of
reference (Jude 7). Some examples of the historical covenant lawsuit and
New Testament types of occurrence now receive further comment.

The second historical notice is topographical. It describes the plain in
which Sodom and Gomorrah were located by a comparison that seems
almost hyperbolic: "Lot looked up and saw that the whole plain of the
Jordan toward Zoar was well watered, like the garden of the LORD, like
the land of Egypt. (This was before the LORD destroyed Sodom and Gomorrah)" (Gen. 13:10). The comparison with "the garden of the LORD"
(i.e., Eden) is important not only as regards the impending judgment
of Sodom and Gomorrah, but also because it occurs later in covenant
lawsuit materials. Through Joel the Lord foretells a devastating locust
onslaught in the day of the LORD (Joel 2:1–2), and describes the land
before and after the judgment: "Before them fire devours, behind them
a flame blazes. Before them the land is like the garden of Eden, behind
them, a desert waste—nothing escapes them" (Joel 2:3). The Edenic comparison can also apply to other nations. The Lord compares Assyria at her
height to the trees of Eden, "I made it beautiful with abundant branches,
the envy of all the trees of Eden in the garden of God" (Ezek. 31:9), but
then recalls how he brought her down. A similar comparison occurs in
a judgment oracle against Egypt (Ezek. 31:1–18), which is also likened
to the trees of Eden: "Which of the trees of Eden can be compared with
you in splendor and majesty? Yet you, too, will be brought down with the
trees of Eden to the earth below; you will lie among the uncircumcised,
with those killed by the sword" (Ezek. 31:18). Nonetheless, although it
occurs in covenant lawsuit evocations of past or impending judgment,
the mention of Eden is a positive thing: the land as it was (or is) before
the judgment is compared to Eden.

Similarly, when the Lord describes how things will be *once his judgment is complete*, he compares the restored land to Eden or "the garden of
the LORD" or "of God." Isaiah predicts, "The LORD will surely comfort
Zion and will look with compassion on all her ruins; he will make her

deserts like Eden, her wastelands like the garden of the LORD. Joy and gladness will be found in her, thanksgiving and the sound of singing" (Isa. 51:3). The Lord foretells a future Edenic restoration through Ezekiel: "They will say, 'This land that was laid waste has become like the garden of Eden; the cities that were lying in ruins, desolate and destroyed, are now fortified and inhabited'" (Ezek. 36:35). Eden has been destroyed, but Eden is also the goal.

In summary, a future object of judgment can be compared to Eden, and a future judgment can be compared to the destruction of Eden (or its "trees," Ezek. 31:16–18); a restored state can also be compared to Eden (e.g., Ezek. 36:35). The Lord's restoration ethos, manifest in these historical events, has an eschatological trajectory: it points toward an ultimate Edenic restoration found at the end of Revelation. There one sees a river that flows from the Lord's presence (Rev. 22:2; cf. Gen. 2:10) and trees of life (Rev. 22:2; cf. Gen. 2:9), which reads literally, "and on this side and on that of the river, a tree of life, yielding twelve fruits"—apparently multiple trees because of a vastly increased blessing to be had, when the Lord restores all things.

The Lord's judgment on Sodom and Gomorrah has eschatological implications, but the prelude to it also has implications for the last days. The prelude to the judgment episode includes Abraham's hospitable reception of three "men" before his tent at Mamre (Gen. 18:1–7), the Lord's birth announcement to Abraham and Sarah (Gen. 18:9–15), and Abraham's intercession for the cities of the plain (Gen. 18:16–22). We consider these items seriatim.

Abraham's Hospitable Reception of Three "Men"

It is important not to forget that Abraham was a wealthy man in his own context, one who could be considered a king even if he did not yet possess the land.[16] Nonetheless, he behaves reverentially toward the three men and provides for their foot washing and meal. The righteous Lot (2 Peter 2:7) behaves in the same way toward the two angels (Gen. 19:1–3). One would rather not carry interpretation too far but it is worth note that this submissive service is not unlike the service of Christ, who in his earthly ministry washed his disciples' feet and fed the hungry. These ideas are

---

16 Cf. Cyrus Gordon, *The Common Background of Greek and Hebrew Civilizations* (New York: W. W. Norton, 1965), 288–89.

stated in a prefatory way because they introduce an even more Christ-like behavior on Abraham's part when he intercedes for the sinful cities.

The Lord's Birth Announcement to Sarah

The Lord—whose identity in the passage Abraham seems to have intuited or suspected and whom he seems to understand as such when he addresses him as the "Judge of all the earth" (Gen. 18:25)—makes a promise to Abraham: "I will surely return to you about this time next year, and Sarah your wife will have a son" (Gen. 18:10). Because Sarah is too old to bear children (Gen. 18:11), and her husband is also very old (Gen. 18:12), she hears the Lord's promise with doubt (Gen. 18:12). She finally amens the Lord, however, as Hebrews tells us:

> And by faith even Sarah, who was past childbearing age, was enabled to bear children because she considered him faithful who had made the promise. And so from this one man, and he as good as dead, came descendants as numerous as the stars in the sky and as countless as the sand on the seashore. (Heb. 11:11–12, author's translation)

The birth of this child of promise was facilitated by a yielded faith—an amening of what God said he would do. The birth of the Son of God was also facilitated by a yielded faith—that of Mary—an event considered more fully when we discuss the new covenant. At this point we outline the announcement to Abraham and Sarah because it resembles other birth announcements in the ancient Near East and in the Bible:

Important Birth Announcements

Ugaritic	"Behold, the virgin will give birth to a son"	*hl glmt tld b[n]*
Genesis 18:10	"And behold, a son to Sarah"	והנה בן לשרה
Judges 13:3	"You are barren and childless, but you are going to become pregnant and give birth to a son"	הנה־נא את־עקרה ולא ילדת והרית וילדת בן
Isaiah 7:14	"The virgin will conceive and give birth to a son"	והנה העלמה הרה וילדת בן

The announcements seem at first glance to be somewhat disparate but they have two things in common: they promise the birth of a son to a virgin (who has not yet given birth) or to a barren woman (who also has not given birth). The one factor that cements the union of these cases is the involvement of a supernatural agency in each promised birth. In the Ugaratic example, a union between the moon god Yarih and the virgin goddess Nikkal is in view.[17] In Sarah's case it seems clear that a woman "past the age of childbearing" would need supernatural help to produce a child. In Samson's birth announcement narrative one learns the mother-to-be is barren, and the announcement by an angel seems to imply some supernatural involvement to change her barren state. Finally, in the Emmanuel promise of Isaiah the virgin birth is foretold, and subsequent revelation explains the fulfillment of this promise when the Holy Spirit produces the incarnate Son in Mary's womb (Matt. 1:18–23).

The promise the Lord made to Sarah is the earliest of these recorded divine promises. It seems fitting that the Lord's promise to Abraham and Sarah has historical pride of place. It had ontological precedence as a realized idea in the mind of God—since God imagined it before the creation. Its historical precedence may have provided the foundation for its occurrence in Ugaritic mythology, since the spirits who produce mythology have always mimicked and distorted what God has done before them—or what God has thought before them, to the extent that they may know it by God's permission.

Abraham's Intercession for the Cities of the Plain

Before the judgment on Sodom and Gomorrah, Abraham tries to bargain with the Lord to avoid it. That episode is prefaced by the account of the three men and the birth announcement just considered. It is clear from the narrative that two men, who set off for the cities (Gen. 18:22), are angels, because they are identified as such (Gen. 19:1). The third man is apparently the Lord, since Abraham identifies him as Judge of all the earth, and clearly the one Abraham addresses is in a position to decide the criteria of judgment.

Since the third man is the Lord, we may have here one of the closest approaches to Docetism in the Bible (another would be Jacob's wrestling with God). What some erroneously attributed to God when they argued that in Christ God only *appeared* to be a man but in fact was not, may in this Old Testament case be closer to the truth. There is no way to fathom

---

17   Cf. discussion in Niehaus, *God at Sinai,* 237–39. Ugaritic *hl* is a functional equivalent to Hebrew הנה, and emphasizes the sentence it introduces; cf. Cyrus Gordon, *Ugaritic Textbook* (Rome: Pontifical Biblical Institute, 1965), 109 (12.7).

the totality of what one reads in this account. We are told, however, that the man Abraham soon calls the Judge of all the earth appears before his tent and accepts his hospitality, which includes arrangements for foot washing and a meal—Oriental courtesies that all three men accept (Gen. 18:1–8).

Abraham's appeal to the Lord is well known. As part of that appeal, his concern for his own relatives is important. Although he has redeemed Lot (and apparently his family) before (Gen. 14), maybe the most notable thing now is this: Abraham shows concern *not only* for his relatives—for Lot and his family—he is concerned for *any who are righteous* in the cities. The foundation of his appeal is his correct understanding of God's own righteousness—that is, God's own *faithfulness to his own character*:

> Will you sweep away the righteous with the wicked? What if there are fifty righteous people in the city? Will you really sweep it away and not spare the place for the sake of the fifty righteous people in it? Far be it from you to do such a thing—to kill the righteous with the wicked, treating the righteous and the wicked alike. Far be it from you! Will not the Judge of all the earth do right? (Gen. 18:23–25)

Abraham has understood God's righteousness: God will not sweep away the wicked with the righteous. The "Judge of all the earth" will do what is "right." Abraham's appeal foreshadows something he could not foresee, Jesus' own statement about the righteousness of God. Jesus gives an example of God's justice in an analogous eschatological context, in what is commonly called the parable of the weeds:

> The kingdom of heaven is like a man who sowed good seed in his field. But while everyone was sleeping, his enemy came and sowed weeds among the wheat, and went away. When the wheat sprouted and formed heads, then the weeds also appeared. The owner's servants came to him and said, "Sir, didn't you sow good seed in your field? Where then did the weeds come from?" "An enemy did this," he replied. The servants asked him, "Do you want us to go and pull them up?" "No," he answered, "because while you are pulling the weeds, you may uproot the wheat with them. Let both grow together until the harvest. At that time I will tell the harvesters: First collect the weeds and tie them in bundles to be burned; then gather the wheat and bring it into my barn." (Matt. 13:24–30)

The parable reassures us that, in an ongoing world, the Lord will not destroy the wicked with the righteous. When the eschaton comes, however, God will separate them and take them to their different destinies.

Abraham has therefore correctly understood or intuited the Lord's righteous nature. He is a just Judge and will not work a premature judgment on the unrighteous that would compromise or destroy the righteous along with them. The case of Sodom and Gomorrah, however, is virtually eschatological—at least for those cities. Their inability to pass an extraordinarily low bar the Lord allows for the postponement of their judgment—ten righteous inhabitants—shows that, much like the inhabitants of the Promised Land later, they are without faith; it is not in their nature. Not even ten people in Sodom and Gomorrah can amen the character and standards of God, even as those were apparent under common grace, and so the time has come for their judgment.[18] So the Lord does send his angels, to use Jesus' terminology—namely, two of them in Genesis 18–19—to separate out the good grain (Lot and those with him) so they may be spared the fiery judgment that God sends on the unrighteous (or to use Jesus' terminology, the weeds).

The virtue of stating such parallels is not to show that one can produce parallels. Rather, the existence of parallels shows that God works consistently vis-à-vis his creation, and this consistency can be seen in what he does (as in the case of Sodom and Gomorrah) and what he says he will do (in the parable of the weeds). And so he is called "Jesus Christ . . . the same yesterday and today and forever" (Heb. 13:8).

ABRAHAM AND ABIMELEK

The last topic of this chapter—the prophetic nature of the life of God's people in the here and now—involves an important matter for the church: how God's people, the true children of Abraham, made to be God's people in the sixth step of the Major Paradigm in the new covenant, can and should represent God prophetically in the world of common grace until the Lord returns to judge that world. The Abraham-Abimelek episode touches on these ideas.

Two things stand out in Abraham's encounter with Abimelek. One has to do with God's interaction with the king. The other has to do with prophecy. God's interaction with the king implies a common grace work

---

18   Cf. Romans 1:18–31 where Paul addresses the same idea in terms of ongoing worldly judgment in the flow of history.

of the Holy Spirit, and this has its eschatological aspect. What God tells the king regarding Abraham teaches about prophecy and what it can entail, and this has its Christological aspect.

The Eschatological Aspect

God graciously keeps Abimelek from the sin of having another man's wife. Elohim, the name used for God in Genesis when he is presented as God of all people (cf. Gen. 1:1, "In the beginning Elohim created the heavens and the earth," author's rendering), speaks to Abimelek and reveals what Abraham and Sarah have done to him.[19] The king complains that he has taken Sarah "with a clear conscience and clean hands" (Gen. 20:5). God knows this of course and responds: "Yes, I know you did this with a clear conscience, and so I have kept (the verb חשׂך) you from sinning against me. That is why I did not let you touch her" (lit. "I did not give you [לא נתתיך] to touch her," Gen. 20:6). The verb (חשׂך) and the action are important. Two other contexts mention the Lord's "keeping" someone from sin: By means of Abigail's plea, the Lord keeps David from slaughtering Nabal and his men (cf. 1 Sam. 25:2–28) so that David declares, "The *LORD* . . . has *kept* [חשׂך] his servant from doing wrong" (1 Sam. 25:39, emphases added). David also pleads, "Keep [חשׂך] your servant also from willful sins" (Ps. 19:13a [19:14a MT]).

The biblical statements that God can keep one from sin are important because fallen humans often have difficulty keeping themselves from sin, *especially when they are aware of what is sinful.* That is part of Paul's great argument in Romans 6–8 regarding the inability of the law to create in people the standard of behavior it demands of them (cf. especially Romans 7), and the subsequent statement: "for what the law was powerless

---

19 Abraham's subsequent confession of this ruse to Abimelek reveals something we have noted about laconic reporting: "And when God had me wander from my father's household, I said to her, 'This is how you can show your love to me: Everywhere we go, say of me, "He is my brother"'" (Gen. 20:13). Abram first played this trick with Pharaoh in Genesis 12. The next report of such a ruse on his part comes in Genesis 20. Only in that later case do we receive the *further information* reported in Genesis 20:13. This seems a good parallel to Genesis 2:17 ("you must not eat from the tree of the knowledge of good and evil") compared with Genesis 3:3. In the latter case, the woman adds the information "and you must not touch it" (i.e., the tree of the knowledge of good and evil). In both cases, data reported by the narrator are supplemented later by a person involved in the narrative, and both are, consequently, cases that show the laconic nature of the first report. Cf. discussion, in volume 1 of *Biblical Theology*, 97.

to do because it was weakened by the flesh, God did by sending his own Son in the likeness of sinful flesh to be a sin offering" (Rom. 8:3). Paul tells us further that "if by the Spirit you put to death the misdeeds of the body, you will live" (Rom. 8:13b), and the major part of the discussion in Romans 8:1–17 is devoted to how, after the work of Christ, one may live according to the Spirit and ironically, having been set free from the law, be able to fulfill the law (Rom. 8:1–4).[20] This issue is discussed more fully when we consider the dynamic of life under the new covenant. What matters now is that we recognize *who it is* that can restrain people from sin. Under the new covenant it is by the power of the Spirit that we can "live according to the Spirit" (Rom. 8:4) since we have "the Spirit of Christ" (Rom. 8:9). The Spirit is the one who makes it possible to live a life that is not under the dominion of sin. If this is so under the new covenant, it may not be an unwarranted suggestion that the Spirit was also the one who kept Abimelek, or could keep David, from sin. David prays, "Keep [חשׂך] your servant also from willful sins; / may they not rule over me" (Ps. 19:13). He also says, "Do not . . . take your Holy Spirit from me" (Ps. 51:11). The Spirit who "came to" David every day (1 Sam. 16:13) did not dwell in him but, David hoped, would nonetheless keep him from sins so they would not rule over him. David hopes and prays to avoid the experience of being ruled by sin, and the idea of being ruled by sin sounds very much like what Paul delineates in Romans 7 (cf. esp. Rom. 7:7–23).

If, then, we ask which person of the triune God had the role of keeping Abimelek, David, or anyone else in the Old Testament from sin, the most likely answer seems to be the Holy Spirit. Abraham's contretemps with Abimelek evokes the first mention of such divine intervention, but one finds the concept later in David's prayer. The relative rarity of the idea in the Old Testament and under the Mosaic covenant is consistent with the dynamic difference between the old covenant and the new, portrayed vividly by Paul in Romans 6–8.[21]

---

20   As Paul says, "Therefore, there is now no condemnation for those who are in Christ Jesus, because through Christ Jesus the *law of the Spirit* who gives life has set you free from the law of sin and death. For what the law was powerless to do because it was weakened by the flesh, God did by sending his own Son in the likeness of sinful flesh to be a sin offering. And so he condemned sin in the flesh, in order that the righteous requirement of the law might be fully met in us, who do not live according to the flesh but *according to the Spirit*" (Rom. 8:1–4, emphases added).

21   The issue anticipated here is discussed much more fully in chapter 5 of volume 3.

The Holy Spirit is the one who through the word sustains all things and without whom life would not be possible. He is also most likely—according to his role as one who can restrain people from sin—the person who holds back secret power of lawlessness in the world: "For the secret power of lawlessness is already at work; but the one who now holds it back will continue to do so till he is taken out of the way" (2 Thess. 2:7).[22] Some have objected to the idea that God could "take" his Spirit out of the way, but we already know the Spirit departed from Saul (1 Sam. 16:14) and David, aware of this, pleads with the Lord: "Do not cast me from your presence / or *take* [the verb לקח] your Holy Spirit from me" (Ps. 51:11, emphasis added). We anticipate, then, an eschatological scenario in which the Lord will *take* his Spirit out of the way: the Spirit will no longer restrain the power of lawlessness; rather, *anomia* will run rampant and open the door to such beings as the Antichrist and his prophet, and their false signs and wonders at the end of the age.

The Christological Aspect

God tells Abimelek something about Abraham in Genesis 20, and what he says has a Christological aspect. It is important to remember that Jesus was a prophet. The word "prophet" occurs for the first time when God says to Abimelek, "Now return the man's wife, for he is a prophet, and he will pray for you and you will live. But if you do not return her, you may be sure that you and all who belong to you will die" (Gen. 20:7). Afterward, "Abraham prayed to God, and God healed Abimelek, his wife, and his female slaves so they could have children again, for the LORD had kept all the women in Abimelek's household from conceiving because of Abraham's wife Sarah" (Gen. 20:17–18). Clearly, Abraham's prayer makes possible the further life of Abimelek and his folk (v. 7a), and apparently one form their deliverance takes is God's healing them so they can reproduce (v. 18). Maladies can have physical or spiritual causes; they can be brought about naturally, or by demons or, as here, by God. We know the Lord can heal any malady, even death. Unquestionably he can heal a malady he himself has imposed, and that is what we find in this passage. Three facts stand out here. First, the passage that contains the first use of the word prophet also contains the first example of divine healing; second, healing comes about because the prophet prays; and, third, and perhaps most important, the prayer that brought healing was

---

22   Cf. further discussion in *ANETBT*, 136.

ordained by God (cf. v. 7). This is related to the more general concept voiced in Ephesians that the Lord has prepared good works in advance for his people (Eph. 2:10). That truth is not as clear in the Old Testament as it is in the New, although there are glimpses of it in certain historical scenarios (e.g., in commissions given to prophets, of which 1 Kings 19:15–16 is a good example).[23]

The Christology of such a case is apparent from several factors. First, Abraham is a prophet and therefore a type of Christ who was the prophet *par excellence*. Second, God gives a warning about sin, both verbally and in the form of a physical affliction, and at God's initiative the prophet can heal the affliction in connection with repentance on the part of the one warned. In Abraham's case his own deceptive act was the occasion of God's warning affliction to the king, and in this Abraham is *not* like Christ. But this weakness or flaw in him highlights an aspect of Christology already noted: it is his office that makes an Old Testament individual Christological, and not his character. Abraham is a type of Christ by virtue of being a prophet, not because he is perfect in virtue. The Lord justified Abraham because of his faith, not because of any moral perfection or attractiveness he may or may not have possessed. Third, although one is first told explicitly in Genesis 20 that Abraham is a prophet, the fact that he is a prophet has already been made apparent from two things: (1) he has heard from the Lord and has been given direction/instruction (i.e., *torah*) by the Lord (even before the Lord cut a covenant with him); and more important (2) he has mediated a covenant from the Lord to his household, a household that will expand to become the Israel of a later covenant and beyond that to become the household of faith, the Israel of God under the new covenant. His being a covenant mediator prophet places him in a small but distinguished company of such prophets, through whom the Lord worked pivotally as history unfolded: Adam, Noah, Abraham, Moses, David, and the last and greatest of them all, Jesus.

---

23 Cf. discussion in chapter 14.

CHAPTER FOUR

GOD'S ONE COVENANT WITH ABRAHAM

How many covenants did God make with Abraham? Readers of the Bible for many generations have thought God made one covenant with Abraham, and so they have spoken of "the Abrahamic covenant." More recently, some scholars have proposed that God made more than one covenant with Abraham, and they find in Genesis 15, 17, and 22 sufficient material to invite or bolster such an understanding. Those chapters offer enough data, some of them overlapping, to make the construction of an argument for two Abrahamic covenants possible.[1] We will see that such arguments are in a sense inductive, leading toward a conclusion by a selection and reassembly of biblical data. Procedurally, this is not much different from the method of scholars who, for example, construct two flood accounts ("J" and "P") out of the repetitive material offered in Genesis 6–8.[2] In both cases there is sufficient material, with a mix of

---

1   See for example Paul R. Williamson, *Sealed with an Oath: Covenant in God's Unfolding Purpose* (Downers Grove, IL: Inter Varsity Press, 2002), 89–91; Scott Hahn, *Kinship by Covenant: A Canonical Approach to the Fulfillment of God's Saving Promises* (New Haven, CT: Yale University Press, 2009), 101–35.

2   I would be quick to affirm, however, that Williamson does not espouse the Documentary Hypothesis, although Hahn, with his canonical approach, seems comfortable working with it. The concept of canonical criticism, as evinced by Childs and practiced by

---

This chapter is an adaptation of my article, "God's Covenant with Abraham," *JETS* 56, no. 2 (2013): 249–71. It argues that the Lord made only one covenant with Abram. The question—How many covenants did the Lord make with Abram?—has become increasingly important in scholarship of the Abrahamic covenant. Moreover, a proper understanding of the Abrahamic covenant is part of a larger issue—a proper understanding of the biblical covenants and how they relate and function.

overlapping data and distinctive data, to make the reconstruction possible. This, however, does not mean that the reconstruction is correct, since such an approach may be flawed on other grounds.[3]

We can suggest another approach, which does not follow an inductive course but rather a deductive one. A deductive approach begins with what the Bible actually tells us about the number of God's covenants with Abraham. Accordingly, we note that the Bible only ever refers to "the Lord's covenant (singular) with Abraham."[4] We affirm that this datum should be the governing consideration in any subsequent analysis. In other words, rather than taking Genesis 15, 17, and 22 and seeing whether one might construe two or even three covenants from them, let us take the biblical affirmation of the Lord's *covenant* (singular) with Abraham as the idea by which we understand the materials of the Genesis chapters. If we do, the result will be that their data may properly be seen as all part of one covenant.[5]

It is probably fair to say that people have heretofore thought the Lord made a covenant with Abram in Genesis 15 and then over time added supplemental information, including name changes, requirements, and promises in Genesis 17 and 22.[6] We reaffirm that older understanding, which is still held by many. Part of our procedure will be to recognize that the Lord subsequently behaved in a similar fashion in the two special grace covenants that established the Old Testament and the New Testament forms of God's kingdom, that is, the Mosaic covenant and the new

---

him and others, is I believe deeply flawed, and will be addressed in an article, "Canonical Criticism: A Modern Folly" (forthcoming).

3   For example, a documentary analysis of the flood narrative produces two distinct accounts but shares the foundational flaw of the whole literary critical approach: a lack of regard for what is now understood of style (including the use of divine names) and the relation of style to authorship in the ancient Near East.

4   That is, in Exodus 2:24, Levitcus 26:42, 2 Kings 13:23, 1 Chronicles 16:16, Psalm 105:9, and Acts 3:25. Cf. my own earlier discussion in Niehaus, "Covenant and Narrative, God and Time." *JETS* 53, no. 3 (2010): 535–59, esp. 542–50.

5   Recognition that the covenantal data are presented as parts of a historical and narrative sequence contributes to such an understanding, a principle that has already been noted.

6   Cf. Dumbrell, *Covenant and Creation*, 77, who affirms this view and says in his summary discussion of Genesis 17: "This chapter is merely a reaffirmation of the material of Gen. 12 and 15." Cf. likewise the more extensive discussion by Gordon Wenham, *Genesis 16–50*, WBC 2 (Dallas: Word, 1994), 28–32, esp. 29 (regarding Genesis 17); 96–118 (regarding Genesis 22).

covenant, respectively. In both cases, after the covenant was made (or cut, to use the biblical term), the Lord added subsequent requirements and promises—for example, in the new covenant the Lord added the requirement of baptism (as a covenant sign) after the cutting of the covenant, just as he had added the Sabbath requirement (as a covenant sign, Exod. 31:16) after the cutting of the Mosaic covenant, and the requirement of circumcision (as a covenant sign) after the cutting of the Abrahamic covenant. Such matters are considered in more detail below.

THE LORD'S SINGULAR COVENANT WITH ABRAM

We have noted that the Bible only refers to the Lord's covenant with Abraham in the singular. The few relevant passages deserve attention in their own right because of their importance for the issue at hand.

The Lord's Covenant with Abraham, Isaac, and Jacob

The Old Testament refers in several places to the Lord's covenant with the patriarchs, and it is a simple but important matter to understand how this can be so. How can the Lord refer to his "covenant" (in the singular) with father, son, and grandson? We read in Exodus 2:24 that "God heard their groaning and he remembered his covenant with Abraham, with Isaac, and with Jacob." Shortly thereafter the Lord refers to his singular covenant with the patriarchs: "I appeared to Abraham, to Isaac, and to Jacob as God Almighty. . . . I also established my covenant with them to give them the land of Canaan, where they resided as foreigners" (Exod. 6:3–4). We are told in 2 Kings 13:23 that "the Lord was gracious to them and had compassion and showed concern for them because of his covenant with Abraham, Isaac, and Jacob. To this day he has been unwilling to destroy them or banish them from his presence." First Chronicles 16:16 refers parallellistically to "the covenant he made with Abraham, the oath he swore to Isaac" as does Psalm 105:9.[7] Similarly in the New Testament, Peter declares, "And you are heirs of the prophets and of *the covenant God made with your fathers. He said to Abraham*, 'Through your offspring all peoples on earth will be blessed'" (Acts 3:25, citing Gen. 12:3; 18:18; and 22:18). One thing becomes quickly clear as we consider these statements. They not only refer to God's covenant with Abraham in the singular;

---

7   "Oath" can be a synecdoche for covenant and has been often recognized as such.

they also refer to God's covenant with Abraham, Isaac, and Jacob in the singular. Peter makes the same point when he refers to "the covenant God made with your fathers" and lest there be any lack of clarity as to who the "fathers" are, he qualifies that covenant by adding: "He said to Abraham, 'Through your offspring all peoples on earth will be blessed,'" thus indicating, to use the Old Testament phrasing, the "covenant [God] made with [the fathers] Abraham, Isaac, and Jacob."[8] It is highly significant also that Peter identifies this patriarchal "covenant" by synecdoche with the promise of universal blessing first made before the Abrahamic covenant was cut (in Genesis 12) and reaffirmed after it was cut (in Genesis 22). The promise was made before the covenant was cut, and then subsequently the promise was made part of the covenant. Its inclusion/containment in the covenant is stated in Genesis 22, along with all the other promises of the Abrahamic covenant, thus indicating the unity of the covenant (see below).

Peter's statement deserves further comment. It is in fact nicely parallellistic, and when we understand the parallelism we understand something about the phraseology of the Abrahamic covenant. He makes the following equation:

a	b	c
the covenant	God made	with your fathers

b′	c′	a′
He said	to Abraham	through your offspring all peoples on earth will be blessed

Peter parallels the promise of universal blessing with "the covenant [God made with your fathers]." God first promised this blessing to Abram

---

8   We find a variant phrasing in In Leviticus 26:42, where God says, "I will remember my covenant with Jacob and my covenant with Isaac and my covenant with Abraham, and I will remember the land." As we have noted, God did indeed have a covenant with each of the patriarchs, but the covenant he had with Isaac and the covenant he had with Jacob were only *reaffirmations* of the covenant he cut with Abraham—that is, they were all the same covenant—and so the usual expression is, for example, "his covenant with Abraham, with Isaac, and with Jacob" (Exod. 2:24).

when he initiated special relations with him, or "engaged" him as we have
characterized his action, in Genesis 12:3b. The promise is repeated in
Genesis 22:18 (by the Lord to Abraham), and 26:4 (by the Lord to Isaac
in reaffirmation/reconfirmation of the Abrahamic covenant).[9] This is the
background to Peter's statement. That is why he can equate what God
"said *to Abraham*" with "the covenant God made *with your fathers*," since
the promise entailed in the covenant was repeated to Abraham's offspring
(e.g., Isaac) in a reconfirmation of the Abrahamic covenant.

We must note further that when the Lord made this promise to Isaac
it was in the context of other promises of the Abrahamic covenant:

> For to you and your descendants I will give all these lands and will con-
> firm the oath I swore to your father Abraham. I will make your descen-
> dants as numerous as the stars in the sky and will give them all these
> lands, and through your offspring all nations on earth will be blessed.
> (Gen. 26:3b–4)

Three major promises of the Abrahamic covenant are repeated here:
"I will give all these lands" (Gen. 26:3b; cf. Gen. 15:18; repeated in Gen.
17:8); "I will make your descendants as numerous as the stars in the sky
(Gen. 26:4a; cf. Gen. 15:5, repeated in Gen. 22:17); and "through your
offspring all nations on earth will be blessed (promised in Gen.12:3 and
affirmed as part of the covenant in Gen. 22:18). Since these promises
of universal blessing and of numerous offspring and possession of the
land all occur in the one covenant reconfirmation with Isaac, and the
Lord promised and repeated them to Abraham in Genesis 15, 17, and
22, it makes perfect sense to understand that, as they were all included
in the one covenant reconfirmation with Isaac, so they were all included in God's one covenant with Abraham before.[10] In the covenant

---

9 It is echoed when Abraham blesses Isaac (Gen. 27:29a), a blessing that also echoes
Genesis 12:3 (Gen. 27:29c). I say "reaffirmation" and "reconfirmation" because of the
verb used when the Lord says: "I will confirm [והקמתי] the oath I swore to your father
Abraham" (Gen. 26:3). I use reaffirmation and reconfirmation interchangeably. Neither of
them equates to a covenant *renewal* however, which is a divinely initiated, formal cutting
of a (special grace) renewal covenant. See chapter 1 and also chapter 5 for the discussion
of covenant making and sustaining idioms.

10 All three are also grouped together when the Lord reconfirms the covenant with
Jacob: "I am the LORD, the God of your father Abraham and the God of Isaac. I will give
you and your descendants the land on which you are lying. Your descendants will be like
the dust of the earth, and you will spread out to the west and to the east, to the north and

reconfirmation with Isaac, the Lord groups all three things under the heading of "the oath I swore to your father Abraham," and it is well understood that "oath" in covenantal matters can serve as synecdoche (*pars pro toto*) indicating the covenant as a whole, so that the Lord is saying in effect, "the covenant I swore/made with your father Abraham."[11] It also makes perfect sense for Peter to mention God's promise of universal blessing to Abraham and refer to it as the singular "covenant God made with your fathers" (Acts 3:25). He selects the promise of universal blessing as *pars pro toto* for the Abrahamic covenant (which had other promises and also had requirements) because that is the relevant part of the Abrahamic covenant on the occasion at which he speaks: the universal blessing promised to Abraham has begun with Pentecost—the outpouring of the Spirit on all flesh through faith in Christ.[12]

We have noted before that the material in Genesis 12:1–3 initiates the Lord's relations with Abram, but it is not yet the Abrahamic covenant because the Abrahamic covenant is "cut" in Genesis 15:18.[13] In Genesis 12:1 we read the Lord had told Abram to leave his homeland, and in Genesis 12:2–3 he made certain promises to Abram. We do not yet have a covenant, however, but only the start of a pre-covenantal relationship. Put another way, all of this is part of the Lord's "engagement" with Abram. When God finally "cuts" a covenant with Abram (Gen. 15:18), the historical prologue of that covenant refers back to this pre-covenantal relationship (or "engagement"): "I am the Lord who brought you out of Ur of the Chaldeans to give you this land to take possession of it" (Gen. 15:7, referring back to Gen. 12:1.7).[14]

---

to the south. All peoples on earth will be blessed through you and your offspring"—that is, land for the descendants (28:13), numerous offspring (28:14a), and universal blessing (28:14b).

11 Suzerains in Assyrian tradition, for example, often noted that when they had conquered a kingdom and brought it into vassal status, they made the newly created vassal king "swear the oath of the great gods," that is, the deities that were witnesses to the newly made suzerain-vassal treaty. Cf. Noel Weeks, *Admonition and Curse: The Ancient Near Eastern Treaty/Covenant Form as a Problem in Inter-Cultural Relationships* (Edinburgh: T&T Clark, 2004), 38–50; cf. earlier A. K. Grayson, *Assyrian Royal Inscriptions*, 2 vols. (Wiesbaden: Harrassowitz, 1972), 1:103; 2:13.

12 By which faith people are saved—we are saved—and so become Abraham's offspring, since, like him, we "believed in the Lord, and he counted it to him as righteousness" (Gen. 15:6; cf. Gal. 3:6).

13 Cf. above, chapter 2; and also Niehaus, "Covenant and Narrative," 543–44.

14 Failure to understand the difference between a pre-covenantal relationship, which

As we have noted, the fact that God reconfirms with Isaac and Jacob the covenant he originally made with Abraham explains how a biblical writer (Moses in Exod. 2:24) or speaker (Peter in Acts 3:25) can refer to the Lord's covenant with Abraham, Isaac, and Jacob (or "with your fathers," Acts 3:25) in the singular. A covenant and its reconfirmation(s) form one legal package.

The same is true of a covenant and its *formal renewal* as has already been observed of the Adamic and Noahic covenant complex. So later the

---

may include promises and commands, on the one hand, and a covenantal relationship, which takes the prior relationship to a different level entailing different privileges and responsibilities, on the other, has led to some misunderstandings of the relationship between Genesis 12:1–3 and Genesis 15. So Gerard van Groningen, *From Creation to Consummation* (Sioux Center, IA: Dordt College Press, 1996), 1: 212–13, comments on Genesis 12:1–3, "Three important factors should be recognized. First, Yahweh God did establish a specific relationship with Abraham when he called him. Second, this relationship included various integral elements. Third, this relationship served as an administrative and redeeming means. These three in combination certainly lead to one conclusion: Yahweh God initiated and established his covenant in a substantial manner with Abraham. Ratifying 'ceremonies' were included in the reiteration and explication of the various elements (Gen. 15, 17, 22, 26)." This analysis fails at the outset because it does not recognize that while Yahweh appeared in Genesis 12 to initiate a special grace relationship with Abram, and while he gave him commands and promises, these things altogether *do not constitute a covenant*. The Lord did *the same thing with Israel* (gave them promises and instructions, and even redeemed them from Egypt) *before* they agreed to enter into covenant with him at Sinai. Before Sinai, the Lord had certainly initiated a relationship with Israel, but until the covenant was cut at Sinai, the covenant did not exist. What existed was a pre-covenantal relationship, which was a good thing, certainly, but not yet a covenant. So the covenant cutting in Genesis 15 does not ratify a covenant made in Genesis 12, any more than the covenant cutting in Exodus 20 ratifies a covenant made in the preceding chapters of Exodus. In both cases, the Lord initiates a relationship and thus "engages" the vassal-to-be. He then later cuts the covenant and, to carry on the analogy, "marries" the vassal (cf., e.g., Ezek. 16:8, "Later I passed by, and when I looked at you and saw that you were old enough for love, I spread the corner of my garment over you and covered your naked body. I gave you my solemn oath and entered into a covenant with you, declares the Sovereign LORD, and you became mine"). In each case also, when the Lord cuts the covenant, he refers back to the pre-covenantal relationship in the historical prologue of the newly made covenant (the historical prologue, we note, recalls the relations between the suzerain-to-be and the vassal-to-be *before they entered into covenant*), for example, "I am the Lord who brought you out of Ur" (Gen. 15:7, referring back to Gen. 12:1), and, "I am the Lord who brought you out of Egypt" (Exod. 20:2, referring back to Exod. 12:31–42, etc.)

Lord makes a covenant with Israel at Sinai, and he makes another covenant with Israel on the plains of Moab (i.e., Deuteronomy). The latter is a renewal of the former, as the many repetitions of its stipulations (with the Decalogue as the parade example) and the literary/legal form of Deuteronomy make clear. Although the Lord made both the Sinai covenant and its renewal (the Moab covenant), and although those are indeed two covenants, the Lord also subsequently refers to them as one, namely, "The covenant [singular] I made with their forefathers when I took them by the hand to lead them out of Egypt" (Jer. 31:32; cf. Heb. 8:7–13). They are referred to in the singular because a covenant and its renewal function as one legal package, and both are binding on the vassal.[15]

For clarity's sake we repeat the following points: (1) the Lord *does not renew* the Abrahamic covenant but rather reconfirms it with Isaac and with Jacob; the original covenant and its reconfirmations constitute one legal package ("the covenant with the fathers"); (2) the Lord *does renew* the Sinai covenant with the subsequent generation on the plains of Moab, and that renewal is enshrined in Deuteronomy; the Sinai covenant and its renewal (Deuteronomy) also constitute one legal package (the Mosaic covenant or the law).[16]

Covenant renewal is a formal process in which the constituent covenant elements appear (and not just, e.g., some important promises from an earlier covenant, such as one finds when the Lord reconfirms the Abrahamic covenant with Isaac and Jacob), along with some sort of formal ratification (e.g., a statement to the effect that *it is a covenant*, as at Deut. 29:1 and, earlier, for the Adamic covenant renewal, Gen. 9:16).

These considerations lead to another conclusion: there are only two covenant renewals in the Bible. The Lord renews the Adamic covenant with the Noahic covenant, and he renews the Sinai covenant with the Moab covenant (Deuteronomy). Only the suzerain in the ancient Near East could renew a covenant. The vassal could not and never did

---

15   Cf. the discussion in Niehaus, "Covenant and Narrative," 547–48.

16   The view stated here of the Abrahamic covenant as it relates to Isaac and Jacob differs from the view I held earlier and published in the articles cited, where I argued that those encounters involved covenant renewals. As I have noted in the present work, God's repetitions, to Isaac and Jacob, of the three major promises of the Abrahmic covenant do not formally constitute covenant renewals—the form criticism of those episodes does not warrant their classification as such. By contrast, the form criticism of Deuteronomy clearly warrants its classification as a renewal covenant, and the same may be said of the Noahic covenant vis-à-vis the Adamic covenant.

presume to do so. He had no legal authority to do so. The covenants/ treaties were after all, the "words" of the suzerain/great king. The vassal could not take it upon himself to renew those words, since they were not his words. Likewise in the Bible only the Lord can renew one of his covenants. Humans cannot presume to do so. It is customary among scholars to call humanly initiated reaffirmations of commitment to (especially) the Mosaic covenant "covenant renewals," but this is not true to the facts.

A COVENANT WITH SUPPLEMENTS

We noted above the following concept: the Lord made a covenant with Abram in Genesis 15 and then over time added supplemental information, including name changes, requirements, and promises in Genesis 17 and 22. We observed that the Lord subsequently behaved in a similar fashion in the two special grace covenants that established the Old Testament and the New Testament forms of God's kingdom, that is, the Mosaic covenant and the new covenant, respectively. This behavior seems to be part of God's pedagogical way with his people and may be outlined broadly as follows:[17]

Covenant	Covenant Making	Further Covenant Torah
Abrahamic	Genesis 15	Genesis 17, 22
Mosaic	Exodus 20–24	Exodus 25–Deuteronomy
New	Matthew 27–28	Acts–Revelation

When the Lord makes his covenant with Israel through Moses, he also prepares a temple for his presence, because the goal of the covenant is to establish relations between him and Israel such that they may be his people and he may be their God and dwell among them.[18] The better fulfillment of this so-called covenant formula occurs in the

---

17   In this analysis, Deuteronomy, the renewal covenant, is included for convenience under the heading, "Further Covenant *Torah*"; Matthew 27–28 is used as one Gospel example, again for convenience, of "Covenant Making" for the new covenant.

18   For this covenant formula, cf. Rolf Rendtorff, *The Covenant Formula: An Exegetical and Theological Investigation*, trans. Margaret Kohl (Edinburgh: T&T Clark, 1998), a detailed presentation of the formula, its variants, and its occurrences, although unfortunately from a higher critical perspective.

New Testament, where the temple presence of the Lord is the individual believer and the church corporately. In both cases, the Lord's temple presence can occur once the covenant has been cut. But even in his covenant with Abram, the Lord anticipated such a reality when he caused Abraham to go to Moriah with Isaac and initiate the symbolic sacrifice on a mountain that would be the future site of the Davidic/Solomonic temple (and cf. David's anticipatory acquisition of, and altar building *cum* sacrifice on, the threshing floor of Araunah the Jebusite, 2 Sam. 24:18–25). Likewise in his covenant with David, the Lord also anticipated the temple and, subsequent to the covenant making, gave instruction for it. The Lord behaves according to the same pattern in all four cases, and this behavior can also be diagrammed as follows:

Covenant	Covenant Cutting	Temple Matters
Abrahamic	Genesis 15:18	Genesis 22
Mosaic	Exodus 20–24	Exodus 25–40
Davidic	2 Samuel 7:1–17	1 Chronicles 28:11–19
New	Matthew 27–28	Acts 2:1–4

In the Abrahamic administration no temple is built, so there are no instructions for temple building. Also in the new covenant no instruction for temple building appears but that is because the Lord himself constitutes as temples those made in his image and likeness. However, the Lord does give certain instructions in those cases. In the Abrahamic, he tells Abraham *where to go* for the sacrifice. In the new, he tells the people *what to do*—namely, wait—for the temple institution. In the Mosaic covenant, on the other hand, the Lord gives instructions for the temple construction and furnishings, and the same is true of the future temple in the case of the Davidic covenant, as David makes clear in 1 Chronicles 28:11–19. It should be noted that the Davidic covenant does not replace the Mosaic but is rather a special administration having to do with the royal line under the Mosaic covenant, as David himself was always under the Mosaic law. Nonetheless, the Davidic covenant does entail a *change of temple*, from the tabernacle to the to-be-built Solomonic temple. Moreover, the temple is built by one who is a son of David and whose name means "His peace." The Christology of these facts should be clear: the new covenant also entails a *change of temple*, and the one who builds that temple is also a son of David and is the "Prince of Peace," the one who promises a peace the world cannot understand.

ENGAGEMENT, COVENANT, AND SUPPLEMENTAL TORAH: THE OVERLAP BETWEEN GENESIS 12, 15, 17, AND 22

We have characterized the Lord's initiation of personal relations with Abram in Genesis 12 as an engagement. Before the Lord revealed himself to Abram in Genesis 12:1, he was indeed Abram's suzerain—just as he was suzerain to everyone on the planet. All people were in Abram's day—and are in our day—vassals to the Lord under the Adamic and Noahic covenants. Those covenants are ongoing and will continue until the Lord returns to establish a new heaven and a new earth. Once he does so, the covenants that governed the old heaven and old earth will no longer function—for example, we will no longer be fruitful and multiply (Gen. 1:28; 9:1) but will be like the angels in heaven who neither marry nor are given in marriage (Matt. 22:30); the shedding of human blood (Gen. 9:6) will no longer be an issue, because in the new world there will be no killers but we will reflect the Lord's glory and be like him, who, unlike Satan, was not a murderer from the beginning (John 8:44).

Genesis 12, then, marks an irruption by the Lord to initiate *personal* relations with Abram. This initiation of relations is not yet a covenant, but it does contain commands and promises. As Abram's suzerain under common grace, the Lord has every right to give him commands (e.g., "leave your homeland," "go to the land I will show you"). As the Lord of creation, he also has every authority to give promises and later to fulfill them. The promises he makes in Genesis 12 are taken up again in Genesis 15 and 22, and moreover there is overlap between promises in these chapters and Genesis 17. The overlapping of statements is consistent with the understanding that Genesis 12 is the Lord's start of pre-covenantal relations with Abram; Genesis 15 is the cutting of the covenant; Genesis 17 and 22 offer supplemental *torah* in the context of further revelation by the Lord as he encounters Abraham later in his life and even leads him through certain life experiences (e.g., the Moriah episode). The overlap of promises may be listed as follows:

"I will bless"	12:2			22:17
Numerous descendants	12:2	15:5	17:2b.4–5	22:17
Land as possession	12:7	15:18–21	17:8	22:17
Universal blessing	12:3			22:18

The overlap of elements should make several things clear. First, the promise of numerous descendants is made in Genesis 12 and repeated in Genesis 15, 17, and 22. The sharing of the promise by the passages is consistent with the idea that the Lord made only one covenant with Abraham, a covenant that bade fair to realize the promise the Lord had made in Genesis 12 (before the covenant was cut). Likewise, the promise of land made in Genesis 12:7 is repeated in Genesis 15 and 17 (and 22), and this suggests that Genesis 15 and 17 do not enshrine different covenants but that Genesis 17 reaffirms and adds further data to the covenant cut in Genesis 15.

One may argue that Genesis 22 presents us with something that implies a different covenant from the one cut in Genesis 15. That something is the reiteration of the promise that all nations will be blessed through Abraham (Gen. 12:3 // Gen. 22:18). However, we have already noted that the promise of universal blessing and the promises of numerous offspring and possession of the land all occur in the one covenant reconfirmation with Isaac (Gen. 26:3b–4) and again in the one covenant reconfirmation with Jacob (Gen. 28:13–14). It makes sense to understand that, as they were all included in each of the individual covenant reconfirmations with Isaac and Jacob, so they were all included in God's one original covenant with Abraham before. The same is true of the statement of the Lord's blessing on Abram/Abraham (Gen. 12:2 // 22:17). The blessing in Genesis 22:17 prefaces and includes two promises already made in Genesis 15 and 17. The first part of the blessing, Genesis 22:17b ("I will surely bless you and make your descendants as numerous as the stars in the sky") repeats the promise of Genesis 15:5. The second part of the blessing in Genesis 22:17c ("Your descendants will take possession of the cities of their enemies") gives point to the promise made in Genesis 15:18 and 17:8. These are then followed by the third part of the blessing: "through your offspring all nations on earth will be blessed" (Gen. 22:18). Because all three things are included under a single act—the Lord's blessing— and because they establish connections not only with Genesis 12 but also with Genesis 15 and 17, it seems reasonable to associate them all as material relevant to a single Abrahamic covenant just as, again, all three of them occur later in each of the individual covenant reconfirmations with Isaac (Gen. 26:3b- 4) and Jacob (Gen. 28:13–14). Finally and perhaps most conclusively, we note that this threefold blessing comes under the aegis of the *oath* the Lord swears in Genesis 22:16a: "I swear by myself, declares the LORD." This again parallels the statement of the threefold promise under the heading of the oath (synecdoche for covenant) the Lord swore to Abraham as reported in the covenant reconfirmation with Isaac (Gen. 26:3b–5). In fact, Genesis 22 gives us both an oath and, under it, a summary of the three great Abrahamic promises forecast in Genesis 12, and so it forms a sort of *inclusio* for the Abrahamic material from the initial promises of Genesis 12, through the covenant cutting of Genesis 15 and the supplemental data of Genesis 17, to the summary statement of the Abrahamic covenant's triple promise, now concluded with an oath.[19] Once we understand that we are dealing with a narrative corpus that reports God's covenantal activity with Abraham, we understand also that Genesis 22:18 rounds off that corpus with a divine oath. By the same token, the self-imprecatory covenant cutting passage of Genesis 15:17 is not, as Lohfink reasoned, an oath, but a ceremony symbolizing the cutting of the covenant.[20] God's oath appears later, in Genesis 22:18.

---

19   One of my students put the matter quite well in a recent paper: "By God's oath in Genesis 22, we understand that all of the promises of Genesis 12 have been made into part of God's covenant with Abraham" (Anna Moseley Gissing, "Divine-Human Covenants: A Survey," submitted to Dr. J. J. Niehaus in partial fulfillment of requirements for NT/OT 795: Seminar in Biblical Theology, April 30, 2012).

20   Norbert Lohfink, *Die Landverheissung als Eid*, Stuttgarter Bibelstudien 28 (Stuttgart: Verlag Katholisches Bibelwerk, 1967). Lohfink views all of the material from a higher critical perspective and because of that is unable to appreciate the unity of the Abrahamic narrative materials, let alone the original unity of Genesis 15 (cf. 45–48 on the passage's structure; cf. on Genesis 15 as narrative: "Gn 15 ist nicht Erzählung im strengen Sinn des Wortes. Das Gewicht liegt ganz auf Jahwereden, die zusammengestellt sind. Es wird mit vorgeprägtem Sprachmaterial, vor allem aus dem Kult, gearbeitet" 114; author's translation: "Gn 15 is not narrative in the strict sense of the word. The weight lies on Yahweh speeches, which have been compiled. It has been crafted with speech material that has been shaped, above all from the cult"). His laborious study ends up conflating categories and thus misunderstanding the solemnizing ritual of Genesis 15:17 as evidence that the idiom, *krt brt*, means "oath" in the passage: "Wir können zusammenfassend sagen, daß sich *krt berît* nicht vom Grundsinn her, sondern erst in gegebenem Zusammenhang als 'Bund schliessen' (nämlich, 'Bund durch Eidablegung schliessen') verstehen läßt. Die eigentliche Bedeutung ist die der Selbst-oder Fremdverpflichtung, meistens durch Eid—in dem Fall, von dem der Ausdruck hergenommen ist, durch Eid unter Setzung des Selbstverfluchungssymbols der zu durschreitenden zerteilten Tiere. 'Verheißen' allein heißt *krt berît* nicht, es meint immer die Verstärkung und Absicherung einer Verheissung oder Zusage durch Eid oder ähnliches," 107; author's translation: "Summarizing, we can say, that *krt berît* may be understood not from its root sense, but only in a given context as 'conclude a covenant' (namely, 'conclude a covenant by oath swearing'). The proper meaning is that of self-obligation or obligation of a foreigner, mostly by an oath—in the case, from which the expression is taken, by oath under the placement of the self-imprecatory curse symbol of the dismembered beasts that must be passed between. By itself *krt berît* does not mean 'promise,' it always means the reinforcement and securing of a promise or

THE COVENANT OF CIRCUMCISION

When Stephen gives his testimony before the Sanhedrin—a salvation history review that upbraids his fellow Jews for being no better than their fathers who persecuted the prophets—he comments that God "gave Abraham the covenant of circumcision" (Acts 7:8). By now we have seen enough of terminological usage in the Bible (e.g., Exod. 2:24 as compared with Lev. 26:42, above) to know Stephen's words need not imply that Genesis 17 enshrines a different covenant from the one the Lord cut in Genesis 15. We know every case of a term's or a phrase's usage should be evaluated in light of a proper understanding of its other occurrences. In Stephen's case, his evocation of circumcision as a reminder of Israel's distinctness and privilege vis-á vis the nations is simply an allusion by synecdoche (part for the whole) to the whole Abrahamic covenant (which has been mentioned in the singular in the examples already noted). We should further note that Stephen's address, as a brief synopsis of salvation history, cannot help but be laconic, so we should not expect it to offer a full portrayal of the Abrahamic covenant in all of its aspects. It would thus be a mistake to interpret the scope of the Abrahamic covenant by his allusion to it as "the covenant of circumcision." Stephen's speech simply refers to the one Abrahamic covenant by its sign, circumcision.

GALATIANS 3 AND THE ABRAHAMIC COVENANT

Paul's argument in Galatians 3 makes it clear that he thought of only one Abrahamic covenant. He argues that the Mosaic law which was given after Abraham does not set aside the Abrahamic covenant: "What I mean is this: The law, introduced 430 years later, does not set aside the covenant previously established by God and thus do away with the promise" (Gal. 3:17). It should be noted that Paul virtually equates the Abrahamic

---

commitment by oath or something similar." Cf. further, "Der Ausdruck b^{e}rît in Gn 15,18 kann nicht mit 'Bund,' 'Vatergottreligion' oder 'Verheißung' übersetzt werden, sondern verlangt die Übersetzung 'Eid,'" 117; author's translation: "The expression b^{e}rît in Gn 15,18 can not be translated with 'covenant,' 'ancestral god religion' or 'promise,' but demands the translation, 'oath.'" Even of one goes so far as to think the ritual cutting involved in covenant making implies—or at the utmost symbolizes—an oath, the cutting is an act and the oath is a word, and in the Abrahamic materials they are both clearly, and separately, portrayed—the cutting in Genesis 15:18, the oath in Genesis 22:18.

covenant and the promise of the Spirit because the great salvation promise of the Abrahamic covenant, the blessing to all the nations, comes
when they receive the Spirit through faith in Christ. The passage at hand
makes this clear:

> He redeemed us in order that the blessing given to Abraham might come
> to the Gentiles through Christ Jesus, so that by faith we might receive the
> promise of the Spirit. Brothers, let me take an example from everyday
> life. Just as no one can set aside or add to a human covenant that has
> been duly established, so it is in this case. The promises were spoken to
> Abraham and to his seed. Scripture does not say "and to seeds," meaning
> many people, but "and to your seed," meaning one person, who is Christ.
> What I mean is this: The law, introduced 430 years later, does not set
> aside the covenant previously established by God and thus do away with
> the promise. For if the inheritance depends on the law, then it no longer
> depends on the promise; but God in his grace gave it to Abraham through
> a promise. (Gal. 3:14–18)

We note an important parallelism in verse 14:

a	b	c
the blessing given to Abraham	might come to the Gentiles	through Christ

c′	b′	a′
by faith	we might receive	the promise of the Spirit

The parallelism shows clearly enough that "the blessing given to Abraham" is paralleled by and thus identified with "the promise of the Spirit."
Paul shows that "the blessing // Spirit" "might come to the Gentiles // we
might receive" "through Christ // by faith." This blessing was promised
as one of several "promises" (Gal. 3:16) of the Abrahamic covenant. We
turn now to those promises.

Paul mentions both "the promises . . . spoken to Abraham" (v. 16)
and "the inheritance . . . God in his grace gave . . . to Abraham through
a promise" (v. 18). The promises are those made to Abraham that are
relevant to Christ, who received them: many offspring (through faith),

blessing to the nations (accomplished by the Spirit who through faith in Christ produces the "offspring") and kingship (Christ, the royal offspring *par excellence*).[21] The singular "promise" mentioned in verse 18 is that of the Spirit, whose work and gracious nature Paul emphasizes in Galatians (cf. 3:1–5). Both "the promises" and the paramount "promise" are made in the Abrahamic covenant—a singular covenant which, as Paul says, is not set aside by the Mosaic law but continues until its fulfillment in Christ.

Since Christ has fulfilled it, the Abrahamic covenant no longer continues as a functioning covenant. The logic of this statement should be obvious but further support for it can be found in the discontinuation of circumcision as a covenant sign. At this point it will be useful to review the Genesis 17 statements about circumcision:

> Then God said to Abraham, "As for you, you must keep my covenant, you and your descendants after you for the generations to come. This is my covenant with you and your descendants after you, the covenant you are to keep: Every male among you shall be circumcised. You are to undergo circumcision, and it will be the sign of the covenant between me and you. For the generations to come every male among you who is eight days old must be circumcised, including those born in your household or bought with money from a foreigner—those who are not your offspring. Whether born in your household or bought with your money, they must be circumcised. My covenant in your flesh is to be an everlasting covenant. Any uncircumcised male, who has not been circumcised in the flesh, will be cut off from his people; he has broken my covenant." (vv. 10–14)

It is clear from the above (and esp. v. 14) that an uncircumcised male cannot be a member of the Lord's covenant with Abraham.[22] Circumcision,

---

21   The "promises" to Abraham have an initial, prefigurative fulfillment in the Old Testament: the many offspring that appear in the days just before the Exodus, the Promised Land—the Old Testament form of God's kingdom on earth—acquired by the Conquest, and the "kings" promised to Sarah and Abraham, that foreshadow Christ's kingship.

22   The phrase "everlasting covenant" (Gen. 17:13) could be translated in a different and better way. As has been noted, the Hebrew word עולם can mean "everlasting," but fundamentally means of indeterminate but long duration (e.g., "Then his people recalled the days *of old* (עולם), the days of Moses [and] his people," Isa. 63:11). Whether עולם means "everlasting" or simply chronologically remote is determined either by its immediate context (as in Isa. 63:11) or by some other biblical statement that sheds further light on it (as Paul's rejection of circumcision for the church does in the case of Gen. 17:13 and Lev. 12:3). Cf. Niehaus, "Covenant and Narrative," 542n23.

then, is necessary for membership in the Abrahamic covenant. But the teaching of the new covenant repudiates circumcision. If then the sign required for membership in the Abrahamic covenant (Gen. 17:10) has been abrogated (Gal. 5:10–12), it follows that membership in the Abrahamic covenant is no longer possible.[23] Rather, one seeks admission to the new covenant in which all of the promises made in the Abrahamic covenant have been fulfilled and thus, in a sense, "live on," as Christ lives and as believers live in him.

We note finally that the circumcision of the Abrahamic covenant symbolizes its *conditional* aspect, being itself a requirement and symbolic of the result if covenant members would break the commands and decrees of the Abrahamic covenant. We do not know what those "commands, decrees, and instructions" were, but we know from Genesis 26:5 that Abraham received them: "I will make your descendants as numerous as the stars in the sky and will give them all these lands, and through your offspring all nations on earth will be blessed, *because* Abraham obeyed me and did everything I required of him, keeping my commands, my decrees and my instructions" (Gen. 26:4–5, emphasis added). Isaac's receiving of the so-called triple promise of the Abrahamic covenant is clearly conditional on Abraham's obedience. Moreover, the Lord uses terms here that are also found later in the Mosaic covenant. Those terms, "obeyed me" [שמע בקול], "in everything I required" [lit. "kept my charge," שמר מש־רה] "commands" [מצות], "decrees" [חקות] and "instructions" [or, "laws," תורת]," are all terms used later of the requirements of the Mosaic covenant. It thus seems reasonable to suggest that they foreshadowed and would also be found in that later covenant, which no one has thought to call unconditional. Circumcision likewise, though it is primarily the sign of the Abrahamic covenant, could easily become symbolic of the conditional aspect of the Mosaic covenant, as it had done by Paul's day, not only because the Mosaic law required it (though as a sign of the Abrahamic covenant, Lev.

---

23   Cf. Niehaus, "Covenant and Narrative," 550. Paul renounces circumcision in the strongest possible terms: "Mark my words! I, Paul, tell you that if you let yourselves be circumcised, Christ will be of no value to you at all. Again I declare to every man who lets himself be circumcised that he is obligated to obey the whole law. You who are trying to be justified by the law have been alienated from Christ; you have fallen away from grace" (Gal. 5:10–12). Although his emphasis is on the circumcision required by the Mosaic covenant (Lev. 12:3), he precludes admission to both the Mosaic covenant and the Abrahamic covenant when he abrogates circumcision. This is so because circumcision is still required by the law as a sign of the continuation of the Abrahamic covenant, and is thus part of the law, so if one takes on part of the law (circumcision), one thereby takes on all of the law.

12:3, since the Sabbath was the sign of the Mosaic covenant, Exod. 31:16–17), thus making it clear that those under the law were also under the still ongoing Abrahamic covenant, but also because it anticipated the many more "commands, decrees, and instructions" of the Mosaic covenant.

Moreover, we get a general statement of those requirements, or an allusion to them, when the Lord considers Abraham before Sodom and Gomorrah: "For I have chosen [lit. "known"] him, so that he will direct [lit. "command," the word from which "commandment" comes] his children and his household after him to keep the way of the LORD by doing what is right and just [lit. "righteousness and justice"], *so that* the LORD will bring about for Abraham what he has promised him" (Gen. 18:29, emphasis added). The fact that the fulfillment of the promises depends in some sense on Abraham's obedience is clearly stated here and not to be avoided. It depends on *his* obedience, however, and not the obedience of every subsequent member of Abraham's household. Similarly, the new covenant depends upon the Son's obedience, and not the obedience of all its subsequent "children," in order to come into being. Moreover, the "righteousness and justice" the Lord requires Abraham to command his household are the same terms the Lord later uses in covenant lawsuit against those who broke the Mosaic covenant ("He looked for *justice*, but saw bloodshed; / for *righteousness*, but heard cries of distress," Isa. 5:7c, emphases added; cf. Isa. 56:1, Amos 5:7; 6:12). As we reaffirm later, the Abrahamic covenant has a conditional aspect notwithstanding its mighty promises. It also has an unconditional aspect. Likewise every divine-human covenant has both conditional and unconditional aspects.[24]

ROMANS 4 AND THE ABRAHAMIC COVENANT

Paul's memorable argument in Romans 4 also makes a case for the idea that the Lord made only one covenant with Abraham. He states that circumcision was a sign of the righteousness Abraham had by faith before he was circumcised. This statement connects the circumcision of Genesis 17 with the faith-righteousness of Genesis 15 in a way that indicates there is only one Abrahamic covenant:

> We have been saying that Abraham's faith was credited to him as righteousness. Under what circumstances was it credited? Was it after he

---

24 Cf. discussion in chapter 1, pages 17–18.

was circumcised, or before? It was not after, but before! And he received circumcision as a sign, a seal of the righteousness that he had by faith while he was still uncircumcised. So then, he is the father of all who believe but have not been circumcised, in order that righteousness might be credited to them. And he is then also the father of the circumcised who not only are circumcised but who also follow in the footsteps of the faith that our father Abraham had before he was circumcised. (Rom. 4:9b–12)

First, it is clear that circumcision, which is indicated in a *pars pro toto* expression as the Lord's covenant in Genesis 17 ("This is my covenant with you and your descendants after you, the covenant you are to keep: Every male among you shall be circumcised," Gen. 17:10), is not a sign of a different covenant from the one cut in Genesis 15, but rather a *sign of the righteousness he had by faith*, with which Abram *entered* the covenant made in Genesis 15.

Looking ahead, we find the same *pars pro toto* usage with regard to the Sabbath and the Mosaic covenant:

Observe the Sabbath, because it is holy to you. Anyone who desecrates it is to be put to death; those who do any work on that day must be cut off from their people. For six days work is to be done, but the seventh day is a day of Sabbath rest, holy to the LORD. Whoever does any work on the Sabbath day is to be put to death. The Israelites are to observe the Sabbath, celebrating it for the generations to come as a lasting covenant. It will be a sign between me and the Israelites forever, for in six days the LORD made the heavens and the earth, and on the seventh day he abstained from work and rested. (Exod. 31:14–17)

Just as the Lord referred to circumcision, the sign of the Abrahamic covenant, as a synecdoche for his covenant with Abraham, so he refers to the Sabbath, the sign of the Mosaic covenant, as a synecdoche his covenant with Israel:

"*This is my covenant* with you and your descendants after you, the covenant you are to keep: *Every male among you shall be circumcised.*" (Gen. 17:10, emphases added)

"*The Israelites are to observe the Sabbath*, celebrating it for the generations to come *as a lasting covenant.*" (Exod. 31:16, emphases added)

The usage is entirely consistent: in both cases the covenant sign is mentioned as a synecdoche for the covenant itself, and in both cases the covenant sign is to be implemented for all subsequent generations who are party to the covenant. When the Lord through Moses refers to the Sabbath as the covenant in Exodus 31, therefore, he is not referring to the Sabbath as a different covenant from the one he cut with Israel in Exodus 24. Likewise, when the Lord refers to circumcision as the covenant in Genesis 17, he is not referring to a different covenant from the one he cut in Genesis 15.

If we ask why the Mosaic covenant still requires circumcision, we note again that it symbolizes the new reality: God's people continue now not only under two common grace covenants, the Adamic and Noahic—as does everyone else in the world—they also now continue under two special grace covenants, the Abrahamic and the Mosaic. The two special grace covenants would continue until they would be fulfilled and terminated by the new covenant. The two common grace covenants would continue until the end of the old world (our current world) that continues under their provisions and requirements.

Returning to Paul's argument in Romans 4, Paul makes it clear that both the faith-righteousness and the covenant sign and seal of it (circumcision) figure in Abraham's father-relation to those who would be saved by faith, whether circumcised or not. Paul's chiastic statement (Rom. 4:11b–12a) illustrates the point:

a	b	c
He is the father	of all who believe	but have not been circumcised

a	c'	b'
He is the father	of those who have been circumcised	and also believe

Circumcision is not the sign of a different Abrahamic covenant, but the sign of the faith with which Abram entered the one and only Abrahamic covenant, cut in Genesis 15. As mediator of that covenant, he is the father both of those who, like him, would be justified by faith without circumcision (as in Gen. 15), and those who, like him, would be circumcised (as per Gen. 17), but have the faith Abram had when the covenant was cut (in Gen. 15). Those who have such faith are the true offspring of Abraham, being saved by a faith like Abraham's, as Paul argues in Galatians.

THE ABRAHAMIC COVENANT:
UNCONDITIONAL *AND* CONDITIONAL

Our consideration of circumcision in Genesis 17 and also the Lord's statements in Genesis 18:19 and 26:5 have naturally opened the question of conditionality in the Abrahamic covenant. By contrast, what has been called the self-imprecatory passage between the pieces of Genesis 15 seems to imply unconditionality: the Lord himself will take the place of the fallible vassal and pass between the pieces and thus guarantee the continuation of the covenant. This contrast can be easily misleading and has caused some to see two different covenants in Genesis 15 and 17.

In the title to this section, we used the phrasing "Unconditional *and* Conditional" rather than "Unconditional *or* Conditional" because it is not either/or, it is both/and. The Abrahamic covenant is both unconditional and conditional. It is unconditional in the sense that the Lord, having instituted it, will see it through until it has accomplished its purpose. It will not fail. It is conditional in the sense that any individual who participates in it may drop out of it by covenant breaking. That is, the individual may fail.[25] For the Abrahamic covenant to be both unconditional and conditional, however, two things must also be true. The first is that Genesis 15, 17, and 22 are all part of one covenant the Lord made with Abraham—a covenant with supplements, as we have said. The second is that materials contained in that one covenant can be shown to require Abraham's obedience (and likewise the obedience of other and subsequent members of the Abrahamic covenant) to divine conditions.[26]

---

25   Of course God is in a different sense the *conditio sine qua non* of every divine-human covenant just as he is the ground of all being (*Seinsgrund*), so Paul notes in Athens quoting the Greek philosopher Epimenides, "'For in him we live and move and have our being'" (Acts 17:28).

26   We stipulate as to the unconditional aspect of the Abrahamic covenant, indicated by the so-called oath passage in the Genesis 15 cutting. For earlier discussion of these ideas and of the presence of conditions in the Abrahamic and Davidic covenants, cf. David N. Freedman, "Divine Commitment and Human Obligation: One Covenant Theme," *Int* 18 (1964): 426 , who says, "The fate of individual kings or claimants was not guaranteed, but in the end the divine promise would be fulfilled," speaking of the Davidic covenant); cf. also Bruce K. Waltke, "The Phenomenon of Conditionality within

We believe the Bible makes it very clear that the Lord made only one covenant with Abraham, and this chapter has been devoted to showing the several decisive biblical statements in that regard. The course of that discussion has encountered data that raise the conditional aspect of the Abrahamic covenant and we have considered those briefly. We now aim to explicate further how the Lord made various requirements of Abraham (and other covenant members) within the context and as part of the Abrahamic covenant. To facilitate our discussion we explore the results of the largest article by an evangelical scholar on the topic.

Ronald Youngblood some years ago made a well-substantiated case for the conditional aspect of the Abrahamic covenant, while also recognizing its unconditional aspect in much the same terms as we have stated above.[27] He identified fifteen passages in the Old Testament that, he said, indicate the conditionality of the Abrahamic covenant.[28] In our judgment the first four of these are mistaken, and it will be worthwhile to discuss them in passing.

The first exemplar is the set of commands in Genesis 12: "Leave your country ... and go" (Gen. 12:1), and "be a blessing" (Gen. 12:2). Youngblood himself recognizes that "formalizing a covenant (Genesis 15) assumes previous (Genesis 12) as well as present and future relationships."[29] This is in line with our understanding that Genesis 12 gives us data regarding the pre-covenantal relationship the Lord initiated with Abram. Accordingly, Yahweh's commands to Abram in Genesis 12 are commands given in the context of the common grace (Adamic and Noahic) covenants under which Abram was the Lord's vassal, as was (and is) everyone on the planet. They are not commands or conditions given under the Abrahamic covenant because the Abrahamic covenant did not yet exist.

The second exemplar is Genesis 12:7 in which we read that Abram

---

Unconditional Covenants," in *Israel's Apostasy and Restoration: Essays in Honor of Roland K. Harrison*, ed. A. Gileadi (Grand Rapids: Baker, 1988), 129, who says, "YHWH explains [in Gen. 18:19] that his grant extends only to those within Abraham's household who behave ethically").

27   Ronald Youngblood, "The Abrahamic Covenant: Conditional or Unconditional?" in *The Living and Active Word of God: Essays in Honor of Samuel J. Schultz*, ed. Morris Inch and Ronald Youngblood (Winona Lake, IN: Eisenbrauns, 1983). Youngblood notes that "a covenant that is everlasting from the divine standpoint may in the course of time be broken by sinful human beings," 41. We would only disagree that the Abrahamic covenant, though of long duration (עולם) is not everlasting (עולם); cf. page 82.

28   Ibid., 36–38.

29   Ibid., 36.

"built an altar . . . to the LORD" at Shechem. Youngblood remarks, "In so doing he acknowledged Yahweh as his God and further demonstrated his intention to serve him."[30] However, this altar building also takes place under the common grace regime established by the Adamic and Noahic covenants. Although Abram's act shows the acknowledgement and intention noted by Youngblood, they are not acts that fulfill any conditions of the Abrahamic covenant, since that covenant had not yet been cut.

The third exemplar occurs in Genesis 14:22–23 where Abram vows to "the LORD, God Most High," that he will not accept anything from the king of Sodom. Youngblood comments that "such an oath presupposes obedience as well as commitment."[31] Although this may be the case, it is still obedience to the Lord with whom Abram is in covenant under the Adamic and Noahic covenants. Again, the Abrahamic covenant has not yet been cut (Gen. 15:18).

Finally, Youngblood cites the Lord's command in Genesis 15:9–10: "The LORD said to him, 'Bring me a heifer, a goat, and a ram, each three years old, along with a dove and a young pigeon'" which Abram then cuts, arranging the halves opposite each other.[32] This case comes closest to being an example of obedience (i.e., fulfillment of a condition or requirement) under the Abrahamic covenant, since it is part of the preparation for the covenant's ratification. However, precision requires our recognition that here, too, Abram is operating as the Lord's vassal under the Adamic and Noahic covenants since, although his treatment of the animals (at the Lord's command) *prepares* for the ratification of the Abrahamic covenant, the covenant has not yet been ratified. Obviously the preparation for the ratification comes before the ratification, and the covenant does not exist until it has been ratified.[33]

The Lord states conditions, or those things in which he requires obedience, in the *torah* that follows the covenant cutting of Genesis 15 (much as he does later in the Mosaic covenant and in the new covenant). Genesis 17 and 22 are the obvious places to look for such conditions, and Youngblood's next four exemplars come from Genesis 17: the Lord requires Abram to "walk before me and be blameless" (v. 1), he tells Abram, "as for

---

30 Ibid., 37.

31 Ibid.

32 Ibid.

33 Of course it existed in God's mind before the creation and in God's experience before the creation, too, since all times are present before God. But we are speaking of its existence within the flow of human history.

you, you must keep my covenant" (v. 4), he obligates Abraham and the males in his household and his descendants to be circumcised (vv. 9–14), and after the Lord commands circumcision we are told of "Abraham's prompt obedience" to the command (vv. 23–27).[34] On the understanding that Genesis 17 gives us further *torah* of the one Abrahamic covenant cut in Genesis 15, these four data establish the conditional aspect of that covenant.

Perhaps the clearest statement of conditionality comes in Youngblood's ninth exemplar, in which God said of Abraham, "I have chosen him, so that he will direct his children and his household after him to keep the way of the LORD by doing what is right and just, *so that* the LORD will bring about for Abraham what he has promised him" (Gen. 18:19, emphasis added). Youngblood quotes J. Barton Payne, who understands that Abraham had to "walk obediently, in subjection to God's revealed will, if he was to receive the fulfillment of the divine promises."[35] This is no mere legalistic fulfillment, however. God, being outside time, knew that when Abram first expressed faith (Gen. 15:6) the faith he expressed was real because from God's point of view the works that flowed from Abram's faith (and showed his faith to be real) had already been done.[36] For God outside time, the events of Genesis 17 and 22 were long past, and indeed the eschaton was (and is) already over since, as Paul says, we have already been seated with Christ in the heavenly realms (Eph. 2:6). So the Lord's election of Abram to become his vassal under the Abrahamic covenant took into account the fruitful (and therefore true) faith

---

34   Youngblood, "The Abrahamic Covenant," 37–38.

35   Ibid., 39, quoting J. Barton Payne, "Covenant (in the Old Testament)," *Zondervan Pictorial Encyclopedia of the Bible*, eds. C. M. Tenney et al. (Grand Rapids: Zondervan, 1975), 1:1008.

36   We say "expressed faith" and *if this is right* we agree with Meredith Kline, "Abram's Amen," *WTJ* 31:1 (Nov. 1968): 1–11. We must add, however, that it is not certain that Abram actually said "amen" to the Lord in Genesis 15. Whether Abram spoke or not, the Lord knew the reality of his faith, and we are nowhere told that Abram knew the Lord credited his faith to him as righteousness. Kline notes: "As for the over-all development of the usage of הֶאֱמִין, it can be readily understood how, starting with the specific, concrete meaning 'declare Amen,' the internalized meaning of 'believe' or 'believe in' could arise" (5). We add, however, that the use of the form in Exodus 14:31 is not so likely to be delocutive, that is, expressed out loud, because the hymn of Exodus 15, which Kline takes as the expression of Israel's amen (2), only occurred later as we will argue (chap. 7). There is no evidence that insists one think Abram actually *said* "amen" to the Lord—in contrast to internally "amening" or believing—in Genesis 15.

that the Lord knew in advance (and simultaneously in retrospect) would characterize (and for God simultaneously in retrospect characterized) the life of Abram/Abraham.[37]

Youngblood's next two exemplars come from Genesis 22. The first is the command-fulfillment sequence wherein the Lord tells Abraham to take his son to Moriah and sacrifice him there (v. 2) and this is followed by "his prompt obedience." Youngblood remarks: "That such obedience springs from divinely implanted faith in no way negates its reality, its force or its significance."[38] The second exemplar is the Lord's comment on Abraham's obedience, which states that the Lord will bless him and make his descendants as numerous as the stars, will give his descendants possession of their enemies' cities, and will fulfill the promise that through Abraham's offspring all nations on earth will be blessed "because you have obeyed me." The Lord's "triple promise" as Youngblood terms it now comprises the promises made in Genesis 12, 15, and 17 under one concept: Abraham's obedience to the Lord. [39]

Youngblood also notes, as we have above, that the Lord repeats this triple promise to Isaac and states again that it is grounded in Abraham's obedience ("because Abraham obeyed me and kept my requirements, my commands, my decrees, and my laws," Gen. 26:4–5). The Lord's statement to Isaac forms Youngblood's twelfth exemplar.[40] We have discussed this passage above and recognized it was a reconfirmation with Isaac of the Abrahamic covenant—the "oath" the Lord swore to Abraham which included the three covenant promises (or the triple promise) found in Genesis 15, 17, and 22.

Youngblood's thirteenth and fourteen exemplars are more questionable. They come from the realms of covenant curse (Deut. 28:15–68) and covenant lawsuit (Jer. 4:1–2), respectively.[41] However, the covenant

---

37 Cf. the discussion in Niehaus, "Covenant and Narrative," 550.

38 Youngblood, "The Abrahamic Covenant," 39.

39 Ibid.

40 Ibid., 40.

41 I submit that there are two major types of prophet in the Bible, and especially in the Old Testament: *covenant mediator* prophets, each of whom mediates a covenant from God with respect to himself and contemporary and future people (e.g., Adam, Noah, Abraham, Moses, David, and Jesus), and *covenant lawsuit* prophets or messengers, who bring God's lawsuit against his people (but also bring exhortations to repentance and promises of restoration and hope, and messianic predictions) when they have broken the covenant (the broken covenant being the Mosaic covenant), for example, Micaiah, Elijah, Elisha, the writing prophets, and in the New Testament, John the Baptist; Jesus

to which they most immediately relate is the Mosaic covenant, not the Abrahamic. Regarding Deutereonomy 28:15–68, Youngblood notes that the promises made to the patriarch could be annulled by national apostasy.[42] Regarding Jeremiah 4:1–2, he connects national obedience under the Mosaic covenant with fulfillment of the Abrahamic blessing:

> "If you put your detestable idols out of my sight
>   and no longer go astray.
> and if in a truthful, just and righteous way
>   you swear, 'As surely as the LORD lives,'
> then the nations will be blessed by him
>   and in him will they glory." (Jer. 4:1–2)

There is, however, a more appropriate way to understand these two exemplars. The body of curses in Deuteronomy 28:15–68 show what consequences will befall Israel if they are disobedient to the Mosaic covenant. The conquest of the land is to be fulfilled under that covenant. Therefore the Mosaic covenant is the instrument by which the Lord will realize the promise of the land made in the Abrahamic covenant.[43] With regard to Jeremiah 4:1–2, it is clear that if Israel had—or could have—obeyed the conditions of the Mosaic covenant, the Abrahamic blessing to the nations would have been realized because of their obedience. Of course they did not and could not—and their failure, as we learn from the New Testament, came about because no one can be justified by obedience to the law. Israel had no hope of fulfilling the law, which, however, had the

---

shows himself in Matthew 23 to be the last and greatest lawsuit prophet under the Mosaic covenant (as he was "born under the law," Gal. 4:4), before he mediates the new covenant.

42   The promise of the land should, then, be seen as conditional. In fairness to Youngblood he is quoting George Shama on this point, and noting that Shama at that time was counselor at the Jordan Mission in the United Nations (and thus perhaps implying that Shama was tendentious and overstated the case), he concludes that Shama's "understanding of the relationship between the Abrahamic and Sinaitic covenants is surely on the right track" (Youngblood, "Covenant," 40).

43   Although a chapter on the singularity of the Abrahamic covenant may properly explore the matter of unconditionality and conditionality (since both qualities seem to appear in the materials of Genesis 15, 17, and 22), a discussion in detail of the ways the promises of the Abrahamic covenant play out, and perhaps in particular how the promise of the land is fulfilled, must be taken up later in this work as we examine the subsequent covenants. Youngblood offers a brief discussion of "Multpile Fulfillments of the Land Promise," 41–42.

pedagogical function of showing them their need for Christ to fulfill it on their behalf.

The fifteenth and final exemplar is a New Testament refection on Abraham's obedience: "By faith Abraham, when called to go to a place he would later receive as his inheritance, obeyed" (Heb. 11:8). As noted above, however, the Lord's call to Abram to leave his homeland and Abram's obedient response took place in Genesis 12, before the Abrahamic covenant had come into existence (had been cut), so it cannot be cited as an example of Abraham's obeying a condition under the Abrahamic covenant. Youngblood comments, "Obedience language presupposes the withholding of promised blessing in the absence of obedience."[44] This seems to be a fair conclusion, but it still applies to obedience to commands given by the Suzerain of the world before the Abrahamic covenant was cut. We would add, as indicated above, that the Lord already knew Abraham's faith was true (as he knew the obedience that would flow from it) before Abraham was born.

Our twofold proposition, which must be among the simplest of propositions, should be clear. The Abrahamic covenant was unconditional because the Lord would see it through (it would not fail); on the other side of the same coin, the Abrahamic covenant was also conditional (any member of it could fail). Youngblood has done us a service by pointing out and discussing several evidences of conditionality in the Abrahamic covenant, and even his errors, as in his first four (and fifteenth) exemplars, are instructive: they remind us not to categorize data as being part of a covenant when the covenant has not yet been cut. We can be grateful that the Lord's magnificent and unprecedented covenant with Abraham did not depend on fallible humans for its success, even though individuals might drop out of it through rejection (as, e.g., Esau rejected his birthright, Gen. 25:34).[45] The Abrahamic covenant would accomplish all that it should, no matter what human failures might (and would) occur along the way.[46]

---

44 Youngblood, "The Abrahamic Covenant," 41.

45 And so it is Jacob and not Esau who receives the blessings of international dominion, rule (perhaps implicitly royal), and the blessing/curse formula ("May those who curse you be cursed/and those who bless you be blessed," Gen. 27:29, cf. Gen. 12:3a) that hark back to the Abrahamic narrative corpus and its pre-covenantal promises.

46 Because every good and perfect gift comes from above (James 1:17) we credit God and God alone even with Abram's ability to amen the Lord and be obedient to the requirements—or the conditional aspect—of the covenant named after him.

THE COVENANT OF GRANT CONCEPT
AND THE DAMAGE IT HAS DONE

Moshe Weinfeld has argued that Genesis 15 enshrines a "covenant of grant," which he says is unconditional.[47] His proposal has arguably muddled discussion of the Abrahamic covenant even while appearing to clarify it, and it has led some scholars to think there is more than one Abrahamic covenant. Although Weinfeld has identified a real type of grant covenant in the ancient Near East, and although certain aspects of the Lord's covenant with Abraham resemble that type (as he has ably demonstrated), the Abrahamic covenant is not a mere grant and is different in two major respects, as we shall see. We will argue that Weinfeld's discussion of the Abrahamic covenant has three major flaws: (1) it uses a higher critical perspective, which inevitably misunderstands the relationship between the Abrahamic covenant and Deuteronomy; (2) it does not recognize the limits of the "covenant of grant" genre; and (3) although it recognizes that the Abrahamic covenant is both unconditional and conditional, it fails to understand the *goal* of its unconditionality, namely, the promise of blessing to all nations (a goal to be accomplished by the Lord's sacrifice of himself—as he symbolically shows by his theophanic passage between the pieces, an act that establishes the unconditional aspect of the covenant).[48]

Since Weinfeld takes a higher critical view of the biblical materials, he is comfortable seeing different sources for and hence different theologies in Genesis 15 and Deuteronomy. Under such an approach, Genesis 15 contains an unconditional covenant of grant (analogous to royal grants

---

47 M. Weinfeld, "The Covenant of Grant in the Old Testament and in the Ancient Near East," *JAOS* 90 (1970):184–203. I have argued elsewhere that Genesis 15 is a narrative account with the structural elements of a second millennium BC suzerain-vassal treaty but that it also contains a "grant" of lands to conquer (Niehaus, "Covenant and Narrative," 543, and pp. 57–61 of this volume). In other words, the passage is more complex than Weinfeld acknowledges. Likewise, Dennis J. McCarthy, *Treaty and Covenant*, Analecta Biblica 21A (Rome: Biblical Institute Press, 1978), 88, disagreeing with Weinfeld in his discussion of the Abba-AN text from the first half of the seventeenth century BC, remarks, "Treaty and grant, therefore, are not simply discreet phenomena. They lie along a continuum in which one leads over into the other." Cf. in a similar vein Noel Weeks, *Admonition and Curse*, 50–51. Cf. more comprehensively Kenneth A. Kitchen, *Treaty, Law, and Covenant in the Ancient Near East*, vols. 1–3 (Wiesbaden: Harrassowitz, 2012).

48 Cf. further Moshe Weinfeld, *Deuteronomy and the Deuteronomic School* (Oxford: Oxford University Press, 1972), 74–81.

in Ugarit and elsewhere in the ancient Near East) whereby the Lord guarantees the gift of land, whereas Deuteronomy contains conditions for possession of the land and comes from a different hand.[49] The key issue, then, is the basis on which the land will be possessed by Abraham's descendants. Weinfeld sees both the Abrahamic covenant and the Davidic covenant as covenants of grant, and although we will not explore the Davidic covenant here, we note Weinfeld's comment on both covenants:

> The covenant of promise itself was never formulated as conditional (cf. Gen 15; 2 Sam. 7). But Deuteronomy and the Deuteronomic school made both the grant of the Land and the promise of dynasty conditional on observance of the law—in their view the most dominant and fateful factor in the history of Israel.[50]

According to Weinfeld, both the Abrahamic covenant and the Davidic covenant are grant-type covenants and both were originally unconditional. Although as we have already stated we will not take up the issue of the Davidic covenant here, we do note that according to Weinfeld the Priestly source added to the Genesis 15 covenant (= "JE") an implication of dynasty in its royal promise in Genesis 17; and this later, Priestly account of the Abrahamic covenant was, like that in Genesis 15, unconditional.[51]

One would think that the flaws of a higher critical approach to the Pentateuch had been sufficiently exposed even by the time Weinfeld composed his book.[52] A better way to view the materials, consistent with

---

49 A higher critical approach, of course, opens the door to seeing later biblical data (like Deuteronomy) as contradictory to Genesis 15. It also renders biblical theology impossible, and the rise of canonical criticism, for example, has attempted to give the higher critic a way out of this impasse so that he, too, can do a theology of a whole book, or even of the whole Old Testament, and not just a theology of, for example, "D." We, however, are not bound by such strictures if we believe that all of Scripture is "God-breathed." Such a view of the Bible does not entail a "unity of the covenants" in the classic sense meant by covenant theology, but it does enable us to read the Bible as a coherent whole, accept as relevant its perspicuity, and be grateful for its unified and true program of salvation, unfolding through history by a program or plan of interconnected covenants culminating in the new covenant.

50 Weinfeld, *Deuteronomy and the Deuteronomic School*, 81

51 Ibid., 80.

52 Cf. Cyrus Gordon, "Higher Critics and Forbidden Fruit," *CT* 4 (November 23, 1959): 3–5; Umberto Cassuto, *The Documentary Hypothesis* (Jerusalem: Magnes, 1961);

their being "God-breathed" and true, is to understand that the Mosaic covenant was the instrument by which the promise of land to Abraham was to be fulfilled. It was the Mosaic covenant that constituted Abraham's descendants a people with a unified constitution and commission, rather than just an ethnic collection of tribes in Goshen. Under the aegis and terms of the Mosaic covenant God's people, by conquest, would fulfill the Abrahamic land promise.

The fact that the land had to be conquered if it was to be possessed constitutes another problem for Weinfeld's approach. The examples of the "covenant of grant" genre he adduces are all royal grants of land to people (citizens, vassals) who have in effect earned such a gift by their loyalty to the king. In such cases, no warfare is required for the grantee to possess the land. He simply walks in, as it were, and enjoys ownership of it.

The fact that Israel will have to conquer the land in order to possess it marks a major difference between the covenants of grant in the ancient Near East and the conquest commission implied in the Abrahamic covenant. We are not (yet) in a position to ask Abraham what he thought when the Lord promised that his offspring would possess the lands delineated in Genesis 15:18–20, but it probably does him no injustice to assume he understood warfare would be involved—that the inhabitants of the land would not simply recognize that Israel had been given the land by a "grant" and surrender it to them without a fight. There is a better analogy than that of a royal land grant to the Lord's gift of territory in Genesis 15:18–20.[53] As we have noted, the annals of the Assyrian monarch, Tukulti-Ninurta I, report the king's claim that the gods gave him

---

cf. subsequently K. A. Kitchen, *Ancient Orient and Old Testament* (Chicago: InterVarsity Press, 1973), K. A. Kitchen, *The Bible in Its World* (Downers Grove, IL: InterVarsity Press, 1978); G. Herbert Livingston, *The Pentateuch in Its Cultural Environment* (Grand Rapids: Baker, 1987); and, more generally, K. A. Kitchen, *On the Reliability of the Old Testament* (Downers Grove, IL: InterVarsity Press, 2000); cf. perhaps ironically, earlier, H. H. Rowley, *The Growth of the Old Testament* (London: Hutchinson's University Library, 1950), 46: "That it [the Wellhausen view] is rejected in whole or in part is doubtless true, but there is no view to put in its place that would not be more widely and emphatically rejected. . . . The Graf-Wellhausen view is only a working hypothesis, which can be abandoned with alacrity when a more satisfying view is found, but which cannot with profit be abandoned until then."

53   This remains so even though, as Weinfeld has pointed out, there are many conceptual and phraseological parallels between the ancient near eastern covenant of grant and the Lord's transactions with Abraham. Cf. M. Weinfeld, "The Covenant of Grant," 184–203.

certain lands in prospect, to conquer and bring under the rule of Assyria and her gods. This theology was hardly uncommon in the ancient Near East and it provides a more precise analogy to what happens in Genesis 15, which is no mere grant for Abram (and/or his descendants) to walk in and enjoy the land in perpetuity. Like the gift of land to Tukulti-Ninurta I by his gods, the gift of the land to Abram by the Lord in Genesis 15 requires that the land be conquered if it is to be possessed, as subsequent revelation makes clear.[54] In other words, the *realization* of the gift of land at any *particular* point in time turns out to be *conditional*. The generation that came out of Egypt with Moses failed to achieve it (although Joshua and Caleb woud later achieve it, e.g., Num. 14:30–38; 26:65; 32:12) because they lacked faith that the Lord would both fight for them and empower them to wage the needed warfare. In any case, the unqualified royal grant explanation of Genesis 15:18–20 should be abandoned, because the land must be conquered by Abraham's obedient descendants in order to be possessed, and the sort of covenant of grant to which Weinfeld appeals does not appear to be a genre that imposed warfare on the grantee in order for him to possess the land.

The third problem with Weinfeld's presentation is that, although it recognizes the Abrahamic covenant is unconditional (and yet entails conditions!), it fails to understand one important aspect—indeed, what is arguably the main goal of its unconditionality—namely, the promise of blessing to all nations, which is fulfilled through the new covenant. He comments:

> In its original setting the promise of the Land was unconditional, although it presupposed—as we have indicated—loyalty and the fulfillment of some obligations and duties (see Gen. 18:19; Ps. 132:12); the covenant of promise itself was never formulated as conditional.[55]

Since Weinfeld cites Psalm 132:12, we note that Psalm 132:11–12 seems quite ironic in this regard:

> The LORD swore an oath to David,
>   a sure oath he will not revoke:
> "One of your own descendants

---

54 Cf. volume 2, chapter 2, and the earlier discussion in Niehaus, "Covenant and Narrative," 244–46; *ANETBT*, 78–79.

55 Weinfeld, *Deuteronomy and the Deuteronomic School*, 81.

I will place on your throne.
If your sons keep my covenant
and the statutes I teach them,
then their sons will sit
on your throne for ever and ever." (emphases added)

We have already observed that the Abrahamic covenant is unconditional in the sense that God will see it through until it accomplishes all
that it should; it will not fail (and the same is true of the Davidic covenant, cf. Ps. 132:11). But it is conditional in the sense that an individual
may forfeit his place in it; the individual may fail (and the same is true
of the Davidic covenant, cf. Ps 132:12). The Abrahamic covenant does not
come to an end if an individual member of it betrays (i.e., is disobedient
to) the Lord. The individual may indeed "forfeit the gift" of the covenant (as did Esau) but the covenant goes on through history, blessing
its other members and culminating in its ultimate fulfillment (in the
new covenant).[56] Its fulfillment in the new covenant is the key point that
Weinfeld has not understood. He recognizes the self-imprecatory nature
of the ceremony in Genesis 15:18 and understands that it is in effect a
statement of unconditionality. But he attaches the unconditionality of the
Abrahamic covenant to the *land*. Since the Lord in Genesis 15 ratifies a
covenant to which he adds supplemental *torah* in Genesis 17 and 22, the
oath passage (as it is usually called) of Genesis 15:17 should be seen not
simply as rendering unconditional the promise of land that follows it in
Genesis 15:18–21, but also the promises of an heir and many descendants
made earlier in Genesis 15:4–5 (and cf. later in Gen. 22:17), and indeed
proleptically rendering unconditional the promises of royal offspring and
blessing to all nations made in the subsequent Abrahamic covenantal
torah of Genesis 17 and 22.[57] The Lord would see to it that all of these
promises would be fulfilled, even though individual members of the fu-

---

56   We emphasize once more that God knew in advance that *Abraham* would not
disobey and thus forfeit the covenant and its promises at its outset; he also knew this in
retrospect, and could comment to Isaac how "Abraham obeyed me and did everything I
required of him, keeping my commands, my decrees and my instructions," Gen. 26:5).

57   We should note that, although the promise that Abram's descendants would *receive* the land is unconditional (i.e., they have to conquer it, so in that sense the fulfillment
of the promise was *conditional*, but the Lord would *see to it* that they did eventually
conquer it, so in that sense the *promise itself was unconditional*: the Lord would see to
it that the Conquest took place), Israel's subsequent *retention* of the land would *not* be
unconditional, as the Mosaic covenant would make clear.

ture covenant community might forfeit them through disobedience; and indeed generations of Israel would forfeit the land and the royal promise, and many ethnic Israelites would forfeit a place in the global blessing because they would not accept the Messiah through whom it would come. This, then, is another and more important sense (in addition to the implicit conquest mandate of Genesis 15) in which the pagan covenant of grant and the Abrahamic covenant are profoundly different. In the pagan covenant of grant there may be a curse, but if there is, it is directed against one who would violate the vassal's rights.[58] In the Abrahamic covenant cutting, by contrast, there is a curse, but the Suzerain pledges to *take it upon himself*. Weinfeld, and, so far as I can see, those who have accepted his characterization of the Abrahamic covenant in Genesis 15 simply as a covenant of grant on the pagan model, have not taken this difference sufficiently into account as a distinguishing characteristic. The Lord's "self-imprecatory oath passage" reminds us of ancient near eastern suzerain-vassal treaty ratification, but (since, as far as we know, no ancient near eastern suzerain ever took it upon *himself* to ratify a treaty by walking between the pieces) what the Lord does by submitting himself to this symbolic ritual makes the Abrahamic covenant truly *sui generis*.

Weinfeld's use of ancient near eastern royal grants (which he has chosen to call unconditional) as a sort of hermeneutical key to Genesis 15 has won a large number of adherents, so that its validity seems to be considered virtually axiomatic.[59] The analogous data that he presents from the ancient Near East certainly seem to demonstrate that Genesis 15 and the related Abrahamic materials in Genesis have aspects of a grant-type relationship. It should be clear from the conquest mandate, which Genesis 15 implies (as noted above), and from the Suzerain's act of self-imprecation, that it cannot properly be considered a mere covenant of grant. It should also be clear that it is unhelpful to characterize the

---

58   Weinfeld, "The Covenant of Grant," 185. This of course resonates with Genesis 12:3, where, however, the curse against any hostile party ("whoever curses you I will curse") is a promise, since the covenant has not yet been cut. The curse ceremony of the actual covenant cutting, by contrast, is a *self-imprecatory* act, quite different from what we find in the ancient near eastern covenant of grant, and more akin to what we find in ancient near eastern suzerain-vassal treaty ratifications (where, however, it is the vassal who passes between the pieces).

59   Cf. S. E. Loewenstamm, "The Divine Grants of Land to the Patriarchs," *JAOS* 91 (1971): 509–510; J. van Seters, *Abraham in History and Tradition* (New Haven, CT: Yale University Press, 1975), 259; Thomas E. McComiskey, *The Covenants of Promise* (Grand Rapids: Baker, 1985), 63; B. K. Waltke, "The Phenomenon of Conditionality," 123–39, esp. 127–30.

Abrahamic covenant simply as unconditional and to link that concept with the covenant of grant as Weinfeld does with regard to both the Abrahamic and the Davidic covenants.

A full exploration of Weinfeld's influence in this matter is well beyond the scope of our biblical theology but his influence should, I believe, be noted in the work of three more recent scholars, two of whom have written major books on the covenant idea. Paul Williamson and Scott Hahn in their books on the biblical covenants have both adopted Weinfeld's covenant of grant characterization of Genesis 15, and, following Weinfeld, think of it as unconditional. However, since they (correctly) see conditions in Genesis 17, they both conclude (mistakenly I believe and unlike Weinfeld) that Genesis 17 reports a different, because conditional, covenant. [60] In their separation of Genesis 15 and 17 into two fundamentally different covenants, Williamson and Hahn follow T. Desmond Alexander. Alexander characterizes the supposed two covenants in Genesis 15 and 17 in this way: "Whereas the promissory covenant of Genesis 15 is unconditional, the establishment or ratification of the covenant of circumcision is dependent upon Abraham's continuing obedience to God."[61]

SUMMARY

Those who, like Alexander, see two different covenants (unconditional and conditional, respectively) in Genesis 15 and 17 seem not to have understood how the *one* covenant the Lord made with Abraham can be

---

60   Cf., Paul Williamson, *Sealed with an Oath*, 89, who characterizes the unconditional/conditional difference between the Genesis 15 covenant and the Genesis 17 covenant in other language amounting, however, to the same thing: Genesis 15 is "unilateral," Genesis 17 is "bilateral"; Scott Hahn, *Kinship by Covenant*, characterizes Genesis 15 as an unconditional grant type treaty ("God unconditionally binds himself to the various elements of his promissory oath," 102), and Genesis 17 as a conditional suzerain-vassal type treaty ("Both Deuteronomy and Genesis 17 are of the same covenant type, that is, they resemble the so-called 'vassal treaty,'" 115). Weinfeld, following classical higher criticism, had simply considered Genesis 15 ("JE") and Genesis 17 ("P") to be earlier and later reports or versions of the same covenant, and thus combined them for purposes of discussing the Abrahamic covenant diachronically from a documentary point of view.

61   T. Desmond Alexander, *From Paradise to the Promised Land* (Carlisle: Paternoster, 1995), 52; cf. his discussion, 48–62. Williamson followed Alexander in this contradistinction of Genesis 15 and 17, and Hahn subsequently followed Williamson (cf. Hahn, *Kinship by Covenant*, 10).

both unconditional and conditional. Moreover, they have apparently failed to appreciate the significance of what the Bible itself says about the Abrahamic covenant.

As we have shown above, the Bible only ever refers to the Lord's covenant with Abraham in the singular. It can even refer to the Lord's covenant with Abraham, Isaac, and Jacob, or "with the fathers," in the singular. It does so because the Lord in fact made only one covenant with Abraham and then reconfirmed it with his descendants. The statements of the Old Testament (e.g., Exod. 2:24) and the New Testament (e.g., Acts 3:25) agree on these points without exception.

We have allowed such biblical data to guide us as we considered the narratives of Genesis 12, 15, 17, and 22 that report the Lord's covenant-related interactions with Abraham. Those reports extend from the promises of Genesis 12 through the covenant cutting of Genesis 15 and the supplemental *torah* of Genesis 17 to the resumptive and summary mention of the triple promise under the finally reported oath of Genesis 22.

Once we take the biblical statements of the Lord's singular covenant with Abraham at face value and allow them to govern our analysis we find that the scope of the narrative material, Genesis 12–22, becomes clear as regards the Abrahamic covenant. It begins with commands (12:1–2) and promises (12:2–3) made under common grace, proceeds to the cutting of a covenant (Genesis 15), which evokes the earlier command in its historical prologue (15:7; cf. 12:1); it continues with a reaffirmation of the Genesis 15 covenant along with supplemental *torah* (Genesis 17—a pattern of supplemental *torah* given after covenant cutting later apparent in the Mosaic and the new covenants), and concludes with a divine oath that repeats the triple promise and thus summarizes and concludes the narrative material of the Abrahamic covenant. We speak here of the narrative material in its scope, which provides a history of the Lord's interactions with Abraham as regards the covenant while affirming again that the Lord's one and only covenant with Abraham is actually cut and thus comes into being in Genesis 15. Such conclusions are made possible by an acceptance of what the Bible says about the number of covenants the Lord made with Abraham (namely, one), and also by an appreciation of the difference between an actual covenant cutting (Genesis 15) on the one hand, and a comprehensive narrative of covenant-related dealings (Genesis 12, 15, 17, and 22) on the other.

We can be grateful that the Lord's covenant with Abraham was both unconditional and conditional. Its unconditionality showed his commitment to the accomplishment of its ultimate salvific purpose, the universal blessing available to all nations by the Spirit. Its conditionality showed he was still the holy God with holy and kingdom requirements that would not be dismissed by cheap grace. Finally, we can be grateful that the Lord did see the Abrahamic covenant through to its fulfillment in and by Christ, so that those who have the faith of Abraham may know salvation by that same faith. The Abrahamic covenant no longer functions as a covenant (e.g., we are no longer required to be circumcised), but its great promise has been fulfilled and continues to be fulfilled every day by those who are and those who become the children of Abraham, and who know the circumcision of the heart by the promised Holy Spirit.

CHAPTER FIVE

IDIOMS OF COVENANT INSTITUTION

I t was noted in chapter 1 that the idioms "to give [נָתַן] covenant" and
"to carry out/put into effect [הֵקִים] covenant" were used with regard
to the Noahic covenant. The idiom "to cut a covenant" (כָּרַת בְּרִית) was
not used with regard to the Noahic covenant. A reason was proposed
for the non-use of that idiom: the idiom symbolizes the possibility that a
member might be "cut out" of the covenant or "cut off" from membership
in the covenant. Obviously such an idiom would be inappropriate to the
Noahic covenant. It is a common grace covenant and one cannot be cut
off from participation in it. We know very well that one may be a murderer, or in other ways God knows but did not state for the record (cf. Isa.
24:1–5), violate the Noahic covenant yet not be cut off from membership
in it. A person may be a murderer, for instance, and escape justice as it
might be administered under the common grace institutions for his or
her whole life. Of course we all die, but if one dies a natural death, that
is in fulfillment of the original curse of the Adamic covenant (Gen. 2:17)
and not because of any sin defined by and committed under the common
grace covenants.[1] On the other hand, the increase of human violation
of the common grace covenantal package *will* lead to a final judgment,
when God will judge the world primarily because of the *lack of faith* of
its inhabitants, which has produced all their godlessness (Luke 18:8).[2]
When faith is no longer possible—because sin has so increased that the

---

1   Obviously there is a death penalty for the shedding of human blood, stated in
the Noahic covenant, but that is a different matter from the general sentence of death on
all humanity.

2   That lack of faith or amening God also leads to the pollution of the world, which
is the fruit of humanity's rampant failure of faith, and so Isaiah declares:

consciences of all are seared—there will be no point in continuing the common grace covenants, and God will put an end to the world they govern, and with that world the covenants themselves. The eschatological situation will parallel the situation Joshua found when he invaded the Promised Land.[3]

We also noted that the use of the idioms for covenant institution ("to cut") and covenant reaffirmation/reconfirmation ("to give," "to carry out/ make effective," etc.) in the rest of the Old Testament is consistent with what we would later in the Abrahamic covenant narrative data. The same is true subsequent to the Abrahamic covenant. A survey of the idioms in the Old Testament shows that the verb כרת ("to cut") is used only of covenants once the special grace program is underway (at the institution of the Abrahamic covenant in Genesis 15, and then subsequently) and *only when a covenant is created*; moreover, this category can include the creation of renewal covenants. By contrast, the verbs נתן ("to give," "go on giving") and הקים ("to carry out," "sustain," "[re]confirm") are used when the confirmation or carrying forth (but not the formal renewal) of *an already existing covenant* is in view, and the same is true if the *existence* of the covenant is *envisioned or future*. A few other verbs are also used infrequently in connection with covenant institution, for example, שים ("to place," "set"), עבר ב ("to cross over into"), לקח ב ("to take into"), and בא ("to enter into," "to bring into" [Hiphil]).[4]

"The earth is defiled by its people;
   they have disobeyed the laws,
   violated the statutes
   and broken the everlasting covenant.
Therefore a curse consumes the earth;
   its people must bear their guilt.
Therefore earth's inhabitants are burned up,
   and very few are left." (Isa. 24:5–6)

3   We noted further that since the Lord was preparing to put a covenant into effect with Noah, and since the idiom "to cut a covenant" was inappropriate to the nature of that covenant, the Lord used the other covenant idioms, "to give covenant" and "to carry out/ put into effect covenant." The idiom using "to carry out/put into effect" also alludes to the continuation of a prior relationship, as Dumbrell correctly noted, and thus alludes to the Adamic covenant—as the parallel between Genesis 1:28 and Genesis 9:1–3 also indicates.

4   The following study has to do only with idioms of covenant institution and maintenance. Readers may compare Gentry and Wellum, *Kingdom through Covenant*, 717–78—an appendix that offers an analysis of ברית in a variety of usages, including idioms of covenant violation or abandonment. The following study (composed before

There now follows a review of all the Old Testament instances of these usages. The usages occur in the Pentateuch, the Historical Books, Job, Psalms, and the Prophets. The data are very straightforward for the most part, although two cases in Ezekiel 16 will require careful discussion before we can suggest what we believe to be a proper understanding of them.

THE PENTATEUCH

We note again that the idiom כרת ברית ("to cut a covenant") is used because it symbolizes the fact that someone party to the covenant can lose membership in that covenant through disobedience, and we begin with the Pentateuchal cases of the idioms under discussion, considering the Mosaic books *seriatim*.

Genesis

After the Lord cuts his covenant with Abram in Genesis 15:18, there are four other cases of covenant institution in Genesis, and all of them use the idiom כרת ברית. These are the cutting of Abraham's covenant with Abimelek (with two mentions, Gen. 21:27, 32), Isaac's covenant with Abimelek (Gen. 26:28; cf. also in that verse the use of "oath" [אלה] as synechdoche for and in parallel with "covenant": "let there be an oath between us . . . and let us cut a covenant with you," author's translation), and Laban's covenant with Jacob (Gen. 31:44). In each case the creation of a previously nonexistent covenant is at issue.

Exodus

There are five cases in Exodus where the issue of covenant institution is raised, and one case in which the carrying out (but not the renewal) of an already existent covenant is in view. The latter is a reference to the Lord's covenant with Abraham, Isaac, and Jacob, and to the fact that the Lord reaffirmed this covenant through the generations, using the idiom הקים ברית ("I also established my covenant with them to give them the

---

the Gentry and Wellum work came to my attention) focuses on instances of covenant making and sustaining, and offers more extensive contextual discussion of the passages in which they occur.

land of Canaan, where they resided as foreigners," Exod. 6:4). Although the Lord cut the covenant originally with Abram, he subsequently also assured Abram that he was continuing to "give" it (נתן, Gen. 17:2) and "sustain" it (הקים, Gen. 17:7, 19, 21; and cf. discussion in chap. 1) and we are here told that he also "sustained" it (NIV, "established" it) with Isaac and Jacob. This is consistent with what the Lord says to Isaac: "Stay in this land for a while, and I will be with you and will bless you. For to you and your descendants I will give all these lands and will *confirm the oath* I swore to your father Abraham" (Gen. 26:3, emphasis added). In other words, by giving these lands to Abraham's offspring the Lord will "sustain" (i.e., show to be valid by putting into effect) the oath (והקמתי את־השבע, with "oath" as synecdoche for "covenant") he swore to Abraham: it is a promise of the eventual carrying out of what the Lord swore to do, not a renewal of the Abrahamic covenant per se, for it shows that that covenant is still in force and Isaac is living under it when the Lord says these things to him.[5]

The five mentions of covenant *institution* in Exodus are of two types: mention of the covenant the Lord is making with Israel (two cases), and the idea that Israel is not to make a covenant with any of the inhabitants of Canaan (three cases). To take the latter first, the Lord warns his people three times not to cut a covenant with the inhabitants of the land and all three warnings use the idiom כרת ברית (Exod. 23:32; 34:12, 15). The idiom is also used when he inscribes the new tablets of the law to replace the ones that were broken, indicating that the Lord is cutting once more (the participle is used) the covenant that had been symbolically destroyed when the tablets were destroyed (Exod. 34:10). The idiom is also used in the finalizing of that process ("Then the LORD said to Moses, 'Write down these words, for *in accordance with these words I have made a covenant* with you and with Israel,'" Exod. 34:27, emphasis added). The Lord in this case is creating once more a covenant with the original party

---

5   Readers familiar with my past articles will realize that this view of the Lord's covenantal dealings with Isaac (and Jacob) differs from what I previously thought when I saw the Lord's reiteration of his promises to Isaac and Jacob as *renewals* of the Abrahamic covenant. As I now consider the matter, I believe the use of biblical terminology conduces more naturally to the view expressed above. The Lord "confirmed" (to use the more usual translation) to Isaac and Jacob his earlier promises to Abram by repeating those promises. But the mere repetition of the promises was not a formal renewal of the Abrahamic covenant, which was still in force—for Isaac and Jacob, as circumcised individuals, lived as members of that ongoing covenant. Cf. chapter 4, n17.

(namely, Israel) that had in effect been destroyed, not renewing with descendants a covenant that had continued in force with a prior generation. The latter does take place, however, when the Lord cuts the covenant of Deuteronomy (cf. Deut. 29:1) with the offspring of that generation whose bodies fell in the desert (cf. Heb. 3:17).

Leviticus

The book of Leviticus contains only one case of ברית used in conjunction with any of the idioms under discussion, and it occurs in Leviticus 26. There the Lord promises, "If you follow my decrees and are careful to obey my commands" (Lev. 26:3), "I will look on you with favor and make you fruitful and increase your numbers, and I will continue to carry out/sustain my covenant (הקים ברית) with you" (Lev. 26:9, author's translation). This is quite simply the Lord's declaration that he will maintain, or continue in effect, his covenant with Israel if they are obedient.[6]

Numbers

The book of Numbers also contains only one case of the idiomatic usages under discussion, and it has to do with the Lord's promise to Phineas as a result of the latter's zeal against the transgressors of the Mosaic covenant at Baal Peor. The background to this promise is found in Numbers 18, and in particular we note the Lord's promise to the Levites under the Mosaic covenant: "Whatever is set aside from the holy offerings the Israelites present to the Lord I give to you and your sons and daughters as your perpetual share. It is an everlasting covenant of salt before the LORD for both you and your offspring" (Num. 18:19). Here the verb "to give" is used, although the object of it is not, syntactically, the "covenant of salt," but rather the provisions included by that covenant. Subsequently, however, the verb is used in connection with that covenant: "Therefore [i.e., because of Phineas' zeal against the breakers of the Mosaic covenant, which turned Yahweh's wrath away from Israel] tell him I am making [lit. "giving"] my covenant of peace with him (הנני נתן לו את־בריתי שלום). He and his descendants will have a covenant of a lasting priesthood, because he was zealous for the honor of his God and made atonement for the Israelites" (Num. 25:12–13). The covenant of peace here is explained by the statement that Phineas and his descendants will have a covenant

---

6   Cf. *BDB*, 879.

of a lasting priesthood. The covenant of peace, being a covenant of a lasting priesthood, is thus also the covenant of salt (or a subdivision of it), which was an emphatic characterization of the priestly arrangement already existing within the Mosaic covenant (as per Numbers 18). If our understanding of the idiom is correct, the sense of the Lord's statement is that he will continue *giving* this covenant (i.e., keeping it in force) for many generations (עולם, although not *eternally*, since the Mosaic priesthood does not last forever)—namely, the priesthood of Phineas and his descendants, a priesthood which already existed by that covenant of salt, which was part of the Mosaic covenant. Moreover, and to be very clear on this point, no covenant making/cutting idiom was needed with regard to the priestly covenant of salt, because when the Mosaic covenant was "cut," every provision it contained and would contain in its further *torah*, including the covenant of salt, was implicitly "cut" with it.

Deuteronomy

Since it is often considered the Pentateuchal covenantal book *par excellence,* it seems fitting that Deuteronomy contains more mentions of covenant cutting, along with a couple of cases of covenant "confirming," than the books that preceded it. Deuteronomy contains three references to the Horeb covenant, two references to the covenant Yahweh swore with the fathers, one warning to make no covenant with the inhabitants of the land, and two references to the covenant (in essence, Deuteronomy) that he is making with the present generation.

There are three historical references to the Horeb covenant, and all use the idiom כרת ברית, reflecting on the fact that the Lord cut the covenant at that place (Deut. 5:2, 3; 29:1 [28:69 MT]). The Lord refers to the covenant that he "swore to your fathers" (נשבע, Deut. 7:12; cf. 7:2) and promises to carry it out/sustain it (הקים) if they remember him (Deut. 8:18). One more time he warns his people not to make any covenant with the inhabitants of the land (כרת ברית, Deut. 7:2). And finally, he speaks of the renewal covenant (in essence, Deuteronomy) he is now cutting with the new generation of Israelites (כרת, Deut. 29:1, 12, 14 [28:69; 29:11, 13 MT]). We note also that the people "enter into (lit. 'cross over into,' עבר) the covenant of Yahweh your God—and into his oath (אלא)," using the latter covenant component perhaps for emphasis or in *merismus* = "the *covenant by oath* of Yahweh your God" (Deut. 29:12; cf. v. 14, using the participle of כרת in both cases). The ones who do so are the children of those whose bodies fell in the desert, the children who, under Joshua, will undertake the conquest.

THE HISTORICAL BOOKS

Joshua

Joshua contains seven references to covenant. One reference is to the Mosaic covenant (Josh. 7:11, in which the Lord speaks of Israel's transgressing the covenant that he commanded [צוה] them—possibly a synecdoche whereby the whole is stated for the part, i.e., covenant for command-ments/stipulations, but the reference seems to be to Deut. 29:1 [28:69 MT], "These are the words of the covenant the Lord commanded [צוה] Moses to make [לכרת] with the children of Israel," author's translation). Five references are to Israel's ill-considered treaty with the Gibeonites (Josh. 9:6, 7, 11, 15, 16). One reference is to the covenant Joshua makes with Israel and then adds to the Book of the Law (Josh. 24:25–26). All except the first use the idiom כרת ברית. The last case (in Joshua 24) is of interest because it is sometimes thought of as an example of covenant renewal. Such, however, cannot be the case, on the understanding that only the Lord can truly renew a divine-human covenant.[7] Any so-called covenant renewal initiated by humans is merely a human recommitment to a covenant to which the human is legally party *whether or not* he chooses to renew his commitment to it. The same is true of couples who renew their marriage vows: in the Lord's sight they are and continue to be married whether or not they renew their marriage by a ceremony on their own initiative.

Judges

Judges contains only one covenant reference using any of the idioms under discussion. Yahweh's angel warns Israel to make (כרת) no covenant with the inhabitants of the land (Judg. 2:2), a reiteration of the warning already seen in Exodus and Deuteronomy.

1 Samuel

The book of 1 Samuel contains six references to covenant institution, all but one of them using the verb כרת. References that use the verb are as follows: the covenant proposed by the men of Jabesh to Nahash the Ammonite (two mentions, 1 Sam. 11:1, 2); the covenant Jonathan cuts

---

7   As noted and discussed in chapter 4.

with David (1 Sam. 18:3), referred to later with the verb בא ("to enter into," here in the Hiphil), "show kindness to your servant, for you have *brought him into* a covenant with you before the Lord" (1 Sam. 20:8), evidence that the verb "to enter into" can be used of a covenant institution; כרת is also used of another covenant Jonathan makes with "the house of David" (1 Sam. 20:16), including Jonathan's having David "reaffirm his oath" (ויוסף . . . להשביע, lit. "added to cause [David] to swear" = "caused [David] to swear again," 1 Sam. 20:17), apparently referring back to the covenant cut in 1 Samuel 18:3; and כרת is used of a third covenant made between Jonathan and David, that David would be king and Jonathan would be next to him (1 Sam. 23:18).

2 Samuel

The book of 2 Samuel contains five references to covenant institution, and four of these use the verb כרת. The first two refer to Abner's covenant with David (2 Sam. 3:12, 13). The next two refer to Israel's vassal covenant with David (2 Sam. 3:21; 5:3). The fifth mention of covenant institution refers to God's "everlasting covenant" with David, and uses the verb שים, "to place / put in place" (in poetical verse, "If my house were not right with God, / surely he would not have *made* with me [lit. "put in place for me"] an everlasting covenant," 2 Sam. 23:5).

1 Kings

The book of 1 Kings contains only two references to covenant institution using the word "covenant" and both employ the idiom כרת ברית: the treaty made between Hiram of Tyre and Solomon (apparently a parity treaty, 1 Kings 5:12), and Ahab's treaty with Ben-Hadad (apparently a suzerain-vassal treaty after Ahab's defeat of Ben-Hadad, 1 Kings 20:34). We note also, however, the Lord's conditional promise to Solomon: "As for this temple you are building, if you follow my decrees, observe my laws and keep all my commands and obey them, I will carry out / sustain with you my word (והקמתי את־דברי אתך) which I spoke to David your father" (1 Kings 6:12, author's translation), a clear allusion to the Davidic covenant and a promise to "sustain it."[8]

---

8   We note that Solomon's tenure of the blessings of the Davidic covenant is thus made conditional upon his obedience, although the continuation of the Davidic covenant

2 Kings

The book of 2 Kings contains seven references to covenant institution, all using the idiom כרת ברית. The first describes Israel's vassal treaty with Joash, to make him king (2 Kings 14:4). The second is a case of a humanly initiated covenant with the Lord, when, after Athalia's execution, Jehoiada the priest makes a covenant between Yahweh, the king and the people, "that they would be the Lord's people" (2 Kings 11:17a). Jehoiada follows that act by instituting a vassal treaty between the king and the people (2 Kings 11:17b). The next three mentions of covenant institution are references back to the Mosaic covenant, in the context of a historical review illustrating how the people of the northern kingdom failed to obey that covenant and were thus conquered and exiled by the king of Assyria (2 Kings 17:15, 35, 38).

1 Chronicles

First Chronicles contains only one mention of covenant institution, and it is the vassal treaty made by Israel and David at Hebron (1 Chron. 11:3 // 2 Sam. 5:3) and uses the idiom כרת ברית.

2 Chronicles

Second Chronicles contains seven cases of covenant institution, five of which use the idiom כרת ברית. The first mention of covenant institution without the verb כרת regards Asa's covenant with Israel to seek Yahweh, and it uses the verb בא ("to enter into," 2 Chron. 15:12: "They entered into a covenant to seek the LORD, the God of their ancestors, with all their heart and soul"). This is the sort of covenant that some would call a covenant renewal, but again, we proceed on the understanding that only the Lord can renew any covenant he has made; any human attempt at so-called covenant renewal in the Old Testament is only a decision on the part of some of God's people to demonstrate their renewed zeal to obey the Mosaic covenant by making a covenant to do so on their own initiative. Whether they feel the onset of such zeal or not, however, and whether or not they do anything about it, they are still living under the Mosaic covenant, which is still in force when they make or enter into the

---

itself is not. Cf. further Niehaus, "God's Covenant with Abraham," 268; and discussion in chapter 4.

covenant they initiate.⁹ We will see a good example of this sort of distinction when we consider Jeremiah 34 in detail. Before then we consider the remaining exemplars of covenant making in 2 Chronicles.

The second mention of covenant institution in that book uses the verb כרת, but not the whole expression כרת ברית. The Lord says to Solomon, "I will establish your royal throne, as I cut with David your father (כאשר כרתי לדויד אביך) when I said, 'You will never fail to have a man to rule over Israel'" (2 Chron. 7:18, author's translation). This interesting example shows that the verb כרת alone could be used in place of the whole expression כרת ברית. Moreover, there was no literal cutting of animals in the making of the Davidic covenant, so we see that the verb כרת or the idiom כרת ברית (as below in 2 Chron. 21:7) could mean simply to create a covenant, without enacting the covenant ratifying ceremony the idiom originally denoted. After all, if the Bible says the Lord made a covenant, then, he has made a covenant.

The third case is a reference to the covenant the Lord made with David and also uses the verb כרת (2 Chron. 21:7). The fourth uses a unique idiom: Jehoiada of Judah *takes* Azariah and the other commanders of units of one hundred *into covenant* with him, using the expression לקח בברית ("to take into covenant," 2 Chron. 23:1). After that the narrative reports what is apparently a vassal treaty: "The whole assembly made a covenant (כרת ברית) with the king at the temple of God" that "the king's son should reign after him, as the LORD promised concerning the descendants of David" (2 Chron. 23:3, author's translation). It is a vassal treaty that takes the people as subjects of the king's son, and the legal basis of it is noted here as well, that is, the Lord's promise to David in the earlier Davidic covenant.

The penultimate covenant making reported in 2 Chronicles involves Hezekiah's desire to make a covenant with the Lord to take away his wrath from the people after their predecessors had neglected the service of the temple (כרת ברית, 2 Chron. 29:10). The final covenant mentioned is the one Josiah makes with the Lord. This is another passage

---

9   That is, they live in a state legally governed by the Mosaic covenant. They themselves are still members of that Mosaic covenant if they have not, in God's sight, been cut off from that covenant through unrepentant disobedience. On the other hand, if some of them are cut off, and if the covenant they undertake proves to be an insincere act on their part (as seems to be the case in Jer. 34:12–16), they will be judged and punished for breaking both covenants: the Mosaic covenant, and the covenant they undertook in order to affirm their intent to obey the Mosaic covenant (cf. as an example, Jer. 34:18–19).

misunderstood as a covenant renewal, and the NIV translation reflects this misunderstanding: "The king stood by his pillar and renewed the covenant in the presence of the LORD—to follow the LORD and keep his commands, statutes, and decrees with all his heart and all his soul, and to obey the words of the covenant written in this book" (2 Chron. 34:31). The "book" referred to is the Book of the Law found by Hilkiah when he was renovating the temple. Josiah read that book (usually considered to be Deuteronomy), and in response to it instituted what reform he could, cleansing the temple and making the covenant mentioned in verse 31. On the grounds outlined above, however, that covenant is not a renewal but only a recommitment on the part of the king and those would join him to obey the Mosaic covenant. The idiom used is כרת ברית.

Ezra-Nehemiah

There are three covenant making episodes mentioned in Ezra-Nehemiah—one in Ezra and two in Nehemiah. The one in Ezra records Shekanaiah's proposal to Ezra that the people make a covenant with their God to put away their foreign wives and their offspring according to the law (כרת ברית, Ezra 10:3). This humanly initiated covenant to commit to the obedience of one part of the Mosaic covenant is very much like the covenant we will consider in Jeremiah 34.

The first covenant making episode in Nehemiah has to do with the Lord's covenant with Abraham: "You found his heart faithful to you, and you made a covenant with him to give to his descendants the land of the Canaanites, Hittites, Amorites, Perizzites, Jebusites, and Girgashites. You have kept your promise because you are righteous" (כרת ברית, Neh. 9:8). We note here that the ground of the Lord's covenant keeping is his own righteousness, that is, his faithfulness to his own nature (and thus to the covenant that is an expression of that nature) and its embodiment of standards of faithfulness and mercy—in short, grace and truth/troth.

The second covenant making episode in Nehemiah uses covenant-related terms that allow one to infer that a covenant making episode is underway. In Nehemiah 9, the Israelites separate themselves from foreigners and review their history: they recollect the many instances of the Lord's faithfulness and of their own sins. They resolve to walk according to the Mosaic covenant and they apparently make a covenant on their own initiative to do so: "In view of all this, we are making a binding agreement, putting it in writing, and our leaders, our Levites and our priests are affixing their seals to it" (Neh. 9:38 [10:1 MT]). The phrase translated by NIV as "we are making a binding agreement" is literally "we are cutting a trustworthy [agreement] and (sub)scribing [to it]" (אנחנו כרתים אמנה וכתבים).[10] The verb "to cut" apparently indicates the covenant making nature of the proceedings (cf. the use of the verb alone noted above, 2 Chron. 7:18). Their action is then summarized as follows: they "bind themselves with a curse and an oath to follow the law of God given through Moses the servant of God and to obey carefully all the commands, regulations and decrees of the LORD our Lord" (Neh. 10:29 [10:30 MT]). The phrase translated "bind themselves with a curse and an oath" is literally "enter into a curse and an oath" (ובאים באלה ובשבועה). This is a case of two covenantal elements, the curse and the solemnizing oath, used in synechdoche for the covenant as a whole. The idiom for entering into (בא) the covenant is one we have encountered and will encounter again.

JOB

Job offers two statements of covenant making, both using the familiar idiom כרת ברית. In the first, Job tells us, "I have made a covenant with my eyes / not to look lustfully at a young woman" (Job 31:1). In the second, the Lord addresses Job out of the theophanic storm and asks in the context of a series of rhetorical questions whether Leviathan "will . . . make an agreement with you, for you to take it as your slave for life (כרת ברית, Job 41:4; note NIV "agreement" is Hebrew ברית, "covenant"; possibly also "vassal" is a better translation than "slave" in this context for Hebrew עבד). Both of these cases are, of course, figurative expressions in a poetic opus.

PSALMS

Perhaps remarkably, statements of covenant institution occur only three times in the Psalms. All three use the idiom כרת ברית.[11] The first is apparently a reference to the Mosaic covenant: "Gather to me this consecrated people, who made a covenant with me by sacrifice" (Ps. 50:5). The second

---

10   *BDB* translates "*we are plighting faith* (make a sure covenant)," 53.

11   Curiously, there appears to be no use of the expressions נתן ברית ("to give covenant") and הקים ברית ("to carry out/sustain covenant") in the Psalms.

portrays Yahweh's foes planning to make a treaty against the Lord and, implicitly, his people: "With one mind they plot together; they form an alliance against you" (יכרתו עליך ברית, Ps. 83:5 [83:6 MT]). The final occurrence is in reference to the Davidic covenant: "You said, 'I have made a covenant with my chosen one, I have sworn to David my servant'" (Ps. 89:3 [89:4 MT]), and the Lord promises that this covenant is trustworthy: "I will maintain [lit. "keep," "guard"] my love to him forever, and my covenant with him will never fail" (Ps. 89:28 [89:29 MT]). The last statement is significant, not as a report of covenant institution, but as a declaration by the Lord of the reliability of the covenant. The declaration actually reads in Hebrew, "My covenant is trustworthy for him" (ובריתי נאמנת לו), "trustworthy" being a better translation than NIV's "will never fail."[12] The fulfillment of this covenant by Jesus, the King of kings, whose kingship is everlasting and unimpeachable, shows how the promise of kingship in the Davidic covenant was indeed trustworthy and, we can now gratefully say, has been realized.

THE PROPHETS

Among the prophets, all of the major prophets (Isaiah, Jeremiah, Ezekiel), but only Hosea among the minor prophets, mention covenant institution, and as we consider these cases we also take into account the prophecy of Daniel 9.

Isaiah

In Isaiah, there are four cases of apparent covenant institution, and two special cases where the Lord speaks of "giving" his servant for a covenant of the people. The latter two cases merit particular attention.

Three cases of covenant institution in Isaiah use the idiom כרת ברית. The first concerns a "covenant with death" that the people are accused of making, so the scourge will not find them: "You boast, 'We have entered into a covenant with death'" (lit. "We have cut a covenant with death," Isa. 28:15). The most important covenant institution of which Isaiah speaks is the institution of the new covenant. The passage is deservedly famous and we reproduce it here:

---

12 Cf. *BDB*, 53.

> Come, all you who are thirsty,
> come to the waters;
> and you who have no money,
> come, buy and eat!
> Come, buy wine and milk
> without money and without cost.
> Why spend money on what is not bread,
> and your labor on what does not satisfy?
> Listen, listen to me, and eat what is good,
> and you will delight in the richest of fare.
> Give ear and come to me;
> listen, that you may live.
> I will make an everlasting covenant with you,
> my faithful love promised to David.
> See, I have made him a witness to the peoples,
> a ruler and commander of the peoples.
> Surely you will summon nations you know not,
> and nations you do not know will come running to you,
> because of the LORD your God,
> the Holy One of Israel,
> for he has endowed you with splendor. (Isa. 55:1–5)

The Lord promises to make at some indefinite future time "an everlasting covenant with (lit. "for") you (pl.)" (ואכרתה לכם ברית עולם, Isa. 55:3). This future covenant is qualified by the parallel phrase "my faithful love promised to David." The latter phrase is literally "the sure/trustworthy graces/mercies of David" (חסדי דוד הנאמנים). The term translated "grace" (חסד) is a standard covenant term, often coupled with "truth/troth/faithfulness" (אמת). The promise thus makes an allusion to the Lord's covenant with David and states in effect that the Lord's covenant cutting with David (in 2 Sam. 7:1–17)—and the "graces" it entailed—foreshadows, and will be fulfilled in, a future covenant which the Lord has yet to cut. The only subsequent divine-human covenant the Bible records is the new covenant, in which Christ does indeed fulfill the promises to David in a way no other ever could (cf. Acts 12:34). It is also significant that the Lord says: "I have made him a witness to the peoples" (v. 4). This statement reads literally: "I have *given him* [as a] a witness to the peoples [עד לאומים נתתיו]." This prophecy foreshadows the fact that Christ is "the faithful witness" (Rev. 1:5). The use of the idiom also anticipates the promises about the servant that the Lord makes in Isaiah 42 and 49, the two cases of נתן used in connection with the servant and the new covenant, which we consider below.[13]

The "everlasting covenant" just noted is also the "everlasting covenant" the Lord promises (later in Isaiah) to make (כרת) with his people in the future, sometime after their return to their ruined land: "In my faithfulness I will reward my people / and make an everlasting covenant with them" (Isa. 61:8). In that day, the Lord says, "you will be called priests of the LORD, / you will be named ministers of our God" (Isa. 61:6); or, as Peter later says, we have become "a royal priesthood" in the new covenant (1 Peter 2:9) in fulfillment of what they failed to be under the Mosaic covenant ("Now if you obey me fully and keep my covenant . . . you will be for me a kingdom of priests and a holy nation," Exod. 19:5–6). The Lord further promises, "Their descendants will be known among the nations / and their offspring among the peoples. / All who see them will acknowledge / that they are a people the LORD has blessed" (Isa. 61:9), a prophecy that begins to be fulfilled in the book of Acts (cf. Acts 2, esp. v. 47).

In addition to Isaiah's four uses of the covenant idiom כרת ברית, there is one statement of a future covenant that employs no verb (i.e., it occurs in a verbless clause, Isa. 59:21). We quote the verse and the verse that precedes it as well because it identifies the Savior associated with the promised covenant:

> "The Redeemer will come to Zion,
>> to those in Jacob who repent of their sins,"
>> declares the LORD.

> "As for me, this is my covenant with them," says the LORD. "My Spirit, who is on you, will not depart from you, and my words that I have put in your mouth will always be on your lips, on the lips of your children and on the lips of their descendants—from this time on and forever," says the LORD. (Isa. 59:20–21)

After a recognition that there is no truth or justice among the people (Isa. 59:1–15), the Lord resolves to supply the need for an intercessor and for salvation himself: "He saw that there was no one, / he was appalled that there was no one to intervene; / so his own arm achieved salvation

---

13   Cf. also the messianic incarnational prophecy of Isaiah 9:6: "For to us a child is born / to us a son is *given*" (emphasis added).

for him, / and his own righteousness sustained him" (Isa. 59:16). His own righteousness—that is, his conformity or faithfulness to his own nature—sustained him. That decision results in the promises quoted above. The first promise is that the Lord will provide a "Redeemer" (v. 20), and the term (גאל) means more exactly "kinsman-redeemer." It evokes the idea that this divine Redeemer will be of the same family as those he redeems, a note sounded earlier in Isaiah (e.g., Isa. 44:23), and it points clearly to Christ. Associated with the advent of this kinsman-redeemer is the promised covenant: "As for me, this is/will be my covenant with them" (זאת בריתי אותם, v. 21, author's translation). In that covenant, "my Spirit, who is on you, will not depart from you." The use of the preposition "on" (על) is consistent with what we have seen of the relation of the Spirit to people in the Old Testament: he comes "on" or "to" people and may temporarily be in them so they can accomplish some task, but he never dwells in them. Now, however, under the promised covenant, the Spirit who has been "on" them will not depart from God's people. Moreover, the words the Spirit produces will show that the Spirit, in that future covenant, will be an indwelling and constant presence in God's people—"my words that I have put in your mouth will always be on your lips, on the lips of your children and on the lips of their descendants—from this time on and forever" (v. 21). Under the Mosaic covenant, people could take the Lord's word into their mouths and meditate on them (e.g., Ps. 1:2). In the future covenant, the *Lord himself* will put his words in their mouths, and if those words never depart (v. 21), then the Spirit who produces them (cf. John 6:63) will never depart from dwelling in the people and producing those words.

We noted that there are two passages in which the Lord says he will make his servant to be a covenant for the people. These remarkable promises indicate that the promised servant will embody all that a covenantal relationship between God and his people could be. The first promise occurs in the context of verses applied in the New Testament to Christ (Isa. 42:1–4 // Matt. 12:18–21), and they sound themes we have noted before:

> This is what God the LORD says—
> the Creator of the heavens, who stretches them out,
>> who spreads out the earth with all that springs from it,
>> who gives breath to its people,
>> and life to those who walk on it:
> "I, the Lord, have called you in righteousness;
>> I will take hold of your hand.

> I will keep you and will make you
>> to be a covenant for the people
>> and a light for the Gentiles,
> to open eyes that are blind,
>> to free captives from prison
>> and to release from the dungeon those
>>> who sit in darkness." (Isa. 42:5–7)

We have already noted verse 5 in connection with our discussion of the role of the Spirit in sustaining human life under common grace. We note also that the Lord's promise of salvation follows his self-identification as Creator. The Bible sounds this theme a number of times. That is the true significance of Genesis 1:1, as John 1 makes clear: the God who created all things is also the Lord who can redeem all things. His power as Creator establishes beyond refutation his authority as Redeemer. The Lord calls this Redeemer "in righteousness" and that means he has called him in a way that faithfully represents his true nature, for he is both love and Redeemer. He then says: "I will make you to be a covenant for the people" (lit. "I will give you for a covenant of the people, וְאֶתֶּנְךָ לִבְרִית עָם"). The promise uses the verb נָתַן, used in idiom נָתַן בְּרִית, which we have thus far encountered in the institution of the Noahic covenant and then in statements of the Lord's continuing to give or sustain some covenant he has cut. Here, however, it is used of the Lord's giving the servant *to be* a covenant of the people. The point is not the act of covenant institution but rather the ontological definition by which the servant's being articulates the nature of the covenant. We know from Jeremiah 31 that this covenant will also be cut. There is one more promise of the servant to consider before we reflect on the reason for the use of this verb in both of these covenant promises.

The second promise using the verb נָתַן occurs in Isaiah 49, another of the Servant Songs. The Lord states his intention to extend his salvation through this servant: "I will also make you a light for the Gentiles, / that my salvation may reach to the ends of the earth" (Isa. 49:5). He then says,

> "In the time of my favor I will answer you,
>> and in the day of salvation I will help you;
> I will keep you and will make you
>> to be a covenant for the people,
> to restore the land
>> and to reassign its desolate inheritances,

to say to the captives, 'Come out,'
and to those in darkness, 'Be free!'" (Isa. 49:8–9)

The Lord promises, "I will give you for a covenant of the people" (Isa. 49:8), and the promise reiterates the phrasing of Isaiah 42:6 ("I will give you as a covenant of the people," ואתנך לברית עם). We noted above that the operative verb is used about the institution of the Noahic covenant, and we noted the reason for it in that case: the Lord was indicating that a covenant was in view, one that he would sustain as he still does today and will until the renewal of all things. The reason the same idiom is used now in regard to giving the *servant* as a covenant for the people is similar. God's gift of the servant is an *ongoing* gift. The gift is given every time someone comes to faith in Christ. Jeremiah 31 uses the idiom כרת ברית for the cutting of the new covenant, and that idiom is appropriate because the Son was indeed "cut" when he was crucified. The Son was also "given," however (e.g., John 3:16), and he continues to be given, for example, "Whoever has the Son has life" (1 John 5:12): God gives us his Son constantly in ongoing life—so Paul can say, "I no longer live, but Christ lives in me" (Gal. 2:10). He does not live for one instant, but goes on living, as Christ goes on living, and being given, in him. The Lord's prophecy through Isaiah adumbrates this dynamic truth of life under the new covenant: The Son who is life is God's *ongoing gift* of life *in those who believe*. He is the *once crucified* but risen and *constantly given* Christ in us, the hope of glory (Col. 1:27).

The usage here also reflects back on Isaiah 55. There we noted God's promise: "I have made him a witness to the peoples" (v. 4), and observed that this statement reads literally, "I have *given him* [as] a witness to the peoples" (עד לאומים נתתיו). The prophecy foreshadows the fact that Christ is "the faithful witness" (Rev. 1:5), and we can now understand God's giving of this servant as a faithful witness always. The Son continues to work salvation in the earth and as he does he faithfully represents the Father—who continues to give the Son as a witness to God's salvific and holy being and doing. In this sense too, the Son continues to "amen" what the Father is saying and doing. So he is the *faithful* witness. Finally, the same idea appears in the statement of Isaiah 49:6: "I will also make you a light for the Gentiles, / that my salvation may reach to the ends of the earth." The Hebrew reads literally, "I will also *give* you as a light for the Gentiles" (ונתתיך לאור גוים). We see this fulfilled by Christ in the new covenant: "the true light that gives light to everyone was coming into the world" (John 1:9). If he gives light, he continues to give light and he thus continues to be the *given* light who *gives* light to everyone. The Father continues to give this light—which is the (servant) Son—and will continue to give him to those who are being saved, until the end of all things.

Jeremiah

Jeremiah offers seven cases of the idiom כרת ברית. Three of them occur in the passage that promises the new covenant (Jer. 31:31–33). One of them occurs in another promise of a future divine-human covenant in Jeremiah 32, and the remaining three appear in Jeremiah 34, where the covenant Hezekiah made with the people to release the slaves according to the law is at issue; in that passage, the verb בא is also used of the covenant into which they entered to free those slaves. There is also one case of the idiomatic use of הקים with "oath" as synecdoche for covenant.

We consider the last mentioned case first, from Jeremiah 11:

> This is the word that came to Jeremiah from the LORD: "Listen to the terms of this covenant and tell them to the people of Judah and to those who live in Jerusalem. Tell them that this is what the LORD, the God of Israel, says: 'Cursed is the one who does not obey the terms of this covenant— the terms I commanded your ancestors when I brought them out of Egypt, out of the iron-smelting furnace.' I said, 'Obey me and do everything I command you, and you will be my people, and I will be your God. Then I will fulfill the oath I swore to your ancestors, to give them a land flowing with milk and honey'—the land you possess today." (Jer. 11:1–5)

The context makes it clear that the Mosaic covenant and obedience to it are the subject of the oracle, and the phrase, "I will fulfill the oath" (v. 5), is a combination of "oath," in synecdoche for covenant, and the verb הקים—"I will *fulfill* the oath I swore to your ancestors" (emphasis added).

We turn now to the cases using the idiom כרת ברית. After reviewing the sins of Judah and the coming Babylonian captivity, the Lord promises to return the people to their land, and he also promises a later divine-human covenant:

> "I will give them singleness of heart and action, so that they will always fear me and that all will then go well for them and for their children after them. I will make an everlasting covenant with them: I will never stop doing good to them, and I will inspire them to fear me, so that they will

never turn away from me. I will rejoice in doing them good and will as-
suredly plant them in this land with all my heart and soul." (Jer. 32:39–41)

It is significant that the Lord begins this promise by saying, "I will
give them singleness of heart and action, so that they will always fear
me" (v. 29), followed by the promise of the land (v. 41). This is similar
language to what we find in Ezekiel 36: "And I will put my Spirit in you
and move you to follow my decrees and be careful to keep my laws. Then
you will live in the land I gave your ancestors; you will be my people,
and I will be your God" (Ezek. 36:27–28). The reason for the similarity
is that the same scenario is projected in each case, and in Jeremiah 32 it
is clearly presented in the context of a future divine-human covenant.
Since we know that the only divine-human covenant subsequent to the
ministry of Jeremiah is the new covenant, that is the covenant in view.
The "everlasting covenant" (ברית עולם) the Lord promises to "make"
(כרת) for them (the future generation) in Jeremiah 32:40 is that new
covenant. One feature of that everlasting, or new, covenant is that it is
indeed everlasting: it will never pass away and is thus unlike its predecessors (which are also called עולם, often translated "everlasting" but
meaning really "temporally hidden/beyond perceiving/out of sight," i.e.,
"of very long duration"). Another feature is that, as the Lord says, "I will
never stop doing good to them" (lit. "I will not turn away from [after]
them," v. 40b); the Lord also promises, "I will inspire them to fear me
(lit. "I will be giving my fear into their hearts"), so that they will never
turn away from me" (v. 40c). Here again we have the verb נתן used with
the sense of ongoing giving, which will be a feature of the new covenant:
the Lord will continually give a proper fear of himself into his people's
hearts, with the result that they will not turn away from him as they did
under the Mosaic covenant. In the words of Ezekiel 36:27, "I will put [lit.
"I will give," אתן] my Spirit in you and move you to follow my decrees
and be careful to keep my laws." Less clearly in Jeremiah, more clearly
in Ezekiel, we have here the promise of the indwelling Holy Spirit, a new
feature in the new covenant that creates a wholly different dynamic from
that of life under the Mosaic covenant.[14]

The last case of covenant institution idioms in Jeremiah occurs in
Jeremiah 34, and the idioms used have to do with the covenant Hezekiah
and the people cut with the Lord, to free the Hebrew slaves according to
the requirement of the Mosaic covenant:

---

14 Cf. further chapter 5 of volume 3.

The word came to Jeremiah from the Lord after King Zedekiah had made a covenant with all the people in Jerusalem to proclaim freedom for the slaves. Everyone was to free their Hebrew slaves, both male and female; no one was to hold a fellow Hebrew in bondage. So all the officials and people who entered into this covenant agreed that they would free their male and female slaves and no longer hold them in bondage. They agreed, and set them free. But afterward they changed their minds and took back the slaves they had freed and enslaved them again. (Jer. 34:8–11)

The idiom used for Hezekiah's covenant institution is כרת ברית: "he cut the covenant" (v. 8, author's translation). For their part, the officials and the people "entered into" the covenant (בא, v. 10). The two subsequent mentions of covenant establishment in this passage use the usual idiom כרת ברית. The Lord thereby reminds them (ironically), "I made a covenant with your ancestors when I brought them out of Egypt, out of the land of slavery" (v. 13). He next refers to the covenant they made with him, to free their slaves, and then broke: "you even made a covenant before me in the house that bears my Name" (v. 15). It is important to note that here once again we have a case, not of covenant renewal, but of a covenant made under human initiative to obey some portion of the Mosaic covenant—much like the covenant cut by Josiah to obey the words of Deuteronomy, as noted in 2 Chronicles 34.

Finally, we note that the Lord's judgment on them for this covenant breaking draws on the symbolism of covenant cutting. The covenant cutting ceremony mentioned here in Jeremiah 34 is the one we saw before in Genesis 15, and the Lord's judgment pronouncement explains its symbolism:

> "Those who have violated my covenant and have not fulfilled the terms of the covenant they made before me, I will treat like the calf they cut in two and then walked between its pieces. The leaders of Judah and Jerusalem, the court officials, the priests and all the people of the land who walked between the pieces of the calf, I will deliver into the hands of their enemies who want to kill them. Their dead bodies will become food for the birds and the wild animals." (Jer. 34:18–20)

"My covenant" here indicates the Mosaic covenant, which they ought to have obeyed all along. "The covenant they made before me" indicates the covenant Hezekiah and the others cut on their own initiative, to release the slaves according to the law. The Lord will judge them for breaking both covenants.

Ezekiel

Ezekiel offers three statements of covenant initiation using the verb כרת, two statements of ongoing covenant support using the verb קום, and two cases using the verb בא. We will examine these cases, not in the sequence of their occurrence in Ezekiel but rather in their historical sequence.

The earliest covenant referred to is (apparently) the Mosaic covenant, and the Lord refers to it by using the metaphor of marriage in Ezekiel 16. First, the Lord gives a history of Jerusalem (the object of the covenant lawsuit in the pericope) and it is expressed as the personal history of a female. Jerusalem was born of an Amorite father and a Hittite mother (v. 3); her cord was not cut and she was not washed (v. 4); she was thrown out into the open field, "for on the day you were born you were despised" (v. 5). The Lord passed by, saw her kicking in her blood, and commanded her to live (v. 6); he made her grow like a plant of the field, and she entered puberty: "your breasts had formed and your hair had grown, yet you were stark naked" (v. 7, author's translation). Then we read: "Later I passed by, and when I looked at you and saw that you were old enough for love, I spread the corner of my garment over you and covered your naked body. I gave you my solemn oath and entered into a covenant with you [ואבוא בברית אתך], declares the Sovereign LORD, and you became mine" (v. 8). The Lord's sense of timing is worth note in this metaphor. First, he underwrote her life ("commanded her to live") and then her development ("made her grow"); he entered into a covenant relationship with Israel only when, in the passage of time, she had developed to a point at which she could realistically be part of such a relationship (when she was "old enough for love"). There is a mystery here one cannot fathom because one cannot know enough. But the Lord, who knows the heart, knows the inner condition of people, and thus knows when they may be reached by his offer of love. He causes them to live and to grow until they are ready for such a relationship. The same principle obviously applies to the Lord's timing of the incarnation and the new covenant (and the marriage of Christ and the church) to which it would lead.

The next covenant institution mentioned is the Babylonian king's treaty with the royal seed of Jerusalem in Ezekiel 17 and it employs the idiom כרת ברית: "Then he took a member of the royal family and made a treaty with him, putting him under oath" (v. 13). The latter phrase,

"putting him under oath" (lit. "and he brought him into an oath," ויבא
אתו באלה), is reminiscent of Mesopotamian emperors' claims that they
made defeated foes "swear the oath of the great gods," that is, enter into
a suzerain-vassal treaty, and that is the sort of treaty indicated here, with
the oath-entering employed in the narrative as a synecdoche for covenant
making, and used parallelistically with "made a treaty (lit. "cut a treaty/
covenant") with him."

The next exemplar to consider also uses the verb בא but in a different
phrase. To facilitate our understanding of this exemplar we quote some
of the context (the Lord is speaking through the prophet):

> You say, "We want to be like the nations, like the peoples of the world, who
> serve wood and stone." But what you have in mind will never happen. "As
> surely as I live," declares the Sovereign LORD, "I will reign over you with
> a mighty hand and an outstretched arm and with outpoured wrath. I will
> bring you from the nations and gather you from the countries where you
> have been scattered—with a mighty hand and an outstretched arm and
> with outpoured wrath. I will bring you into the wilderness of the nations
> and there, face to face, I will execute judgment upon you. As I judged
> your ancestors in the wilderness of the land of Egypt, so I will judge you,
> declares the Sovereign LORD. I will take note of you as you pass under my
> rod, and I will bring you into the bond of the covenant. I will purge you
> of those who revolt and rebel against me. Although I will bring them out
> of the land where they are living, yet they will not enter the land of Israel.
> Then you will know that I am the LORD." (Ezek. 20:32–38)

The predicted scenario is parallel to the wilderness wanderings that
followed the Exodus, and as the Lord judged his people then he will judge
them in this future wilderness after their exodus from the nations of their
exile. The phrase in question is found in the Lord's declaration, "I will
bring you into the bond of the covenant" (והבאתי אתכם במסרת הברית,
v. 37). The first thing to note is that this is a similar sort of statement to
the one we just saw in Ezekiel 17:13, "and he brought him into an oath"
(ויבא אתו באלה). There "oath" was used as synecdoche for (and in parallel
with) "covenant," because the oath was part of the covenant institution
and indeed "oath" is sometimes used in this way by itself (as *pars pro
toto*).[15] The word "bond" is far less common, but we find a similar and at
least implicit synecdoche in Psalm 2:

---

15   On covenant and oath, cf. Gordon P. Hugenberger, *Marriage as a Covenant:*

> Why do the nations conspire
>   and the peoples plot in vain?
> The kings of the earth rise up
>   and the rulers band together
>   against the LORD and against his anointed, saying,
> "Let us break their chains
>   and throw off their shackles." (Ps. 2:1–3)

The word translated "chains" (NIV) we render "bonds" (מוֹסְרוֹתֵימוֹ, cf. מֹסֶרֶת, Ezek. 20:37). Psalm 2 portrays a rebellion of vassals against the Lord and his anointed king (in this case probably Solomon but with a forward looking messianic nuance). The kings and rulers band together to throw off the "bonds" of their suzerain-vassal relationship with the Lord's anointed king. In other words, we have here a case of the concept bonds being used as a synecdoche for treaty/covenant. But the use of the term as a synecdoche for covenant is unusual (the rarity of the occurrence would seem to indicate it was not a *terminus technicus* for a part of a treaty/covenant—although, as has been aptly said, absence of evidence is not evidence of absence), and the context in Psalm 2 suggests that the word is used because of the irksomeness of the suzerain-vassal relationship and the requirements it makes of the vassal kings and rulers (note the parallel "their cords/shackles," עֲבוֹתֵימוֹ). When, therefore, the Lord says "I will bring you into the bond of the covenant" (Ezek. 20:37), he is not using a term typically used of some formal component of a covenant, but rather a term apparently meant to evoke the unpleasant effect (to the vassal) of some aspect of the covenant relationship—presumably the requirements it places on the vassal. This line of reasoning leads us to agree in large part with Keil and Delitzsch, who wrote of the Lord's promised contending with Israel:

> This contending is more precisely defined in Ezekiel 20:37 and Ezekiel 20:38. I will cause you to pass through under the (shepherd's) rod. A shepherd lets his sheep pass through under his rod for the purpose of counting them, and seeing whether they are in good condition or not (vid., Jer. 33:13). The figure is here applied to God. Like a shepherd, He will cause His flock, the Israelites, to pass through under His rod, i.e., take them into His special care, and bring them "into the bond of the covenant"

A Study of Biblical Law and Ethics Governing Marriage Developed from the Perspective of Malachi (Leiden: Brill, 1994), 168–215.

(מסרת, not from מסר, Raschi, but from אסר, for מאסרה, a fetter); that is to say, not "I will bind myself to you and you to me by a new covenant" (Bochart, Hieroz. I., 508), for this is opposed to the context, but, as the Syriac version has rendered it, *b-mardûtâ* (in disciplina), "the discipline of the covenant."[16]

I think Keil and Delitzsch have the right idea when they identify the bonds as some sort of discipline the Lord will exercise to purify his people from their idolatry. I also agree that no new covenant is in view because everything in the passage points to some employment of "the covenant"—that is, of the already existing covenant that had to do with the wilderness experience and its judgments under Moses. However, Keil and Delitzsch saw the bond of the covenant, not as the structured environment of the stipulations that bind or constrain the vassal, but rather as a combination of the covenant punishments and the covenant promises.[17] Given the somewhat figurative nature of the prediction, one cannot insist on one value or the other. It does seem, though, that the emphasis in the pericope is on a stern discipline ("There, face to face, I will execute judgment upon you," v. 35) which is, to be sure, an aspect of love (cf. Prov. 3:12), but not one whose face seems loving at the time.

The final two instances of the idiom in Ezekiel have to do with a "covenant of peace" the Lord will cut with his people at some unspecified future date. The first promise occurs in the context of the promised "David" who will rule over the people:

> I will save my flock, and they will no longer be plundered. I will judge between one sheep and another. I will place over them one shepherd, my servant David, and he will tend them; he will tend them and be their shepherd. I the LORD will be their God, and my servant David will be prince among them. I the LORD have spoken. I will make a covenant of peace with them and rid the land of savage beasts so that they may live in the wilderness and sleep in the forests in safety. I will make them and the

---

16   Keil and Delitzsch, *Commentary on the Old Testament: Ezekiel, Daniel*, vol. 9, 281–82, who reference Samuel Bochart, *Hierozoïcon* (London: Martyn and Allestry, 1663).

17   Ibid., 282: "By this we are not merely to understand the covenant punishments, with which transgressors of the law are threatened, as Hvernick does, but the covenant promises must also be included. For not only the threats of the covenant, but the promises of the covenant, are bonds by which God trains His people; and אסר is not only applied to burdensome and crushing fetters, but to the bonds of love as well (vid., Sol 7:6)."

places surrounding my hill a blessing. I will send down showers in season; there will be showers of blessing. The trees will yield their fruit and the ground will yield its crops; the people will be secure in their land. They will know that I am the LORD, when I break the bars of their yoke and rescue them from the hands of those who enslaved them. (Ezek. 34:22–27)

Although we quote material surrounding the relevant verse (v. 25) for context, we reserve detailed comment on the context for later. For now, we note that the idiom כרת ברית is used, and from all prior usage this indicates that the creation of a new covenant is in view. The same is the true in the second mention of this covenant of peace three chapters later in Ezekiel:

My servant David will be king over them, and they will all have one shep-herd. They will follow my laws and be careful to keep my decrees. They will live in the land I gave to my servant Jacob, the land where your an-cestors lived. They and their children and their children's children will live there forever, and David my servant will be their prince forever. I will make a covenant of peace with them; it will be an everlasting covenant. I will establish them and increase their numbers, and I will put my sanc-tuary among them forever. My dwelling place will be with them; I will be their God, and they will be my people. Then the nations will know that I the LORD make Israel holy, when my sanctuary is among them forever. (Ezek. 37:24–28)

In Ezekiel 34, David was mentioned as shepherd and prince (vv. 23–24). Now he is mentioned as king and shepherd (37:24). His unending rule over his people, expressed partly in terms of the royal shepherd typology of the Bible and the ancient Near East, is announced in the context of the covenant of peace the Lord will cut with his people (34:25; 37:26).[18]

Before we leave these passages some comment is in order about the "David" they promise. Theologians usually understand this to be a Chris-tological statement: the Lord is not promising to resurrect David and have him rule over a future people under a new covenant; rather, one like David, whom David foreshadows and of whom David is a type, will be that future shepherd, prince and king, and so he is, namely, Jesus. This

---

18   The combination of land promise and the Lord's everlasting dwelling with his people would be consistent with the land being the Promised Land in the new earth, in other words, from Revelation 21 onward.

understanding is good and serviceable as far as it goes. But the Lord's reference to David has more to tell us. We recall that the name, David, comes from the root דוד, "to love." If we also note that the vowel pattern in the name David is a passive one, we understand the name means "the beloved." This, I would submit, is exactly what the Father pronounces over the Son when the latter comes up out of the baptismal waters: "You are My beloved Son, in whom I am well pleased" (Mark 1:11 NKJV, lit. "You are My son, the beloved," σὺ εἶ ὁ υἱός μου ὁ ἀγαπητός). In other words, if one thinks Hebraically, the Father is saying, "You are my Son, the David." The same nuance is implied in any of the passages that refer to Jesus as the beloved (e.g., Matt. 17:5 // Mark 9:7 // Luke 9:35, and of course the passages synoptic with Mark 1:11; the same nuance seems to me implicit in the parable of the vineyard, Mark 12:6, Luke. 20:13). The somewhat hidden import, then, of the David promises of Ezekiel 34 and 37 is this: the Beloved will indeed come and be the shepherd, prince, and king of his people, and to some extent then at least the prophecy will be fulfilled that "they will know that I am the LORD" (Ezek. 34:27; cf. 37:27–28). Finally, the Lord's sanctuary will be "among them forever" (Ezek. 37:28) because he will make *them* his sanctuary, dwelling within them as per the promise of Ezekiel 36:27. And again, this promise has its eschatological nuance (Rev. 21:22).

The final covenant exemplars we consider in Ezekiel use the idiom "to carry out/sustain covenant" (הקים ברית). Although they occur early in his book, we believe they refer to the later covenant of peace the Lord promises to cut with a future people:

> This is what the Sovereign LORD says: "I will deal with you as you de-
> serve, because you have despised my oath by breaking the covenant. Yet
> I will remember the covenant I made with you in the days of your youth,
> and I will establish an everlasting covenant with you. Then you will re-
> member your ways and be ashamed when you receive your sisters, both
> those who are older than you and those who are younger. I will give them
> to you as daughters, but not on the basis of my covenant with you. So I will
> establish my covenant with you, and you will know that I am the LORD.
> Then, when I make atonement for you for all you have done, you will
> remember and be ashamed and never again open your mouth because of
> your humiliation, declares the Sovereign LORD." (Ezek. 16:59–63)

Perhaps the first matter to address is the identity of the older and younger sisters. Commentators have long taken these to be the other nations, and we concur with this view.[19] The second and more important matter to consider is the nature of the covenant the Lord is promising here. We cannot agree with the view that Lord means a renewal of the Mosaic covenant when he says, "I will establish an everlasting covenant with you" (v. 60b).[20] He does precede that statement with a recollection of the Mosaic covenant: "yet I will remember the covenant I made with you in the days of your youth" (v. 60a), and Keil and Delitzsch are right in pointing out that he will return his people from exile because of his own faithfulness to that covenant (e.g., Lev. 26:45).[21] However, the promised covenant is one in which atonement will be made for their their sins, but astoundingly not by animal sacrifice as under the Mosaic covenant but by the Lord himself: "When *I make atonement* for you for all you have done" (v. 63, emphasis added). Now, the Lord makes that atonement when he enacts the new covenant: "God presented Christ as a sacrifice of atonement, through the shedding of his blood—to be received by faith" (Rom. 3:25; cf. Heb. 2:17). Although people pray in the Old Testament

---

19 Cf. Keil and Delitzsch, *Ezekiel, Daniel*, 231, who state the view well: "This shame will seize upon Israel when the establishment of an everlasting covenant is followed by the greater and smaller nations being associated with it in glory, and incorporated into it as children, though they are not of its covenant. The greater and smaller sisters are the greater and smaller nations, as members of the universal family of man, who are to be exalted to the glory of one large family of God." Cf. likewise A. B. Davidson, *The Book of Ezekiel* (Cambridge: Cambridge University Press, 1896), 117n61. The Israelite covenant the nations are not part of is, of course, the Mosaic covenant, which has characterized Israel up until the new covenant.

20 Keil and Delitzsch *Ezekiel, Daniel*, 230–31, take this view: "The covenant which God concluded with Israel in the day of its youth, i.e., when He led it out of Egypt, He will establish as an everlasting covenant. Consequently it is not an entirely new covenant, but simply the perfecting of the old one for everlasting duration." This view is untenable, however. Hebrews makes it clear that the new covenant is not a perfecting of the Mosaic covenant, which was passing away (Heb. 7:18; 8:6–13; cf. Col. 2:14). Cf. further discussion chapter 2 of volume 3.

21 Cf, Keil and Delitzsch, "The remembrance of His covenant is mentioned in Leviticus 26:42 and Leviticus 26:45 as the only motive that will induce God to restore Israel to favour again, when the humiliation effected by the endurance of punishment has brought it to a confession of its sins." However, the commentators conflate here the Abrahamic covenant (mentioned in Lev. 26:42) and the Mosaic (mentioned in Lev. 26:45). The Lord will remember *both* and, being faithful to both, will restore his people to the land, which was promised in the Abrahamic (cf. Lev. 26:42) and fulfilled under the guidelines of the Mosaic (cf. Lev. 26:46). Both the Abrahamic covenant and the Mosaic covenant were in force when Ezekiel prophesied.

that the Lord will make atonement for/forgive his people (Deut. 21:8; 2 Chron. 30:18; Ps. 79:9), and even express confidence that he will do so (Deut. 32:43; Pss. 65:3 [65:4 MT]; 78:38), nowhere else do we find the Lord stating that he will atone for the sins of his people, as here.[22] Moreover, it is not on the basis of the Mosaic covenant ("not on the basis of my covenant with you," Ezek. 16:61), but because of the new covenant that the Lord will put into effect ("So I will establish my covenant with you," Ezek. 16:62) that he will do this.[23]

---

22   Negatively, cf. Jeremiah's prayer regarding his opposers: "But you, LORD, know / all their plots to kill me. / Do not forgive [כפר] their crimes / or blot out their sins from your sight. / Let them be overthrown before you; / deal with them in the time of your anger" (Jer. 18:23).

23   Cf. Davidson, *Book of Ezekiel*, 117n61, "The glory of receiving Samaria and Sodom and her other sisters and nationalities for daughters shall not accrue to Jerusalem as the result of her former covenant with Jehovah, for that covenant of his she broke. It shall be like the new covenant itself, something altogether additional, an act of God's goodness in no way depending on former relations (v. 62)." So also Walter Eichrodt, *Ezekiel*, trans. Cosslett Quin (Philadelphia: Westminster Press, 1975), 220: "We catch a glimpse of the New Testament fulfillment by which the covenant is to be brought into effect; it witnesses to a power of divine love, as yet hardly discernible." Some, however, have taken a different view of this covenant; cf. Georg Fohrer, *Ezechiel* (Tübingen: Verlag J. C. B. Mohr [Paul Siebeck] 1955), 92–94, citing A. Bertholet: "Doch Jahwes Barmherzigkeit ist größer als seine Gerechtigkeit. Daher wird er sich an den alten Bund erinnern und einen ewigen Bund aufrichten, wie der Verfasser in der Sprache von P sagt. . . . Doch zeigt sich an dieser Stelle, daß das Word trotz der Verheißung von demselben Geist wie 6 8–10 16 44–58 getragen ist. Es ist bezeichnend, 'daß diese Verheißung, weit entfernt von der evangelischen Auffassung von der herrlichen Freiheit der Kinder Gottes, die "ein lustig fröhlich Herz" haben" (Luther), letzten Endes nur Beschämung wirkt (63)' (A. Bertholet)"; author's translation: "But Yahweh's mercy is greater than his justice. Therefore he will remember the old covenant and raise up a new covenant, as the author in the language of P says . . . but it appears at this point, that in spite of the promise, the word is carried in the same spirit as 6 8–10 16 44–58. It is significant, 'that this promise, far removed from the evangelical conception of the glorious freedom of the children of God, who "have a happy, joyful heart" (Luther), works only shame in the end (63).'" But this mistakenly understands the shame Israel will feel at their past sins as the whole effect of the promised covenant. Who among us does not feel shame for past sins when we recall them, while at the same time living in a grateful and unprecedented (for us) freedom from them? As Paul says, "When you were slaves to sin, you were free from the control of righteousness. What benefit did you reap at that time from the things you are now ashamed of?" (Rom. 6:20–21). Cf. Eichrodt, *Ezekiel*, 217–18, "The writer here saw how to unmask the self-righteous pride which he knew for the besetting sin of his own people. Did he then

We now consider the idiom הָקִים בְּרִית, used twice in this pericope. These occurrences can be understood in the same way we have understood them up to this point: they do not indicate the cutting or making of a covenant but rather the putting into effect or sustaining of a covenant that has already been cut. We submit that Ezekiel 34:25 and 37:26 (and Isa. 51:3; 61:8; and Jer. 31:31–34) tell us of the *cutting* of this everlasting, new covenant, which does indeed accomplish the atonement mentioned in Ezekiel 16 and Hebrews 1. Once that atonement has been accomplished, however, the Lord will "put into effect," that is, render effective in the life of his people the newly cut covenant (Ezek. 16:60, 62). The alternate translation of verse 63 helps bring clarity to this proposal: the Lord will put the covenant into effect (vv. 60, 62) "when/once I *have made* atonement for all you have done" (v. 63, author's translation and emphasis; cf. NASB, OJB, WYC). Only after the Lord has put that covenant into effect (v. 60), and in particular after Pentecost, will Israel begin to receive the other nations (the "sisters" mentioned in v. 61). Finally, the Lord has said of those nations: "I will give them to you as daughters, but not on the basis of my covenant with you" (v. 61). That is, he will not bring the

---

substitute the ceaseless torture of backward-looking remorse for the joy and freedom of forgiveness? Such an assertion can be made only by one who has ceased to experience that alternation between deep shamefulness and joyful trust which makes up even the Christian life." Cf. also Helmut Lamparter, *Zum Wächter Bestellt: der Prophet Hesekiel* (Stuttgart: Calwer Verlag, 1968), 120: "Der tiefe Gedanke, daß gerade die Erfahrung der Vergebung Gottes in die Tiefe der Erkenntnis der Sünde führt, ist in v. 63 zum Ausdruck gebracht (vgl. Ps. 130, 4)"; author's translation: "The profound thought, that the very experience of God's forgiveness leads to the depths of recognition of sin, is brought to expression in v. 63 (cf. Ps. 130, 4)." The silencing prophesied by Ezekiel in verse 62 may show, as Eichrodt suggests, "the way in which such incomprehensible mercy strikes us dumb and leaves us without a word to say" (*Ezekiel*, 217). It may also suggest a cessation of the sort of behavior (mostly characterized as a prostitute's solicitation, so "you will . . . never again open your mouth," v. 62) in which sinful Israel used to indulge (cf. vv. 15–34). Cf, further, Alfred Bertholet, *Das Buch Hesekiel* (Freiburg: J. C. B. Mohr [Paul Siebeck], 1897), 90. Bertholet also sees the covenant promised here as only a further development of the old covenant—"nur als die weitere Fortentwicklung des alten Bundes," 89; author's translation: "only as the further, continued development of the old covenant." Among more recent commentators, cf. Douglas Stuart, *Ezekiel* (Dallas: Word, 1986), 143–44, who views the covenant promise here as fulfilled in the new covenant; Daniel I. Block, *The Book of Ezekiel, Chapters 1–24* (Grand Rapids: Eerdmans, 1997), 516–20, who views it as the same new covenant we find in in Jeremiah 31:31–34, but thinks both prophecies refer to a renewal of the Sinai covenant.

nations into the new covenant on the basis of the Mosaic covenant—"my covenant with you"—which was a covenant made with ethnic Israel and which established them as a nation-state. Rather, the Lord will make that covenant of peace (Ezek. 34:25; 37:26) and put it dynamically into effect, and that covenant will be not only for Israel but for all people.

Daniel

We treat Daniel under the heading of the Prophets even though the Hebrew Bible groups his book under the Writings. There is only one covenant making episode in Daniel and it has to do with the treaty/covenant made by the one usually understood to be the Antichrist: "he will confirm a covenant with many for one 'seven'" (Dan. 9:27). The idiom used here is not used anywhere else in the Old Testament: הגביר ברית (translated "to confirm covenant," but lit. "to make strong [a] covenant" or "to make [a] covenant prevail").[24] Further discussion of this passage will appear when we take up eschatology proper.[25]

Hosea

Hosea offers three statements of covenant institution and all three use the idiom כרת ברית. The first has to do with a future covenant the Lord will cut with his people and with the created order; the second has to do with false covenants made by Israel; and the last has to do with Ephraim's covenant with Assyria.

We take the last case first. In it the Lord is calling Israel to account for their perfidy and violence, and promises a covenant lawsuit and judgment against them (11:12–12:1 [12:1– 2 MT]). He rebukes them for indulging in legal and commercial relations with foreign nations: "Ephraim feeds on the wind; / he pursues the east wind all day / and multiplies lies and violence. / He makes a treaty with Assyria/and sends olive oil

---

24 *BDB*, 149, sees the idiom as implied in Psalm 12:5 (English 12:4): "May the LORD silence all flattering lips / and every boastful tongue—those who say, / 'By our tongues we will prevail [נגביר ללשננו]; / our own lips will defend us—who is lord over us?'" The apparent inference is, "We will make [נגביר] *a covenant* with/for our tongues," but this seems an interpolation based solely on the usage in Daniel 9:27 and with no other supporting evidence. I have found no other translation that adopts *BDB*'s reading.

25 Cf. especially chapter 8 of volume 3.

to Egypt" (12:1 [12:2 MT]). The standard idiom for initiating a treaty/covenant is used (כרת ברית).

Earlier in the book, and in the context of an oracle of coming judgment, the Lord characterizes Israel as follows:

> They make many promises,
>> take false oaths
>> and make agreements;
> therefore lawsuits spring up
>> like poisonous weeds in a plowed field. (Hosea 10:4)

The heart of the verse reads literally "to swear falsely, to cut a covenant" (אלות שוא כרת ברית), i.e., deceptive oath taking and the making of false agreements are rampant [with the infinitives used apparently for emphasis, for which usage in covenant lawsuit, cf. Jer. 7:9]). The reference here may be to international treaties, or to covenants initiated by Israel and made with God, or to contracts agreed upon, and then reneged upon, by Israelites among themselves.[26] If the result of their false agreements is lawsuits (משפט, Hosea 10:4b), it seems likely that contracts are the issue.[27]

Finally, the first use of כרת ברית in Hosea has to do with a future covenant the Lord will make for his people with the created order. The passage is worth quoting at length:

---

26 Commentators have differed on their interpretation of this verse. For instance, Keil and Delitzsch argue, *Commentary on the Old Testament, Minor Prophets*, vol. 10, 129: "כרת ברית, in connection with false swearing, must signify the making of a covenant without any truthfulness in it, i.e., the conclusion of treaties with foreign nations—for example, with Assyria—which they were inclined to observe only so long as they could promise themselves advantages from them." Calvin thought the covenant making had to do with a covenant they had made with God: "Here again the Prophet no doubt reproves them for renewing their covenant with God perfidiously; for it was a mere dissimulation" (cf. http://www.sacred-texts.com/chr/calvin/cc26/cc26016.htm). We have no Old Testament evidence of a contract made between human parties and then reneged upon, but we do have, apparently, the use of *brt* ("covenant contract") as a Canaanite loan word in an Egyptian inscription recording a contract between a boss and his labor force from the fourteenth century BC; cf. Kenneth A. Kitchen, "Egypt, Ugarit, Qatna, and Covenant," *UF* 11 (1980), 453–64.

27 This is not clearly supporting evidence for the "contract" interpretation, however. Translations differ: "judgment springs up like hemlock" (NKJV); "judgment sprouts like poisonous weeds" (NASB); "lawsuits break out like poisonous weeds" (HCSB).

"In that day," declares the LORD,
  "you will call me 'my husband';
  you will no longer call me 'my master.'
I will remove the names of the Baals from her lips;
  no longer will their names be invoked.
In that day I will make a covenant for them
  with the beasts of the field, the birds in the sky
  and the creatures that move along the ground.
Bow and sword and battle
  I will abolish from the land,
  so that all may lie down in safety.
I will betroth you to me forever;
  I will betroth you in righteousness and justice,
  in love and compassion.
I will betroth you in faithfulness,
  and you will acknowledge the LORD." (2:16–20)

A few salient points are worth noting in this passage. First, the Lord says they will in that future day call him not "my master" (בעלי, lit. "my baal/my lord," with a probable allusion to their present Baalism). Rather, they will call him "my husband" (אישי, lit. "my man"), indicating that future covenant (v. 18, and cf. Christ as the husband of the church). Second, the marriage language just noted anticipates the promise the Lord makes three verses later, that he will "betroth" his people, with the result that they will "know" him—not, as NIV renders, "acknowledge," since a more intimate relationship is prefigured here (vv. 19–20). We remember that betrothal leads to marriage, which is a covenant, and the covenant the Lord promises to make for them with the created order (v. 18) appears in the context of the more intimate relationship that God has foretold between himself and his people. The juxtaposition of these two things is, it seems to me, not far removed from their combination under the new covenant, as Paul says: "The creation itself also will be delivered from the bondage of corruption into the glorious liberty of the children of God. For we know that the whole creation groans and labors with birth pangs together until now" (Rom. 8:21–22). Finally, betrothal (ארש) involved paying a price for the bride, and we know the Lord paid that price on the cross.[28]

---

28 Cf. *BDB*, 76–77.

CONCLUSION

At the outset of this chapter we undertook a survey of the idioms relating to covenant creation or covenant confirmation in the Old Testament. This survey has produced results that we believe are clarifying for translation and understanding. The survey has shown that the verb כרת ("to cut") is only used of covenants once the special grace program is underway (i.e., at the institution of the Abrahamic covenant in Genesis 15 and then subsequently), and *only when a covenant is created*; moreover, this category of covenant creation can include the creation of renewal covenants. By contrast, the verbs נתן ("to give," "to go on giving") and הקים ("to carry out," "to sustain") are used when the confirmation or carrying forth (but not the renewal) of *an already existing covenant* is in view, and the same is true even if the existence of the covenant is envisioned as future. A few other verbs are also used infrequently in connection with covenant institution, for example, שׂים ("to place, set"), עבר ב ("to cross over into"), לקח ב ("to take into"), and בא ("to enter into" [Qal], "to bring into" [Hiph.]). The *hapax* הגביר (lit. "to make strong," "cause to prevail") is an expression probably used not of covenant institution but of rendering an existing covenant powerful and effective (cf. vol. 3, chap. 8).

I submit now a motto I had almost placed at the beginning of this chapter: where interpretation is possible, disagreement is inevitable. Not everyone will, perhaps, agree with the results of this survey. Nonetheless, the survey has applied in a consistent way certain translation values (in particular for נתן ברית and הקים ברית), which seem to have considerable explanatory power in the pericopes in which they are used. If this approach has been correct, passages such as Ezekiel 16 in particular communicate to us much more clearly, and also somewhat differently, than they do in current translations. The relation between the "everlasting covenant" that the Lord will render effective in Ezekiel 16 and the "covenant of peace" that he promises to "cut" in Ezekiel 34 and 37 in particular becomes clear. If the Occam's razor principle can be a standard for us, this way of understanding the covenant idioms does seem to produce the simplest picture and seems to be consistent with good sense and clarity. If it offers the simplest explanation of the biblical data (as I believe it does), it is by that standard likely to be correct. Our considerations regarding Ezekiel 16, 34, and 37 are also consistent with what what we have affirmed on other grounds elsewhere: the new covenant is not a renewal of the Mosaic covenant.

The data surveyed are also (and somewhat incidentally) consistent with another important distinction: the difference between divinely initiated covenants and humanly initiated covenants—or, to put it another way, between divine-human covenants and human-divine covenants.[29] What have often and seemingly somewhat casually been called covenant renewals—those initiated by people with God—are better understood as human expressions of renewed commitment to an existing covenant. The covenant at issue is always the Mosaic covenant. The several human attempts to recommit to that covenant or to some part of it (e.g., by Joshua in Joshua 24 and subsequently by Jehoiada in 2 Kings 11, by Ezra in Ezra 10, and one might add such efforts as the covenant made by Zedekiah in Jeremiah 34 and the covenant made by Asa in 2 Chronicles 15) were not renewals of the Mosaic covenant, which in each case was still legally in place and in force. At best they illustrate what Paul says about human nature under the law in Romans 7. Those who make these covenants agree that the law is holy and good and although they have wandered from it, they still desire to be obedient to it. That zeal leads them to recommit to it, and when the zeal is sufficient among the people or, one might say, when it attains critical mass, they actually undertake a covenant making ceremony—presumably thinking that such a large symbolic step will somehow cement the effectiveness of their resolution. What Jeremiah 34 reports, however, shows us the other half of Paul's argument in Romans 7: though they agree that God's law is holy and good—and though they may recommit to it (or some part of it) by a covenant of their own making on their own initiative—they end up doing what they did not want to do and break the law again. The failed covenant of Jeremiah 34 is actually a good illustration of this principle: no one can be justified by works of the law because the law, by revealing God's standard yet not imparting the power (the Holy Spirit) to obey it, only provokes sin and effectively puts a weapon into the enemy's hands—"the certificate of debt consisting of decrees against us, which was hostile to us" (Col. 2:14); "for," as Paul

---

29 The following observations are a refinement, and to some extent a corrective, to comments I made a few years ago in the article "An Argument against Theologically Constructed Covenants." In that article, I followed the general usage that considers humanly initiated covenants of the sort discussed below to be *covenant renewals*. The distinction I now make between the Mosaic covenant on the one hand, and human attempts to reaffirm commitment to that covenant on the other, makes it clear that humans could not renew a divinely given covenant that in any case was still in force when they aimed to recommit themselves to it. Such covenants as, for example, even the one reported in Joshua 24 are not covenant renewals, but only human reaffirmations of commitment to an existing covenant. Only God can renew a covenant he has made.

says, "sin, seizing the opportunity afforded by the commandment, deceived me, and through the commandment put me to death" (Rom. 7:11).

We turn now to the Mosaic covenant—the law—and consider it in terms of the historiographical aspects of its literary deposit, the warfare that prefaced the covenant, its place in the Major Paradigm, the conquest it mandated, and then some aspects of life under it—in particular the experience of the prophets. The last topic is relevant because, in a broad sense, all God's people under the new covenant are prophetic by the work of the Spirit through them, even if they are not all gifted as prophets. In that regard, prophetic life under the old covenant may teach, or at least foreshadow, things about life under the new and final divine-human covenant, through which we are made new creations, and through which we will receive a promised new heavens and new earth in God's good time.

CHAPTER SIX

MOSAIC COVENANT PRELIMINARY

W e move now from the Abrahamic covenant to the Mosaic covenant adumbrated by the earlier patriarchal covenant. It was seen that historiography—the role of narrative—was foundational to understanding the way the Abrahamic covenant materials related to each other.[1] Historiography continues to be a fundamental category for understanding God's covenant making episodes because they are all reported in narrative as parts of a sequence of historical events. The unity of the materials, and thus their internal coherence, is also important both to recognize and to affirm. The Bible, and subordinately but also foundationally the Pentateuch, are as God-breathed data a unity.[2]

A few remarks are in order about biblical historiography and covenants and their renewals pursuant to these comments and preparatory to what will follow. Several things were noted in volume 1 as fundamental to a proper—or *sachgemäss*—view of the Bible's historiographical unity. First, it was noted that the historical literature and indeed all of the literature presented by the Old Testament (and the whole Bible) is *covenantal*. For example, from the beginning Genesis 1:1–2:3 presents a general account of creation and is also an expression of the Creator's covenantal nature. Genesis 2:4–25 provide additional covenantal history and *torah*. Genesis 3 presents the first covenant lawsuit, conducted not by a covenant lawsuit prophet but by the Lord himself—unless one reckons that the preincarnate Son as archetypal prophet with the Spirit of judgment

---

1 In chapter 4.
2 The Sinai covenant and its renewal (Deuteronomy) are likewise, but in a distinct way, a unity.

speaking through him conducted the lawsuit.[3] The rest of the Bible continues to be among other things the literary presentation of life under the Adamic covenant and under its renewal, the Noahic covenant. It is God's historiography, inspired/breathed through human writers up through John's Apocalypse, which culminates in the end of history and the start of a new order. Second, the history the Bible presents is composed on a principle or principles of selectivity. It is whatever the Spirit selected according to his criteria of choice that are both covenantal and relational criteria. Third, and as background to God's special grace program, the Adamic and Noahic covenants form one legal package under which the realm of common grace continues and all humanity have lived, do live, and will continue to live until the Parousia brings the end of the Adamic-Noahic common grace order.

In the special grace domain, and after the institution of the Mosaic covenant, the presentation of covenantal life under that legal arrangement—the Sinai-Moab arrangement—occupies most of the rest of the Bible until the birth and ministry of Christ, which culminate in the cutting of the new covenant on the cross, a cutting validated by the resurrection (cf. Acts 17:31).[4] In the present volume, chapters 9–16 consider different aspects of life under the Mosaic covenant before Christ. The present chapter introduces the process involving Mosaic covenant institution in terms of the Major Paradigm.

MOSAIC COVENANT AND RENEWAL

The Mosaic covenant was cut as has been noted, but that cutting was not a one time affair. The Lord cut the covenant with Israel at Sinai. He subsequently apparently *restored* it (using the idiom כרת ברית) after the

---

3   Cf. detailed discussion in volume 1, chapters 1–3; and also Introduction to this volume.

4   After those events, namely, the crucifixion and the resurrection, the Mosaic covenant ceased to function as a covenant. Many people may have continued to attempt to regulate their lives by its requirements just as they do today, but the fact that they have not recognized Jesus for who he is, and the new covenant in his blood for what it is, does not alter the fact that they have chosen to live under a defunct covenant—or as Paul puts it, "I can testify about them that they are zealous for God, but their zeal is not based on knowledge" (Rom. 10:2; cf. Col. 2:13–14). They would still live under the law unaware that Jesus "canceled the charge of our legal indebtedness, which stood against us and condemned us; he has taken it away, nailing it to the cross" (Col. 2:14). Cf. chapters 2 and 5 of volume 3.

symbolic destruction of the covenant by the shattering of the original tablets, and finally he *renewed* it with the grown children of the faithless generation whose bodies fell in the desert—with those who under Joshua would begin the Conquest.[5] The book of Deuteronomy presents that renewal covenant (cf. Deut. 29:1, again using the idiom כרת ברית). The pattern wherein a suzerain renews a treaty with the son of a departed vassal king was known in the ancient Near East and it appears biblically in the Noahic renewal of the Adamic covenant, and now in the Moab covenant that renews the Sinai covenant.

MOSES THE IDEAL COVENANT MEDIATOR

It is an important historical fact that Moses grew up in Pharaoh's household and "was educated in all the wisdom of the Egyptians and was powerful in speech and action" (Acts 7:22). He was the ideal person for the Spirit to convey God's revelation in covenantal ways: his Egyptian education would have included the sort of diplomatic training that entailed knowledge of such matters as covenant making, covenant renewal, and covenant lawsuit and the forms or *Gattungen* appropriate to them, and Moses gave us materials in all three genres—the covenant made at Sinai, its renewal at Moab, and the great covenant lawsuit poem of Deuteronomy 32.[6]

MOSAIC COVENANT AND THE LAW

It was affirmed at the start of this chapter that the Mosaic covenant was one covenant. This is true in the special sense that a covenant and its

---

5   For the shattering of the original tablets, cf. discussion in chapter 8.

6   This is true even though we have no evidence that Egyptians inscribed suzerain-vassal treaties—which is not to say they had no suzerain-vassal relationships since, after all, they conquered many people; the Amarna Letters show the appeal of client kings to Pharaoh when under attack, using ancient imperial phraseology: "Pharaoh has placed his name in [e.g.] Jerusalem." We do have extant *parity* treaties that Pharaohs made with the Hittites, and we know Egyptians had literature from Mesopotamia (e.g., the "Epic of Sargon"). These archaeological exemplars give a glimpse of a larger legal and literary context in which the Egyptians would, one might reasonably infer, have been cognizant of the legal forms under discussion.

renewal form one legal package. As was noted, the Adamic and Noahic covenants offer a good example of this idea, and the Sinai and Moab covenants offer an even better example—better because more detailed and terminologically indisputable (except from a critical or post-critical perspective). So traditionally the phrase "the Mosaic covenant" has meant all of the material from Sinai on through Deuteronomy. The same is true of the phrase "the law," by which the entire Mosaic corpus is meant. Pauline usage makes these matters clear since he refers to only one Mosaic covenant (e.g., 2 Cor. 3:14) and to only one law (e.g., Gal. 3:17).[7]

THE MAJOR PARADIGM COMPLETE
FOR THE FIRST TIME AFTER THE FALL

Because the Lord not only wages war in order to provide the context for the Mosaic covenant (as arguably he did before the Noahic covenant) but also to establish for the first time after the Fall a temple presence and all that goes with it (e.g., a priesthood and sacrifices and most importantly, the residence of the Lord among his people), the Mosaic covenantal literature is the first after the Fall to show us in a complete form the Major Paradigm.[8] All the elements of that paradigm were present in the Adamic material except for warfare because there was no need for warfare when the covenantal acts of creation took place: God declared all of it to be "very good" (Gen. 1:31). After the Fall, however, God must intrude into human history and into a human environment increasingly alienated from him (cf. Rom. 1:18–23) if he is to establish a covenant with anyone—either a common grace covenant such as the Noahic, or a special grace covenant such as the ones that follow the Noahic—and such intrusions characteristically involve warfare. The

---

7   The expression in Galatians 4:24 is *pars pro toto*: "One covenant is from Mount Sinai and bears children who are to be slaves: This is Hagar." The statement is part of a larger argument already considered in volume 1 and to be discussed further under the topic of the new covenant. Cf. chapter 3.

8   There is no temple presence in the Noahic covenant, even if the structure of the ark may be thought to allude to a temple structure of the cosmos. No temple iterations appear under the common grace covenants (except for lost Eden) because establishment of a temple presence after the fall only happens for a special people under special grace covenants, and as part of the eschatological trajectory of God's special grace program that aims at a final and eternal temple presence (cf. Rev. 21:22).

ultimate goal is stated by the so-called covenant formula, for example, "my dwelling place will be with them; I will be their God, and they will be my people" (Ezek. 37:27).

MOSAIC COVENANT MAJOR PARADIGM ARTICULATION

Below is the Major Paradigm as it finds expression in the Mosaic covenantal materials, and it will serve as a reference point for discussing the Mosaic covenant making process in this chapter and in chapters 7 and 8:

The Major Paradigm

1. God works	Exod. 3:14–15
2. by his Spirit	Num. 11:25
3. through the Word/a prophet-figure	Deut. 34:10
4. to war against and defeat his foe(s)	Exod. 15:8
5. God establishes a covenant with a people	Exod. 24:8
6. God's covenant establishes that people as God's people	Exod. 19:5–6 Exod. 6:7; 22:23
7. God establishes a temple among his people, because he will reside among them	Exod. 25–31 Exod. 25:8

We have observed that theophanies are not initiated by humans but by God.[9] Even when Elijah calls upon the Lord to show his power on Mount Carmel the prophet declares, "LORD, the God of Abraham, Isaac, and Israel, let it be known today that you are God in Israel and that I am your servant and have done all these things at your command" (1 Kings 18:36). The Lord was the initiator: he commanded a contest he would win with theophanic fire, who was arguably the Holy Spirit.[10] So the Lord takes the initiative with Moses and appears to him in a burning bush. It is here that we find the first element of what we have called the Major Paradigm, namely, "God works." God begins to work on and through Moses, and an important part of his commission is the Lord's own self-identification.

---

9   Cf. Niehaus, *God at Sinai: Covenant and Theophany in the Bible and Ancient Near East* (Grand Rapids: Zondervan, 1995), 20.

10   Cf. volume 3, chapter 10.

The Lord Works: His Self-Naming

Before proceeding further it will be worthwhile to examine how the
Lord names himself. The self-naming has commonly been translated
"I AM WHO I AM" (Exod. 3:14a) or the like. The Lord adds: "This is
what you are to say to the Israelites: 'I AM has sent me to you'" (Exod.
3:14b). However, if that is the correct reading (in other words, if the
Masoretic tradition does indeed represent what Moses heard in this
encounter) it is curious that the Lord tells Moses in the next verse, "Say
to the Israelites, 'The LORD the God of your fathers—the God of Abraham, the God of Isaac and the God of Jacob—*has sent me to you*'" (Exod.
3:15, emphases added). The parallelism of these statements is displayed
and discussed below. First we note that "the LORD" here is "Yahweh,"
and Yahweh is a causative form of the verb "to become" (הוה), and that
verb is a parallel form of the verb "to become/be," היה translated "I AM"
in the previous verse.[11] As one considers the parallel forms, these two
verses taken together seem to present an inconsistency. In the first (v. 14)
the Lord identifies himself as "I AM" and tells Moses to tell the people,
"I AM has sent me to you." In the second (v. 15) he identifies himself
as "he causes to be/become" (i.e., "Yahweh") and instructs Moses to
tell the people, "Yahweh has sent me to you." It seems possible that the
name Yahweh, meaning "he causes to be/become," implies a causative
understanding, or as one would say nowadays subtext, for the name
given in verse 14. In other words, if one removes the traditional vowels
in Exodus 3:14, both or either of the two verbs in verse 14a (and the
one in v. 14b) could be read in a causative sense. Depending, then, on
the vowels assumed, the divine self-identification in verse 14a could be
understood in the following ways:

1   I AM/WILL BE who/what I AM/WILL BE

2   I CAUSE/WILL CAUSE TO BE/BECOME
    who/what I AM/WILL BE

3   I CAUSE/WILL CAUSE TO BE/BECOME
    what(ever) I CAUSE/WILL CAUSE TO BE/BECOME[12]

---

11   Cf. *BDB*, 217–19, 222.
12   Cf. discussion in Niehaus, *God the Poet*, 25–26.

The first statement is the traditional rendering and is usually understood as an affirmation of absolute Being and so LXX translated it, "I am the Being" ('Εγώ εἰμι ὁ ὤν).[13] The third statement is an affirmation of the Lord as Creator; thus to paraphrase: "I will create what I will create." The second statement is perhaps the most intriguing since it affirms what theologians call God's aseity (literally, God's "by-means-of-himself-ness," from the Latin, *a se*, "by means of himself"): "I will cause to be/create what I will be." This understanding tells us that God *constantly recreates* himself, which is another way of saying he sustains himself and has no need of any outside means of sustenance. Jesus said the same thing in different words: "For as the Father has life in himself, so he has granted the Son also to have life in himself" (John 5:26). God is the fathomless source of life in himself and his life constantly renews and so continues in existence, and all created life also continues in existence so long as God renews it—a process which, as had been argued, is accomplished by the Spirit through the Word. Finally, the fact of God's self-existence is the supreme example of God's righteousness. This is so because he is always true to himself—faithful to the standard of himself—as he recreates himself. God's righteousness is thus a much more profound concept than has been generally recognized.[14]

One thing to remember is this: the Lord spoke, as far as we know, only one name to Moses in verse 14a—whichever of the three above mentioned possibilities it was. However, he also left a consonantal text that could be read three different but related ways. The Masoretes in due course added the vowels handed down by tradition and this ought to be highly respected. However, it remains true that a pre-Masoretic reader of the consonantal text might have imagined any of the three meanings of the Lord's self-identification in verse 14a or all of them at the same time, especially after reading verse 15, which parallels אהיה in verse 14b with יהוה, each followed by the predicate "has sent me to you":

Verse 14   "say to the Israelites, 'אהיה has sent me to you.'"

Verse 15   "say to the Israelites, 'יהוה ... has sent me to you.'"

---

13   LXX translates the divine name Yahweh as Κύριος ("the LORD") in verse 15, as usual.

14   Cf. discussions of God's righteousness in volume 1, chapter 6; and in volume 3, Appendix E.

It seems quite possible that we have here an example of what could be called "God's wittiness." He said one thing to Moses, but he gave subsequent generations a consonantal text that could accommodate three possible meanings. Moreover, each of those three possible meanings is true. God is absolute Being, he does create whatever he will, and he is the creator/sustainer of himself or, as theology says, he has the incommunicable divine attribute of aseity.[15]

By His Spirit: Theophanic Spirit Effulgence

When the Lord appears to Moses in a fire that does not consume the bush in Exodus 3, the theophanic fire is best understood as a manifestation of the Spirit. We have already identified the glory of God as his Spirit and we have seen the divine presence appear in the form of a firepot passing between the pieces in the ratification of the Abrahamic covenant. The fire here is benign—it does not consume—but in future that holy fire will consume in judgment even as he does in 2 Kings 1:10, 12. When the Lord appears in order to initiate the Mosaic covenant—surely also a benign intent—he appears nonetheless as a *consuming fire* as a warning to the people about the holiness of the one with whom they are about to engage. That glory appears as a consuming fire on Sinai ("To the Israelites the glory of the LORD looked like a consuming fire on top of the mountain," Exod. 24:17), and the Lord identifies himself through his prophet Moses as "a consuming fire" (Deut. 4:24). That Glory-Fire or Glory-Spirit consumes the offering at Aaron's ordination ("the glory of the LORD appeared to all the people. Fire came out from the presence of the LORD and consumed the burnt offering and the fat portions on the altar. And when all the people saw it, they shouted for joy and fell facedown," Num. 9:23–24), and the same fire consumed Elijah's offering on Mount Carmel (1 Kings 18:38). As one might expect, the phrase "consuming fire" appears characteristically of the Lord's coming in judgment.[16] The author of Hebrews admonishes that our "God is a consuming fire" (Heb. 12:29), a statement in keeping with Paul's counsel that we "work out our salvation with fear and trembling" (cf. Phil. 2:12). One statement

---

15   Pagan sources attributed the same quality to certain deities. So an Egyptian poem can call their chief god, the sun god, Amon, the "one who made himself and beheld what he would make." (He "beheld" it, i.e., he *envisioned* it, before he made it.) Assyrians sometimes called their chief god, Ashur, "the builder of himself."

16   Cf. 2 Samuel 22:9 // Psalm 18:8; Isaiah 30:27; 30:30; 33:14.

from Isaiah is particularly evocative in this regard: "See, the Name of the LORD comes from afar, with burning anger and dense clouds of smoke; his lips are full of wrath, and his tongue is a consuming fire" (Isa. 30:27). The Lord pictured here with consuming fire coming from his mouth can also be pictured with a sword coming out of his mouth ("Coming out of his mouth is a sharp sword with which to strike down the nations," Rev. 19:15a). The word of God is also compared with a sword: "For the word of God is alive and active. Sharper than any double-edged sword, it penetrates even to dividing soul and spirit, joints and marrow; it judges the thoughts and attitudes of the heart" (Heb. 4:12). This statement recalls what Jesus said of his own words, that they were Spirit (John 6:63). In sum, the fire is the glory and is the Spirit and the Spirit also takes the form of words in God's mouth—the words of the incarnate Word and of the Bible as we have understood. Indeed, the fiery sword that forbade readmittance to Eden may have been the Spirit as fiery sword-word (Gen. 3:24). He is the one whose words Moses hears and whose fiery appearance attracts his initial interest in Exodus 3.

Through a Prophet-Figure

One later learns that the Lord's Spirit has been *on* Moses: "Then the LORD came down in the cloud, and spoke to him, and took of the Spirit that was upon him (מִן־הָרוּחַ אֲשֶׁר עָלָיו), and placed the same upon the seventy elders; and it happened, when the Spirit rested upon them, that they prophesied, although they never did *so* again" (Num. 11:25 NKJV). One notes here again that even in the case of Moses, the greatest Old Testament prophet (cf. Deut. 34:10), the Spirit was not "in" him but "upon" him, and from this one sees again the greater privilege those under the new covenant have been given as over against those under the Mosaic covenant, including even Moses himself (cf. 2 Cor. 3:7–18).

Because the Lord wages war through a prophet (the fourth step of the Major Paradigm), some further consideration of aspects of Moses' prophetic call is in order. The twofold aspects include a general prophetic dynamic or outline, and Moses' prophetic reluctance (with a forward looking comparison to the same in Isaiah and Jeremiah).

The Outline of Prophecy

The Lord makes it clear enough that he is calling Moses to do prophetic work and he spells it out in the first of four Pentateuchal passages (Exod.

4:10–17; Num. 12:6–8; Deut. 13:1–5; 18:15–22) that give the foundational *torah* regarding prophecy in the Bible:[17]

> Moses said to the LORD, "LORD, I have never been eloquent, neither in the past nor since you have spoken to your servant. I am slow of speech and tongue." The LORD said to him, "Who gave human beings their mouths? Who makes them deaf or mute? Who gives them sight or makes them blind? Is it not I, the LORD? Now go; I will help you speak and will teach you what to say." But Moses said, "Please send someone else." Then the LORD's anger burned against Moses and he said, "What about your brother, Aaron the Levite? I know he can speak well. He is already on his way to meet you, and he will be glad to see you. You shall speak to him and put words in his mouth; I will help both of you speak and will teach you what to do. He will speak to the people for you, and it will be as if he were your mouth and as if you were God to him. But take this staff in your hand so you can perform the signs with it." (Exod. 4:10–17)

One notable thing about the passage is Moses' reluctance to accept his calling and we will say more about that momentarily. The thing to note now is the paradigm of a prophetic dynamic outlined in the Lord's statement of intent. The Lord tells Moses that Aaron "will speak to the people for you, and it will be as if he were your mouth and as if you were God to him" (Exod. 4:16). The following simple diagram illustrates the implicit dynamic:

Moses	God
⇓	⇓
Aaron	Prophet
⇓	⇓
Audience	Audience

The resemblance of this diagram to the earlier illustration of what we have called a prophetic dynamic is noteworthy.[18] As the Bible unfolds,

---

17 Cf. further discussion of the Pentateuchal passages in chapter 9.
18 Cf. volume 1, Prolegomena, 15–20; and chapter 1, 27–31.

it presents more and more of the Lord's work in history and through people, and as it does, the prophetic dynamic becomes visible in greater detail and this is part of the pedagogical progress of Scripture. Here, in the relatively early going, the Lord outlines for Moses what the prophet might expect in days to come. Such an outline is probably needed because Moses' Egyptian upbringing would not have tutored him in the role of a prophet: there was at least no such phenomenon in Egypt.[19] The Hebrews presumably had some knowledge that Abraham was a prophet. Nonetheless, one cannot assume a detailed understanding of prophecy on their part at this stage of redemptive history.

Moses' Prophetic Reluctance

Moses shows considerable reluctance to accept the job the Lord has in mind for him. If one compares his reaction to the Lord's irruption into his life with that of other prophets an interesting and instructive similarity becomes apparent. The fact that the subsequent prophets are not covenant mediators, like Moses, but rather covenant lawsuit prophets under the Mosaic covenant makes no difference, and even enhances the instructional value of what one can see. We consider first the case of Moses, and the following diagram illustrates the matter:

Moses' Prophetic Call (Exod. 3:1–4:17)

Divine initiation	3:4–6	Theophany
Commission	3:7–10	Exodus and Conquest
Moses protests	3:11	Who am I?
	3:13	Who are you?
	4:1	What if the people do not believe?
	4:10	I am not eloquent
	4:13	Send someone else!
Yahweh responds	3:12	I will be with you
	3:14–22	I AM WHO I AM, YAHWEH
	4:2–9	staff turns to snake, hand turns leprous
	4:11–12	Who gave man his mouth?
	4:14–17	Aaron to speak for Moses, etc.

---

19 This remains true even though part of Pharaonic ideology/theology was that Pharaoh was the incarnation of the sun god, and that the god put good ideas into his mind. No Pharaoh records his employing a prophet, and indeed an incarnate god would not seem to need one.

Foremost, the Lord and not Moses initiates the call. It may seem commonplace to note the application of this fact for ministry in any age but then again, we already know most of the things we hear in sermons but can still benefit from hearing them again. The point here is: it is the Lord who calls. No one can say, "I am going to be a prophet"—not, at least, if that person intends or hopes to be a true prophet. Such a call and gift can only come from God. The same should be true in any form of ministry. As Ephesians 2:10 informs us, we are God's workmanship formed for good works that he prepared in advance for us to do. If he prepared them for us, then he calls us to them when he will and gives us what we need to accomplish them.

Moses' call comes with a clear commission (Exod. 3:7–10) to rescue the Lord's people out of Egypt and lead them into Canaan. In the face of such a glorious calling, Moses protests! He comes up with a number of objections, each of which the Lord answers satisfactorily (including the revelation of the divine name in a fruitful apparent ambiguity explored above). Finally, and apparently unable to come up with any more excuses, Moses shows his true attitude and asks the Lord to send someone else. The Lord's response to this is to propose Aaron as Moses' "prophet," and his response provides the first biblical paradigm of a prophetic dynamic.

The conversation just considered between Moses and the Lord finds its counterpart in other prophetic callings, and this is as good a place as any to display those because they have to do with covenant lawsuit prophets under the Mosaic covenant. The prophets in question—or rather, who have questions!—are Isaiah and Jeremiah, and a schema outlines the events:

Event	Isaiah	Jeremiah
Divine initiation	6:1–4 vision	1:4–5 word event
Commission	6:8–13	1:10–19
		1:11a word event
		1:11b response
		1:12 explanation
		1:13a word event
		1:13b response
		1:14–16 explanation
Protestation	6:5 unclean	1:6 only a child
Yahweh's response	6:6–7	1:7–9

The pattern of divine initiation and human response parallels what appeared in the case of Moses. That is so not because one is dealing here with some contrived literary pattern that could almost amount to a *Gattung*/genre. It is so because events *unfolded* as they are *reported to have unfolded* and in a certain sequence that has partly to do with divine initiation, and partly to do with human sinfulness, reluctance, and self-doubt. In other words, the fact that the pattern occurs more than once is consistent with a manifest claim to the historicity of these events in each case: the experiences of Moses, Isaiah, and Jeremiah show the inevitable response of sinful man to the Lord's presence, and they are reported as they happened.[20]

Isaiah's calling and the nature of his commission come under discussion when we consider the prophets who operate under the Mosaic covenant and the same is true for Jeremiah. We note now, however, in passing the wordplay involved in Jeremiah's commission as two specimens of the sort of wittiness the Lord displays from time to time in the Pentateuch (e.g., בבל, בלל in Gen. 11:9, and the divine self-naming considered above) and beyond. In the first case, the Lord asks Jeremiah, "What do you see?" (1:11a) and Jeremiah answers, "I see the branch of an almond tree [שָׁקֵד]" (1:11b). The Lord responds, "You have seen correctly, for I am watching [שֹׁקֵד] to see that my word is fulfilled" (1:12). The wordplay is between "almond" and "watching," which in Hebrew have identical consonants. The allusion is grounded in the fact that the almond is eye-shaped. The second case is perhaps less winsome but it also involves figurative language. The Lord again asks Jeremiah, "What do you see" (1:13) and Jeremiah answers, "I see a pot that is boiling.... It is tilting toward us from the north [מִפְּנֵי צָפוֹנָה]" (1:13b). The Lord responds, "From the north [מִצָּפוֹן] disaster will be poured out on all who live in the land" (1:14). The wordplay here involves a variant form of repetition but is associated with the figure of a boiling pot and it augurs no good for the inhabitants of the land. Both events are called "word events" because both *events* are the *coming* of the *word* of the Lord to the prophet (1:11, 13). The phraseology involved in such reporting, "The word of the Lord came to [someone]" (lit. "the word of the LORD was to [someone], וַיְהִי דְבַר־יהוה אֶל") is often referred to as the "word event formula"—consisting of the verb "to be" + "the word of the LORD" + "to"— and it introduces a number of God's communications to his prophets.[21] Other aspects of prophetic calling

20 The same is true of the *Gattung* that characterizes reports of biblical theophanies, as discussed in *God at Sinai*, 39–42.

21 For example, Elijah (1 Kings 17:2), Jonah (1:1), Haggai ("the word of the LORD was to Zerubbabel by the hand of Haggai the prophet," היה דבר־יהוה ביד־חגי נביא אל־זרבבל,

and tasking are explored when we consider some experiences of select covenant lawsuit prophets under the Mosaic covenant.[22]

To War Against and Defeat His Foe(s)

Under this heading of the Major Paradigm three aspects of God's warfare come under consideration: the signs and wonders done by his Spirit against Pharaoh and the gods of Egypt; the Lord's hardening of Pharaoh's heart or psychological interference with Pharaoh; and his final defeat of the Egyptian forces at the Red Sea (in Hebrew, the "Reed Sea"). The first two are discussed in this chapter; the third is discussed in the following chapter.

The Spirit and Miracles

The Spirit of God is upon Moses and works through him, and since one understands from later revelation that the Spirit does the miracles recorded in the New Testament it would be consistent if the same Spirit did the miracles of the Old Testament.[23] The dynamic outlined in the Major Paradigm is in play: the Spirit works through Moses to speak to God's people and to Pharaoh, and the same Spirit works through Moses' words (warnings, predictions) to do the miracles recorded in Exodus 7–12, all of which are in one way or another acts of war. (The dynamic outlined in the Kingdom Creation Paradigm by which God caused his Spirit to work through a prophet-figure to accomplish kingdom work is likewise in play here).[24] The plagues are the form of God's warfare against Pharaoh and the gods of Egypt as the following chart illustrates:[25]

Hag. 1:1), and Zechariah (היה דבר־יהוה אל, Zech. 1:1); and cf. the phrasing, "The word of the LORD which was to" (דבר־יהוה אשר היה אל) in Hosea (1:2), Joel (1:1), Micah (1:1), and Zephaniah (1:1). In a few instances we read the phrase, "The vision of" a prophet (e.g., Isa. 1:1; Obad.1), or "the burden" [משא] of a message given to the prophet, for example, Nahum (1:1), Habakkuk (in an interesting phrase, "The burden which Habakkuk the prophet saw," המשא אשר חזה הבקוק הנביא, Hab. 1:1; cf. "The word that Isaiah the son of Amoz saw," הדבר אשר חזה ישעיהו בן־אמוץ, Isa. 2:1).

22   In chapters 14 and 15.

23   The signs and wonders of Jesus, mediator of the new covenant, are done by the Spirit in the New Testament; the signs and wonders of Moses, mediator of the old covenant, are done by the Spirit in the Old Testament.

24   Cf. volume 1, page 97; and the Introduction in this volume.

25   This chart is adapted from John J. Davis, *Moses and the Gods of Egypt* (Winona Lake, IN: BMH Books, 1985), 92–160.

Plague	Exodus	Egyptian deity
1 Blood*	7:14–24	Osiris (Nile = his bloodstream)
		Neith (fish)
		Hapi (crocodile)
2 Frogs*	8:1–15	Heqt (fertility)
3 Gnats	8:16–19	Nut (sky goddess)
4 Flies	8:20–32	Nut
5 Livestock (death)	9:1–7	Ptah (Apis bull)
		Hathor (cow = deity of love, beauty)
6 Boils	9:8–12	Serapis (healing)
		Imhotep (medicine)
7 Hail	9:13–34	Nut
8 Locusts	10:1–20	Nut
9 Darkness	10:21–29	Re/Ra
10 Firstborn (death)	11:1–12:30	Re/Ra

The plagues marked with an asterisk are the ones Pharaoh's magicians are able to mimic. The last two judgments are the most signal because they target the sun and the firstborn. The sun was the supreme god of the Egyptian pantheon and the plague of darkness shows Yahweh's supremacy over the sun. The plague on the firstborn is reported in a way that implies its deep significance: "At midnight the Lord struck down all the firstborn in Egypt, from the firstborn of Pharaoh, who sat on the throne, to the firstborn of the prisoner, who was in the dungeon, and the firstborn of all the livestock as well" (Exod. 12:29). The plague on the firstborn probably finds its theological roots in the death of God's firstborn son, Adam (Luke 3:38) for his sin.[26] But the death first mentioned in the tenth plague is that of *Pharaoh's* firstborn son and that had theological significance for Egypt: that son was thought to be the next incarnation of Amon Ra, the sun god. In other words, by means of the ninth and tenth plagues, Yahweh accomplishes judgment on the (supposed) sun god in heaven and on his (supposed) incarnation on earth. When the Lord accomplishes that final judgment on the firstborn, it will complete a cycle of "judgment on all the gods of Egypt" (Exod. 12:12) and it is doubtful any Egyptian would have missed the significance of those last two plagues.

---

26 For discussion along these lines, cf. *ANETBT*, 164–65.

They sent the message, not by words but by acts, that Yahweh was God in heaven above and on earth below, and there is no other.

God's judgment on Egypt and her gods is also warfare against them and it means salvation for Israel. We understand it is the Spirit who moved these things since we have seen elsewhere that the Spirit is the breath of life for all people (cf. Job 34:14–15; Isa. 42:5) and also the one who sustains all things through the word.[27] The Spirit brings judgment as Isaiah remarks: "He will cleanse the bloodstains from Jerusalem by a Spirit of judgment and a Spirit of fire" (Isa. 4:4).[28]

The Spirit produces "signs and wonders" and that phrase first occurs in Exodus 7: "But I will harden Pharaoh's heart, and though I multiply my signs and wonders in Egypt, he will not listen to you" (Exod. 7:3–4). Both halves of verse 3 are important for understanding the warfare the Lord will conduct through his prophet. We take the second half first and note that the signs and wonders the Lord promises to multiply turn out to be very destructive: the plagues that virtually destroy Egypt in the course of proving her deities to be powerless. This important phrase appears a number of times as salvation history unfolds and is used in three large areas of concern: the Lord's signs and wonders done in Egypt and for Daniel in the Old Testament; signs and wonders performed by Jesus and his apostles in the New Testament, generally implicit in the promise made through Joel ("I will show wonders in the heavens and on the earth," Joel 2:30) and paraphrased by Peter ("I will show wonders in the heavens above, and signs on the earth below," Acts 2:19); and false signs and wonders performed by false messiahs, false prophets, and the Antichrist.[29] One striking thing about these signs and wonders—if not the most striking thing—is the differences between them.

---

27   Cf. Hebrews 1:3 and discussion in volume 1, chapter 4.

28   The Spirit also enables judgments: "The person with the Spirit makes judgments about all things, but such a person is not subject to merely human judgments," (1 Cor. 2:15). The judgments made by the person who has the Spirit are not such colossal affairs as the Lord's judgments on Pharaoh and Egypt but they do, like any judgment, involve discernment of what is right or wrong and imply action in accordance with that discernment—for example, rejection of the wrong, which in the Lord's case can take the form of a judgment.

29   The Old Testament notes signs and wonders done through Moses (Deut. 4:34; 6:22; 7:19; 26:8; 29:3; 34:11; Neh. 9:10; Ps. 135:9; Jer. 32:20–21) and signs and wonders done for Daniel (4:2; 6:27). The New Testament shows them associated with Jesus (John 4:48; Acts 2:22 ["wonders and signs"]; 4:30), and with the apostles (Acts 2:43; 5:12; 6:8 [through Stephen]; Acts 14:3 [through Paul and Barnabas]; Acts 15:12 [Paul and Barnabas]; Rom.

One category of difference is that between signs and wonders done by the Lord and signs and wonders done by the "false messiahs and false prophets" and by "the lawless one." The ability of such evil agents to do false signs and wonders may recall the counterfeit miracles performed by Pharaoh's magicians (Exod. 7:11, 12, 22; 8:6). Such biblical data indicate that the devil and his demons, being spirits, are fully capable of producing what seem to be miracles, manipulating things in the material world to whatever extent God allows. By definition signs and wonders are miraculous effects or transformations, things that cannot be done except by some spiritual power, and since the Lord does no evil and does not lie, one can be sure the signs and wonders performed by false messiahs and false prophets and by the Antichrist are not done with the Lord's power or by his Spirit, who is the Spirit of truth.

Another category of difference is that between the signs and wonders done through Moses and those done through Jesus and his followers. The Mosaic signs and wonders are destructive—as Pharaoh's officials ask their master, "Do you not yet realize that Egypt is ruined?" (Exod. 10:7); by contrast the signs and wonders done by Jesus and his followers have mostly to do with healing, or with provision (of food or, at Cana, wine). Of course the Lord provided manna through Moses, and that positive provision is also a sign or a wonder. But the larger contrast between the Mosaic signs and wonders and those of the New Testament remains: the Mosaic miracles are mostly destructive of the power and dominion of God's foes, whereas the New Testament signs and wonders are mostly sustaining or restorative for God's people.

The apparent difference disappears, however, if one considers the purpose of the signs and wonders. Whether the Lord does them through Moses or through Jesus and his followers, he does them for largely the same reasons. In both cases they attest to the truth of the words spoken by the prophet—Moses in the Old Testament and Jesus (and his followers who partake of a prophetic dynamic when they speak words the Spirit gives them or when they do signs or wonders) in the New Testament. Moreover, when the Lord does a sign or a wonder it typically has two aspects: it destroys or diminishes the power of an evil that oppresses one

---

15:19 [through Paul], 2 Cor. 12:12 [through Paul]); and associated with (apparently) Jesus and the church subsequently (Heb. 2:4). The phrase also appears once in a historical retrospective on Moses in Stephen's speech before the Sanhedrin (Acts 7:36). Finally, it is predicated of false messiahs and false prophets (Matt. 24:24; Mark 13:12) and of the "lawless one" (2 Thess. 2:9).

or more of his people, and it heals or liberates one or more of his people. The Lord's signs and wonders through Moses virtually destroyed Egypt and showed their deities to be empty, but those same signs and wonders also liberated the Lord's people to leave the land of their oppressors and worship the true God. Likewise, God's signs and wonders through Jesus and his followers set people free from disease and even demonic powers, and so in doing showed them the nature of the true God and enabled them to worship him in the person of his Son.

Signs and wonders, then, are a two-sided coin. On one side, one finds destruction of the dominion of evil; on the other, one finds an impress of the Lord's dominion, which is salvation. The two go together, because whenever the Lord intends to win a people to himself, he must *win* them to himself and that happens only by warfare of some sort. One reason for the vivid contrast between the Mosaic miracles and the ones in the New Testament is, quite simply, that in Moses' case the Lord was doing miracles to reduce a *visible* and oppressive rule (that of a false incarnate god, Pharaoh), whereas in the case of Jesus and his followers he was doing them to reduce an *invisible* oppressive rule (that of the false "god of this world," Satan)—to destroy the devil's work (1 John 3:8), and thus to save individuals from that sinful oppression. Also and insofar as the miracles proved the truth of the gospel message (cf. John 14:11; Rom. 15:18–19), the Lord did them to build a new form of God's kingdom, the church—just as the signs and wonders performed through Moses led to the Old Testament form of God's kingdom—Israel constituted as a nation under the laws of the Mosaic covenant.

Because God's judgments on Pharaoh and the gods of Egypt are a form of warfare, our considerations imply another issue: the form of God's warfare in the Old Testament and the very different form of God's warfare in the New Testament. When we consider the Conquest, we will give this more attention but for now note the following principle: the *form of God's warfare* depends upon, or is consistent with, the *form of his kingdom*. Under the Mosaic covenant, the form of the kingdom was a people with whom he would create and maintain a state; correspondingly, the form of God's warfare was physical, involving the clash of armed forces, tactics, and weapons like swords and spears. Under the new covenant, the form of God's kingdom is not a nation-state but the church, which is an entity composed by the Spirit and not limited to any one nation and whose commission is to become global; correspondingly, the form of God's warfare under this form of his kingdom is spiritual: "For our struggle is not against flesh and blood, but against the rulers, against the authorities, against the powers of this dark world and against the spiritual forces of evil in the heavenly realms" (Gal. 6:12); "The weapons we fight with are not the weapons of the world. On the contrary, they have divine power to demolish strongholds. We demolish arguments and every pretension that sets itself up against the knowledge of God, and we take captive every thought to make it obedient to Christ" (2 Cor. 10:4–5). The advance of such warfare in the New Testament can be facilitated by signs and wonders, just as the advance of God's kingdom in the Old Testament was facilitated by signs and wonders.[30]

As will appear, the form of God's kingdom conditions not only the form of his warfare but also the form of certain judgments and sentences God commands among his people. Another way of putting this is: God chooses forms of judgment that are appropriate to the form of his kingdom under the Mosaic covenant and appropriate to the form of his kingdom under the new covenant; as the form of the kingdom is different under the two covenants, so the form of the judgments is different. These observations on warfare and judgment are also consistent with the fact that the two covenants are different.[31]

The Hardening of the Heart as Warfare

In addition to signs and wonders, the hardening of the heart, or psychological interference, is another form of divine warfare. The Lord says, "I will harden Pharaoh's heart" (Exod. 7:3a). The first statement of this intent occurs three chapters earlier: "When you return to Egypt, see that you perform before Pharaoh all the wonders I have given you the power to do. But I will harden his heart so that [lit. "and"] he will not let the people go" (Exod. 4:21). After these two statements by the Lord, one finds many occasions on which Pharaoh hardens his heart or Pharaoh and his officials harden their hearts, as well as further statements that the Lord hardens their hearts (and cf. the Lord's hardening of the army's hearts, Exod. 14:17). Three verbs are used in these passages although one is used predominantly, and they seem to overlap in meaning: the usual verb is חזק, "to harden."[32] The other two verbs are קשה, also meaning "to make hard, stiff, stubborn"; and כבד, meaning "to make heavy, dull,

---

30 For example, at Jericho (Josh. 6) and at Gibeon and Aijalon (Josh. 10:12–14).

31 Cf. Jeremiah 31:32 and further discussion in volume 3, chapters 2 and 5.

32 Cf. *BDB*, 304.

unresponsive."[33] If one surveys the hardening passages or verses a certain pattern seems to emerge:

Exodus	Subject	Verb
4:21	Yahweh	חזק
7:3	Yahweh	קשה
8:15	Pharaoh	חזק
8:32	Pharaoh	חזק
9:12	Yahweh	חזק
9:34	Pharaoh and officials	כבד
10:1	Yahweh	כבד
10:20	Yahweh	חזק
10:27	Yahweh	חזק
11:10	Yahweh	חזק
14:4	Yahweh	חזק
14:8	Yahweh	חזק
14:17	Yahweh	חזק

Apparently the verbs חזק and קשה have essentially the same meaning, and both are used in the Lord's initial statements of intent (Exod. 4:21; 7:3). The verb כבד has a slightly different nuance ("to make heavy, dull") but the effect is apparently the same: to render the heart unable to respond positively to the Lord. The difference between being *too dull to see the truth* (or one might say with a different metaphor, to be spiritually blind) on the one hand, and seeing the truth but *hardening oneself against it* on the other hand may capture the idea.

The intriguing thing about the pattern of usage, which is really a pattern of behavior, is this: the Lord states his intention to do the hardening but as events unfold we see that Pharaoh, and even at one point his officials, harden their own hearts. This latter fact would seem to suggest their own responsibility for their response to the Lord and what he is doing through Moses.

The narrative sequence invites the conclusion that Pharaoh had certain predispositions that the Lord confirmed by using him as he did. The Lord used him as he was and "raised him up" and "hardened" him for the Lord's purposes. Mysteriously—however all of this may appear—we are responsible for our choices and so the point is made in many of the relevant verses that Pharaoh *hardened his own heart*, even as also the

---

33   Ibid., 904 (קשה), 458 (כבד).

Lord was at work confirming him in this sin. Between the Lord's stated intention to harden Pharaoh's heart (Exod. 4:21; 7:3) and his conclusive hardening of Pharaoh's heart (Exod. 10:1, 20, 27; 11:10; 14:4, 8) and in judgment "the hearts of the Egyptians" (Exod. 14:17), three of the four relevant verses speak of Pharaoh's own hardening of his heart (Exod. 8:15, 32; 9:34), and one speaks of the Lord's doing so (Exod. 9:12). This seems to suggest a process and even some give-and-take in the process, and if so, it seems entirely realistic. The Lord does work in our lives, or he tries to, and the nature and success of his work can very much depend on what we allow or do not allow him to do.[34]

If one looks further ahead in the Old Testament, one finds other occurrences of the idioms just considered: a reference back to the events of Exodus (כבד, 1 Sam. 6:6), a reference to the people's rebelliousness at Meribah and Massah (קשה, Ps. 95:8; cf. Heb. 3:8, 15; 4:7), a warning against hardening one's heart (קשה, Prov. 28:14), a complaint that the Lord is doing so with his own people (קשה, Isa. 63:17), and the observation that Nebuchadnezzar did so (singularly, אמץ, 2 Chron. 36:13).[35]

One sees a similar behavior on the Lord's part in the Conquest with reference to those in the northern half of the land: "For it was the LORD himself who hardened their hearts to wage war against Israel, so that he might destroy them totally, exterminating them without mercy, as the LORD had commanded Moses" (חזק, Josh. 11:20). From this theological datum, in addition to what has appeared in Exodus, we conclude that such hardening of the heart—or psychological interference—was one of the Lord's ways of waging war or preparing the foe for a coming judgment. The Lord waged that war through a prophet-figure, for his words and deeds toward Pharaoh through Moses produced the hardening of which one reads (arguably the Lord's words through Moses were Spirit as they are through any prophet, cf. John 6:63). That is a preliminary act of war on the Lord's part, both against Pharaoh and the gods of Egypt and later (apparently directly by the Spirit and not through a prophet)

---

34 None of these remarks precludes the idea that God shaped Pharaoh from conception to be what he was; cf. further discussion in chapter 7 of volume 3.

35 Daniel also observes of Nebuchadnezzar (in Aramaic), "But when his heart became arrogant and hardened (ותקפת ורוחה) with pride, he was deposed from his royal throne and stripped of his glory" (Dan. 5:20).

against the Canaanites.[36] A comparable phenomenon appears when one considers the episode of Rahab.[37]

AFTERWORD: MOSAIC COVENANT AND EDEN PROMISED LAND

The Mosaic covenant has implicitly both a restorative and an eschatological agenda, yet neither is realized under the Mosaic covenant. Neither can be realized because the answer to the Lord's wish, "Oh, that [lit. "who would give," מִי יִתֵּן] their hearts would be inclined to fear me and keep all my commands always, so that it might go well with them and their children forever!" (Deut. 5:29 [Heb. 5:25]) is the reality, "Yet the LORD has not given [לֹא נָתַן] you a heart to perceive and eyes to see and ears to hear, to this *very* day" (Deut. 29:4 NKJV [29:3 MT]). Nonetheless, the Mosaic covenant (the law) is given as an earnest of a future glory as well as a pedagogue or guardian of Israel until the appearance of the one who would embody and realize the glory.

The restorative agenda is indicated when the Lord's redemption of Israel is portrayed in a way that alludes to God's original creative act:

> In a desert land he found him,
>   in a barren and howling waste.
> He shielded him and cared for him;
>   he guarded him as the apple of his eye,
> like an eagle that stirs up its nest
>   and hovers over its young,
> that spreads its wings to catch them
>   and carries them aloft.
> The LORD alone led him;
>   no foreign god was with him. (Deut. 32:10–12)

---

36 The ancients had their own form of this concept, in which a god might bind the heart of someone who had been rebellious against the emperor/suzerain; cf. *ANETBT*, 64, and earlier, Niehaus, "The Warrior and His God: The Covenant Foundation of History and Historiography," in *Faith, Tradition, and History: Old Testament Historiography in Its Near Eastern Context*, ed. David Baker (Winona Lake, IN: Eisenbrauns 1994), 299–312.

37 Cf. chapter 10. We note also that the Lord can interfere with a person's psyche for good: "And God said to him [i.e., Abimelech] in a dream, 'Yes, I know that you did this in the integrity of your heart. For I also withheld you from sinning against Me; therefore I did not let you touch her [i.e., Sarah]'" (Gen. 20:6 NKJV); cf. 1 Samuel 25:26.

Key terms "wilderness" (תֹהוּ, v. 10) and "hovered" (יְרַחֵף, v. 11; cf. מְרַחֶפֶת, Gen. 1:2) allude to the Lord's Spirit hovering over the *Urstoff* of God's creative process in Genesis 1:2. They point to the idea that Israel would be the Lord's new creation.

Joel, one covenant lawsuit prophet of the Mosaic covenant, compares the now possessed land to Eden, which however is being devoured by the locust army in judgment: "Before them fire devours, behind them a flame blazes. Before them the land is like the Garden of Eden, behind them, a desert waste— nothing escapes them" (Joel 2:3). The phrase "a desert waste" translates a phrase that also employs a word used in Deuteronomy 32:10 (בְּאֶרֶץ מִדְבָּר וּבְתֹהוּ; cf. Joel 2:3, מִדְבַּר שְׁמָמָה). Both point to "chaos": the first to primordial chaos God shaped into cosmos; the second to a chaos that results from sin and judgment.[38] The first alludes to the creation and thus indicates the restorative aspect of Israel's salvation; the second points to eschatological de-creation and indicates part of the Lord's eschatological agenda. The warfare of the "prophet like Moses" defeats the chaos monster Satan and leads to that eschatological Promised Land. The adumbrating warfare of Moses defeats Egypt-Rahab prior to Israel's entry into their typological Promised Land.

---

38 Cf. further on eschatology and de-creation volume 3, chapter 10.

CHAPTER SEVEN

WARFARE BEFORE THE MOSAIC COVENANT:
RAHAB (EGYPT) IN BATTLE

This chapter continues the fourth part of the Major Paradigm: "to war against and defeat his foes." The last chapter took up two aspects of God's warfare: the signs and wonders done by his Spirit against Pharaoh and the gods of Egypt, and the Lord's hardening of Pharaoh's heart, or psychological interference with Pharaoh. The third aspect of God's warfare is considered here: the Lord's final defeat of the Egyptian forces at the Reed Sea. The heading of the present chapter, Rahab in Battle, draws on a poetical identification of Egypt made at several points in the Old Testament.[1]

The Old Testament references to Rahab apparently all have to do with what happened at the Reed Sea crossing. However, we extend the symbolic name to apply to an earlier battle, one that Pharaoh—unwittingly—waged against the newly born covenant mediator prophet, Moses. In fact, Rahab/Egypt/Pharaoh waged two battles against Moses and Israel. The first was the slaughter of the male children. The second was the Reed Sea pursuit—which however by a *peripeteia* became the Lord's final battle against Pharaoh and Egypt. Because these two battles are *started by Pharaoh* they are considered sequentially in this chapter. The first battle, the slaughter of the male children, adumbrates events in the life of the new covenant mediator. We discuss that "battle" first, and then consider the battle that takes place at the Reed Sea—a battle initiated by Pharaoh though it turns out to be the Lord's final and decisive battle against Egypt/Rahab.

---

1   The Rahab (רהב) that forms the subject of this chapter is not the Rahab (רהב) of Joshua 2 but a mythical dragon figure identified symbolically with Egypt.

RAHAB'S FIRST BATTLE AGAINST THE LORD

Pharaoh waged war against the Lord *before he knew it* and before the Lord acted against Egypt by attempting to destroy the newly born covenant mediator without knowledge of his existence. This seems at first an unlikely statement, but the remarkable parallelism of Pharaoh's effort with Herod's attempt to destroy the recently born mediator of the new covenant, Jesus— without knowing the covenant mediator aspect of Jesus' role—invites consideration of both events. If one asks what prompted both kings to commit the wholesale slaughter of innocent children, one finds their stated motives to be different. The remarkable parallelism nonetheless invites us to consider a possible deeper motive—one shared by the two kings but unknown to either of them. Before we discuss their to-them-unknown motivation, we display the parallelism not only between these two events but more broadly between the lives and careers of the two covenant mediators:

Event	Exodus	Matthew
Birth	1:1–9; 2:1–2	1:1–25
Persecution (all males)	1:8–22	2:16–18
Transport from persecution	2:3–10	2:13–14
Flight from royal peril	2:11–25	2:13–14
Return to God's people	4:18–28	2:19–23
Identity of prophet	3:1–4:17	3:13–17 ("my son")
		4:1–11 (temptations)
		4:12–16 (Isa 9:1–2)
Call of followers	4:29–30a	4:18–22
Initial signs and wonders	4:30b–31; 7:8–12:30	4:23–25
Torah on mountain	20:1–23:19	5:1–7:29
Torah + signs and wonders	25:1–39:42	8:1–25:46
Transfiguration on/from mountain	34:29–35	17:1–9
Covenant institution	24:8	26:28 (blood of cov.)
		27:32–50 (crucifixion)
Covenant ratification meal	24:9–11	26:17–30

Event	Exodus	Matthew
Consecration of temple	40:34–35	[Acts 2:1–4]
Ongoing Presence	40:36–38	28:20

We will have occasion to revisit this schema when we consider the new covenant.[2] For now we focus on the issue of Pharaoh's warfare against the newborn covenant mediator and its parallelism to Herod's behavior much later.

The most remarkable thing about the two cases—the one that prompts a comparison—is the attempt by each king to kill an infant who will be a major covenant mediator in God's special grace program. Neither king is aware of this, although Herod does have the idea that his kingship is threatened by one born to be king according to Micah's prophecy—"But you, Bethlehem, in the land of Judah, / are by no means least among the rulers of Judah; / for out of you will come a ruler who will shepherd my people Israel" (Matt. 2:6; cf. Micah 5:2, 4). Pharaoh's motivation is couched in broader terms: "Come, we must deal shrewdly with them or they will become even more numerous and, if war breaks out, will join our enemies, fight against us, and leave the country" (Exod. 1:10). The common ground, however, is that each king imagines the power he holds—his security—is at risk. Each one tries to eliminate the risk by slaughtering the male children (Exod. 1:22; Matt. 2:16).

Pharaoh has no idea that Moses, the future liberator of Israel from Egyptian oppression and future covenant mediator between the Lord and Israel, is among the male infants he would slaughter.[3] Herod has no

---

2   One consideration will be the strong indication offered by these data that the book of Exodus—as a record the life and redeeming work (with signs and wonders and divine *torah*) of the Lord's covenant mediator, Moses—offers the first exemplar of what would later be called the Gospel genre.

3   We affirm this in accord with the biblical narrative, and *pace* a scholar who is still often cited by liberal scholars, Hugo Gressmann, *Mose und seine Zeit: Ein Kommentar zu den Mose-Sagen* (Göttingen: Vandenhoeck & Ruprecht, 1913). Gressmann's reconstruction of the formation of Exodus 1:1–2:10 includes some bizarre speculations, of which his account of the birth narrative affords a good example: "Von hier aus läßt sich nun die ürsprungliche Exposition der Mose-Sage mit Sicherheit rekonstruieren. Der Pharao fürchtet nicht die Übervölkerung, sondern einzig und allein den Mose, wie noch aus der gegenwärtigen Fassung deutlich zu erkennen ist. Irgendwoher hat er erfahren, sei es aus einem Traum oder aus einer Weissagung, daß in allernächster Zeit ein Hebräisches Weib eines Knaben genesen werde, der bestimmt sei, der gefährlicher Gegner des Pharaos zu werden und him Thron und Leben zu rauben, Darum beschränkt sich der Befehl auf die

idea that the Son of God, who will set his people free from sin and be the mediator of a new covenant, and whose kingdom is *not of this world*, is the one he fears and targets. But the parallelism of the targets and even the mass slaughter meant to destroy the targets suggest a possible source of motivation beyond the kings involved. The first sin in Eden gave legal entrée into the world to Satan and his angels so that he became "the god of this world" (2 Cor. 4:4) and he is also effectively "the ruler of the kingdom of the air, the spirit who is now at work in those who are disobedient" (Eph. 2:2b). If that spirit can be at work in "those who are disobedient" (among whom those Paul addresses were once numbered, Eph. 2:2a)—who were, one might say, fairly ordinary sinners—how much more may he have been at work in Pharaoh, who fancied himself an incarnate god and was thus an early form of Antichrist, or in Herod?

If one dares to consider a more contemporary issue implied by the slaughter of the infants, one may also ask whether the slaughter of infants generally by means of abortion has any resonance with the biblical data just considered. This topic alone could easily occupy a book and we cannot hope to address it fully. On the other hand, it seems remiss not to raise it at all, especially since there are points of contact. Dr. Andrew White in a paper comparing the ancient practice of child sacrifice and the (ancient as well as modern) practice of abortion has noted some suggestive parallels, among which are the issues of control and security discussed above.[4] Child sacrifice was sometimes practiced to gain the

---

Knaben, weil Mädchen überhaupt nicht in Frage kommen, und darum ergeht er zunächst an die Hebammen, da Mose noch nicht geboren ist (anders in der Geburtssage Jesu!)," 5; author's translation: "From here on, the original explication of the Moses saga may be reconstructed with certainty. Pharaoh fears, not overpopulation, but uniquely and solely Moses, as is still clearly discernable from the present version. From somehere he has learned, be it from a dream or from a prophecy, that in the immediate future a Hebrew woman would give birth to a boy who was destined to become the dangerous opponent of Pharaoh and deprive him of throne and life. For that reason the command limits itself to the boys because girls do not enter the question at all, and consequently it is issued to the nursemaids since Moses has not yet been born (differently in the birth legend of Jesus!)" To quote the heroine of the recent television comedy-crime-drama series *Castle*, "Here I am looking for evidence—and all I had to do was just make something up" ("Ghosts," first aired 4/27/2009).

4 Cf. the article by Andrew White, MD, "Abortion and the Ancient Practice of Child Sacrifice," http://bmei.org/jbem/volume1/num2/white_abortion_and_the_ancient _practice_of_child_sacrifice.pdf. All of the data and quotes offered below are taken from this online article.

favor of the gods during a crisis—in other words to assure the security of the state or of an individual. Sometimes it was done to assure the economic security of a family. As Stager and Wolff (cited by White) note,

> Among the social elite of Punic Carthage the institution of child sacrifice may have assisted in the consolidation and maintenance of family wealth. One hardly needed several children parceling up the patrimony into smaller and smaller pieces . . . for the artisans and commoners of Carthage, ritual infanticide could provide a hedge against poverty."[5]

White also mentions the sacrifice of defective children in hopes that they would be followed by children with no birth defects, and he parallels the sacrifice of the unwanted fruit of sacred prostitution with the abortion of unwanted children that result from premarital or extramarital sexual activity. White recognizes he has written "At the risk on the one hand of pointing out obvious parallels and on the other hand of suggesting parallels which some may say are forced." Both risks are probably worth taking because the data provide significant parallels and are thought provoking, and the topic is so important.

I would add one thought that White did not raise in his article, but it touches upon abortion, child sacrifice, and, I believe, implicitly on the wholesale slaughter commanded by Pharaoh and later by Herod. If indeed the spirit at work in those kings was that of "the ruler of the air" (Eph. 2:2)—and we know that Satan was "a murderer from the beginning" (John 8:44)—the same spirit may be the one at work in the child sacrifices and abortions just considered. The reason for the death penalty for murder, as God first announced that penalty, was that "in the image of God / has God made mankind" (NIV, or better, "the human" [הָאָדָם], Gen. 9:6b). God in the Noahic covenant defines murder as destruction of the *imago Dei*. The reason the enemy urges such atrocities as those noted above may be the same: humans are made in God's image. Satan cannot really "get at" God. The closest he can come to hurting God is to maim or destroy the image of God, and any way that "murderer from the beginning" can contrive to do so, he may attempt. It is worth noting that in his attempts Satan cannot be hindered by human culture or institutions alone.[6]

---

5   Cf. L. E. Stager and S. R. Wolff, "Child Sacrifice at Carthage: Religious Rite or Population Control?" *BAR* (Jan/Feb 1984): 45.

6   P. G. Mosca, *Child Sacrifice in Canaanite and Israelite Religion*, PhD dissertation,

RAHAB'S SECOND AND LAST BATTLE AGAINST THE LORD

Pharaoh attempts one last battle against the Lord and Israel at the Reed Sea. The Lord turns that attempt into his own last battle against Pharaoh and Egypt before he leads his people to Sinai for the cutting of a new covenant. One aspect of God's warfare appeared in the previous chapter: the Lord's confirmatory hardening of Pharaoh's heart for the battle of Exodus 14. In this chapter we consider (1) the symbolic value of the Reed Sea battle, and then (2) the outline of its events and also (3) the Lord's projected agenda beyond it.

The Reed Sea Event and Its Symbolic Value

As one considers what happened at the Reed Sea when the Lord directed Moses to raise his staff with the result that the waters parted, the first thing to understand is that there is no warfare here against the sea. As David says, "The earth is the LORD's, and everything in it, / the world, and all who live in it; / for he founded it on the seas / and established it on the waters" (Ps. 24:1–2). Because the Lord created the heavens and the earth and everything in them he has no need to engage any created element in combat in order to make it to do his will.[7]

The sea is not the enemy; Egypt is the enemy. But Egypt *is* elsewhere characterized poetically/figuratively as a *sea dragon* or *sea monster* of some sort. The Lord through Isaiah comments on "Egypt, whose help is utterly useless. / Therefore I call her / Rahab the Do-Nothing" (Isa. 30:7). The identity of Rahab at this point in Isaiah is unclear to a modern

---

Harvard University, 1975, 273–74 (as cited by White), raises the following questions about the Carthaginians, "How could a culture so well developed morally, intellectually and materially tolerate so 'abominable' a custom? How could a sophisticated people sanction what seems to be such a barbaric practice for so long a time? How at the most visceral and critical level could human parents bring about the destruction of their own child?" One could raise similar questions about later cultures, including Germany under the Third Reich—a nation still in many ways at the cultural zenith of the West, in, for example, music, philosophy, linguistics, technology—and biblical studies!—a nation that developed jet fighters with stealth technology and was, in 1945, within a year of developing an atom bomb (with a *transatlantic stealth jet bomber* to deliver it), while at the same time putting Jews and other "undesirables" to death in concentration camps, making lampshades of their skin, etc. The culture—the civilization—in which people may pride themselves provides no sure safeguard against the worst possible sins.

7   Cf. further discussion in chapter 4 of volume 3.

reader, but the Old Testament elsewhere portrays Rahab as a sea monster.[8] Job remarks:

> The pillars of the heavens quake,
>   aghast at his rebuke.
> By his power he churned up the sea;
>   by his wisdom he cut Rahab to pieces.
> By his breath the skies became fair;
>   his hand pierced the gliding serpent. (Job 26:11–13)[9]

The parallelism of the verse suggests the serpent nature of Rahab:

a	b
By his power	he churned up the sea

a′	b′
By his breath	the skies became fair

and

a	b
by his wisdom	he cut Rahab to pieces

a′	b′
his hand	pierced the gliding serpent

The verses celebrate the Lord's power over all nature and hence over any sentient creature that would oppose him. In this case, the apparent foe is Rahab // "the gliding serpent" (b // b').[10] The Lord's "breath" (Job 26:12a) is instrumental and decisive. The word "breath" also means "spirit" or "Spirit"

---

8 Cf., however, Isaiah 51:9–10 and discussion on pages 216–17.

9 Cf. also Job 9:13 in an apparent allusion to the exodus: "God does not restrain his anger; / even the cohorts of Rahab cowered at his feet."

10 We apply the letters b and b' to the whole half verse, understanding that a more detailed analysis is possible, in which "He cut . . . to pieces" could be "b" (// "he pierced"),

(רוח), and the same agent is highlighted in Exodus 15:8: "By the blast of your nostrils / the waters piled up." The word translated "blast" (NIV) could also be translated "breath" and is the same Hebrew word found in Job 26:12a (רוח inevitably evoking the Spirit. Also noteworthy is the description "the gliding serpent," evocative of a description found in Isaiah:

> In that day,
> the LORD will punish with his sword—
> his fierce, great and powerful sword—
> Leviathan the gliding serpent,
> Leviathan the coiling serpent;
> he will slay the monster of the sea. (Isa. 27:1)

In both Job 26:13 and Isaiah 27:1 the serpent is a "gliding serpent" (נחש ברח). One could say all serpents glide and are thus gliding, but there is a larger resonance between these passages because both speak of extraordinarily powerful sea monsters hostile to God. They accord with the serpent idea first seen in Genesis 3 and later given ontological definition as "that ancient serpent called the devil, or Satan, who leads the whole world astray" (Rev. 12:9).

Much later David can praise the Lord in ways that recall the Reed Sea battle and he does not fail to note that the Lord is the creator and rules over the sea:

> You rule over the surging sea;
> when its waves mount up, you still them.
> You crushed Rahab like one of the slain;
> with your strong arm you scattered your enemies.
> The heavens are yours, and yours also the earth;
> you founded the world and all that is in it.
> You created the north and the south;
> Tabor and Hermon sing for joy at your name.
> Your arm is endowed with power;
> your hand is strong, your right hand exalted. (Ps. 89:9–13)

We are told the Lord crushed Rahab and reminded that he is the Creator, and the two points are related. Because the Lord created all things,

---

and consequently "Rahab" would be "c" (// "the gliding serpent"). Such detailed analysis is not necessary, however, for the point being made here.

he is ontologically superior to and also more powerful than all things. Because of that, no created thing can oppose him and triumph over him. The connection of creation and redemption—also of God as creator and redeemer—is a recurrent theme in the Bible. Latterly, it marks the start of John's Gospel.[11] The verses of Psalm 89 present a specimen case of the Lord's ability as creator to redeem his people from a great and powerful foe. They also evoke terms found in Exodus 15. The Lord scattered his enemies with his "strong arm" (lit. "with the arm of your strength," בזרוע עזך , Ps. 89:10b; cf. עז, Exod. 15:2). David says of him: "Your right hand is exalted" (תרום ימינך, Ps. 89:13) and Moses says the Lord's "right hand" was instrumental in destroying the Egyptians (ימינך, Exod. 15:6).[12]

Isaiah, who called Egypt "Rahab the Do-Nothing" (Isa. 30:7) in mockery of her uselessness as an ally, also recalls the Lord's triumph over Rahab at the Reed Sea as he appeals to the Lord for present help:

> Awake! Awake! Clothe yourself with strength,
>   O arm of the LORD;
> awake, as in days gone by,
>   as in generations of old.
> Was it not you who cut Rahab to pieces,
>   who pierced that monster through?
> Was it not you who dried up the sea,
>   the waters of the great deep,
> who made a road in the depths of the sea
>   so that the redeemed might cross over? (Isa. 51:9–10)

Recalling that great event of deliverance, Isaiah uses terms he has also used of a future deliverance: the release of God's people from Babylonian exile and their return to their homeland ("Was it not you who dried up [המחרבת] the sea," Isa. 51:10a; cf. "who says to the watery deep, 'Be dry' [חרבי]," Isa. 44:27).

The two nations Rahab and Babylon, in which the Lord's people experienced oppression and want of a homeland, will one day nonetheless themselves be the objects of God's salvation:

---

11   Cf. discussion in Jeffrey J. Niehaus, *God at Sinai: Covenant and Theophany in the Bible and Ancient Near East* (Grand Rapids: Zondervan, 1995), 286–87.

12   He also alludes to a later event, namely, as we will argue, the Korahite rebellion: "You stretched out your right hand [ימינך] / and the earth swallowed your enemies" (Exod. 15:12, author's translation).

> Glorious things are said of you,
>   O city of God:
> "I will record Rahab and Babylon
>   among those who acknowledge me—
> Philistia too, and Tyre, along with Cush—
>   and will say, 'This one was born in Zion.'"
> Indeed, of Zion it will be said,
>   "This one and that one were born in her,
> and the Most High himself will establish her."
> The LORD will write in the register of the peoples:
>   "This one was born in Zion."
> As they make music they will sing,
>   "All my fountains are in you." (Ps. 87:3–7)

The birth in Zion is the new birth Jesus proclaims to Nicodemus, and the fountains are the Spirit who gives the new birth, and both are said to eventuate from Zion because it is from there that the *torah* of the new covenant goes forth and it is to that place that the nations will *stream* (cf. Isa. 2:2–3; Micah 4:1–2). In addition to that interim fulfillment, the poem may be seen to imply the heavenly Jerusalem and the Lord's throne/temple presence as the source of life-giving waters (Rev. 22:1–2).[13] The psalmist transmits God's ultimate saving intention for all people—the God who does not desire the death of a sinner—and if the Adamic and Noahic covenants have thus far provided a context within which that salvation can be worked out, the Mosaic covenant soon provides the challenging standard and lessons conducive to that great salvation.

Pharaoh's Pursuit and Yahweh's "Rear Guard" Action

As we consider the topic of Pharaoh's last attempt to have his way with Israel at the Reed Sea apart from its symbolic value, there are several observations that would be useful to make, one regarding the quality of the Egyptian pursuit, one regarding the quality of the Lord's response to his foes, and one regarding the Lord's forecast objective. All of these are present in the poetical account of the Reed Sea event in Exodus 15. It has been recognized that the poem, Exodus 15:1–18, presents the outline of the Reed Sea events as a

---

13 Cf. the Eden-temple/river/tree of life complex (Gen. 2:1–10; Ezek. 47:1–12; Rev. 12:1–2), to which the Isaiah/Micah synoptic prophecies seem to allude. Cf. the "already not yet" in John 7:38–39. For further discussion, see chapter 16.

chiastic structure. One methodological point to make before demonstrating a chiastic structure, especially one in material as extensive as this poem, is the importance of labeling the corresponding chiastic elements in a way that is both true to their identity and illustrative of the parallels that really are there. As a preface to the covenant making at Sinai, we present an overview of that chiastic structure followed by comments on the issues noted:

Exodus 15	Theme	Chiasm
1b	Yahweh highly exalted	A
2	Yahweh as salvation—salvation promise in Canaan	B
3–5	Yahweh as prevailing against Pharaoh	C
6–8	Yahweh's shatters Egypt (land from which)	D
9	Foe's attitude toward Yahweh's people (persecution)	E
10	Yahweh's response to foe—sunk in the sea	F
11	Yahweh's praise: incomparable among gods	G (HINGE)
12	Yahweh's response to foe—swallowed by earth	F'
13	Attitude of Yahweh toward his people (led them in love)	E'
14–15	Yahweh's victory terrifies nations (land to which)	D'
16	Yahweh as prevailing against the nations	C'
17	Yahweh will realize salvation promise in Canaan	B'
18	Yahweh as reigning forever and ever	A'

The poem's overall structure begins and ends with the exaltation of the Lord (v. 1) and his exalted reign (v. 18). The hinge verse ("G") also has to do with Yahweh's exaltation—he is unique and incomparable among the gods—and so although we labeled verse 11 with the letter "G" in order to emphasize its distinctive hinge role in the poem, we could just as well have labeled it an "A" element because of its fundamental affinity with verses 1b and 18 (labeled "A" and "A'" above). The concept Yahweh as exalted thus forms the beginning, middle, and end of the poem. That is fully appropriate because he is truly exalted, he has shown himself by the center of the poem to be incomparable among the so-called gods, and he does truly reign forever.

Quality of the Egyptian Pursuit

The Lord's supremacy over the gods is shown by the poem's portrayal of the Egyptian pursuit and the attitude it shows on the one hand, and the Lord's response to it on the other. We consider first the Egyptian pursuit, and in particular the attitude shown by expressions the poem attributes to the Egyptian forces:

> The enemy boasted,
>   "I will pursue, I will overtake them.
> I will divide the spoils;
>   I will gorge myself on them.
> I will draw my sword
>   and my hand will destroy them." (Exod. 15:9)

The enemy boasts of six things he will do to Israel and the operative indicator is not the destructiveness of the intent but its *unfulfilled purpose*. All of the six verbs are in the imperfect tense indicating intent, but also indicating actions not completed. And those actions never are completed because Egypt lacks the power—the *authority*—to complete them. It has been noted before: all authority comes from the Lord, and although the Lord gave Egypt the authority to oppress his people for some time and for his own purposes, he did not grant Egypt the authority to destroy them. He allowed the oppression in order to prepare in them sufficient frustration to welcome the Lord's deliverer (even though he had to "prove" himself by signs and wonders—a phenomenon noticeable also in the career of the much greater covenant mediator, Jesus). Similarly, perhaps, God chose a time that was propitious in other ways to send his Son.[14]

The Quality of the Lord's Response to His Foes

The Lord's response to the Egyptian pursuit shows where the true authority in this episode of deliverance rests.

---

14 Cf. volume 3, chapter 1 and discussion of Matthew's genealogy.

> But you blew with your breath,
> and the sea covered them.
> They sank like lead
> in the mighty waters. (Exod. 15:10)

As contrasted with the six verbs in the imperfect used to characterize the Egyptian presumption, only one verb is used of the Lord: "you blew with your breath" (v. 10a). The word for breath, in this case, is the word that also means spirit or Spirit (רוח), and it is probably right to see a play on that concept in this verse as also in the flanking verse, "By the blast (רוח) of your nostrils the waters piled up" (v. 8a). Elsewhere I have noted the identification of wind and the breath of a god; the comparison here is not unknown in the ancient Near East.[15] Be that as it may, all the Lord has to do is send his wind/Spirit to make the waters of the Reed Sea produce a *decisive result*. Accordingly, the verbs describing the resultant actions of the water and of the Egyptians are also in the perfect tense ("the sea covered them," "they sank," v. 10b, c).[16] Similarly, the verbs of verse 8 are in the perfect tense: "By the blast of your nostrils / the waters piled up. / The surging waters stood up like a wall; / the deep waters congealed in the heart of the sea." Taken together, verses 8–10 form a chiastic pattern in which the Lord's use of the water against Egyptian ambition flanks the statement of Egyptian intent:[17]

Exodus	Theme	Element
15:8	Two lines: Yahweh's control of the water	A
15:9	Three lines: The Egyptian intent	B
15:10	Two lines: Yahweh's use of water to destroy them	A′

Both the subject matter (Yahweh's authority over and use of the water) and the verb tense (the prefect) create a parallel or echoing quality between verses 8 and 10 such that they stand apart, with regard to theme

---

15   Cf. Niehaus, *God at Sinai*, 325–26.

16   Tenses in the rest of the poem vary, as typically in Hebrew and, for example, Ugaritic poetry, but the contrast between the imperfects of verse 9 and the perfects of verses 8 and 10, juxtaposed as they are by their subject matter, naturally strike a reader and produce the effect under discussion.

17   I use the term "lines" instead of giving a detailed poetical analysis according to cola (which is not needed to illustrate the contrast and chiasm) in this analysis.

and verb tense, from verse 9 and thus flank it. Not to make too much of a structural nuance, it does nonetheless seem that the related verses (vv. 8 and 10) that show Yahweh's power over and use of the water flank (or outflank!) the Egyptians and their pretentions, just as the Lord used the water to destroy them from both sides—to surround and cover/enclose them with water, as verses 8 and 10 surround and contain verse 9.[18]

This section was titled "The Quality of the Lord's Response to His Foes," and certainly the foe immediately in view is the army of Egypt. However, the verse that complements this one in the chiastic structure of the poem, Exodus 15:12, mentions another action by the Lord against a foe, and it does not seem to be the same action or the same foe just considered: "You stretched out your right hand, / and the earth swallowed up your enemies" (Exod. 15:12, author's translation).[19] Unless this verse is presenting the drowning of Egyptian forces in a very—and unexpectedly—figurative manner (in which their drowning is portrayed as being swallowed by the earth), the verse does not seem to make a lot of sense in its context. There was, however, another event in which the Lord's foes *were* swallowed up by the earth: the challenge by Korah and his allies often called the Korahite rebellion. Moses gave an account of the rebellion in Numbers 16 and later reflected on it in Deuteronomy 11. In the later reflection, Moses also recalled what happened at the Reed Sea. A comparison of the recollections in Deuteronomy 11 with the relevant verses in Exodus 15 reveals parallels in both the sequence of events and the terminology. The parallels may clarify exactly what the poet and

---

18   Cf. the same "A-B-A'" device in the prophecy of a prophet like Moses, a prophet who will "contain" the glory (Deut. 18:15–19), *God at Sinai*, 224–25.

19   The NIV does a disservice by translating these verses in the present tense because that translation obscures the event in question. We note that the NIV also misleads its readers by titling the extensive poem, Exodus 15:1–18, as "The Song of Moses *and Miriam*," since the text clearly tells us that Moses produced the song (15:1–18). Cf. "The Song of Moses" (ESV); "The Song of Moses and Israel" (NASB); "The Song of Moses" (NKJV), etc. Miriam produced the *one-verse* song introduced in Exodus 15:20 and presented in verse 21: "Then Miriam the prophetess, Aaron's sister, took a timbrel in her hand, and all the women followed her, with timbrels and dancing. Miriam sang to them: 'Sing to the LORD, / for he is highly exalted. / Both horse and driver / he has hurled into the sea.'" The NIV does the same sort of thing with what it calls "The Song of Deborah" in Judges 5 (where, however, as a translation it has more company), whereas we are told that "on that day *Deborah and Barak* son of Abinoam *sang this song*" (Judg. 5:1, emphases added); cf. discussion, chapter 6 of volume 3.

prophet was describing in Exodus 15:12. First, the relevant material from the primary account of the Korahite rebellion:

> Korah son of Izhar, the son of Kohath, the son of Levi, and certain Reu-
> benites—Dathan and Abiram, sons of Eliab, and On son of Peleth—be-
> came insolent and rose up against Moses. . . . Then Moses said, "This is
> how you will know that the LORD has sent me to do all these things—that
> it was not my idea: If these men die a natural death and suffer the fate of
> all mankind, then the Lord has not sent me. But if the LORD brings about
> something totally new, and the ground opens its mouth and swallows
> them and all that belongs to them, and they go down alive into the realm
> of the dead, then you will know that these men have treated the LORD
> with contempt." As soon as he finished saying all this, the ground under
> them split apart and the earth opened its mouth and swallowed them
> and their households, and all those associated with Korah, and all their
> possessions. (Num. 16:1–2, 28–32, author's translation)

Some important terms are used here—key because they bid fair to unlock the mystery of Exodus 15:12. The terms are "earth" (אֶרֶץ, v. 32) and "swallowed" (בלע, v. 32). We note in passing that the verb "create" (ברא, v. 30) is the same verb used in Genesis 1:1, and as many have noted, it is used only with God as subject and indicates a creative act only he can perform. In this case, the act is one of judgment that employs the created earth under divine impetus (which one could also suggest is the work of the Spirit, who undergirds all creation).

Moses recalls this event in Deuteronomy 11 as he admonishes the people to remember that it was not their children but they themselves who saw what the Lord did to his foes:

> Remember today that your children were not the ones who saw and ex-
> perienced the discipline of the LORD your God: his majesty, his mighty
> hand, his outstretched arm; the signs he performed and the things he
> did in the heart of Egypt, both to Pharaoh king of Egypt and to his whole
> country; what he did to the Egyptian army, to its horses and chariots,
> how he overwhelmed them with the waters of the Red Sea as they were
> pursuing you, and how the LORD brought lasting ruin on them. It was
> not your children who saw what he did for you in the wilderness until
> you arrived at this place, and what he did to Dathan and Abiram, sons of
> Eliab the Reubenite, when the earth opened its mouth right in the middle
> of all Israel and swallowed them up with their households, their tents and

every living thing that belonged to them. But it was your own eyes that saw all these great things the LORD has done. (Deut. 11:2–7)

Moses urges the people to recall the *magnalia Dei* in one of his last great speeches to them before they cross into the Promised Land under Joshua's prophetic leadership. Such exhortation and *rhetorical* recall are the best he has to offer them because the covenant under which they had come to live, unlike the new covenant, did not endow them with the Spirit of whom Jesus says, "The Advocate, the Holy Spirit, whom the Father will send in my name, will teach you all things and *will remind you of everything I have said to you*" (John 14:26, emphasis added). Moses' review of the Lord's past works is significant for the matter under discussion because of the sequence of the portrayed events and because of the terminology used. The data are as follows:

Deuteronomy	Event	Terms	Element
11:3–4	Yahweh's deeds against Egypt	י‍ם סוף	A
11:5	Yahweh's deeds in the desert = praise		B
11:6	Yahweh's deeds against Dathan and Abiram	ארץ, בלע	A′

The outline above parallels the sequence of events portrayed in Exodus 15 along with the relevant terminology:

Exodus	Event	Terms	Element
15:8–10	Yahweh's deeds against Egypt	סוף, ים	A
15:11	Yahweh's praise (incomparability)		B
15:12	Yahweh's deeds against [Dathan and Abiram]	ארץ, בלע	A′

The overall parallel structure, with two A elements using the terms ים and סוף, and two A′ elements using the terms ארץ and בלע, indicates that the same sequence of events is portrayed in both cases. The natural conclusion then is that Moses alludes to the Korahite rebellion in Exodus 15:12.

One may object that the poem is introduced as something produced by Moses when he and the people crossed the Reed Sea so that verse 12 could not be referring to the Korahite rebellion that took place later, and that is the way translations usually present it: "*Then* [presumably just after crossing the Reed Sea] Moses and the Israelites sang this song to the LORD" (Exod. 15:1 NIV; cf. NKJV, ESV, NASB, CJB, etc.) However, the Hebrew word translated "then" [אָז] can also mean "that being the case"—in other words, once something has occurred, however long ago it may have occurred.[20] That understanding opens the door to a later date for the production of the "Song of Moses" (Exod. 15:1–18), such that Moses could have composed it after the Korahite rebellion reported in Numbers 16.[21]

The "Song of the Sea" thus gives us a sweeping historical review not only of the Lord's triumph over the pretensions of Egypt but also over falsehood among his own covenant people—one might think of the later and more fully revealed truth of the new covenant that demolishes "every pretension that sets itself up against the knowledge of God" (2 Cor. 10:5). One can see in Exodus 15, as in the plagues of Egypt, those demonstrations of the Lord's insuperable holiness. The same holiness later appears in a more physically benign way that destroys the pretensions of falsehood (more physically benign, but equally destructive of the enemy's work) in the ministry of the new covenant.

The Lord's Forecast Objective

The Lord not only undoes whatever is false and would pretend to divine status (like Pharaoh) and what is untrue and pretends to a prophetic status that God never bestowed in his kingdom administration (like the Korahites), he also prepares and accomplishes salvation for his people. Thus his deliverance is always a two-sided coin. One side is the destruction or the defeat of evil, and that leads to the other side—the deliverance of people from the bondage of evil. The "Song of Moses" displays this pattern.

The poetical progress of the "Song of Moses" illustrates a thematic progress from the destruction of evil to the realization of salvation promises in Canaan in a particular way. The poetical lines in the second half of the poem—the half that deals increasingly with the realization of the

---

20 Cf. *BDB*, 23 (1.c and 2). Cf. the same word in Psalm 2:5: "*That being the case* [אָז], he will speak to them in his wrath" (author's translation).

21 The "Song of Miriam," on the other hand (v. 21), is clearly portrayed as something produced by the prophetess immediately after they had crossed the Reed Sea and witnessed the destruction of the Egyptian forces.

promises—are for the most part longer than those in the first half of the poem. One can illustrate this by using the terminology developed by Frank Cross according to which a "line" or segment (colon) of four to six syllables is termed *breve*, and a colon that is longer is termed *longum*.[22] According to that device, Exodus 15:1b–12, which deals with the Lord's triumph over his foes—and so, past events—consists almost entirely of cola one would term *breve* (with the notable exception of v. 2, which is an expression of faith—"The LORD is my strength and my defense; / he has become my salvation. / He is my God, and I will praise him, / my father's God, and I will exalt him"—and consists of long cola for emphasis). Beginning with verse 13, one finds a transition from *breve* to *longum* in the cola as the topic shifts to how the Lord will lead his people to his "holy dwelling" (v. 13d). All the subsequent cola qualify for the *longum* designation and they carry us through the anguish that will grip all the nations, including Philistia (v. 14), Edom, Moab, and Canaan (v. 16), until the Lord's purchased people pass by (v. 16). The Lord will lead his people to the mountain of his inheritance and plant them there—"the place, Lord, you made for your dwelling, / the sanctuary, Lord, your hands established." (v. 17). The poem concludes (v. 18) with the expansive declaration, "The Lord reigns for ever and ever," which we take as a unicolon (*longum*).[23]

The overall pattern of lengthening cola as the poem progresses from the defeat of foes to the prospect of the Promised Land and the Lord's planting of his people on his holy mountain—evocative of what has been called the covenant formula—even though the latter will also involve conflict with foes, produces a tone of expansiveness appropriate to the prospects Israel may now be on the brink of enjoying thanks to the *magnalia Dei* of which they have been the beneficiaries. That future will also involve a literal expansion into enemy territory, but that is probably not the point here. Rather, the poem is in this formal way celebratory not

---

22 Cf. Frank M. Cross, "Studies in the Structure of Hebrew Verse: The Prosody of the Psalm of Jonah," in *The Quest for the Kingdom of God: Studies in Honor of George E. Mendenhall* , ed. H. B. Huffmon, F. A. Spina, and A. R. W. Green (Winona Lake, IN: Eisenbrauns, 1983), 159. Cf. earlier, F. M. Cross Jr. and D. N. Freedman, *Studies in Ancient Yahwistic Poetry*, SBL Dissertation Series 21 (Missoula, MT: Scholars Press, 1975).

23 One could, alternatively, take it as two cola (thus, *breve/breve*), and if that is correct we have a sort of winding down of the poem in a relatively gentle denouement, which would then echo the *breve/breve/breve/breve*) of 15:1b.

only of Israel's recent liberation, but even more of the broadened prospects—the "great expectations"—that await them.

With regard to those prospects certain terms are used that resonate both with the Lord's past triumph and with the subsequent historiography of the Conquest. Moses declares that in the future, because of the Lord's advance into Canaan with his people, "By the power of your arm they will be as still as a stone" (v. 16a). This echoes the way that, as the Lord's right hand shattered the enemy (v. 6), "they sank to the depths like a stone" (v. 5). Perhaps more important is the promise "the people of Canaan will melt away [נמגו]; / terror and dread will fall on them [ותפל עליהם אימתה ופחד]" (vv. 15b–16a). Joshua 2 shows the fulfillment of this promise when Rahab tells the spies that, after her compatriots heard the report of Yahweh's deeds against Pharaoh and Sihon and Og (Josh. 2:10), "I know the LORD has given you the land, and that terror of you has fallen on us [נפלה אימתכם עלינו], and that all the inhabitants of the land have melted away [נמגו] before you" (Josh. 2:9, author's translation). After the Reed Sea event, the Lord promises not only that terror and dread will "fall on" the enemies (Exod. 15:16a), but that "*I will send my terror* [אימתי] *ahead of you* and throw into confusion every nation you encounter" (Exod. 23:27, emphasis added). We will revisit this aspect of divine interference in the psyche of a foe when we consider the Conquest in greater detail. When we do so we will examine once again the likely identity of the angel the Lord promises to send ahead of his people in the Conquest.[24]

AFTERWORD AND PREFACE: TWO ABRAHAMIC PROMISES FULFILLED BEFORE THE CONQUEST

The Lord promised Abram numerous offspring, a land for that offspring, kings born of his descendants, and a blessing to all the nations. God's irruptive actions up to the point of the Reed Sea crossing have fulfilled *one* promise of the Abrahamic covenant, the promise of judgment on the nation that would enslave them. The covenant mediator prophet, Moses, was instrumental in this work. The Lord had promised Abram numerous offspring as well, and this promise was also fulfilled in Moses' lifetime. Brief comment on these promises follows.

The Lord had promised Abraham that he would judge the nation of

---

24   Cf. Niehaus, *God at Sinai*, 191–95; cf. chapter 3.

their enslavement: "I will punish the nation they serve as slaves, and afterward they will come out with great possessions" (Gen. 15:14). When he commissioned Moses, the Lord declared:

> "I also established my covenant with them to give them the land of Canaan, where they lived as aliens. Moreover, I have heard the groaning of the Israelites, whom the Egyptians are enslaving, and I have remembered my covenant. Therefore, say to the Israelites: 'I am the LORD, and I will bring you out from under the yoke of the Egyptians. I will free you from being slaves to them, and I will redeem you with an outstretched arm and with *mighty acts of judgment*. I will take you as my own people, and I will be your God. Then you will know that I am the LORD your God, who brought you out from under the yoke of the Egyptians.'" (Exod. 6:4–7)

The Lord fulfilled the promise of numerous offspring before their entry into the Promised Land. The Lord had promised Abram: "Look up at the heavens and count the stars—if indeed you can count them. . . . So shall your offspring be" (Gen. 15:5). What was arguably true when Israel still lived in Goshen (cf. Exod. 1:7, "the Israelites were exceedingly fruitful; they multiplied greatly, increased in numbers and became so numerous that the land was filled with them") was apparently even more the case when Israel stood on the plains of Moab. Just before the Conquest, Moses is able to tell the people, "The LORD your God has increased your numbers so that today you are as many as the stars in the sky" (Deut. 1:10).[25]

There was no doubt Lord would fulfill these promises—their fulfillment was present to him and past to him before he created the universe. But in addition to the judgment and exodus promises to Moses—which have been fulfilled—we review two important points. The first is that the Lord refers to his "covenant" (singular) *with the fathers*, a clear indication that the Abrahamic covenant that contained these and other promises and was reaffirmed with Isaac and Jacob is one covenant and not two covenants. The second point is that the Lord's promises to Abraham are the basis for what the Lord has done and will also do for Israel, and of course the true foundation for all of this is the Lord himself: he is a faithful witness to himself and he amens his own nature and all that comes

---

25 As has been recognized, the fact that Israel had been "exceedingly fruitful" and had "multiplied" alludes to the original creation mandate (Gen. 1:28), and hints at the Lord's commitment to the ultimate fulfillment of that mandate by means of a redeemed humanity.

forth from it. So the counsel that is ironic in the mouth of Polonius is nonetheless fulfilled in the Lord:

> This above all: to thine own self be true,
> And it must follow, as the night the day,
> Thou canst not then be false to any man.
> (*Hamlet*, Act 1, Scene 3, 78–81)[26]

Additionally the fulfillment of the land promise is in prospect: "And I will bring you to the land I swore with uplifted hand to give to Abraham, to Isaac, and to Jacob. I will give it to you as a possession. I am the LORD" (Exod. 6:8). Before that event the Lord has conducted one final and decisive battle against Egypt/Rahab. Subsequently he will carry out the final three steps of the Major Paradigm: God will establish a covenant with a people, God's covenant will establish that people as God's people, and God will establish a temple among his people because he would reside among them.

---

26 William Shakespeare, *The Tragedy of Hamlet Prince of Denmark*, ed. Tucker Brooke and Jack Randall Crawford (New Haven, CT: Yale University Press, 1952), 31.

CHAPTER EIGHT

Mosaic Covenant Institution, Restoration and Renewal, Tabernacle and Temple

We have seen how God worked by his Spirit through a prophet-figure—Moses—to wage war against and defeat his foes. The next phases of the Major Paradigm for the Mosaic covenant are the following three items: God will establish a covenant with a people, God's covenant will establish that people as God's people, and God will establish a temple among his people because he will reside among them. This chapter turns to those phases, but in the course of doing so also considers matters of covenant restoration (in Exodus 34) and renewal (in Deuteronomy), as well as the public address nature of Deuteronomy. We also discuss in a concluding note the unconditional aspect of the Mosaic covenant.[1]

At this stage it is important to review some basic ideas about covenant and relationship, and a comparison of the Abrahamic and Sinai covenants may be helpful in this regard. Just as the Lord's "engagement" with Abram led to the "marriage" that was the Abrahamic covenant, so now the Lord's engagement with Israel constitutes an invitation to a new and *previously nonexistent covenant relationship* ("marriage"). That relationship will include the first temple presence of the Lord on earth since Eden. Because of Israel's sins the covenant relationship would be fractured, and because of God's grace it would be restored and renewed. The Lord *restored* the Sinai covenant after Moses broke the first two tablets of the law (following the sin of the golden calf, Exodus 34). He later *renewed* the Sinai covenant with a subsequent generation on the plains of Moab (Deuteronomy) after their parents had lacked the faith needed to enter the Promised Land. The Lord showed patience and

---

1   Cf. anticipatory discussion in Introduction, pages 17–18.

longsuffering with his people in Moses' day, just as he had shown patience with Adam and his wife by maintaining his covenant with them in spite of their covenant breaking. He showed steadfastness in his covenant purpose by renewing the Mosaic covenant on the plains of Moab with a subsequent generation, just as he had shown steadfastness in his covenant purpose by renewing the Adamic covenant with Noah some generations later. The Lord's covenant purpose in the cases of Adam and Noah was to maintain a world in which his program of salvation could begin and proceed. The Lord's covenant purpose in the cases of Sinai and Moab was to provide an essential revelatory and pedagogical step in that salvation program.

With these ideas in mind we turn to our study of the Mosaic covenant—and especially its institution, restoration, and renewal. For expediency, items 5 and 6 of the Major Paradigm are taken together, as they occur together in the Mosaic covenant making account:

5. God establishes a covenant with a people
6. God's covenant establishes that people as God's people

As with the Abrahamic covenant so with the Mosaic covenant a narrative flow presents the Lord's engagement with Israel and his subsequent "marriage" with them in the covenant made at Sinai. A schema illustrates the major components of the narrative:

Exodus 19	Formal Engagement and Preparations for the Covenant
19:3–6	Yahweh's initial offer of covenant relationship to Moses
19:7	Moses brings the offer to the people
19:8	The people agree with the offer
19:9	Moses reports their agreement to Yahweh
19:10–13	Yahweh commands that Moses prepare the people (including approach warning)
19:14–15	Moses prepares the people
19:16–20	Yahweh descends on Sinai and summons Moses
19:21–23	Yahweh repeats approach warning and Moses confirms it
19:24	Yahweh summons Aaron
19:25	Moses repeats the approach warning to the people

Exodus	
20–23:19	The Stipulations of the Covenant
20:1–17	Basic stipulations of the covenant (i.e., the Decalogue)
20:18–21	People's reactions to theophany, and Yahweh's intent
20:22–23:19	Detailed stipulations
Exodus 23:20–33	Blessings, Conquest Mandate, and Provisions
Exodus 24:1–11	Cutting the Covenant and Covenant Ratification Meal
24:1–2	Preparations for approach
24:3–4a	Moses reports the stipulations to the people (3a)
	People swear an oath to obey (3b)
	Moses writes down the Lord's words (4a)
24:4b	Moses builds an altar and twelve pillars (symbolic of the two parties)
24:5–8	Covenant sacrifice (5–6)
	+ second oath of the people (7)
	= cutting (i.e., ratification)
	"This is the blood of the covenant that the LORD has cut with you in accordance with all these words" (8)
24:9–11	Covenant ratification meal

The covenant cutting is followed by a covenant ratification meal. Covenant ratification meals occurred in the ancient Near East and there are examples of them in the Bible. An example of what one may call a "parity" covenant ratification meal has already appeared in Genesis, between Abimelek and Jacob (Gen. 26:26–31). The Sinai covenant ratification meal, by contrast, ratifies a suzerain-vassal covenant and it takes place in the presence of the covenant Lord.

Access to the Lord's covenant meal is restricted—only a few consecrated ones are permitted to approach his Glory-Presence. Those present are the covenant mediator, Moses, and his elders. The counterpart to this arrangement is the Lord's Supper of the new covenant. Displayed below are the parallel elements of those two meals:

Theme	Mosaic Covenant	New Covenant
Blood of the covenant	before the meal	part of the meal
Divine presence	Yahweh (visible)	Jesus (visible)

Theme	Mosaic Covenant	New Covenant
		Father and Spirit (invisible)
Covenant mediator	Moses	Jesus
Guests at the table	elders	disciples
In an elevated location	Sinai	the "upper room"

Unlike the covenant ratification meal of the Mosaic covenant, which takes place after the covenant has been cut, the covenant ratification meal of the new covenant is proleptic: it takes place before the new covenant is cut, that is, before the Lord is crucified.

The background for understanding the covenant ratification meal goes as far back in biblical history as the covenant ratifying meal of Isaac and Abimelek, and the details of that event are worth note: "Isaac then made a feast for them, and they ate and drank. Early the next morning the men swore an oath to each other. Then Isaac sent them on their way, and they went away peacefully" (Gen. 26:30–31). Three items stand out in this brief account: (1) the *sworn oath* indicates the completion of a covenant between the two parties; (2) the *covenant meal* has solemnized the completion of the arrangement; (3) the *peaceful departure* of Abimelek and his party is consistent with the sworn oath and covenant solemnizing meal—because they are now in covenant, the parties can know peace between themselves.

The solemnizing meal of the new covenant draws upon this ancient background. It also appears to have a more spiritual aspect. Not only do Jesus' followers recall his death when they share the Lord's supper—a material act which, as Paul notes, is nonetheless to be taken seriously as a spiritual event (1 Cor. 11:17–32)—the meal itself also apparently symbolizes an inner or spiritual banquet. The Lord says to the church in Laodicea: "Here I am! I stand at the door and knock. If anyone hears my voice and opens the door, I will come in and eat with that person, and he with me" (Rev. 3:20). Whatever it means for the Lord to enter a person and dine with that person, Isaiah seems to have prefigured it:

> Come, all you who are thirsty,
>   come to the waters;
> and you who have no money,
>   come, buy and eat!
> Come, buy wine and milk
>   without money and without cost.

Why spend money on what is not bread,
    and your labor on what does not satisfy?
Listen, listen to me, and eat what is good,
    and you will delight in the richest of fare.
Give ear and come to me;
    listen, that you may live.
I will make an everlasting covenant with you,
    my faithful love promised to David.
See, I have made him a witness to the peoples,
    a ruler and commander of the peoples.
Surely you will summon nations you know not,
    and nations you do not know will come running to you,
because of the LORD your God,
    the Holy One of Israel,
    for he has endowed you with splendor." (Isa. 55:1–5)

This remarkable prophecy adumbrates the *inner meal* promised in Revelation 3:20. It displays in material terms a future *inner* repast that the King of kings—who is the fulfillment of the Lord's "faithful love promised to David"—will provide. The Lord indeed made him "a witness to the peoples" (cf. Rev. 1:5) who began to summon nations that (in the days of his incarnation) he knew not, and to whom such nations would also come running because of the resurrection "splendor" with which God endowed him.

The spiritual banquet enjoyed by members of the new covenant should, arguably, be understood as the nourishing presence of the Spirit of Christ. Just as material food and drink provide the nourishment needed for bodily sustenance and growth, so our spiritual food and drink is the Spirit of Christ, or Christ *within*, who provides our spiritual sustenance and growth. Paul suggests the same in figurative language: "They all ate the same spiritual food and drank the same spiritual drink; for they drank from the spiritual rock that accompanied them, and that rock was Christ" (1 Cor. 10:3–4). In Paul's figurative presentation, that eating and drinking by the human Mosaic covenant members was primarily external—that is, the rock accompanied them as a fellow traveler and supplied them with actual water.[2] But they drank of the rock, and such drink being symbolized by water could be said to be the Spirit. Nonetheless,

---

2   Paul plays upon the occasions on which Moses caused water to come from the rock for the people (cf. Exod. 17:1–7; Num. 20:13).

those who drank once would have to drink again. By contrast, under the new covenant the Spirit is a fount of living water *within* the person always (John 7:38–39). Similarly, although the Lord's Supper is a meal of external elements, the Lord also promises an internal meal that he will share being present *within* us.

If one asks how Christ within us can be dining on himself—because he *is* the meal he *shares* with us—this would appear to be where the promised nourishment understood more exactly as the Spirit can shed light. Since the Spirit is life (cf. John 5:26, 6:63), he nourishes us. Likewise, in a way beyond fathoming, the Spirit nourishes the Son, that is, the Son is alive in and by his own Spirit. From nanosecond to nanosecond the *recreating Spirit* is the agent of the Son's supernal aseity and also of the Father's. Although this mystery is utterly beyond humans, one may say nonetheless that God nourishes himself by his Spirit and also nourishes those whom he enters by the same Spirit (who is also himself), because the Spirit is and gives life (cf. John 6:63; Rom. 8:10–11; 2 Cor. 3:6) and is moreover the "power of an indestructible life" (Heb. 7:16).

This internal aspect appears symbolically in the Last Supper, as becomes clear when one contrasts it with the Mosaic ratification meal. In the Mosaic meal, the people did not drink the blood of the sacrifice but were sprinkled with it. In the new covenant ratification meal, they *drink* the wine that symbolizes *the blood of the sacrificed Son*. In the Mosaic ratification, they ate the flesh of a *bestial sacrifice*. In the new covenant ratification, they eat the bread that symbolizes *the body of the sacrificed Son*. That Son is both sacrifice and suzerain (cf. John 13:13). Only in the new covenant are the sacrifice and the Lord of the covenant *one and the same*, and only in the new covenant is the Lord of the covenant thus (symbolically) internalized. The symbolic internalization of Christ points to the nourishing presence of the Spirit of Christ in us. As Paul says, "So it is written: 'The first man Adam became a living being'; the last Adam, a life-giving Spirit" (1 Cor. 15:45).

THE SINAI COVENANT AND THE EXODUS 34 COVENANT RESTORATION

The Lord cut his covenant once more with Israel—the one made at Sinai and symbolically broken or annulled when Moses came down from the mountain, saw the idolatry into which Aaron and Israel had lapsed, and broke the two tablets of the law. As was noted, there are five mentions of covenant *institution* in Exodus and they are of two types: notice of the covenant the Lord is cutting with Israel (two cases), and the command that Israel is not to make a covenant with any of the inhabitants of Canaan (three cases).[3] Taking the latter first, the Lord warns his people three times not to cut a covenant with the inhabitants of the land and all three warnings use the idiom כרת ברית (Exod. 23:32; 34:12, 15). The idiom is also used when the Lord inscribes two *new* tablets of the law to replace the ones that were broken. The Lord has Moses hew out two new stones, and then the Lord inscribes them (Exod. 34:1, 4, 28b).[4] The significance is as follows: the Lord is cutting once more —the participle is used—the covenant that had been symbolically destroyed when Moses destroyed the tablets (Exod. 34:10). The idiom is also used in the finalizing of that process ("Then the LORD said to Moses, 'Write down these words, for in accordance with these words *I have made a covenant* with you and with Israel,'" Exod. 34:27, emphasis added). The Lord is recreating with the original party (namely, Israel) a covenant that had been—as we have said—symbolically destroyed. The Lord's act shows his commitment to the covenant and also implies the unconditional aspect of the covenant: the Lord will not allow it to end before its purposes have been accomplished.[5] The re-creation of the tablets indicates that the Lord is *reproducing* a covenant just symbolically broken: he is not renewing with descendants a covenant that had continued in force with a prior generation. The renewal of the same covenant with a subsequent generation—with some tweaking appropriate to changed circumstances—is what was understood as covenant renewal

---

3   Cf. chapter 5.

4   As Douglas K. Stuart, *Exodus*, New American Commentary (Nashville: B&H, 2006), 734, notes, although the Lord told Moses to write down various instructions he also gave Moses in this encounter (vv. 10–27), it is the Lord and not Moses who inscribed the tablets ("Moses was there with the Lord forty days and forty nights without eating bread or drinking water. And he [i.e., the Lord] wrote on the tablets the words of the covenant—the Ten Commandments," v. 28), consistent with what the Lord said to Moses earlier, "Chisel out two stone tablets like the first ones, and I will write on them the words that were on the first tablets, which you broke" (Exod. 34:1). The fact that the Lord writes on the new tablets the same Ten Commands that had stood on the old tablets, without nuancing or variation, is consistent with our understanding that this is not a covenant renewal. We note that the restatement of the Decalogue in Deuteronomy, the true renewal covenant, has some tweaking, for example, the proximate ground of the Sabbath is brought home to Israel (from the Lord as Creator of all to the Lord as deliverer of Israel [Exod. 20:8–11 // Deut. 5:12–15]).

5   One might say the same of the Lord's commanding Hosea to take back his faithless wife, as the Lord takes Israel back (Hosea 2–3). Cf. the discussion at the end of chapter 4.

in the ancient Near East and (as has been argued) in the Old Testament. This is not what happens in Exodus 34. It does take place, however, when the Lord cuts the covenant of Deuteronomy (cf. 29:1) with the offspring of that generation whose bodies fell in the desert (cf. Heb. 3:17).[6]

DEUTERONOMY: MOAB RENEWAL OF THE SINAI COVENANT

The Lord does renew the Sinai covenant on the plains of Moab, and the renewal is the book called Deuteronomy. The name of the book comes from the Septuagint mistranslation of Deuteronomy17:18. The Lord gives instruction for any future king in Israel:

> When he takes the throne of his kingdom, he is to write for himself on a scroll a copy of this law, taken from that of the Levitical priests. It is to be with him, and he is to read it all the days of his life so that he may learn to revere the LORD his God and follow carefully all the words of this law and these decrees and not consider himself better than his fellow Israelites and turn from the law to the right or to the left. Then he and his descendants will reign a long time over his kingdom in Israel. (Deut. 17:18–20)

The LXX translator(s) mistook the Hebrew of verse 18, in which the relevant phrase reads, "a duplicate of this law" (author's translation; מִשְׁנֵה התורה הזאת), and translated it "this second law" (LXX, τὸ δευτερονόμιον τοῦτο). Although their translation was wrong, they perhaps inadvertently captured the sense of the matter, for Deuteronomy, as a renewal covenant, is in a sense a "second law" to be bundled with the first law (i.e., the Sinai covenant) for the original vassals' descendants who have been wandering in the wilderness and for their offspring. Together, the Sinai covenant and the Moab covenant form one legal package henceforth understood as such, lived under as such, and called—without differentiation—"the law" by Jesus and the New Testament writers. Because their understanding was correct, the Sinai suzerain-vassal covenant and its renewal should not be separated into two different covenants, even though some ingenious scholars have done so. Like the Adamic and Noahic—or creation and re-creation—covenants the Sinai and Moab covenants together form

---

6   We note the famous episode of Moses' radiant face occurs in this chapter (Exod. 34:29–35). I have discussed this at some length (cf. *God at Sinai*, 226–29), and we consider it afresh when we discuss life under the new covenant (cf. 2 Corinthians 3).

one legal package under which subsequent generations live and under which they are accountable to God. Under the Adamic-Noahic package, all humanity live and are accountable to God in terms of common grace until the end of time (cf. Isa. 24:5). Under the Sinai-Moab package, all Israel were accountable to the Lord in terms of his special grace revelation until that package came to an end *qua* covenant—as it has done with the institution of the new covenant.

Life under the Mosaic covenant will entail warfare against the enemies of God, but it also contains privileges of revelation more broadly experienced than had been the case after the expulsion of our first parents from Eden or after the Flood, or even under the Abrahamic covenant. It entails intimations of a trajectory that aims to restore what was lost. It does so not only by the fact of the Promised Land, which is often described in Edenic ways, but also ultimately through a new covenant and its mediator, in terms of an Edenic synthesis or symbiosis of a new heaven and a new earth.[7]

FORM OF THE RENEWAL COVENANT

We turn now to the form of the "covenant the Lord commanded Moses to make with the Israelites in Moab, in addition to the covenant he had made with them at Horeb" (Deut. 29:1). As has been recognized for some time, the whole book of Deuteronomy is cast in the form of a second millennium BC suzerain-vassal treaty, but it articulates that form in an extended narrative:

Form of the Renewal Covenant Narrative

Element	Deuteronomy 1–34
Title	1:1–5
Historical Prologue	1:6–4:49
General Stipulations	5–11
Detailed Stipulations	12–26
Deposition	31:9, 24–26
Public reading	31:10–13
Blessings	28:1–14
Curses	28:15–68
Witnesses	4:26; 30:19; 31:16–30; 32:1–47

---

7 Cf. further chapter 10 of volume 3.

The data show the covenantal nature of Deuteronomy. Although the book comes closer than any other biblical book to being an actual treaty document, it is more than that. It is a narrative and is presented as such. It enshrines the Moab covenant, just as other biblical narratives enshrine the other divine-human covenants. That is part of the narrative art of biblical presentation. As has been noted, Old Testament historiography—of which covenant reporting forms a part—surpasses its ancient near eastern counterparts considerably in a number of ways. Deuteronomy is a good example, for it offers narrative as well as covenant structure. If one asks what accounts for the literary and aesthetic superiority, not to mention the moral superiority, of the biblical material, it seems reasonable to suggest the role of the Holy Spirit in the composition of the accounts. The same may be affirmed of biblical materials generally (perhaps most obviously the poetry). Deuteronomy, however, offers more than a narrative account and treaty data—it also offers the speeches of Moses.[8]

THE PUBLIC ADDRESS NATURE OF DEUTERONOMY

It was observed at the start of this chapter that Deuteronomy not only embodies the form of a second millennium BC suzerain-vassal treaty, it also contains Moses' final three addresses to the people. This formal aspect of Deuteronomy is also well known. We display it briefly in order to emphasize a point:

Mosaic Final Addresses

Element	Verses
Prologue	1:1–5
First address	1:6–4:43
Second address	4:44–28:68
Third address	29:1–30:20
Epilogue	31:1–34:12

In the first address (1:6 – 4:43), Moses reminds the Israelites how their lack of faith resulted in forty years of wandering in the desert. The second

---

8   Consequently, we may affirm the presence of three genres that constitute Deuteronomy simultaneously, just as we noted several simultaneous literary forms in Genesis 1:1–2:3. Cf. volume 1, chapter 1 of *Biblical Theology*. Cf. further comment below on page 230.

address is the longest. It forms the heart of the book (4:44–28:68). Most of this address (4:44–26:19) is a restatement of various stipulations contained in the previous three books of the Pentateuch. It concludes by describing the blessings God would shower upon Israel if the people obeyed him and the curses that would result if they disobeyed (27:1–28:68). Moses' third address is a general restatement of what the covenant meant (29:1–30:20). This address is closely linked to the last two chapters of the prior address, since both sections present the covenant in terms of blessings and curses. The epilogue (31:1–34:12) records the following: Joshua's appointment as Moses' successor, the "Song of Moses" (which declares God's greatness), Moses' blessing on the various tribes of Israel, and the account of Moses' death and burial.

The nature of these addresses may be summed up largely by these categories: recollection, admonition, and exhortation. Moses repeats *recollections* of God's displayed grandeur as the only possible savior among earthly powers because he is above all earthly powers. He rehearses the failures of Israel as an *admonition* but also an encouragement to both humility and obedience. He *exhorts* the people to covenant faithfulness and to a conquest that will now at last—but only by the Lord's insuperable authority—take place.

Moses' repeated recollections, admonitions, and exhortations contribute in large part to the highly repetitive style of Deuteronomy. The need for such repetition—affirmed by its very God-breathed existence—shows once more the externality of the law. One need not be told again and again what is dynamically alive *at the core of one's being.* The promise of Ezekiel 36:27 is still a long way off for Moses' audience, both in its articulation and in its even more remote fulfillment: "I will put my Spirit in you and move you to follow my decrees and be careful to keep my laws." Equally remote, because the same, is the fulfillment of Deuteronomy 30:6: "The LORD your God will circumcise your hearts and the hearts of your descendants, so that you may love him with all your heart and with all your soul, and live." That promised circumcision by the Lord never gets reported in the Old Testament because it never happens there. It is not mentioned again until the New Testament: "No, a person is a Jew who is one inwardly; and circumcision is circumcision of the heart, by the Spirit, not by the written code" (Rom. 2:29).[9] When God's people were under the Mosaic covenant ("the written code"), God was promising something that was—as a dynamic reality—beyond the purview of the Mosaic covenant.

---

9   Cf. discussion in chapter 13.

Finally, the tri-formal nature of Deuteronomy as narrative, treaty, and a series of addresses may and should recall the tetra-formal nature of Genesis 1:1–2:3 as narrative, treaty, ancient near eastern list form, and the so-called Framework Hypothesis Structure.[10] Polyvalent structures of such sophistication are consistent with the God-breathed nature of the material—words that are Spirit (2 Tim. 3:16; cf. John 6:63).

GOD ESTABLISHES A TEMPLE AMONG HIS PEOPLE BECAUSE HE WILL RESIDE AMONG THEM

The seventh and final phase of the Major Paradigm as regards the Mosaic covenant is now before us: the Lord builds a temple because he wants to dwell among his people. That sequence of events now takes place for the first time since the Fall. A parallel spiritual dynamic is involved in the two cases. The Lord worked by his Spirit through his preincarnate Son to create the world and the Eden-temple. Now, in a fallen world, the Lord works by his Spirit through his prophet to create a tabernacle-temple. The Spirit also works through the prophet's helpers in the tabernacle construction: he gives Bezalel and Oholiab the Spirit-wisdom to do what is needed for its preparation. The same pattern will appear later when the Spirit works through the greater prophet, Jesus, to build the temple of his church. These and other temple-related matters are discussed in the following pages.

Supernal Archetype, Spirit Guidance: The Mosaic Tabernacle

The role of the Spirit in temple construction is arguably primary. The Lord told Moses to construct a tabernacle after the pattern he showed him on the mountain in a Glory-Spirit theophany, and also gave him instructions for its accouterments and for the priestly garments. God's words were Spirit, and Exodus 25–39 portrays the patterns (chaps. 25–30) and their realization (35:4–39:43). The golden calf episode (Exodus 32), the revelation of God's glory to Moses (Exodus 33), and the Lord's reaffirmation of the Sinai covenant with new tablets he inscribed himself, all form a brief but important hiatus in the command-fulfillment narrative of tabernacle

---

10 Because of their clear structure, we focused on the *three* formal aspects—treaty form, list form, and "Framework Hypothesis"—in volume 1, but of course the pericope, like all the biblical covenants, was reported in another or fourth genre, narrative; cf. Niehaus, "Covenant and Narrative," 538–41.

instruction and completion.[11] The progress of those interruptive elements shows a Lord who on the one hand will not tolerate idolatry yet on the other hand will not let the folly of his people undo his covenant purpose. The impartation of a glory that is externally visible (Exodus 33) puts a seal as it were to this intent, and is an outward and visible anticipation of a future inward and invisible glory (2 Cor. 3:7–18).

The Holy Spirit was, then, involved in two obvious ways with the construction of the tabernacle: (1) the Lord in his Glory-Spirit theophany gave Moses instructions for the tabernacle; (2) the Lord also gave Holy Spirit guidance to Bezalel and Oholiab, and to those who worked with them:

> Then the LORD said to Moses, "See, I have chosen Bezalel son of Uri, the son of Hur, of the tribe of Judah, and I have filled him with the Spirit of God, with wisdom, with understanding, with knowledge and with all kinds of skills—to make artistic designs for work in gold, silver and bronze, to cut and set stones, to work in wood, and to engage in all kinds of crafts. Moreover, I have appointed Oholiab son of Ahisamak, of the tribe of Dan, to help him. Also I have given ability to all the skilled workers to make everything I have commanded you: the tent of meeting, the ark of the covenant law with the atonement cover on it, and all the other furnishings of the tent— the table and its articles, the pure gold lampstand and all its accessories, the altar of incense, the altar of burnt offering and all its utensils, the basin with its stand—and also the woven garments, both the sacred garments for Aaron the priest and the garments for his sons when they serve as priests, and the anointing oil and fragrant incense for the Holy Place. They are to make them just as I commanded you." (Exod. 31:1–11)

The Spirit in Bezalel is also the one who has "given ability to all the skilled workers to make everything I [the Lord] have commanded you [Moses]" (v. 6). They prefigure those under the new covenant who, by the gifts of the Spirit, do the work of building the church.

Supernal Archetype, Spirit Guidance: The Jerusalem Temple

Just as the Spirit gave guidance for construction of the Mosaic tabernacle, so he gave guidance for the construction of the Jerusalem temple. As

---

11   For a helpful discussion of the command-fulfillment pattern as regards the Mosaic tabernacle instructions and fulfillments, cf. Umberto Cassuto, *Biblical and Oriental Studies, Volume 2: Bible and Ancient Oriental Texts* (Jerusalem: Magnes, 1975), 31, 78, 122.

he gave Moses and his workers instruction for building and furnishing the tabernacle, so he gave David instructions both for building and furnishing the temple. He gave Moses instructions in a theophany, and he appeared in theophany to David on the future site of the temple, "the place provided by David" (cf. 2 Chron. 3:1–2). His Spirit gave guidance to Moses' coworkers, and his Spirit gave guidance to David:

> Then David gave his son Solomon the plans for the portico of the temple, its buildings, its storerooms, its upper parts, its inner rooms and the place of atonement. He gave him the plans of all that the Spirit had put in his mind for the courts of the temple of the LORD and all the surrounding rooms, for the treasuries of the temple of God and for the treasuries for the dedicated things. He gave him instructions for the divisions of the priests and Levites, and for all the work of serving in the temple of the LORD, as well as for all the articles to be used in its service. He designated the weight of gold for all the gold articles to be used in various kinds of service, and the weight of silver for all the silver articles to be used in various kinds of service: the weight of gold for the gold lampstands and their lamps, with the weight for each lampstand and its lamps; and the weight of silver for each silver lampstand and its lamps, according to the use of each lampstand; the weight of gold for each table for consecrated bread; the weight of silver for the silver tables; the weight of pure gold for the forks, sprinkling bowls and pitchers; the weight of gold for each gold dish; the weight of silver for each silver dish; and the weight of the refined gold for the altar of incense. He also gave him the plan for the chariot, that is, the cherubim of gold that spread their wings and overshadow the ark of the covenant of the LORD. "All this," David said, "I have in writing as a result of the LORD's hand on me, and he enabled me to understand all the details of the plan." (1 Chron. 28:11–19)

David's testimony regarding "all that the Spirit had put in his mind" (v. 11) is also a testimonial of "the LORD's hand on [him]"—the Spirit who "enabled [him] to understand all the details of the plan" (v. 19). The Spirit thus had a consistent role as guide for tabernacle and temple construction. Once the residence is built, he inhabits it.

Tabernacle and Temple as "House"

This section is headed "Tabernacle and Temple as 'House'" because the Mosaic tabernacle and the later Solomonic temple are both "temples" in the ancient near eastern and biblical sense—a "house" or dwelling for the Lord.[12] Agreeably, the account of the Lord's coming to dwell in the tabernacle is paralleled later by the account of his coming to dwell in the temple:

The Lord Invests the Tabernacle (Exod. 40:34–35)	The Lord Invests the Temple (1 Kings 8:10–11)
"Then **the cloud covered the Tent of Meeting,** and the glory of the LORD filled the tabernacle."	"When the priests withdrew from the Holy Place, **the cloud filled the temple of the LORD."**
"*Moses could not enter the Tent of Meeting* because **the cloud had settled upon it,** and the glory of the LORD filled the tabernacle."	"And *the priests could not perform their service* because of **the cloud,** for the glory of the LORD filled his temple."

Given all we have seen, the parallels should not surprise us. One thing is important to understand regarding them. As was noted long ago in cases of parallel theophanic accounts—whose elements were so parallel and consistent that they could be called a *Gattung* or genre, as they have been—the fact that the same elements recur in a *given type of event* does not mean that any of the events reported are contrived or fictional.[13] In the case before us, one finds repeated parallel elements because the Lord's session in the Solomonic temple produced the same theophanic phenomena seen generations before when he invested the Mosaic tabernacle. The Lord's manifest irruption into world-space is attended by such phenomena.

Spirit Advent and Consecration

God's temple investiture is a Spirit advent. The Lord explains: "I have *consecrated* this temple, which you have built, *by putting my Name there forever* (1 Kings 9:3, emphases added). It is understood the Lord's "Name" means his essential nature. We know his holy presence—in other words,

---

12   The Semitic words for temple are loan words from the Sumerian meaning "big house" (Sumerian É.GAL; cf. Akkadian *ekallu*, Hebrew היכל).

13   Cf. Niehaus, *God at Sinai*, 39–42.

that *Name*—is what makes the place holy, or "consecrates" it.[14] The same is true whether the place is the ground Moses may not tread with his sandals (and cf. Josh. 5:15), the tabernacle, or the temple—or us, whom God makes holy or "saints" by his presence within us. That presence is the Spirit (cf. "Where can I go from your Spirit? / Where can I flee from your presence?" Ps. 139:7).[15]

Finally, the initial counterpart to the Mosaic and Solomonic temple investiture under the new covenant is the storm theophany at Pentecost when God's people become for the first time temples of the Spirit and thus, by his internal dwelling, consecrated by God and to God.

Tabernacle, Temple, and God

The Glory-Spirit historically has had a consistent role regarding instruction about, and involvement in, tabernacle and temple construction. He is the Spirit of wisdom who possesses the knowledge by which alone a suitable temple can be built for his own residence. Once the residence is built he inhabits it.[16]

The same was arguably intended for the first man and woman, built by Spirit-wisdom to be suitable temples of the Spirit and in fact animated by, although not inhabited by, the Spirit (Gen. 2:7). The man and woman failed to become temples within the Eden-temple. God by his Spirit graciously under a special grace covenant built a tabernacle and then a temple of stone, but Solomon was right in more ways than one when he said the Most High could not dwell in a temple built by men (cf. 1 Kings 8:27). The temples the Lord most wants are those made by himself, in his image. At the Lord's set time, a second Adam, who was "a life-giving Spirit" (1 Cor. 15:45) would come and bring to fruition that intended work of Spirit-temple building and dwelling.

All of the above is consistent with what was said about God's being a *temple of himself* (on the basis of Ezek. 1:28) and what it means to be fully

---

14   Ibid., 25–26

15   A related figure is the "angel" who will lead the people into the Promised Land, and of whom the Lord says: "My Name is in him" (Exod. 23:21). He prefigures and is supernally the Son—an uncreated "messenger"—who in his incarnate days will have the Spirit (i.e., the Name, the essential nature) without measure (John 3:34). Cf. discussion in chapters 3 and 10.

16   This cluster of ideas was understood in the ancient Near East, although in a distorted and polytheistic way; cf. *ANETBT*, 89–99.

human—fully what God intended us to be, temples *in parallel with himself*. That temple idea has become real on earth under the new covenant. But the parallelism between God and us, accomplished internally under the new covenant, was displayed symbolically, or externally, at Moses' "tent of meeting" that anticipated the Mosaic tabernacle:

> Now Moses used to take a tent and pitch it outside the camp some distance away, calling it the "tent of meeting." Anyone inquiring of the LORD would go to the tent of meeting outside the camp. And whenever Moses went out to the tent, all the people rose and stood at the entrances to their tents, watching Moses until he entered the tent. As Moses went into the tent, the pillar of cloud would come down and stay at the entrance, while the LORD spoke with Moses. Whenever the people saw the pillar of cloud standing at the entrance to the tent, they all stood and worshiped, each at the entrance to his tent. The LORD would speak to Moses face to face, as one speaks to a friend. Then Moses would return to the camp, but his young aide Joshua son of Nun did not leave the tent. (Exod. 33:7–11)

The narrative plays on the words "pillar" (עמוד) and "standing" (עמד) in verse 10 (the word translated "stood" by NIV is different in Hebrew: קום, "arose") but the play is possible because of a spiritual though *external* reality: the people act as the Spirit-presence of the Lord acts—in tandem with him—at least in a temporary and external way.

The people's journey from the consecration of the tabernacle onward was also an external prefiguration of a spiritual reality that would be made possible only under the new covenant, and later called "keeping in step with the Spirit":

> Then the cloud covered the tent of meeting, and the glory of the LORD filled the tabernacle. Moses could not enter the tent of meeting because the cloud had settled on it, and the glory of the LORD filled the tabernacle. In all the travels of the Israelites, whenever the cloud lifted from above the tabernacle, they would set out; but if the cloud did not lift, they did not set out—until the day it lifted. So the cloud of the LORD was over the tabernacle by day, and fire was in the cloud by night, in the sight of all the Israelites during all their travels. (Exod. 40:34–38)

God's presence was what made the tabernacle and later temple holy—consecrated them—and is also what makes us holy. The consecrating work of the Glory-Spirit follows a work of Spirit *instruction* and consequently, through human agency, Spirit *construction* in the cases of tabernacle and temple.

By analogy, all humans, made in God's image, are by Spirit-wisdom *constructed* to be temples, but only those who belong to God under the new covenant become temples of the Spirit. For them, the dynamic is somewhat more complex than what has been seen in the cases of the Mosaic tabernacle and the Solomonic temple. The Holy Spirit inhabits his created images, but then begins to (re)construct the human temples of the new covenant: "Therefore, if anyone is in Christ, the new creation has come: The old has gone, the new is here!" (2 Cor. 5:17). Moreover, that inner reconstruction follows a death of the old man, but has to do with life (Rom. 6:1–4). That sequence in turn anticipates the reduction of the cosmos to death in order that the Spirit-renewed and Spirit-informed life of the new cosmos can arise.

In both of these cases—the human and the cosmic—the Spirit puts to death (cf. Rom. 8:13) and the Spirit brings to life. Only the withdrawal of the Spirit can bring cosmic undoing, because the Spirit through the Word sustains all things. Likewise, only the renewing work of the Spirit can bring life (cf. figuratively Isa. 32:14–20) because the Spirit is life. The one who created the cosmos through the preincarnate Word will not only judge that cosmos through the same Word (2 Peter 3:5–7), as a Spirit of judgment and of fire (cf. Isa. 4:4), but will also bring about a new heavens and a new earth with abundant life through that same Word (Rev. 21:5), who is a life-giving Spirit.[17]

UNCONDITIONALITY OF THE MOSAIC COVENANT

God's eschatological goal—a goal for him already accomplished—becomes possible for humans only because of God's faithfulness to himself. God is faithful to himself—that is, he is righteous—and for that reason he is also faithful to his covenants. One consequence of that faithfulness is that every divine-human covenant is unconditional. A review of that idea is presented now as it bears on the covenant under discussion, the Mosaic covenant.

Prior discussion has shown that the Abrahamic and Davidic covenants were both unconditional (from the Lord's side) and conditional (from the human side). Those two examples are part of a larger pattern. Not

---

17   Cf. further discussion in chapter 10 of volume 3.

only those two covenants, but all divine-human covenants are both un-conditional and conditional. The Lord will see to it that any covenant he makes with and through a human covenant mediator will continue until the covenant has accomplished what the Lord intended it to accomplish. Nothing can prevent that—it is an unconditional commitment. On the other hand, for humans living under any divine-human covenant, every one of those covenants has conditions—in other words, is conditional. Continuation of the covenant is not conditional upon a vassal's obedi-ence, but continuation of the covenant *for the vassal* (i.e., the vassal's own own continuation in the covenant) can be conditional upon that vassal's obedience. The consequences, for the vassal, of breaking the con-ditions are different, however, between the common grace and special grace covenants. In the common grace covenants, one may violate the conditions but not yet be "cut out" of covenant membership. On the other hand, everyone under those covenants dies because of the first Ad-am's transgression of the first condition. (Nonetheless, his transgression did not terminate the covenant—i.e., the continuation of the Adamic covenant was not conditional upon Adam's obedience. God has contin-ued it unconditionally). In the special grace covenants, by contrast, one may violate the conditions and be "cut out" of membership in the cov-enant. This difference between the common grace and the special grace covenants has been discussed.[18] Chapter 4 discussed the unconditional and conditional nature of the Abrahamic covenant and likewise of the Davidic covenant. Here the dual nature of the Mosaic covenant comes under review, and since no one doubts that the Mosaic covenant has its conditional aspect, it is the unconditional aspect that comes into focus.

The record of God's relations with Israel shows how unconditional the Mosaic covenant is, because God continued to keep at least a remnant of Israel as his people. Such was the case when Jesus was "born under the law." Jesus also affirmed the ongoing nature of the law: "For truly I tell you, until heaven and earth disappear, not the smallest letter, not the least stroke of a pen, will by any means disappear from the law until everything is accomplished" (Matt. 5:18). The truth of this statement ap-pears in John's Apocalypse: "Then God's temple in heaven was opened, and within his temple was seen the ark of his covenant. And there came flashes of lightning, rumblings, peals of thunder, an earthquake and a severe hailstorm" (Rev. 11:19). What does that mean?

John's revelation shows that the Mosaic covenant—the law—continues

---

18   Cf. chapter 1 of this volume and also the Introduction.

today and throughout human history, but supernally, as an expression of God's nature. Its supernal presence means the world will be judged by that nature, of which the law is an expression. On that Day the pagans will find themselves judged by that law, whose work some of them even had on their hearts while they lived (Rom. 2:14–16).[19] Paul says, "Now we know that whatever the law says, it says to those who are under the law, that every mouth may be stopped, and all the world may become guilty before God" (Rom. 3:19 NKJV). In other words, the law continues in some sense as a standard by which all shall be judged. Its continuance is supernal; it continues in heaven. At the end all men shall be confronted by it: at its final revelation "all the world" will "become guilty before God." Paul adds, "Therefore by the deeds of the law no flesh will be justified in His sight, for by the law is the knowledge of sin" (Rom. 3:20 NKJV). As the law exposed sin during the life of Israel, it will expose sin on the day of judgment.

Nonetheless, the law, or the Mosaic covenant, has *on earth* fulfilled its purpose as a functioning covenant under which one may live—as *torah* regarding God and sin, and thereby as a pedagogue/guardian to lead us to Christ: "*Why, then, was the law given at all?* It was added because of transgressions until the Seed to whom the promise referred had come" (Gal. 3:19, emphasis added); and again, "So the law was our guardian *until Christ came* that we might be justified by faith. Now that this faith has come, *we are no longer under a guardian*" (Gal. 3:24–25, emphases added). Once the person who was under the law finds pardon and freedom in Christ, he or she can own the reality that "Christ . . . forgave us all our sins, having canceled the charge of our legal indebtedness, which stood against us and condemned us; he has taken it away, nailing it to the cross" (Col. 2:13b–14). The law, or the Mosaic covenant, *as a functioning covenant on earth*, has been canceled by Christ, who fulfilled it for us by his sinless life and atoning death—and so he nailed it to the cross. In other words, the Mosaic covenant has accomplished all God wanted it to accomplish as a covenant under which people lived on earth. Consequently, it no longer functions as a covenant.

Nonetheless, and despite Israel's many sins and God's judgments, God's Mosaic covenant continued in force for those living under it until the completed earthly work of Christ, who like his contemporary Jews was born under the law.

One more point must be clearly understood. The law exposed human

---

19   Cf. discussion in chapter 13.

sin, and human sin abounded under the law. Nonetheless, human sin could not annul the law. That is the unconditional aspect of the Mosaic covenant it shares with every other divine-human covenant.

AFTERWARD: MOSES AND THE PROPHETS

Moses mediated the covenant named after him. No other mediator of a covenant for all God's people would come until Jesus. Nonetheless, God knew his people would need prophetic guidance, and also, unfortunately, prophetic rebuke. So God raised up prophets after Moses, just as he had promised to do. The Spirit would provide guidance for God's people through prophets under the Mosaic covenant. Under the Mosaic covenant, that could only be an external work toward the people—the Spirit speaking and working through individual prophets. That was so notwithstanding that the Spirit could and no doubt did influence people without indwelling them.[20]

The situation under the new covenant would be different. The Spirit would provide guidance *within* God's people under the new covenant. He would lead them into all truth. He would move them to keep in step with himself, and thus avoid sin.[21]

The foregoing considerations have had much to do with the Spirit. The Spirit's work under the old covenant is almost always observed in connection with the prophets. Consequently, our further observations concerning life under the Mosaic covenant will have to do mainly with prophetic standards and prophetic experience. Accordingly, they will include remarks on covenant lawsuit—the main calling of the prophets—and on typology and Christology, as forms of the prophetic.

---

20 Cf. the experience of David: "So Samuel took the horn of oil and anointed him in the presence of his brothers, and from that day on the Spirit of the LORD came powerfully *upon* [Heb. "to," אֶל] David" (1 Sam. 16:13, emphasis added). The Spirit came to him, but did not dwell in him. One might imagine that Israelites of lesser office, or of no formal office, could sometimes experience similar blessing.

21 Moses, the great covenant mediator prophet, showed a great heart—the heart of the Lord—when he said, "I wish that all the LORD's people were prophets and that the LORD would put his Spirit on them!" (Num. 11:29). The Lord would grant that wish, and even more, but only under the new covenant: he would put his Spirit *in* his people and move them to obey his will (cf. Ezek. 36:27). So he would make them all a representative and prophetic people.

CHAPTER NINE

MOSAIC CRITERIA OF PROPHECY, TYPOLOGY, AND CHRISTOLOGY

As noted at the end of the last chapter, this chapter takes up Mosaic criteria for prophecy and matters of prophetic experience, as well as, in the latter part, some adumbrational issues, including Christology, the prophetic quality of blessings and curses, and typology.

A starting point for such a discussion is—what apparently amounted to an existential necessity—that Israel's experience of God's propositional revelation had to be prophetic. It could hardly be otherwise. By their own testimony the people could not abide God's holy presence: "When the people saw the thunder and lightning and heard the trumpet and saw the mountain in smoke, they trembled with fear. They stayed at a distance and said to Moses, "Speak to us yourself and we will listen. But *do not have God speak to us or we will die*" (Exod. 20:18–19, emphasis added). The Lord chose one man to be his covenant mediator prophet. That man was not sinless, but he was God's choice to lead a sinful people. God had shaped him for this purpose.

The Lord liberated Israel from bondage through that prophet. The Lord accustomed Israel to a life's journey and provision under the leadership of that prophet. Moses would have no equal in the history of Israel (Deut. 34:10). But Moses would not live forever. He would not lead them into the Promised Land. The Lord knew the ongoing life of his people required a prophetic element. Even under Moses there had been other prophets, for example, Miriam (Exod. 15:20; Num. 12:1–2), and Aaron (Exod. 4:14–16; Num. 12:1–2).

In his *torah* regarding those and future prophets, the Lord provided guidelines Israel would need in their ongoing life: to understand the nature of prophecy, to be able to distinguish between true prophecy and false prophecy, and to deal with the latter so it would not corrupt the people of God. As the God who superintended their history and provided their *torah*, the Lord gave those guidelines in historical narratives that first preceded, and then followed, the Mosaic covenant institution. Agreeably, in that body of material five passages give the Lord's propositional instruction on the nature of prophecy.

STANDARDS FOR PROPHETS MADE CLEAR UNDER THE MOSAIC COVENANT

The five passages in the Pentateuch and, more specifically, in the Mosaic covenantal corpus, that give the Lord's *torah* about the nature of prophecy and matters pertaining to it are Exodus 4:10–17 (esp. vv. 15–16); 7:1–2; Numbers 12:6–8; Deuteronomy 13:1–5; and 18:9–22 (esp. vv. 15–22). As one progresses through them, the passages reveal more and more, and thus present a small specimen of progressive revelation.

Exodus

An outline of prophecy is presented for the first time in Exodus, in the context of Moses' reluctance to embrace the role of prophet and liberator of a people to which the Lord has called him. One detail worth note is that Moses' sinful avoidance of a commanding truth leads to a further revelation of truth:

> Moses said to the LORD, "O LORD, I have never been eloquent, neither in the past nor since you have spoken to your servant. I am slow of speech and tongue." The LORD said to him, "Who gave man his mouth? Who makes him deaf or mute? Who gives him sight or makes him blind? Is it not I, the LORD? Now go; I will help you speak and will teach you what to say." But Moses said, "O Lord, please send someone else to do it." Then the LORD's anger burned against Moses and he said, "What about your brother, Aaron the Levite? I know he can speak well. He is already on his way to meet you, and his heart will be glad when he sees you. You shall speak to him and put words in his mouth; I will help both of you speak and will teach you what to do. He will speak to the people for you, and it will be as if he were your mouth and as if you were God to him. But take this staff in your hand so you can perform miraculous signs with it." (Exod. 4:10–17)

The Lord gives Moses an elemental outline of the prophetic dynamic that can be displayed as follows:

Moses	God
⇓	⇓
Aaron	prophet
⇓	⇓
Pharaoh	audience

This earliest utterance of a prophetic dynamic in the Bible forms the basis for the prophetic dynamic outlined earlier in this work.[1] The dynamic of the Lord's encounter with Moses is important to note. The Lord first says to Moses, "Now go; I will help you speak and will teach you what to say" (v. 12). When Moses balks at the assignment, the Lord designates Aaron, apparently in Moses' place but not entirely or permanently, since the Lord also says: "You shall speak to him and put words in his mouth; *I will help both of you speak and will teach you what to do*" (v.15, emphasis added). The Lord's promise comports with a dual ministry that follows, in which Aaron plays a part (e.g., "Moses and Aaron brought together all the elders of the Israelites, and Aaron told them everything the LORD had said to Moses. He also performed the signs before the people, and they believed," Exod. 4:29–31a; cf., before Pharaoh, Exod. 7:6–23) but Moses eventually assumes the chief role. Moreover, a more literal translation of the Lord's words better captures the prophetic dynamic involved: "And you shall speak to him, and you shall place (וְשַׂמְתָּ) the words in his mouth; and I will be with your mouth and with his mouth" (v. 15). The dynamic of a source placing the words into the mouth of a prophet is applied figuratively to the case of Moses and Aaron but aptly describes what happens in true prophecy. The Lord's instruction here, therefore, gives a foundational picture of how true prophecy works, and it is noteworthy that it comes only some

---

1   It is reaffirmed in our second Exodus passage, Exodus 7: "Then the LORD said to Moses, 'See, I have made you like God to Pharaoh, and your brother Aaron will be your prophet. You are to say everything I command you, and your brother Aaron is to tell Pharaoh to let the Israelites go out of his country'" (Exod. 7:1–2).

generations after the word "prophet" is first used in the Bible (of Abraham, Gen. 20:7).[2]

Now as then the prophetic gift is associated with miracles: "But take this staff in your hand so you can perform miraculous signs with it" (Exod. 4:17; cf. Gen. 20:7: "Now return the man's wife, for he is a prophet, and he will pray for you and you will live"). If we consider the pedagogical nature of Scripture we get a glimpse here of how the Lord adds detail regarding a doctrine or facet of life under a special grace covenant, namely, the nature and dynamic of prophecy.

Numbers

The Lord adds further detail regarding the nature of prophecy in his rebuke to Miraim and Aaron when they contest Moses' unique prophetic authority:

> [The LORD] said, "Listen to my words: 'When a prophet of the LORD is among you, I reveal myself to him in visions, I speak to him in dreams. But this is not true of my servant Moses; he is faithful in all my house. With him I speak face to face, clearly and not in riddles; he sees the form of the LORD. Why then were you not afraid to speak against my servant Moses?'" (Num. 12:6–8)

The Lord affirms Moses' superiority to other prophets (the "to other prophets" is implied by a comparison: "With him I speak face to face, clearly and not in riddles," v. 8). If the Lord speaks to Moses "face to face," and not "in riddles," he implies he also speaks to others, but "in riddles" and not "face to face." The expression "riddles" (חידות) is also translated "dark speech." The word denotes a "riddle" or "enigmatic saying."[3] The Lord mentions such "riddles" along with other categories of revelation a prophet may receive, namely, "visions" and "dreams" (v. 6). Later prophets are given such revelations: "The vision . . . that Isaiah son of Amoz

---

2   Which may be taken as another illustration of progressive revelation.

3   Cf. *BDB*, 295. The term is used of Samson's riddle to the Philistines, divulged by his Philistine wife (Judg. 14:12, 13, 14, 15, 16, 17, 18, 19), riddles or hard questions put to Solomon by the queen of Sheba (1 Kings 10:1 // 2 Chron. 9:1), riddles proposed by the psalmist (49:4; 78:2), riddles expounded in Proverbs (1:6), a riddle the Lord tells Ezekiel to publish (17:2), Daniel's ability to solve riddles (5:12), and a taunt/riddle against the proud (Hab. 2:6).

saw" (Isa. 1:1); "At Gibeon the Lord appeared to Solomon during the night in a dream, and God said, 'Ask for whatever you want me to give you'" (1 Kings 3:5); and the historian says of Daniel, "Daniel could understand visions and dreams of all kinds" (Dan. 1:17). As for "dark speech," it could be apposite "dreams and visions" in the passage; but the term "speech" is only used elsewhere of verbal statements, and a verbal statement is also what one normally understands by the term "riddle." Perhaps the most outstanding example of such a "riddle" would be the messianic and incarnational prophecy of Isaiah 9:5—a word from the Lord that was, apparently, obscure to Israelites up to and including the time of Jesus' earthly ministry.[4]

Deuteronomy

In addition to the Sinai covenant-related *torah* about prophecy, the Lord gives very specific instruction regarding that gift and institution just prior to Israel's crossing over into the Promised Land under Joshua. The occasion for such instruction in the course of covenant renewal (in Deuteronomy) is the impending future. The Lord's people have been under prophetic leadership for nearly forty years. They would naturally hope for and expect such leadership, or something like, it to continue. It would be perhaps the best Old Testament analogue, after the theophanic tabernacle leadership during the wilderness wanderings, to being led by the Spirit on the national level. The Lord knows they need such guidance. He lays the conceptual foundation—the standards—for it in two passages in Deuteronomy.

The first passage lays down the most stringent punishment for false prophets, and causes one to ask the possible reasons for such stringency:

> If a prophet, or one who foretells by dreams, appears among you and an-
> nounces to you a miraculous sign or wonder, and if the sign or wonder of
> which he has spoken takes place, and he says, "Let us follow other gods"
> (gods you have not known) "and let us worship them," you must not listen
> to the words of that prophet or dreamer. The LORD your God is testing
> you to find out whether you love him with all your heart and with all your
> soul. It is the LORD your God you must follow, and him you must revere.
> Keep his commands and obey him; serve him and hold fast to him. That

---

4   Cf. further discussion of forms of prophetic revelation and experience in chapters 14 and 15.

prophet or dreamer must be put to death, because he preached rebellion against the LORD your God, who brought you out of Egypt and redeemed you from the land of slavery; he has tried to turn you from the way the LORD your God commanded you to follow. You must purge the evil from among you. (Deut. 13:1–5)

A prophet or dreamer may appear among the people and foretell something, and it comes to pass. That is what one would, by now, expect from a prophet of the Lord. Nonetheless, although a true prophet may give an accurate prediction, the presence of this faculty alone is not enough to prove the prophet is a true prophet. What if the person says to "follow other gods" (v. 2b)?

The phrase used here "to walk after" (הלך אחרי) is a covenant idiom that denotes how a faithful vassal follows his suzerain.[5] The idiom occurs in Mesopotamia (in its Akkadian cognate equivalent) with the same nuance, and Israel's history had by now given them an example of it: "You saw with your own eyes what the LORD did at Baal Peor. The LORD your God destroyed from among you everyone who followed [lit. "walked after," הלך אחרי] the Baal of Peor, but all of you who held fast to the LORD your God are still alive today" (Deut. 4:3–4). Those who walked after Baal at Peor—and thus took him as their suzerain—all perished. Those who "held fast" to the Lord were "still alive today." The verb "held fast" (הדבקים, Deut. 4:4) first appears in the Genesis comment on the nature of marriage: "That is why a man leaves his father and mother and is united to [דבק] his wife, and they become one flesh" (Gen. 2:24). To a reader of Hebrew the coincidence is hardly wasted: it points to an ideal of marital relationship between the Lord and his people. The ideal only begins to be realized in a dynamic way under the new covenant when the indwelling Holy Spirit informs both the head (Christ) and the body (the church), who are thus united in a way analogous to the "one flesh" ideal of marriage. Unfortunately, the marital relationship also implies its opposite: just as one can walk after Baal instead of the Lord, one can have an ersatz relationship with spiritual Baal—instead of the Lord—through idolatry (cf. chapter 12).

Because "walking after" other gods means taking/following a different suzerain, it means, ipso facto, "rebellion against the Lord your God." Since the Lord is Israel's king, they commit high treason if they choose

---

5   Israel received a practical lesson in this as they followed the Glory above the tabernacle (Exod. 40:34–38; and cf. discussion in chap. 8); the new covenant counterpart is "keeping in step with the Spirit" (Gal. 5:25).

to have another king (i.e., god) over them. That helps one understand the death penalty for false prophets under the Mosaic covenant. It also explains why the penalty for false messengers under the new covenant is very different. The form of God's kingdom under the old covenant and its form under the new covenant determine the form of God's penalties in each kingdom and under each covenant.

Under the Mosaic covenant, if Israel followed the lead of a false prophet and "walked after" other gods, their behavior could lead to divine enactment of the covenant curses. That would in turn lead to God's dismantling the state—that form of the kingdom. Any prophet who would lead them astray would be committing, in effect, high treason and encouraging them to commit high treason as well. In a nation-state, such a crime is punishable by death. It is a severe punishment, but one that does what it can to safeguard the state from an eruption of treasonous behavior. Likewise, the death penalty for the false prophet can help protect the people from the flourishing of a treasonous—false and idolatrous—spirit and thus help ensure the continuance of that form of God's kingdom, the nation-state of Israel. So again, the form of the punishment fits or is conditioned by the form of the kingdom.

Under the new covenant, the form of the kingdom is not a nation-state but a supranational church. This new form of the kingdom has no death penalty: anathematizing (including exclusion from the church) is the only form of response to false prophecy open to it (provided the false prophet is unrepentant, cf. Matt. 18:15–17). Paul writes of anyone who proclaims a false gospel: "But even if we or an angel from heaven should preach a gospel other than the one we preached to you, let him be under God's curse [lit. "anathema," ἀνάθεμα]! As we have already said, so now I say again: If anybody is preaching to you a gospel other than what you accepted, let him be under God's curse!" (Gal. 1:8–9).

The punishment of a false prophet under the old covenant is determined by the Old Testament form of God's kingdom. It also has eschatological overtones: "You must purge the evil from among you." (Deut. 13:5). The word "purge" is literally "burn" (בָּעַר). One may think forward to the example of Achan and his family who, after being stoned to death, were burned (Josh. 7:25). That was more merciful than Assyrian practice, as their emperors sometimes boasted they burned a city full of rebellious vassals alive.[6] But merciful or not, these examples of burning, to purge

---

[6]   Cf. Jeffrey Niehaus, "Joshua and Ancient Near Eastern Warfare," *JETS* 31, no. 1 (1988): 45; Niehaus, *ANETBT*, 150.

evil from among God's people, adumbrate an eschatological judgment when, as Peter says: "The day of the Lord will come like a thief. The heavens will disappear with a roar; the elements will be destroyed by fire, and the earth and everything done in it will be laid bare" (2 Peter 3:10), and as John reports in his eschatological vision: "Anyone whose name was not found written in the book of life was thrown into the lake of fire" (Rev. 20:15). Obviously, the thematic coherence of such biblical statements—such as the connection between Deuteronomy 13:5 and Revelation 20:15—does not depend on how much a person (even Moses) under the old covenant could know of any future parallel or analogy or iteration of the same principle.

Noted already, and to be explored later, is the identification of God's judgment fire as the Holy Spirit, as Isaiah intimates, "When the Lord has washed away the filth of the daughters of Zion, and purged the blood of Jerusalem from her midst, by the spirit [or "Spirit"] of judgment and by the spirit [or "Spirit"] of burning" (Isa. 4:4 NKJV), and compare John's eschatological portrayal in which "from the throne proceeded lightnings, thunderings, and voices. Seven lamps of fire were burning before the throne, which are the seven Spirits [or, as often suggested, "the sevenfold Spirit"] of God" (Rev. 4:5 KNJV). If the association of eschatological judgment fire and the Spirit is correct, such data as those found in Deuteronomy 13:5 and Joshua 7:24 anticipate in the natural realm a supernatural and ontological reality.

Deuteronomy 18 presents the last guidelines for prophecy of the renewal covenant. The Lord gives not only *torah* regarding prophecy, but also a prophecy of a future prophet who will be like Moses. The verses fall conveniently into three sections: what is proscribed (18:9–14), what is promised (18:15–19), and what is prescribed (18:20–22).

What Is Proscribed

Moses starts by warning the people against forms of revelation that are not allowed. The passage shows how people in that day hoped to discern the future, or the will of the gods. It also contains a clue regarding a spiritual dynamic that can be involved in that illegitimate pursuit of knowledge:

> When you come into the land which the LORD your God is giving you, you shall not learn to follow the abominations of those nations. There shall not be found among you anyone who makes his son or his daughter

pass through the fire, or one who practices witchcraft, or a soothsayer, or one who interprets omens, or a sorcerer, or one who conjures spells, or a medium, or a spiritist, or one who calls up the dead. For all who do these things are an abomination to the LORD, and because of these abominations the LORD your God drives them out from before you. You shall be blameless before the LORD your God. For these nations which you will dispossess listened to soothsayers and diviners; but as for you, the LORD your God has not appointed such for you. (Deut. 18:9–14 NKJV)

Before telling his people how the Lord will provide prophetically in the future, the Lord tells them what avenues of supernatural revelation are proscribed. Not so long ago, comments of this sort may have seemed bizarre—as though one could get in touch with a supernatural realm by any means at all. But our culture (if the singular noun still applies) has been undergoing changes that have made various forms of spirituality and various ways of being in touch with an otherworldly realm seem plausible. But why would one want such contact in any age? Arguably, there is one reason—human insecurity. Ever since the Fall, human beings, separated from God, cannot help but experience insecurity because we were meant to find our security in God, who is not only supernal but also and as such the ground of our being as well as the only possible provision for our ongoing existence (cf. Heb. 1:3). Nonetheless, although God sustains all things by the word of his power, not all things exist in communion and fellowship with him. The Spirit may sustain them but he does not dwell in all of them. Consequently, humans in a fallen condition naturally seek whatever security they can find—money, power, or as here, knowledge of the future. The operative although unspoken assumption seems to be that if one knows the future, one can do something to prepare for it.

The Lord knows his people need reassurance about their provision and their future, and he is willing to provide it. After all, the Lord carried them "on eagles' wings" and brought them to himself (Exod. 19:4; cf. Deut. 32:11). He also knows, however, the ways of seeking knowledge of the future practiced by the peoples around Israel can lead to no good and can put people in touch with no supernatural power at all, or perhaps with an evil power.[7] In any case, the Lord wants true guidance for

---

7   The word translated "medium" in Deuteronomy 18:11 (אוֹב) apparently had a common meaning "ghost" (cf. BDB, 15). However, the same term appears in Leviticus 20:27: "A man or woman who is a medium or spiritist among you must be put to death." The

his people. Sorcerers, mediums, wizards, and necromancers are not the way to get it.

What Is Promised

The Lord knows his people need guidance from above. By ruling out some forms of guidance he is not excluding all possible forms of supernatural direction. What he promises now is actually an archetype of all the prophetic guidance they have so far had through Moses, and also of any guidance they will later have through prophets of the Mosaic covenant:

> The LORD your God will raise up for you a Prophet like me from your midst, from your brethren. Him you shall hear, according to all you desired of the LORD your God in Horeb in the day of the assembly, saying, "Let me not hear again the voice of the LORD my God, nor let me see this great fire anymore, lest I die."And the LORD said to me: "What they have spoken is good. I will raise up for them a Prophet like you from among their brethren, and will put My words in His mouth, and He shall speak to them all that I command Him. And it shall be that whoever will not hear My words, which He speaks in My name, I will require it of him." (Deut. 18:15–19 NKJV)

The promised prophet will be like Moses (v. 15). That would have meant more to its first hearers than it would first mean to us. Subsequently we are told: "There has not arisen a prophet since in Israel like Moses, whom the LORD knew face to face" (Deut. 34:10). Since the Lord raised up other prophets who imparted guidance or instruction (i.e., *torah*) to his people, and since the Lord raised up prophets who worked remarkable signs and wonders (e.g., Elijah and Elisha), one might ask what more would be required for a prophet to be "like Moses"? Moses had one qualification shared by no other prophet until Christ: Moses

---

Hebrew of this verse begins literally, "A man or woman *in whom* there is an אוֹב." We know that there are only two sorts of spirit—apart from a person's own spirit—that can be "in" a person, as reported in the Bible: the Holy Spirit or an evil spirit. The implication of Leviticus 20:27 seems to be that a medium, if he or she is a true medium—that is, truly in touch with some spirit—is dealing with an unclean spirit. If so, this would add some weight to the judgment expressed by the Lord on such people (and cf. the judgment on false prophets in Deut. 13:5, who may also, at least sometimes, prophesy by false spirits; cf. 1 Kings 22:21–22).

mediated a covenant for all the Lord's people. They would not be the Lord's people unless they lived under that covenant. The Mosaic covenant had brought them into a covenantal relationship with the Lord. It had provided *torah* by which they were to live. The same cannot be said of the Davidic covenant—even though David, like Moses, was a covenant mediator prophet—because the covenant David mediated was a covenant narrowly focused on the royal line. Moreover, David himself still lived under the Mosaic covenant, and the creation of the Davidic covenant did nothing to change that. Subsequently, David was judged under the Mosaic covenant—although the Lord did show him extraordinary mercy.

Once more, no prophet like Moses arose until Christ, who, like Moses, mediated a covenant under which all the Lord's people would live, and in terms of which they must live if they are to be reckoned God's people, "the Israel of God" (Gal. 6:16), "the household of faith" (Gal. 6:10 NKJV). Accordingly, Peter, when he addressed the crowd after healing a lame beggar at the temple, confidently identified the prophet promised in this passage with Christ: "For Moses said, 'The Lord your God will raise up for you a prophet like me from among your own people; you must listen to everything he tells you'" (Acts 3:22).

This last and greatest covenant mediator prophet not only mediated the final divine-human covenant in the course of fallen human history by the shedding of his blood (and so we have come "to Jesus the mediator of a new covenant, and to the sprinkled blood that speaks a better word than the blood of Abel," Heb. 12:24)—he also preexisted all other prophets, and has always been the archetype of all prophets.

One more feature of this remarkable passage deserves notice. The reason given for the coming of the promised prophet was the inability of the people to endure the Lord's presence on Sinai: "Just as you desired of the LORD your God on the day of the assembly, when you said, 'Let me not hear again the voice of the LORD my God, or see this great fire any more, lest I die'" (Deut. 18:16 ESV; cf. Exod. 20:18–19). The Lord approved this request (v. 17) because he understood the root of it: the inability of fallen people to endure the divine glory. The discussion of the "Isaiah Apocalypse" noted this issue as it was highlighted in Isaiah 24:23: once sin has been done away with, the Lord's elders (and by synecdoche all God's people) will be able to endure the divine glory—no longer mitigated by "dark cloud," or even by the Lord incarnate as he walked among us.[8]

---

8   This also has been, of course, a major theme in the book *God at Sinai*: the Lord's work in *Heilsgeschichte* to bring about a state of affairs in which, once again as in Eden, he

Although, then, Deuteronomy 18:15–19 contains a messianic prophecy, and although it delineates or suggests certain characteristics of the promised prophet that will make him unique (he will, implicitly, mediate a new covenant for all the people since, to be like Moses, he will have to be a covenant mediator on such a scale; he will in his own person provide the Lord's answer to the problem created by sin—the people's inability to endure the Lord's unmitigated glory), nonetheless he will have characteristics shared by ontologically lesser covenant lawsuit prophets, characteristics Moses himself shares with them: He will be a man, he will be an Israelite, he will be a prophet, he will speak God's words, and the Lord himself will require it of his people if they disobey him. The final section of the passage under consideration implies one further quality of a prophet in Israel.

What Is Prescribed

Moses returns to the *near* future after giving the people a glimpse of that "prophet like Moses" whose advent lay in the far future—after centuries of disaster and hope, centuries that would provide the pedagogy Israel would need (Gal. 3:24) to bring them to a place at which some of them could accept the prophet Moses had described to their ancestors. As Moses turns to the near future, he gives the people final *torah* regarding false prophets who would come:

> But the prophet who presumes to speak a word in My name, which I have not commanded him to speak, or who speaks in the name of other gods, that prophet shall die. And if you say in your heart, "How shall we know the word which the LORD has not spoken?"—when a prophet speaks in the name of the LORD, if the thing does not happen or come to pass, that is the thing which the LORD has not spoken; the prophet has spoken it presumptuously; you shall not be afraid of him. (Deut. 18:20–22 NKJV)

In addition to a death penalty for a false prophet, this last portion of *torah* provides two things: standards by which a prophet may be assessed and an attitudinal requirement. The standards of assessment show a prophet to be false: (1) if he speaks in the name of other gods, or (2) if he speaks a word that is not from the Lord. How may Israel know whether

---

could be among his people with no interference from human sinfulness—a state in which his people might not only endure his glory but also shine like the sun in his presence.

or not a word is from the Lord? If a prediction does not come to pass, it is not from the Lord (v. 20). Moses had already provided a standard echoed here: if a prophet counsels following another god, he is not from the Lord (Deut. 13:5). That provision is reaffirmed, and Moses now offers a supplementary criterion.[9] The pedagogical soundness of repeating earlier *torah* and then adding to it is obvious. A required attitude is also given the people: they are told they need not "fear" such a prophet. "Fear" is used here, as often, to mean "revere, pay high respect to." Once more, Moses affirms the death penalty for a false prophet.

The *torah* about prediction is fundamental. The prophetical books preserved in the literature of the old covenant clearly show that covenant lawsuit addresses (containing for the most part reviews of Israel's past behavior and indictments on the basis of such reviews) form the bulk of the prophetical material, and predictions are in the minority. Predictions occur mostly as warnings of coming judgments (because of the sins documented in the lawsuits) or less often (but perhaps more importantly), as promises of hope, restoration, and messianic redemption. Nonetheless, although they are in the minority, preditions are very important, and Moses has now given criteria for their evaluation.

Taken as a whole the passage, Deuteronomy 18:9–22, gives a final account of what the Lord's people should avoid and what they can expect by way of a prophet in days to come, after Moses has been taken from them:

1. The prophet will be Israelite (vv. 15, 18)
2. He will speak the word the Lord commands him (v. 18)
3. He will not speak in the name of other gods (v. 20)
4. Supernatural knowledge of the future, that is, prediction, could be a sign of the prophet's authenticity and authority (v. 22)

The passage offers clear evaluative criteria for a prophet. It also includes the last and greatest messianic prophecy in the Mosaic corpus. Although Moses had been, and subsequent prophets would also to some extent be, the Lord's solution to the disconnect made by sin between Israel and her holy God, the true solution would only come in the person of the prophet promised in this passage, who would like Moses be a mediator of a covenant for all the people, and who would be able to say

---

9   Supplementary, although implied by its inverse, "If a prophet, or one who foretells by dreams, appears among you and announces to you a sign or wonder, and if the sign or wonder spoken of takes place" (Deut. 13:1–2a).

of himself: "He who has seen me has seen the Father" (John 14:9 NKJV). The promise of another covenant mediator prophet implies ineluctably the promise of another covenant—a promise made explicit only later, in the prophecies of Isaiah, Jeremiah, and Ezekiel.[10] One sees here, once again, a developmental principle: as the history of the Lord's covenantal dealings with his people unfolds, the revelation that records and presents that history displays certain ideas and doctrines with greater clarity through time. This is apparently the Lord's pedagogical way with his people, showing them more of what is to come—and thus more of *his own nature*—as time and experience prepare them to receive it. Paul expresses the penultimate realization of the fruit of this pedagogical tendency as an ontological reality: "but we have the mind of Christ" (1 Cor. 2:16).

The Pentateuchal standards for prophecy have led to a prophecy of the Christ. That prophecy can be a stepping stone to a brief discussion of Christology and typology, with some illustrations, and that discussion will conclude this chapter.

ADUMBRATIONS I: CHRISTOLOGY AND TYPOLOGY

We take up the matters of Christology and typology in chapter 19 but now offer some preliminary thoughts on those topics in the context of prophecy. The undertaking is legitimate because as Vos noted typology and its subset Christology are oblique forms of prophecy. We begin with Christological reflections on the "prophet like Moses."

The Prophet like Moses

One of the things Deuternomy 18:15–21 showed God's people was that there *would be* another prophet like Moses. The promise invited the consideration: what could make a prophet "like Moses"? It was understood that, although subsequent prophets received the Lord's words for the people and conveyed them to the people, and although some subsequent prophets also did signs and wonders, none of them could have been "like Moses" in some important way, since it is also clear that no prophet like Moses arose in Israel—Moses, "whom the Lord knew face to face" (Deut. 34:10). The statement indicates a degree of intimacy with the Lord that

---

10 The promise of a new covenant is hinted at in, for example, Hosea and Amos, but not stated explicitly as such.

no subsequent prophet enjoyed until the incarnate Son who could say he was one with the Father. Nonetheless, once we know that the Son is the future "prophet like me" of whom Moses spoke, we catch a glimpse of one explicitly Christological figure—namely, this same Moses—who was a prophet like the Son as (with due account for an ontological difference) the Son was a prophet like Moses.[11] The fact is established, then, or at least indicated, that one who holds a prophetic office could be considered a foreshadowing of Christ or, as theologians say, a type of Christ.

As Geerhardus Vos reminded us, typology and Christology are forms of prophecy.[12] Classically, important volumes appeared in the nineteenth century on these topics not only exploring things in the Old Testament that the authors considered typological or Christological but also establishing criteria by which one could hope to discern or decide what things in the Old Testament could justly be called typological and what could not, and what people in the Old Testament could justly be called Christological and what people could not.[13] In the latter case, it has made sense to argue that anyone in the Old Testament who held any of the offices Christ is known to have held, or to hold, could be called a type of Christ. This is consistent with the case of Moses and the promised prophet like Moses. It also makes sense in terms of divinely given roles.

When God gave prophets, priests, and kings among people, and especially among his covenant people, he was giving on the human plane functions that he himself always has filled and does fill. It was understood that Adam was a prophet who meditated the creation covenant, a priest set to keep and do the service of the Garden-temple, and a king who was commanded to rule over and develop the earth. These roles, *mutatis mutandis*, show up subsequently in the history of God's covenant people under special grace. But God is Suzerain over all and the Son is the great High Priest at the right hand of the Father always making intercession

---

11   The Son was a man like Moses, but his ontological difference lay in what he affirmed of himself, for example, "For as the Father has life in himself, so he has granted the Son also to have life in himself" (John 5:26). Jesus' claim to aseity showed he was ontologically different from—and superior to—any other prophet, even Moses.

12   Geerhardus Vos, *Biblical Theology: Old and New Testaments* (1948; reprint, Grand Rapids: Eerdmans, 1991), 144–46.

13   For typology, cf. Patrick Fairbairn, *Typology of Scripture* (1847; reprint, Grand Rapids: Kregel, 2000); for Christology, cf. E. W. Hengstenberg, *Christology of the Old Testament* (1839; reprint, Tampa: MacDonald Publishing, 1972); cf. further Vern S. Poythress, *The Shadow of Christ in the Law of Moses* (Phillipsburg, NJ: Presbyterian & Reformed, 1991).

for his people, and he is also the prophet promised by Moses, and as such mediated the new and better covenant (Heb. 8:6; cf. 12:24), and moreover is the archetype of all prophets as the Word through whom the Father by the Spirit spoke the creative fiats to establish the first form of his kingdom by what would become recognizable in human history as a prophetic paradigm. Also, the preincarnate Son was the Word who by the Spirit from the Father mediated the creation covenant to Adam by creating Adam into it—that creation covenant Adam then mediated to all generations. Although it cannot be demonstrated, it would be consistent if the Son also had a priestly role before the creation and subsequently interceding for the created order and for humans within that order—as well as being with the Father and the Spirit the ruler of all and the one who mediates God's Spirit-presence and thus also God's self-revelation in the realm of common grace, and that is also a prophetic role.

The observations just made would also be consistent with a larger pattern observed in the matter of heavenly-earthly correspondences. No divinely created thing exists or could exist without first being an idea in the mind of God. The whole created order therefore is patterned after ideas internal to the being of God. As has been noted, human ideas that are genuinely "new" among people and not merely derivative by some combination of preexisting data in the created order—such ideas (as, e.g., Cain's idea of a city) have a supernal source. As was also noted, much human art and other forms of creativity owe God as their source, however much the art or other created products may draw upon data in the already created order, and however much the art or other created products may be distorted in the creative process by the nature of the human artist or creator who produces them.

If one remembers that, for example, the Lord told Moses to make the earthly tabernacle after the pattern (παράδειγμα, i.e., "paradigm," Exod. 25:8, LXX) he revealed from heaven on Sinai, one can appreciate the implications that have been noted and explored.

The Bronze Serpent

Taking the idea of a paradigm for purposes of illustration, we can make the following point about an event in Numbers: the Lord has Moses make a "paradigm" that is Christological, although its Christology does not appear in its Old Testament context but is made clear in the New Testament. This case is an example of Mosaic Christology that has nothing to do with the roles of prophet, priest, or king, but has much to do with divine healing. In Numbers 21 one reads the following notable account:

> They traveled from Mount Hor along the route to the Red Sea, to go around Edom. But the people grew impatient on the way; they spoke against God and against Moses, and said, "Why have you brought us up out of Egypt to die in the wilderness? There is no bread! There is no water! And we detest this miserable food!" Then the LORD sent venomous snakes among them; they bit the people and many Israelites died. The people came to Moses and said, "We sinned when we spoke against the LORD and against you. Pray that the LORD will take the snakes away from us." So Moses prayed for the people. The LORD said to Moses, "Make a snake and put it up on a pole; anyone who is bitten can look at it and live." So Moses made a bronze snake and put it up on a pole. Then when anyone was bitten by a snake and looked at the bronze snake, he lived. (Num. 21:4–9)

Why would looking at a facsimile of a venomous serpent produce healing in those who looked? The obvious answer is the Lord said it would, and because he does not lie, he made it so. But there is a deeper answer. Before we address it we note the story does not end here. Later Jesus tells Nicodemus, "Just as Moses lifted up the snake in the wilderness, so the Son of Man must be lifted up, that everyone who believes may have eternal life in him" (John 3:14–15). Jesus creates the following parallel:[14]

Serpent	Son of Man
Lifted on pole	Lifted on cross
Bitten people look	Sinners see and believe
People healed	People receive eternal life

The parallel between the bronze serpent and the Son of Man is counterintuitive because one normally does not associate Jesus with a serpent. It succeeds because of parallel symbolism: a bronze serpent lifted up to public view on a pole represents God's punishment for Israel's sin. The Son of Man lifted up to public view on a cross also represents God's

---

14 Vos does not discuss this parallel at all. He would probably have called it symbolic as well as typological (cf. Vos, *Biblical Theology*, 144–46). He does refer to it, in association with a number of other passages, as one "fulfillment of Old Testament prophecy" pointed out by Jesus to authenticate "his own messianic character" (359).

punishment for Israel's sin—for *all* sin. It fulfills the statement, "God made him who had no sin to be sin for us, so that in him we might become the righteousness of God" (2 Cor. 5:21). As Peter says, "He himself bore our sins in his body on the cross, so that we might die to sins and live for righteousness; by his wounds you have been healed" (1 Peter 2:24; cf. Isa. 53:4–6). In other words, Christ on the cross symbolized God's punishment for the sin of all, and not less so because the Son himself "knew no sin." God nonetheless made him "to be sin"—symbolically to represent the punishment of others' sin, on the cross, just as the bronze serpent had represented God's punishment of others' sin as it was raised up, on the pole. In the Mosaic example, Israelites were healed. In Jesus' parallel case, as Isaiah prophesied, "by his wounds" we also "have been healed."

But why does looking at a bronze serpent heal God's people? And how does it parallel believing in Jesus? Understanding faith is essential to answering those questions. Faith—belief/believing—is an inner act of amening who God is and what he does. Those who looked on the bronze serpent—and who looked because the Lord *had said to look if they wanted to be healed*—were amening the Lord and his appointed means of healing/salvation, and so God honored their amening (their faith), and they were healed. Those who "look at" the Son on the cross (implicitly in Jesus' comparison because of the parallel with the Mosaic example) are also amening the Lord and his appointed means of healing/salvation.[15] God will honor that amening with healing: they will "have eternal life in him" (John 3:15; and cf. again 1 Peter 2:24). In Moses' day the healing/salvation was from the serpent's bite. In Jesus' day, and for all days afterward until the eschaton, the healing/salvation is also from the serpent's bite—but the serpent is "that ancient serpent called the devil, or Satan, who leads the whole world astray" (Rev. 12:9).[16]

ADUMBRATIONS II: PROPHETIC BLESSINGS AND CURSES

Blessings and curses are widely familiar terms in biblical studies. Analysis of the Hittite treaty form and recognition of its importance for Old

---

15 Or, one might say, those who properly *regard* or *own the meaning of* the Son on the cross.

16 Cf. also "The *sting of death is sin*, and the power of sin is the law. But thanks be to God! He gives us the victory through our Lord Jesus Christ" (1 Cor. 15:56–57, emphasis added); and discussion in chapter 5 of volume 3.

Testament studies, and in particular for the study of the Pentateuch, probably accounts for this. The blessing and curse sections of ancient near eastern treaties and biblical covenants have drawn attention partly (1) because the genres are interesting (who is not interested in curses?) and partly (2) because the presence of blessing sections has suggested a Mosaic date for some Pentateuchal materials (e.g., Deut. 28:1–15), or has been seen to be consistent with such a date. Blessing sections are a known feature of second millennium treaties but, so far, have not been found in their first millennium counterparts.

When the Lord pronounced those blessings and curses he was in a position to know not only what he would do in case of Israel's obedience or disobedience, but also that he could do those things. For that matter he already knew he *had done them* in a day future for Israel but eternally present before himself.

But what of those cases in which human beings uttered blessings or curses? How could a person who blessed someone know that the words of blessing he uttered were not mere wind—and the same might be true of any curse he pronounced? When God pronounces a blessing or a curse he knows it is not mere wind (although it is Spirit!) because he can make it happen. He also knows when he utters it *how* he has enacted it in the future, because for him the future is also present and past. A human being is not in this situation. Nonetheless, we see that blessings and curses uttered by human beings in the Old Testament do come to pass. Since they involve future events, the person who uttered them—unlike God—cannot bring them to pass, and since they typically come to pass some time after the one who uttered them is dead, it would seem there are only two ways to account for their fulfillment. Either (1) they are merely human utterances the Lord chooses to honor and bring to pass, or (2) they are spoken by the Holy Spirit and must therefore come to pass, because the Holy Spirit is the Spirit of truth and knows and can do all things.[17]

If a person is led to utter blessings or curses by the Spirit so that they are utterances of the Spirit—the view taken here—then they are virtually a form of prophecy as their eventual fulfillment shows. Three cases of blessing and/or curse are now considered. They are uttered by humans, apparently on their own initiative but, we propose, with the omniscient and omnipotent Spirit involved: (1) Noah's pronouncements after Ham's sin, (2) Isaac's blessing on Jacob, and (3) Joshua's curse on anyone who

---

17   Cf. Isaiah 44:24: "Ich bin der HERR, der alles tut" (Luther). Cf. earlier: Ἐγὼ κύριος ὁ συντελῶν πάντα (LXX); Ego sum Dominus, faciens omnia (Vulgate).

would rebuild Jericho. We turn to this issue—the prophetic nature of blessings and curses—now because the Mosaic covenant revelations open the door to prophecy and the prophetic in several aspects, and they do so much more than revelatory data found under the previous covenants.

Noah's Pronouncements after Ham's Sin

The first case is what Noah says after the sin of Ham. This was discussed in its context in volume 1. We now consider it in regard to one important particular not mentioned there but taken up here because the Conquest is soon to come. Noah blessed Shem, and the implications of that blessing were noted. Noah blessed Japheth, and we saw from our locus in history that the blessings involved (God would extend the territory of Japheth, and Japheth would dwell in the tens of Shem) would also come true. Noah cursed Canaan, and that was understood partly in terms of the *Gattung* of household judgment found in the Bible and the ancient Near East. However, there is a more particular reason why Ham's son, Canaan, and not Ham himself, is the object of Noah's curse: "The lowest of slaves will he be to his brothers" (Gen. 9:25). The reason is that—like Shem and Japheth—Canaan will figure largely in the history of God's people. His land will be the Promised Land, and Shem's descendants will have a great deal to do with Canaan—for centuries—in a future the Lord has prepared for them.

Isaac's Blessing on Jacob

Isaac blesses Jacob, and his blessing also may be called prophetic because it helps move history toward the fulfillment of Noah's curse on Canaan:[18]

> Ah, the smell of my son
>> is like the smell of a field
>> that the LORD has blessed.
> May God give you heaven's dew
>> and earth's richness—
>> an abundance of grain and new wine.

---

18 Cf. the Lord's statements regarding prophetic words: "So is my word that goes out from my mouth: It will not return to me empty, but will accomplish what I desire and achieve the purpose for which I sent it" (Isa. 55:11); "Then the LORD said to me, 'You have seen well, for I am watching over my word to perform it'" (Jer. 1:12 ESV).

> May nations serve you
>> and peoples bow down to you.
> Be lord over your brothers,
>> and may the sons of your mother bow down to you.
> May those who curse you be cursed
>> and those who bless you be blessed. (Gen. 27:27b–29)

Jacob fooled Isaac into granting this blessing, but it is nonetheless powerful and effective.[19] The blessing has to do, for the most part, with things the Lord will fulfill in Canaan after the Conquest—rich fields watered with the dew of heaven, abundance of grain and new wine, and the vassaldom of nations. Isaac expresses them as wishes or hopes ("May God give you," "May nations serve you") and that is the language of blessing by a human, whose blessing is both a pronouncement and—because, from the human point of view, it is contingent on God's favorable response—a prayer. The Lord will fulfill these paternal blessings, and because the Bible records their fulfillment one can see their prophetic nature. But no prophecy comes by the will of man: "For prophecy never had its origin in the human will, but prophets, though human, spoke from God as they were carried along by the Holy Spirit" (2 Peter 1:21). The fruition of Isaac's blessing shows the Lord fulfilled it, and also suggests Isaac was "carried along by the Holy Spirit" as he spoke the words over Jacob.

One more thing to note is the last pronouncement: "May those who curse you be cursed/and those who bless you be blessed" (Gen. 27:29). It is a clear echo of the Lord's own blessing on Abram when he made his first overtures to him—overtures that would lead to the cutting of the Abrahamic covenant with its promise of land for a future generation (Gen. 12:3a). The Lord expressed it then as a sure blessing. Isaac expresses it now as a human blessing—as a hope, but also because he was carried along by the Spirit, a hope the Lord would fulfill. From God's point of view, Isaac's blessing had long ago been fulfilled by the Spirit, who had worked in the Conquest before the creation of the world.

Joshua

Our third case is the curse Joshua utters over anyone who undertakes to rebuild Jericho:

---

19 For a discussion of the role of deception in God's way of things see chapter 11.

> At the cost of his firstborn son
> will he lay its foundations;
> at the cost of his youngest
> will he set up its gates. (Josh. 6:26b)

The curse is drastic because Jericho's conquest has a symbolic value. Jericho was the firstfruits of the Conquest, and so it, and everything in it, were devoted to the Lord (Hebrew חרם, Josh. 6:17; cf. 6:24). Achan's transgression of this ban would bring God's judicial process and the execution of Achan and his family, and that is an issue of justice to be explored later.[20] But the curse Joshua pronounced on anyone who would rebuild Jericho did come to pass: "In Ahab's time, Hiel of Bethel rebuilt Jericho. He laid its foundations at the cost of his firstborn son Abiram, and he set up its gates at the cost of his youngest son Segub, accordance with the word of the Lord spoken by Joshua son of Nun" (1 Kings 16:36). The verse reports the fulfillment of Joshua's curse. It also adds information. In the original account we were only told, "At that time Joshua pronounced this solemn oath" (Josh. 6:26a). One finds clearly stated now what one could only surmise in Joshua 6:26: Joshua's curse was not just his own, but was "the word of the Lord spoken by Joshua son of Nun."[21] In other words, it was the Spirit speaking prophetically through Joshua when he pronounced the curse.

The biblical explanation of Joshua's curse affirms our proposal: when someone utters a blessing or a curse, the words may be Spirit, and thus powerful and effective. Such was obviously the case with Joshua's curse in Joshua 6:26. It would seem to be the case in any humanly uttered blessing or curse (in the OT) that later comes to pass. If one looks back once more to Noah's curse on Canaan, one can see it was also most likely a prophetic curse produced through Noah by the Spirit who knew for a certainty Canaan would one day be the slave of his brothers—just as he knew Shem would one day enjoy a special relationship with the Lord, and Japheth would one day dwell in the tents of Shem.

---

20   Cf. the discussion in Niehaus, *ANETBT*, 138–161, esp. 153. Cf. the judicial process parallel displayed between Genesis 3 and Joshua 7, in volume 1, 109.

21   One may—one should—think of Eve's supposed "addition" in Genesis 3:2 to what the Lord had said in Genesis 2:17, and of Abraham's additional information regarding his ruse in Genesis 20:13, and of the Lord's addition in Genesis 26:5 to what he had said to Abram/Abraham in Genesis 12–22. Cf. volume 1, 97.

ADUMBRATIONS III: THOUGHTS ON TYPOLOGY

Some criteria were noted that would enable one to understand whether an Old Testament figure should be called a type of Christ. Those long recognized criteria serve us well and simplify the work of Christology because they remove any subjective element. If, for example, any king under the Mosaic covenant was a type of Christ merely by virtue of his office—whether or not he was virtuous—there need be no qualms about saying Ahab was a type of Christ, however unlike Christ he was in other respects.

The case is not so simple when it comes to the larger category of typology. Unless we restrict the identification of type-antitype relations to those the New Testament designates as such, the field is open to the discovery—or the unbridled invention—of all sorts of correspondences. A classic example is the identification of the scarlet thread Rahab must hang outside her window (Josh. 2:18.21) as a foreshadowing (or a symbol or type) of the blood of Christ.[22]

One piece of typology can serve us well, even if it is not identified as such in the New Testament. It includes an example of Christology no one would dispute. People easily recognize that Joshua is a type of Christ; Joshua and Jesus even share the same name (LXX renders Joshua in, e.g., Josh. 1:10 as Ἰησοῦς, i.e., Jesus). Joshua is a type of Christ (1) as a prophet and (2) as a leader of the people into the Old Testament form of God's kingdom, the Promised Land. The following parallels are clear:

Joshua (Ἰησοῦς)	Jesus (Ἰησοῦς)
People of God	People of God
Warfare (physical)	Warfare (spiritual)
Kingdom (land)	Kingdom (church)/eternal

Christology anchors typology in this example, and the pattern replicates what was seen in the case of Moses, although in that case we had to deal with a covenant mediator prophet (which Joshua was not) and the establishment of a covenant people (which Joshua did not do, nor was he tasked with it). But just as the Lord waged war through Moses to establish a covenant people and a temple presence, so the Lord would wage war through Joshua to establish a land for the Old Testament form of the

---

22 Cf. chapter 2 of volume 3 for fuller discussion, including discussion of the foundation and criteria of typology.

kingdom, a nation-state. That form of the kingdom would be governed by the covenant Moses mediated, and indwelt by the temple presence the Lord established through Moses. In a similar way, the New Testament form of the kingdom—the church—would be established by the covenant mediation of the "prophet like Moses" and governed by new covenant *torah*, and would itself be the temple inhabited by the Lord of the covenant (cf. 1 Cor. 3:16).

The New Testament form of the kingdom would accomplish a missional purpose members of the Old Testament form of the kingdom could not accomplish, because the Spirit did not indwell them and empower them. That issue is discussed in a separate chapter that also considers the conquest itinerary of Paul.[23] For now we turn to the conquest itinerary of Joshua and what it tells us of the faith or lack of faith of the Canaanites, and how that scenario anticipates the eschaton.

---

23 Cf. chapter 16.

CHAPTER TEN

THE MOSAIC COVENANT CONQUEST

The Major Paradigm in its post-Fall articulations introduced the element of warfare because of the inevitable resistance God's irruptions into a fallen world would produce, and this is true especially if the irruptions were judgment acts. Divine advance initiated in the Major Paradigm would always produce resistance en route to the realization of such stages of the dynamic as covenant formation, people formation, and temple building for the Lord's dwelling among a people. Even when the time was not yet for a temple and a divine residence, the divine initiative was an intrusion, and the warfare, if only suggested by association as between, for example, Genesis 14 and 15 (a warfare between God's elect and the alliance of Babylon), was real and significant nonetheless. It appears full blown against Pharaoh and the gods of Egypt—just as it later would to discerning eyes in the ministry of Christ and his crucifixion, the act of war sealed victoriously by a resurrection that showed the covenant "cut" on the cross to be true, and so its promises also would prove true.

After the new covenant came into being, however, another sort of warfare would begin: the spiritual warfare of the advance of the kingdom that had been established by the warfare of the Major Paradigm—that is, the ongoing warfare of the church that would demolish false arguments and bring people into a now established kingdom. Likewise prefiguratively, after the cutting of the Mosaic covenant by the warfare of the Major Paradigm another sort of warfare would begin: the physical warfare by armed and organized Israelites against the inhabitants of the Promised Land who were coming under judgment and would be replaced.

As one considers the conquest of the Promised Land from a theological point of view a few things are paramount, and these points form the topics of this chapter. First, one must keep firmly in mind that the

Conquest under Joshua, although fought by men, was not merely human warfare. It was a divine judgment. Second, although the Lord had long-term goals in mind for the land, retention of the land in the short term was contingent upon Israel's obedience to the Mosaic covenant. That was the legal arrangement under which Israel had become a form of the kingdom of God and under which she received a specific mandate for conquest. Third and related to the second point, the Lord would treat his people just as he had treated the Canaanites before them if they turned to a lifestyle like that of the Canaanites—the land would "vomit them out" just as it had "vomited out" the pagan inhabitants of the land (cf. Lev. 18:25–26; 20:22). Fourth, Joshua and Israel would win their battles *only* because the Lord fought for them (cf. Josh. 10:42) and this fourth principle harks back to the theme that the Conquest was a judgment. Evidence suggests that the divine warrior who led the conquest was the preincarnate Son—the angel of the LORD promised in Exodus 23. Fifth and finally for our purposes, faith would play an important role in the Conquest, and Rahab (cited as an example of faith in Hebrews) has a good deal to teach on this matter—and faith as a criterion also has eschatological implications. The present chapter concludes with discussion of Rahab's faith, her covenant with the spies, her deception, and with a look toward the New Testament, the role of deception in divine judgments.

THE CONQUEST AS A JUDGMENT

Consideration of the Conquest as a judgment may start with some comment on what the Conquest was not. The Conquest was not an act of aggression in merely human terms. The Conquest was not—all appearances to the common grace eye notwithstanding—a war of genocide. The Conquest was not even, to appeal to a humanly contrived way of justifying war, a "just war" on the human plane.

Just as western civilization is indebted to the church for much of its cultural heritage—the beginnings of musical notation, drama, even other arts and sciences—it is also indebted to thinkers of the early church for what is commonly known as just war theory. What began apparently with Augustine has been developed over the centuries and used at times to justify and at times to disqualify the war efforts of nations.

Among the principles of just war theory, three are important for the present purpose, which is to elucidate the nature of the Conquest and even to correlate it successfully though in an unexpected way with just war theory. First, a war can only be just if it redresses some wrong or responds to some offense. Second, the response must be proportional to the offense or to the injury suffered. Third, a war can only be just if it discriminates between combatants and non-combatants.[1]

If one considers the Conquest in light of the criteria of just war theory in human terms it does not fare so well. First, the Canaanites had in no way offended or injured the Israelites. They had been living in their own land minding their own business. Second, the question of proportionality is nullified by the absence of the first criterion. If there was no offense there can be no question of a response in proportion to the offense. Third, the Conquest did not at all discriminate between combatants and non-combatants. It did just the opposite. Regarding the inhabitants of the land the Lord commanded Israel: "You must destroy them totally. Make no treaty with them, and show them no mercy" (Deut. 7:2). Thus the Conquest fails all three of these important criteria that would qualify it as a just war.

What happens, though, if one considers the first criterion from a different point of view? What if the question is not, Did the Canaanites offend Israel, but rather, Did the Canaanites offend God? From that vantage point things look quite different. First, the Canaanites did offend God. After declaring a long list of sexual sins the Canaanites routinely committed (Lev. 18:20–24), the Lord said, "Do not defile yourselves in any of these ways, because this is how the nations that I am going to drive out before you became defiled. Even the land was defiled; so I punished it for its sin, and the land vomited out its inhabitants" (Lev. 18:25–26). Second, one may now see the Conquest for what it was—a divine judgment. Therefore—and since as Abraham indicated the "Judge of all the earth" will do what is right (Gen. 18:25)—the Lord's response to the offense is in fact proportional. The inhabitants of the land have rejected the Lord of life (as Joshua 2 shows), and so God will eliminate them entirely.[2] Third and consequently, there can be no distinction between combatants and non-combatants for all of them have been offenders. The Lord instructs Moses and Israel as follows:

When the LORD your God brings you into the land you are entering to possess and drives out before you many nations—the Hittites, Girgashites,

---

1   Cf. discussion and resources at http://www.justwartheory.com.

2   This leaves unanswered the question of, for example, infants who were too young to know right or wrong. Scripture at this point gives readers an opportunity to trust the Lord—that as Judge of all the earth he will do what is right. He alone knew what those infants would grow up to be had they been allowed to live and he alone knows their eternal destiny.

Amorites, Canaanites, Perizzites, Hivites and Jebusites, seven nations larger and stronger than you—and when the LORD your God has delivered them over to you and you have defeated them, then you must destroy them totally. Make no treaty with them, and show them no mercy. Do not intermarry with them. Do not give your daughters to their sons or take their daughters for your sons, for they will turn your children away from following me to serve other gods, and the LORD's anger will burn against you and will quickly destroy you. This is what you are to do to them: Break down their altars, smash their sacred stones, cut down their Asherah poles and burn their idols in the fire. For you are a people holy to the Lord your God. The LORD your God has chosen you out of all the peoples on the face of the earth to be his people, his treasured possession. (Deut. 7:1-6)

The verses show a mandate for utter destruction. They also show one reason for the mandate: preservation of God's people from sin, so they may be a holy people. Intermarriage and idolatry are related, and foreseen, snares. Canaanite idolatry was a manifest reason for the coming judgment (whose root and invisible cause, however, was lack of the possibility of faith among the Canaanites). Idolatry—which spiritually and thus properly understood seems commonplace enough in our day—is an offense to God because it is a warped devotion, and thus also a distorted development of humans made in God's image. As God foresees, intermarriage with the inhabitants (if any are left to survive) will lead to idolatry—the worship of false gods (vv. 3-4). The mere existence of idolatrous apparatus would become a snare to his people. So when they have taken the land they are to destroy all such apparatus—the altars, sacred stones, Asherah poles, and idols (v. 5).[3]

LAND RETENTION CONTINGENT IN THE NEAR TERM

The Lord promised the land to Abraham, and being faithful to his promise, he would give it to Abraham in the person of his offspring (for the principle, cf. Heb. 7:9-10). But nothing in that promise said the land

---

3   Another important and related factor in God's judgment was the rampant sexual liberties taken by Canaanites, which are prevalent today and are now, as they were then, abuses of the divine image (cf. Lev. 20:10-24). Illicit sexual behavior in the form of cult prostitution as part of Baal worship was thus also, implicitly, part of the Lord's judgment on Canaanite idolatry.

could *never be lost*. When the Lord cut the Mosaic covenant with his people, he made two things very clear: (1) his people would inherit the land because the Lord fought for them, and (2) they could lose the land through disobedience.

The possibility of such forfeiture is found not only in the subsequent covenant lawsuit prophets of the Mosaic covenant. It is articulated clearly enough in both the Sinai covenant and its renewal, the Moab covenant (Deuteronomy).

Some of the Sinai covenant curses found in Leviticus make this point. After a series of three warnings that the Lord would punish the people's sins seven times over if they reject his decrees, abhor his laws, and violate his covenant (cf. Lev. 26:14–26) the Lord utters a fourth warning:

> If in spite of this you still do not listen to me but continue to be hostile toward me, then in my anger I will be hostile toward you, and I myself will punish you for your sins seven times over. You will eat the flesh of your sons and the flesh of your daughters. I will destroy your high places, cut down your incense altars and pile your dead bodies on the lifeless forms of your idols, and I will abhor you. I will turn your cities into ruins and lay waste your sanctuaries, and I will take no delight in the pleasing aroma of your offerings. I myself will lay waste the land, so that your enemies who live there will be appalled. I will scatter you among the nations and will draw out my sword and pursue you. Your land will be laid waste, and your cities will lie in ruins. Then the land will enjoy its Sabbath years all the time that it lies desolate and you are in the country of your enemies; then the land will rest and enjoy its Sabbaths. All the time that it lies desolate, the land will have the rest it did not have during the Sabbaths you lived in it. (Lev. 26:27–35)

The Lord's admonitions start with a dire prospect: "You will eat the flesh of your sons and daughters" (v. 29), a warning repeated in Deuteronomy (28:53–57), stated again by Jeremiah (19:9), and reported as fulfilled in Lamentations (5:10). The high places and idols Jeremiah later inveighs against are foretold here, long before the people had even seen the land where their descendants would practice false worship in those places (Lev. 26: 30). The violation of the land Sabbath ordinance is foreseen as well (Lev. 26:34) with the ironic conclusion that their removal from the land will enable it finally to enjoy its Sabbaths (Lev. 26:35).[4]

---

4   It is noteworthy that these curses are as devastating as any we find in the Moab covenant, and are in fact repeated in that later renewal covenant, something that often

This curse also is later fulfilled (2 Chron. 36:21). All the fulfilled curses, as noted in the previous chapter, assume the stature of prophecy.

Forfeiture of the land is an item in the Moab covenant. That covenant contains a large body of curses (Deut. 28:15–68) that include items found in the curse list of Leviticus 26 and adds others.[5] The curses of Deuteronomy conclude with a prospect of exile:

> Then the LORD will scatter you among all nations, from one end of the earth to the other. There you will worship other gods—gods of wood and stone, which neither you nor your ancestors have known. Among those nations you will find no repose, no resting place for the sole of your foot. There the LORD will give you an anxious mind, eyes weary with longing, and a despairing heart. You will live in constant suspense, filled with dread both night and day, never sure of your life. In the morning you will say, "If only it were evening!" and in the evening, "If only it were morning!"—because of the terror that will fill your hearts and the sights that your eyes will see. The LORD will send you back in ships to Egypt on a journey I said you should never make again. There you will offer yourselves for sale to your enemies as male and female slaves, but no one will buy you. (Deut. 28:64–68)

The curses of Deuteronomy 28 include the futility curses noted before as well as other forms of irony. For example, the irony of affliction with the diseases suffered by the Egyptians—diseases the Lord used to help liberate his people: "The LORD will afflict you with the boils of Egypt and with tumors, festering sores and the itch, from which you cannot be cured" (Deut. 28:27) and again, "He will bring upon you all the diseases of Egypt that you dreaded, and they will cling to you" (Deut. 28:60). The irony is strong. Irony is fundamental to the nature of a curse because a curse reverses what ought to be—that is, the blessed state in which a covenant-obedient person could expect to live (cf. Deut. 28:1–14).[6]

One of the ironies stated in the curses of Deuteronomy is that "the LORD will send you back in ships to Egypt on a journey I said you should

---

goes unremarked by scholars who want to see the later covenant as more harsh than its predecessor. Cf. Hahn, *Kinship by Covenant*, 75–77, 115.

5   Among them are such futility curses as were noted in volume 1 of *Biblical Theology*, chapter 3 (Deut. 28:30, 31, 32, 33, 38, 39, 40, 41).

6   Cf. further discussion of material and spiritual blessings under the old and new covenants in chapter 2 of volume 3.

never make again" (Deut. 28: 68a). The notable thing about this curse is not so much that it is ironic, but that the form of its irony is return to a former state. It shares this quality with the first curses ever pronounced upon humans by the Lord:

> By the sweat of your brow
>> you will eat your food
> until you return to the ground,
>> since from it you were taken;
> for dust you are
>> and to dust you will return. (Gen. 3:19)

History informs us the Lord's curse upon the man—he would "return to the ground" from which he was taken—applied also to the woman. The curse embodies a principle of return just noted in Deuteronomy: "I will send you back in ships to Egypt."

That journey would be one the Lord said his people "should never make again." If the Lord does not desire that anyone should perish (cf. 1 Tim. 2:3–4), he also does not desire that someone should fall into sin. That is not what he intended for Adam and his wife, and it is not what he intended for people under the Mosaic covenant. But he would apply the same judicial principle to both, and both would return to the place from which he took them.[7] Those covenant judgments are parallel in principle to the undoing of heaven and earth—their return to a formless state—in the last judgment. All judgments signify a move in that direction—from life to death, from cosmos to chaos, from creation to decreation—as the Lord withdraws his Spirit-support of those who reject him.[8]

CANAANITE BEHAVIOR EARNS CANAANITE JUDGMENT

The people of the Lord conquer the land but nonetheless they may falter and fall into sexual sin and idolatry. If they do they become like the Canaanites who inhabited the land before them. In that case the Lord will treat them like those Canaanites. Two passages make this especially clear.

---

7   This can involve a symbolic aspect, since most of the people were exiled to Babylon, not Egypt; accordingly, their return from Babylon would be characterized as a second exodus (cf. poetically, Hosea 2:14–15; Isa. 44:27–28).

8   See chapter 10 of volume 3.

God told his people that indulgence in sexual activities without boundaries—and so, in ways God never intended—was one factor that would lead to the destruction of the Canaanites (Lev. 18:20–24). The Lord would use his people as a judgment instrument against the inhabitants of the land. However, if Israel became like the Canaanites, they would suffer the same fate (Lev. 18:25–26).

Similarly, if they turned away from the Lord to worship the idols of Canaan the Lord would judge them as he had judged the Canaanites: "If you ever forget the LORD your God and follow other gods and worship and bow down to them, I testify against you today that you will surely be destroyed. Like the nations the LORD destroyed before you, so you will be destroyed for not obeying the LORD your God" (Deut. 8:19–20).

The parallelism illustrates a broader principle regarding sin: the more one sins, the more one's inner nature becomes conformed to one's sin. For example, one may lie so habitually that it becomes virtually impossible to be truthful or to see things honestly. Satan apparently represents the epitomy (or the nadir) of that condition. Such conformity is a movement away from conformity to the Lord and so, as conformity to God's nature is ever increasing righteousness, a move in the opposite direction (a move away from conformity to God's nature) is by definition an ever increasing conformity to what is not God's nature—an ever increasing unrighteousness. Sin in this way perverts the image of God and turns it increasingly into something it was not meant to be. The Lord does not want this for his people. Nonetheless, if they ignore him and go their way in sin, and become conformed to the sinful nature of those they dispossessed, the Lord will dispossess them (ironically) by the same judgment he used them to impose on the Canaanites.

THE LORD FIGHTS FOR ISRAEL

Initially—at the Jordan crossing and the conquest of Jericho—things look more positive. The sin of Achan notwithstanding, the Conquest makes a good start with the occupation of the southern half of the Promised Land. The account concludes, "All these kings and their lands Joshua conquered in one campaign, because the LORD, the God of Israel, fought for Israel" (Josh. 10:42).[9] The idea could hardly be stated more clearly: Joshua conquered because the Lord fought for Israel. One may ask, How did the

---

9   I have argued that the Hebrew phrase translated "in one campaign" by NIV would

Lord fight for Israel? One finds he did so in several ways: (1) he sent fear into their hearts (as per Rahab's testimony, Josh. 2:11; cf. Exod. 23:27: "I will send my terror ahead of you and throw into confusion every nation you encounter. I will make all your enemies turn their backs and run"); (2) he hardened their hearts so they would resist Israel and by doing so would seal their own doom (Josh. 11:20); and (3) he worked signs and wonders—to bring down the walls of Jericho, or to lengthen the daylight over Aijalon in order to give his people more time to pursue and defeat the foe (Josh. 10:12–14), or to rain down hailstones on the Amorite forces so that more of them were killed by the hail than by the swords of the Lord's people (Josh 10:11).

The Lord's warfare was foretold on the eve of the Conquest when Moses told Israel:

> You may say to yourselves, "These nations are stronger than we are. How can we drive them out?" But do not be afraid of them; remember well what the LORD your God did to Pharaoh and to all Egypt. You saw with your own eyes the great trials, the miraculous signs and wonders, the mighty hand and outstretched arm, with which the LORD your God brought you out. The LORD your God will do the same to all the peoples you now fear. Moreover, the LORD your God will send the hornet among them until even the survivors who hide from you have perished. Do not be terrified by them, for the LORD your God, who is among you, is a great and awesome God. The LORD your God will drive out those nations before you, little by little. You will not be allowed to eliminate them all at once, or the wild animals will multiply around you. But the LORD your God will deliver them over to you, throwing them into great confusion until they are destroyed. (Deut. 7:17–23)

Moses reminds the people the Lord will fight for them, and they need the reminder. Moses had promised their parents the Lord could wage the needed warfare for them and enable them to conquer the land (cf. Num. 14:1–9), but that earlier generation had lacked faith ("The LORD said to Moses, 'How long will these people treat me with contempt? How long will they refuse *to believe in me*, in spite of all the signs I have performed among them?'" Num. 14:11, emphasis added; cf. Heb. 3:16–19). The Lord now reminds another generation of his past signs and wonders (Deut.

---

be better rendered "once." Cf. Jeffrey Niehaus, "Pacam ehat and the Israelite Conquest," *VT*, vol. XXX, fasc. 2 (April 1980): 236–39.

7:17–19)—that ought to bolster their faith. Jesus later does a similar thing with his disciples:

> *Believe me* when I say that I am in the Father and the Father is in me; or at least *believe* on the evidence of the works themselves. Very truly I tell you, whoever *believes in me* will do the works I have been doing, and he will do even greater things than these, because I am going to the Father. (John 14:10–12, emphases added)

On the eve of the great work that would found the church and initiate the "conquest" of other nations by bringing them into the church, Jesus reminds the disciples just who he is—because he is the one who will bring about the coming kingdom advance. In case they find it hard to accept his claim—that he and the Father who can do all things are *one*—he reminds them of the works they have seen him do. If he can do those works, he can also enable those who believe in him to do such works—and even greater works of kingdom advance.[10]

THE ANGEL OF THE LORD IN THE VANGUARD

The Lord promises to wage war for Israel. From a New Testament perspective one knows the Lord is a triune God. The Old Testament is not so clear on that matter. Nonetheless, one may get a glimpse of the person of the preincarnate Son in several passages that parallel "the angel of the Lord" with "the Lord" or "God."[11] In the matter of the Conquest, the Lord's "angel" was apparently instrumental in God's warfare as the Lord promised Moses he would be:

> See, I am sending an angel ahead of you to guard you along the way and to bring you to the place I have prepared. Pay attention to him and listen to what he says. Do not rebel against him; he will not forgive your rebellion, since *my Name is in him*. If you listen carefully to what he says and do all that I say, I will be an enemy to your enemies and will oppose those who oppose you. My angel will go ahead of you and bring you into the land of

---

10 For a similar appeal to the evidence of past works, cf. Matthew 16:5–12; and cf. Paul's validation of the gospel (Rom. 15:18–19), as entailing signs and wonders and kerygma. The author of Hebrews affirms the same, reflecting also on Israel's past unbelief (2:1–4).

11 Cf. discussion in chapter 3.

the Amorites, Hittites, Perizzites, Canaanites, Hivite and Jebusites, and I will wipe them out. Do not bow down before their gods or worship them or follow their practices. You must demolish them and break their sacred stones to pieces. Worship the LORD your God, and his blessing will be on your food and water. I will take away sickness from among you, and none will miscarry or be barren in your land. I will give you a full life span. (Exod. 23:20–26)

There are many important promises here. The less important ones are those of blessing on the people's food and water, the removal of sickness from among them, full term and successful pregnancies, and long lifespans (vv. 25–26). They are less important because they are contingent: all those blessings will be Israel's if they worship the Lord exclusively (vv. 24a, 25a), which will also entail destruction of pagan religious apparatus (v. 24b).

The contingent promises have to do with life once the land has been conquered. The more important promises are those upon which the possibility of the contingent promises rests. In particular, the more important promises will make the conquest of the land possible. Those promises have to do with the Lord's "angel." The term "angel" is put in quotation marks because the term may not in this case designate a created being (i.e., an angel). The term "angel" in Hebrew (מלאך) denotes primarily a messenger or one who "goes" (from the root, לאך, "to go") for someone else.[12] The same is true of the Greek noun transliterated "angel" (ἄγγελος). In either language, an angel can be a human messenger or a heavenly messenger—but the important thing for our discussion is that an angel is a messenger. It is important because a messenger can be a Being who was not created—the preincarnate Son.

What the Lord says about him has opened the possibility that this promised angel is the preincarnate Son. Most importantly the Lord says, "*My Name is in him*" (emphasis added, v. 21). We have noted the "Name" in the ancient world stood for the nature of the one named. People thought that was true of gods and hoped it would prove true of children to whom their parents gave theophoric names. In some wonderful cases, the latter proved true: Isaiah means "Yahweh is salvation" and Isaiah's book has been justly called the Gospel of the Old Testament. Ezekiel's name means "God strengthens," and that dynamic was often enough true of that prophet's encounters with God. When it comes to

---

12 The root is commonly used for "going" in Ugaritic, whereas in Hebrew the common verb for "going" is הלך. The two, however, seem genetically related.

the Lord, he told Israel, "You are to seek the place the LORD your God will choose from among all your tribes to put his Name there for his dwelling. To that place you must go; there bring your burnt offerings and sacrifices, your tithes and special gifts, what you have vowed to give and your freewill offerings, and the firstborn of your herds and flocks" (Deut. 12:5–6). For the Lord to put his Name there meant he would be present there and this promise was fulfilled at the dedication of the Solomonic temple after which the Lord told Solomon: "I have consecrated this temple, which you have built, by putting my Name there forever. My eyes and my heart will always be there" (1 Kings 9:3b). The Lord's statement makes the equivalence clear: "my Name" = "my eyes and my heart/my nature," and we have noted that divine presence also signifies the Spirit.[13]

If then the Lord himself is present in the temple, and if he calls that presence his Name, it would seem to follow that, when he says "my Name is in" the angel promised in Exodus 23:21, he is declaring that he himself, the Lord, is in that angel. Analogously, the "angel" would then be a temple—a residence—of the Spirit (cf. Ezek. 1:28), that is, God himself, who is a temple of himself. This looks like an Old Testament equivalent of what Paul says about Jesus in the New Testament:

> For God was pleased to have *all his fullness dwell in him*, and through him to reconcile to himself all things, whether things on earth or things in heaven, by making peace through his blood, shed on the cross. (Col. 1:19–20, emphasis added)

We know that Jesus was a temple (John 2:19) who had the Spirit without measure (John 3:34), and so his incarnate presence was consistent with his eternal and supernal reality.

RAHAB: COVENANT, FAITH, AND THE ESCHATON

As indicated at the outset, this chapter will conclude with some observations on Rahab the prostitute: the covenant she makes with the two Israelite spies, the faith that motivated her to do so, and the implications of her faith—or rather of its uniqueness—for the Conquest judgment and for the eschaton.

---

13   Cf. chapter 3, page 83; cf. Ps. 139:7, "Where can I go from your *Spirit*? / Where can I flee from your *presence*?" (emphasis added).

Faith and Rahab's Declaration

Rahab appears in the honor role of faith in Hebrews 11: "By faith the prostitute Rahab, because she welcomed the spies, was not killed with those who were disobedient" (Heb. 11:31). Now faith is amening God, who he is and what he has done, what he does, and what he will do—those things that illustrate his nature among people, so that David can imply human accountability when he says: "The heavens declare the glory of God / the skies proclaim the work of his hands" (Ps. 19:1) and Paul can boldly declare: "Since the creation of the world God's invisible qualities—his eternal power and divine nature—have been clearly seen, being understood from what has been made, so that people are without excuse" (Rom. 1:20).

Those are statements about the realm of common grace. But Rahab is privileged to have access to more special information. She can say: "We have heard how the Lord dried up the water of the Red Sea for you when you came out of Egypt, and what you did to Sihon and Og, the two kings of the Amorites east of the Jordan, whom you completely destroyed" (Josh. 2:10). Rahab knows what the Lord has done for his people in acts of special grace: he has delivered them from Egypt and begun a Conquest with the defeat of Sihon and Og.[14]

Rahab's Covenant

Rahab makes an agreement with the two spies. Not so obvious perhaps is the covenantal structure of her agreement. One may say "covenantal" because the elements of a second millennium BC treaty are embedded in the narrative of Joshua 2. The following display shows the alternation of covenant elements and narrative elements that make up the passage:

---

14 The mere fact that Og's sarcophagus was made of iron indicates he was king of some stature and implies that his kingdom was strong and affluent; cf. Deuteronomy 3:11 in which the Hebrew term usually translated "bed" or "bedstead" (עֶרֶשׂ) can also be translated "sarcophagus" as per *BDB*, 793; and cf. Phoenician inscriptions on sarcophagi: Donner, H. U. W. Röllig, *Kanaanäische und Aramäische Inschriften*, 3 vols. (Wiesbaden: Harrasowitz, 1971–1976). To date, only CEV ("coffin"), GNT ("coffin"), and NET ("sarcophagus") among English translations translate in this sense.

Structure of Joshua 2

Verse	Genre and Content
Verse	*Genre and Content*
1	**Narrative** introduction: Joshua sends two spies
2–7	**Narrative**: Rahab's action on behalf of the spies
4ab	She has hidden them on her roof
4b–5	She lies to the king about them
8–14	**Covenant**
8–11	Historical Prologue
9	Yahweh has given them the land (Canaanites afraid)
10	Yahweh dried up the Reed Sea, defeated Sihon and Og
11	Yahweh is God of heaven and earth (Canaanites afraid)
12–13	Stipulations
12a	Israel to swear (השבע) to show grace (חסד) for Rahab's grace (חסד)
12b–13	Israel to give sign of troth (את אמת) they will spare Rahab's family
14	Oath and Stipulations
14a	Oath: "Our lives for your lives"
14b	Stipulations: "Do not tell our business (and we'll show grace [חסד])
15–16	**Narrative**: Rahab's action on behalf of the spies
15	Lets them down by a rope through the window
16	Advises them to head for the hills and hide for three days
17–21a	**Covenant**
17–20	Stipulations
17	Apodosis: Spies' oath not binding
18a	Protasis: If scarlet cord is in the window
18b	Protasis: If family is in the house
19a	Protasis: If anyone goes into the street
19b	Apodosis: his blood is on his own head—spies are innocent
19c	Apodosis: Anyone in house—his blood is on spies' heads
19d	Protasis: if a hand is laid on him
20a	Protasis: If you tell what we're doing
20b	Apodosis: we're released from the oath you made us swear
21a	Oath: "Agreed. Let it be as you say."
21b–22	**Narrative**: Rahab's action and the spies
21b	She sends them away and ties the cord
22	They follow her advice and head for the hills and hide three days
23–24	**Narrative** conclusion: Spies return to Joshua (INCLUSIO)

This analysis reveals a chiastic pattern in the account:

Theme	Verse(s)	Chiastic element
Joshua and spies	1	A
Rahab narrative	2–7	B
Covenantal elements	8–14	C
Rahab narrative	15–16	B′
Covenantal elements	17–21a	C′
Rahab narrative	21b–22	B″
Joshua and spies	23–24	A′

It is important in a chiastic display to label the elements of a poem or a narrative in a way that does justice to them but also brings out the chiastic resonances between them. If the display of Joshua 2 does those things, it also shows the dynamic interplay between action and covenant articulation, and has all the hallmarks of being true to the nature of human interaction.

The narrative has another formal aspect. It includes the elements of a second millennium BC international treaty, including a historical prologue, stipulations, and oath elements. The divine-human covenants in the Old Testament are couched or presented to us in narratives. The same is true here, and in this case the covenantal elements alternate with purely narratival data. The purpose of this may be to show how the covenantal arrangement arose out of the flow of events: out of the words and deeds that gave rise to the evolution of a covenantal arrangement.

To one who is familiar with ancient near eastern historiography it must be striking that so much historical narrative space is devoted to a prostitute—even a prostitute who was instrumental in the first great coup of the Conquest. No Hittite, Assyrian, or Babylonian emperor, and no Pharaoh (for example) ever noticed such a person in his annals. The Spirit's inclusion of such a narrative shows the Lord cares about people who, in the grand sweep of history, would not be noticed by historiographers. Gunkel held a common view when he said history writing arose out of an organized society, and had mostly to do with major players and events. The Lord's history shown in the Bible—the "Annals of the Great King"—is more comprehensive. It does not focus on the personal lives of the movers and shakers of the extrabiblical world in Old Testament times. It does have room for the occupations and concerns of common people who matter in his sight—such as Rahab or the widow of Zarephath.

Rahab's Deceptions

Rahab's lies to her ruler deserve attention because they imply a biblical role for deception. Deception becomes relevant for divine judgments and eschatology. As a created act, deception has ontology, as will be discussed in the next chapter.

How does the Bible characterize Rahab's behavior? Two things stand out. The author of Hebrews praises Rahab because "she welcomed the spies [and] was not killed with those who were disobedient" (Heb. 11:31). Her action was one of faith. However, as Joshua reports, Rahab did more than welcome the spies: she told three lies about them to the king (Josh. 2:4b–5a) and misdirected the troops he sent to apprehend them (Josh. 2:5b–7). How can one understand her deceptions in covenantal terms?

False testimony is declared to be a sin under the Mosaic covenant, but Rahab was not under that covenant when she spoke. But someone may reasonably object that, even under the common grace covenants, people know or sense that lying is not right.[15] Nonetheless, people may think it justifiable, under special circumstances, to tell a lie. Corrie ten Boom, who deceived the Nazis to save Jews hidden in her house, is often cited as an example.[16] One may say that—sometimes—the end justifies the means. That was the case with her, and perhaps by extension with Rahab. Corrie ten Boom protected some descendants of those who had been God's people under the Mosaic covenant. Rahab protected those who were serving the Lord millennia before under the Mosaic covenant. Because Rahab was not under that covenant, she had no divinely given law about the wrongness of bearing false witness, and so she just did the best she could.[17]

Such arguments make their point, and some may find them compelling. But the result of Rahab's behavior—effective implementation of a divine judgment—implies a more important question. The Lord may not take credit for her deception, but he used it to advantage. What about those cases in which the Lord himself uses deception to bring about a judgment? The Conquest was a judgment. One would rather not say the Lord may deceive, although it seems David comes close to saying so:

---

15   The Lord testified that Noah was a righteous man (Gen. 7:1), and it is hard to imagine his righteousness did not include honesty, since God is the truth and God is also righteous—true to himself.

16   Cf. Corrie ten Boom, *The Hiding Place* (Grand Rapids: Chosen, 1971).

17   Cf. Paul's comment on coveting before the law was given (Rom. 7:7–8).

> To the faithful you show yourself faithful,
> To the blameless you show yourself blameless,
> To the pure you show yourself pure,
> But to the crooked you show yourself shrewd. (Ps. 18:25–26)

The phrase "you show yourself shrewd" is one verb in Hebrew (תתפתל,
Ps. 18:26 // 2 Sam 22:26 [18:27 // 2 Sam 22:27 MT]). Fundamentally it
means "to be twisted," and it only occurs a few times.[18] It is used to describe Rachel's struggle with her sister: "I have had a great struggle (lit.
"with mighty wrestlings"; I have twisted/wrestled [נפתולי אלהים נפתלתי])
with my sister, and I have won" (Gen. 30:8, a case of אלהים as a plural
abstract). It is used in Job to describe the wily: "He catches the wise in
their craftiness, / and the schemes of the wily (נפתלים) are swept away"
(Job 5:13). In Proverbs, Wisdom can say: "All the words of my mouth are
just; / none of them is crooked (נפתל) or perverse" (Prov. 8:8). Although
the term is used mostly in a pejorative sense—to indicate some sort of
trickery for bad ends—it is not always so (at least one may grant the
Lord's "wiliness" is not for a bad end).

But if the Lord is "wily" with respect to the "crooked," what does that
tell us about God? It seems to mean he gives the crooked what they deserve. Somewhat in the spirit, perhaps, of Jesus' saying that those who
live by the sword will die by the sword, Psalm 18 declares that those who
live by deception—whose lives are so characterized by deception they
can be called "crooked"—will be undone by deception.[19]

But how does the Lord "show [himself] shrewd?" God apparently
can show himself shrewd in more ways that one: (1) he can give counsel
that leads an enemy to destruction; (2) he can allow an evil spirit to deceive someone, and thereby lead to a person into judgment. Two cases
of the former (one during the Conquest and one during the period of
the judges) and one case of the latter (during the reign of Ahab) appear
in the next chapter.

---

18   All of the cases are discussed here. The verb is attested only in the Niphal and
(in Ps 18:26) the Hithpael (cf. BDB, 836). The adjective translated "crooked" also means,
fundamentally, "twisted," and likewise occurs only a few times (Deut. 32:5; Pss. 18:27; 101:4;
Prov. 2:15; 11:20; 17:20; 19:1; 22:5; and 28:6) (cf. BDB, 786).

19   Although the deception is, somehow, by God.

CHAPTER ELEVEN

MOSAIC COVENANT AND BEYOND: DECEPTION AND THEODICY

As was noted deception has an ontology and this is ineluctably the case because deception is an intellectual product and thus itself relies on beings. If thoughts or words have ontology, then deception has ontology.[1] Perhaps Hitler and his Reich offer the most powerful examples in the last century of deception and its ontology—extending to the religious: "Hánds falten, Köpfe senken, jetzt an Adolf Hitler denken" (author's translation: "Fold hands, bow heads, think now on Adolf Hitler"). This prayer or meditation is cited as an example of deception in modern times and an apparent substitute for the Lord's Prayer at the start of what one would call a grade school class in Nazi Germany. The substitution makes perfect sense if one understands Hitler was a prefiguration of Antichrist, a false Messiah whose idea or image one could hold in prayer or meditation—an "antichrist," to use the term as John does ("Dear children, this is the last hour; and as you have heard that the antichrist is coming, even now many antichrists have come. This is how we know it is the last hour," 1 John 2:18). The topic of antichrist, as a particular form of deception, is discussed later.[2] It is closely related to the idea of deception now to be explored, and in particular, how God relates to deceptions that serve his own ends. Both God and the spirit of antichrist relate to deception but, as one should expect, in diametrically opposite ways.

---

1   Not, however, the almost shadow ontology that Barth claims for *das Nichtige* or its concrete form. Cf. chapter 4 of volume 3. Our words continue to exist in the mind of God long after their sound has passed away: "But I say to you that for every idle word men may speak, they will give account of it in the day of judgment. For by your words you will be justified, and by your words you will be condemned" (Matt. 12:36–37 NKJV).

2   In chapter 8 of volume 3.

The first point to affirm, perhaps, is that God is "true" and "the truth." Jesus declares he is the way, the truth and the life (John 14:6), and John says: "The Spirit is the truth" (1 John 5:6; cf. "the Spirit of truth," John 14:17; 15:26; 16:13). John also affirms: "We know also that the Son of God has come and has given us understanding, so that we may know him who is true. And we are in him who is true by being in his Son Jesus Christ. He is the true God and eternal life" (1 John 5:20; cf. Rom. 3:4). The Bible affirms that God—Father, Son, and Holy Spirit—is both "true" and "the truth." It is important to remember these affirmations, because there are times when God appears to be the author of untruth or deception, and one ought to understand those occasions as well as one may.[3] God is not untruth, as ontologically he cannot be, but God can use untruth as an agent of judgment, and his ability to do so is part of the subject matter of this chapter.

Some elementary distinctions are important at the outset.[4] First, a lie does not necessarily produce a deception. One person may lie to another, but if the one who hears the lie does not believe it—amen it—he has not been deceived. No deception has been practiced successfully upon him. Second, a person may tell someone a half-truth, but with the intent to deceive. If the hearer amens the half-truth, he has been deceived. For example, Abraham tells Abimelek that Sarah is his sister (and she is his half-sister, cf. Gen. 20:12) but omits to tell him she is also his wife. Abimelek embraces the half-truth and so he is deceived. Third, a person may deceive without telling a lie or a half-truth. That is, a person may deliberately make an ambiguous or polyvalent statement, leaving open the possibility that the hearer of the statement will take it in a way that is not consistent with the truth that lies behind the ambiguity or

---

3   Jeremiah even thought at one point that God had deceived him into his calling: "You deceived me, Lord, and I was deceived; you overpowered me and prevailed. I am ridiculed all day long; everyone mocks me" (Jer 20:7). Jeremiah's complaint is natural considering it follows yet another abuse by an opponent (Passhur had him put in the stocks overnight, Jer. 20:1–6). For Jeremiah's experience of resistance and abuse in his calling, cf. chapter 15. His frustrated outcry should not be taken as an accurate description of the Lord, however, even though Jeremiah was a prophet, because prophets, when they only speak as men, can make mistakes (cf. Nathan's mistaken advice to David, 2 Sam. 7:3; cf. discussion, chapter 17).

4   For the term "deception" in what follows, we use the Merriam-Webster online dictionary's definition 1b, "the fact or condition of being deceived." Cf. http://www.merriam-webster.com/dictionary/deception. Likewise, to deceive is to produce a state of deception—not merely to attempt to produce a state of deception.

polyvalence and makes one understanding of the statement true, and this is obviously akin to a half-truth, although it not quite as simple as a half-truth. For example, the Shunammite woman answers Gehazi's enquiry about her family's health with an ambiguous/polyvalent answer, "Shalom," which could mean: (1) "They are well," or (2) "Peace be to you," or simply (3) "Peace," in the sense of, "I'm in a hurry and don't want to talk with you about my purpose in coming here" (cf. pp. 289–91). If Gehazi interprets her answer in the first or second way, he has been deceived by her ambiguous/polyvalent statement, because her family is not at all doing well—her son is dead—and she is probably not merely expressing a wish for Gehazi's well-being. The crucial point in all such cases and any others one might imagine is this: It is useful to distinguish between (1) a deception, which is a product, and (2) whatever produces the deception. One may accomplish a deception—leading someone to embrace a falsehood—by a variety of means. One may deceive (1) by means of a lie, (2) by means of a half-truth, or (3) by means of an ambiguous/polyvalent statement. The following discussion explores these distinctions in some relevant biblical passages. The issue at hand is one of human deceptions and how God uses them. This obviously has eschatological implications. Because God is somehow involved, we turn to what may be the one unambiguous principial statement on the issue, pronounced by the warrior and covenant mediator prophet, David.

GOD AND DECEPTION: A GUIDING PRINCIPLE

When David prayed for the Lord's salvation from his enemies, he also presented a theophanic portrayal of the Lord who came to save him (Ps. 18:6–15). Dramatic as that judgment intrusion was, and however much it adumbrates God's eschatological coming, David's poem contained something just as important: revelation of a judgment ethos that—sometimes at least—operates when God judges one or more people:

> To the faithful you show yourself faithful,
> To the blameless you show yourself blameless,
> To the pure you show yourself pure,
> But to the crooked you show yourself shrewd. (Ps. 18:25–26)

As Jesus said, only one is good (Matt. 9:17). Those who are "faithful," "blameless," and "pure" therefore are so with two qualifications.

First, no one is perfectly so. Second, no one is so in any degree without the Lord's help. Nonetheless, there are those in the world who are, as David says, "faithful," "blameless," and "pure." Otherwise his statement would be meaningless. The Lord treats those people according to the faithfulness or "amening" of God's nature according to which they are so. Under common grace one can be faithful to God's nature in some degree although not to a saving degree (as Paul indicates, Rom. 2:12–16). Nonetheless, there is another class of people who are "crooked," and to them the Lord shows himself—or proves to be—"shrewd."[5] The Hebrew words for "crooked" (עִקֵּשׁ) and "shrewd" (the verbal root, פתל) are much the same in meaning. The fundamental sense in each case is "twisted."[6] The concept is the opposite of what one would call, to use an old phrase, "straight and true."

How does the Lord show himself "shrewd" with a person he would judge? One can hardly hope for an exhaustive answer to that question! Exploration of one Old Testament passage in particular (1 Kings 22) and one New Testament passage (2 Thessalonians 2) may be suggestive.[7]

What about human deceptions God apparently *approves or makes use of*? Discussion of them is also in order. Two cases are especially notable because of their historical importance: Jacob's ruse in Genesis 27, and Rahab's lie in Joshua 2 (discussed in parallel with the Gibeonite deception in Joshua 9 as an exploration of the faith issue). Elisha's deception of the Aramaeans also comes under review (2 Kings 6). If the Lord "approves" any such it would be in accord with the ethos stated in Psalm 18:25–26.

There are cases of human deception the Lord may not use but tolerate, and they become part of a larger narrative in which the Lord is providentially involved—to the benefit of the deceivers (e.g., Abram's/Abraham's ruse in Genesis 12 and 20, the deception by Jacob's sons in Genesis 34, and the Shunammite woman's replies in 2 Kings 2).

The following study takes these three categories—(1) cases in which the Lord shows himself shrewd against those he will judge, (2) cases of human deception God apparently *approves or makes use of*, and (3)

---

5   Cf. another, similar statement about God: "He mocks [יליץ] proud mockers [לצים] / but shows favor to the humble and oppressed" (Prov. 3:34). The same principle appears as follows: as God treats the crooked shrewdly, he treats the mockers (scornful ones) with mockery (scorn).

6   Cf. discussion in chapter 10, pages 279–80.

7   Along with some ancillary passages: the Lord's ambushes at Ai (Joshua 8), and possibly against the Benjamites (Judges 20).

human deception the Lord tolerates that also become part of a larger narrative in which the Lord is involved to the benefit of the deceivers. The categories are considered in reverse order, from the categorically least important to the categorically most important.

Human Deception the Lord Tolerates (Part 1): Deception by Abraham

Two outstanding cases of deception are provided by Abram/Abraham—one before and one after the Abrahamic covenant is cut in Genesis 15. Christians who—say, in a Bible study—find consolation for their shortcomings when they consider the missteps of Abraham, our father in the faith as he is often called, tend to forget one qualifying difference. Notable as Abraham was for his faith, he did not have the Holy Spirit dwelling within him. He thus lacked that inner spiritual help toward the level of faithfulness to the Lord the church now has (cf. Ezek. 36:27; John 14:17). Although the Lord could say Abraham "obeyed me and did everything I required of him, keeping my commands, my decrees, and my instructions" (Gen. 26:5), and although the Lord credited Abram's faith to him as righteousness (Gen. 15:6), Abram could falter in his faith, just as he did even after the Lord changed his name.[8] The name change was a change of credentials and not a change of fallen nature—although it prefigured the change of nature believers will experience when the Lord gives them a new name (cf. Rev. 2:17).[9]

Early and late demonstrations of the patriarch's faltering faith occur when Abram and Sarai go down to Egypt in Genesis 12, and again when Abraham and Sarah enter the kingdom of Gerar in Genesis 20. Abraham uses the same ruse with both kings; the results play out in parallel fashion:

Genesis 12:10–20		Genesis 20:1–18	
Verse		*Verse*	
11	about to enter Egypt	1	in Gerar
	"Tell them you're my sister"	2a	"She is my sister"
15	Sarai taken to Pharaoh's palace	2b	Abimelek sends for Sarah

---

8   Paul tells us that Abraham did not weaken in his faith regarding God's promise of a son, but that does not mean Abraham never faltered in his faith (cf. Rom. 4:19–21).

9   Cf. likewise the "new name" foretold for God's corporate people embodied by the New Jerusalem (Isa. 62:2) and the association of the two by name—individual and city of God (Rev. 3:12).

Genesis 12:10–20		Genesis 20:1–18	
Verse		*Verse*	
17	Lord afflicts Pharaoh and his household with diseases	18	Lord closes wombs of the king's household
18–19a	Pharaoh reproaches Abram	9–10	King reproaches Abraham
20	Pharaoh sends Abram and Sarai away with rich gifts	15	King offers land to Abraham

Parallelism between narratives is not proof of a doublet. One can find for example many parallel accounts of Assyrian attacks against and conquest of cities, and the parallels exist because the Assyrian kings took much the same actions when they attacked any city so that the accounts of them are parallel in description and phraseology. Likewise here, Abram took much the same approach when he and his wife entered Gerar as he had taken when they entered Egypt.[10] After what one may charitably call the imperfect success of the approach Abram took in Egypt, one might wonder that Abraham took the same approach later in another land.[11] A current popular aphorism says: "One definition of insanity is making the same mistake repeatedly and expecting a different result." Abram was not insane. But he did, at some challenging moments, falter in his faith.

It is instructive to note that the Lord intervened, in both Egypt and Gerar, and made up for the patriarch's lack of faith—on the earthly level, a lack of trust in the Lord to protect him and his wife; supernally considered, a lack of owning or amening the Lord's nature and the protections it could be trusted to produce. In both cases the Lord afflicted the king's household as a sign, and in Abimelek's case God even spoke to him in a dream and warned him not to take Sarah (Gen. 20:3–7). As for Abraham's faith faltering, it is important to affirm what faith is: amening God's nature and what God is doing. Had Abraham amened the Lord who is trustworthy, he would not have resorted to a ruse to ensure his own safety (cf. Gen. 12:12–13). The Lord's intervention in each case, to correct

---

10 His son Jacob, like a chip off the old block, did the same with (presumably) Abimeleck's successor of the same name, and received a similar rebuke (Gen. 26:7–11).

11 Not to mention that by his own confession (Gen. 22:13) he told her to use the same ruse wherever they went.

what Abraham had done and change the patriarch's course, shows this to be true.[12]

Abram had more lessons to learn about the Lord's trustworthiness—his covenant faithfulness when looking out for his chosen vassal. Through those lessons Abraham would grow in his faith to the point at which he trusted the Lord would restore his son Isaac to him even if by a resurrection (cf. Heb. 11:17–19)—and this from someone who earlier tried to fulfill the promise of Isaac through his Egyptian handmaid (cf. Gen. 16:1–4). Abraham did not have the Holy Spirit dwelling within him. That would be the privilege of a new covenant toward which the Abrahamic covenant would point, and for whose inception it would provide the start of a special grace covenant program. Nonetheless, Abraham can stand as an encouragement today, not because of his failures, but because of his growth in faith: he was ready to make a sacrifice few could bring themselves to offer.

Abraham's grandson also practiced deception, of a sort one can hardly approve. The way he manipulated his father and abused his brother could easily be seen as grasping and unworthy by civilized human beings. Nonetheless, the Lord apparently used it.[13]

Human Deception the Lord Tolerates (Part 2): Deception by Jacob's Sons

The second example of deception tolerated (apparently) by the Lord involves Jacob's sons. Jacob's sons may have inherited some penchant for deception from their notorious father. After the rape of Dinah by Shechem, Shechem and his father, Hamor, come to Jacob and his sons and ask that they give Dinah to Shechem as his wife (Gen. 34:6–12). The account seems to make it clear that Shechem really does have his heart set on Dinah (cf. Gen. 34:2.9) even though he took her in a way not culturally approved.[14] However, Hamor's proposal for an alliance of the two groups has a hidden motive:

---

12 One could imagine the Lord wanted Abraham to make these mistakes and thus learn from them, but one cannot know that. Abraham's mistakes were the fruit of a lack of faith, and whatever is not of faith is sin (Rom. 14:23); one cannot easily say the Lord wanted the patriarch to sin. Certainly the Lord allowed the mistakes and they became by God's grace learning opportunities.

13 Cf. below, "Human Deception That God Apparently Approves or Makes Use of (Part 1): Deception by Jacob," pages 291–93.

14 To put it mildly. The statement "he took her and raped her" (Gen. 34:2) provides

So Hamor and his son Shechem went to the gate of their city to speak to
the men of their city. "These men are friendly toward us," they said. "Let
them live in our land and trade in it; the land has plenty of room for them.
We can marry their daughters and they can marry ours. But the men will
agree to live with us as one people only on the condition that our males be
circumcised, as they themselves are. Won't their livestock, their property
and all their other animals become ours? So let us agree to their terms,
and they will settle among us. (Gen. 34:20–23)

Because the account is laconic, there is no way to know how much
Jacob and his sons knew or intuited about the motives of Shechem and
his father. Shechem's motives were apparently mixed because Shechem
loved Dinah but was also part of a plan to absorb Jacob's clan and property into his own.

However much Jacob and his sons knew, the progress of the account make it clear they responded to Shechem's marriage proposal
(Gen. 34:6–12) in the spirit of Psalm 18:26 ("To the crooked you show
yourself shrewd"):

Because their sister Dinah had been defiled, Jacob's sons replied deceit-
fully as they spoke to Shechem and his father Hamor. They said to them,
"We can't do such a thing; we can't give our sister to a man who is not
circumcised. That would be a disgrace to us. We will enter into an agreement with you on one condition only: that you become like us by circumcising all your males. Then we will give you our daughters and take your
daughters for ourselves. We'll settle among you and become one people
with you. But if you will not agree to be circumcised, we'll take our sister
and go." (Gen. 34:13–17)

After Hamor and the men of his city undergo circumcision, and when
they are still prostrate and recovering from the operation, Jacob's sons
Simeon and Levi put them all to the sword. They justify their deed with
a rhetorical question: "Should he have treated our sister like a prostitute"
(v. 31).

A modern person might question the extreme nature of their response. They inflict a penalty far more severe than what the Mosaic law
later imposed for rape of an unbetrothed virgin (cf. Deut. 22:28–29);

---

a case of the verb "take" (Heb. לקח) used not only of marriage but also of rape; cf. the
discussion of Genesis 6:1–4 in volume 1, chapter 5, 164–68 (esp. 168).

their wholesale looting of the city afterwards sounds like the treatment dished out by Assyrian suzerains to rebellious vassals: "They seized their flocks and herds and donkeys and everything else of theirs in the city and out in the fields. They carried off all their wealth and all their women and children, taking as plunder everything in the houses" (Gen. 34:28–29).[15]

Just as questionable is the key component of their ruse: circumcision. Jacob and his sons underwent circumcision as a sign of membership in the Abrahamic covenant. Now they use it as a tool for fooling people they would slaughter—surely a questionable use of a divinely given sign that ought to have been held by them in great reverence. The Lord does not rebuke it, and that may indicate a divine attitude that the heart is more important than even a covenant sign. The Lord's silence on the matter either indicates a refusal to take sin into account at this stage of his revelatory involvement in human history (cf. Rom. 5:13: "To be sure, sin was in the world before the law was given, but sin is not charged against anyone's account where there is no law"), or it indicates divine approval of the action: tacit endorsement of a judgment on pagans carried out by his covenant people.

Human Deception the Lord Tolerates (Part 3): Deception by the Shunammite Woman

In a discussion of the Lord and prophetic experience, other aspects of Elisha's encounter with Shunammite woman will come under consideration.[16] Now the subject is *deception by way of ambiguity or polyvalence*, and the woman's trip to Elisha gives examples of it: her response to her husband as she sets out to see the prophet (namely, "Shalom"), and her identical response to Gehazi when he enquires about the well-being of the Shunammite and her family (2 Kings 4:23.26). Her interaction with her husband comes first:

> The child grew, and one day he went out to his father, who was with the reapers. He said to his father, "My head! My head!"
> His father told a servant, "Carry him to his mother." After the servant had lifted him up and carried him to his mother, the boy sat on her lap

---

15   For discussion of household punishment of rebellious vassals with biblical and extrabiblical examples, cf. *ANETBT*, 138–61.

16   Cf. chapter 14, pages 359–61.

until noon, and then he died. She went up and laid him on the bed of the
man of God, then shut the door and went out.

She called her husband and said, "Please send me one of the servants
and a donkey so I can go to the man of God quickly and return."

"Why go to him today?" he asked. "It's not the new Moon or the
Sabbath."

"That's all right," she said. (2 Kings 4:18–23)

The husband orders his afflicted son be taken to his mother. He knows
the boy is sick and naturally has reason for concern. When his wife
emerges from the house some time later, and has her donkey prepared
for travel, one could imagine the husband's concern would only grow.
When he asks why his wife is going to see the man of God it is presumably not a casual question. His wife responds with one word: "Shalom,"
that is, "Peace." The word is completely unclear, and perhaps NIV tries to
convey this by translating it with "that's all right," which could convey the
idea that in fact everything is all right; or "Shalom" might just be a way
of saying, "Good-bye, I don't have time to talk right now," or the like; it
could even be an expressed wish—in the midst of a hasty departure—for
her husband's well-being (since the word can mean "good health") during
the remainder of the day. The ambiguity also suggests the woman is not
prepared to tell her husband what has happened to their son. It is a sort
of practical obscurantism—in effect, a deception. She chooses not to trust
her husband with some very important information.

Her response to her husband could be the product of haste. Her interaction with Gehazi is perhaps more likely one of distrust:

When he saw her in the distance, the man of God said to his servant Gehazi, "Look! There's the Shunammite! Run to meet her and ask her, 'Are
you all right? Is your husband all right? Is your child all right?'"

"Everything is all right," she said. (2 Kings 4:25–26)

The account is a good example of laconic reporting: although the
prophet's command to his servant is recorded, the servant's relaying of
the prophet's words to the woman is not. But her answer makes it clear
the question was delivered.

She answers Gehazi as she answered her husband: "Shalom." Here,
as with her husband, she does not give a straight answer. Her response
is almost invited, because the servant used the same word in his que-
ries (lit. "Is it peace/soundness [השלום] with you? Is it peace/soundness

[הֲשָׁלוֹם] with your husband? Is it peace/soundness [הֲשָׁלוֹם] with your child?" (v. 26). As Gehazi's behavior with Naaman soon afterward shows, he is not always to be trusted. The woman puts him off, and that may show some sensitivity on her part to his nature, although one cannot be sure. More importantly, she is intent on seeing the prophet, the "man of God," and will not be delayed (cf. v. 24). She seems to feel Elijah is her only hope. When Elisha sends Gehazi to attempt the boy's healing, she stays with Elisha and will only go back with him (v. 30).

Maybe the Shunammite deceives her husband out of mere haste and impetuousness; maybe she deceives Gehazi for the same reasons. In both cases, she does not pause to trust her enquirers with the truth. She reserves that for the prophet. Her behavior is deceptive by way of ambiguity/polyvalence at some level in each encounter. Do impetuousness and haste sufficiently account for her behavior?

Because of the outcome, we suggest she is moved by faith—an inner amening of what she senses or hopes God will do: raise her son from the dead by the hand of the prophet. What the author of Hebrews says of Abraham (regarding the soon to be sacrificed Isaac) may also be true of her: She reckoned "God was able to raise him up, even from the dead, from which he also received him in a figurative sense" (Heb. 11:19 NKJV). The Shunammite received her son back from the dead, not figuratively but literally. Like Rahab before her, she used deception, yet the Lord did not condemn her deception: He *tolerated* her deception, and beyond that he honored her faith.

Human Deception That God Apparently Approves or Makes Use Of (Part 1): Deception by Jacob

A category of deception that comes closer to divine approval now comes under review. The first example is that of Jacob and his mother. Complicit with his mother's lead, Jacob deceives his father Isaac and robs his brother of his birthright. Rebekah is unquestionably the instigator (Gen. 27:6–10), and she also provides the cover Jacob needs for the deception to work (Gen. 27:15–16). Nonetheless, Jacob enters fully into the scheme:

> He went to his father and said, "My father."
> "Yes, my son," he answered. "Who is it?"
> Jacob said to his father, "I am Esau your firstborn. I have done as you told me. Please sit up and eat some of my game, so that you may give me your blessing."

Isaac asked his son, "How did you find it so quickly, my son?"

"The LORD your God gave me success," he replied.

Then Isaac said to Jacob, "Come near so I can touch you, my son, to know whether you really are my son Esau or not." (Gen. 27:18–21)

The conversation is remarkable in one way: how Jacob accounts for the quickness with which he accomplished what his father wanted—"The LORD your God gave me success" (v. 20b).[17] The statement is not only an outright lie. It is a lie that invokes the Lord's name for its validation. Moreover, it lays the foundation for Isaac's blessing on the firstborn son, who is thus robbed of his primogeniture:

> Your dwelling will be
> > away from the earth's richness,
> > away from the dew of heaven above.
> You will live by the sword
> > and you will serve your brother.
> But when you grow restless,
> > you will throw his yoke
> > from off your neck. (Gen. 27:39–40)

This is a very qualified blessing, but it fulfills what the Lord told Rebekah before she gave birth:

> Two nations are in your womb,
> > and two peoples from within you will be separated;
> one people will be stronger than the other
> > and the older will serve the younger. (Gen. 25:23)

God foretells what will become of Esau. Other biblical data show God is not only forecasting for two people what he (being outside time) knew before the foundation of the world. He is making a statement of predestination. The Lord later declares through his messenger: "'Was not Esau Jacob's brother?' declares the Lord. 'Yet I have loved Jacob, but Esau I have hated, and I have turned his hill country into a wasteland and left

---

17   I recall Rev. Peter Gomes, sometime Plummer Professor of Christian Morals and Pusey Minister in Harvard Memorial Church, refer to Jacob in a sermon as "that combination of Yankee horse trader and Hebrew chutzpah." Not a bad description.

his inheritance to the desert jackals'" (Mal. 1:2b–3). Paul famously takes up that judgment:

> Not only that, but Rebekah's children were conceived at the same time by our father Isaac. Yet, before the twins were born or had done anything good or bad—in order that God's purpose in election might stand: not by works but by him who calls—she was told, "The older will serve the younger." Just as it is written: "Jacob I loved, but Esau I hated." (Rom. 9:10–13)

Paul's argument comes under consideration as part of the new covenant discussion. For now it is reaffirmed: God is omniscient and outside time. Consequently, he knew Esau's nature before he created the world, and his judgment regarding Esau had to do not with Esau's works ("before the twins were born or had done anything good or bad") but with the faithless nature of the man. Paul makes a germane asseveration: "For those God *foreknew* he also predestined to be conformed to the image of his Son" (Rom. 8:29a, emphasis added).[18]

As part of that determination, God was apparently prepared to allow Jacob, at his mother's instigation, to rob his brother of his birthright and even to mislead his father by a lie that used the Lord's name as a spurious validation regarding faux-Isaac's success as a hunter. This *may* hark back to the idea already noted regarding one principle by which the Lord deals with those he would judge (Ps. 18:26). Not to mention that Esau sold his birthright for a mess of pottage (Gen. 25:34a)—an act that receives the following evaluation: "So Esau despised his birthright" (Gen. 25:34b). The Lord, then, may have allowed a deception because it brought about a *just result* for faithless Esau—whose faithlessness is made clear by his untrue estimate of his birthright and of the Lord, by whose providence he was the firstborn. The historian faults him for the former, and his fault in the latter is obvious. In terms of faith, he fails to amen both the Lord and the honor provided for him in God's providence. This may be a case of what Jesus explained in the parable of the minas: "I tell you that to everyone who has, more will be given, but from the one who has not, even what he has will be taken away" (Luke 19:26).[19]

---

18   Cf. chapter 7 of volume 3, "Foreknowledge, Election, and Predestination."

19   What such a person—Esau—"had not" was faith, as the faithfulness of the other servants in Jesus' parable implies. Cf. verse 17: "Because you have been faithful in a very little, you shall have authority over ten cities."

Human Deception That God Apparently Approves or Makes Use Of (Part 2): Rahab and the Gibeonites

The book of Joshua offers two famous cases of deception. Both involve people who want to ally with God's people. Both try to do so via deception. The Lord approves or makes use of both attempts, one way or another. Faith, or lack of it, is an important component in both cases. Partly for that reason they receive special attention now. Rahab's lying behavior and her salvation have been discussed in the previous chapter. Her case is the more important because of the way it illustrates her faith. The other case is that of the Gibeonites, whose faith is more dubious.

The cases offer elements of comparison and contrast. Both Rahab and the Gibeonites are aware of a threat, as they consider what the God of Israel has done and will or may do. Consequently both lie, and as a result both become associated with God's people. Rahab, however, affirms her faith to the Lord's people. The Gibeonites never do. The key points are as follows:

Rahab (Joshua 2)	Gibeonites (Joshua 9)
A hasty deception 2:3–4	An elaborate deception 9:3–5
Lies to the king 2:4–5	Lie to the Israelites 9:6
Fear with faith 2:10–11	Fear without faith 9:24

First, both parties commit acts of deception. Rahab's deception appears to have been the more urgent and spontaneous of the two and that seems inevitable given the different circumstances of the deceiving parties, since the Gibeonites were some distance from any immediate threat and had more time to prepare their ruse. However, the difference may also have something to do with the impetuousness of a nascent faith on Rahab's part, and the more deliberate calculation of deceivers on the part of the Gibeonites. The deception Rahab practiced did involve some work—the camouflaging of the spies with stalks of flax on her roof—but nothing like the extensive preparations of the Gibeonites. Their work was elaborate—several verses show the care to which they went to make all their accouterments look like those of a people who had traveled a long and hard journey. A more important difference in the two cases: Rahab lied to her king and by doing so took on a great risk *for the sake of the Israelites*, whereas the Gibeonites *lied to the Israelites*.

The contrast suggests the two parties have profoundly different attitudes. Both have heard the report of Israel's successes, and both are driven by fear of the God of Israel. The fear is appropriate in both cases. Fear drove Rahab to her affirmation of faith: "We have heard how the Lord dried up the water of the Red Sea for you when you came out of Egypt, and what you did to Sihon and Og, the two kings of the Amorites east of the Jordan, whom you completely destroyed. When we heard of it, our hearts melted in fear and everyone's courage failed because of you" (Josh 2:10–11a). Rahab follows this confession of her fear ("*our* hearts melted with fear") with a statement of faith: "For the Lord your God is God in heaven above and on the earth below" (Josh. 2:11b). The essential point is the contrast between Rahab—whose statement is the declaration of a new faith—and the Gibeonites—who never make such a declaration. Fear drives Rahab to affirm and cast her lot with the people of Israel and their God, whereas it drives the Gibeonites to rely on their own devices to deceive the Israelites into an alliance. Rahab takes the first step in casting off the old mythological pantheon under which she had grown up as she affirms the reality of the one true God: "The Lord your God is God in heaven above and on the earth below" (Josh. 2:11b). Consequently the author of Hebrews characterizes Rahab's deception as an act of faith (Heb. 11:31). Rahab's faith is a true faith and so it is not inconsistent with works (cf. James 2:5). Her faith *produced* works as all faith must. Moreover, as has been noted, the Lord used her deceptions to advance his own kingdom work. This would appear to be in the spirit of Psalm 18:25–26.

Human Deception That God Apparently Approves or Makes Use Of (Part 3): Elisha and the Arameans

One might reckon a prophet who produces a deception does so as part of a divine judgment and that seems to be the case with Elisha.[20] The prophet Elisha has, by a miracle, imposed blindness on a host of Aramean would-be conquerors who have come to Dothan to capture him (cf. 2 Kings 6:8–18). Then he misleads them:

> Elisha told them, "This is not the road and this is not the city. Follow me, and I will lead you to the man you are looking for." And he led them to Samaria. After they entered the city, Elisha said, "LORD, open the eyes of these men so they can see." Then the LORD opened their eyes and they

---

20 Although the "old prophet" in the northern kingdom (1 Kings 13:11–31) might be a counterexample; but the case is not simple and deserves investigation in its own right.

looked, and there they were, inside Samaria. When the king of Israel saw them, he asked Elisha, "Shall I kill them, my father? Shall I kill them?" "Do not kill them," he answered. "Would you kill those you have captured with your own sword or bow? Set food and water before them so that they may eat and drink and then go back to their master." So he prepared a great feast for them, and after they had finished eating and drinking, he sent them away, and they returned to their master. So the bands from Aram stopped raiding Israel's territory. (2 Kings 6:19–23)

It looks as though there are two acts of deception in the narrative. The first seems to be an outright lie: Elisha tells the Arameans they have come by the wrong road to the wrong city. However, his words can be counted as truth if they are uttered in this sense: "The is not the road [by which you must travel to deal with me] and this is not the city [in which you will deal with me]." In that light his words could be half-truths or partial truths that do not state his full intention, much as Sarai's words to Pharaoh at Abram's request were half-truth. When the whole truth is not stated, the result can be misdirection or deception—that is, as we have understood it, a state of being deceived. Nonetheless, there is a difference between saying what is not true on any understanding (a lie) and saying only some of the truth (a partial truth open to misunderstanding). Elisha continues with another statement that could be considered truth, but likewise only in a qualified way: "I will lead you to the man you're looking for."[21] Of course he himself is the man, so no further "leading" is necessary, but he leads the enemy to Samaria and *only there* is the prophet revealed to them. This may count as a fulfillment of his promise, "I will lead you to the man you are looking for" (v. 19). It would appear the Lord is not displeased with all this or is at least willing to tolerate it—as he tolerated Abram's ruse—since he now works another miracle through Elisha: he restores the Arameans' sight and they find themselves in their enemy's capital (v. 20).[22]

---

21   Of course one could understand his statement in a nuanced way: "I will lead you to [the place where you can see] the man you are looking for," but even if that was in the prophet's mind he was probably the only person who understood the words in that laconic sense.

22   We note the Lord had already provided horses and chariots of fire around Elisha for his protection (2 Kings 6:15–17). That is not gratuitous information. The Lord presumably could have used them to influence the Arameans away from Elisha (cf. Jesus' ability to appeal for angelic legions for protection, "'Put your sword back in its place,'"

Another datum is noteworthy, that is, the command-fulfillment sequence of the narrative suggests Elisha's "clout" with the Lord: "Elisha said, '*LORD, open the eyes of these men* so *they can see.*'" / "Then *the LORD opened their eyes* and *they looked*" (emphasis added).[23] If the Lord was displeased with Elisha's ruse, this would not be the way to show his displeasure. By the Lord's miracle they are able to see what Elisha promised in the midst of his trickery, that he would lead them to the man they were looking for. What follows is an act of victorious magnanimity. On Elisha's advice the king does not slaughter his enemies but prepares a feast for them; and after they have feasted, they return home and hostilities come to an end (vv. 22–23).

How is one to evaluate this account? How does one understand the meaning of the prophet's statements and what the Lord does or does not do about them?

The understanding suggested above, that Elisha's statements are partial truths, is probably the best way to understand the episode. If, however, one takes them as outright lies, a couple of possibilities may occur to one:

1a   Elisha lies without being sure what the consequence of his lies will be.

1b   Since he lies, the Lord, who is the truth, cannot be pleased, but tolerates the lies anyway, and even uses them to his people's advantage.[24]

Or

Jesus said to him, "For all who draw the sword will die by the sword. Do you think I cannot call on my Father, and he will at once put at my disposal more than twelve legions of angels? But how then would the Scriptures be fulfilled that say it must happen in this way?" Matt. 26:52–54). In both cases the Father seems to have intentions that preclude the active assistance angelic forces could provide.

23   It is a classic command-fulfillment pattern, but this can only be meant as a way of showing the power and effectiveness of Elisha's request (cf. James 5:16b and the example of Elisha's mentor, Elijah, James 5:17–18), since Elisha does not have the authority to command the Lord to do anything. Cf. also Elijah's resurrection of the widow of Zarephath's son, where the authoritative covenant idiom שמע לקול is used: "The LORD *paid heed* to Elijah's cry, and the boy's life returned to him, and he lived" (1 Kings 17:22, author's translation).

24   Cf. Joseph's statement regarding his brothers' sinful behavior: "As for you, you meant evil against me, but God meant it for good, to bring it about that many people should be kept alive, as they are today" (Gen. 50:20 ESV).

2a   Elisha lies with some prophetic inkling or even some clearer direction from the Lord, and leads the foe to Samaria in obedience to
that instruction.[25]

2b   By the same token, then, the Lord has directed Elisha to mislead and
shown himself to be "shrewd" with the foe toward whom, however,
he intends to show mercy.

If one accepts the first set of interpretations, one finds the Lord prepared to use someone's deceptions to advance his kingdom work in some
fashion. (There are other cases that show this principle more clearly,
one involving Rahab in Joshua 2 and another involving a lying spirit in
1 Kings 22). But this view is not without some difficulty in Elisha's case.
It seems wrong to credit Elisha with an outright lie when he need not
have resorted to such a thing (cf. 2 Kings 6:15–17). Not to mention that
one would expect better of the prophet.[26] If one accepts the second set of
interpretations, one also encounters some difficulties. Like the first view,
it credits Elisha with lying; moreover, it makes God the author of the
lie. Although one cannot insist upon the correctness of the second set
of interpretations, it does appeal to one well-documented characteristic
not only of biblical narrative but of narratives in general: the narratives
are laconic. On that understanding, then, the Lord instigates a deception
in order to deliver his people, and in particular his prophet, from a foe.[27]
The best antidote to the concern that God seems to be the author of a
lie appears to be what David wrote in Psalm 18:25–26. Nonetheless, that
appeal may not feel satisfactory to some, and it may not be satisfactory.
When all is said and done, the most redeeming way of understanding
the prophet's statements would seem to be that they are *partial statements of the truth*. This understanding avoids the untenable concept
that God authors a lie. God himself can, however, present *partial data*,
which his foes are free to understand however they will, and he may
have led his prophet to do this. One may add that their blindness gives

---

25   In the latter case (the Lord's directing), the text would be laconic, and the reader
left to imagine the possibility of such a thing.

26   But cf. the "old prophet" in 1 Kings 13:11–31. It is not obvious, however, that the
old prophet has the stature or character of Elisha.

27   It must also be noted that Elisha struck the Aramaeans blind only by the Lord's
power and thus consent, which would be consistent with the Lord's involvement in the
ruse from the beginning. Had the foe not been blinded, there could have been no ruse.

them little choice but to trust the apparent meaning of what they hear, but they do still have choices. The choice they make means they will experience God's mercy.

There are cases in which it is more or less obvious the Lord is "showing himself shrewd" in a judgment. In those cases there can be no doubt the Lord himself is the initiator of the device by which he chooses to accomplish a judgment. Four cases of the sort are considered now. Two of them involve direct counsel from the Lord, and they are ambushes. Two of them involve divine permission for an evil and deceptive entity to do what it wants, and their successes result in divine judgments.

GOD SHOWS HIMSELF SHREWD IN JUDGMENTS

The Lord himself does not lie. In judgment, however, he can "show himself shrewd" (Ps. 18:26b). Two cases of what one may call God's tactical "shrewdness" involve ambushes. Now an ambush is not exactly a lie. An ambush offers a visual reality that is incomplete and thus potentially misleading. It conceals some of the truth. It probably ranks with what one would call on the verbal level *withholding some of the truth* or *stating only part of the truth*—as Abraham did when he said Sarah was his sister: a half-truth, since she was his sister but also his wife. God's ambushes in Joshua 8 and Judges 20 rely on concealment. The deceiving party only shows half of his "hand." The other half, or part, is hidden so the deception can work.

God Shows Himself Shrewd in Judgments (Part 1): The Case of Ai

Israel defeats the troops of Ai (Josh. 8:1–29) before whom they had previously retreated (Josh. 7:2–6). The Lord had withheld victory because of Achan's sin (cf. Josh. 7:1–12). Once that sin is acknowledged and punished, the Lord tells Joshua: "Do not be afraid; do not be discouraged. Take the whole army with you, and go up and attack Ai. For I have delivered into your hands the king of Ai, his people, his city and his land" (Josh. 8:1–2). The verb is important. The Lord says, "I have delivered" (נתתי) Ai into Israel's hands. Soon after, when Joshua addresses the troops, he says, "The LORD your God will give it [i.e., Ai] (ונתתיה, converted perfect of the same verb as at v. 2) into your hand" (Josh. 8:7b). For the Lord outside time, the conquest of Ai has *already happened* and he can announce it to Joshua as a *fait accompli*; for Joshua and Israel within the flow of time, the conquest of Ai is *still future* and remains a promise until they conquer it with the Lord's help.[28]

Divine help comes in part by way of an ambush the Lord instructs Joshua to set: "Set an ambush behind the city [Ai]" (Josh. 8:2b). So Joshua divides his forces and sends thirty thousand men to set the ambush behind Ai. With his remaining forces Joshua lures the fighting men out of Ai. When those in ambush reveal themselves—and the combined Israelite forces encircle the foe—Israel wins the victory. As per the ban, they leave no survivors except the king of Ai, whom they capture and execute and whose body they impale (Josh. 8:22–29).

The Lord helps Israel, in part, by having them set an ambush. The other "part"—if the account offers one—involves an individual action. Joshua holds up a javelin as a signal for the hidden forces to come forth (Josh. 8:18–19). It is also a signal for the fighting to continue until the people of Ai have been exterminated (Josh. 8:26). Joshua does it at the Lord's command: "The LORD said to Joshua, 'Hold out toward Ai the javelin that is in your hand, for into your hand I will deliver the city.'So Joshua held out toward the city the javelin that was in his hand" (Josh. 8:18). The gesture looks like a signal and nothing more. It recalls the victory by Joshua and Israel over the Amalekites. In that battle the Israelites under Joshua were successful as long as Moses held up his rod over the fray (Exod. 17:8–16). The parallel is not complete because the account does not say Israel's success in battle against the army of Ai depended from moment to moment on the upholding of Joshua's javelin, as was the case with Moses' staff (Exod. 17:11). The connection in the prior case between holding up the staff and victory invites one to consider the Lord may have been behind Joshua's action at Ai in a similar way. It is the same Lord who commands Joshua to extend his javelin to start the battle with Ai, and to continue to extend the javelin (and thus the battle) until Ai has been exterminated. In Joshua's case the extermination proves to be complete, whereas in Moses' case completion was only promised. The Lord said, "Write this on a scroll as something to be remembered and make sure that Joshua hears it, because I will completely blot out the name of Amalek from under heaven" (Exod. 17:14). Both are cases of judgment, either partial (Amalek at the time) or complete (Ai). At Ai the Lord accomplishes it by means of an ambush.

---

28 A similar phenomenon was noted with regard to the gift of land in Genesis 12 ("To your offspring I *will give* this land," Gen. 12:7, emphasis added) and Genesis 15 ("To your descendants I *have given* this land," Gen. 15:18, emphasis added). Cf. discussion chapter 1, page 38.

God Shows Himself Shrewd in Judgments (Part 2):
The Case of the Benjamites' Rape

An ambush destroys some Benjamites after they rape a Levite's concubine in Benjamite territory (Judg. 20:1–48). A modern reader would easily think this account a relic of a barbaric age. It is better seen as a divine judgment against inhuman behavior. Any such judgment prefigures in one way or another God's eschatological judgment against the world. One element of prefiguration is God's "dealing shrewdly" with those he judges (cf. 2 Thess. 2:11–12).

The present narrative tells how a Levite from the hill country of Ephraim took a concubine from Bethlehem and stopped with her at Gibeah to spend the night on his way home (Judg. 19:1–22). An old man from Ephraim who lived in the town saw them in the town square and invited them to spend the night in his house. The evil men of the city pounded on the door of their elderly host and demanded the Levite for themselves, for they wanted to have sex with him (Judg. 19:22). Their behavior recalls the account of the angels who stopped for the night at Lot's house (Gen. 19:1–9). The host calls upon them not to commit such a gross affront to hospitality and offers his own daughter and the Levite's concubine instead (Judg. 19:23–24).[29] The men at first refuse, but do end up taking the concubine and having their way with her all night; after this treatment she dies (Judg. 19:25–28). The Levite takes his dead concubine home. There he cuts up her body, sends the parts to the tribes of Israel, and urges them to help him take some appropriate action (Judg. 19:29–30). Most of the rest of Israel join forces to attack Gibeah. They must, however, also contend with the Benjamites who not only do not join their effort but stand against them in defense of their own. The Lord counsels Israel to fight against the Benjamites (Judg. 20:18, 23b) but Israel must suffer two failed engagements with Benjamite forces (Judg. 20:19–25) before the Lord grants them success.

Success comes by way of an ambush. The narrative does not say the Lord instructed them to set the ambush, but he does tell them: "Go, for tomorrow I will give them into your hands" (Judg. 20:28b), and the next thing one reads is: "Then Israel set an ambush around Gibeah" (Judg. 20:29). The summary of their success follows: "The LORD defeated Benjamin before Israel" (Judg. 20:35a). One has here the sort of

---

29 The offer of the concubine is presumably made with the Levite's agreement but we are not told so.

promise-fulfillment sequence often found in prophetic narratives (cf. 1 Kings 17:1–7), and since the Lord is the one who made the promise and took its accomplishment on himself, it seems opportune to compare these events with the sequence of events in the Lord's judgment of Sodom and Gomorrah. Both events are divine judgments and they have parallel elements:

Genesis 19	Judges 19–20
Angels arrive 19:1	Levite and concubine arrive 19:15
Lot invites them to stay 19:2a	Old man invites them to stay 19:20a
Objection:	Objection:
They'll overnight in the square 19:2b	They have their own provisions 19:19
Host's insistence: 19:3a	Host's insistence: 19:20b
They stay; he supplies their needs 19:3b	He will supply their needs 19:21
Men demand sex with angels 19:4	Men demand sex with Levite 19:22
Host offers daughters 19:8a	Host offers daughter and concubine 19:24
Appeal to hospitality ethos 19:8b	Appeal to hospitality ethos 19:23
Men struck blind 19:11	Men abuse concubine 19:25
God's judgment 19:24	God's judgment 20:35

The parallelism is almost as notable as the perversion that drives the wicked in both places. The lust of men, young and old, for angels (thought to be men) in Sodom and Gomorrah is thwarted by a miracle from the Lord. The homosexual lust at Gibeah is not thwarted by the Lord—it is assuaged by a sacrificial concubine.[30] The Lord does not seem to be as actively involved in the Levite's case as he was in the case of the angels, perhaps because the angels were heavenly emissaries on a direct mission from the Lord. The offenders outside Lot's house are

---

30 Irrespective of the context, lust is at root a distortion—an abuse of the *imago Dei*. That is the heart of the matter. Any sin is an abuse of the *imago Dei*, whether the sin only harms the perpetrator (in the first instance) or whether it also harms someone else. Even a sin that seems to harm only the sinner inevitably harms other people because the sin makes the sinner a less authentic person—one who amens God less or not at all in his or her being—for human interactions.

thwarted by a supernaturally induced blindness in order to facilitate the angels' mission to Lot. By contrast, the offenders outside the old man's house are allowed to satisfy themselves, though not in quite the way they had wanted. Nonetheless, the omniscient Lord does become actively involved, because he gives the Benjamites into the avengers' hands. Vengeance is the Lord's, but he uses human agents to accomplish it. It remains unspoken whether the Lord inspired the ambush or just used it. One's choice between those possibilities depends on whether one views the Lord's proleptic statement—that he has given the abusers into the hands of the avengers—as (1) a statement implying God's invention of the ambush plan, and his moving the avengers to a successful ambush, or (2) a statement of his impending use of a humanly devised ambush.

God Shows Himself Shrewd in Judgments (Part 3): Micaiah and the Prophets of Ahab

Ahab plans to attack and recapture the Levitical city of Ramoth Gilead (1 Kings 22:1–4). After the manner of ancient near eastern monarchs, he consults his god—nominally Yahweh—for guidance about the battle. When pagan emperors reported successful campaigns in their annals, they typically claimed they consulted their god(s) and received (as per Assyrian tradition for example) a "firm yes." Ahab's experience is no different. He consults the prophets of the Lord and they say with one voice: "Go . . . for the LORD will give it into the king's hand" (1 Kings 22:6b). But the prophecy is a lie, as Micaiah, whom Ahab reluctantly summons to prophesy (at the insistence of his ally, Jehoshaphat) reports:

> Micaiah continued, "Therefore hear the word of the LORD: I saw the LORD sitting on his throne with all the multitudes of heaven standing around him on his right and on his left.
> And the LORD said, 'Who will entice Ahab into attacking Ramoth Gilead and going to his death there?' One suggested this, and another that.
> Finally, a spirit came forward, stood before the LORD and said, 'I will entice him.'
> 'By what means?' the LORD asked.
> 'I will go out and be a deceiving spirit in the mouths of all his prophets,' he said. 'You will succeed in enticing him,' said the LORD. 'Go and do it.'"
> (1 Kings 22:19–22)

Micaiah's experience is remarkable and will be considered later.[31] Before us now are the divine judgment by which Ahab was led astray to his death, and the nature and role of the "lying spirit" in the process.

Micaiah's audience before Ahab is unique for what it reveals about goings on behind the scenes, when God allows an evil spirit to have its way in order to work a judgment on someone. There is another, more succinctly portrayed case of spiritual maleficence apparently coming from God's presence: "Now the Spirit of the LORD had departed from Saul, and *an evil spirit from the LORD tormented him*" (1 Sam. 16:14, emphasis added). There is no question in Saul's case of the nature of the attacking spirit (רוח רעה) that comes "directly from the Lord" (מאת יהוה).[32] If one considers the laconic report in 1 Samuel in light of the more fulsome account in 1 Kings, one may suggest a similar process underlay the Lord's mission—or *permission*—of an evil spirit to afflict Saul. Whether the heavenly process is the same in both cases or not, both cases show God working a judgment by allowing an evil spirit to act within whatever limits the Lord has established—although those limits have not been revealed.[33]

The Lord may then, apparently, let an evil entity do what it wants in order to produce a judgment. The action of that evil entity is tantamount to a judgment on the receiver of the action. The evil entity can be human, and the Lord may even empower and bring that entity—for example, Assyria, as a judgment instrument against Israel (cf. Isa. 10:5–6.15), or Babylon, as a judgment instrument against Judah (cf. Hab. 1:5–6)—but with Saul and Ahab the agents are evil spirits. There can be no doubt concerning the evil of the "lying spirit" that informs Ahab's prophets: a better translation could be "spirit of deception." The phrase shows the nature of the spirit.[34]

---

31 Cf. chapter 14, pages 346–49.

32 Cf. the same phrase used of a prophecy that comes straight from the Lord: "We have heard a message *directly from the LORD* (מאת יהוה)" (Obad. 1, author's translation, emphasis added).

33 Cf., however, the case of Job, where the limits set on the evil spirit are made clear (Job 2:6). Job's experience is ineluctably a judgment on him because it refines him. The Lord is like a refiner's fire, and when he refines *but does not consume* in judgment, it is a work of the Spirit who burns away whatever is evil so that whatever is good may shine forth (cf. even after death, 1 Cor. 3:15). As has been noted, the Lord's very theophanic presence in a redemptive situation also ipso facto judges the human; cf. Niehaus, *God at Sinai*, 24. The 2 Samuel 24 // 1 Chronicles 21 parallel apparently offers another case of an evil entity "from the Lord" allowed to do its work as a divine judgment (see p. 307n39).

34 Cf. the remarkable and, to the present writer, outrageous interpretation that the

That last statement deserves a little elaboration. Because whatever is not of faith is sin—and because faith is amening God and his deeds and words—any falsehood is by definition sin: a disagreement with God on the true nature of any thing.[35] Any "spirit of deception" is therefore a spirit *out of accord* with God and how God sees things. In the case of Ahab, for example, God knows that, *contrary to the lying spirit's prophecy*, he is *not* going to give Ramoth Gilead into Ahab's hands.

But what of the prophets who allowed the lying spirit to speak through them? The account assumes a spirit was actually speaking through them, so they had a spiritual experience. They were prophets of the Lord (cf. 1 Kings 22:7–8). They gave a prophecy supposed to be from the Lord (cf. 1 Kings 22:6). But what sort of men were they? Apparently they had sold themselves out to say whatever would please their king. Pleasing the monarch—which usually meant giving a favorable oracle—was the goal of an ancient near eastern seer.[36] Ahab's prophets were, apparently, similarly motivated. Jehoshaphat asked for another prophet of the Lord, and that may mean he sensed their falsehood. What the Lord later says through Jeremiah could well apply to Ahab's prophets:

> I did not send these prophets,
>   yet they have run with their message;
> I did not speak to them,
>   yet they have prophesied.
> But if they had stood in my council,
>   they would have proclaimed my words to my people
> and would have turned them from their evil ways
>   and from their evil deeds. (Jer. 23:21–22)

"lying spirit" of 1 Kings 22 is the Holy Spirit: Simon J. DeVries, *1 Kings* (Nashville: Thomas Nelson, 1985), 260–68; cf. earlier Simon John DeVries, *Prophet against Prophet: The Role of the Micaiah Narrative (1 Kings 22) in the Development of Early Prophetic Tradition* (Grand Rapids: Eerdmans, 1978), 19.

35 This issue was raised in the Prolegomena in volume 1 and is taken up more fully in chapter 4 of volume 3. It is a determinative matter for the Lord's irruption in eschatological judgment, when he also allows a strong delusion to grip the ungodly, preparatory to a final judgment.

36 Note how Nebuchadnezzar, aware of this, sets a high bar for his seers: They must *tell* his dream, and then explain it. Only when they can tell the dream (rather than having the king tell it to them) can the king be sure their explanation of it has come from heaven (Dan. 2:1–11).

The Lord portrays prophets who have not stood in his council ("But which of them has stood in the council of the LORD / to see or to hear his word? / Who has listened and heard his word?" (Jer. 23:18). Ahab's prophets were apparently such men who did not stand in the Lord's council to see or hear his word and are contrasted vividly with Micaiah, who in a revelatory experience, "stood" in the Lord's council in that he was privileged to see the council and hear the Lord's words when the Lord opened heaven to his view (1 Kings 22:19–20).

Ahab's prophets *were* prophets of the Lord but their spiritual condition was such that, when they had *the spiritual experience of a lying spirit* wanting to speak through them, they could not tell it was a false spirit. They freely let pass through their lips a false prophecy. The words of that prophecy were spirit—a lying spirit—and the prophecy would lead Ahab to his death (1 Kings 22:29–38). The episode is a judgment scene, appropriately unfolding on a threshing floor (1 Kings 22:10 // 2 Chron. 18:9).[37] The Lord uses an evil spirit, letting it do what it wanted to do, in order to work a judgment. The Lord did not produce the lie, but he allowed it and used it.

The Lord later spoke some words through Ezekiel that seem to explain a situation like the one just considered:

> Therefore say to the house of Israel, "Thus says the Lord GOD: 'Repent, turn away from your idols, and turn your faces away from all your abominations. For anyone of the house of Israel, or of the strangers who dwell in Israel, who separates himself from Me and sets up his idols in his heart and puts before him what causes him to stumble into iniquity, then comes to a prophet to inquire of him concerning Me, I the LORD will answer him by Myself. I will set My face against that man and make him a sign and a proverb, and I will cut him off from the midst of My people. Then you shall know that I am the LORD." (Ezek. 14:6–8 NKJV)

The words of the Lord show just what happened to Ahab—who was at best double minded under the influence of his Baal-devoted wife Jezebel, who built a Baal altar and worshiped Baal (1 Kings 16:31–32). The Lord answered Ahab (to quote Ezekiel's prophecy) "by myself" [בִי], as

---

37   A threshing floor—where wheat and chaff were separated—was a fitting ancient near eastern symbol for a place of judgment or discernment. Cf. Judges 6:37; 2 Samuel 24:16, 18, 21, 24 (// 1 Chron. 21:18, 21, 22, 28); Psalm 1:4; Jeremiah 51:33; Hosea 13:3; Daniel 2:35; and Matthew 3:12 (// Luke 3:17).

the Lord told him, through Micaiah, just how things stood. The Lord's words are always Spirit. When the Lord spoke through Micaiah, the words Ahab heard were Spirit—the Lord himself—answering Ahab. The Lord says further:

> "And if the prophet is induced to speak anything, I the LORD have induced that prophet, and I will stretch out My hand against him and destroy him from among My people Israel. And they shall bear their iniquity; the punishment of the prophet shall be the same as the punishment of the one who inquired, that the house of Israel may no longer stray from Me, nor be profaned anymore with all their transgressions, but that they may be My people and I may be their God," says the Lord GOD. (Ezek. 14:9–11 NKJV)

1 Kings 22 does not show how God dealt with the false prophets— although Micaiah's answer to Zedekiah (1 Kings 22:24–25) mentions obscurely a punishment that awaits him—but the principle the Lord reveals to Ezekiel in days of Babylonian greatness could be assumed to apply at any time, and to apply beyond any worldly judgment, that is, eternally, as the New Testament makes clear.[38] The Lord declares, "If the prophet is induced to speak anything, I the Lord have induced that prophet" (v. 9), and that comports with what appeared in 1 Kings 22: the Lord *did* induce Ahab's false prophets, by a lying spirit he allowed to deceive both the prophets and their king. Had the Lord not allowed it, it would not have happened.[39]

God Shows Himself Shrewd in Judgments (Part 4): The Man of Lawlessness

Discernment of evil can only come by the Spirit of truth who shows a spiritual falsehood for what it is. The Antichrist will be discussed in more detail under the rubric of the new covenant and life under it. It is worth

---

38   Cf. Luke 10:16, "He who hears you hears Me, he who rejects you rejects Me, and he who rejects Me rejects Him who sent Me"—with obviously eternal implications.

39   A parallel instance, in which *the Lord is said to do something* but the same act is portrayed in more detail with *Satan himself* as the agent, occurs in the 2 Samuel 24 // 1 Chronicles 21 parallel: "Again the anger of the LORD burned against Israel, and he incited David against them, saying, 'Go and take a census of Israel and Judah.'" (2 Sam. 24:1) // "Satan rose up against Israel and incited David to take a census of Israel" (1 Chron. 21:1).

noting now that just as the Lord allowed a spirit of deception to speak persuasively through prophets who were nominally his but only pretended to be his (in Ahab's Israel), so at the end of days the Lord will allow a spiritual deception to be spoken to and embraced by the many, through one who will not only be a prophet (and who has a special prophet of his own) but claims to be God himself (cf. Rev. 13; 16:13–14; 2 Thess. 2:3–4). Paul describes a spiritual event that allows the coming of the "lawless one": "For the secret power of lawlessness is already at work; but *the one who now holds it back will continue to do so till he is taken out of the way*" (2 Thess. 2:7, emphasis added).[40] He then says:

> The coming of the lawless one will be in accordance with how Satan works. He will use all sorts of displays of power through signs and wonders that serve the lie, and all the ways that wickedness deceives those who are perishing. They perish because they refused to love the truth and so be saved. For this reason *God sends them a powerful delusion* so that they will believe the lie. (2 Thess. 2:9–11, emphasis added)

Paul does not give the amount of detail provided in 1 Kings 22, but the broad outline of events he describes is similar to what appeared in the case of Ahab and the false prophets. The epitome of false prophecy comes at the end, not only with words ("the lie") but also with deeds ("all sorts of displays of power through signs and wonders that serve the lie"). Just as the signs and wonders of Christ served the truth (cf. John 10:38; 14:11), so the signs and wonders of Antichrist serve the lie. The false words and false miracles together are the *gospel of the Antichrist*. That parallels Paul's account in Romans 15, in which the words of gospel proclamation coupled with signs and wonders are called effectively the full gospel:

> I will not venture to speak of anything except what Christ has accomplished through me in leading the Gentiles to obey God by what I have *said and done*—by the power of *signs and wonders*, through the power of the Spirit of God. So from Jerusalem all the way around to Illyricum, I have *fully proclaimed the gospel of Christ*. (Rom. 15:18–19, emphases added)

Paul combines the two—"what I have said and done" and "the power of signs and wonders"—and referring to both he declares: "So . . . I have

---

40 I have agreed with interpreters who understand that "the one who now holds it back" is the Holy Spirit; cf. *ANETBT*, 135–36.

fully proclaimed the gospel of Christ." Centuries before, the same combination of words and wonders brought the widow of Zarephath to acknowledge the Lord when she told Elijah (after the Lord had resurrected her son): "Now I know that you are a man of God and that the word of the LORD from your mouth is the truth" (1 Kings 17:24). The Lord prefigured there what he would do in his work of kingdom progress in the new covenant: God would expand the kingdom by words and deeds, by proclamation of the saving work and nature of Christ, and by signs and wonders that showed the proclamation to be true (cf. Heb. 2:1–4).[41]

It follows naturally and inevitably that Antichrist would mimic the Lord's pattern. God's pattern of a proclamation accompanied by spiritual endorsement was made for those in God's image to receive; Satan knows that, so he empowers Antichrist not only with a false gospel but also with false signs and wonders to complete the package. Satan appeals to human ontology—that is, on the basis of the way the Lord has formed humans to be recipients of God's truth and power. We are made in the image of One who is Word and Spirit. So we are made to receive *words* of the Father and the *works* of the Spirit through the Son.[42]

CONCLUDING THOUGHTS

The Lord is true and *is the truth*. Nonetheless, he can let evil spirits deceive others as part of a judgment, and he can let his people to do the same. God let a lying spirit produce a false prophecy that brought about a judgment on Ahab. He let Rahab—who was becoming one of his people—fool her king and facilitate a judgment on Jericho. Moreover, the Lord may let someone who is coming under judgment receive partial information, and the actions the person takes on the basis of that information lead to his or her judgment. As regards the Lord, then, David's verses pronounce a hermeneutical principle by which God's people may rightly understand what could otherwise seem to be questionable behavior on God's part:

---

41   The same was true even earlier of the Mosaic signs and wonders that showed the Lord's words through Moses to be true, and the same is true today as many accounts from the mission field attest.

42   Those works, of course, also include the inner work of the Spirit. That work endures forever in the redeemed person, whereas signs and wonders, amazing as they can be, accomplish their task and then become history.

> To the faithful you show yourself faithful,
> To the blameless you show yourself blameless,
> To the pure you show yourself pure,
> But to the crooked you show yourself shrewd. (Ps. 18:25–26)

Our study may in some small way "justify the ways of God to men," or at least some of those ways. [43] One truth affirmed by such a study is surely the adage: things are not always what they appear to be!

Satan is in that category, and as Satan has an ontology, deception has ontology. This point was affirmed at the outset. It is repeated here after many examples of how effective deception can be. Only things that *are* can produce effects. As words are spirit, so acts are spirit as *realia* produced by a spirit. Finally, God sustains all that, so the mystery of God's goodness as sustainer of evil remains. Satan, who *is himself the lie* of godhood apart from God, has an ontology only because God sustains him.

Finally, a brief comment on God's righteousness is in order lest one suppose God is unrighteous in some of his behaviors noted above. It is impossible for God to be unrighteous, because righteousness is conformity to a standard, and in the Bible the standard of righteousness is always God and only God: true righteousness is always conformity to God's nature, and God is always in conformity to himself.[44]

---

43   Cf. John Milton, *Paradise Lost*, ed. Merrit Y. Hughes (New York: Odyssey Press, 1935), 9 (book I, line 26).

44   True righteousness is at issue here, not any merely human righteousness, which is not conformity to God but to some humanly asserted standard that can only be unrighteous (not in conformity to God). Cf. Isaiah 64:6 (NKJV): "But we are all like an unclean *thing*, / And all our righteousnesses *are* like filthy rags." Cf. volume 3, Appendix E.

CHAPTER TWELVE

MOSAIC COVENANT AND BEYOND: IDOLATRY AND FRUIT

Deception as a tool of judgment was the subject of the last chapter. Deception as a factor of idolatry is the subject of this. Siddhartha, as Hesse portrays that character, poses the question: "Waren nicht die Götter Gestaltungen, erschaffen wie ich und du, der Zeit untertan, vergänglich?"[1] The gods were not immortal—they would perish, as would their idols. Bluntly put, idols are not what they appear to be. Idols of gods and goddesses in the ancient world were, as the Old Testament calls them, fakes or falsehoods. Even under the old covenant with all its materiality, idolatry was understood to be *first an internal affair* (cf. Ezek. 14:6–8). Idols in the church age are the same—according to Paul greed is idolatry (Col. 3:5). Idolatry plays in important role as a challenge in the life of God's covenant people under any covenant because it offers a substitute for the true God of covenant. The first case of idolatry arguably occurred when our first parents exalted themselves above God and took the fruit, thus violating the first covenant. The one who invites us to idolatry is of course "the god of this world" (2 Cor. 2:4) who, under God's permission, is the false suzerain who gained legal entrée and dominion by the sin of the first Adam, and whose dominion is terminated by the second Adam. The ultimate idol, apparently, will be the image that the beast sets up in the temple just before the end (Rev. 13:11–15). Worship of the beast will be as close as Satan gets to being worshiped, in his own right, by the world.

Idolatry elevates something a human has created or adopted *within*—an idea—to the exalted status of a god in one's life. That work of false

---

1   Hermann Hesse, *Siddhartha* (Frankfurt: Suhrkamp Verlag, 1969), 9. Author's translation: "Were the gods not also creations, made like you and me, subject to time, perishable?"

creation parallels the manufacture of an idol made of wood, stone, or metal for worship (Isa. 44:12–17). An inner ontology of falsehood produces an outer counterpart—a false god.

IDOLATRY INTERNAL IN THE FIRST INSTANCE

People tend to think of an idol as a statue of some god or goddess, and a statement like's Paul's about greed as merely figurative and based on the physical fact of idolatry. The truth is actually the other way around. Idolatry is always an internal move of the spirit. Ezekiel portrays idolatry's inner nature indisputably: "For anyone of the house of Israel, or of the strangers who dwell in Israel, who separates himself from Me and *sets up his idols in his heart* and puts before him what causes him to stumble into iniquity, then comes to a prophet to inquire of him concerning Me, I the LORD will answer him by Myself" (Ezek. 14:7 NKJV [emphasis added]; cf. NASB, NIV, HCSB, OJB). An alternate translation could be "taking his idols into his heart," or "taking his idols to heart" (perhaps but not decisively closer to the Hebrew, ויעל גלוליו אל־לבו, ESV; cf. YLT). On the first understanding, the person creates or "raises up" an idol in his heart; he then "puts before him" a physical, realized form of his idolatrous idea—a material idol—and that further "causes him to stumble into iniquity." On either translation idolatry is fundamentally an interior affair—a love affair with falsehood.

IDOLATRY AS SIN

Understood more fundamentally, idolatry is sin because it *does not amen* God. Affirmation that a humanly formed object—an idea—is God claims an ontology for something that cannot live up to it. And God does not affirm it, although he sustains its existence. The same is true of the physical product of an idolatrous idea. An idol is not *nothing* in an absolute sense, for it exists—if only as a block of wood shaped to look like a man or a woman, or an animal. Nor can an idol be nothing spiritually: an idol involves the worshiper with spirits said to be behind the idolatry (cf. Deut. 32:16–17; 1 Cor. 10:20). Those spirits are also not nothing. They are empowering forces for the idols.[2] Yet compared to God an idol is

---

2   It is remarkable that NIV (2011), in what appears to be its increasingly slipshod

nothing. Isaiah can apostrophize idols: "You are less than nothing" (Isa. 41:24). But David asks, "How long will you love delusions and seek false gods?" (Ps. 4:2, lit. "fakes," "deceptions," Hebrew כֹּזָב).[3] Now nothing *in an absolute sense* cannot be false or a fake or a deception. Nothing in an absolute sense is simply the absence of something, and in our case particularly God. Because God is omnipresent and sustains all creation, there can be no such thing as absolute nothingness, for there is no thing without God's undergirding—not even such an invisible thing as the space-time continuum, and certainly not Satan or demons. The concept of nothingness or "das Nichtige" comes up for discussion and rejection in chapter 4 of volume 3, but we affirm for now the rhetorical quality of a statement, such as the Lord makes through Isaiah, that idols are "less than nothing."

When on the other hand the Lord calls idols "false," he does truly say they are lies or deceptions. A lie is also not *nothing* but rather a mis-representation of *something*, of a reality—whether the reality is God or something God has created, or even an idea in the mind of the Creator, or a creature, or something a creature has created.

Biblical characterization of idolatry in fact alludes to the created or-der. The Lord says of idolaters: "Their molten images are wind and con-fusion" (Isa. 41:29). The combination of "wind" (רוח) and "confusion" (תהו) evokes Genesis 1:2: "Now the earth was formless (תהו) and empty, darkness was over the surface of the deep, and the Spirit (רוח) of God was hovering over the waters." Idols, by a poetic turn, are the opposite of God's creative process. He created cosmos out of chaos. Idols—or the spirits behind them—tend by nature to reduce cosmos to chaos, whether it be the created order or the individual who is disordered by worshiping an idol. The spirit behind the whole enterprise is Satan. He has come to destroy (John 10:10). He is the primordial author of sin and of the ἀνομία of sin (cf. 1 John 3:4, "all sin is lawlessness"). Sin produces and is the essence of chaos. Nonetheless and in the profoundest sense, all sin—all

---

translation policy, translates Hebrew שֵׁדִים ("demons") as "false gods" in Deuteronomy 32:17. Only GNT, TLB, and (of course) NIRV do likewise. The translation misses the point, namely, the object of sacrifice; it also shows no sign of appreciating cognate evidence. NIV 2011 does, inconsistently as it would appear, translate "demons" in 1 Corinthians 10:20 (δαιμονίοις).

3 For other passages that use the Hebrew term the same way, see Psalm 40:4 and Amos 2:4. Cf. the similar term שֶׁקֶר ("deception") also used of idols/false gods in Jeremiah 10:14; 13:25 (possibly); and 51:17.

failure to amen God—has union with an alternative that it *does and must* amen—an idol. So Isaiah can say, "Their molten images are wind (רוח) and confusion (תהו)."

Once one affirms with Isaiah the *less-than-nothingness* of idols on the one hand, but also rejects their *ontological nothingness* on the other, and once one agrees with the old covenant prophets that idols are fakes or deceptions, and once one recognizes the satanic power behind them, then one can turn to another aspect of idolatry. Just as idols—or rather the powers behind them—are opposed to God, as falsehood is *by defini-tion* opposed to the truth, those beings carry the enterprise further and want to substitute themselves for God in suzerainty over people, and especially, if possible, over God's chosen people. That substitution is not merely a ritual matter on some high place, or even in the temple, but is ineluctably a spiritual event. The nature of the event becomes clear if one understands the intended relation between God, as a husband, and Israel, his wife. The relationship clarifies the nature of a demonic or idolatrous substitution—one the Lord and the prophets do not tolerate.

WHO WILL BE HUSBAND?

The Lord is sometimes called Israel's husband. His covenant people are, accordingly, his bride or wife. The husband-wife relationship that is fig-urative in the Old Testament becomes more dynamic in the New Tes-tament. It becomes more dynamic under the new covenant for spiritual reasons well understood by Christians.[4] However, even if the relation-ship is more dynamic under the new covenant than it could possibly have been under the old covenant, it was nonetheless real before the new covenant came into existence on earth.[5] In Ezekiel 16, the Lord vividly portrayed his own witness of Israel's growth from infancy to young wom-anhood and then described his choice of her for his bride—a figurative account of his taking her into the Sinai covenant. The account resonates with a biblical truth—the Bible also views marriage as a covenant. It can do so because of the nature of God's relationship with his people. That relationship born of God's ideational and creative work is the founda-tion of the prophets' use of marriage as a figure for the Lord's covenant

---

4   Cf. also the brief discussion in volume 1, 87–89.

5   Of course the new covenant always existed and does exist as a present reality in the mind and experience of God.

relationship with his elect. The problem with idolatry on this level is that it offers itself as—and insists upon being—a substitute for the Lord as husband of his people. That blasphemous idea informs the drama of Hosea's calling (see pp. 317–20).

Idolatry, Marriage, and Fruit

Related to the concept of marriage is the concept of fruit. That is obvious in the natural realm but it is also true—in a sense more substantially and enduringly true—in the spiritual realm: more substantially and enduringly there because it is the spiritual (the "unseen" things) that are truly *substantial and enduring.*[6] Heaven and earth will pass away, but the Lord's words, *which are Spirit,* will never pass away. The spiritual fruit of marriage is therefore of paramount importance.

A husband marries a wife, and once that marriage has been consummated, fruit in the form of a child or children becomes a legitimate possibility. If, however, the wife becomes an adulteress, there may also be fruit in the form of a child or children, but such fruit is considered illegitimate.

The same concepts apply in the spiritual realm. The Lord becomes the husband of a people. Once he has done so he may reasonably expect fruit from them. If they are faithful to their marriage to him, the fruit they bear will be legitimate or good fruit. If, however, they are unfaithful and commit adultery with some different lover or lovers, the fruit they bear will be illegitimate or bad fruit. So the Lord says through Isaiah in the vineyard parable: "Then he [i.e., the Lord, the planter of the vineyard] looked for grapes, but it yielded only bad fruit" (Isa. 5:2). Instead of (implicitly) good fruit, the vineyard produced only bad fruit.

The prophetic epitome of this figurative thinking is probably the situation in Hosea 1–3. The Lord calls his prophet into ministry with a strange and challenging command: "Go, marry a promiscuous woman and have children with her, for like an adulterous wife this land is guilty of unfaithfulness to the Lord" (1:2). The phrase "promiscuous woman" is literally "a woman of harlotries" (אשת זנונים). Some understand the phrase (because it is a plural abstract) as figurative, so it means not a literally adulterous woman but rather a woman who is an idolatress.[7]

---

6   Cf. 2 Corinthians 4:18: "So we fix our eyes not on what is seen, but on what is unseen, since what is seen is temporary, but what is unseen is eternal."

7   Whether or not the woman is an adulteress or an idolatress, she should by law have been refused and not taken as a wife. The challenge to Hosea therefore remains the

But the first time the word זנונים appears in the Old Testament, it is used of literal pregnancy: "Tamar your daughter-in-law has played the harlot; furthermore she *is* with child by harlotry [זנונים]" (Gen. 38:24 NKJV). If a person can become pregnant by זנונים, it is more than an abstract term.

The Lord therefore commands Hosea to marry a promiscuous woman whose promiscuity in marriage means adultery and who gives him children of her promiscuity. She bears him illegitimate or bad fruit (cf. Isaiah's vineyard parable): "Go, take yourself a wife of harlotry / And children of harlotry, / For the land has committed great harlotry / *By departing* from the LORD" (1:2 NKJV). As a husband in Israel, Hosea had a right to expect legitimate or good fruit to come from his marriage. Instead, because of his wife's unfaithfulness, he receives bad fruit.

The Lord has put his prophet into a place in the natural that parallels the Lord's place in the spiritual vis-à-vis his people. It does not take much imagination to see this was a hard calling. Who would want it? Nonetheless, it is an exalted privilege to be put in parallel with the Lord. Abraham had this privilege when the Lord called him to offer his only son, whom he loved, to God—and then rescued him from the grievous trial by providing a substitute. Hosea's case is not unlike Abraham's: Hosea also must undergo a relational challenge one would not choose, but in his case (as with Abraham on Moriah) there is a Christological component: Hosea will take Gomer back, and the Lord will take Israel back. Moreover, the Lord will do so by betrothing her, which involves paying a bride price.[8] That is what the Lord later does when he lays down the price of his Son for Israel's redemption and betrothal.

Before that happens, the Lord deals prophetically with an intolerable substitution of idols for himself in the marital relationship with his people. It is intolerable to God not only as a denial of ontological reality, and thus also an affront to his Being (and hence his brief judgment: "I am not I AM to you" [ואנכי לא אהיה לכם], 1:9, author's translation), but also because of what it does to his people: idolatry produces spiritual fruit in a way his people are not yet in a position to understand. The following outline makes the problem clear:

---

same in either case, although the command to marry a woman who will literally give him illegitimate children would obviously be more existentially challenging, and this is more likely the case.

8   The Hebrew word often translated "betroth" is ארש. It involves or can involve paying a bride price; cf. *BDB*, 77.

Legitimate Scenario		Actual Scenario	
Yahweh	Hosea	Lover(s)	Lover(s)
⇓	⇓	⇓	⇓
Israel	Gomer	Israel	Gomer
⇓	⇓	⇓	⇓
Good fruit	Good fruit	Bad fruit	Bad fruit

The alternate realities show what the Lord called for and hoped for from his marriage with Israel, and what he instead got. He hoped she would bear good fruit—the obedience of faith—and in so doing would represent the Lord's nature and what it meant to be the Lord's people on earth (cf. Deut. 4:5–8). Instead, Israel went after false lovers and produced bad fruit. Agreeably the Lord caused his prophet to endure in the *natural* realm what the Lord had to endure in the *spiritual* realm: Hosea had to see his wife prove unfaithful again and again, and see her illegitimate children—the fruit of her unfaithfulness—abounding in his own household.

The question remains: Who were Israel's lovers (2:5)? Hosea makes it clear enough they were the Baals: "She said, 'I will go after my lovers, / who give me my food and my water, / my wool and my linen, my olive oil and my drink'" (2:5), and so the Lord says, "I will punish her for the days / she burned incense to the Baals; she decked herself with rings and jewelry, / and went after her lovers, / but me she forgot, declares the LORD" (2:13). The people, then, went after false gods. They worshiped idols and mistakenly imagined those "gods" were the givers of abundance. That is exactly what the Lord foretold through Moses. After the Lord had blessed Israel with prosperity (Deut. 32:13–14),

> Jeshurun grew fat and kicked. . . .
> Then he forsook God who made him,
> And scornfully esteemed the Rock of his salvation.
> They provoked Him to jealousy with foreign gods;
> With abominations they provoked Him to anger.
> They sacrificed to demons [שׁדים], not to God,

To gods they did not know,
To new gods, new arrivals
That your fathers did not fear. (Deut. 32:15–17 NKJV)

When Israel worshiped other gods, they were in fact worshiping demons. Both Moses in the Old Testament and Paul in the New (1 Cor.
10:20) make it clear that the power behind idolatry is demonic. Accordingly, Israel was bringing herself under the influence of demonic powers
when she engaged those lovers. The result of demonic influence is the
spiritual relationship considered above that produces bad spiritual fruit.
That truth is indicated less clearly in the Old Testament than in the New
Testament; in the Old Testament it is, for the most part, only suggested
by the sort of figurative language being explored here.

By engaging with demonic powers through idolatry, Israel was committing adultery in the spiritual realm, just as a married woman might
commit adultery in the natural realm. The cases can now be outlined in
a way that shows the parallelism between the natural and the spiritual:

	Legitimate Scenario		Actual Scenario	
Husband	Yahweh	Adulterer	Idol / Demonic power
⇓	⇓	⇓	⇓
Wife	Israel	Wife	Israel
⇓	⇓	⇓	⇓
Good fruit	Good fruit	Bad fruit	Bad fruit

The Old Testament uses physical harlotry and adultery as figurative
language for idolatry. The spiritual nature of idolatry gave rise to the use
of such language for its illustration. No modern disinclination to accept
spiritual reality of this sort should interfere with anyone's understanding.
The Bible is a spiritual book—a God-breathed book whose words are
Spirit—about spiritual things. The outline presented above is no arbitrary concoction, but a dynamic portrayal of what the Spirit reveals in
Deuteronomy 32:15–17 and 1 Corinthians 10:20.

The question naturally arises: What exactly was *going on* in the spiritual realm when Israel, or an Israelite, was unfaithful via idolatry to the Lord of the national marriage covenant? Paul tells us those who worship idols (in the Corinthian context, pagans) "offer their sacrifices to demons . . . and I do not want you to have fellowship with demons" (1 Cor. 10:20). It seems obvious that demons inspired false/idolatrous worship and benefitted from it in some way (or else presumably they would not have inspired it). One can probably infer that, as Satan's desire was to "be like God" (cf. Isa. 14:14), and as he tempted our first parents with that same lure, his angels also crave that same exaltation, to whatever degree they can attain it. Power held by one person over another is a profoundly spiritual reality. It affects the spirit of the person who has the power as well as the spirit of the subordinate person. There is no reason to assume things are different in principle in the spiritual world. Just as a human spirit is purified and exalted, and also humbled in service, by the Holy Spirit when one gives oneself to God, so the opposite things are true when one gives oneself to the worship of demons via idolatry. What then of those worshipers? What happens to them when they engage with false gods, that is, idols? The warning, or portrayal, offered by Scripture is that they become like what they worship: "Those who make them will be like them, and so will all who trust in them" (Pss. 115:8; 135:18).[9] Whatever that means, it would seem to entail an increasing conformity of the human nature to the nature of the false god, that is, to the demonic nature. One sees the converse if one considers the result of true worship: "But whenever anyone turns to the Lord, the veil is taken away. Now the Lord is the Spirit, and where the Spirit of the Lord is, there is freedom. And we all, who with unveiled faces contemplate the Lord's glory, are being transformed into his image with ever increasing glory, which comes from the Lord, who is the Spirit" (2 Cor. 3:16–18).

Paul's comments in 2 Corinthians 3 come in the context of an illustration of the superiority of life under the new covenant to life under the old covenant: "Now if the ministry that brought death, which was engraved in letters on stone, came with glory, so that the Israelites could not look steadily at the face of Moses because of its glory, transitory though it was, will not the ministry of the Spirit be even more glorious?" (2 Cor. 3:7–8).[10] Paul can say so because, under the new covenant, the Lord's people have

---

9   Cf. G. K. Beale, *We Become What We Worship: A Biblical Theology of Idolatry* (Downers Grove, IL: InterVarsity Press, 2008).

10   This important passage will be examined in detail later, when we discuss the new covenant.

the Spirit dwelling within them (as Ezekiel had promised, Ezek. 36:27). Such was not the case under the Mosaic covenant.

Consequently, whatever fruit bearing the Lord may have looked for from his people under the old covenant, it could only approximate what would be possible under the new covenant. The Spirit, who is portrayed as a river of living water and promised as such to followers of Jesus—a promise fulfilled at Pentecost and always thereafter—was never a river of living water within anyone under the Mosaic covenant. Arguably Psalm 1 portrays figuratively the relation of the Spirit to the person under the old covenant. It shows the best one could hope for under the Mosaic state of affairs. Psalm 1 portrays the person who is not an idolater, and who consequently bears good fruit.

PSALM 1 AND THE SPIRIT

The first Psalm offers a picture of the faithful person who lives under the Mosaic covenant, and the picture shows both the unique blessing of life under that covenant—a blessing unattainable to those who were outside it, who did not have the benefit of the Lord's *torah*—but also implicitly, as one knows now from a new covenant perspective, the limitations of such a relationship. Of one who does have that *torah*, David says:

> But his delight is in the law of the LORD,
>   And in His law he meditates day and night.
> He shall be like a tree
>   Planted by the rivers of water,
>   That brings forth its fruit in its season,
>   Whose leaf also shall not wither;
> And whatever he does shall prosper. (Ps. 1:2–3 NKJV)

Three points stand out in David's poem. First, the ideal or model person under the Mosaic covenant does what the prophet leader Joshua was told to do. He "meditates day and night" in the law and as a result whatever he does is successful (cf. the Lord's guidance in Josh. 1:8: "Keep this Book of the Law always on your lips; meditate on it day and night, so that you may be careful to do everything written in it. Then you will be prosperous and successful"). Second, the source of the person's spiritual fruitfulness is important. It is the law. But the situation of the one who meditates on that law, which is external to him but becomes internalized by his ingestion of it, is like that of a tree planted by/beside streams of water—streams that are also external to the tree but internalized by it to produce growth and fruit. Third, the person is like a tree that has been *trans*planted (Hebrew שָׁתוּל). The word "transplanted" has an important nuance that is easily missed in the ubiquitous translation "planted." Transplanted indicates that the tree once grew in a *different environment*—implicitly one less conducive to growth and life and fruitfulness, since it is the *trans*planted person who now has those qualities. Once these points have been noted, one can better understand what the Psalm says about a faithful—non-idolatrous—person under the Mosaic covenant.

Portrayed poetically and in a figure, the faithful person under the Mosaic covenant is one who at some point in his or her life has come dynamically under that covenant. In other words, at some point in that person's life he or she took the step of faith and amened or "owned" the covenant relationship for himself or herself. Obviously a biologically male descendant of Abraham took that step some time after circumcision. Once that happened, the person experienced the sort of blessing the old covenant had to offer—meditation on the law with its attendant internal benefits. The dynamic of that relationship is portrayed in a figure with the streams of water analogous to the law, and the person analogous to the tree:

Streams	Law
⇓	⇓
Tree	Person
⇓	⇓
Physical fruit	Spiritual fruit

One must remember, however, that the law is *external to the person*, as the streams are external to to the tree. The streams represent the law but that would be spiritually impotent unless we recognize that the law is also Spirit, for the law is God-breathed (θεόπνευστος, 2 Tim. 3:16) and like Jesus' words the words of the law are Spirit (πνεῦμά, cf. John 6:63). Under the Mosaic covenant, then, the Spirit is external to the person and works effectively through the law. That law is at best an expression of the Spirit. And this, to use a common expression, is "as good as it gets" under the old covenant. It is not a bad thing to have that much, that is, the Spirit working through the law to encourage growth, freshness, and fruitfulness.

Obviously it is better to have the Spirit (the "streams of living water," John 7:38) on the inside than on the outside. That is one's privilege under the new covenant. Once one knows and is part of the new covenant, the tree, water, and fruit illustrations of Psalm 1 vividly show the contrast between life under the old covenant and life under the new covenant—or put more simply, the blessings and the limitations of life under the old covenant as they can be seen from a new covenant perspective. Paul addresses the same contrast, using the figurative language of the veil of the temple and the glory of the Spirit in 2 Corinthians 3.

SPIRITUAL INFLUENCE: IDOLATRY, DEMONS, AND THE SPIRIT

Moses and Paul made it clear that those who worship idols worship demons. Demonic influence moves them to that worship. On the other hand, the Holy Spirit moves people to worship the true God (cf. 1 Cor. 12:3). Psalm 1 presents figuratively the person's quotidian relation to the Holy Spirit under the old covenant. The figurative language of adultery used to characterize idolatry in the Old Testament presents the person's relation to idols or false gods. Both relations appear external in their Old Testament presentations. But the Holy Spirit could also be "in" someone for a task under the old covenant, and there is no reason to think demons could not be "in" someone in the days of the old covenant or before, just as the ministry of Jesus and his followers showed they could be. God's reservation of the crucifixion-ratification of the new covenant as the precondition of the Pentecost donation of the Spirit and the constitution of believers as temples of the Spirit does not mean that in some parallel fashion demons could not indwell people before Pentecost. Ezekiel's characterization of idolatry as *ab initio* an internal matter should be a warning to anyone anywhere about the dangers of idolatry in light of such biblical data.

CHAPTER THIRTEEN

THE HEART AND THE OLD COVENANT

The discussion of Psalm 1 that concluded the previous chapter antic-ipates issues raised in this chapter. One of those is the problem with the old covenant. The problem with the Mosaic covenant (the "fault" with it, to use the language of the book of Hebrews) was that, although it set a godly standard, it did not give the human covenant member power to live up to that standard. At such a juncture the need for God's power becomes obvious. We know the covenant law was an articulation of God's own na-ture. Humans, although made in the *imago Dei*, are polluted by sin. What-ever is not of faith is sin (Rom. 14:23b). Moreover, the law even provokes sin ("*The sinful passions aroused by the law* were at work in our bodies, so that we bore fruit for death," Rom. 7:5, emphasis added). A person in such a condition—that is, a person under the law—has no hope of conforming to God's nature even as that nature is expressed in the law. He cannot amen it consistently in his daily life. Only God's Spirit within a person can enable a human to conform to God's nature. An inner reformation by the Spirit is a necessary precursor to one's living up to that standard (cf. Rom 8:13b: "If by the Spirit you put to death the misdeeds of the body, you will live").[1] Because God's nature is also the standard of righteousness, Paul can articulate justly the hopelessness both of life under the law and of the fallen human condition: "What shall we conclude then? Do we have any advantage? Not at all! For we have already made the charge that Jews and Gentiles alike are all under the power of sin. As it is written: 'There is no one righteous, not even one'" (Rom. 3:9–10; cf. Eccl. 7:20).

The Old Testament has different ways of noting Israel's failure to

---

1   There will be much more to say about the contrast between life under the law and life in the Spirit when we discuss the dynamics of life under the new covenant.

conform to the Lord's standard (the law). The Old Testament writers use more colorful or figurative language than a review of broken laws that one might find in a covenant lawsuit, although covenant lawsuits are not without striking imagery.[2] Relevant figures employed relating to the old covenant deficiency include circumcision (the circumcision of the heart), and having the law written on the heart—states of being unknown to old covenant saints. Relevant to the law written in/on the heart, Paul's characterization of pagans in Romans 2:12–16 comes under discussion as it relates to the new covenant promise of Jeremiah 31. Because these *figurae* are the major ones that deal with the new covenant and life under it vis-à-vis the old and life under it, they form the organizing core of the present chapter.

CIRCUMCISION

One way of profiling the issue of human failure to conform to God's standard is to express it in terms of circumcision. Circumcision under the Abrahamic covenant signified an individual's submission to the terms of that covenant. We do not have an exhaustive account of what those terms were. We only know that, according to the Lord, "Abraham obeyed me and did everything I required of him [lit. "kept my charge"], keeping my commands, my decrees and my instructions" (Gen. 26:5). The terms "charge" (משמרת) "commands" (מצות) "decrees" (חקות) and "instructions" (תרות) are all used later to describe the Lord's requirements under the Mosaic covenant.[3] Moreover, the covenant idiom in the expression "Abraham obeyed me" (lit. "Abraham paid heed to my voice") is also used later of Israel under the Mosaic covenant (e.g., שמע לקול, Exod. 15:26 [before Sinai, but regarding the Lord's commands and decrees that Israel must obey]; שמע בקול, Num. 14:22; Deut. 4:30). Circumcision then, as the sign of the Abrahamic covenant, signified the possible "cutting off" of an individual who broke that covenant or, put another way, it indicated the conditional aspect of the Abrahamic covenant.[4]

Although it was the Sabbath, and not circumcision, the Lord designated

---

2   Cf. for a grand example what has been called the Great Indictment of Isaiah 1 with its figures of a wounded and untreated body, a hut in a melon field, and a besieged city.

3   For example, "charge" (משמרת, Lev. 8:35; Num. 1:35 and passim; Deut. 11:1); "commands" (מצות, Exod. 20:6; Num. 15:22; Deut. 4:2 and passim); "decrees" (חקות, Exod. 27:21; Lev. 3:17 and passim; Deut. 6:2); and "instructions" (תרות, or "instruction/law" [תורה], Exod. 24:12; Lev. 26:46; Num. 5:29.30; Deut. 1:5 and passim).

4   Cf. discussion in chapter 2.

as the sign of the Mosaic covenant (Exod. 31:13; cf. Ezek. 20:12), nonetheless the Mosaic law also required circumcision on the eighth day even though circumcision was not a sign of the Mosaic covenant, and this is an indication that the Abrahamic covenant was still in force, and any member of the Mosaic covenant was also required to become a member of the Abrahamic covenant. For any male individual, the signs of the two covenants were undertaken in the historical order of the covenants to which they pertain, since the person would be circumcised as an infant on the eighth day (sign of the Abrahamic covenant) and only later would choose to observe the Sabbath (sign of the Mosaic covenant). Circumcision then not only stood for the consequence of disobeying the "charge," "commands," "decrees," and "instructions" of the Abrahamic covenant (Gen. 26:5), but also came to stand for the consequence of disobeying the Mosaic covenant that more fully articulated and encoded those requirements. For we take it as indicated by the historical shift in the perceived significance of circumcision, that the Mosaic law included and expanded upon the requirements of the Abrahamic covenant just as it included and expanded upon the death penalty of the Noahic covenant.[5] So later Paul could say, "I declare to every man who lets himself be circumcised that he is obligated to obey the *whole* law" (Gal. 5:3, emphasis added). The law required circumcision, which was the sign of the Abrahamic covenant, and if one "took on" circumcision one also, by the same token, "took on" the whole body of the law, of which circumcision was one requirement (*pars pro toto*).

It was not possible for anyone to live up to the high standard of the Mosaic covenant. Jesus later made that unarguably clear in the Sermon on the Mount, in which he showed the depth of both the apodictic laws and the casuistic laws of the Mosaic covenant. The depth of the law, clarified at last by Jesus, showed the depth of human sin and the concomitant hopelessness of the human condition.

CIRCUMCISION OF THE HEART

Because of its importance as a covenant sign—a sign of the faith with which Abram had entered the Abrahamic covenant—circumcision of the heart is one figure the Lord uses to portray the hopeless spiritual condition of people. It is clear that God's people under the Mosaic covenant had uncircumcised hearts, and it would become clear that only the Lord could perform the needed circumcision, and that he would not do it under the old covenant.

---

5   Cf. volume 1 of *Biblical Theology*, 205–208.

The matter of heart circumcision appears in three important documents: the original Sinai covenant (Leviticus), the Moab renewal of that covenant (Deuteronomy), and the Lord's covenant lawsuit based on the Mosaic covenant (Jeremiah).

Uncircumcised Heart in the Sinai Covenant (Leviticus)

The Lord's people apparently had uncircumcised hearts under the Sinai covenant. When the Lord foretold in that covenant that his people would go into exile because of their sin, he also foretold that, even when he would undertake to bring them back from exile, they would still have uncircumcised hearts:

> But if they will confess their sins and the sins of their ancestors—their unfaithfulness and their hostility toward me, which made me hostile toward them so that I sent them into the land of their enemies—then when their uncircumcised hearts are humbled [i.e., in exile] and they pay for their sin, I will remember my covenant with Jacob and my covenant with Isaac and my covenant with Abraham, and I will remember the land. (Lev. 26:40–42)

The Lord foretold that his people would be exiled because of their unfaithfulness (26:33–39), epitomized perhaps by their ignoring the land Sabbath sign (26:43). They had that prophetic warning in the *torah* of the Sinai covenant, but they ignored it. They ignored it because they had "uncircumcised hearts"—as they obviously still would have even after experiencing the punishment of exile.

Uncircumcised Heart in the Moab Covenant (Deuteronomy)

The Leviticus prophecy notwithstanding, the people's hearts remained uncircumcised. That is clear because the Lord commanded his people to circumcise their hearts when he renewed the Sinai covenant on the plains of Moab: "Circumcise your hearts, therefore, and do not be stiff-necked any longer" (Deut. 10:16). He did so in the context of telling them that, although heaven and earth belong to him (10:14), he had set his affection on their fathers and chosen them alone out of all the nations (10:15). One would think such assurances from God himself would have motivated the people to try, at least, to circumcise their hearts.[6]

---

6   It should be remembered that the generation on the plains of Moab was more

Uncircumcised Heart in Covenant Lawsuit (Jeremiah)

Accordingly, the Lord was just when he brought covenant lawsuit against those who egregiously broke his covenant, and in the course of doing so he told that later generation to circumcise their hearts:

> Circumcise yourselves to the LORD,
>   circumcise your hearts,
>   you people of Judah and inhabitants of Jerusalem,
> or my wrath will flare up and burn like fire
>   because of the evil you have done—
>   burn with no one to quench it. (Jer. 4:4)

The Lord once more commands his people to circumcise their hearts. That can only mean two things: their hearts are uncircumcised (as they have been throughout their history), and the Lord is not doing the circumcising. This is consistent with the nature of the old covenant. Under the old covenant, the people must fulfill the law, and they must circumcise their own hearts. Neither is possible. Under the new covenant, the Lord fulfills the law for us, and he circumcises our hearts.

Verdict in Jeremiah: Israel like the Nations

The Israelites had the covenant sign of circumcision and were subjected to it before they could chose to be or not, and before any of them had done anything good or bad. But that physical circumcision could not produce a heart circumcision. Accordingly, the Lord made it clear through Jeremiah that those Israelites—like the pagans—who were circumcised in the flesh were not circumcised in their hearts:

> "The days are coming," declares the LORD, "when I will punish all who are circumcised only in the flesh—Egypt, Judah, Edom, Ammon, Moab and all who live in the wilderness in distant places. For all these nations are really uncircumcised, and even the whole house of Israel is uncircumcised in heart." (Jer. 9:25–26)

The Lord's word through Jeremiah is actually devastating in its implications, for it classes Israel with the pagans. The point of the Lord's

---

faithful—more willing to trust the Lord for the Conquest—than their parents had been. Nonetheless, they still had uncircumcised hearts.

judgment is that the Israelites have become like the pagans in their behavior, and so will be judged like the pagans. Ironically, circumcision
meant as a sign of Israel's membership in a divine covenant (again, the
Abrahamic covenant), has become merely a sign that they are like the
pagans who also practice circumcision. The pagans have physical circumcision but are uncircumcised in heart. The Lord's people are in the
same condition.

BRIEF SUMMARY: HEART UNCIRCUMCISION
UNDER THE MOSAIC COVENANT

The examples from Jeremiah are two of only four figurative uses of circumcision in the Old Testament. Apart from those verses (just considered), every other use of the verb having to do with circumcision signifies
literal circumcision.[7] The examples make it clear that, under the Mosaic
covenant, circumcision of the flesh did not guarantee circumcision of the
heart, and possession of the law could not produce a circumcised heart.

Accordingly, the Lord's call through Jeremiah was a call to something
the people under the old covenant *could not accomplish.* Jesus makes
this ontological reality—ontological because sin is a part of our nature
and of the nature of a being—clear in the Sermon on the Mount. Even
if—like Saul before he became Paul—an Israelite might imagine he was
righteous under the law, Jesus' sermon taught that the requirements of
the law run far deeper—so deep that no mere human being after the Fall
could ever fulfill them.

PROMISED CIRCUMCISION OF THE HEART

The Lord knows this of course and so he promises through Moses toward
the end of the Mosaic covenant renewal that one day, after his people
return from exile, he will perform the needed but humanly impossible
circumcision:

---

7   The mentions of literal circumcision are Genesis 17:10, 13, 23–27; 21:4; 34:15, 17,
22, 24; Exodus 12:44, 48; Leviticus 12:3; Deuteronomy 10:16; Joshua 5:2–5, 7, 8; and above,
Jeremiah 9:25. The verb is used with a different meaning in Psalm 90:6 (grass is "cut
down," Polel); Psalm 118:10–12 (the Lord will "cut off" the nations," Hiphil); and Psalm
58:7 (Heb., 58:8—a prayer that the wicked be "cut off," Hithpolel).

Even if you have been banished to the most distant land under the heavens, from there the LORD your God will gather you and bring you back. He will bring you to the land that belonged to your ancestors, and you will take possession of it. He will make you more prosperous and numerous than your ancestors. The LORD your God will circumcise your hearts and the hearts of your descendants, so that you may love him with all your heart and with all your soul, and live. (Deut. 30:4–6)

The Lord himself will perform that circumcision of the heart so necessary if one is to love him with all one's heart and soul—the first and greatest commandment (Matt. 22:37–38). The Deuteronomic promise is paralleled by a later promise of the Spirit in Ezekiel where, at some future date after their exile, the Lord would put his Spirit in his people and move them to obey his *torah*. The following display shows the parallel:

Deuteronomy	Ezekiel
Exilic situation (Deut. 30:1–4)	Exilic situation (Ezek. 36:22–23)
Return from exile (Deut. 30:3–5a)	Return from exile (Ezek. 36:24)
Blessings in the land (Deut. 30:5b)	Blessings in the land (Ezek. 36:25)
Promise of heart circumcision (Deut. 30:6)	Promise of Spirit (Ezek. 36:26–27)

Heart circumcision and the indwelling of the Spirit are parallel, and that is part of the parallel structure of these revelations. The parallel is inevitable because it is the indwelling Spirit who performs the heart circumcision (Rom. 2:29). In both Deuteronomy and Ezekiel, the promises are to be fulfilled *at some indefinite future date*, that is, after the exile. It follows that the events they describe—having one's heart circumcised by the Lord, and having the Lord put his Spirit within one—have *not yet been part* of Israel's experience under the Mosaic covenant. Any other biblical statements regarding, for example, someone under the old covenant having the Spirit in him must consequently be understood in a qualified way in light of what the Lord has promised through Ezekiel.[8]

Paul makes it clear that the circumcision commanded in Jeremiah and promised in Deuteronomy has only now been accomplished: "A person is not a Jew who is one only outwardly, nor is circumcision merely outward and physical. No, a person is a Jew who is one inwardly; and circumcision is circumcision of the heart, by the Spirit, not by the

---

8   Cf. discussion, volume 1, 70–74.

written code. Such a person's praise is not from other people, but from God" (Rom. 2:28–29).[9]

Paul says the needed circumcision of the heart is performed by the Spirit and *not by the written code.* That is so because the written code (the law) *could never perform it.* As Paul tells us, this inner circumcision—that which was always needed, but was unattainable under the old covenant—has only come now through the work of Christ:

> In him you were also circumcised with a circumcision not performed by human hands. Your whole self ruled by the flesh was put off when you were circumcised by Christ, having been buried with him in baptism, in which you were also raised with him through your faith in the working of God, who raised him from the dead. (Col. 2:11–12)

The phrase "not by human hands" (Col. 2:11) is used elsewhere to indicate a supernal origin (e.g., the "stone" that brings down the heritage of world imperial systems or—put another way—the human idea of empire, Dan. 2:34, 45; the heavenly tabernacle, Heb. 9:11). Paul speaks of an inner circumcision performed by Christ, and that is the same as the circumcision of the heart performed by the Spirit (Rom. 2:29a) as the Spirit and the Son work together—more particularly, as the Spirit works through the Son in a believer to perform the circumcision. Moreover, as Stephen explains in his prophetic address to the Jewish council, that circumcision never happened under the old covenant: "You stiff-necked people! Your hearts and ears are *still uncircumcised. You are just like your ancestors*: You always resist the Holy Spirit" (Acts 7:51, emphasis added).

Paul says, "Your whole self ruled by the flesh was *put off* when you were circumcised by Christ, *having been buried with him in baptism*" (Col. 2:11b, emphases added). In other words, freedom from the rule of the flesh only comes once one has been buried with Christ in baptism and one has been circumcised by Christ. Burial and circumcision of that sort come only after the full revelation and work of Christ in the new covenant. It is not as though God had done the same things in some

---

9   It is an act of will to imagine that what Paul says here could apply to Jews before the new covenant, especially in view of his contrast between the Spirit and "the written code" (i.e., the law, v. 29). Everything he says about the law goes against such an understanding. Cf. Romans 7 and Colossians 2; cf. likewise the author of Hebrews.

different way under the old covenant and just not mentioned it. We are never told that.[10]

The divine act of circumcision—so far beyond human ability to accomplish, yet so desperately needed by us all—is put in another way in the Old Testament: the Lord promises he will write (or put) his law in our hearts.

THE LAW IN THE HEART

The Lord promises in Jeremiah 31 that he will write his law on his people's hearts in a new covenant. The natural reading of the promise is that the Lord has *not yet done* this writing, for two obvious reasons: it is given as a future promise, and it is given in terms of a new covenant that "will *not be like* the covenant / I made with their forefathers when I took them by the hand / to lead them out of Egypt" (Jer. 31:32, emphasis added). The other occurrences of this idea—the law in the heart—in the Old Testament are consistent with this understanding.

STATEMENTS THAT THE LAW IS IN THE HEART

There are three statements in the Old Testament to the effect that the law is in the heart of (or within) someone. One passage addresses a righteous individual (Ps. 37:30–31) and another addresses the people of God (Isa. 51:7–8)—both under the Mosaic covenant. One of the passages is messianic. So it speaks of a future person and a future condition (Ps. 40:6–8).

A RIGHTEOUS INDIVIDUAL UNDER THE MOSAIC COVENANT

David characterizes the righteous individual in a wisdom Psalm. He urges the godly person not to fret about or envy the wicked, who will

---

10   What Paul says here is consistent with what he said in Romans 6–8 regarding death to the old self through baptism, and the fact that we are now free, and need not be slaves to sin any longer (unlike the man under the law portrayed in Romans 7); we can now to put to death the deeds of the flesh by the power of the Spirit (as per Rom. 8:13; cf. Rom. 8:1–16). Cf. discussion in chapter 5 of volume 3.

wither like grass (37:1–2). He encourages one to trust in the Lord and do good (v. 3), delight in the Lord (v. 4), commit one's way to the Lord and trust him (v. 5), along with other admixtures of exhortation to good, and portrayals of the ultimate fate of the wicked, which continue to the end of the Psalm. Toward the end of the poem David says of the righteous:

> The mouth of the righteous speaks wisdom,
> And his tongue talks of justice.
> The law of his God is in his heart (בלבו);
> None of his steps shall slide. (Ps. 37:30–31 NKJV)

A fair reading of this statement, even in its context, admits that the phrase "the law of God is in his heart" is ambiguous in one important respect: we are not told how the law *got* there. This is no small matter. Anyone may "get something by heart" and so have it, in that sense, in his or her heart. But that sort of knowledge does not guarantee a life that *conforms* to the knowledge one has acquired. Nonetheless, in this case it does seem that the person who has the law in his heart is righteous, so that wisdom and justice come forth from him. This would, however, be consistent with the portrayal of the blessed person in Psalm 1, who meditates on the law day and night. In other words, a person under the old covenant could internalize the law by such meditation and live a righteous life relative to others who did not do so. Such a person could be a conveyor of wisdom and justice and his steps would not slide. Nonetheless, the poem does portray a man under the law, and so it must also be true of that man as it was of Paul and his fellows under the old covenant that the law was "the charge of our legal indebtedness, which *stood against us* and *condemned us*" and which Jesus "has taken . . . away, nailing it to the cross" (Col. 2:14, emphasis added). One understands that wisdom statements (such as we find in this poem) under the old covenant only go so far, and seem to go farther than they actually can because the ideal simplicity and purity of a poetic statement in such a doctrinal case confronts one with an ideal and indeed a pursuable maxim, and yet does not exhaustively present things as they are—and in this case one can see that it does not, because the New Testament statements pertaining to the condition of man under the law are quite different. For example, Romans 7 paints no such picture of rosy success.

RIGHTEOUS PEOPLE UNDER THE MOSAIC COVENANT

The Lord also addresses righteous people under the Mosaic covenant in the days of Isaiah. Eschatological evocations of Eden (cf. 51: 3–6) follow a retrospective on Israel's origins that harks back to Abraham (cf. vv. 1–2) and reminds Israel of that righteous patriarch. The Lord then addresses righteous people in Isaiah's day as those who have the law in their hearts in a historical/eschatological context that also has a wisdom flavor:

> Listen to Me, you who know righteousness,
> You people in whose heart is My law (תורתי בלבם):
> Do not fear the reproach of men,
> Nor be afraid of their insults.
> For the moth will eat them up like a garment,
> And the worm will eat them like wool;
> But My righteousness will be forever,
> And My salvation from generation to generation.
>   (Isa. 51:7–8 NKJV)

After evocations of the past and the future, the Lord speaks through Isaiah to a present generation as well as perhaps to future generations to encourage them. The people addressed, then, consist of those who "know righteousness" and "in whose heart" is the Lord's law (v. 7). One must admit that this statement also is ambiguous, and in the following way: one may "know" righteousness as one "knows" the law, and the same person may have the law in his heart *by such knowledge*, as was noted regarding the blessed person in Psalm 1. These are good things. They are not, however, statements that the Lord has *put the law* in anyone's heart or *written it* on anyone's heart by his Spirit, both of which are spoken of to old covenant believers as future events.

One should add that having the law in one's heart in such a manner, that is, by internalizing it *oneself*—even if the Lord did not "put" it there or "write" it there—is not only a good thing, but would probably not happen under the old covenant without the help of the Spirit. Just as the Spirit came to David every day and worked on and through him, and just as the Spirit even worked on and through Cyrus so the Lord could call him his "Messiah" (Isa. 45:1), so the Spirit could help a faithful Israelite who sought to internalize God's law and live by it.[11] Nonetheless, that is

---

11 The Spirit could certainly work on someone's heart under the old covenant, for

not the same as having the Lord put or write his law in one's heart by the indwelling Spirit, and the Old Testament statements fall short of mandating an interpretation that the Lord did so under the old covenant. Any insistence that these verses require us to understand that the law was put into or written on anyone's heart by the Spirit under the Mosaic covenant is eisegetical, because there are no statements to the effect that he ever did so under the old covenant, and there are *promises* to the effect that he *would do so* in some indefinite future and under a covenant that would "not be like" the Mosaic covenant (Jer. 31:32).[12]

THE LAW WITHIN: A MESSIANIC PORTRAYAL

The third passage to consider is a messianic portrayal that presents the Messiah's words:

> Sacrifice and offering
> You did not desire;
> My ears You have opened.
> Burnt offering and sin offering
> You did not require.
> Then I said, "Behold, I come;
> In the scroll of the book it is written of me.
> I delight to do Your will, O my God,
> And Your law is within my heart." (Ps. 40:6–8 NKJV)

The messianic nature of these verses is established by their use in

---

example, God gave Saul another heart (1 Sam. 10:9), God puts wisdom in Solomon's heart (1 Kings 10:24), God put plans for Jerusalem in Nehemiah's heart (Neh. 2:12), and he even forms the hearts of all mankind (Ps. 33:15; cf. discussion of election and foreknowledge in chapter 7 of volume 3).

12   Indeed the wisest advice one can get stemming from the old covenant *torah* says: "Keep my commands and you will live; / guard my teachings as the apple of your eye. / Bind them on your fingers; / *write them on the tablet of your heart*" (Prov. 7:2–3, emphasis added). Cf. exhortations to apply one's heart to instruction from the Lord's law (Prov. 22:17–21; 23:12). More generally, the Lord enjoins Jerusalem to wash the evil from her heart (Jer. 4:14), but the people have stubborn and rebellious hearts (Jer. 5:23). The Lord will give them a heart to know him, in a promised future (Jer. 24:7) and will give them singleness of heart and action (Jer. 32:39; cf. Ezek. 11:19; 36:26), but that will be under "an everlasting covenant" that he has yet to make with them (Jer. 32:40).

Hebrews as part of the argument that the new covenant replaces the old. After quoting Psalm 40:5–8, the author of Hebrews writes this: "Previously saying, 'Sacrifice and offering, burnt offerings, and *offerings* for sin You did not desire, nor had pleasure *in them*' (which are offered according to the law), then He said, 'Behold, I have come to do Your will, O God.' *He takes away the first that He may establish the second*" (Heb. 8:8–9 NKJV, emphasis added). Since the person involved in Psalm 40 is the Messiah, there is no question that he had the law in his heart. Nonetheless, the Hebrew actually reads, "And your law is in the midst of my inward parts (בתוך מעי)."[13] We know the law was present in the Messiah's inner being, not because he memorized it, but because the Spirit of whom the law is an articulation was in him without limit (John 3:34).[14] The Messiah was in that respect the forerunner of a people who would also have the Spirit-written law within, under the new covenant promised by the Lord through Jeremiah.

THE LAW WRITTEN IN/ON THE HEART: THE NEW COVENANT

The most famous passage to use the language of the law written on the heart is the Lord's promise of a new covenant in Jeremiah. It is important to quote the passage at length from its context in Hebrews because in this New Testament location the contrast between the old covenant and the promised new covenant is made most clearly. Agreeably the author continues his discussion of the superiority of Jesus' (Melchizedek) priesthood over the priesthood of the old covenant:

> But the ministry Jesus has received is as superior to theirs as the covenant of which he is mediator is superior to the old one, since the new covenant is established on better promises. For if there had been nothing wrong with that first covenant, no place would have been sought for another. But God found fault with the people and said:
>
> "The days are coming, declares the LORD,
>   when I will make a new covenant

---

13 Cf. *BDB*, 588–89.

14 We cannot know how much Bible memorizing Jesus did, but if it was foretold of us that the Lord would write his law on our hearts, how much more thoroughly would that be true of his Son?

with the people of Israel
and with the people of Judah.
It will not be like the covenant
I made with their forefathers
when I took them by the hand
to lead them out of Egypt,
because they did not remain faithful to my covenant,
and I turned away from them,
declares the LORD.
This is the covenant I will establish with the house of Israel
after that time, declares the LORD.
I will put my laws in their minds
and write them on their hearts.
I will be their God,
and they will be my people." (Heb. 8:6–10; cf. 10:16)

The Lord promises he will write his law on the hearts of his people. Since that is a future and open-ended promise, it had not yet taken place when Jeremiah wrote. In other words, like the promise that the Lord would circumcise the people's hearts (Deut. 30:6), and the promise that the Lord would put his Spirit in his people (Ezek. 36:27), the promise that the Lord would put his laws in his people's minds and write them on their hearts was a promise made to God's people under the Mosaic covenant and yet it was something the Lord *had not yet done* but would do at some unspecified future date, under a new covenant.

There was no way the people could do such things for themselves; they could not put themselves in God's place and do them. The sinful creature lacks the power to put sin to death in himself by himself. Even if he manages to conform outwardly to the law, as Paul apparently did (cf. Phil. 3:6), he covers up a sinful inner being. That is why, for instance, Paul says, "No, a person is a Jew who is one inwardly; and circumcision is circumcision of the heart, by the Spirit, not by the written code" (Rom. 2:29). The needed transformation could not be accomplished under or by "the written code" (i.e., the Mosaic covenant).

Another way of expressing the new and different spiritual life under the new covenant is alluded to in Jeremiah 31:

"It will not be like the covenant
I made with their forefathers
when I took them by the hand

> to lead them out of Egypt,
> because they broke my covenant,
>   though I was a husband to them,"
> declares the LORD. (Jer. 31:32)

The expression for "I was a husband" in this verse is actually "I was a lord" (בעלתי). It is an implicit allusion to Hosea 2: "'In that day,' declares the LORD, / 'you will call me "my husband [that is, "my man, אישׁ"]; / you will no longer call me "my master [that is, "my lord/owner, בעל"]'" (v. 16). Under the old covenant, the Lord was "master" or "owner."[15] Under the new covenant, the Lord will be "husband" (cf. Eph. 5:23–33; Rev. 21:9)—a much more intimate relationship because of the indwelling Spirit.

A NEW TESTAMENT CONUNDRUM?

Paul portrays God's coming judgment on those who have had the law and those who have not (i.e., the Gentiles) and he uses the phrase "the work of the law written in their hearts," language close to that of Jeremiah 31:33:

> For as many as have sinned without law will also perish without law, and as many as have sinned in the law will be judged by the law (for not the hearers of the law *are* just in the sight of God, but the doers of the law will be justified; for when Gentiles, who do not have the law, by nature do the things in the law, these, although not having the law, are a law to themselves, who show the work of the law written in their hearts, their conscience also bearing witness, and between themselves *their* thoughts accusing or else excusing *them*) in the day when God will judge the secrets of men by Jesus Christ, according to my gospel. (Rom. 2:12–16 NKJV)

Paul apparently portrays in a straightforward manner some Gentiles who have "the work of the law written on their hearts" [τὸ ἔργον τοῦ νόμου γραπτὸν ἐν ταῖς καρδίαις αὐτῶν]—just as one might argue that most people have some sense of right and wrong, for example, that bearing false witness is wrong under common grace. However, Paul's phrasing is evocative of Jeremiah 31:33, and that apparent allusion to Jeremiah's prophecy of a new covenant seems to pull one in another

---

15   Cf. the allusion to this reality in Isaiah 1:3: "The ox knows its master, / the donkey its owner's [בעליו] manger, / but Israel does not know, / my people do not understand."

direction. The "other direction" is to take the work of the law written on the Gentiles' hearts as pertaining to members of the new covenant—and so, Gentile believers.[16]

Although the echo of Jeremiah's phrase could suggest the Gentiles Paul has in mind are believers, there are elements of the context that seem to make that interpretation unlikely. The parallel statements in this passage may help one understand who is who:

verse 12

a	b	c	d
For as many as have sinned	without law	will also perish	without law
a'	b'	c'	d'
as many as have sinned	in the law	will be judged	by the law

verse 14

a	b	c	d
when Gentiles,	who do not have the law,	by nature	do the things in the law,
a'	b'	c'	d'
these,	although not having the law,	are	a law to themselves

The two verses understood together, in what we believe is the right way, resolve the identity question of verse 14. The present reading of verse 12 understands two classes of people: those who sin but do not have the law, and those who sin and do have the law. The first class will perish without the law, and the second class will be judged by the law. Clearly those who perish without the law are not believers, and in particular apparently are Gentiles. A comparable reading of verse 14 understands the first class of people is still under discussion: Gentiles who do not have the law (// those who sin but do not have the law in v. 12). Those people, though they do not have the law, are "a law unto themselves."[17] Can Paul

---

16   Cf. Eckhard J. Schnabel, *Der Brief des Paulus an die Römer, Kapitel 1–5* (Giessen: SCM R. Brockhaus, Witten Verag, 2015). This view has had a place in the history of interpretation ultimately as a minority view from Ambrosiaster and Augustine to Barth and Wright (cf. Schnabel, 295 n18).

17   Cf. the historically pre-Christian Aristotle, *Nichomachean Ethics*, who says, "The

be describing here Gentile believers? That seems very unlikely. Believers under the new covenant are not elsewhere called "a law unto themselves" by Paul or anyone else. Nor should they be. What Christian would say: "I am a law unto myself"? Anyone who keeps in step with the Spirit because he lives by the Spirit cannot be a law unto himself. The "law of Christ" (Gal. 6:2) at work by the Spirit in him (cf. "the law of the Spirit," Rom. 8:2) is his law—he is not his own law, "a law unto himself."[18]

An important part of Paul's statement is the phrase "by nature" in verse 14. Regarding this expression Schnabel writes, "The adverbial expression

---

refined and well-bred man, therefore, will be as we have described, being as it were a law to himself." Aristotle's phrase, νόμος ὢν ἑαυτῷ, is the same as Paul's, ἑαυτοῖς εἰσιν νόμος, the only differences being the participle and the singular in Aristotle and the word order. Cf. "Aristotle on Wit, and Conscience vs. Law," https://sniggle.net/TPL/index5.php?env try=10Oct09. Schnabel however says, "The formulation then they are a law to themselves (οὗτοι . . . ἑαυτοῖς εἰσιν νόμος) is not to be interpreted from Aristotle, but against the background of the contrast between the fact, that the Gentiles do not possess the law from birth, and the remarkable fact, that (many) Gentiles embody the law." The German text reads, "Die Formulierung dann sind sie selbst Gesetz (οὗτοι . . . ἑαυτοῖς εἰσιν νόμος) ist nicht von Aristoteles her zu erklären, sondern auf dem Hintergrund des Kontrasts zwischen der Tatsache, dass die Heiden das Gesetz nicht von Geburt an besitzen, und der bemerkenswerten Tatsache, dass (manche) Heiden das Gesetz verkörpern" (Schnabel, 297). His rejection of the parallel with Aristotle relies at least half, however, on his preferred understanding of φύσει ("von Geburt an," i.e., "from birth"), which is one of the points at issue. The other part of the argument relates to the idea that these Gentiles "embody" ("verkörpern") the law, which is something Paul never says (see p. 340).

18 The only other people described as a "law unto themselves" in the whole Bible (*in translation* however) are the Babylonians: "They are a feared and dreaded people; / they are a law to themselves (ἐξ αὐτοῦ τὸ κρίμα αὐτοῦ ἔσται)" (Hab. 1:7; cf. Rom. 2:14, ἑαυτοῖς εἰσιν νόμος). The Greek phrasing is different in these two cases, however, and for a reason. Habakkuk speaks of ruthless Babylonians. The Babylonians are self-adjudicating (αὐτοῦ τὸ κρίμα αὐτοῦ, in *effect*, "a law unto themselves" in the negative way people usually understand that phrase, and so commonly translated). They act out of what is perversely built into their own nature—by lives of a sinful distortion of what a human should be, even under common grace (cf. discussion volume 1, 149–50). The Gentiles of whom Paul writes, by contrast, also do not know God's law but sometimes do what it requires and so figuratively are a law unto themselves, in a different and better sense. They also act out of what is built into their own nature—by lives that, though fallen, still allow God's common grace work to be beneficially effective within themselves. There is one way in which both cases are the same: both the bad Babylonians and the good pagans act out of some principles (bad or good) built into themselves, but they do not act out of God's indwelling Spirit.

'by nature' (φύσει) should not be connected with the subsequent phrase (τὰ τοῦ νόμου ποιῶσιν), but rather with the preceding verb (ἔχοντα). Paul speaks of Gentiles, who do not have the law 'from birth.'"[19] The Gentiles in view (on Schnabel's understanding) are Christians: "Paul speaks in 2:14 of Gentile Christians, who do not have the law from birth, but who nevertheless in their attitude toward its demands are in a comprehensive (not partial) manner in accordance with and thus embody the law and in the final judgment will be declared not guilty (2:13)."[20]

Now to take "by nature" with the first phrase—"when Gentiles, who do not have the law by nature"—diminishes the fullness of the parallelism shown above between "by nature do the things in the law" and "are a law to themselves." That is not a decisive argument against the proposed different understanding of "by nature," but it is also fair to say that to interpret "by nature" as meaning "from birth onward" ("von Geburt an/ aus") is a rather curious reading. One should also note Paul never says these people "embody" ("verkörpern") the law.

On the usual understanding of Paul's series of statements the rest of the portrayal follows: "Their conscience also bearing witness, and between themselves *their* thoughts accusing or else excusing *them* in the day when God will judge the secrets of men by Jesus Christ, according to my gospel" (vv. 15b–16). Everyone will have to give an account before God at the last judgment (Rom. 14:12), and Paul's portrayal of what goes on in a soul who is going to "perish without the law" on that day seems a plausible characterization of what will be going on inside such a person.[21]

The expression "the work of the law written on their hearts" (v. 15) is also not identical with "*I will write* my law on their hearts" (Jer. 31:33). The

---

19   Schnabel, *Der Brief des Paulus an die Römer*, 296. The German text reads: "Das Adv. 'von Natur aus' (φύσει) ist nicht mit der folgenden Wendung (τὰ τοῦ νόμου ποιῶσιν) zu verbinden, sondern mit dem vorausgehenden Verb (ἔχοντα). Paulus spricht von Heiden, die das Gesetz nicht 'von Geburt an' haben."

20   Ibid., 297. The German text reads: "Paulus spricht in 2,14 von Heidenchristen, die das Gesetz von Geburt aus nicht haben, seinen Forderungen in umfassender (nicht partieller) Weise in ihrem Verhalten jedoch entsprechen und so das Gesetz verkörpern und im Endgericht freigesprochen werden (2,13)."

21   Cf. Martin Luther, *Commentary on Romans*, trans. J. Theodore Mueller (Grand Rapids: Zondervan, 1954), 60: "Men will finally be judged by their own thoughts, which either accuse them of guilt or defend them according to the good which they have done; for then not words or works, which might deceive, but their own innermost thoughts witness concerning them publicly, just as these now witness in them, telling them what they are and what they have done."

law as an expression of God's nature is also an expression of God's Spirit, and the words of the law are Spirit. The Spirit expressive of the law can work in a person under common grace without dwelling in that person.[22] If Cyrus was the Lord's "messiah," he was also anointed by the Spirit and that anointing was not for nothing: Cyrus' gifts should naturally be attributed to that same Spirit, otherwise the anointing/messiahship amounts to nothing. The Spirit-lawgiver did his "work" in Cyrus. The same Spirit-lawgiver can work in any person who like Cyrus does not know the Lord (cf. Isa. 45:4–5). Paul's phrasing therefore is *analogous* to that of Jeremiah 31:33 because the work of the Spirit in a nonbeliever can be analogous to his work in a believer under the new covenant: in both cases the Spirit-lawgiver does "work" in the individual but he does not indwell the person in both cases but only in the latter. In the latter—the new covenant believer—the Spirit-lawgiver does what Ezekiel prophesied: "And I will put my Spirit in you and move you to follow my decrees and be careful to keep my laws" (Ezek. 36:17). The Spirit does this to a limited extent in pagans—limited because he does not indwell them—and no doubt this is why Paul enjoins: "I urge, then, first of all, that petitions, prayers, intercession and thanksgiving be made for all people—for kings and all those in authority, that we may live peaceful and quiet lives in all godliness and holiness. This is good, and pleases God our Savior, who wants all people to be saved and to come to a knowledge of the truth" (1 Tim. 2:1–4). We know the Spirit convicts regarding sin, righteousness, and judgment and so the Spirit is the one who may move anyone "to be saved and to come to a knowledge of the truth" (v. 3). The same Spirit should naturally be understood as the one who does the other things Paul mentions: affecting kings and those in authority in a way that will mean a government that produces a peaceful environment for the people (v. 2), just as the Spirit anointed Cyrus and moved him to restore God's people to their homeland. Pagan kings and rulers so affected thus evidence "the *work* of the law written in their hearts" (Rom. 2:15, emphasis added).

---

22 Cf. Murray, *The Epistle to the Romans*, 2 vols. (Grand Rapids: Eerdmans, 1959–1965), 1:74–75: "Paul does not say that the law is written upon their hearts. He refrains from this form of statement apparently for the same reason as in verse 14 he had said that the Gentiles 'do the things of the law' and not that they did or fulfilled the law. Such expressions as 'fulfilling the law' and 'the law written upon the heart' are reserved for a state of heart and mind and will far beyond that predicated of unbelieving Gentiles." Cf. likewise Hodge, *Commentary on the Epistle to the Romans* (Grand Rapids: Eerdmans, 1950), 65–66.

Understood in the traditional way, the sequence of Paul's points in Romans 2:12–27 is as follows: Paul describes how it really is/will be for Gentiles who under common grace "do the things of the law" but not always. When they stand before God on that day, they will both accuse and excuse themselves knowing that in terms of mere works they did sometimes do what the law required though not always; yet that will not be not enough to save them (vv. 14–16). Paul's statements are not hypothetical, but rather a spiritually insightful and prophetic statement of how things are and will be for that class of people—even how they are today when pagans' consciences conflict within them.

Paul next addresses Jews who mistakenly think they are acceptable before God because they have the law (vv. 17–24). Finally, Paul goes on to talk about the only circumcision that counts, and those he describes in verses 26–27 are Gentile Christians who are not circumcised in the flesh but have had the circumcision of the heart by the Spirit (vv. 28–29). Those are the true Jews, the Israel of God.[23]

----

23   Schnabel, *Der Brief des Paulus*, 317, understands the Gentiles of verse 27 as Gentile Christians and we agree. We note that, although the word φύσις occurs in both verses 14 and 27, that alone does not mean both verses are talking about the same people: "Indeed, when Gentiles, who do not have the law, do *by nature* (φύσει) things required by the law, they are a law for themselves, even though they do not have the law" (v. 14) and "The one who is not circumcised *physically* (ἡ ἐκ φύσεως ἀκροβυστία) and yet obeys the law will condemn you who, even though you have the written code and circumcision, are a lawbreaker" (v. 27). Paul uses the word in two different senses and is talking about two different classes of people. The same word can carry more than one sense and application in the same passage and this is well known; cf. the older and newer meanings of Hebrew נֶפֶשׁ, "throat/neck" and "soul/self/life" in Jonah 2: "The waters engulfed me up to the *neck*" (v. 5); "as my *life* was fading away" (v. 7). Here Paul uses φύσις in the sense of "by nature, naturally" (i.e., from within, v. 14) but also in the sense of "physically" (v. 27). Certainly the parallelism in verses 28 and 29 by which Paul explains the nature of the person in verse 24 shows he is a Gentile Christian:

a	b	c
For a person	is *not* a Jew	who is one outwardly,
a′	b′	c′
and true circumcision	is not something	visible in the flesh.

On the contrary,

a	b	c
a person	*is* a Jew	who is one inwardly,
a′	b′	c′
and circumcision	is of the heart—	by the Spirit, not the letter.

CONCLUSION

The Lord promised his people under the old or Mosaic covenant that (1) he would circumcise the hearts of his people at some unspecified future date after their exile (Deut. 30:6), (2) he would write his law in their hearts in the context of a new covenant *unlike* the Sinai covenant at some unspecified future date (Jer. 31:31–34), and (3) he would put his Spirit in them at some unspecified time after their exile and thereby move them to obey his laws and requirements (Ezek. 36:27).

Occam's razor dangles before us and invites us to accept the simplest construction that accounts for these statements harmoniously. Accordingly, the Lord would make the new covenant (Luke 22:20) in the context of which he would put his Spirit into his people (John 14:17) and his Spirit would circumcise their hearts (Rom. 2:29) and move them to obey him.

A great dynamic privilege belongs to members of the new covenant because God has given them his Spirit by whom they can grow to be more like their Master and Teacher to the extent that they allow that Spirit to work and bear fruit in them. Their lives can be unfruitful *if* they choose a path of immaturity by routinely quenching the Spirit. In that case, they resemble the person under the law Paul portrays so memorably in Romans 7.

CHAPTER FOURTEEN

THE LORD AND PROPHETIC EXPERIENCE:
THE NON-WRITING PROPHETS
AND MODELED MINISTRY

INTRODUCTION

The Old Testament prophets—even the greatest of them, Moses—did not have the Spirit dwelling within them. Nonetheless, they are as close as humans came under the old covenant—at least in the recorded history of life under the old covenant—to representing the nature of God on earth because the Spirit was with them and often entered them and worked through them.

The Lord identifies himself as the potter through the prophet Isaiah: "This is what the LORD says—your kinsman Redeemer, your shaper [lit. "your potter," יֹצֶרְךָ] from the womb" (Isa. 44:24, author's translation). The Lord formed Israel in/from the womb, much as a potter shapes clay. That is consonant with Paul's declaration: "But who are you, a human being, to talk back to God? Shall what is formed say to the one who formed it, 'Why did you make me like this?' Does not the potter have the right to make out of the same lump of clay some pottery for special purposes and some for common use?" (Rom. 9:20–21).

The Lord is the potter or shaper of his prophets and all people. The Old Testament offers some detailed examples of prophetic formation—some of the Potter's work—through particular experiences. They are worth examining for four reasons. First, they show the Lord's sovereign activity as potter—that is, what agents or circumstances he may use to do his shaping. Second, they also show how the pot reacts to the potter's hand—usually a matter of compliance tantamount to yielding, although sometimes not without complaint. Third and more importantly, they show the nature of God—one who in covenant faithfulness to those he has made and called as covenant lawsuit messengers not only uses them and works through them but also simultaneously shapes them out of an insuperable purpose. Finally and accordingly and most importantly, they imply an eschatological trajectory: conformity to the nature of God is necessary if one is to abide in his presence—the ultimate goal for God's people—and God's formation of his prophets offers glimpses of formative processes that help move the individual toward that conformity under the old covenant.

The non-writing prophets in particular—and their shaping or spiritual formation—form the subject matter of this chapter. The formation of the writing prophets is the subject of the next chapter. Of course the Lord also shaped his covenant mediator prophets, Abraham, Moses, and David, through what he did with and for them and what he allowed them to experience at the hands of both beneficent and hostile people. Jesus himself, the greatest mediator of the final divine-human covenant in space-time, was shaped by his Father during the course of his years among us:

> During the days of Jesus' life on earth, he offered up prayers and petitions with fervent cries and tears to the one who could save him from death, and he was heard because of his reverent submission. Son though he was, he learned obedience from what he suffered and, once made perfect, he became the source of eternal salvation for all who obey him. (Heb. 5:7–9)

Jesus was shaped—"he learned obedience"—as he grew, and that shaping had to do with submission (v. 7b), and all of that was from and to his Father. The Son's experience is the example nonpareil of the principle affirmed in Hebrews: "The Lord disciplines the one he loves, and he chastens everyone he accepts as his son" (Heb. 12:6; cf. Prov. 3:12).[1] Because *all* things in what we call the Old Testament were written for our instruction (Rom. 15:4), we could undoubtedly also take the Lord's covenant mediator prophets as models for our education. However, since his covenant lawsuit prophets played a role more closely analogous to what the church has in fact experienced in its history (if only because there are no covenant mediator prophets after the Son), the experience and formation of the covenant lawsuit prophets form the subject of this and

---

1   The discipline to which Hebrews 12:5–11 appeals is that administered—however perfectly or imperfectly on any occasion—by a human father to his son. It is not unrelated to the perfect example offered by Jesus and his Father—a formative discipline applied by a perfect Father to a sinless Son.

the next chapter. The non-writing prophets to be considered are Micaiah, Elijah, and Elisha. Consistent with the correlation between prophetic ministry under the old covenant and prophetic ministry under the new covenant, the chapter concludes with examples of modeling involving Elijah, Jesus, Peter, and Paul.

God the Shaper and Prophetic Experience: Ahab and Micaiah

Micaiah's encounter with Ahab and Ahab's false prophets was explored in chapter 11. Ahab's prophets were subject to the work of a "lying spirit," but apparently unable to discern its deceptive nature. With all the confidence that comes with being an acknowledged prophet of Yahweh, they allowed that spirit to speak through them.[2] The only true prophet on that occasion, Micaiah, was privileged to view the heavenly court. He witnessed the Lord and his council (presumably a scenario like that of Job 1–2), and saw the Lord invite council members to give their thoughts in a planning session. The Lord's gracious invitation to them is like his invitation to pray: he invites those made in his image to be a part of his decision making process, even though eschatologically considered and thus also from before the creation of all things, his decisions have always been made, are always being made, and will always be made. The question before them in Micaiah's vision was how to bring the Lord's judgment on Ahab (1 Kings 22:19–20).

Micaiah's visionary account is the first on record of a prophet who was allowed to see God's heavenly council and its process. It may be fair to suppose his visionary encounter was in some way transformative—it gave a boldness that can attend clarity—since Micaiah's handling of himself and the situation before two enthroned kings is magisterial.

The other Old Testament revelation of the Lord in the juridical presence of his angels—the "sons of God" in Job 1–2—shows a deliberative process that takes place between the Lord and Satan. Because the spirit the Lord allowed to deceive Ahab and his prophets foreshadows the strong delusion the Lord will send at the end, and because Satan is the father of deceptions and involved in the eschatological scenario, something of the ontology of Satan is now explored.

The term "Satan" occurs with the definite article in Job (lit. "the Satan," Job 1:6, 7, 8, 9, 12; 2:1, 2, 3, 4, 5, 6, 7), and some have taken this to mean

---

2   Spiritual boldness is right if it is in the *Spirit*—but with them it was not. Cf. discussion on pages 350, 352–54.

that one sees here, not a fallen angel called Satan but simply a heavenly officer of the court, "the accuser-adversary" (the literal sense of the word Satan)—in other words, a heavenly prosecuting attorney after the pattern of some ancient near eastern courts, and of courts down to the present day.[3] That view is unlikely for the following two reasons. First, the presence of the definite article may simply emphasize the adversarial and accusatorial nature of Satan, who is later called "the accuser of our brethren" (Rev. 12:10). Second, not only is the term Satan used with the definite article in Hebrew (so, in addition to Job, 1 Chron. 21:2; Zech. 3:1.2), but the Greek transliteration in the New Testament almost always occurs with the definite article (i.e., ὁ σατανᾶς, "the Satan").[4] Wherever the term occurs in the New Testament it refers to Satan (and is routinely so translated), and the being it denotes is not an official of the heavenly court doing his duty but a sinful being opposed to God and bent on the destruction of God's image. He is the one who entered Judas to make him betray Christ (John 13:27), who filled the heart of Ananias and made him lie to the Holy Spirit (Acts 5:3), who would block the progress of the gospel (1 Thess. 2:18), and with whom the man of lawlessness is in accord (2 Thess. 2:9); he is the one who leads the whole world astray (Rev. 12:9), and whom Jesus saw fall like lightning from heaven (Luke 10:18); he is the one who wanted to sift Peter (Luke 22:31), much as he had asked the Lord's permission to sift Job long before.

Another term used for this being in the New Testament similarly almost always occurs with the definite article (ὁ διάβολος, "the devil," which also means "the accuser" and from which our words "diabolical"

3　So for example Walther Eichrodt, *Theology of the Old Testament*, trans. J. A. Baker (Philadelphia: Westminster Press, 1967), 2:205–209. Eichrodt argues for a later evolutionary development (perhaps under Persian influence) of this original "Satan concept . . . to anchor the ethical opposition between good and evil in the metaphysical order" (209).

4　The term occurs without the definite article in cases of direct address, as one would expect (Matt. 4:10 // Mark 1:13; Matt. 16:23 // Mark 8:33 [where Jesus calls Peter "Satan" to indicate the true, Satanic nature of Peter's misguided wish, which is closer to Satan's third temptation of Christ than it is to God's plan for his Son]). It occurs without the definite article in three other cases: Mark 2:23 (Satan cannot cast out Satan), Luke 22:3 (Satan enters Judas), and 2 Corinthians 12:7 (Paul was given a thorn in the flesh, a messenger of Satan). All other occurrences (29 in number) are with the definite article: Matthew12:26 (2x); Mark 1:13; 3:26; 4:15; Luke 10:18; 11:18; 13:16; 22:31; John 13:27; Acts 3:5; 26:18; Romans 16:20; 1 Corinthians 5:5; 7:5; 2 Corinthians 2:11; 11:14; 12:7; 1 Thessalonians 2:18; 2 Thessalonians 2:9; 1 Timothy 1:20; 5:15; Revelation 2:9, 13, 24; 3:9; 12:9; 20:2, 7.

and "devil" derive).[5] He is the "father of lies" (John 8:44) who "prowls around like a roaring lion looking for someone to devour" (1 Peter 5:8).

It is clear that "the Satan," or "the devil," has been an opponent to God from the beginning. He is "that ancient serpent called the devil, or Satan" (Rev. 12:9). The terminology does not present an evolutionary development of a human metaphysical thought, but characterizes the one Milton called the "Archfiend" who, ever since his calamitous fall (and for some time before, apparently), has been diametrically opposed to God and those made in his image. The Bible consistently identifies him not merely by his role, but more substantially by his ontology.

Micaiah, who had a revelation of the Lord and his angelic council, and who was incarcerated for faithfully reporting it (1 Kings 22:26–27), saw not Satan but a lying spirit. The role of that spirit and the role of deception in divine judgment were discussed in chapter 11. What remains to consider is Micaiah's experience and its possible effects. This is the first clear-cut case of what has been termed "the word-controversy genre," which is a genre not because it is a literary invention but because it reports a type of encounter that happened all too often between the Lord's prophets and those to whom they were sent. Because such encounters occurred a number of times—as we know because they were reported a number of times—the ensemble of accounts does amount to what one may appropriately call a genre.[6] The basic outline of the genre appears in the contretemps between Ahab and Micaiah:

Word-Confrontation Genre Outline	1 Kings 22
Event	*Reference*
Prophet gives a word/words from Yahweh	vv. 17, 19–23
Challenge to the prophet	v. 24
Sentence on the challenger by the prophet	v. 25

---

5   It occurs without the definite article six times: John 6:70 (Jesus with a veiled reference to Judas: "one of you is a devil"); Acts 13:10; 1 Timothy 3:11; 2 Timothy 3:3; Titus 2:3; Revelation 20:2. It occurs with the definite article 28 times: Matthew 4:1, 5, 8, 11; 13:39; 25:41; Luke 4:2, 3, 6, 13; 8:12; John 8:44; 13:2; Acts 10:38; Ephesians 4:27; 6:11; 1 Timothy 3:6, 7; 2 Timothy 2:26; Hebrews 2:14; James 4:7; 1 Peter 5:8 (effectively: ὁ ἀντίδικος ὑμῶν διάβολος); 1 John 3:8, 10; Jude 9; Revelation 12:9, 12; 20:10.

6   The same is true of what I and others have called the *Gattung* (genre) of theophanic encounters reported throughout the Bible. Cf. Niehaus, *God at Sinai: Covenant and Theophany in the Bible and Ancient Near East* (Grand Rapids: Zondervan, 1995), 30–42.

The genre is simple. Sadly, it was recorded often enough during Israel's rebellious history. In the case before us, Micaiah gives two words from the Lord. The first is, "I saw all Israel scattered on the hills like sheep without a shepherd, and the LORD said, 'These people have no master. Let each one go home in peace'" (1 Kings 22:17 // 2 Chron. 18:16). The phrase is characteristic of anyone, but especially God's people, in a leaderless state (Num. 27:17; Matt. 9:36; and cf. Isa. 14:13 [Babylon]). A shepherd was an ancient near eastern figure for a king, and in the Bible for the Lord, the King of kings, and King more particularly of Israel.[7] The second word from the Lord exposes the deception practiced by the lying spirit on Ahab's prophets (vv. 19–23).

That revelation prompts a sarcastic rebuke (= the *challenge*) from Zedekiah, one of the prophets: "Then Zedekiah son of Kenaanah went up and slapped Micaiah in the face. 'Which way did the spirit from the LORD go when he went from me to speak to you?' he asked" (v. 24). The implication is obviously that if Ahab's prophets have prophesied by a lying spirit, so has Micaiah—an implication that, if true, would invalidate everything Micaiah has said.

Micaiah's response constitutes the *sentence*: "You will find out on the day you go to hide in an inner room" (v. 25). The meaning of this may not be exactly clear but it does not sound good. Maybe it foretells an attempt to hide in the face of a future invasion. One important thing to understand about the sentence a prophet of the Lord pronounces in response to a challenge is this: The sentence is not some vindictive wish on the part of the prophet. It is a sentence the Lord pronounces through the prophet against those who challenge his messenger. It is the inverse of the principle stated by Jesus: "Anyone who welcomes you welcomes me, and anyone who welcomes me welcomes the one who sent me. Whoever welcomes a prophet as a prophet will receive a prophet's reward, and whoever welcomes a righteous man as a righteous man will receive a righteous man's reward" (Matt. 10:40–41). The opposite is also true: anyone who rejects the Lord's messenger—be that messenger a disciple or a prophet—rejects not only the messenger but also the one who sent him. Since that "one" is the Lord, whoever rejects the Lord's prophet rejects the Lord. Such was the case of those who challenged the Lord's covenant lawsuit prophets under the old covenant, and the Lord's response was to pronounce sentence on those rejecters. Some of those challenges will be considered in detail in discussions of the ministries of the Lord's writing prophets under the Mosaic covenant.

---

7 Cf. *ANETBT*, 34–55.

God the Shaper and Prophetic Experience: Elijah, Before Carmel and After

The prophetic contest on Mount Carmel—one could call it a theomachy if Baal had been a god—is one of the more dramatic events of the Old Testament. The background to the encounter includes Elijah's first challenge to Ahab and his time with the widow of Zarephath. The foreground includes his flight from Jezebel and his journey to Horeb and encounter with the Lord. All of these episodes contain valuable lessons.

Elijah's First Challenge to Ahab

It has often been noted that Elijah appears suddenly and without any prior introduction in the biblical narrative. He challenges Ahab: "As the LORD, the God of Israel, lives, whom I serve, there will be neither dew nor rain in the next few years except at my word" (1 Kings 17:1). The most notable thing about this laconic report may not be the dramatic prediction, but the boldness with which Elijah delivers it. He seems to have no fear of the royal person. This is an important theme that occurs later, before Mount Carmel and after.

The Wadi Kerith and the Widow of Zarephath

The Lord then tells Elijah to hide in the wadi Kerith—presumably to protect himself from royal retribution (cf. 1 Kings 18:10)—where he drinks from the stream and receives food that ravens bring to him. This provision has its instructional aspect. The raven was an unclean bird according to the law (Lev. 11:15; Deut. 14:14), but Elijah must humble himself to accept food from its beak because that is how the Lord wants to sustain him. That lesson prepares the prophet to receive food at the hands of an "unclean" foreign woman, the widow of Zarephath (1 Kings 17:10–16). Later under the new covenant, the Lord teaches Peter a similar lesson. He lowers a sheet from heaven that contains "all kinds of four-footed animals, as well as reptiles and birds" (Acts 10:12). The voice from heaven commands Peter to kill and eat but Peter replies, "Surely not, Lord! . . . I have never eaten anything impure or unclean" (Acts 10:14). This happens three times and then the vision is taken away. Peter subsequently understands the meaning of this experience when he is called to share the gospel with Cornelius and his household: "You are well aware that it is against our law for a Jew to associate with or visit a Gentile. But God has shown me that I should not call anyone impure or unclean" (Acts 10:28). Peter's mission is evangelistic and part of the early realization of the Abrahamic promise that "all peoples on earth / will be blessed through you" (Gen. 12:3b). Those who were unclean God now declares clean.

In Elijah's case, the mission is also evangelistic although there is no indication he realizes it. Once the wadi dries up because of the drought Elijah foretold, the Lord tells him: "Go at once to Zarephath in the region of Sidon and stay there. I have commanded a widow there to supply you with food" (1 Kings 17:9). The subsequent narrative tells nothing of the Lord's having "commanded" the widow, and the word used (צוה) does basically have that meaning. The verb "ordained" may therefore capture the meaning better: the Lord has ordained that this particular widow provide for Elijah. The end result is apparently salvific. Once the widow's son has been raised from the dead she declares: "Now I know that you are a man of God and that the word of the LORD from your mouth is the truth" (1 Kings 17:24). The narrative concludes with the same combination of *words* ("the word of the LORD") and *signs and wonders* (the resurrection of her son) that Paul later in Romans characterizes as a full proclamation of the gospel:

> I will not venture to speak of anything except what Christ has accomplished through me in leading the Gentiles to obey God by what I have said and done—by the power of signs and wonders, through the power of the Spirit of God. So from Jerusalem all the way around to Illyricum, I have fully proclaimed the gospel of Christ. (Rom. 15:18–19)

Paul considers the combination—words plus signs and wonders—to be the work of the power of the Spirit and the full proclamation of the gospel of Christ. Elijah's experience with the widow and the resurrection of her son foreshadows this new covenant reality.

The background just discussed implies a spiritual combination worthy of two considerations. First, the prophet's supernatural experience with the widow of Zarephath—miraculous provision of food and a biblically unprecedented resurrection—could only deepen the prophet's trust in the Lord for the miraculous. Second, receiving provision at the hands of (if not by the power of) an unclean foreign woman might counteract any pride successful miracle working could produce.[8] If this combination was

---

8   Cf. Paul's admonition: "What do you have that you did not receive? And if you did receive it, why do you boast as though you did not?" (1 Cor. 4:7).

operative, it would prepare him for the coming encounters with Ahab, the people, and the prophets of Baal.

Elijah and Mount Carmel

When one considers those three encounters, one sees an exposition of Elijah's authority. The authority is enshrined in the narrative of 1 Kings 18, much as God's authority was enshrined in the narrative of Genesis 1. Each narrative is heavily informed with what has been called "the command-fulfillment sequence." The elements are as follows in 1 Kings 18:17–40:

Command-Fulfillment Elements in the Carmel Episode

Verse	Event	Characterization
17	Ahab challenges Elijah	
18	Elijah responds	
19	Elijah's challenge to Ahab (call the prophets)	Command
20	Ahab's response (he calls the prophets)	Fulfillment
21a	Elijah's first challenge to the people	
21b	People response (nil)	
22–24a	Elijah's second challenge to the people	Suggests contest
24b	People's response	Agree on contest
25	Elijah tells Baal prophets to choose a bull	Command
26	Baal prophets' response	Fulfillment
27	Elijah taunts the Baal prophets	
28–29	Baal prophets' response	Continue
30	Elijah summons the people to himself	Command
31	The people come to Elijah	Fulfillment
33–34a	Elijah commands the people re water	Command
34a	The people obey	Fulfillment
34b	Elijah's third command to the people	Command
34b–35	The people obey, the water flows	Fulfillment
36–37	Elijah calls to the Lord	Request
38	The Lord responds	Fulfillment
39	The people respond	Acclamation
40a	Elijah orders execution of the Baal prophets	Command
40b	The people respond	Fulfillment

The analysis shows Elijah in full control of events as they unfold. He commands and his commands are obeyed. Ahab confronts Elijah as the episode begins and in effect judges him: "Is that you, you troubler of Israel?" (1 Kings 18:17b). This is the king who scoured the earth for Elijah and who had authority to make other kings swear that they could not find him—a fugitive and potential expatriate—in their kingdoms (cf. 1 Kings 18:10).[9] Ahab was not suzerain to all the other kingdoms, but the idiom used shows he had considerable clout with them. They would not lightly dismiss his demand to disclose Elijah's presence and hand him over if they had him. Nonetheless, the prophet shows no fear before such a formidable king but rather rebukes him: "'I have not made trouble for Israel,' Elijah replied. 'But you and your father's family have. You have abandoned the LORD's commands and have followed the Baals'" (1 Kings 18:18). From that point on Elijah is in command of the process. And the process is literally a *Prozess*—a trial by which the powers of darkness are shown to be not God as the inability of Baal to find his voice [קוֹל] or produce thunder shows (1 Kings 18:29; contrast 1 Kings 19:12).[10]

However, it is the Lord who is truly in command of events, and Elijah makes it clear before everyone that whatever authority he has shown in the unfolding of events on Mount Carmel, it has all come from the Lord:

At the time of sacrifice, the prophet Elijah stepped forward and prayed: "O LORD, the God of Abraham, Isaac, and Israel, let it be known today that you are God in Israel and that I am your servant and have done all these things at your command. Answer me, O LORD, answer me, so these people will know that you, LORD, are God, and that you are turning their hearts back again." Then the fire of the LORD fell and burned up the sacrifice, the wood, the stones, and the soil, and also licked up the water in the trench. (1 Kings 18:36–38)

---

9   The idiom "made them swear" (הִשְׁבִּיעַ), which is used by Obadiah when he tells Elijah of Ahab's global search for him is used of treaty swearing in the Old Testament, for example, Joshua 23:7a: "Do not associate with these nations that remain among you; do not invoke the names of their gods or cause [anyone] to swear by them." NIV incorrectly translates the verb as "swear" when it should be translated "make/cause to swear"—that is, take them under oath as vassals in a suzerain-vassal treaty relationship. So Assyrian emperors often boast that they made defeated kings "swear the oath of the great gods"— that is, the gods who were witnesses to and oversaw the new suzerain-vassal treaties.

10   For discussion of the translation "roaring, crushing sound/voice" superior to "still small voice" or "gentle whisper," cf. J. Lust, "A Gentle Breeze or a Roaring, Thunderous Sound?" *VT* 25 (1975): 110–15.

The prophet who had grown humble and powerful in the ministry the Lord gave him makes it clear to everyone where his authority comes from. Whatever he has called for has been at the Lord's word, and he now calls upon the Lord to fulfill that word, and so to have the last word. The Lord answers by fire. Now the prophets of Baal had called on their god, "But there was no response, no one answered, no one paid attention" (1 Kings 18:29b). The statement, "There was no response," is actually, "There was no voice" (קוֹל). The term is important under the circumstances. It can also be translated "thunder," and it was encountered and discussed with regard to the proper translation of Genesis 3:8. The same term is used for the "thunders" on Mount Sinai during the Lord's storm theophany there (Exod. 19:16). Baal was the storm god of the pagans. So when one reads "there was no voice," one understands that the "voice/thunder" one would expect if a summons to Baal were to produce any result has not taken place. The message would not be lost on Elijah's audience. The Lord by contrast *does* respond and that presence of a response sends an even more powerful message. Not only is Baal *not* a god; the Lord *is* God: "When all the people saw this, they fell prostrate and cried, 'The LORD—he is God! The LORD—he is God!'" (1 Kings 18:39). The Lord did a wonder that was also a sign to bring a pagan woman to himself. Now the Lord does a sign and a wonder to turn his people—who in their Baal worship had become effectively pagans—back to himself. The wonders are signs and that can hardly be overemphasized. They point a person to the Lord, and in the case of the Mount Carmel episode, his readiness to provide such a sign shows he is unwilling to see any lost who could be saved.[11]

Elijah and His Flight from Jezebel

The prophet who apparently moved with such effortless authority in the Mount Carmel episode—the prophet who could rebuke a powerful king who had spared no effort to find him among the nations and call him to account—shows a different attitude when Ahab's queen, the infamous, unscrupulous, and powerful Jezebel threatens him with death after he slaughters the prophets of Baal. She sends a messenger with the word: "May the gods deal with me, be it ever so severely, if by this time

---

11   Cf. 1 Kings 18:19: "Now summon the people from all over Israel to meet me on Mount Carmel." One assumes not all came or could come, but the Lord's salvific desire for all his people seems clear enough.

tomorrow I do not make your life like that of one of them" (1 Kings 19:2). Elijah's response to her is quite different from his response to Ahab earlier: "Elijah was afraid and ran for his life" (1 Kings 19:3). The unpointed verb in the report (וירא) is ambiguous. The consonants could read "[Elijah] was afraid" or "[Elijah] saw."[12] The report of Elijah's condition after he fled, however, is unambiguous: "He came to a broom bush, sat down under it and prayed that he might die. 'I have had enough, Lord,' he said. 'Take my life; I am no better than my fathers'" (1 Kings 19:4, author's translation). That is probably not the statement of a man who had rationally weighed his circumstances and decided it would be prudent to leave. Although departure on the heels of such a threat could be a reasonable choice, it also seems the prophet is depressed and does not feel able to stand up to the queen as he had stood up to her husband before.

If this understanding is correct, it would be consistent with other examples of an unworthy timidity on the part of a person or people of God just after they have seen the Lord do some great thing. Israel feared the Canaanites after the spies' report, despite all they had seen the Lord do in Egypt and against Pharaoh's army, and notwithstanding any encouragement (Num. 13:26–33; 14:1–4). Peter, after being bold enough to trust he could walk to the Lord on the sea, suddenly felt overwhelmed by the wind and waves, and fear replaced his faith (Matt. 14:22–31). That may be the case with Elijah now. Every thing he did on Mount Carmel was done by the Lord, and as the prophet effectively stated, he could not have had any authority except what was given from above. It may be that the Lord has, in the present case, withdrawn some of that spiritual support. As a result, Elijah's spirit is not what it was. He looks to himself as he evaluates his situation ("I am no better than my fathers," 1 Kings 19:4b), rather than to the Lord for prophetic and perhaps salvific authority against an evil queen. He does pray to the Lord, but only for escape by death (1 Kings 19:4a). The spiritual question is paramount. Why would the Lord allow his prophet to fall back onto his own resources and face the discouragement and fear that inevitably come when one who has relied on the Lord falls into the error of relying, to some extent, on himself instead? The answer seems to be: precisely so the prophet could learn from the experience. The implications for God's people in ministry are worth taking into account. They can help illuminate what we go through, especially if we are privileged to have God work through us in some unusual way.

We noted that Jezebel sent a messenger to Elijah with a death threat

---

12 Translations differ: "was afraid" (NIV, NASB, NRSV); "saw" (NKJV, MSG, CJB).

(1 Kings 19:2). The account bears further examination, because the word for "messenger" and the word for "angel" are the same (מַלְאָך). The Greek word for messenger and for angel is also the same, and our word "angel" comes from it (ἄγγελος). But Jezebel's messenger is not the only מַלְאָך. After her death threat, an angel of the LORD appears to Elijah. The angel provides for him and encourages him on his way. After Elijah complains to the Lord that he is no better than his fathers (1 Kings 19:4), he lies down under a broom tree and falls asleep. The angel then comes:

> All at once an angel touched him and said, "Get up and eat." He looked around, and there by his head was some bread baked over hot coals, and a jar of water. He ate and drank and then lay down again. The angel of the LORD came back a second time and touched him and said, "Get up and eat, for the journey is too much for you." So he got up and ate and drank. Strengthened by that food, he traveled forty days and forty nights until he reached Horeb, the mountain of God. There he went into a cave and spent the night. (1 Kings 19:5b–7)

A Hebrew reader can hardly miss the recurrence of the word "messenger/angel" (מַלְאָך) used both for Jezebel's human messenger and the Lord's heavenly messenger. The juxtaposition would seem to be deliberate—Jezebel's threat could have been narrated without using the word "messenger"—and points to a deeper theological idea. An outline shows the comparison and contrast:

Kingdom of Israel	Kingdom of Heaven
Human Royalty (Jezebel)	Heavenly Royalty (Yahweh)
Human messenger (מַלְאָך)	Heavenly messenger (מַלְאָך)
Threat of death and end of work	Provision of sustenance for life and continuation of work

If one admits that spirits can move people—be it the Holy Spirit or an evil spirit—and if one adds the biblical truth that those who worship idols really worship demons, one sees a spiritual possibility behind the diagram. Jezebel was a committed worshiper of Baal and Asherah. It would not be unreasonable to infer that demons informed not only her religious thought and feeling, but other aspects of her policy as well (cf. even in the church, 1 Tim. 4:1). Her death threat is in sympathy with the one who comes to kill, steal, and destroy, and if Jesus could address his opponents as children of the devil, Jezebel would also be a good candidate for that title. The fact that the false prophetess at Thyatira is later called Jezebel—who teaches Satan's deep secrets—as spiritual heir to the queen of Israel also points in the same direction: Jezebel is not a pawn but a dark queen on the chessboard of the land. A power beyond her whom she does not know moves her. She and her agents, including her "angel," play their roles in an ongoing contest between the Lord and his kingdom and the devil and his.

Consequently the outline shows a conflict between two kingdoms: the kingdom of Israel and the kingdom of Yahweh. The two ought to be in concert—Israel ought to be an extension of the heavenly kingdom—but because Israel's monarchy is false, they are opposed. Behind the human monarchy lies a power of deeper opposition: the opposition between the kingdom of darkness and the kingdom of light, between death and life. Elijah is caught up in a profound warfare that spans almost all human history—however much or little he may know of its spiritual dimensions.

Elijah and Horeb

An angel provides for Elijah so he may continue on the journey he has begun, that is, to Horeb, the mount where the Lord originally gave the covenant to Moses for his people. I have written about that encounter at greater length elsewhere, but a brief review may be helpful now.[13] The narrative before us implies two sets of parallels. One set displays theophanic encounters of Moses and Elijah on Horeb:

Set #1

Theme	Exodus // 1 Kings
God commands Moses to prepare for theophany	Exod. 33:19–34:3
God commands Elijah to prepare for theophany	1 Kings 19:11a
God appears to Moses	Exod. 34:5–7
God appears to Elijah	1 Kings 19:11b–13
Moses asks God to "be with us"	Exod. 34:8–9
Elijah complains, "I am the only one left"	1 Kings 19:14
God restores covenant, will destroy idolaters and idols	Exod. 34:10
God will anoint leaders to destroy idolaters and notes seven thousand covenant faithful	1 Kings 19:15–17 1 Kings 19:18

13   Cf. *God at Sinai*, 245–49.

The Lord's faithfulness to his covenant people is apparent in both cases, even if, as in the later case of Elijah, the Lord must judge those who are unfaithful. In fact, that is part of his covenant faithfulness—faithfulness to his own nature, which we have understood is God's righteousness.[14] There are, however, noteworthy differences. First, Moses asks the Lord to appear to him and "show me your glory" (Exod. 33:18). The Lord agrees and also uses the occasion to fashion another set of tablets to replace those Moses broke. Elijah by contrast does not request a theophany. Rather, the Lord speaks to him and—apparently unexpectedly—tells him to prepare for one. Second, in Moses' encounter, the Lord reaffirms his recently made covenant with Israel despite their fractiousness. In Elijah's case, the Lord prepares further covenant lawsuits (through the person of Elisha) and further judgments (through the persons of Jehu and Hazael) on Israel, a people who have had the covenant for a very long time but shown themselves largely unfaithful to it.

There is another set of parallels in the encounter. It has to do with the Lord's repeated questions and commands to Elijah:

Set #2

Theme	1 Kings 19
Yahweh's word: "What are you doing here, Elijah?"	19:9b
Yahweh's word: "What are you doing here, Elijah?"	19:13b
Elijah's reply: "I have been very zealous. . . . I alone am left"	19:10
Elijah's reply: "I have been very zealous. . . . I alone am left"	19:14
Yahweh theophany	19:11b–13a
Yahweh commands out of theophany	19:15–18

The repetitions are noteworthy, and may have to do with pedagogy. The Lord puts the same question two times (vv. 9b, 13b), and Elijah gives the same answer both times (vv. 10, 14). The third parallel is actually an expansion or an exposition, that is, first the Lord appears, then he gives a revelation that apparently motivated the theophany. A reader can hardly fail to notice the parallels, and they are probably emphatic. The Lord is unrelenting in his probing and Elijah is pertinacious in his complaint. The Lord's persistence wins through: it provokes the prophet's complaint, but also answers it. Much later one finds a similar parallelism of question

---

14 Cf. further discussion in volume 3, Appendix E.

and answer between Jesus and Peter. As William Barnes noted long ago: "The divine question is repeated in order that the divine lesson may be repeated and impressed upon the prophet. Cf. our Lord's threefold question to St. Peter, 'Lovest thou me' (John xxi.15, 16, 17)."[15]

There is more to say about this theophanic encounter. The Lord speaks to Elijah not with a "still, small voice" (the traditional translation), but with a "roaring, thunderous sound/voice." The proposed translation would be consistent with other storm theophanies the Bible records, but that is not a good enough reason to choose the translation. Rather, good lexical evidence supports it.[16] The Lord has a voice. That distinguishes him from Baal, who can make no response when his prophets try to invoke him. Because he is no god, Baal has nothing to say. That became obvious when his prophets tried to summon him: "There was no sound/thunder/voice" (קוֹל, 1 Kings 18:29b). By contrast, when the Lord appears, there is a "voice" (קוֹל, 1 Kings 19:12).

What matters most is not the volume of the voice, but the fact that the Lord has a voice. That issue is at the core of this theophany and accounts for the way it is portrayed. We are told the Lord was not "in" (or perhaps better, "as," with the preposition taken as *beth essentiae*) the earthquake, wind, or fire. One could expect those phenomena in a powerful Baal theophany (i.e., a storm). Such attendant storm theophany phenomena accompanied the Lord when he appeared on Sinai.[17] Nonetheless, the phenomena are just that—attendant. The Lord is not to be confused with or identified *as the storm*. Unlike a storm—unlike Baal—the Lord can speak: his "voice" (קוֹל) is not "thunder" (קוֹל) although it can be a "thunderous voice" (קוֹל). The Lord does what Baal cannot do, that is, he gives verbal, propositional revelation—*torah* from which his prophet and people may benefit.

God the Shaper and Prophetic Experience: Elisha and the Shunammite Woman

A Shunammite woman offered Elisha hospitality. In response, the prophet declared she would have a son (2 Kings 4:16). Because (in its

---

15   W. E. Barnes, *The First Book of Kings* (Cambridge: Cambridge University Press, 1911), 158.

16   As we affirm in agreement with Lust, "A Gentle Breeze or a Roaring, Thunderous Sound?" Cf. discussion in *God at Sinai*, 248.

17   Cf. discussion in *God at Sinai*, 247–48.

literary form) his promise resembles the Lord's promise of a son to Sarah when she was old and barren, it may be some very good destiny awaited the child. However, the young boy dies suddenly one day on his mother's lap, after being out with his father and the reapers (2 Kings 4:18–20). The mother lays his body on the bed, in the room she had provided for Elisha, and sets off to see the prophet. The account offers two points of spiritual interest. The first is the woman's response of *shalom* to her husband and to Gehazzi, when they ask about her journey (2 Kings 4:23.26). The second is Elisha's commissioning Gehazzi to run ahead of him and lay his staff on the dead boy's body (2 Kings 4:29)—an action that does not bring the boy to life. We explored these matters in chapter 11 and will comment further on Elisha's instruction to Gehazzi below.

What concerns us now is one other remarkable fact. Although Elisha is a prophet, he does not know why the woman has come to him. When Gehazzi would deny her access to Elisha, the prophet admonishes: "Leave her alone! She is in bitter distress, but the LORD has hidden it from me and has not told me why" (2 Kings 4:27). The woman then blurts out questions that are both accusatory and revelatory: "'Did I ask you for a son, my Lord,' she said. 'Didn't I tell you, "Don't raise my hopes?"'" (2 Kings 4:28). Elisha apparently knows from the questions that her son is dead, and he does ultimately bring the boy back to life. Before that, the encounter between the woman and the prophet can be instructive. Elisha does not know why the woman has come to him. He can see she is distressed, but the Lord has not revealed why. If the prophet is to know the cause of her distress, and the reason for her coming, she will have to tell him. And she does. The Lord's reticence has made that necessary, and it may be part of the Lord's healing ministry to the woman. The Lord keeps his prophet in ignorance, so the woman is compelled to unburden herself of the agony she bore on her journey to him. The catharsis she wins by that confession could not have been hers had the Lord simply told the prophet what was wrong.

From such a case one may justly take a lesson: God sometimes wants statements from people—confessions of one sort or another (as with Adam, Eve, Hagar, and the Shunammite)—not because he lacks data they can provide, but because he is at work in some way for their good. The good may be a blessing or even a covenant lawsuit, but it will be a form of ministry that can only take place once the person involved has told his or her story.[18]

---

18 A comparable case is that of Achan in Joshua 7 who, although he has been

People who minister in some form of the Lord's revelatory gifting today may take comfort from these facts. If one is a prophet and accustomed to receiving revelation from God about a person to whom one is ministering, one need not worry, if in a given case one does not hear from the Lord. The lack of revelation may have nothing to do with any shortcoming on the part of the minister, just as Elisha's failure to hear from the Lord regarding the Shunammite woman apparently had nothing to do with any shortcoming of his. After all—as Paul aptly declares in a rhetorical question—who is sufficient for the works God calls his people to do (2 Cor. 2:16)? But if the Lord withholds information from the minister, it may be that God wants the person receiving the ministry to unburden himself or herself, or to confess something he or she needs to confess. The resultant catharsis is part of the Lord's ministry to the person. It is important to remember: it is the Lord's ministry. His Spirit is the one who truly does the work.

The case of Elisha and the Shunammite is the third of three prophetic cases we have considered of divine shaping or forming among the covenant lawsuit prophets of the Mosaic covenant. They give only glimpses of some of the spiritual formation the Lord accomplished among those men. There is another type of formation for ministry to consider before the conclusion of this chapter, and it has to do with modeling. The Lord can work in a certain way to accomplish something through one prophet, and form him by so doing. A subsequent prophet or prophets when called upon to do a similar work may model their ministry approach or method on the example set by their forerunner. The resurrections performed by Elijah, Elisha, and Paul, and those performed by Jesus and Peter, illustrate this principle.

God the Shaper and Modeled Ministry: Elijah and the Widow of Zarephath Revisited

When Elijah entered Zarephath and encountered the widow—although he was a prophet—he probably had no idea a resurrection lay in the future. When the widow accosted him about her dead son, she probably had no idea a truth encounter was coming. However, the history of Elijah

---

providentially taken by lot as the guilty party, is still called upon to "give glory to God" and confess what he has done (Josh. 7:19). He gives glory by being brought to the point of confession (which is agreeing with God, *confiteor*) and then making the confession.

suggests the Lord had been preparing both of them for that encounter.[19] When her son dies, she asks two questions that will lead to the truth encounter, and the second one is very revealing. The NIV unfortunately obscures both questions: "She said to Elijah, 'What do you have against me, man of God? Did you come to remind me of my sin and kill my son?'" (1 Kings 17:18). This unfortunate translation obscures her very first words. She says literally, "What to me and to you"—that is (paraphrased): "What do we have to do with each other" (hardly, "What do you have against me," NIV). The second highly interpretive move by NIV comes with the second question: "Did you come to remind me of my sin." The Hebrew reads literally, "Have you come to me to cause [someone] to remember my sin [להזכיר את־עוני]." The NKJV captures the sense of these questions somewhat better: "What have I to do with you, O man of God? Have you come to me to bring my sin to remembrance, and to kill my son?"

The widow's question is natural for a pagan. She knows Elijah is a man of Elohim; and his God is the God of Israel. But, assuming she holds a typically pagan point of view, the God of Israel would, to her way of thinking, be like any other deity: he would have his attention on his own national dominion. He could easily fail to notice something going on in another country. That is the point of Elijah's subsequent taunt to the prophets of Baal: "Cry aloud, for he *is* a god; either he is meditating, or he is busy, or he is on a journey, *or* perhaps he is sleeping and must be awakened" (1 Kings 18:27 NKJV). The pagan gods were humans writ large, apparently immortal and considerably more powerful than humans, but all too human in other ways—committing adultery, getting drunk, oversleeping, finite. According to such a point of view, the Lord's attention would be mostly on his own country, but could also turn to his prophet Elijah—at least from time to time—in another country. When his attention was on Elijah, God might sooner or later happen to notice the widow and, noticing her, be reminded of some sin or sins she had committed. The account does not reveal any details of the widow's sin. Whatever it was, she did not like the idea of Elijah's presence calling it to the Lord's attention. If a god—even a foreign god—became aware of her sin and took offense to it, that could lead to some form of punishment. In this case, she imagines, it may have led to the "putting to death" of her son. So she asks whether Elijah came to her "to put my son to death"

---

19   We have seen the Lord prepare Elijah for the unclean foreign woman by using ravens to feed him and noted the Lord ordained the woman's positive reception of the prophet.

(1 Kings 17:18). Obviously Elijah has not killed her son. Her son died apart from Elijah's presence. How, then, can she connect him with her son's death? The connection makes perfect sense if her thoughts followed the pattern just outlined: the prophet's presence drew the attention of his God to himself and to his surroundings; that same God then noticed the widow, recalled her sin, and punished her by putting her son to death.

This moment is the start of a truth encounter for her, because she is about to have her theology, pagan and fragmentary as it is, overturned and replaced by the truth. When Elijah raises her son from the dead she can acknowledge: "Now I know that you are a man of God and that the word of the LORD from your mouth is the truth" (1 Kings 17:24). Her confession is the end result of a process than began when she first met Elijah. Two things we can document prepared her for that confession. First, she had been blessed by signs and wonders—the miraculous pro-vision of flour and oil—at the start of their relationship. Second, she had been *convicted*—that is, made aware of her sin (and that conviction would probably be a work of the Spirit)—after her son's death. Nonetheless, it is only after the unprecedented miracle of her son's resurrection that she is totally convinced, not only of the supernatural reality of God, but also of the truth of his words through his prophet. We may recall how Paul characterizes a powerful combination of words and works. According to Paul, the combination of words and signs and wonders is "the full proc-lamation of the gospel of Christ" (cf. Rom. 15:18–19). According to the widow, the wonder of the resurrection convinced her that the prophet's words were truth. One cannot know, but one may imagine those words included some accounts of the nature and acts of Israel's God.

Finally, the word translated "the truth" (אמת) actually appears without a definite article here and has covenantal overtones. It is one member of a word pair "grace and truth" (cf. John 1:17) used of covenant relations (e.g., Exod. 34:6; Josh. 2:12). Additionally, the Hebrew term has a nuance not only of truth but also of *troth*—that is, covenant faithfulness. The widow says, "I know that the word of Yahweh in your mouth is truth/troth." The word of Yahweh is trustworthy. Long before, Rahab, who joined the Lord's covenant people, asked for a sign of their own cove-nant faithfulness (אמה) from the two spies (cf. Josh. 2:12). The widow's confession now may mark her own entry into covenant fellowship with Elijah and his God.

A display outlines the narrative of this prophetic encounter from the beginning of the woman's relationship with Elijah up to what may justly be called her statement of faith:

Illness and death of only son	17:17
Woman seeks and rebukes prophet	17:18
Prophet's response and prayer	17:19–21
Resurrection of son	17:22
Restoration of son to mother	17:23
Mother's reaction	17:24

The pattern of events is paralleled by a pattern of events in Elisha's ministry, as a comparison with the resurrection he performs will show.

God the Shaper and Modeled Ministry: Elisha and the Shunammite Woman Revisited

Unlike Elijah, who provided food miraculously for the widow of Zarephath who agreed to receive him, Elisha is asked to sojourn in her house by a Shunammite woman, who provides him a furnished room. She wants him to be her guest. Even when he asks whether he can do a favor for her, in view of her hospitality, she declines: "I dwell among my own people" (2 Kings 4:13b NKJV). Her answer is enigmatic to us and probably ranks as an example of laconic narrative left without explanation. Since monarchs were happy to impose taxes (as much as even a tenth of grain, wine, and flocks, cf. 1 Sam. 8:15–17), maybe a tax exemption is in view. [20]

Elisha is prepared to provide some good thing for the Shunammite woman but her reply suggests that, being one who lives among her own people (i.e., a citizen), she does not need his intercession with the king or army commander (cf. 2 Kings 4:13) for any special favors (including perhaps a tax exemption). Whether or not taxes or the possibility of being tax-exempt are involved, her reply does indicate she considers herself to be well enough provided for within the legal structure of her own society.

---

20   Other explanations have been ventured. Cf. Herbert Lockyer, *All the Women of the Bible* (Grand Rapids: Zondervan, 1967), 207: "Would she like the prophet to further her interests by securing a position for her husband at the court, or in the army, seeing he had influence both with the king and the captain of the host? Her reply was characteristic of the humility of her nobility. 'I dwell among mine own people,' or 'in the midst of my people I am dwelling far from the court and courtly interests. My husband and I are humble commoners, quietly living in the country, and do not seek the company of exalted personages.'" Any explanation, however, including our "tax exemption" offered above, remains speculative.

Nonetheless, Elisha summons her and prophesies that she will have a son (2 Kings 4:15–16). Since true prophecy is not a product of human will or hope but of the Spirit, it is understood this prediction is from the Lord and will come to pass.

Two spiritually instructive events inform the Shunammite episode, as was noted at the outset of this chapter. First, the woman's answer of *shalom* to her husband and then to Gehazzi when they enquire about her journey (2 Kings 4:23.26); second, Elisha's instruction to Gehazzi to run ahead of him and lay his staff on the dead boy's body (2 Kings 4:29)—an action that does not bring the boy to life. We now explore Elisha's instruction to Gehazi, and then the resurrection Elisha performs. The point of the exploration is to show what sorts of formation may be going on, or intended, in the disciple and the prophet. A comparative outline of resurrections in the Old Testament and the New follows that discussion.

Elisha's Command to Gehazi

Elisha told Gehazi to run ahead of him and use the prophet's staff to do whatever could be done to help the boy: "Tuck your cloak into your belt, take my staff in your hand and run. Don't greet anyone you meet, and if anyone greets you, do not answer. Lay my staff on the boy's face" (2 Kings 4:29). The staff does no good, and that ought to raise some questions about Elisha's instruction and its purpose. Four possibilities come to mind:

1. Elisha does not know whether laying the staff on the boy will do any good, but he sends Gehazi to use the staff just in case it may work.
2. Elisha does not know whether laying the staff on the boy will do any good, but surmises it may do good if Gehazi has the faith necessary for the Lord to work through him.
3. Elisha knows the staff will do no good, but he is testing Gehazi's obedience.
4. Elisha knows the staff will do no good, but he wants Gehazi to learn a lesson: there is nothing magical about the staff; what counts is a true prophetic connection with the Lord.

Comments on the possibilities:

1. According to the first proposal Elisha would be operating out of ignorance—taking a "shot in the dark." That is not a likely scenario

for a prophet in such an important matter, although it is possible (cf. Nathan's mistaken advice to David in 2 Samuel 7).

2.   According to the second proposal, the prophet knows or senses that, if his apprentice has faith—that is, if the Lord wants to heal the boy in this manner and Gehazi can amen it—the attempt will succeed. Gehazi will have grown in faith toward a prophetic ministry.

3.   According to the third proposal, the prophet thinks Gehazi ought to be tested. As the episode with Naaman soon shows, Gehzai does have serious character flaws—he is greedy and mendacious, and he probably has some contempt for someone the Lord has just healed, apparently because he was a foreigner (cf. 2 Kings 5:19b–27).

4.   According to the fourth proposal, the prophet wants to instruct his helper. That may be the most likely explanation. Staffs had been important in the past in connection with the Lord's miraculous work—for example, Moses' staff in the crossing of the Reed Sea (Exod. 14:16) and at the defeat of Amalek (Exod. 17:8–16); and cf. Joshua's javelin at the battle of Ai (Josh. 8:18–26; see discussion in chapter 11). Nonetheless, it is the Lord who works, and not the wooden staff. Among a people whose fathers could worship Gideon's ephod, and who had shown themselves prone to idolatry, Elisha's apprentice may need the sort of lesson such a failure would provide.

The use of a staff because it was a prophet's staff—and thus endowed somehow with mystical power—is close to magic. The attraction of magic lies partly in its mystery, since one cannot really know what makes it work, and partly in the control or illusion of control it gives to the one who wields it. As subsequent events prove, Gehazi would have to learn that the best solution to human problems does not lie in our exercise of control but in the Lord who alone can raise the dead—in "the God who gives life to the dead and calls into being things that were not" (Rom. 4:17).

The Ministry of Resurrection

Not many have been called to raise the dead. Nonetheless, the biblical accounts of resurrection can help us understand some basic, ordinary things about ministry and discipleship. A disciple follows the pattern set by his master. Accordingly, comparative outlines show points of resemblance between various resurrections reported in the Bible. The first set compares resurrections performed by Elijah and Elisha.

Comparison of Resurrections by Elijah and Elisha

	1 Kings 17:7–24	2 Kings 4:8–37
Initial encounter with woman	17:7–12	4:8–10
Initial blessing for blessing	17:13–16	4:11–17
Illness and death of only son	17:17	4:18–21
Woman seeks and rebukes prophet	17:18	4:22–28
		[Gehazi's errand
		4:29–31]
Prophet's response and prayer	17:19–21	4:32–33
Resurrection of son	17:22	4:34–35
Restoration of son to mother	17:23	4:36
Mother's reaction	17:24	4:37

The parallels show what one ought to expect. A student (learner, disciple, μαθητής) patterns himself after his master—a principle Jesus taught his disciples (but in the context of another matter, Matt. 10:25). Elisha was not present when Elijah raised the widow of Zarephath's son. Nonetheless, there is a high degree of parallelism between the two prophets' resurrection ministries. This suggests Elisha's master told him about the miracle. Presumably Elijah would have told his disciple many things the senior prophet had seen the Lord do in his ministry. The parallel may also suggest the double portion Elisha received after Elijah's ascension: Elijah stretched out on the widow of Zarephath's son three times, whereas Elisha did so two times on the Shunammite's son.[21] This inheritance pattern ranges more widely in the Bible, backward to Moses and Joshua and forward to John the Baptist and Jesus and beyond.[22] Along these lines there is another instructive parallel. It can be shown by comparing the examples noted above with the resurrection of Eutychus performed by Paul.

---

21 One does not want to push the interpretive point too far. However, if Elisha did indeed receive twice the anointing Elijah had (cf. 2 Kings 2:9), it would be consistent that he would perform a resurrection more efficiently. Since half of three is one and one half, and since Elisha could hardly have stretched himself out on the dead boy *one and one half* times, he did so two times. As further study shows, the inheritance idiom Elisha uses when he asks Elijah for the double portion is consistent with this understanding. Cf. chapter 16.

22 Cf. chapter 16 and implications for ministry in the church.

Comparison of Resurrections by Elijah, Elisha, and Paul

	1 Kings 17:19–22	*2 Kings 4:32–35*	*Acts 20:7–12*
Prophet in upper room	17:19	4:32	20:7–8 [Eutychus' death, 20:9]
Prophet cries to God	17:20	4:33	
Prophet stretches out	17:21 (3x)	4:34–35 (2x)	20:10 (1x)
Life returns	17:22	4:34b–35	20:10–11

Jesus performed resurrections before Paul raised Eutychus. A natural question may occur: Why does Paul *not* perform a resurrection one of the ways Jesus did?[23] The Bible offers no explanation. It may be that Paul—who knew his Old Testament well—tried to help Eutychus by the method he knew the great prophets of the old covenant had used when confronted with similar situations. He modeled his ministry on theirs. If that explanation is correct, the following would also be true: Paul probably heard accounts of the resurrections Jesus performed, but Paul's default way of doing what was wanted when confronted with the crisis of Eutychus was to take as his model the prophets he knew so well from his immersion in the materials of the old covenant. God honored his choice. One could even say God led him to it. Peter's reaction when faced with a similar situation is consistent with this line of thought.

Peter ranged from being a person who could boldly declare who Jesus was (Matt. 16:16) to a person that same Jesus, figuratively, called Satan (Matt. 16:23)—from a man who healed a cripple at the temple and ignited controversy for the name of Christ all over Jerusalem (Acts 3:6) to a man Paul rebuked for cowardly behavior before the Judaizers at Galatia (Gal. 2:11). The Christian who looks at Peter may be encouraged because his vicissitudes can look very like our own. Peter was nonetheless the rock on whom Christ would build his church, and he was a disciple who could learn from his master. One example of his discipleship at work is Tabitha's resurrection, as it parallels a resurrection performed by Jesus.

---

23 We note Jesus raised the synagogue ruler's daughter and Lazarus in different ways. The difference points to a ministry reality: there is *no one way* to do a healing or any other work of the Spirit. The only way to do it is the way the Spirit is doing it. This too is amening the Lord.

Comparison of Resurrections by Jesus and Peter

	Mark 5:37–43	Acts 9:39–42
Enters room	5:40b	9:39
Sends folks out	5:40a	9:40a
Takes by the hand	5:41 (before)	9:41a (after)
Prays		9:40b
Command	5:41 "Talitha koum"	9:40 "Tabitha, rise"
Resurrection	5:42	9:40c–41a
Command of secrecy	5:43	
Word spreads		9:42

As has been noted, when one displays a chiasm—and especially a chiastic structure that covers an expanse of narrative material—it is important to label the elements of the chiasm in a way that makes clear a parallel structure that really is there. The same principle is true when one sets out to show parallels between two events, as we have done with these resurrection narratives. When it comes to Jesus and Peter, not only are many of the key elements similar (entry into a room, dismissal of others, taking by the hand), but the name of the dead girl—*Tabitha*—is only *one letter different* from the word Jesus uses to address the dead girl—*talitha* (an Aramaic vocative), and the command is the same: "Get up!" In God's providence, this was probably not a coincidence. It looks like a demonstration of God's wittiness. And why not? A joyful event is about to take place. And the discovery of such a thing shows that—as has often been seen before—a demonstration of parallels does not have to be just a mechanical exercise. It can open one's eyes to dynamics of spiritual life that are part of the multifaceted brilliance of the biblical data—and of their main Actor and Author. One could search ancient near eastern inscriptions and histories in vain for comparable demonstrations of interest in the spiritual dynamics of an ordinary person—or ordinary people—in connection with divine activity. Apparently that is because the Bible records revelations of a god who really exists—who really is God—and who has a deep interest in the welfare of his creatures.[24]

---

24 Including animals (cf. Jonah 4:11).

CONCLUSION

Because the Lord is the potter or shaper of all people, it follows that he is also the shaper of his prophets. A number of Old Testament examples have shown the Lord shaping those people. Not only the Lord's sovereign activity as potter, but also the ways the pot reacted to the potter's hand are on display. Not only are God's actions manifest but also his nature. The Lord is one who, in covenant faithfulness to those he made and whom he called as covenant lawsuit messengers, not only used them and worked through them but also simultaneously shaped them out of an insuperable love.

Jesus himself was shaped by his Father during his years among us as the author of Hebrews reminds us (Heb. 5:7–9). If Jesus was shaped and "learned obedience," the same ought to be be true of us, because a servant is not greater than his master. The Son's life experience is the supreme example of a principle affirmed in Hebrews: "The Lord disciplines the one he loves, and he chastens everyone he accepts as his son" (Heb. 12:6; cf. Prov. 3:12).

The Lord shaped the prophets by putting them through various challenges. Those challenges included his irruption into their lives and his call on their lives, and he shaped them as long as they lived on this earth. He also shaped them by other prophets as a matter of discipleship. Moreover, that shaping could go on over a longer span of time than a prophet's life: the resurrections performed by Elijah and Elisha shaped Paul, for instance.

The Lord uses what he will to shape his covenant people. What Paul knew of Elijah and Elisha he knew only by words, yet those words were God-breathed and Spirit, and the Lord who is Spirit used them to shape Paul. Accordingly, anyone can be shaped by words in any book because those words too are spirit—the articulated spirit of the author, be the author good or bad.

The next chapter explores the work and experience of more prophets—the writing prophets—of the Mosaic covenant. It takes into account a particular sort of "prophetic experience"—the so-called word-confrontation genre. It also considers the calls of Hosea and Isaiah and how they anticipate the new covenant. It sets the phenomenon of old covenant prophecy in a historical-theological perspective that anticipates the new covenant.

CHAPTER FIFTEEN

THE LORD AND PROPHETIC EXPERIENCE: THE WRITING PROPHETS

After considering the lives and ministries of some non-writing proph-ets, and how their work looks forward to the Lord's work in his church, it may be helpful to step back briefly for a broader view that can put both their work and the work of the later writing prophets into a proper historical-theological perspective before we move on to consider some of the formative experiences of writing prophets that can also be instructive to the church. The perspective developed now can summarize the phenomenon of old covenant prophecy, and will also be reviewed under the heading of eschatology.

A HISTORICAL PATTERN AND ITS IMPLICATIONS

Human history has shown a recurring pattern: (1) God reveals himself in a covenant relationship with humans; (2) humans drift away from the good standards God has revealed and into increasing sin and unrigh-teousness; (3) God brings judgments on those who have rebelled; (4) God reveals himself once more in a covenant relationship with humans.

That pattern, *mutatis mutandis*, informs the trajectory of the biblical data. It played out in the primordial history, which culminated in the Noahic flood followed by a renewal covenant. It also played out in Israel's history, which culminated in Babylonian exile and restoration to their homeland—but ultimately in, not a renewal covenant, but a new cove-nant. It is also playing out in post-resurrection history, with a waxing and waning of Christianity that is still in process, which will culminate in a final judgment and a new heaven and a new earth.[1]

---

1 A similar pattern has appeared in smaller segments of history, for example, the

The Old Testament prophets provide a view of that same pattern—or part of it—unfolding during the historical segment known as the history of Israel. Biblical historiography, as well as the production of prophetical books, shows the development of God's people through time. That development was one of increasing apostasy and unrighteousness, to be followed by judgment (phases 2 and 3 of the pattern outlined above).

The Lord's response to the increase of unrighteousness included, first, non-writing prophets, and then as the problem broadened, the writing prophets.[2] The non-writing prophets considered in the last chapter were active in the ninth-century BC. The writing prophets considered in this chapter were active during the eighth- and seventh-centuries BC.

Why did the Lord follow a period of non-writing prophets with a period of writing prophets? It is here proposed that, as sin increased in both kingdoms, the Lord moved from raising up prophets like Elijah, Elisha, and Micaiah, who were *ad hoc* ministers from time to time, to raising up prophets like Isaiah, Jeremiah, Ezekiel, and the Twelve, who would compose broader and more formal covenant lawsuits as a matter of record (in the books named after them).[3]

Non-writing prophets and writing prophets were primarily covenant lawsuit messengers under the old covenant form of God's kingdom—the nation-states of Judah or Israel. They were sent to address sins and sinners under the Mosaic covenant and, if possible, lead them out of their sin. The new covenant form of God's kingdom is the church, and it has no covenant lawsuit prophets. The Lord's people under the new covenant have the Spirit dwelling within them, and he convicts them of sin, righteousness, and judgment and also leads them into the truth. So they need no covenant lawsuit messengers to do, from the outside, what the Spirit does from within.[4]

---

period of the Judges, and revivals throughout church history. In those cases, the Lord did not reveal himself after judgment by making another covenant, but his activity was meant to restore and advance his kingdom.

2   For the idea of broadening unrighteousness ("adultery") subsequently, cf. Jeremiah 3:6–10.

3   This statement applies generally to the Twelve, with obvious exceptions like Jonah and Nahum, whose prophecies had to do with Assyria.

4   This is not to deny that, on rare occasion, the Lord may deliver a covenant lawsuit message of some sort through a prophet in the church. However, it seems clear that prophecy in the church is meant primarily to edify (cf. 1 Cor. 14:4b). The letters to the churches in Revelation may be taken as covenant lawsuit material, but they are exceptional in the New Testament—perhaps meant as warning and guidance for the church

Both the non-writing prophets and the writing prophets of the Mosaic covenant also offer examples of prophetic reach beyond the nation-state form of God's kingdom. So Elijah went to save a widow in Zarephath, and Jonah went to save a pagan capital. Both were adumbrations of the Lord's salvific gospel ministry through his prophetic people, the church.

HISTORY, BIOGRAPHY, AND AUTOBIOGRAPHY

Biblical historiography has given us many chapters from the lives and encounters of Elijah and Elisha. The same cannot be said so uniformly of the writing prophets. With the notable exceptions of Hosea (whose calling is fraught with relational challenge that may fairly be said to color his whole book) and Jeremiah (whose book is arguably autobiographical except for a final chapter that summarizes and recapitulates some points), the major and minor prophets of the Old Testament have not told a great deal *about themselves*. Nonetheless, what they offer is substantial. Isaiah's book is not autobiographical but it does contain important events from his life—most notably for our purposes, his existential encounter with the Lord and his challenge to Ahaz. Amos does not contain much autobiography, but does show (in what is arguably an autobiographical passage) a word-controversy with a priest. Jeremiah offers even more. One can see the hand of the great Potter at work in the lives of his prophets.

Prophets of the Mosaic covenant—both writing and non-writing—were not, like Moses, covenant mediator prophets, but rather covenant lawsuit prophets or messengers. Israel had the law, and prophets of Isaiah's and Jeremiah's category brought no *new* law, no *new covenant*—even if they could foretell a new covenant the Lord would one day make with his people. Instead, they had the unwelcome task of confronting God's people with the truth that they had broken the law—the Mosaic covenant—the Lord had already given them. The writing prophets, like the non-writing prophets, had a divinely appointed task that aroused opposition and persecution. Their calling also meant that what they said and wrote had more to do with sins God's people had already committed—and with indictments corresponding to those sins—than with prediction per se.

From what has been said, it follows that two major areas of concern deserve consideration and are explored in this chapter: first, the role of

throughout her subsequent history—and the Lord has not produced similar covenant lawsuits for the church after the closure of the canon.

the Lord's call in shaping each prophet; and second, the role of the covenant lawsuit experience—namely, people's opposition to the prophet and his lawsuit—in shaping the Lord's prophets. The writing prophets are in view in this chapter, and for sake of illustration the calls experienced by Hosea and Isaiah are considered, and then the covenant lawsuit/word-confrontation experiences of Amos and Jeremiah.

THE LORD SHAPES HIS PROPHETS:
PROPHETIC CALLS AND HOW THEY SHAPE THE PROPHETS

Word-confrontations forced on the Lord's prophets shaped them because words and experience do shape us, whether we want them to or not, and words that amount to an existential threat provoke formative reactions. There are two writing prophets whose elective shaping comes not so much by existential threat as by the nature of their call. Foundational themes in the call of Hosea and Isaiah show up in the prophecies each produces, and this is indication of the formative influence of the call of each prophet.

Prophetic Calls and How They Shape the Prophets: Hosea

The Lord called Hosea to marry a "woman of harlotries." It was noted that although the term "harlotries" (זנונים) could be used metaphorically for idolatry, its first use was for literal prostitution (Gen. 38:24). The same is true in the Old Testament for the word group as well. On the other hand, such terms are used both literally and figuratively in Hosea's own book. I believe we have seen the literal usage in Hosea 1:2. Subsequently the Lord uses the term figuratively of Israel's idolatrous relations with her "lovers" (i.e., the Baals): "Let her remove the adulterous look from her face / and the unfaithfulness from between her breasts" (Hosea 2:2); "A spirit of prostitution leads them astray; / they are unfaithful to their God" (4:12b); "A spirit of prostitution is in their heart; / they do not acknowledge the Lord" (5:4b). Although those are figurative uses—signifying idolatry rather than literal harlotry—the latter phrase, "a spirit of prostitution" (רוח זנונים), is important because of its resonance with another false spirit reported in the Old Testament.

When Micaiah reported to Ahab and Jehoshaphat at the gates of Samaria, he informed them that he had seen the divine council in which the Lord had given "a deceiving spirit" (lit. "a spirit of deception," רוח שקר)

permission to go and speak a lie through Ahab's prophets that would lead him to his death (1 Kings 22:19–23). It was noted that the Spirit could not do this without the Lord's permission because all authority comes from God, including the authority to exercise power, even deceptively, on earth. This does not mean the Lord is the author of falsehood, but he does allow evil entities to have their way sometimes. The "spirit of prostitution" that leads Israel astray (Hosea 4:12; 5:4) is likely also an evil spirit, and that would be consistent with what Moses and Paul say about the demonic power that inspires idolatry.

The parallelism between idol worship and prostitution/adultery has been noted.[5] That dynamic parallelism underlies the usage both literally and figuratively in Hosea not only of "harlotries" (זְנוּנִים) but also of the root verb "to practice prostitution" (זנה). That is why the verb can be used both for literal prostitution—as Hosea tells his wife after taking her back: "You must not be a prostitute" (תִזְנִי 3:3)—and figuratively for idolatry—"Your mother [i.e., Israel] has played the harlot" (זָנְתָה 2:5 [2:7 MT], author's translation).[6] Should anyone doubt that the same term may be used both literally and figuratively in one book, or even in one passage, an example from another book may be helpful. The word usually translated "life" or "soul" (נפש) is used both literally and figuratively in Jonah 2: "The engulfing waters threatened *me*" (NIV; literally, "The waters came up around my *throat*," עַד־נֶפֶשׁ 2:5a [2:6a MT], author's translation); "When my *life* [נפשי] was ebbing away, / I remembered you, LORD" (i.e. figurative usage, 2:7 [2:8 MT]).[7]

Adultery and Its Children

God allowed Hosea to have experiences that must have shaped him in powerful ways. The prophet must marry a faithless wife and have illegitimate children in his own home. That parallels the Lord, who has a faithless wife (Israel) and spiritually illegitimate children. But what about the law, which commands that an adulterous woman be put to death (Lev. 20:10)? The parallelism explains why the Lord has Hosea marry a woman who should have been executed by law rather than married by

---

5   In chapter 12.

6   For other cases of its figurative use, that is, for idolatry in the same book, cf. Hosea 4:12, 13, 15; 9:1 (Qal), 4:10, 18; 5:3 (Hiphil).

7   For other uses of terms in more than one sense in the same pericope, cf. Isaiah 7:9b (אמן) and Jeremiah 23:2 (פקד).

the prophet. The Lord can make an exception to his law for his purpose, and he does so in this case.[8]

We have taken the view that the Lord told Hosea to marry an adulterous woman. He would have to suffer the consequence of having children of adultery in his own household. People who live in one of the most adulterous ages in human history may nonetheless find it hard to comprehend the challenge of such an experience, especially if one has never committed adultery oneself or had it committed by a spouse. That is so quite apart from the fact that all people have committed spiritual adultery since, for example, even excessive desire for money is idolatry (Col. 3:5).

People are naturally shaped in certain ways by what they go through. Having to endure a faithless wife and be a legal father to children of adultery would challenge and shape the prophet. Hosea's subsequent prophecies seem to bear witness to that shaping, because many of the judgments the Lord pronounces through him are couched in terms of marital or childbirth imagery. A seriatim presentation makes the point:

> Rebuke your mother, rebuke her,
>   for she is not my wife,
>   and I am not her husband.
> Let her remove the adulterous look from her face
>   and the unfaithfulness from between her breasts.
>   (2:2 [2:4 MT])

The Lord's rejection of Israel as his wife is couched in sexually graphic terms. He follows it with the threat: "Otherwise I will strip her naked / and make her as bare as on the day she was born" (2:3)—an utterance that evokes the use of nakedness as a figure for divine judgment already noted in Habakkuk 2:15–17, and also the account of the Lord's choice and marriage of Jerusalem in Ezekiel 16.[9]

Within two verses there is another use of adulterous language: "I will not show my love to her children, / because they are the children of adultery [זְנוּנִים]. / Their mother has been unfaithful [חָזְנָה] / and has conceived them in disgrace" (2:4–5a [2:6–7a MT]).

---

8   The law expressed God's nature, but not exhaustively so. What look like exceptions to God's law can in fact be seen as *fuller expressions* of his forgiving nature—as here, and cf. John 8:3–11.

9   For discussion of Habakkuk 2:15–17, cf. volume 1, 226–27. For discussion of Ezekiel 16, cf. chapter 5 of this volume, page 160.

Two chapters later, the Lord uses the same language in a statement of deep irony:

> I will not punish your daughters
>> when they turn to prostitution,
> nor your daughters-in-law
>> when they commit adultery,
> because the men themselves consort with harlots
>> and sacrifice with shrine prostitutes—
>> a people without understanding will come to ruin! (4:14)

Here the usage appears to be quite literal: the Lord indicts his people not only for the figurative prostitution and adultery of idolatry, but also for literal acts of prostitution and adultery they have committed and continue to commit. Both sorts of prostitutes—the secular (זנה) and the sacred (קדשה)— are mentioned (v. 14b).[10]

The Lord also rebukes them for the illegitimate children they bear ("They have dealt treacherously with Yahweh; / they give birth to illegitimate children," 5:7, author's translation), and as a result his judgment will come upon them:

> Even if they rear children,
>> I will bereave them of every one.
> Woe to them
>> when I turn away from them. . . .
> But Ephraim will bring out
>> his children to the slayer.
> Give them, O LORD—
>> what will you give them?
> Give them wombs that miscarry
>> and breasts that are dry. (9:12–14)

The judgment is pronounced both as a divine decision (vv. 12, 13b) and as a prayer from the prophet (v. 14). The latter is suggestive when it comes to prophetic formation because the prophet is motivated to ask not for judgment in general terms but specifically for a divine interruption of the "wife's" ability to produce and suckle children. He calls for the Lord to

---

10   Possibly hinting at the underlying motive for using a shrine prostitute, as a cultic justification for satisfying sexual desire.

ban motherhood in Israel, literally—or figuratively, that is, putting a stop to idolatry by divine judgment—or perhaps both, because the children produced by such mothers are illegitimate. The sentiment could naturally have roots in the prophet's experience in his own household.

Among the Lord's last statements of judgment through his prophet are two more oracles couched in terms of childbirth imagery. One is figurative and one is painfully literal. First, the figurative:

> Pains as of a woman in childbirth come to him,
>> but he is a child without wisdom;
> when the time arrives,
>> he doesn't have the sense to come out of the womb. (13:13)

Birth pangs are used figuratively here for incipient judgment. The first mention of them had to do with the Lord's judgment on our first mother (Gen. 3:16a), and subsequently the Spirit uses the idea figuratively in a number of judgment portrayals: foreign kings seized by "pain like that of a woman in labor" at God's favor toward Jerusalem and what it implies for them (Ps. 48:6), the mighty men of Moab (Jer. 48:41) and Edom (Jer. 49:22) on a day of judgment, Jerusalem before Babylonian captivity (Micah 4:10), and the world before the eschaton (Matt. 24:8; Rom. 8:22). The further indictment of Israel is that, even when such warnings of impending judgment come upon him, he does not understand their significance—like a baby who doesn't "have the sense to come out of the womb."

Hosea's next judgment statement is one of the more graphic in the Bible. It portrays pregnant mothers literally under judgment:

> The people of Samaria must bear their guilt,
>> because they have rebelled against their God.
> They will fall by the sword;
>> their little ones will be dashed to the ground,
>> their pregnant women ripped open. (13:16)

The judgments progress in severity: Israelites (adults presumably, since they are the ones who have "rebelled against their God") will fall by the sword but also their "little ones" who are presumably not yet of age—and not engaging in the adulterous behavior of their parents—"will be dashed to the ground." Moreover, "their pregnant women will be ripped open" showing a judgment on the unborn. The Lord himself will not exactly do this. He is not the agent. In fact, he condemns Ammon for doing this very thing to the pregnant women of Gilead (Amos 1:13). But the ones the Lord brings in fulfillment of his covenant curses will execute this horrible judgment. As was noted, one way the Lord judges an individual or a nation is by allowing an evil entity to have its way against that person or state. That will be the case with Israel.

The foregoing review should make it clear that marital and childbearing imagery, along with indictments of adultery and harlotry both literal and figurative (i.e., both physical and spiritual) play a notable role in the indictments and judgments Hosea, as a covenant lawsuit messenger, brings against the Lord's people. Although the Spirit works through the prophets or "carries them along" (cf. 2 Peter 1:21), it is nonetheless true that the Spirit works through prophets who are individuals. Each of those prophets has his own personality, his own literary and poetic gifting, and his own background, and all those factors play a role in both the propositional content and the aesthetic quality of his prophecies. Bishop Lowth was right when he ranked the major prophets in descending order according to their talent and skill *as poets*—Isaiah first, Jeremiah second, and Ezekiel third.[11] In addition to gifting, come those experiences a poet or prophet undergoes, and the way(s) they form him and contribute to the quality and content of his poetry.

In Hosea's case it seems clear the Lord caused the prophet to undergo a difficult life as husband of an adulterous woman and head of a household peopled with illegitimate children. Those experiences conditioned some of the utterances—the comparisons and the judgments—he brought against Israel. Still those utterances and judgments were not his own, but the Lord's. They were "God-breathed." Yet the Spirit did not operate alone. The Spirit worked with what was *in the prophet, as a man*, just as he works today in us and through us, operating within the limitations of those through whom he works, sometimes accommodating himself to those limitations, sometimes raising us to a higher level of accomplishment than anyone would expect given our limitations. One could reasonably doubt, for example, that Isaiah could have produced such exalted poetry *qua poetry* as he did—not to mention the revelatory content—had the Spirit not taken his natural poetic gifts and exalted them to a previously unknown level.

---

11   Robert Lowth, *Praelectio Vicesima Prima: Prophetarum Singulorum Proprii Characteres* in *De Sacra Poesi Hebraeorum*, (1753; reprint, Whitefish, MT: Kessinger Publishing, 2009), 281–85.

Prophetic Calls and How They Shape the Prophets: Isaiah

Some consider Isaiah's call to be his conversion experience. Although the report of Isaiah 6 would be consistent with that view, there are not sufficient data to confirm the interpretation. Beyond any doubt, however, Isaiah's call ranks with those of Moses and Paul for the sheer drama it offers a reader and for the life-changing influence it had on the prophet. One thing that stands out is the contrast Isaiah suddenly appreciates between the Lord's holiness and his own sinfulness:

> In the year that King Uzziah died, I saw the LORD, high and exalted, seated on a throne; and the train of his robe filled the temple. Above him were seraphim, each with six wings: With two wings they covered their faces, with two they covered their feet, and with two they were flying. And they were calling to one another:
>
>> "Holy, holy, holy is the LORD Almighty;
>> the whole earth is full of his glory."
>
> At the sound of their voices the doorposts and thresholds shook and the temple was filled with smoke. "Woe to me!" I cried. "I am ruined! For I am a man of unclean lips, and I live among a people of unclean lips, and my eyes have seen the King, the Lord Almighty." (6:1–5)

The seraphim and their relation to the four living creatures of Revelation 4 form the subject of a later discussion, but one can suggest in advance: although the creatures of Revelation 4 are routinely paralleled with the living creatures of Ezekiel 1, they are—according to form and function—more likely to be seraphim than cherubim.

The function of the angels is important. They surround the Lord's heavenly throne and declare his holiness (the so-called *trisagion*, the "thrice holy" they proclaim). The reaction of Isaiah is also important. The holiness of the Lord makes him aware of his own unholiness, and he declares himself unclean. The Lord provides a symbolic but effective solution to Isaiah's "godly sorrow": a seraph takes a coal from the altar and touches his "unclean" lips with it and so purifies them (and him) for a prophetic call that he is about to own.[12]

---

12   Keil and Delitzsch may be right in deriving the name "seraphim" (lit. "burning ones") from this symbolic act, but we do not know enough to be sure of this. The reason

What effect, beyond producing a state of mind amenable to a prophetic calling, did this encounter have on Isaiah? How did the encounter shape or begin to shape the prophet? No doubt it qualified him in ways one cannot know: it worked or began to work changes in his inner being that could only mean growth in understanding of himself and the world around him as well as growth in holiness—having the mind of God and thus God's point of view by the Spirit of God.

One evidence of Isaiah's transformation is his abundant use of the phrase "the Holy One of Israel" as he speaks of the Lord. Outside the book of Isaiah, the phrase occurs only five times, and one of those (2 Kings 19:22) is a copy of material from Isaiah's own book (or vice-versa—his prophecy regarding Sennacherib, Isa. 37:23). Three of them come from Psalms that apparently predate Isaiah (Pss. 71:22; 78:41; and 89:18), and one of them comes from Jeremiah (51:5). The other twenty-two occurrences of the phrase (twenty-three including the already mentioned Isa. 37:23) come from the book of Isaiah.[13] This is an extraordinary fact considering the widespread use of stock phrasing in the Old Testament and the ancient Near East—and surely this particular phrase was a candidate for wide use among biblical writers. One cannot account for its relative neglect by other biblical authors, but its abundant use by Isaiah can plausibly be traced to the overwhelming nature of a call to ministry that confronted him dramatically with the Lord's holiness and what that meant for his own fallen condition. The humbling work accomplished in the prophet may have put him in a frame of mind not only to declare the Lord's holiness again and again, but also to express such an important spiritual truth as one finds later in his book:

> For this is what the high and exalted One says—
>   he who lives forever, whose name is holy:
> "I live in a high and holy place,
>   but also with the one who is contrite and lowly in spirit,
> to revive the spirit of the lowly
>   and to revive the heart of the contrite." (57:15)

---

for the name could just as well be ontological (rather than functional, as they suggest) in some way we cannot understand in our present condition.

13   The phrase appears in Isaiah 1:4; 5:19, 24; 10:20; 12:6; 17:7; 29:19; 30:11, 12, 15; 31:1; 37:23; 41:14, 16, 20; 43:3; 45:11; 47:4; 48:17; 49:7 (2x); 54:5; 55:5; 60:9, 14. One might note that it occurs similarly in all three of the "three Isaiahs" imagined by some scholars (ten times in Isaiah 1–39, nine times in Isaiah 41–54, and three times in Isaiah 55–66). Apparently all three Isaiahs had the same view of the Lord's holiness.

and again

> This the one I regard:
> one who is of a poor and contrite spirit,
> and who trembles at my word. (66:2, author's translation)

Such information is important not only for Isaiah and his calling, but also for a proper approach to biblical revelation and to the living and supernal Lord who continues to reveal himself to those who humble themselves before him. In Isaiah's case, a dramatic encounter with the Lord of glory led him to see and amen with greater clarity One who was Lord of Israel and of his own life. Whether or not this was a conversion experience, it is true that anyone at any time is brought into a saving relationship with the Lord only by amening who he is and all that goes with that holy presence—including some degree of self-recognition on the individual's part (an awareness the Bible calls conviction). As it is the Spirit under the new covenant who convicts regarding sin, righteousness, and judgment, so for Isaiah it was the Glory-Presence of the Lord who is also Spirit that brought about such conviction. When the Lord called Isaiah to be a prophet, he not only called him to be a prophet, he began to *form* him to be a prophet—a humble person who trembled at God's word.

THE LORD SHAPES HIS PROPHETS:
THE WORD-CONFRONTATION GENRE

The Lord could shape his prophets by the manner of their calling. He could also shape them in and through opposition to their work. Because the prophets encountered opposition so often, the word-confrontation genre occurs a number of times in the records of their divinely ordained and divinely shaped ministries. As Micaiah was exemplary for word-confrontation among the non-writing prophets, Amos and Jeremiah are exemplary among the writing prophets.

Word-Confrontation Genre: Amos

The Lord sends Amos from the south to the north in the days of Jeroboam II, much as he had sent an unnamed "man of God" from the south to the north in the days of Jeroboam I (cf. 1 Kings 13).[14] Amos reports a confrontation with the priest Amaziah. The confrontation has all the elements of the acknowledged genre:

Word-Confrontation Genre Outline	Amos 7
Event	*Verses*
Prophet gives a word/words from Yahweh	10–11
Challenge to the prophet	12–13
Refutation of the challenge, by the prophet	14–15
Sentence on the challenger, by the prophet	16–17

Amos apparently gives a fairly full account of the confrontation and its development. Amaziah reports to king Jeroboam II (v. 10) some of the words of Amos' prophecy (v. 11). Amaziah challenges Amos to return to his place in the south and prophesy and earn his living there (v. 12). The implication is that Amos is somehow a prophet for hire—that he earns his living as a prophet. The charge has an implicit and unintended irony: it was precisely kings like Ahab and queens like Jezebel who had cadres of prophets who "ate at the table" of the ruler (cf. 1 Kings 18:19), and in this as in other things they patterned themselves after ancient near eastern kings (cf. Dan. 2:1). Amos refutes the implication: "I was neither a prophet nor the son of a prophet, but I was a shepherd, and I also took care of sycamore-fig trees" (v. 14). But what does it mean to be a son of a prophet?

It is important to be clear on the meaning of Amos' statement because he is indeed a prophet. By saying he was not a son of a prophet, he seems to allude to a pattern of prophetic discipleship in which *he never took part*. There are very few data on this concept.[15] The only place one gets a

---

14   The account includes the southern prophet's bizarre and fatal encounter with the unnamed "old prophet" in the north—a gem of laconic reporting! Apparently the old prophet was of dubious character—his lie led to his brother prophet's death—but nonetheless the Lord spoke words of prophecy through him.

15   The student would do well to be chary of scholars who write about "prophetic guilds" in the Old Testament as though a prophetic guild was a generally understood and well-documented type of organization. There is no evidence at all that anything like a medieval "guild" for prophets ever existed in Israel. The only evidence that comes close is not evidence for a guild, which is an institution for learning a trade, but rather for prophetic *discipleship*, which is a spiritual and ministerial calling, and it occurs in 2 Kings 2.

look at what it means to be a son of a prophet is in the events leading up to the apotheosis of Elijah, when the "sons of the prophets" at Bethel and Jericho come out to Elisha and tell him what he already knows: the Lord will take his master from over him that day (2 Kings 2:3, 5). Now Elisha is a true prophet—the disciple and successor of Elijah as the events of 2 Kings 2 show. If therefore the sons of the prophets share with Elisha a prediction he already knows, it seems clear that those sons of the prophets have prophetic anointing and are receiving a word from the Lord.

There is no evidence for such a thing as a medieval "guild" or "guilds" of prophets in the Old Testament. On the other hand, the New Testament may offer an analogy or parallel to the sons of the prophets: the disciples of Jesus. It is well known that the Hebrew term "son" can also mean "disciple." Moreover, Jesus was certainly a prophet—*the* prophet foretold by Moses (Deut. 18:15–19; cf. Acts 3:22–23). The following diagram illustrates the parallel:

Prophet	Jesus
Instruction	Instruction
Anointing	Anointing
"Son(s)" of prophet	Disciple(s) of Jesus
Kingdom work	Kingdom work

There will be occasion to revisit this dynamic pattern of spiritual instruction and commission when we consider the new covenant. A liberty is acknowledged here, namely, imputing to the sons of the prophets at Jericho and Bethel those aspects of discipleship one sees later in the ministry of Jesus—the instruction and the anointing. The latter (the anointing) is not actually reported in either case but is a given, because a true prophet can only prophesy by the Spirit, and the ministries to which Jesus sent his disciples could only be accomplished by the Spirit (e.g., healing, deliverance, and even gospel proclamation as part of that ministry, and on the analogy of John 6:63 and Acts 1:8; cf. John 14:17).

The meaning of Amos' refutation of Amaziah's imputation is consequently twofold. First, he was not a prophet or did not pretend to the office before the Lord sovereignly elected him to it. Second, he had no prophetic discipleship experience before his calling nor (apparently) after it. As for the sentence the Lord delivers through Amos, it suits its object:

> Your wife will become a prostitute in the city,
> and your sons and daughters will fall by the sword.

> Your land will be measured and divided up,
> and you yourself will die in a pagan country. (7:17)

The judgments on Amaziah's offspring and land (the middle verses) are flanked by judgments on his wife and himself. Now Amaziah was a priest—probably the high priest at Samaria (cf. Amos 7:10)—so the judgment on him and his wife is full of irony. His wife will become a prostitute and he himself will die in a pagan (lit. "unclean") land. The prospects for both Amaziah and his wife are "unclean." That judgment would carry a special sting for one who is a priest and for whom ritual cleanness—and one apparently could expect no deeper cleanness of Amaziah—would be especially offensive. On the other hand, it is appropriate for a man who led God's people into unclean worship.[16]

Word-Confrontation Genre: Jeremiah

Jeremiah was the most autobiographical of the covenant lawsuit prophets, and he underwent severe persecution because of his warnings about the coming Babylonian conquest of Judah.[17] The Lord knew Jere-

---

16 In other words, idolatry, which both the Old Testament and the New tell us involves the worship of demons, that is, "unclean" spirits (cf. Deut. 32:17 [NKJV, NASB, and HCSB, which correctly translate Hebrew שֵׁדִים as "demons"], 1 Cor. 10:20; demons are routinely referred to in the New Testament as unclean spirits, e.g., Matt. 10:1; 12:43; Mark 1:23, 26, 27; 3:11; 5:2; Acts 5:16; 8:7; etc.). One sees in the sentences pronounced on Amaziah and his wife, perhaps, the sort of biblical reality that may have formed part of the conceptual background for Dante when he composed the first third (the *Inferno*) of his *Commedia Divina*. The sense of justice one sees in Amos 7—making the punishment fit the crime—characterizes the imaginative judgments one finds in Dante's hell. In such a work, one sees true imagination—the poetic imagination—following the conceptual lead of the divine imagination in principle if not literally.

17 Arguably both the first person and third person portions of Jeremiah were produced by the prophet—whether directly composed or dictated to Baruch, his amanuensis (cf. 36:4). The shift between first person and third person passages in Jeremiah appears to be analogous to an ancient near eastern phenomenon; the same shift is found in Assyrian annals, and even to some extent in Hittite treaties and Ugaritic letters. Much of this material—in particular Jeremiah, the Assyrian annals, and the Hittite treaties—falls in the domain of covenant related literature: either treaties, or covenant lawsuit material, or covenant-based historiography. In all of these realms—Hebrew, Assyrian, and Hittite—the shift remains unexplained. Nonetheless, it was apparently a stylistically acceptable literary device for several centuries. If this proposal is correct, then the words of Jeremiah

miah would face strong opposition, so he assured the prophet when he commissioned him:

> Get yourself ready! Stand up and say to them whatever I command you. Do not be terrified by them, or I will terrify you before them. Today I have made you a fortified city, an iron pillar and a bronze wall to stand against the whole land—against the kings of Judah, its officials, its priests and the people of the land. They will fight against you but will not overcome you, for I am with you and will rescue you. (1:17–19)

The Lord had already assured Jeremiah his youth would be no obstacle to his ministry (1:7–8). The episode of his calling has been discussed in parallel with the callings of Moses and Isaiah.[18] The Lord now reassures Jeremiah, but the reassurance contains a challenge: "Do not be terrified by them, or I will terrify you before them." The Lord foretells the sort of opposition the prophet will face—opposition from the kings, officials, priests, and people. The prophet is subsequently persecuted by Judah's kings (e.g., 36:1–26), officials (e.g., 38:1–6), priests (e.g., 20:1–6), prophets (e.g., 28:1–17) and by the people (e.g., 11:8–23)—and by priests, prophets, and people together (e.g., 26:1–8). The present chapter examines three word-confrontation scenarios from his confrontational ministry.

Word-Confrontation at Anathoth

Since the people of Jeremiah's hometown want to kill him, his career illustrates, as well as any, one truth spoken by Jesus: "A prophet is not without honor except in his own town and in his own home" (Matt. 13:57).

Word-Confrontation Genre Outline	Jeremiah 11
Event	*Verses*
Prophet is given a word/words from Yahweh	1–17
Challenge to the prophet (revealed by Yahweh)	18–19, 21
Appeal to Yahweh, by the prophet	20
Sentence on the challenger, by the prophet	22–23

Because they do not like what Jeremiah has had to say, the men of

---

51:64 should be taken at face value: "Thus far are the words of Jeremiah" (NKJV). Jeremiah 52 then functions essentially as a short recapitulation of what has gone before (1–51).

18   Cf. chapter 6.

Anathoth have told him not to prophesy (11:21a). And they plan to murder him (11:19, 21b). It was noted—but cannot be emphasized enough—
that a sentence on those who resist the Lord's prophet is never a prophet's
own vindictive hope. It is the Lord's judgment. It may seem otherwise
when one first reads what Jeremiah says to the Lord at Anathoth:

> "Because the LORD revealed their plot to me, I knew it, for at that time
> he showed me what they were doing. I had been like a gentle lamb led to
> the slaughter; I did not realize that they had plotted against me, saying,
>
> > 'Let us destroy the tree and its fruit;
> >   let us cut him off from the land of the living,
> >   that his name be remembered no more.'
> > But you, O LORD Almighty, who judge righteously
> >   and test the heart and mind,
> >   let me see your vengeance on them,
> >   for to you I have committed my cause."
>
> Therefore this is what the LORD says about the people of Anathoth who
> are threatening to kill you, saying, "Do not prophesy in the name of the
> LORD or you will die by our hands"—therefore this is what the LORD Al-
> mighty says: "I will punish them. Their young men will die by the sword,
> their sons and daughters by famine. Not even a remnant will be left to
> them, because I will bring disaster on the people of Anathoth in the year
> of their punishment." (11:18–23)

Jeremiah seems to call vindictively to the Lord for vengeance on his
enemies, but that may not be the case because he prefaces his cry with an
affirmation: the Lord is one who judges righteously and who tests both
heart and mind (v. 20a). Moreover—consciously or unconsciously—he
shows prophetic affinity with the Suffering Servant promised by Isaiah:
"He was led like a lamb to the slaughter" (Isa. 53:7).[19] Like Jesus, he commits his cause to the Lord ("to you I have committed my cause," v. 20b; cf.
the authorities' mocking but true assertion, "He trusts in God. Let God
rescue him now if he wants him," Matt. 27:43; and cf. Luke 23:46)—but his
cause is in fact the Lord's cause. The Lord's answer shows this to be true.
He tells Jeremiah what he will do to those who have resisted his prophet
and thereby himself: "I will punish them. Their young men will die by

---

19 Cf. "I had been like a gentle lamb led to the slaughter" (11:19)

the sword, their sons and daughters by famine. Not even a remnant will be left to them, because I will bring disaster on the people of Anathoth in the year of their punishment" (11:22–23). Like the Lord's judgment on Canaan, the judgment pronounced on the whole town of Anathoth may seem inordinate. But humans are in no position to assess the mind of the Lord or his rationale for what he does. One can understand some fundamental ideas: (1) God is the Judge of all the earth, and (2) he will do what is right (Gen. 18:25). When it comes to individual cases, however, humans are in no position to judge. In some cases, God's judgment may obviously be just. In other cases, it may not obviously be just. In such cases, one does better to amen the Lord—to trust God's revealed nature—than to play the judge oneself, which is another way of wanting to be like Elohim.

Word-Confrontation in Jerusalem with Passhur

Passhur was an official in charge of the temple of the Lord. He heard Jeremiah prophesying disaster for Jerusalem and the surrounding towns (20:1; cf. chap. 19), and as retribution he had the prophet beaten and put in the stocks overnight:

Word-Confrontation Genre Outline	Jeremiah 19–20
Event	*Verses*
Prophet gives a word/words from Yahweh	19:1–15; cf. 20:1
Challenge to the prophet	20: 2
Refutation of the challenge, by the prophet	20: 3
Sentence on the challenger, by the prophet	20:4–6

Being put in the stocks overnight may seem more like a comic episode than a serious affliction, but in an Iron Age society it was no joke. A person put in the stocks could undergo serious abuse. Short of that, the mere detention of the Lord's prophet showed contempt for the Lord himself—or perhaps more charitably, lack of faith that this prophet really was the Lord's prophet. The sentence on the perpetrator is accordingly severe: "For this is what the LORD says: 'I will make you a terror to yourself and to all your friends; with your own eyes you will see them fall by the sword of their enemies,'" 20:4); and again: "And you, Pashhur, and all who live in your house will go into exile to Babylon. There you will die and be buried, you and all your friends to whom you have prophesied lies," (20:6). Without sounding sententious, one could observe that the Judge of all the earth is not one to be trifled with.

Word-Confrontation in Jerusalem with Hananiah

Jeremiah is challenged later by the prophet Hananiah and they encounter one another in the temple before both priests and people:

Word-Confrontation Genre Outline	Jeremiah 27–28
Event	*Verses*
Prophet gives a word/words from Yahweh	27:1–22
Challenge to the prophet	28:1–4, 10–11
Refutation of the challenge, by the prophet	28:12–14
Sentence on the challenger, by the prophet	28:15–16

Hananiah is a prophet (Isa. 28:1), and in the temple before Jeremiah and the people he prophesies that the Lord will restore within two years all that Nebuchadnezzar has taken from Jerusalem, including prince Jehoiakin, the captive people, and the articles of the Lord's house (Jer. 28:3–4). He also prophesies that the Lord will break the Babylonian yoke, and as a demonstration he breaks a symbolic wooden yoke Jeremiah had made at the Lord's instruction (vv. 10–11, cf. 27:1–7). Although Hananiah's prophecy contradicts the Lord's prophecy given through Jeremiah in Isaiah 27, Jeremiah does not respond defensively or aggressively. He says: "Amen! May the LORD do so! May the LORD fulfill the words you have prophesied by bringing the articles of the LORD's house and all the exiles back to this place from Babylon" (Jer. 28:6). But he reminds everyone of other prophets' predictions of international disaster (28:7–8) and then adds: "But the prophet who prophesies peace will be recognized as one truly sent by the LORD only if his prediction comes true" (28:9).

Three things stand out in Jeremiah's response. First, past prophets have predicted disaster for many kingdoms. That confirms what has been said: the chief role of covenant lawsuit prophets was to bring warnings and indictments. If Israel and the nations were being faithful to God, there would be virtually no need of their prophetic ministry. Second, Jeremiah hopes Hannaniah is right (28:6). The prophet may have to prophesy disaster, but he does not want to see it come. Third, Jeremiah does not try to defend himself or his record; he only reminds everyone of the Mosaic standard of prophecy: "If what a prophet proclaims in the name of the LORD does not take place or come true, that is a message the LORD has not spoken. That prophet has spoken presumptuously, so do not be alarmed" (Deut. 18:22). Jeremiah's righteousness is apparent in all three matters—in other words, he conforms to God's nature in three ways: (1)

he is obedient in his role of covenant lawsuit messenger; (2) like God, he does not want to see sinners perish; (3) he nonetheless adheres to God's standard of prophecy. The Lord has called him to a prophetic role, and unfortunately he must predict disaster.

The Hannaniah episode is not yet over. After he leaves Hannaniah, another word of the Lord comes to Jeremiah:

> Go and tell Hananiah, "This is what the LORD says: You have broken a wooden yoke, but in its place you will get a yoke of iron. This is what the LORD Almighty, the God of Israel, says: I will put an iron yoke on the necks of all these nations to make them serve Nebuchadnezzar king of Babylon, and they will serve him. I will even give him control over the wild animals." (28:13–14)

Jeremiah conveys the word to Hannaniah and, along with it, the Lord's death sentence on the false prophet (28:15–16). His death is then reported (28:17). The message was not Jeremiah's, but the Lord's. The death sentence is not Jeremiah's, but the Lord's. The one who rejected the Lord's prophet has not only rejected the Lord's prophet, but has also rejected the Lord.

Significance of the Word-Confrontations

The significance of word-confrontations for the prophets' contemporaries would have been clear. They were the Lord's messengers, and if one rejected them, one rejected the One who sent them. Paul taught that these and other matters of life under the old covenant were written for our instruction. The principle enshrined in the old word-confrontations becomes clear in Jesus' teaching (as the word-controversies are the converse of Matt. 10:40–42). That is what matters to us. We have not to do with covenant lawsuit prophets, but with Jesus, the life-giving Spirit whose Spirit-Gospel convicts us regarding sin, righteousness, and judgment. Those who reject his messengers reject him, and those who reject him reject the One who sent him.

NEW COVENANT PROMISE AND PROPHETIC EXPERIENCE

The covenant lawsuit prophets of the Mosaic covenant had to experience opposition and persecution, but sometimes they got to experience wonderful and redemptive revelations of the Lord's future intent. One such revelation appears in their predictions of another covenant for all God's people—a covenant that would be different in fundamental ways from the Mosaic covenant. Jeremiah calls it the "new covenant" (Jer. 31:31) and an "everlasting covenant" (Jer. 32:40). Isaiah and Ezekiel call it the "covenant of peace" (Isa. 54:10; Ezek. 34:25; 37:26) and "everlasting" (Isa. 55:3; Ezek. 16:60). Although the Lord termed almost every covenant he made with people after the Adamic covenant (which is not even called a covenant) an "everlasting covenant"—for example, the Noahic (Gen. 9:16), the Abrahamic (Gen. 17:7, 13, 19; 1 Chron. 16:17), the Sabbath as a sign of the Mosaic (Exod. 31:16; cf. the bread of the Sabbath apparently associated with it, Lev. 24:8), the Davidic (2 Sam. 23:5) and the new covenant (Heb. 13:20)—we know the Hebrew word commonly translated "everlasting" (עולם) does not always mean everlasting, so the meaning has to be be understood from the context in which it occurs. [20] Agreeably, reiteration of some key covenantal points is in order as we depart the prophets of the Mosaic covenant, because only one divine-human covenant is truly everlasting, and it is the one foretold by Isaiah, Jeremiah, and Ezekiel.

Accordingly, the Noahic covenant does not last forever because the Noahic ends when the earth it governs passes away; the Abrahamic covenant no longer functions because the sign of admission to and membership in it (namely, circumcision) has been abrogated; the Mosaic covenant, as the author of Hebrews says, was faulty and passing away (8:7–13; cf. 10:9), and as Paul says, Christ canceled it on the cross (Col. 2:14). The Davidic covenant is called everlasting, although its "sure mercies" are associated with the everlasting (new) covenant prophesied by Isaiah (Isa. 55:3). This will come under discussion when we consider the Davidic covenant, but for now it is affirmed that the Davidic covenant has been fulfilled in Christ. So there is no room for other kings of Israel who, like David, would live under the Mosaic covenant, and no further fulfillment of the Davidic covenant by human kings on earth.

The prophecies of Jeremiah 31:31–34 and Ezekiel 16:60–63 are remarkably parallel as they anticipate this new covenant.[21] Isaiah, Jeremiah, and Ezekiel, then, were privileged to report this covenant to come. The new

---

20   Cf. also the Lord's "covenant of salt," which he makes for the Aaronic priesthood, "a covenant of salt forever" (Num. 18:19).

21   As A. B. Davidson, *The Book of Ezekiel*, 116–17 notes: "The Lord will substitute for the old covenant which was broken an 'everlasting' covenant, cf. ch. xxxvii. 26; Is. liv. 9, 10, lv. 3; Jer. xxxi. 35, 36; xxxii. 40, xxxiii. 20–22. The covenant will be everlasting because he will forgive their sins (Jer. xxxi. 34), and write his law (v. 33), and put his fear

covenant was already implied in the promise of a prophet like Moses (Deut. 18:15) but has received fuller articulation through subsequent covenant lawsuit prophets. God shows his consistency here: just as he promised a savior when he brought the first covenant lawsuit in Genesis 3, so later he promises a new and better covenant when his prophets bring his covenant lawsuits to Israel—when, like Adam, his people had broken the Lord's commandments—their covenant with the Lord.[22] Those covenant lawsuit prophets are like the Lord in another way: they bring a new covenant promise in the midst of a present covenant disaster. How much of this parallelism they understood we do not know. But they experienced in their own limited and human way, although also moved by the Spirit, something of the conflict the Lord must have felt when, in faithfulness to his own nature—in his righteousness—he brought that first lawsuit and with it the promise of redemption.

CONCLUSION

Jesus the Son who brought and *who was* the new covenant (Isa. 49:8, "I . . . will make you to be a covenant for the people," lit. "I . . . will give you [as] a covenant for the people," ואתנך לברית עם) validated the relevance of covenant lawsuit prophetic experience for his own followers when he said, "Blessed are you when people insult you, persecute you and falsely say all kinds of evil against you because of me. Rejoice and be glad, because great is your reward in heaven, for *in the same way they persecuted the prophets* who were before you" (Matt. 5:11–12, emphasis added). He also stated a fundamental principle: "Blessed are those

---

(xxxii. 40) in their hearts; giving them a new heart and putting his spirit within them (Ezek. xxxvi. 26)."

22 There is thus some parallelism between the Adamic covenant and the Mosaic, and the parallelism we are considering exists because both covenants had commands. Neither covenant is of itself *salvific*, however. In each case, a covenant was made, and in each case the covenant contained conditions that, if violated, would mean the implementation of covenant curses. Nonetheless, in each case the covenant continued even after the failure of the vassal to do the work required by the covenant. So Adam and his descendants continued after their exile from Eden; so Israel continued after their exile from the Promised Land. Cf. discussion in the Introduction to volume 2. Agreeably we add: The Lord did not save Israel by the Mosaic covenant, any more than he saved Noah by the Noahic covenant. The Lord saved Noah, and then made a covenant with him. The Lord saved Israel, and then made a covenant with them.

who are persecuted *because of righteousness*, for theirs is the kingdom of heaven" (Matt. 5:10, emphasis added).

The enemies of God persecuted the prophets and would persecute Jesus and his followers "because of righteousness"—that is, because in their persons and work they *conformed to the nature of God* who is *the standard of what a human should be* and whose words and acts were the standard of prophetic deeds and utterance. God's enemies consitutionally react with *hostility to righteousness* because they are in their own *Dasein antithetical to God's nature*. Jesus, by stating this principle, stated the ground of hostility—and hostilities—by the kingdom of darkness against the kingdom of light, as God's kingdom irrupts into the world. The next chapter explores some aspects of that conflict as it appears in the missional failure of Israel under the old covenant, a failure also addressed by the covenant lawsuit prophets of that covenant.

CHAPTER SIXTEEN

THE MISSIONAL PROMISE AND FAILURE OF THE MOSAIC COVENANT

The irruption of God's kingdom into the world by gospel proclamation and signs and wonders has not ceased. The sort of news reported from the mission field in, for example, Colombia is far from unusual in today's world, and it gives a glimpse of the most powerful sort of power encounter that can take place through the church: the power encounter that brings a person out of the darkness and into the wonderful light of Christ.[1] But what the article says of Colombia is also true elsewhere. The spiritual unity of the church and revival, including miracles of healing, deliverance, and gifts of the Spirit are happening in Colombia and around the world. In a land now famous (or infamous) for the chaos its drug lords produce in the lives of people, a superior Lord is winning some people into a more enduring kingdom.

Both Testaments prefigure such events, and even give a glimpse of what they would look like through the ministry of Jesus and the apostles. But the Old Testament generally presents a very different state of affairs. There, in spite of the Lord's revelations of himself, and in spite of

---

1 Cf. "Revival Breaks Out amidst Civil War," *Everyhome Magazine*, June 2014 (Colorado Springs, CO: Every Home for Christ), 11–12.

This chapter was occasioned by the seriously flawed view that the new covenant is a renewal of the old. The view has implications for Pentecost, viewing the endowment of the Spirit then as emphatically an endowment for missions and ignoring the implications of John 14:17. My attention was first drawn to this view by Scott Hafemann (personal conversation). Cf. N. T. Wright, *Justification* (Downers Grove, IL: InterVarsity Press, 2009), 246, who says of Pentecost, "This is the renewal of the covenant. That is why there now needs to be a Gentile mission."

his gracious creation of a covenant people after rescuing them from the grip of one of the world's greatest and most oppressive powers, we find him appealing again and again through the covenant lawsuit prophets to a stiff-necked and rebellious people. What accounts for this difference?

The Mosaic covenant began with a power and glory of divine presence unknown—or at least unreported—in the ancient world since Eden, when God was present with his people but also, after the Fall, appeared in storm theophany to judge them. God's judgment came with a promise: the woman's seed would bruise the serpent's head, a promise that was fulfilled by the resurrection and continues to be fulfilled as the Spirit of Christ advances the church in Colombia and around the world.

The combination of present judgment and future promise first occurred in Genesis 3, but was subsequently to appear often in those prophets who were covenant lawsuit messengers under the Mosaic covenant. The very need for such covenant lawsuit prophets shows the failure inescapably bound up with the Mosaic covenant. In that Mosaic covenant failure lies the answer to the question, Why does one not see the sort of spiritual dynamism and advance of God's kingdom among the nations in the Old Testament that one sees in the new? It will be helpful to understand what the Mosaic covenant (the "law") could and could not do for an old covenant believer, and what the Spirit *can* do for a new covenant believer, before one considers what the Spirit can do *through* a new covenant believer in fulfillment of the Great Commission.[2]

WHAT THE LAW COULD AND COULD NOT DO

As Paul wrote, "The law is holy, and the commandment is holy, righteous and good" (Rom. 7:12). Nonetheless, the law, although it imparted God's standard, did not impart God's Spirit who alone could help God's people obey the law. That was the defect of the Mosaic covenant. That is why the author of Hebrews wrote: "If there had been nothing wrong with that first covenant, no place would have been sought for another" (8:7). Of course fault was also found with the people because they did not (could not)

---

2   The issue of the spiritual difference between the old covenant and the new has been touched on at several points, and will be discussed more fully in chapter 2 of volume 3. We consider it now with special reference to the issue of mission and the people's representation of God in his world. It is remarkable how many students today do not understand this difference.

obey the law (8:8). But that was precisely the problem with life under the Mosaic covenant—that was what was "wrong with that first covenant"—and Paul demonstrates the problem memorably in Romans 7: that is, the person who lives under the law agrees that it is holy, righteous, and good, yet lacks the power to fulfill it.

The work of Christ and the mission of the Holy Spirit make life under the new covenant dynamically superior: "What the law was powerless to do because it was weakened by the flesh, God did by sending his own Son in the likeness of sinful flesh to be a sin offering. And so he condemned sin in the flesh, in order that *the righteous requirement of the law might be fully met in us, who do not live according to the flesh but according to the Spirit*" (Rom. 8:3–4, emphasis added) and again, "For if you live according to the flesh, you will die; but *if by the Spirit you put to death the misdeeds of the body*, you will live" Rom. 8:13, emphasis added). "The power of sin is the law" (1 Cor. 15:56) but by the power of the Spirit in the new covenant, "We know that our old self was crucified with him so that the body ruled by sin might be done away with, that *we should no longer be slaves to sin*" (Rom. 6:6, emphasis added). We in Christ do not live perfectly but we ought to affirm with the apostle: "Sin shall no longer be your master, *because you are not under the law, but under grace*" (Rom. 6:14, emphasis added). We stress these points because they are at the foundation of the Christian life and also because they should make obvious the error of those who teach that the new covenant is a renewal of the old (Mosaic) covenant. The new covenant is indeed, as its given name naturally conveys, *new—"not like* the covenant / [God] made with their forefathers / when [he] took them by the hand / to lead them out of Egypt" (Jer. 31:32, emphasis added)—and life under it is governed by an utterly different dynamic than life under the old covenant: that of the promised Holy Spirit, who enables us to obey God's standards to a degree Old Testament believers could not do, and to be the witnesses to the world that Old Testament believers almost always failed to be.[3]

The Lord did not send Israel on an evangelistic mission, but he certainly wanted Israel to be his witnesses to the world:

---

3   For the Old Testament promise of the Spirit and the very different life his indwelling would produce, cf. Ezekiel 36:27: "I will put my Spirit in you and move you to follow my decrees and be careful to keep my laws." Further discussion of these matters appears in chapter 5 of volume 3.

See, I have taught you decrees and laws as the Lord my God commanded me, so that you may follow them in the land you are entering to take possession of it. Observe them carefully, for this will show your wisdom and understanding to the nations, who will hear about all these decrees and say, "Surely this great nation is a wise and understanding people." What other nation is so great as to have their gods near them the way the LORD our God is near us whenever we pray to him? And what other nation is so great as to have such righteous decrees and laws as this body of laws I am setting before you today? (Deut. 4:5–8)

The Lord knew that if Israel obeyed the Mosaic covenant it would make them winsome in the eyes of the world around them, and more importantly show the winsomeness of Lord who saved them and gave them his great and wonderful law. Yet the very existence of the book of Deuteronomy implied that such would not be the case.

Deuteronomy constituted a renewal on the plains of Moab of the covenant the Lord had made with Israel at Sinai nearly forty years before. The Lord made this covenant renewal once the generation with whom he had made the covenant at Sinai had all passed away (except for Moses and Joshua). That generation had died in the wilderness because of their unfaithfulness: "Who were they who heard and rebelled? Were they not all those Moses led out of Egypt? And with whom was he angry for forty years? Was it not with those who sinned, whose bodies perished in the wilderness? And to whom did God swear that they would never enter his rest if not to those who disobeyed?" (Heb. 4:16–18).[4] The Lord knew that, as Israel had been disobedient in the past, they could and would be disobedient in the future. Nonetheless, he graciously renewed the Sinai covenant with them on the plains of Moab, with the hope expressed in Deuteronomy 4 through Moses.

That hope would not be fulfilled under the old covenant. There were rare exceptions of pagans who came to faith, such as Rahab the Canaanite prostitute and Ruth the Moabitess, both of whom became members of the Mosaic covenant community—the former appearing in the honor

---

4   Cf. the comments by Paul earlier: "Moreover, brethren, I do not want you to be unaware that all our fathers were under the cloud, all passed through the sea, all were baptized into Moses in the cloud and in the sea, all ate the same spiritual food, and all drank the same spiritual drink. For they drank of that spiritual Rock that followed them, and that Rock was Christ. But with most of them God was not well pleased, for their bodies were scattered in the wilderness" (1 Cor. 10:1–5 NKJV).

roll of faith in Hebrews (Heb. 11:31), the latter becoming the ancestress of David (Ruth 4:16–17). There was the exceptional case of Nineveh, which repented at the preaching of Jonah and was spared God's judgment for a time under common grace, although there is no indication that the people of Nineveh ever entered the Mosaic covenant. Encouraging as those examples may be, the Old Testament makes it clear that God's people did not win the nations over to the Lord, nor did they even, on the whole, make an impression on them, as Moses hoped they might, by their obedience to the God-given law. To an outsider they looked like any other nation, as the boast of the Assyrian field commander suggests:

> Do not let Hezekiah mislead you when he says: "The LORD will deliver us." Have the gods of any nations ever delivered their lands from the hand of the king of Assyria? Where are the gods of Hamath and Arpad? Where are the gods of Sepharvaim? Have they rescued Samaria from my hand? Who of all the gods of these countries have been able to save their lands from me? How then can the LORD deliver Jerusalem from my hand? (Isa. 36:18–20)

To an Assyrian field commander, the Hebrews looked like any other polytheistic nation ripe for Assyrian conquest.[5] This was a partial fulfillment of the prophetic assessment of Israel made ironically at the end of Deuteronomy in the song the Lord told Moses to take up as a witness against his people. They rejected the God who made them (32:15) and made him jealous with their foreign gods (32:16), so he would bring judgment on them by a foreign nation (along with other judgments, 32:19–25).[6]

---

5 The field commander also attributes his campaign against Judah to the Lord ("Have I now come up without the LORD against this land to destroy it? The LORD said to me, 'Go up against this land, and destroy it,'" Isa. 36:10). This is a propaganda ploy on his part, although his statement contained a theological truth he may have partly understood (since pagans did think the gods of nations could punish the nations subject to them), but was not in a position fully to understand.

6 The covenant lawsuit form of Deuteronomy 32 may be set forth simply as follows:
1 Call to witnesses ("heaven and earth"), who will witness the unfolding lawsuit (Deut. 32:1–2).
2 Statement of the case (including identification of Suzerain, Deut. 32:3–6).
3 Suzerain's faithfulness to the covenant = historical review (Deut. 32:7–14).
4 Indictment(s) (Deut. 32:15–18).
5 Sentence pronounced (Deut. 32:19–29).

OLD COVENANT FAILURE, NEW COVENANT PROMISE

Just as the old covenant did not give people the power to obey it—and accordingly progress in God as a nation-state under him—it agreeably did not endow them with power to be God's witnesses to the nations around them. The endowment of that power would only come, as promised, under the new covenant: "But you will receive power when the Holy Spirit comes on you; and you will be my witnesses in Jerusalem, and in all Judea and Samaria, and to the ends of the earth" (Acts 1:8). This is the fulfillment of what Paul called the promise of the Spirit ("that the blessing of Abraham might come upon the Gentiles in Christ Jesus, that we might receive the promise of the Spirit through faith," Gal. 3:14) implicit in the Lord's promise to Abraham: "In you all the families of the earth shall be blessed" (Gen. 12:3).

That mission of the Spirit makes the believer a temple of the Spirit, and being temples of the Spirit has something to do with the advance of God's kingdom through us. No person is ever called a temple of the Holy Spirit in the Old Testament. Jesus is the first one to apply the term to a human,

---

The form corresponds to the covenant form in which it is rooted, presented here as the genres appear, *mutatis mutandis*, in the Old Testament:

Covenant	*Covenant Lawsuit*
	Witnesses (to unfolding lawsuit)
Title = Yahweh as King	Title = Yahweh as Judge
Historical Prologue (Yahweh's good deeds)	Historical Review (Yahweh's good deeds)
Stipulations	Indictments (broken stipulations)
Witnesses (to terms of the covenant)	
Blessing	Promise of restoration
Curse	Judgment pronounced

Only in biblical covenant lawsuits (as contrasted with pagan covenant lawsuits) do promises of restoration or salvation occur along with judgment announcements. The Lord set that pattern in the first covenant lawsuit in Genesis 3, where he brought judgments but also promised a savior, and subsequent biblical covenant lawsuits display the same combination of judgment and grace. Like the covenants themselves, the Lord's covenant lawsuits also display his character, which is both uncompromisingly holy and gracious. Hence the oft noted pattern of alternating doom and salvation in the oracles of the prophets. For some Hittite and Assyrian covenant lawsuits, cf. Jeffrey J. Niehaus, *Amos* in volume 1 of *The Minor Prophets: An Exegetical and Expository Commentary: Hosea, Joel, and Amos*, ed. Thomas Edward McComiskey (Grand Rapids: Baker, 1992), 318–20.

when he identifies himself as a temple (John 2:19). It seems it was God's plan not to have the Spirit reside in people until the Spirit resided in the Son and accomplished his earthy mission. Perhaps that was so they could be justified by faith in the risen and ascended Christ—justified by faith in the now fully revealed Christ—and only then receive the Spirit of Christ who began to sanctify them. Whatever God's reason, it is only after the ascension that people are called temples of the Spirit. The Spirit's advent at Pentecost was apparently the start of such an endowment, even if it also had the effect of enabling the recipients to speak in the tongues of foreigners present. The constitution of people as temples and the first great missional work of the church thus coincide. That also makes perfect sense if we consider the biblical use of water as a metaphor for the Spirit, and how that water metaphor relates to the temple and blesses the nations.

The association of water and the Spirit is well known, but one occurrence of it has special importance for the human temple: "'Whoever believes in me, as Scripture has said, rivers of living water will flow from within him.' By this he meant the Spirit, whom those who believed in him were later to receive. Up to that time the Spirit had not been given, since Jesus had not yet been glorified" (John 7:38–39). Those who would receive the Spirit would become temples of the Spirit, and from them the Spirit-water would flow. That dynamic is a key to understanding two eschatological temple passages, Ezekiel 47 and Revelation 22. The Lord shows both Ezekiel and John essentially the same vision of a future, eschatological temple reality. That vision shows the pattern of our being:

Thematic Parallels	Ezekiel 47	Revelation 22
Water flows from temple/throne of God and the Lamb	v. 1	v. 1
Fruit trees/tree of life grows along the river	v. 12	v. 2
Leaves will not wither, nor fruit fail	v. 12	v. 2
Will bear every month, because water from the sanctuary flows into it/them	v. 12	v. 2
Fruit for food [implicitly], leaves for healing [of the nations, Rev.]	v. 12	v. 2

The eschatological temple vision shows water flowing from the Lord's presence. The water nourishes trees, whose fruit is for food and whose leaves are for *healing of the nations* (Rev. 22:12). The eschatological picture is in one sense a restoration of what was lost at Eden, as another schematic shows:

Parallel Themes	Ezekiel 47	Revelation 22	Genesis 2
River flows from temple/throne of Lamb	v. 1	v. 1	v. 10
Tree of life	v. 12	v. 2	v. 9

The eschatological scenario replicates and amplifies the original Eden scenario. The Son of Man does indeed come to restore what was lost. The restoration involves, and is partly accomplished by, fulfillment of the Abrahamic promise (Gen. 12:3; 18:18; 22:18) reiterated to Isaac (Gen. 26:4) and Jacob (Gen. 28:14)—the Abrahamic blessing to all nations that comes by the Holy Spirit, through faith in Christ.

The temple scenarios pictured above make an important point for missions: "On each side of the river stood the tree of life, bearing twelve crops of fruit, yielding its fruit every month. And the leaves of the tree are for the *healing of the nations*" (Rev. 22:2, emphasis added). For the nations to receive that supernal and final healing, which comes about as sin is destroyed and all things are restored, they must first know the fulfillment of the Abrahamic promise on earth and in this life. They can do so when members of the church—the temples of the Spirit—allow the Spirit to bring healing through them for the nations: the healing that comes with knowledge of the Savior who is head of the church, for example: "Believe in the Lord Jesus, and you will be saved" (σωθήσῃ, which can also be translated, "you will be healed" [i.e., of your sins], Acts 16:31; cf. Rom. 10:9–10).[7] It is no accident that healing and salvation are so closely associated in the New Testament, for example, "He himself bore our sins in his body on the cross, so that we might die to sins and live for righteousness; by his wounds you have been healed" (1 Peter 2:24, quoting Isa. 53:5).

It should be clear from the above that it is only under the new covenant that God's people have the power of the Spirit both to represent God better in their personal lives and to represent him evangelistically to the nations—to allow the Spirit to flow through them as temples and bring healing to the nations.[8] The Great Commission—which has no

---

7   The Greek verb σῴζω can mean save (in the technical, soteriological sense) but also heal, cure, make well, for example, Matthew 9:22; Mark 10:52; Luke 17:19; and James 5:15.

8   And so they echo the Eden temple and anticipate the eschatological temple presence of the Lord—as well as being patterned after his incarnate presence—and so the Son

counterpart in the Old Testament—and the promise of the Spirit fulfilled at Pentecost with its concomitant promise of evangelical witness, which also has no counterpart in the Old Testament, also make this clear.

MISSION AND THE FORM OF GOD'S KINGDOM IN THE TWO COVENANTS

The spiritual conclusions stated above are also consistent with the differing forms of God's kingdom under the old covenant and under the new. The form of God's kingdom under the old covenant was a nation of people—fundamentally an ethnic unity—who by means of the Conquest began to become a nation-state with its own laws and was often under attack from other nation-states or empires. People under that covenant and in that state were called on to show God's nature by their obedience to God's covenant, but they were not called on to travel to other lands and make converts to the Lord of their covenant. By contrast, the form of God's kingdom under the new covenant is the church, not a nation-state and not an ethnic unity, but rather an entity composed of increasingly various ethnicities (*ethnoi*) and finding its place in many nations—an entity, in other words, *unlike a state*. It does not have geographical boundaries, it does not have the sort of laws used to govern a state (e.g., it has no death penalty) and it does not employ the sort of warfare used to conquer territory and thereby execute God's judgment on those who occupy that territory, as was the case with the old covenant form of God's kingdom. It is, however, incumbent upon the church to let the nations know of God's coming judgment on all nations.

If one asks what the average Israelite probably thought of his or her role vis-à-vis the nations, any answer one tries to give would be mostly speculation. That is inevitable. None of us can speak with perfect knowledge about our own contemporaries. Even our own family members inevitably remain to some extent unfathomed by us because each of us is bound up in his or her own skin. How much greater, then, the challenge if we are asked to explain the attitudes of a person or persons who lived three millennia ago in a very different world—different materially, culturally, and spiritually.

God's kingdom under the old covenant has been characterized as a

---

on earth was the sinless ectype of the divine type who is the paradigm for all true temples (cf. Ezek. 1:28).

nation-state. Historians like to say that nationalism, at least in the form it has been known in modern times, was largely aroused by the tumult of such combined forces as the Enlightenment (which, although it was congenial to the cosmopolitanism of a Goethe, was also instrumental in undercutting the international vision of a Christian church) and the Romanticism that arose contemporaneous with the American and French revolutions. It is also true, however, that some sense of national or ethnic pride resided in ancient Rome; and even as far back as the days of ancient Israel and before, the Egyptians and Assyrians (to cite two examples) had a strong sense of ethnic and cultural identity and superiority. There is evidence for such attitudes even within the Old Testament. Note the comment by Naaman the Syrian when told by Elisha to bathe in the Jordan: "Are not Abana and Pharpar, the rivers of Damascus, better than all the waters of Israel? Couldn't I wash in them and be cleansed?" (2 Kings 5:12); and also the remark by Gehazi: "My master was too easy on Naaman, this Aramean, by not accepting from him what he brought" (2 Kings 5:20). One may see also in Jonah's reluctance to bring salvation to Nineveh some sense of Israelite identity and some tinge of Israelite resentment at the historical power and success of the brutally oppressive nation Assyria.

If one reckons that ancient Israelites may have had sentiments like those of Jonah, one can well imagine that any sense of representing God winsomely to the nations would not have been predominant among them, even though the Lord had made it clear that he wanted such representation. The history of Israel is sufficient testimony of their failure to honor the Lord when it came to even more fundamental instructions of the Mosaic covenant—such as for instance the first commandment.[9]

SUMMARY OBSERVATIONS

The Lord made it clear first to the patriarchs and then to Israel during the final formulation of the Mosaic covenant and subsequently through

---

9   Such facts and observations notwithstanding, it does appear the Lord established and has maintained the idea of ethnic/national boundaries:

"When the Most High gave to the nations their inheritance,
    when he divided mankind,
he fixed the borders of the peoples
    according to the number of the sons of God" (Deut. 32:8 ESV).

the prophets, that he wanted his people to show the nations around them the true and winsome character of the Lord. They could only do so by demonstrating in their own lives what it looked like to live according to the Lord's standards—in other words, *to be righteous*. That would have represented the Lord to the nations.

Such a task, however, was beyond them. The seemingly endless ups and downs of God's people under the Mosaic covenant, the apparently unavoidable historical cycle of failure, intervention by the Lord to set them right, and failure again, all leading eventually and seemingly inexorably to the Lord's judgment on, first, the northern kingdom, and then Judah—the whole canvas of Israel's history shows what Jesus made sharply clear in the Sermon on the Mount: the law set an impossibly high standard for Israel, and they needed the Son of God to fulfill it for them. It was a standard *only he* could fulfill because it was, after all, an expression of the Lord's own covenantal and perfect nature—of his righteousness also because he always conforms to his own nature, or, put another way, is always true to himself.

The inability of Israel to represent the Lord faithfully within their own boundaries, let alone carry anything like a saving message from him beyond those boundaries to other nations—with the singular case of the unwilling Jonah apparently the exception that proved the rule—showed the need for some future hope for the nations, a hope that Israel herself could not provide. The prophets give voice to that future hope, and especially Isaiah:

> A bruised reed he will not break,
> and a smoldering wick he will not snuff out.
> In faithfulness he will bring forth justice;
> He will not falter or be discouraged
> Till he establishes justice on earth.
> In his teaching the islands will put their hope. (42:3–4)

And again:

> I, the Lord, have called you in righteousness;
> I will take hold of your hand.
> I will keep you and will make you
> to be a covenant for the people
> and a light for the Gentiles,
> to open eyes that are blind,

> to free captives from prison
> and to release from the dungeon those who sit in darkness.
>   (42:6–7)

The literature of the Old Testament shows (1) the global promise the Lord made to Abraham, (2) how Israel could never deliver on that promise, and (3) how one future individual, the Servant who would be all that Israel failed to be, would fulfill that promise. It remained for the New Testament to make clear just how the Servant would do so—by his Spirit through his fellow servants, the church.

ELISHA'S DOUBLE PORTION AND ITS PROMISE

One memorable Old Testament passage touches on the expansive promise of the new covenant. It adumbrates that future hope in an oblique way, and it shows a principle or a pattern of divine activity that has occurred with signal prophets. A point of departure for considering the pattern can be found in the relationship of Elijah and Elisha.

Elisha made a bold request of his master—he asked for a double portion of Elijah's Spirit. One ought to capitalize "Spirit," because in fact Elijah had no proprietary spirit to give: the Spirit who had been operating through him was the Lord's Spirit. Elisha apparently got what he asked for. After Elisha duplicates Elijah's miracle of stopping the Jordan in its flow (2 Kings 2:14; cf. 2:8) the "sons of the prophets" at Jericho conclude, "The spirit of Elijah is resting on Elisha" (2 Kings 2:15). But again, that "spirit of Elijah" is the Spirit. The Holy Spirit was likely alluded to at the parting of the Reed Sea and, it was surmised, was the One through whom Moses was able to part those waters (ברוח קדים, Exod. 15:8; cf. ברוח אפיך, 14:21; and cf. probably another such allusion, Gen. 8:1). The same Spirit now parts the Jordan waters—or better, stops their flow—for Elijah and later for his successor.

When Elisha asks for a double portion of Elijah's Spirit, he is using inheritance language from the Mosaic covenant:

> If a man has two wives, and he loves one but not the other, and both bear him sons but the firstborn is the son of the wife he does not love, when he wills his property to his sons, he must not give the rights of the firstborn to the son of the wife he loves in preference to his actual firstborn, the son

of the wife he does not love. He must acknowledge the son of his unloved wife as the firstborn by giving him a double share of all he has. That son is the first sign of his father's strength. The right of the firstborn belongs to him. (Deut. 21:15–17)

The ethos of the Lord's instruction is this: If, for example, a man has three sons, he is to divide the inheritance into four parts, and the first-born son will inherit two of those parts, while the other two brothers inherit only one part each. In that way the firstborn son gets twice as much of the inheritance as either of the others—that is, a double portion. Elisha, according to Deuteronomy 21:17, asks for the portion of the firstborn son.

Questions naturally arise such as, who is the father who will bestow the inheritance? and who are the sons? The answers that make the most sense are that God is the Father, and Elijah and Elisha are the sons. A hint in this direction is Elisha's own declaration at Elijah's assumption: "My father! My father! The chariots and horsemen of Israel" (2 Kings 2:11). The exclamation is ambiguous, but that should present no obstacle to understanding. Perhaps Elisha in some ways considers Elijah to be his father. He is after all Elijah's son, or disciple, just as the sons of the prophets at Bethel and Jericho (2 Kings 2:3, 5) are (presumably) disciples of some more seasoned and approved prophets.[10] On the other hand, God is also their Father and the Father of his people, as one is told in Deuteronomy (cf. Deut. 1:31; 32:18), the same book from which the inheritance language is drawn. God then, as the Father of Elijah and Elisha, places his Spirit on them for works of ministry. However, Elijah was chronologically the first of the two prophets, and Elisha the second. Elijah was also Elisha's father or discipler. It is very bold then for Elisha to ask for a double portion of the Spirit. He is, after all, only the disciple; with respect to God the Father he is, so to speak, not the first son but the second. And yet, although he is only the disciple and the second son vis-à-vis God, he asks for the portion of the first son—the double portion—and he receives it. This conclusion is consistent with the inheritance language employed, even if it seems unexpected: After all, Elisha is not literally God's son. On the other hand, the relationship of the prophet to God and the disposition of God's Spirit is obviously Christological.

---

10   Cf. discussion in chapter 15.

The correctness of this understanding is suggested by the reports of prophecies and miracles performed by the two prophets. When they are examined all together, it turns out that twice as many prophecies and twice as many miracles are reported for Elisha than for his great predecessor, as the following display shows.

Elijah and Elisha: Double Portion (2 Kings 2:9; cf. Deut. 21:17)

Elijah prophecies — *Verses*
1. three-year drought — 1 Kings 17:1
2. condemns Ahab regarding Naboth — 1 Kings 21:17–24
3. Ahaziah's death — 2 Kings 1:4, 16
4. double portion — 2 Kings 2:9

Elisha's prophecies — *Verses*
1. Victory over Moab — 2 Kings 3:14–19
2. Syrian plans revealed — 2 Kings 6:8–23
3. much food, but an officer dies without eating — 2 Kings 7:17–20
4. seven-year famine — 2 Kings 8:1–3
5. Ben-Hadad's death — 2 Kings 8:10
6. Hazael to ravage Israel — 2 Kings 8:12
7. Hazael to be king — 2 Kings 8:13
8. Jehoash's defeat of Syrians — 2 Kings 13:14–20

Totals indicate double portion:
Elijah: 4
Elisha: 8

Elijah's miracles — *Verses*
1. fed by ravens — 1 Kings 17:2–6
2. flour and oil — 1 Kings 17:6
3. resurrection — 1 Kings 17:17–24
4. Mt. Carmel fire — 1 Kings 18:16–40
5. 2 × 50 soldiers consumed by fire — 2 Kings 1:10–13
6. parts Jordan — 2 Kings 2:8
7. apotheosis — 2 Kings 2:11

Elisha's miracles	*Verses*
1. parts Jordan	2 Kings 2:14
2. waters healed	2 Kings 2:19–22
3. two bears kill youths	2 Kings 2:23–25
4. widow's oil	2 Kings 4:1–7
5. resurrection	2 Kings 4:8–37
6. purifies stew with flour	2 Kings 2:38–41
7. feeds one hundred	2 Kings 4:42–44
8. Naaman healed	2 Kings 5:1–19
9. Gehazi leprous	2 Kings 5:20–27
10. ax head floats	2 Kings 6:5–7
11. servant sees angels	2 Kings 6:17
12. Syrian soldiers blinded	2 Kings 6:18
13. Syrian soldiers sighted	2 Kings 6:20
14. resurrection of dead man who touches Elisha's bones	2 Kings 13:20–21

Totals indicate double portion:
Elijah: 7
Elisha: 14

Someone may object that both prophets probably issued more prophetic statements and performed more miracles than the historian recorded. As John says of Jesus, "Jesus performed many other signs in the presence of his disciples, which are not recorded in this book. But these are written that you may believe that Jesus is the Messiah, the Son of God, and that by believing you may have life in his name" (John 20:30–31). One may freely concede the point. But what John said of his own account illustrates an acknowledged and important point about historiography. A historical writer composes his work with some principle of selectivity. He does not report everything he knows, but selects from among his data for some purpose. John's purpose was "that you may believe that Jesus is the Messiah, the Son of God, and that by believing you may have life in his name" (John 20:31). When the composer of the Elijah/Elisha accounts wrote his history, one purpose he apparently had was to show that Elisha did receive *twice as much* of the Spirit as Elijah had received—as may be inferred from the datum that he illustrated the double portion by reporting *twice as many* works of the Spirit for Elisha as he did for Elisha.

It was said at the start of this section that Elisha's inheritance "touches upon the expansive promise of the new covenant" and "shows a principle or a pattern of divine activity that has occurred with signal prophets." If one broadens the concept from that of a double portion to that of a large amplification more generally, the prospect of divine activity becomes obvious.[11]

The principle broadly stated is this: there are times of prophetic succession when the successor accomplishes more by way of kingdom advance than his predecessor. The following chart illustrates the idea in a simple way:

Prophetic Succession Pattern

Moses	Elijah	John the Baptist	Jesus
⇓	⇓	⇓	⇓
Joshua	Elisha	Jesus	Church

The first pair, Moses and Joshua, may seem curious. After all, the Lord did works through Moses that Joshua never equaled: he set his people free from Egypt's yoke by signs and wonders, and led them to a place where they could worship him and enter into a covenant with him. Joshua never did any of that. There is, however, one area of kingdom advance in which Joshua outdid his great mentor: the Conquest. Although it was given to Moses to conquer some land east of the Jordan—territories of the Amorite kings, Sihon (Num. 21:21–31) and Og (Num. 21:32–35)—the bulk of the Promised Land was left for Joshua to conquer.

The same is true of the great covenant mediator Jesus, the "prophet like Moses," vis-á-vis his successors, the church. Jesus did the hard work of mediating the new covenant in his blood—a covenant that would set his people free from the yoke of sin and death. No successor could possibly do that. But it was left to the church to expand the kingdom of God more than Jesus did or could have done as a man in his short span of ministry. Had it been God's intent, Jesus could have accomplished all the church has accomplished and more. But such was manifestly not God's plan. As Jesus said, "Very truly I tell you, whoever believes in me will

---

11 I first heard the following idea from a Vineyard pastor who spoke at a conference on Long Island in the early 1990s. I forget the pastor's name, but the principle struck me at the time and I have shared it with my students for over two decades.

do the works I have been doing, and he will do even greater things than these, because I am going to the Father" (John 14:12).

If one considers the middle two pairs of the set, the same principle applies. It was after all the double portion allotted to Elijah's successor, Elisha, that set us on this interpretive course. Likewise, however, although Jesus could say that no man born of woman was greater than John the Baptist (Luke 7:28a), Jesus was nonetheless the more anointed prophet. John considered himself unworthy to undo the sandals of his great successor (Mark 1:7; Luke 3:16; John 1:27; cf. Matt. 3:11) who, unlike John—who baptized with water for repentance—would baptize with the fiery Holy Spirit (taking "the Holy Spirit and fire," Matt. 3:11, as a hendiadys). He would empower his followers to live a repentant lifestyle, to be greater even than John the Baptist (Luke 7:28b), and to advance God's kingdom in an unprecedented manner globally and by the Spirit.

Jesus declared, "Truly I tell you, among those born of women there has not risen anyone greater than John the Baptist; yet whoever is least in the kingdom of heaven is greater than he" (Matt. 11:11). One overcomes the shock value of this statement if one understands one thing: the "least in the kingdom of heaven"—the weakest member of the church (cf. 1 Cor. 12:22)—is a temple of the Holy Spirit. That is more than any Old Testament saint, including John the Baptist, could say. With regard to that one truth, any member of the new covenant form of God's kingdom is greater than anyone under the old covenant.[12] That, however, is not a matter of works but of ontology—a new ontology (cf. 2 Cor. 5:17) created by the Spirit under a new covenant.

---

12 The "kingdom of heaven" comes to earth in the ministry of the new covenant (cf. Matt. 3:2; 4:17; 10:7). Jesus often talks of the kingdom of heaven not only as something that has come near (Matt. 4:17; 10:7; cf. Matt. 3:2), but also as something future (Matt. 5:19, 20; 7:21; 8:11). Ladd is surely correct when he identifies the kingdom of heaven as the presence and rule of the Lord—manifestly so in the ministry of Christ who speaks of the kingdom as *present*: "From the days of John the Baptist until now, the kingdom of heaven has been subjected to violence, and violent people have been raiding it" (Matt. 11:12, author's translation). The same presence and rule of the Lord also appear subsequently in the Spirit-informed and Spirit-led church. Cf. George Eldon Ladd, *A Theology of the New Testament* (Grand Rapids: Eerdmans, 1974).

CHAPTER SEVENTEEN

THE DAVIDIC COVENANT AND DAVID

David lived under the Mosaic covenant and was a prophet under that covenant. The Lord made a separate covenant with David, however, and that covenant is the subject of this chapter.

The Lord's covenant with David is one of the major divine-human covenants and resembles the others in the following ways: (1) it was initiated by the Lord and not at human request; (2) it was made through a human covenant mediator; (3) it is, like all the divine-human covenants, both unconditional and conditional; and (4) the dynamic of its creation illustrates the Major Paradigm. Nonetheless, the Davidic covenant is *sui generis*. It is unique in one way, that is, it has to do with the royal line exclusively. Consequently it is a covenant with an extraordinarily narrow focus.

The Davidic covenant shows God's unfolding purpose. The Lord promised royal offspring to Abraham in Genesis 17. Deuteronomy 17 gave more details regarding a future king and what he should and should not do. The Davidic covenant gives further focus to the Abrahamic promise and the Deuteronomic instruction, because the Lord finds in David a man *after his own heart* to occupy the royal office (1 Sam. 13:13; cf. Acts 13:22). The data show a progressive revelation of God's royal plan. Jesus fulfills these promises and instructions and thereby brings ultimate clarity to their intent. Abraham rejoiced to see his day (John 8:56); Jesus fulfilled the law (Matt. 5:17); and he is the promised Son of David.[1]

The present chapter explores the Davidic covenant and its relation to the Major Paradigm. It also considers David as a prophet and worshiper

---

1 As the Son of David he is also, *par excellence* a man after the Lord's heart (cf. Matt. 3:17).

of the Lord. David's life and nature, as a prophet and poet, accordingly come into view. One may see that part of the chapter as a further install-ment on the issue of prophetic experience.[2] David's compositions, as covenant literature, also come under consideration, as do typology and Christology, before considering some aspects of the new covenant, which is prefatory to volume 3.

THE DAVIDIC COVENANT

The Davidic covenant is one of three covenants anticipated by the Abra-hamic covenant. The other two are the Mosaic covenant and the new covenant.[3] However, the Davidic covenant background is not only Abra-hamic. The Lord's promise to Abraham (Gen. 17:6) and Sarah (Gen. 17:16) that kings would come from them finds narrower focus in Deuteronomy 17, where future kings of Israel are foretold, and the Lord commands any future king to have a copy of God's law and be familiar with it so he may not forget any of its provisions and by so doing stray and lead the people astray.

Deuteronomic Provisions

Inasmuch as it has to do with a future king, the Mosaic covenant also anticipates the Davidic covenant. The Deuteronomic provisions show the Lord's care for a future king and for his people:

> When you enter the land the LORD your God is giving you and have taken possession of it and settled in it, and you say, "Let us set a king over us like all the nations around us," be sure to appoint over you a king the LORD your God chooses. He must be from among your fellow Israelites. Do not place a foreigner over you, one who is not an Israelite. The king, moreover, must not acquire great numbers of horses for himself or make the people return to Egypt to get more of them, for the LORD has told you, "You are not to go back that way again." He must not take many wives, or his heart will be led astray. He must not accumulate large amounts of silver and gold. (Deut. 17:14–17)

---

2   The topic of chapters 14 and 15.

3   The Abrahamic, Mosaic, and Davidic covenants, of course, all anticipate and prepare the way for the new covenant.

The Lord, creator of time and outside time, knows Israel will one day ask for a king "like all the nations around" them (v. 14; cf. 1 Sam. 8:19–20). He knows a future king will "acquire great numbers of horses for himself" (v. 16; cf. 1 Kings 10:26) from "Egypt" (v. 16; cf. 1 Kings 10:28), and "accumulate large amounts of silver and gold" (v. 17; cf. 1 Kings 10:14), and have "many wives" (v. 17; cf. 1 Kings 11:1–3), who will lead his heart astray (v. 17; cf. 1 Kings 11:4). Solomon and kings after him committed those errors with increasingly disastrous consequences.

To keep any future king from error, the Lord instructs a king to provide himself with a copy of the Lord's covenant with Israel and become familiar with it:

> When he takes the throne of his kingdom, he is to write for himself on a scroll a copy of this law, taken from that of the Levitical priests. It is to be with him, and he is to read it all the days of his life so that he may learn to revere the LORD his God and follow carefully all the words of this law and these decrees and not consider himself better than his fellow Israelites and turn from the law to the right or to the left. Then he and his descendants will reign a long time over his kingdom in Israel. (Deut. 17:18–20)

As Deuteronomy reminds us, the Levitical priests were custodians of the covenant document in the tabernacle and in the temple-to-be. The Lord's covenant was handled in this regard much like international suzerain-vassal treaties in the ancient Near East, where both the suzerain and the vassal had a copy of the treaty in the temple of their chief gods, along with a provision for regular reading (cf. Deut. 31:10–13). In Israel's case, the king is to write his own copy. The personal involvement by the king—the king functions as scribe—could be meant to help inculcate the law on the king's heart.

The Lord foresaw that his people would want a king to rule over them like the other nations. The laconic context in Deuteronomy 17 does not tell what the Lord also knew—that his people's desire for such a king would be sin (cf. 1 Sam. 8:7) and that the first man to hold the office would be a model of failure in faith (and thus of rejecting the Lord, 1 Sam. 15:23).

The Lord's forecast of royalty in Deuteronomy 17 makes it clear, for those who knew the passage after Saul became king, that accommodation to Israel's erroneous wish was foretold to be part of the Lord's future dealings with his people. It also gave sufficient instruction for any future monarch to avoid error. It did not prophesy a king who would be a man after the Lord's own heart. It did indicate that tenure of the royal office would be contingent upon—or conditional upon—obedience to the Mosaic covenant: He must not "turn from the law to the right or to the left. *Then* he and his descendants will reign a long time over his kingdom in Israel" (Deut. 17:20, emphasis added).

Unconditionality and Conditionality

The issue of unconditionality and its implied opposite is worth review because it has occasioned a good deal of debate. Our discussion will be followed by some consideration of the relation between unconditionality and the quality of the covenant mediator prophets. Both topics are germane to the Davidic covenant.

An approach proposed earlier offers a way of accounting for the apparent fact that the Davidic covenant—like the Abrahamic covenant in which it is rooted—is both unconditional and conditional. It is *unconditional* because the Lord is committed to carrying it through until it has accomplished what he created it to accomplish; it is *conditional* because any member of it may fall out of covenant fellowship through disobedience.

We consider now the conditional aspect. The provision already noted in Deuteronomy 17:20 clearly implies the possibility of failure by a member of the Davidic covenant. Psalm 132 makes the same point even more clearly:

> The LORD swore an oath to David,
>   a sure oath he will not revoke:
> "One of your own descendants
>   I will place on your throne.
> *If your sons keep my covenant*
>   *and the statutes I teach them,*
> *then* their sons will sit
>   on your throne for ever and ever."
>   (vv. 11–12, emphases added)

The Lord promised *unconditionally* to place one of David's descendants on the throne (v. 11). There is no way to limit that promise so that it may not include God's Son who, as Isaiah prophesied, will sit on the throne of David (9:1–7, and esp. vv. 2, 6, and 7; cf. Matt. 4:12–16). But the *conditional* aspect foretold in Deuteronomy is stated in no uncertain terms in verse 12: tenure of the throne by any of David's descendants—in other words, his participation in the Davidic covenant—depends on the descendant's obedience to the Mosaic covenant. Now only Jesus, Son of David, was perfectly obedient, and so only he holds the throne forever.[4] Solomon understood the Davidic covenant in the same conditional way, as is shown by his prayer to the Lord after the dedication of the temple: "Now LORD, the God of Israel, keep for your servant David my father the promises you made to him when you said, 'You shall never fail to have a successor to sit before me on the throne of Israel, *if only* your descendants are careful in all they do to walk before me faithfully as you have done" (1 Kings 8:25, emphasis added). This incidentally is information supplemental to the original Davidic covenant passage (2 Sam. 7:1–17), which did not state any such condition.[5]

Basis of Covenant Unconditionality and the Davdic Covenant

At this point we may consider in a summary way the issue of how the covenant mediators relate to the unconditionality of the covenants they mediate. These considerations will conclude with remarks on David and the Davidic covenant, but will begin with a consideration of the overall problem.

We have argued that all the divine-human covenants are unconditional and they are also all conditional. They are unconditional in that the Lord will not let any vassal disobedience annul any of God's covenants. They are conditional in that every one of them contains one or more conditions for the vassal. This fundamental distinction is true of all the divine-human covenants. It leaves open, however, the question, how do the covenant mediators relate to the unconditionality of the covenants that they mediate? In other words, what if the covenant mediator breaks the covenant in some way or is found to be wanting? Does such failure on his part mean the end of the covenant? Or does the Lord's mercy to him and continuation of the covenant nonetheless illustrate the

---

4   Not to mention ontological considerations. For more detailed discussion of the dual nature (unconditional and conditional) of the Abrahamic and Davidic covenants, cf. chapter 4.

5   Cf. the issue of laconic reporting in the first instance, followed by later supplemental data, as evidenced in, for example, Genesis 2 vis-à-vis Genesis 3, Genesis 9 vis-à-vis Isaiah 24, Genesis 12 vis-à-vis Genesis 20, and Acts 9 vis-à-vis Acts 22. Cf. discussion in volume 1, 97–98; cf. Jeffrey J. Niehaus, *When Did Eve Sin?*, forthcoming.

unconditionality of the covenant? These questions matter because one might assume the following: the failure of the covenant mediator could mean the failure of the covenant. As regards the Davidic covenant in particular, if David failed—as he did—and was "cut off" from the covenant before he had viable offspring, the covenant made with him and through him with his offspring could not continue.[6] Of course such was not the case because, although David failed, he was not "cut off," and although his first child by Bathsheba died, David was not left without viable offspring. In addition to David, the cases of the other covenant mediators deserve consideration. As we consider them, we look back to the previous covenants and forward to the new covenant and its mediator, Jesus.

When we consider the covenant mediator prophets, it becomes immediately apparent that Adam and David failed, and each one failed in a way that could have led to his exclusion from the covenant he mediated and to the failure of that covenant (because of the death of the covenant mediator before he had any children). By contrast, neither Noah, Abraham, Moses, nor Jesus failed in such a way as to be excluded from the covenant he mediated. At least that distinction is what the biblical record shows. This is quite apart from the fact that none of the covenant mediators from the Fall onwards was without sin except for Jesus. If sinless perfection were the prerequisite for being a covenant mediator, only the first Adam, before the Fall, and the second Adam, after the Fall, fulfill that condition. It is clear, nonetheless, that the Lord kept all of these covenants going despite the failure of those covenant mediators who failed, and certainly despite their sinfulness.

What of those who did not fail—that is, who are not reported as having failed in such a way as to break the covenant they had mediated? In several cases, the quality of the mediator seems to form the basis for the Lord's election of him for the role of covenant mediator. This appears to be the case with Noah, Abraham, and David, and it is certainly the case with Jesus.

The Lord says to Noah, "Go into the ark, you and your whole family, because I have found you righteous in this generation" (Gen. 7:1). Noah's singular righteousness seems to form the basis of his election, both to salvation and to the role of covenant mediator. Even if we grant that proposition, however, it remains true that Noah could have no righteousness unless God had created him as one who could want to be, and who would

---

6   David failed the Mosaic covenant by committing adultery. That failure should have led to his death before he had a son and thus also to the failure of the Davidic covenant.

be, righteous (cf. James 1:17, Heb. 12:9; and discussion in vol. 3, chap. 7). Consequently the Lord elects as righteous those he has created to be righteous. We submit that Noah's righteousness, like anyone's, is consonant with his faith, or his amening God. Consequently also, if God keeps the Noahic covenant going, he does so not because Noah was righteous, but because God has his own eschatological reason to keep the covenant going. He will keep it in effect until the time has come when there will be no more faith on the earth (Luke 18:8). At that time, there will be no point in maintaining the old common grace order, and God will conclude it and usher in the new heavens and the new earth. So the uncondtiionality of the Noahic covenant does not depend on Noah's righteousness. It depends on God's purpose for the covenant. It is also true that in his grace God created Noah to be a righteous man.

What about Abraham? Here we are confronted with a more direct statement of apparent causality:

> "I swear by myself, declares the LORD, that *because you have done this* and have not withheld your son, your only son, I will surely bless you and make your descendants as numerous as the stars in the sky and as the sand on the seashore. Your descendants will take possession of the cities of their enemies, and through your offspring all nations on earth will be blessed, *because you have obeyed me.*" (Gen. 22:16–18, emphases added)

The Lord's continuation of and fulfillment of the Abrahamic covenant seem to be contingent on Abraham's obedience. However, the Lord's statement in Genesis 15:18 that, once he has cut the covenant with Abram, he *has given* the land to Abram and his descendants, states that part of the covenantal promise package as a *fait accompli*, some time before the statements of Genesis 22. As we have noted, the Lord is outside time and knows Abraham's whole life already. Therefore, he knows that when Abram "amens" him (Gen. 15:6), Abram's faith is real. The Lord's statement in Genesis 22 is therefore a corroboration of Abraham's faith. But as such it is a corroboration of *what the Lord made Abram to be*: Abram would be the man of faith, who amened the Lord at the outset and whose life (for the most part!) amened him to the end. If, then, the Lord corroborated all that, he stated that he based the fulfillment of the Abrahamic covenant promises on what the Lord, as the Father of Abraham's spirit, had made Abraham to be. But the Lord made Abraham to be the person through whom the Lord would make the Abrahamic covenant. The Lord therefore maintains the Abrahamic covenant on the basis of the Lord's own work and purpose. The real ground of the Abrahamic covenant's unconditionality is not therefore Abraham's obedience after all—considered merely on the human, or what we might call intermediate (between man and God) plane—but more immediately, the ground of the covenant's unconditionality is the righteousness of the Lord who in forming Abraham to be the faithful and obedient covenant mediator was actually being true to himself. This principial merging of covenant mediator and covenant Lord becomes most clear in the one perfect example of it, the covenant mediator Jesus, who was formed by the Father to be the "faithful [i.e., amening] witness" (Rev. 1:5) and God's obedient covenant mediator. But when the Lord made that new covenant with its unconditional aspect, he did so through and on the basis of the covenant mediator whom he had formed for the work. Nonetheless, that covenant mediator was the Lord himself (cf. John 14:9). Agreeably, Jesus affirmed that his words and deeds were not his own, but his Father's. The same was true as regards Abraham's own faithful obedience corroborated by the Lord in Genesis 22, because whenever Abraham obeyed, he was amening the Lord, that is, doing what the Father was doing (although, of course, Abraham was not without sin as Jesus was).

The same principles apply to the case of David. David failed terribly, and yet the Lord kept him in the covenant and thus kept the covenant going. The Lord did not show such grace to some later kings in the Davidic line, whom the Lord judged and cut off (e.g., apparently Amon, 2 Kings 21:19–21; Jehoiakin, 2 Kings 24:8–16). But the Lord did nonetheless maintain the Davidic covenant, even if some of the royal line were unfaithful. As regards David, we read that he was "a man after [the Lord's] heart." The Lord says to Saul: "But now your kingdom will not endure; the LORD has sought out a man after his own heart and appointed him ruler of his people, because you have not kept the LORD's command" (1 Sam. 13:14). This statement certainly seems to say the Lord's choice of David as king was contingent upon David's being a man after the Lord's heart. If that is a fair understanding, the case of David and the quality of his heart are nonetheless no different in principle from the case of Abraham and his faithful obedience. Like Abraham, David was the man the Lord had shaped him to be (cf. Ps. 139:13) for the Lord's own purposes, one of which was that David should be the mediator of a Davidic covenant that was unconditional, not because David was good, but because the Lord had eschatological purposes for the Davidic covenant and would maintain it until his Son, the "David" *par excellence*, fulfilled it.

Davidic Covenant Narrative

As we turn to consider the Davidic covenant proper, we see that a narrative houses that covenant (2 Sam. 7:1–17), just as narratives house the other divine-human covenants of the Bible. In this narrative, one can see more clearly the unconditional aspect of the Davidic covenant. Before reviewing the covenant narrative itself, the material that precedes it deserves attention. The prior narrative is important because it provides a background that makes sense of David's desire to build a house for the Lord. David's victorious warfare in the Lord's cause is schematized in 2 Samuel 1–5:

	Warfare before the Covenant	Various Campaigns
1	Defeat of Amalekites	2 Samuel 1:1
2	Defeat of Israel under Ish-Bosheth	2 Samuel 2:8–4:12
3	Defeat of Jebusites in Jerusalem	2 Samuel 6:6–8
4	Defeat of Philistines	2 Samuel 5:17–25
	Summary Statement	2 Samuel 7:1

The summary of the warfare account also introduces the covenant narrative: "After the king was settled in his palace and the Lord had given him rest from all his enemies around him . . ." (2 Sam. 7:1). That is important, because what David now wants is *what a king in the ancient world would want* after his god had given him success in war.

So the covenant narrative begins: "He said to Nathan the prophet, 'Here I am, living in a palace of cedar, while the ark of God remains in a tent.' Nathan replied to the king, 'Whatever you have in mind, go ahead and do it, for the LORD is with you'" (2 Sam. 7:2–3). Probably most ancient near eastern readers would have understood these statements, and even to a modern reader they communicate well enough. David wants to build a house for the Lord out of thankfulness for success in war and the establishment of peace—because the Lord has made all that possible. David finds it improper under the circumstances that he should live in a palace of cedar, while the ark of the Lord sits in a relatively humble tent.

David's statement, then, implies a commonly understood ethos in the ancient Near East. When a king came home from a victorious campaign, he would thank his god for his success. He would build a new temple, or refurbish a temple that was dilapidated or, if that was not needed, devote some of the booty to his god.[7]

David expresses a culturally normal desire. Nathan understands David's wish as an ancient near eastern man would understand it. Nathan does not respond as a prophet—his answer is not a word from the Lord by the Spirit—but as any man of his day would probably respond: "Whatever you have in mind, go ahead and do it, for the LORD is with you" (v. 3). But the Lord soon makes it clear he has another plan in mind. His word comes to Nathan as a corrective for David, and it also functions as a historical prologue for an unfolding covenant:

> That night the word of the LORD came to Nathan, saying: "Go and tell my servant David, 'This is what the LORD says: Are you the one to build me a house to dwell in? I have not dwelt in a house from the day I brought the Israelites up out of Egypt to this day. I have been moving from place to place with a tent as my dwelling. Wherever I have moved with all the Israelites, did I ever say to any of their rulers whom I commanded to shepherd my people Israel, "Why have you not built me a house of cedar?" Now then, tell my servant David, 'This is what the LORD Almighty says: I took you from the pasture and from following the flock to be ruler over my people Israel. I have been with you wherever you have gone, and I have cut off all your enemies from before you.'" (2 Sam. 7:4–9)

The Lord makes two corrections—statements that challenge David to a change of outlook. The first comes when he asks David, "Are you the one to build me a house to dwell in?" (v. 5), with the implicit answer no. The second comes when he tells David the Lord has never asked for a house to live in (vv. 6–7). Underlying both correctives is the unspoken fact that the Lord needs no one to build a house for him and has therefore never asked anyone to build him one since—as Solomon says later—"will God really dwell on earth? The heavens, even the highest heaven, cannot contain you. How much less this temple I have built!" (1 Kings 8:27). The Lord may also be addressing another issue: David's assumption of a cultural norm. Other kings built or renovated temples or made gifts to their gods as acts of gratitude once they achieved victories. The Lord may be prising David away from conforming to the pattern of this world. Strong evidence for that comes when the Lord tells David why he may not build a temple: "But this word of the LORD came to me: 'You have

---

7   Cf. *ANETBT*, 70–71, 81.

shed much blood and have fought many wars. You are not to build a house for my Name, because you have shed much blood on the earth in my sight'" (1 Chron. 22:8). Any other ancient near eastern king would build a temple for his god precisely *because*—he thought—he had shed much enemy blood in holy warfare for his god. The Lord tells David that criterion does not apply in his case. Rather, the Lord says, "Behold, a son shall be born to you, who shall be a man of rest; and I will give him rest from all his enemies all around. His name shall be Solomon, for I will give peace and quietness to Israel in his days. He shall build a house for My name" (1 Chron. 22:9–10a NKJV). His name will be Solomon (שְׁלֹמֹה), which means "his peace," and the Lord will grant peace (שָׁלוֹם) in his day.[8] The fact that the Lord had given David success in war and rest from warfare (cf. 2 Sam. 1:1–7:1) does not alter any of this. Nor is there any contradiction. The Lord chooses a man of peace to build his temple, because the Lord understands Christology and so designates a man of peace to foreshadow the Prince of Peace, whose warfare (in his days among us) will not involve bloodshed. The fact that Solomon declined in his faithfulness to the Lord also does not disqualify him from being a Christological figure.

Nonetheless, on a higher level David's thought is acceptable. A human pattern of temple building after victory—also attributed to gods by pagans—is grounded in a supernal reality. After the Fall, whenever the Lord establishes a temple presence among humans, he does it after warfare that clears a way for the temple, and so temple building has a place in the Major Paradigm.

The Lord follows his challenges to cultural norms with a reminder of his personal history with David. The historical review constitutes both the historical prologue of the covenant and a statement of choice. It alludes to the Lord's election of David (2 Sam. 7:9), and to the success the Lord gave him in battle (v. 8, corresponding to the warfare background in 2 Sam. 1:1–7:1). As a specimen of valued phraseology, the Lord's statement, "*I took you from the pasture and from following the flock* [lit. "from after the flock"] *to be ruler over my people Israel*," was used later by Amos when he rebuked Amaziah, the priest at Samaria: "I was neither a prophet nor the son of a prophet, but I was a shepherd, and I also took care of sycamore-fig trees. But *the LORD took me from tending the flock* [lit. "from after the flock," as at 2 Sam. 7:8] and said to me, 'Go, prophesy to

---

8   The Christology of Solomon and his temple-building has been discussed in chapter 4, and is briefly reviewed on pages 444–45.

my people Israel'" (Amos 7:14–15, emphasis added). David was a prophet
before Amos, and both statements are examples of prophetic election.

David was a king, and that is the focus of the Davidic covenant. Pursuant to the historical prologue, the Lord offers not stipulations but promises. The first set of promises has to do with the Lord's people and the
peaceful conditions they will enjoy under their king (2 Sam 7:10–11), who
receives the promise of a great name (v. 9).[9] The second set of promises
addresses David's desire to build a house for the Lord but adds promises
regarding the royal offspring who will build that house:

> The LORD declares to you that the LORD himself will establish a house
> for you: When your days are over and you rest with your fathers, I will
> raise up your offspring to succeed you, who will come from your own
> body, and I will establish his kingdom. He is the one who will build a
> house for my Name, and I will establish the throne of his kingdom forever.
> I will be his father, and he will be my son. (2 Sam. 7:11–14a)

After the well-known wordplay on the term "house," which can mean
either temple (as in vv. 5, 7, 13) or household—or, as befits a monarch, dynasty (v. 11)—the Lord promises that David's offspring will be the Lord's
adoptive son (v. 14a; cf. Ps. 2:7).

The Lord makes a great promise when he says, "I will establish the
throne of his kingdom forever" (v. 13b). As regards the unconditional
aspect of the Davidic covenant, it is important to understand just what
this means. The Lord is not promising here an eternal earthly united
kingdom (Judah-Israel). He is promising an eternal throne. Or is he? We
find here the Hebrew term that can mean forever or eternal, but can also
mean simply of long duration (עוֹלָם). The promise is thus ambiguous.
As, however, the promise of a Davidic son on the throne cannot exclude
the Son, so the promise of an eternal throne and kingdom also cannot
exclude the Lord's throne and his eternal kingdom. What Israel later
misunderstood as a carte blanche for themselves (cf. Jer. 7:4), was actually
a charter of salvation through great David's greater Son.

What could be called the curse portion of the narrative now follows,

---

9   The Lord also promised to *make* Abram's name great (וַאֲגַדְּלָה שְׁמֶךָ, Gen. 12:2), and
the promise to David may echo that. However, only David and the Lord are actually said
to have a "great name" (שֵׁם גָּדוֹל, 2 Sam. 7:9 [David]; 1 Sam. 12:22; 1 Kings 8:42; 2 Chron.
6:32; Ps. 99:3, and variants on the same [Yahweh]). The phraseological difference is slight
but may be meaningful.

but it is also ameliorated with promises. Regarding the promised off-spring who is to build the temple, the Lord says:

> "When he does wrong, I will punish him with the rod of men, with flog-gings inflicted by men. But my love will never be taken away from him, as I took it away from Saul, whom I removed from before you. Your house and your kingdom will endure forever before me; your throne will be established forever." Nathan reported to David all the words of this entire revelation. (2 Sam. 7:14b–17)

The Lord will punish the Davidic son when he does wrong, but he adds, he will not take his love (חסד) from him as he took it from Saul. We know what it looked like when the Lord took his love from Saul: "Now the Spirit of the Lord had departed from Saul, and an evil spirit from the Lord tormented him" (1 Sam. 16:14). The dynamic involved in this epi-sode is discussed later in this chapter. The important point to be noted now is that the Spirit of the Lord departed Saul. The Spirit had enabled Saul to have military success (cf. 1 Sam. 11:1–11), and was a demonstration of the Lord's love or, better, *grace* toward him. Once the Spirit left Saul, he was without spiritual cover; consequently he was defenseless against the enemy. The episode also has ramifications for temple abandonment to be considered later.[10]

The Lord's promise that he will not take his love from David's offspring when he does wrong is not tantamount to a promise that the Lord will not respond to such disobedience in some way. The Lord's response will be to raise up against him troublesome adversaries as he later does against Solomon (1 Kings 11:14, 23,25). In all those verses, the term "adversary" is Hebrew שָׂטָן. The Lord will raise up "satans" against a disobedient Davidic son. The pattern anticipates God's allowing Satan's adversarial role against the Son of David who had no sin but became sin for us. The warning of 2 Samuel 7:14 seems tantamount to the curse portion of the covenant nar-rative. As was the case in the Mosaic covenant, the Lord warned of a curse for disobedience. The implementation of the Mosaic curses was meant to turn God's people back to repentance (cf. Amos 4:6–12; Jer. 3:8–10). The Lord was prepared to enact curses against his disobedient people, yet not entirely destroy them. The same is the case with the promise now in the Davidic covenant: the Lord would punish the disobedient seed of David, but not destroy him. One can take that as a promise particularly aimed

---

10   Cf. chapter 3 of volume 3.

at David's own son (i.e., Solomon), since in fact the Lord did later bring more drastic curses upon kings in the Davidic line.

A Throne "Forever"

The prospect of judgment raises the question of the meaning of the term translated "forever" (עולם) in this passage. It seems likely that, in the first instance, it should be understood just as עולם in the Noahic covenant narrative was understood. It signifies a very long time, but not forever. The Davidic monarchy *qua* monarchy over the geopolitical state of Israel had a definite terminus—it did not endure "forever." Nonetheless, the throne and kingdom of the Son *par excellence* do endure forever.

Literary-Legal Form of the Covenant

We are now in a position to display the elements of the covenant narrative in 2 Samuel 7, and we can see they conform to the elements of a second millennium BC Hittite international treaty, although in a simplified way:

2 Samuel 7:1–17	Covenant Elements in the Narrative	
7:5–7	Title	the Lord identified
7:8–9	Historical prologue	the Lord's election of David
7:10 –16	Blessings	National security, Davidic dynasty
7:14b	Curses	Chastening of son

The presence of a historical prologue and blessings establishes the affinity of the covenant with the second millennium BC international treaty genre.[11] This is historically suitable because David ruled at the hinge of the millennia. The Davidic covenant, like the other biblical covenants, is also an expression of the nature of God. Any reader subsequent to David would have been comfortable with the literary/legal form (the genre) simply because it was the form also used in God's prior biblical covenants. From a modern perspective, the consistency of the covenant form as an expression of God's nature evokes a foundational biblical fact: "Jesus Christ is the same yesterday and today and forever" (Heb. 13:8).[12]

---

11   Cf. discussion in Niehaus, "Covenant and Narrative," 553–55.

12   The elements of the second millennium suzerain-vassal treaty form in this pericope make the narrative comparable to the other Old Testament narrative accounts of

It was noted the Lord would punish the disobedient seed of David but stop short of destroying him (2 Sam. 7:14–15). That was taken as a promise specially aimed at David's immediate son (Solomon) since in fact the Lord did later bring more drastic curses upon kings in the Davidic line. In light of this historical reality, it is worth considering a misunderstanding of the Davidic covenant that made it easier for God's people who lived under those later kings to sin and—erroneously—imagine they could do so without incurring a drastic judgment.

JUDAH'S MISUNDERSTANDING OF THE DAVIDIC COVENANT

Jeremiah's ministry was as difficult as it was partly because of a popular misunderstanding of the Davidic covenant. The episode in Jeremiah dubbed a Temple Sermon by commentators illustrates the misunderstanding. Jeremiah addresses people coming to the temple:

> Do not trust in deceptive words and say, "This is the temple of the LORD, the temple of the LORD, the temple of the LORD!" If you really change your ways and your actions and deal with each other justly, if you do not oppress the foreigner, the fatherless or the widow and do not shed innocent blood in this place, and if you do not follow other gods to your own harm, then I will let you live in this place, in the land I gave your ancestors for ever and ever. But look, you are trusting in deceptive words that are worthless. (Jer. 7:4–8)

The divinely commanded "sermon" has two major components: (1) the people are routinely violating the Mosaic covenant under which they all live (vv. 6, 9–11); (2) they mistakenly place confidence in the temple of

---

divine-human covenants. This is manifestly so in any fair reading of the passage, notwithstanding the remarkably generous—or grant-like—quality of the covenant. By now this merging or sharing of qualities ("suzerain-vassal" plus "grant") should come as no surprise since, as McCarthy noted decades ago, the ancient Near East offers a range or a spectrum of treaty types, and so one should avoid simplistic and mutually exclusive classifications of the biblical covenants as either vassal type or grant type (the Abrahamic and Davidic covenants both contain suzerain-vassal and grant aspects). Cf. D. J. McCarthy, *Treaty and Covenant*, Analecta Biblica 21A (Rome: Pontifical Biblical Institute, 1978), 88: "Treaty and grant, therefore, are not simply discreet phenomena. They lie along a continuum in which one leads over into the other."

the Lord (v. 4). Because of their presumption, the Lord rebukes them as robbers: "Has this house, which bears my Name, become a den of robbers to you? But I have been watching! declares the LORD" (v. 11). Jesus later takes up the accusation: "'It is written,' he said to them, 'My house will be called a house of prayer,' but you are making it 'a den of robbers'" (Matt. 21:13; cf. Mark 11:17; Luke 19:46). They are robbers in both cases because they deprive the Lord of honor they should render him.[13] Jesus' audience would have understood the implication. Their behavior is preparing the same doom for them that befell Judah long ago. They would be dispossessed by a great empire, and lose both temple and land (cf. Jer. 7:12–15).

But what was it—that is, this confidence in the "temple of the Lord"? It was a popular misunderstanding of the Davidic covenant temple promise. The Lord promised David's son would build the temple for his Name, and possess a throne and a kingdom that would last "forever" (עולם, 2 Sam. 7:16a) and people wrongly thought the promised temple, throne, and kingdom were the ones they knew in Jerusalem and Judah. They had forgotten the Lord's words to Solomon:

> If you or your descendants turn away from me and do not observe the commands and decrees I have given you and go off to serve other gods and worship them, then I will cut off Israel from the land I have given them and will reject this temple I have consecrated for my Name. Israel will then become a byword and an object of ridicule among all peoples. (1 Kings 9:6–7)

An earthly Davidic throne and kingdom would not last forever, as Jeremiah warned them. It did not last forever, as God's people learned to their cost. So the prophet clarifies: "You are trusting in deceptive words that are worthless" (Jer. 7:8).

The Davidic covenant would not trump the Mosaic covenant. Because God's people had a lifestyle of Mosaic covenant violation, they risked losing temple and land. Nonetheless, true repentance is possible: "Reform your ways and your actions, and I will let you live in this place" (Jer. 7:3b).

The verse bears closer examination because of a Hebrew feature that eludes translation. In Jeremiah's day, Hebrew was written without vowels. The absence of vowels produces an ambiguity in verses 3 and 7, and the ambiguity is theologically important. The Hebrew phrase in question (ואשכנה

---

13 Any pecuniary "robbing" money changers and dove sellers in Jesus' day may have done was only a manifestation of a deeper robbery they were committing.

אתכם במקום הזה, v. 3b) has been translated, "I will let you live in this place" (lit. "I will cause you to dwell in this place"). If, however, one takes the direct object marker (את) as a preposition (also את), one would translate: "I will dwell with you in this place."[14] That is a good promise, but it entails its opposite. If the people do not repent, the Lord warns: "Therefore, what I did to Shiloh I will now do to the house that bears my Name, the temple you trust in, the place I gave to you and your ancestors. I will thrust you from my presence, just as I did all your fellow Israelites, the people of Ephraim" (v. 15). This is a clear warning of temple abandonment. Because the people pay no heed, the Lord does later abandon his temple (cf. Ezek. 8:6, 10–11) in fulfillment of the Temple Sermon warning he gave through Jeremiah.

MESSIANIC PROMISE AND THE DAVIDIC COVENANT

It must be clear from the foregoing that the Davidic covenant was not unconditional regarding a Davidic kingdom or throne—in the world as God's people knew it. Accordingly, the traditional understanding of the Lord's promises to David in 1 Samuel 7 has been that they are ultimately fulfilled by Christ and his royal rule. That understanding is correct and not arbitrary—as it might seem if one read only the Davidic covenant narrative and wanted to see the Son of David/Son of God implied by it. Isaiah makes it clear that the Davidic "son" *par excellence* is the incarnate Son and his throne the Davidic throne.

Isaiah 9 and the Davidic Covenant

Isaiah foretells the Davidic Son in an incarnational prophecy memorable in itself and memorably set to music by Händel:

> For to us a child is born,
>   to us a son is given,
>   and the government will be on his shoulders.
> And he will be called
>   Wonderful Counselor, Mighty God,
>   Everlasting Father, Prince of Peace.

---

14 The ambiguity occurs also in verse 7b: The Lord says that if his people repent and are obedient, "then I will let you dwell in this place / then I will dwell with you in this place" (author's translation; Hebrew ושכנתי אתכם במקום הזה).

> Of the greatness of his government and peace
> there will be no end.
> He will reign on David's throne
> and over his kingdom,
> establishing and upholding it
> with justice and righteousness
> from that time on and forever.
> The zeal of the LORD Almighty
> will accomplish this. (Isa. 9:6–7 [9:5–6 MT])

The foremost thing about the prophecy is its incarnational quality. The son to be given will have a fourfold name, and each element of that name points to the child as an incarnation of "the mighty God." First, the name has an historical aspect. It evokes the Lord's warfare for his people in the past: "God the Hero," more commonly translated "the mighty God" (אל גבור), occurs in reflections on the Lord's warfare for Israel against Egypt in both Deuteronomy ("the great God, the Hero, and the dreadful/awesome," האל הגדל הגבר והנורא, Deut. 10:17) and Jeremiah ("the great God, the Hero," האל הגדול הגבור, Jer. 32:18). The root of the noun translated "wonder" (פלא) is used in connection with divine deliverance, both in reflections on the salvation from Egypt ("wonders," נפלאת, Exod. 3:20, 4:21 and passim; Deut. 4:34 and passim) and at the birth announcement of Samson, who will also be a savior. When Manoah asks the name of the angel who foretells the birth, the angel responds: "Why do you ask my name? It is wonderful (פלאי)" (Judg. 13:18). Agreeably, the name revealed in Isaiah 9 has to do with warfare and alludes to the Lord's wondrous past acts of salvation. It suggests the Son to be born will wage a warfare that will mean salvation for his people.

Something of that warfare and the spiritual nature of it appears earlier in Isaiah's prophecy. Isaiah says of those dwelling in Zebulun and Naphtali (Isa. 9:1 [8:23 MT]):

> The people walking in darkness
> have seen a great light;
> on those living in the land of deep darkness
> a light has dawned (Isa. 9:2 [9:1 MT])

The "light" is the son whose birth is announced three verses later. The New Testament identifies that light as Jesus at the onset of his preaching ministry in Zebulun and Naphtali (Matt. 4:15):

> The people living in darkness
>   have seen a great light;
> on those living in the land of the shadow of death
>   a light has dawned. (Matt. 4:16)

Before Isaiah foretells the child, he implies the warfare nature of his ministry:

> For as in the day of Midian's defeat,
>   you have shattered the yoke that burdens them,
> the bar across their shoulders,
> ʼthe rod of their oppressor. (Isa. 9:4)

The allusion to Midian's defeat evokes the *manner* of their defeat (cf. Judges 7), and also has spiritual implications. A synopsis of the event makes this clear. Three hundred Israelites overcame a superior Midianite force. They did so by attacking in the dark—sounding trumpets and shattering clay pots that contained torches. That war onset, combined with the visual impact of numerous *lights in the darkness*, threw the foe into confusion and led to their defeat (Judg. 7:15–25). The allusion to light—and in particular to light in the darkness, as at Isaiah 9:1—is no accident. The prophesied Son, who will accomplish the future victory, will also be "a light shining in the darkness" ("The light shines in the darkness, and the darkness has not overcome it," John 1:5) who by his ontology as Holy Spirit incarnation *is* the shining forth—"The Son is the radiance of God's glory" (Heb. 1:3)—the ἀπαύγασμα of luminous glory that overcomes the darkness. Those who believe in him will also become "the light of the world" ("You are the light of the world," Matt. 5:14) by virtue of accepting into themselves the same "light"—the Holy Spirit—whom the Son had without measure in his earthly ministry. As Paul says of "the light of the gospel of the glory of Christ" (2 Cor. 4:4): "We have this treasure in earthen vessels, that the excellence of the power may be of God and not of us" (2 Cor. 4:7). Like the Son—and evocative of the clay pots of Judges 7—we are clay pots who contain that light.

A few more remarks are in order about Isaiah 9:5. The name in which one can see so much of the incarnate Lord has been, contrarily, understood as a sentence name—a relatively common phenomenon in the ancient Near East and in the Bible—but that is not the better way to take it.[15] Rather, the name has the following structure:

---

15   If it were taken as a sentence name, the participle (יוֹעֵץ), usually translated as

Structure of Isaiah 9:5

| A Wonder (is) Counselor | God (is) Hero |
| Father of Eternity | Prince of Peace |

In other words, there are two verbless clauses followed by two bound phrases. That structure is obviously more balanced, or has a higher level of order, than a sentence name interpretation would allow. It is less likely that a higher level of order would arise accidentally out of a misinterpretation of a sentence name than that a higher level of order was intended in the first place. A sentence name interpretation then would dissolve the higher level of order originally offered in the prophecy.

On the other hand, there is no reason to suppose Isaiah or any of his contemporaries understood the full message of this verse. The ambiguity that allows a sentence name understanding makes that clear in our day. Unless the Lord had made his meaning unmistakably obvious to the prophet and his contemporaries (and one is not told that he did), the full meaning of the verse would only be understood after the incarnation it adumbrates had taken place and was itself understood. These seem reasonable conclusions when one considers Jesus' self-identification in John 8. When Jesus claimed equality with God (an equality Isaiah's prophecy avers), his contemporaries were prepared to stone him (John 8:48–59). In other words, no one in Jesus' day understood the prophecy correctly. That should be no surprise, since even Sanhedrin members could assert, "A prophet does not come out of Galilee" (John 7:52).

The fourfold name also adumbrates the triune nature of God, because it shows aspects later associated with the Father ("Father of Eternity"), the Son ("Prince of Peace") and the Spirit ("A Wonder [is] Counselor"). One may also see the salvific nature of God expressed in the phrase "God the Hero/Warrior," because all three persons of the triune God are involved in a spiritual warfare that informs the earthly ministry of the Son. As the Major Paradigm maintains, the Father caused his Spirit to work through

---

a substantive, would be taken simply as a participle, with "the Mighty God" (אל גבור, lit. "God the Hero") as subject: "The Mighty God, Father unto eternity and Prince of peace *is planning* a wonder." Another sentence name translation could be: "A wonderful counselor *is* the mighty God, the everlasting Father, the ruler of peace." For the former, cf. https://yourphariseefriend.wordpress.com/2012/02/08/fifth-response-to-dalton-lifsey-isaiah-956-67/. For the latter, alternative sentence name, cf. http://jewsforjudaism.org/knowledge/articles/answers/jewish-polemics/birth-of-jesus/who-is-the-child-in-isaiah-95-6/.

THE DAVIDIC COVENANT AND DAVID   431

the incarnate Son to wage war—be that warfare kerygma, healing, or deliverance.

Finally, as regards the name of Isaiah 9:5, the promised Son will reign on David's throne and uphold it *by his own nature* ("with justice and with righteousness")—fulfilling thus the "righteousness and justice" required of Abraham (Gen. 18:19) and of Israel under the Mosaic covenant (Isa. 5:7) but impossible for them to attain. The Son will uphold, and reign from, the Davidic throne from that time on and forever. That "forever" will be truly forever (עולם) and not just "for a long time" (עולם): "of the greatness of his government and peace / *there will be no end*" (v. 7, emphasis added).

Psalm 89 and the Davidic Covenant

The eternality of the Davidic royal rule is declared at some length in Psalm 89. The Psalm shows the unconditional aspect of the Davidic covenant:

> I will sing of the LORD's great love forever;
> > with my mouth I will make your faithfulness known
> > through all generations.
> I will declare that your love stands firm forever,
> > that you have established your faithfulness in heaven itself.
> You said, "I have made a covenant with my chosen one,
> > I have sworn to David my servant,
> 'I will establish your line forever
> > and make your throne firm through all generations.'"
> (vv. 1–4)

The Hebrew of verse 4 is particularly important. It reads literally, "For eternity I will establish your seed (עד־עולם אכין זרעך) and build your throne for generation plus generation (ובניתי לדר־ודור כסאך)."

It would make sense to understand the singular term "seed" here as the same seed of Abraham Paul talks about when he understands the promise of a seed to Abraham (Gen. 12:3; 22:18) as a promise of Christ (Gal. 3:16)—the singular seed through whom all nations would be blessed (although, of course, all God's children are included corporately in that seed, being "in Christ"). God does unquestionably establish ("build") that throne, not to last on earth for a king of Israel or Judah "for all generations," but to endure forever with a King upon it *for the beneficent rule of* "generation plus generation."

The psalmist continues to portray emphatically the nature of the Lord's unconditional promise:

> Once you spoke in a vision,
>   to your faithful people you said:
> "I have bestowed strength on a warrior;
>   I have raised up a young man from among the people.
> I have found David my servant;
>   with my sacred oil I have anointed him.
> My hand will sustain him;
>   surely my arm will strengthen him.
> The enemy will not get the better of him;
>   the wicked will not oppress him.
> I will crush his foes before him
>   and strike down his adversaries.
> My faithful love will be with him,
>   and through my name his horn will be exalted.
> I will set his hand over the sea,
>   his right hand over the rivers.
> He will call out to me, 'You are my Father,
>   my God, the Rock my Savior.'
> And I will appoint him to be my firstborn,
>   the most exalted of the kings of the earth.
> I will maintain my love to him forever,
>   and my covenant with him will never fail.
> I will establish his line forever,
>   his throne as long as the heavens endure." (89:19–29)

The first part (vv. 19–25) of this notable passage reports in a poetically expansive way the revelation the Lord gave to Nathan (2 Sam. 7:4), and has to do with that great name and national peace and security the Lord promised David (2 Sam. 7:9b–11). The next verse reiterates the adoptive sonship the Lord promised David's offspring (2 Sam. 7:14 // Ps. 89:26), but the following verse promises much more for the son than the Lord had promised David. The Lord promised David he would make the son's name "like the names of the greatest men on earth" (2 Sam. 7:9b). But now he promises "I will appoint him to be my firstborn, / the most exalted of the kings of the earth" (v. 27). The poetry outstrips what the Lord had promised in the Davidic covenant narrative. It prefigures, or gives a glimpse of, the Son of David *par excellence*, the Son of God who is truly "the most exalted of the kings of the earth." Understood in that way, the verse also tells something about the legal nature of that Father-Son relationship. The Son who fulfills this portrait, in a way no mere mortal ever could, will be *appointed* God's firstborn. That is not to say his firstborn status implies a time when he *was not*—as an Arian might argue—but rather, his firstborn status is appointive. We are not told he was "born" in heaven. Rather, we are told God *appointed* him firstborn and thus heir of all creation or, as Paul later puts it: "for of him and through him and to him are all things" (Rom. 11:36a NKJV). Finally, the Lord says, "I will establish his line forever, / his throne as long as the heavens endure" (v. 29). His "line" becomes all the children of this Great King and so it includes the church: "If we endure, we will also *reign with him*" (2 Tim. 2:12, emphasis added), and "Blessed and holy are those who share in the first resurrection. The second death has no power over them, but they will be priests of God and of Christ and will *reign with him* for a thousand years" (Rev. 20:6, emphasis added).[16]

The next three verses expound on the Davidic covenant warning of punishment ("If his sons forsake my law . . . , I will punish their sins with the rod, / their iniquity with flogging" vv. 30–32; cf. "When he does wrong, I will punish him with a rod wielded by men, with floggings inflicted by human hands" 2 Sam. 7:14)—a restatement of the conditional aspect of the covenant. If the Davidic sons forsake God's law (the Mosaic covenant) the Lord will punish them, even though they are kings under the Davidic covenant. But the poet follows those lines with a yet stronger affirmation of the covenant's unconditional aspect:

> but I will not take my love from him,
>   nor will I ever betray my faithfulness.
> I will not violate my covenant
>   or alter what my lips have uttered.
> Once for all, I have sworn by my holiness—
>   and I will not lie to David—
> that his line will continue forever
>   and his throne endure before me like the sun;
> it will be established forever like the moon,
>   the faithful witness in the sky." (89:33–37)

---

16 For the "thousand years," see chapter 10 of volume 3.

The opening promise "but I will not take my love (חסד) from him" (v. 33) echoes the promise made to David through Nathan: "But my love (חסד) will never be taken away from him" (2 Sam. 7:15). After that, the grand nature of the similes ("endure before me like the sun . . . forever like the moon") must either be taken as hyperbole or as a statement of a fact not yet realized, and in the normal course of human history incapable of being realized. The poetic figure of the sun and moon does foretell the Son's faithful witness to the Father: "His line . . . will be established forever like the moon, the faithful witness in the sky" (vv. 36–37). Just as the moon witnesses to the sun by reflecting its light, so the Son witnesses to the Father by reflecting his glory (Heb. 1:3; Rev. 1:5).

The unrealizable nature of such a promise in human terms is brought home at the Psalm's conclusion:

> But you have rejected, you have spurned,
>> you have been very angry with your anointed one.
> You have renounced the covenant with your servant
>> and have defiled his crown in the dust. . . .
> You have exalted the right hand of his foes;
>> you have made all his enemies rejoice.
> Indeed, you have turned back the edge of his sword
>> and have not supported him in battle.
> You have put an end to his splendor
>> and cast his throne to the ground. (89:38–39, 42–44)

The psalmist expresses his own assessment of things when he declares, "You have renounced the covenant with your servant." He (mistakenly) takes the outward signs of disaster to mean the Lord has renounced the Davidic covenant—which, whatever he may think, is still in place and eventuates in Christ. Nonetheless, because the Lord is also judging, the lines do show at the psalmist's moment in history the very opposite of the Davidic promise: the Lord has not exalted the horn of the Davidic king and has not protected his people from their enemies (vv. 21–24), but rather exalted the hand of his foe and not supported Israel's king in battle (vv. 42–43). The Lord has not caused his throne to endure forever (vv. 36–37), but rather has cast it to the ground (v. 44). Such inevitable failure in the course of the history of God's people pointed toward a fulfillment of the Davidic promise no Israelite could have imagined. But Isaiah foretold it in his prophecy of the Son.

Psalm 2 and the Davidic Covenant

Only the Messiah *par excellence*—one who was not only anointed with the Spirit as David was, but who had the Spirit without limit—could fulfill what could seem to be the hyperbolic expectations of the promised seed of David. Psalm 2, a Psalm recognized as messianic by the New Testament, is rooted in the Davidic covenant and gives a glimpse of what that seed of David would be like. The linkage of 2 Samuel 7 and Psalm 2 can be seen by way of their thematic parallels:[17]

Thematic Analysis of the Davidic Covenant and Comparison with Psalm 2

Theme	2 Samuel 7:1–17	Psalm 2
Security from foes	v. 11	vv. 1–6
Yahweh establishes throne forever	v. 13b	vv. 6, 8–12
Yahweh = father		
king = son	v. 14	v. 7
chastening	v. 14	—

There are four major components to consider in this outline (security from foes, an eternal throne, a father-son relationship, and a threat of chastening) and they can be taken seriatim.

The theme of security from foes, a promise made in 2 Samuel 7:11, finds a counterpart in the promise of extended rule in Psalm 2:

> Why do the nations conspire
>   and the peoples plot in vain?
> The kings of the earth rise up
>   and the rulers band together
>   against the LORD and against his anointed, saying,
> "Let us break their chains
>   and throw off their shackles."
> The One enthroned in heaven laughs;
>   the LORD scoffs at them.
> He rebukes them in his anger
>   and terrifies them in his wrath, saying,
> "I have installed my king
>   on Zion, my holy mountain." (vv. 1–6)

---

17 Cf. Niehaus, "Covenant and Narrative," 253–55.

The kings and rulers of the earth want to sunder the chains and throw off the shackles of the Lord and his anointed, his Messiah (מָשִׁיחַ). Both Saul and David were anointed at the Lord's command, and any king of Israel could be considered the Lord's "anointed." Even pagans could be in this category. Cyrus was called the Lord's anointed/messiah—and that by the Lord himself (Isa. 45:1). The Lord commanded Elijah to anoint (מָשַׁח) Hazael king over Aram (1 Kings 19:15). The idea that— in the first instance in Psalm 2—the anointed king is Solomon seems reasonable. The royal Messiah, however, will ultimately be Christ, who is the Lord's anointed *par excellence*.

In its historical context, the scenario presented by the Psalm is one of vassal kings and rulers wanting to throw off the yoke of their suzerain and his god. In the ancient Near East, a conquered king and his kingdom came into a state of vassaldom to both the conquering king/suzerain and the suzerain's god.[18] The Lord laughs at the presumption of those pagan rulers, and rebukes and terrifies them in his wrath. He displays the hopelessness of their efforts by reminding us that it is he, the Lord, who has installed his king on his holy mountain, Zion.

The Lord's asseveration is tantamount to a declaration of the Zion throne's imperturbability, and implies a broader and unshakable rule. That declaration forms the second theme in our outline—Yahweh establishes the throne forever. The Messiah declares it:

I will proclaim the LORD's decree:

> He said to me, "You are my son;
>   today I have become your father.
> Ask me, and I will make the nations your inheritance,
>   the ends of the earth your possession.
> You will break them with a rod of iron;
>   you will dash them to pieces like pottery." (vv. 7–9)

The Lord's declaration of sonship in verse 7 ("You are my son; / today I have become your father") states the third theme, that of the father-son relationship. It is taken up in the New Testament and claimed for Jesus as an aspect of the Son's superiority to angels: "For to which of the angels did God ever say, 'You are my Son; / today I have become your Father'"

---

18   So, for instance, Assyrians reckoned the tribute they received from vassals to be the tribute due to their chief god, Ashur. Cf. *ANETBT*, 81.

(Heb. 1:5a). That statement is linked to the promise of the Davidic covenant in the second half of the verse in Hebrews: "Or again, 'I will be his Father, and he will be my Son'" (Heb. 1:5b; cf. 2 Sam. 7:14). The sonship promised in 2 Samuel 7 was only an adoptive sonship, but it prefigured the incarnational sonship of the Christ, the Messiah or Anointed One *par excellence*—who also preexisted as the Son in eternity, and who was and is the model of all sonship—just as his Father is the model of all fatherhood, and the triune God the model of all family.[19]

Jesus is therefore affirmed as the promised Davidic king *par excellence* whose throne will endure forever (agreeable to the extent and unchallengeable authority of his rule as expressed in vv. 8–9)—that "rule with an iron scepter" also attributed to Christ eschatologically (Rev. 12:5; 19:15).[20]

The fourth and final theme noted in the Psalm is the chastening of the son (2 Sam. 7:14). Solomon experienced the Lord's chastening because he took foreign wives and built places of worship for their gods. Nonetheless, the chastening forewarned in the Davidic covenant finds no counterpart in Psalm 2. That is reasonable. If the Psalm is about Solomon and his accession to the throne, omission of any negative note would be understandable. If the poem was a celebratory composition, a negative note would naturally find no place in it. One cannot prove it was an occasional poem, but such an explanation would be consistent with the absence of any warning for the Messiah in Psalm 2.

The Psalm does conclude with a warning, but it is to the rulers of the earth. There has been some unwillingness on the part of translators to acknowledge its patent sense:

> Now therefore, be wise, O kings;
> Be instructed, you judges of the earth.
> Serve the LORD with fear,
> And rejoice with trembling.
> Kiss the Son, lest He be angry,
> And you perish in the way,

---

19   Cf. Royce Gordon Gruenler, *The Trinity in the Gospel of John: A Thematic Commentary on the Fourth Gospel* (Grand Rapids: Baker, 1986), 12–13; Jeffrey J. Niehaus, "Covenant: An Idea in the Mind of God." *JETS* 52, no. 5 (2009), 228–29.

20   A similar quality of rule is also promised to the one who overcomes evil and does the Lord's will in the church at Thyatira (cf. Rev. 2:26–27), a church noted for its infatuation with evil.

When His wrath is kindled but a little.
Blessed are all those who put their trust in Him.
(vv. 10–12 NKJV)[21]

Although some have cast doubt on the phrase "kiss the Son" (cf. RSV, NRSV, "kiss his feet"), the best evidence supports it.[22] Kissing an idol was a way of paying homage to a deity in the ancient Near East. The Old Testament tells of people who kissed the idol of Baal: "Yet I will leave seven thousand people alive in Israel—all those who are loyal to me and have not bowed to Baal or kissed his idol" (lit. "kissed him" [נָשַׁק לוֹ], 1 Kings 19:18). Assyrian annals record an analogous idea: conquered vassals were said to have kissed the feet of the conqueror as a way of paying homage to him. Apart from such ancillary data, the mistaken translation of the Septuagint (followed in turn by the Vulgate) actually points to a Hebrew *Vorlage* that would have been the same as the Hebrew we now have.[23]

---

21 I quote the NKJV version to avoid the unhelpful paraphrase of NIV: "and your way will lead to your destruction" (v. 12a). In the Hebrew, there is no possessive pronoun associated with "way," and NIV's "lead to your destruction" is a paraphrase of "you perish." Translators inevitably take interpretive steps in ambiguous cases, as does NKJV (though less egregiously) by inserting the preposition "in" ("in the way"). The word "way" is an adverbial accusative, translatable as "in the way" or "from the way," that is, "in your way of life," or "from your way of life," or "from the way of life," or even "from the way of the Lord." Likewise, the phrase "when his wrath is kindled but a little" (vs. 12b) could just as well be rendered "for his wrath is quickly kindled (cf. NIV, "for his wrath can flare up in a moment"). The ambiguities are fruitful, and translations should, as much as possible, not obscure them for readers who have no Hebrew.

22 Many translations of an evangelical bent translate "kiss the Son" (ASV, ESV, and cf. OJB) or paraphrase it, for example, "pay homage to the Son" (HCSB, NASB).

23 LXX translates δράξασθε παιδείας as "embrace discipline"; Vulgate translates "aps prehendite disciplinam," that is, "grasp discipline." There are two Hebrew verbs that look identical: נָשַׁק ("to kiss") and נָשַׁק ("to handle," cf. the associated noun, נֶשֶׁק, "equipment"). The LXX translators mistook the former verb ("to kiss") for the latter ("to hold, handle") and so translated "grasp, embrace." That was their first mistake. Their second mistake was apparently to translate the Aramaic word for "son" (בַר) as "discipline/instruction," that is, παιδεία. Apparently the word παις ("lad") lies behind παιδείας, and somehow LXX chose παιδείας for the occasion—maybe to make sense of what seemed a strange expression; or maybe παιδείας is an inner Septuagintal corruption in transmission of παις. Whatever the process, the relation between the two Greek nouns is obvious, as is their affinity to Aramaic בַר ("son"). Finally, the use of an Aramaic word presents no problem in a poem by David. He had hegemony over Aramaean territories (2 Sam. 8:5–8), and a poet could well interject a foreign word for some poetic reason—in this case as Keil and Delitzsch

THE DAVIDIC COVENANT
AND THE COVENANT CUTTING IDIOM

It was observed that the Adamic or Creation covenant came into existence without the use of the usual covenant making idiom "to cut a covenant" or even the term "covenant." The point was also made that absence of a term does not ipso facto mean absence of what the term denotes.[24] The same idea applies to Noah as a prophet, who is never called a prophet, and to the Trinity, a term that does not occur in Scripture at all. The Davidic covenant narrative, like the Adamic covenant narrative, does not use the terms "to cut a covenant" or "covenant." However, subsequent biblical statements do attest to the "covenant" the Lord "made/cut" with David, as noted below:

1   2 Chronicles 7:18
    "I will establish your royal throne, as I covenanted with (lit. "cut for": כרתי ל) David your father when I said, 'You shall never fail to have a man to rule over Israel.'"

2   2 Chronicles 13:5
    "Don't you know that the LORD, the God of Israel, has given the kingship of Israel to David and his descendants forever by a covenant of salt (ברית מלח)?"[25]

---

suggest for euphony (E. Delitzsch, *Psalms* in C. F. Keil and E. Delitzsch, *Commentary on the Old Testament*, vol. v [Peabody, MA: Hendrickson, 1996], 98). Cf. Jeremiah's declaration of a whole sentence in Aramaic for poetic and theological reasons (10:11).

24   It was also noted that the usual idiom has to do exclusively with the special grace covenants and that there was good reason for this; cf. chapters 1 and 5.

25   Salt was regarded as a valuable ingredient of meals and consequently of sacrifices offered under the Mosaic covenant (Lev. 2:13). Since covenant ratification was apparently often solemnized by a covenant meal, a natural connection apparently arose between salt and covenant cutting. Moreover, sharing a meal implied friendship. (Compare the Arabic expressions, "There is salt between us"; "He has eaten of my salt," indicating a hospitality that cemented friendship). It could also be used as a metaphor for service to a sovereign, for example, to "eat the salt of the palace" (Ezra 4:14; cf. perhaps "the four hundred and fifty prophets of Baal and the four hundred prophets of Asherah who eat at Jezebel's table," 1 Kings 18:19b). Because salt is also a preservative, it could easily become symbolic of an enduring covenant. So offerings to the Lord were to be by a statute forever: "a covenant of salt for ever before the LORD" (Num. 18:19). In light of these ideas, Jesus' remark has

3   2 Chronicles 21:7
Nevertheless, because of the covenant (ברית) the Lord had made
with [lit. "cut for": כרת ל), David the LORD was not willing to destroy the house of David. He had promised to maintain a lamp for
him and his descendants forever.[26]

4   Psalm 89:3 [89:4 MT]
You said, "I have made a covenant (lit. "cut a covenant": כרתי ברית)
with my chosen one, I have sworn to David my servant."

5   Jeremiah 33:21
Then my covenant (בריתי) with David my servant—and my covenant with the Levites who are priests ministering before me—can
be broken and David will no longer have a descendant to reign on
his throne.[27]

6   One should also note 2 Chronicles 23:3
The whole assembly made a covenant with the king at the temple of
God. Jehoiada said to them, "The king's son shall reign, as the Lord
promised concerning the descendants of David.

The narrative that enshrines the institution of the Davidic covenant
(2 Sam. 7:1–17) portrays no ritual cutting—says nothing of blood shed to
create the covenant—and speaks of no oath. However, just as Psalm 89:3b
could say the Lord had "sworn to David my servant," and just as Psalm
32:11 can tell us the Lord "swore an oath to David"—even though no oath
is reported in 2 Samuel 7—so later passages can tell us the Lord "cut a
covenant with/for David," although no cutting was mentioned in the
covenant institution narrative. The cited instances provide subsequent
divine commentary on what happened in 2 Samuel 7. They also show

---

covenantal implications: "Have salt in yourselves, and be at peace one with another"
(Mark 9:50).

26 The term still routinely translated "lamp" (ניר) should be translated "yoke," indicating sovereignty, and this has been understood for decades, although translations show
no knowledge (or acceptance) of it. Cf. Paul Hanson, "The Song of Heshbon and David's
NIR," HTR 61:5 (1968): 297–320. Assyrians used the same term (niru) to characterize their
suzerainty; cf. ANETBT, 79–80.

27 For "covenant with the Levites," cf. Numbers 25:12–13, Yahweh's covenant of priesthood with Phineas and his descendants; and see the discussion in chapter 5.

that, later in Israel's history, the covenant cutting idiom could be used to describe a case in which, although a covenant had come into being, it had done so without any literal cutting. Our contemporary idiom to "cut a check" may illustrate the idea for our day. In summary:

1   Clearly, in later usage "to cut a covenant" did not necessarily mean there was a symbolic ritual passage between cut-up animals.

2   The idiom always, however, had the sense of "to ratify, to bring into existence" a covenant as a legal arrangement.

The Noahic covenant was a prior covenant brought into existence without a cutting ceremony, but in that case the absence of such a ceremony had to do with the common grace nature of the covenant.[28]

DAVID A PROPHET

David was a prophet because the Lord anointed him and spoke to and through him. He was, moreover, a covenant mediator prophet through whom the Lord gave the covenant named after him. The Spirit of the Lord came upon David when Samuel anointed him (1 Sam. 16:13), and although that anointing was in the first instance an anointing for royal rule, the Lord also spoke prophetically through David:

> These are the last words of David:
> "The oracle of David son of Jesse,
>   the oracle of the man exalted by the Most High,
> the man anointed by the God of Jacob,
>   Israel's singer of songs:
> 'The Spirit of the LORD spoke through me;
>   his word was on my tongue.'" (2 Sam. 23:1–2)

Notable is the parallelism of Spirit and word. It harks back to the Spirit who worked through the Word in creation, as per the Major Paradigm, and looks forward to Jesus' statement that his words were Spirit (John 6:63).[29]

---

28 Cf. discussion in chapters 1 and 5.

29 Cf. discussion in volume 1, Prolegomena, 8–11.

In the New Testament, Peter calls David a prophet as he addresses the crowd at Pentecost:

> Brothers, I can tell you confidently that the patriarch David died and was buried, and his tomb is here to this day. But he was a prophet and knew that God had promised him on oath that he would place one of his descendants on his throne. Seeing what was ahead, he spoke of the resurrection of the Christ, that he was not abandoned to the grave, nor did his body see decay. (Acts 2:29–31)

Speaking by the Spirit, Peter alludes to the Davidic covenant promise (v. 30) and then to David's own prophetic words about his royal offspring—namely, Jesus—that he would not see corruption (v. 31; cf. Ps. 16:10). David "saw what was ahead" (v. 31), and in this he was like those others in what one may call the Honor Role of Faith, who "did not receive the things promised; they only *saw them* and welcomed them from a distance" (Heb. 11:13).[30] As has been noted, this phenomenon is one in which *faith and sight combine* even though what is seen by faith is not visible to the natural eye.

DAVIDIC COVENANT IN RELATION TO THE MAJOR PARADIGM

Although David wanted to build a house for the Lord, his offspring would accomplish that task, and the Christology of Solomon as temple builder has already been noted. We turn now to consider David as a covenant mediator prophet with regard to the Major Paradigm:

Davidic Covenant Articulated by the Major Paradigm

God works	1 Samuel 16:13
by his Spirit	1 Samuel 16:13
through the Word/a prophet-figure	Acts 2:29–31
to war against and defeat his foe(s)	2 Samuel 2–5
God establishes a covenant with a people	[2 Samuel 7:1–17]

---

30 Although Hebrews 11:1 defines faith as assurance of what is unseen, the same chapter speaks of past believers who died without receiving what was promised but only "saw" those things "from a distance." Cf. discussion of faith and seeing, including their relation to the creation, in volume 1, Prolegomena, 19–20.

God's covenant establishes that people
as God's people   [2 Samuel 7:8–11]
God establishes a temple among his people,   [2 Samuel 7:13a]
because he will reside among them   [1 Kings 6–8]

Four items must be put in brackets, because the Davidic covenant differs in important ways from other special grace covenants: (1) God does not establish a covenant with a people by the Davidic covenant, (2) the covenant he does "cut" does not establish a people as God's people (as sons of Abraham began to be under the Abrahamic covenant, and as Israel was formed to be with more laws under the Mosaic covenant), and (3 and 4) it does not order the covenant mediator to make a temple for the Lord to occupy, and so be among his people (as the Lord had commanded Moses to do). When the Lord makes the Davidic covenant, he institutes a covenant focused on the royal line. That is a narrow focus. To be sure, the covenant has implications and even promises for the people over whom the king rules. Nonetheless, it is *with David* that the Lord makes the covenant, and the covenant has to do *with David and his royal offspring*. The Lord does promise to give peace to his people, but it is expressly in that context that he will protect David from his enemies (vv. 10–11), make it possible for David's son to become king in turn ("I will make one of your sons king and will keep his kingdom strong" v. 12) and finally build the temple (v. 13a).[31] In other words, national security is promised as a context in which a peaceful transition can take place from David to his son and in which the temple can be built—and these are core goals of the Davidic covenant. The Lord does not establish Israel as his people by this covenant for he had already done that in the Abrahamic and Mosaic covenants.[32] The Davidic covenant is not a new covenant for the people as a whole,

---

31   The promise to make David's name great (v. 9b) ironically echoes the false ambition of those who set about to build the Tower of Babel: "Then they said, 'Come, let us build ourselves a city, with a tower that reaches to the heavens, so that we may make a name for ourselves and not be scattered over the face of the whole earth'" (Gen. 11:4). Fallen humans opposed to God can only produce warped versions of what God would intend because, though they sin, they are made in God's image and are bound by their nature come up with distortions of God's ideas.

32   Israel was God's people before Sinai, as is made clear by the Lord's demand: "Let my people go" (Exod. 5:1; 7:16; 8:1, 20, 21; 9:1; etc.). At Sinai they became his people under another and different covenant—the Mosaic covenant with its laws and requirements, etc.

for they remain under the Mosaic covenant—as does David himself—
and they will incur covenantal judgments if they disobey the Mosaic
covenant—as will David himself.

THE TEMPLE BUILT BY THE SON

The Lord's temple will be built by the son of David, and the symbolic significance of the son's name that means "his peace" has been noted.[33] The
name is evocative of the "Prince of Peace" encountered in the fourfold
name of Isaiah 9:5 who will also rule on David's throne. It should also
recall Jesus' promise: "Peace I leave with you" (John 14:27). As Prince
of Peace, he can promise and give a peace that is no mere absence of
conflict (often rather the contrary) but an inner restoration undertaken
by the Spirit.

One sees then a certain Christology in the promised son of David.
He will be king over the Lord's people, he will be a prophet, and he will
build the temple.[34]

According to the clear and usual standard for Christology, David
himself is a type of Christ by his offices. He is a king, a prophet, and
intriguingly, a shepherd like Moses, the covenant mediator prophet
before him.

When the Lord allowed Moses to go through a shepherding experience away from Egypt for forty years, and when he allowed David to grow
up a shepherd before making him king, he knowingly drew on or alluded
to the shepherd typology of the ancient Near East according to which
kings styled themselves shepherds.[35] However, the relationship between
a shepherd and his sheep—as a calling among men—is also rooted in

---

33 In chapter 4; cf. Jeffrey J. Niehaus, "God's Covenant with Abraham," *JETS* 56, no. 2
(2013): 254–55.

34 Solomon's prophetic standing is established because the Lord reveals himself to
him and speaks good to him for his kingdom (1 Kings 3:5–15)—and cf. the so-called word-
event formula typically applied to prophets, also applied to Solomon: "The word of the
LORD came to Solomon," 1 Kings 6:11; for the formula, cf. Genesis 15:1 (Abram), 1 Samuel
15:10 (Samuel), 2 Samuel 7:4 (Nathan), 24:11 (Gad), 1 Kings 13:10 (the old prophet), 1 Kings
17:2; 18:1 (Elijah), 2 Kings 20:4 (Isaiah), Jeremiah 1:4 (Jeremiah), Ezekiel 3:16 (Ezekiel),
Hosea 1:1 (Hosea), Joel 1:1 (Joel), Jonah 1:1 (Jonah), Micah 1:1 (Micah), Zephaniah 1:1
(Zephaniah), Haggai 2:20 (Haggai), Zechariah 1:1 (Zechariah). Solomon is *ipsis factis*
a prophet.

35 Cf. *ANETBT*, 34–55.

the divine nature and is a particular expression of it—or, perhaps better, is patterned after an archetype and also is and resembles an ectype. The archetype is the nature of God who always has, and does, and will stand in a shepherding relation to his people—until he and they are made one in the way he will make us one in the new heaven and the new earth. The ectype is the incarnate Son (cf. Heb. 1:3) who could justly call himself "the Good Shepherd" (John 10:11). He also is the Lamb who was slain who becomes one with his sheep—who are called to offer themselves as living sacrifices to the same lamb who sacrificed himself for them. Pastors who are called to shepherd display this resemblance perhaps more obviously that do others in the body of Christ.

We also know the name "David" means "beloved"—a reality that comes to full expression as Jesus emerges from the baptismal waters: "And a voice from heaven said, 'This is my Son, whom I love [lit. "the beloved," ὁ ἀγαπητός]; with him I am well pleased'" (Matt. 3:17). The Greek term "beloved" exactly translates the name "David," so the translation, "This is my Son, the David," would not be inappropriate. On the same understanding, Ezekiel's prophecies were not merely Christological, but literal (Ezek. 34:23–24; 37:24–25). The relations discussed above appear in the following simple chart:

Name	Significance	Realized in Christ
David	"beloved"	"My Son the beloved" (Matt. 3:17)
Solomon	"his peace"	"My peace I give you" (John 14:27)

It is also a pertinent consideration that in both cases—that of Solomon and that of Christ—the son/Son builds the temple, which in the latter case is the church. The concept of the Davidic son/Son as temple builder and the implications of "house/temple" will be further considered under discussion of the new covenant.[36]

The discussion of David would not do justice to the prophet without considering something about the dynamic of prophecy as David experienced it. This topic could have been taken up under the rubric of prophetic experience.[37] It is reserved for this place as part of an overall discussion of David. David's prophetic gifting first shows up in the form of his gifting as a harpist.

---

36 In chapter 10 of volume 3.
37 In chapters 14–15 of this volume.

DAVID AND THE DYNAMIC OF PROPHECY:
COMPOSER/HARPIST/WORSHIPER

Many Psalms are attributed to David, and the Old Testament portrays David not only as a composer of poems but also as an instrument player and organizer of worship groups. Two things are foundational to all this: (1) David was anointed by God and (2) David worshiped God. David's playing for Saul offers data for subsequent consideration:

> Now the Spirit of the LORD had departed from Saul, and an evil spirit from the LORD tormented him. Saul's attendants said to him, "See, an evil spirit from God is tormenting you. Let our lord command his servants here to search for someone who can play the lyre. He will play when the evil spirit from God comes on you, and you feel better." So Saul said to his attendants, "Find someone who plays well and bring him to me." One of the servants answered, "I have seen a son of Jesse of Bethlehem who knows how to play the lyre. He is a brave man and a warrior. He speaks well and is a fine-looking man. And the LORD is with him." Then Saul sent messengers to Jesse and said, "Send me your son David, who is with the sheep." So Jesse took a donkey loaded with bread, a skin of wine and a young goat and sent them with his son David to Saul. David came to Saul and entered his service. Saul liked him very much, and David became one of his armor-bearers. Then Saul sent word to Jesse, saying, "Allow David to remain in my service, for I am pleased with him." Whenever the spirit from God came on Saul, David would take up his lyre and play. Then relief would come to Saul; he would feel better, and the evil spirit would leave him. (1 Sam. 16:14–23)

"Now the Spirit of the LORD had departed from Saul, and an evil spirit from the LORD tormented him" (v. 14). One has here in a small specimen a dynamic that takes place later, when the Lord abandons the Jerusalem temple, and later still when the Lord withdraws his Spirit from restraining the "man of lawlessness"—apparently the Antichrist. In every case, the Lord's presence, or Spirit (cf. Ps. 139:7 for the parallelism and identification of the two: "Where can I go from your Spirit / Or where can I flee from your presence?") provides a spiritual cover or bulwark against a spiritual foe. Once that presence or Spirit has been withdrawn, whoever the Spirit had covered is left open to attack by an evil spiritual power. That is what happens to Saul.[38]

---

38 None of that, however, proves that Saul was at any point a temple of the Spirit.

Saul apparently agrees that having someone play for him could assuage the unwelcome effects he has begun to experience. That is not to suggest Saul understands the spiritual dynamics in which he will now play a part, for we are not told that he does and it is probably not likely he does. We are not told that he understands what may transpire in the spiritual world, once a skilled player comes to attend him and play for him. But he senses such a player could bring some relief, and so it turns out. But what causes the relief?

It seems two explanations are possible. Either the music itself brings some sort of emotional or psychological relief, or David's performance somehow involves an act of deliverance—that is, it causes the evil spirit to leave. As is known, music can calm a person or excite a person. The saying "Music soothes the savage beast" is not groundless.[39] However, we are not told David's music simply calmed Saul's emotions. Rather, "Whenever the spirit from God came on Saul, David would take up his lyre and play. Then relief would come to Saul; he would feel better, *and the evil spirit would leave him*" (1 Sam. 16:23, emphasis added). Since the evil spirit was the one who caused Saul to feel poorly, it would seem unlikely that Saul's feeling better would cause the evil spirit to leave. Rather, David's playing caused the evil spirit to leave, and as a result Saul felt better. The advent of the evil spirit *made Saul feel badly*. The departure of the evil spirit *removed the cause* (namely, *the spirit*) of Saul's afflicted condition, and the king's mood improved.[40]

It is important to parse this event so nicely (to use that word in an older sense), since it is too easy for a modern person to pass over what is going on in this passage because of its spiritual implications.[41] If one

---

The Spirit can be with, bless, and empower someone for kingdom work without residing in that person. Cf. discussion in volume 1 of *Biblical Theology*, chapter 4.

39   The adage is actually a slight paraphrase Congreve's line: "Music has charms to soothe a savage beast." Cf. William Congreve, *The Mourning Bride* (1697), act 1, scene 1.

40   A modern book or movie cannot be a hermeneutical key for our passage, although such a work may offer some parallel insight: Gandalf's deliverance of King Theoden from the evil, intimate spirit-presence of Saruman, as portrayed in the movie *The Two Towers* may come to mind for Tolkein aficionados. Cf. J. R. R. Tolkein, *The Peoples of Middle Earth: The History of Middle Earth, Book 12* (New York: HarperCollins, 1997), Appendix B, 17: "Théoden. He is called Théoden Ednew in the lore of Rohan, for he fell into a decline under the spells of Saruman, but was healed by Gandalf, and in the last year of his life arose and led his men to victory at the Hornburg, and soon after to the Fields of Pelennor, the greatest battle of the Age."

41   As an illustration of the case in point, I was once approached by a student at the

takes the spiritual data of the Bible seriously as fact, one admits the existence and activity of evil spirits and, of course, of Satan himself. On such an understanding, there are evil spirits who may be—who seem to be—fallen angels. When one reads a New Testament report of Jesus casting out an evil spirit, one is not reading an ancient writer's attempt to explain—in the only way he knew how—God's healing of a mental disorder. One takes the report at face value, and one does well to do so. As Peter warns God's people: "Your enemy the devil prowls around like a roaring lion looking for someone to devour" (1 Peter 5:8).

It follows that something more than delightful music must have been filling the air when David played for Saul. Since it was David who played, it is possible that his play was no mere musical improvisation or repetition of some popular tune, but an act of worship. If it was, the possibility arises of a spiritual presence opposed to the evil spirit afflicting Saul. Psalm 22 may offer some help in identifying that presence. Below are two translations of the relevant verse:

> Yet you are enthroned as the Holy One;
> you are the one Israel praises. (v. 3)

A more literal translation would be:

> You are the Holy One enthroned [amid/   ואתה קדש יושב
> upon] the praises of Israel   תהלות ישׂאראל

The verse is genuinely ambiguous. The NIV rendering, however, obscures some important detail. First, there is in the Hebrew no second "you" (as in "*you are* the one Israel praises"), although NIV's repetition of the pronoun could be justified if the pronoun were doing double duty, as happens in Hebrew poetry and in general language usage.[42] Second, the whole sentence, "You are the one Israel praises," is a paraphrase of the words "praises of Israel." A more literal translation, true to the NIV's intent, would be "you are the praises of Israel." The paraphrase may do

---

Harvard Divinity School Library and asked if I knew where to find the Old Testament passage about a king of Israel who had a mental disorder and was depressed.

42   For example, as in such a sentence as, "You are a baker and a homeowner," that is, "You are a baker and *you are* a homeowner," where the first (and only) "you are" does double duty. We note that there is also no verb "to be" in verse 3, but this is quite common in Hebrew sentences.

justice to David's intent, but that is not unquestionably the case.[43] If we translate in the alternate way we have offered, there are also things to explain. First, there is no "amid" or "upon" in the Hebrew and the whole phrase "praises of Israel" is taken as an adverbial accusative—hence we supply a preposition, either "amid" or "upon" (to explain adverbially, *where*). Second, the translation we offer produces an enjambment ("You are the Holy One enthroned / upon the praises of Israel"), something that seldom occurs in Hebrew poetry although it does occur. One could avoid this difficulty by assuming the word "enthroned" actually belongs to the second half of the verse, hence: "You are the Holy One, / you are enthroned upon the praises of Israel." If we do so the resultant syllable count is: 5:8, instead of the slightly more even 7:6 that results if we keep "enthroned" in the first half of the verse (or if we follow Stuart's not infrequent practice of deleting the first *waw* [ו] as secondary, we get an even more even 6:6).[44] However, the syllable count issue is not necessarily an impediment to our translation because some variety of the range 5:8 is commonly attested in Hebrew poetry.[45] Finally, another translation possibility is "You inhabit the praises of Israel."

If either of the suggested translations is appropriate (i.e., "enthroned upon/amid" or "inhabit")—and they seem to fall within the range of reasonable proposals for the verse—that has spiritual implications. The New Testament makes it clear that deliverance from an evil spirit is a work of the Holy Spirit (e.g., "But if it is by the Spirit of God that I drive out demons, then the kingdom of God has come upon you," Matt. 12:28). If it is true, according to the suggested renderings of Psalm 22:3, that the Holy One is enthroned amid or inhabits the praises of his people, that could mean the Holy Spirit (God's presence) is especially palpable or

---

43 NIV essentially follows LXX, although the latter is more periphrastic ("But you dwell among the holy ones/the praise of Israel": σὺ δὲ ἐν ἁγίοις κατοικεῖς, / ὁ ἔπαινος Ισραηλ), and cf. Jerome (Vulgate: "But you dwell in the holy [place], / the praise of Israel": Tu autem in sancto habitas, laus Israel).

44 Cf. Douglas K. Stuart, *Studies in Early Hebrew Meter*, Harvard Semitic Monograph Series, 13 (Missoula, MT: Scholars Press, 1976), 79.

45 The foregoing discussion of syllable count understands that the metrical criteria for scansion in Hebrew poetry developed toward the end of the nineteenth century by German scholars is not likely to correspond realistically to the way Hebrew poetry was read in the days of, say, David or Isaiah. Someone somewhere once made the point—quite validly it seems to me—that, had the tradition of scanning Vergil, for example, not been handed down to us along with his poetry, it is unlikely modern scholars would have figured it out. Cf. Stuart, *Studies*, 1–49.

potently present where genuine worship of God is going on. There may be no need to make a case for this dynamic to members of Pentecostal or charismatic churches, although there are many Christians who have not had such experiences, just as we do not all have the same spiritual gifts, and there are some who even (unfortunately in my view) argue strongly that such a Christian experience is not possible.

Be that as it may, if David was singing praises to the Lord when he played before Saul, and if the Holy Spirit did presence himself more powerfully in response to his worship, that sequence of events could explain the departure of the evil spirit. Just as evil spirits would depart because of the work of the Holy Spirit when Jesus delivered someone, so here the work of the Holy Spirit could have resulted in the departure of the evil spirit that was afflicting Saul. Since David's ministry was repeated ("Whenever the spirit from God came on Saul, David would take up his lyre and play," v. 23a) the deliverance was never permanent—the evil spirit was after all "from the Lord" (v. 14)—nonetheless, the Lord honored the worship David offered with a noticeable result in his ministry to Saul: "Then relief would come to Saul; he would feel better, and the evil spirit would leave him" (v. 23b).

The observation made above about the character of David's musical performance in Saul's presence—namely, that it was worshipful—would be consistent with what is known of David's later poetical compositions, including hymns, and his later involvement in the organization of the Lord's worship. David may have already been a composing poet when he first visited Saul. Although, for example, David was still only a shepherd when Saul summoned him, it could be that Psalm 8 dates from that period of his life as some have suggested—although the hymn is so full of mature reflection in its praise that internal evidence from it can hardly be used to insist on an origin from David's adolescence or young manhood. He could have composed it when he was a youth and later, as king, taken it up and assigned it (or even revised it and assigned it) "For the director of music. According to *gittith*" (Psalm 8, title [8:1 MT]). Or David could have composed it as king and assigned it for worship then. In any case, David composed poems for worship. Much later Amos could remark sarcastically—to an audience whose spiritual orientation was very different from that of David—"You strum away on your harps like David and improvise on musical instruments" (6:5). David could take a vigorous part in the worship of God's people: "David and all Israel were celebrating with all their might before the LORD, with castanets, harps, lyres, timbrels, sistrums, and cymbals" (2 Sam. 6:5; cf. 1 Chron. 13:8).

David not only took part in but also gave directions for worship. "David told the leaders of the Levites to appoint their fellow Levites as musicians to make a joyful sound with musical instruments: lyres, harps and cymbals" (1 Chron. 15:16). Intriguingly we are also told "David, together with the commanders of the army, set apart some of the sons of Asaph, Heman, and Jeduthun for the ministry of prophesying, accompanied by harps, lyres, and cymbals" (1 Chron. 25:1). The connection between worship and prophesying will be discussed shortly. Before that, we consider another passage in which the two are associated:

> He stationed the Levites in the temple of the LORD with cymbals, harps and lyres in the way prescribed by David and Gad the king's seer and Nathan the prophet; this was commanded by the LORD through his prophets. Hezekiah gave the order to sacrifice the burnt offering on the altar. As the offering began, singing to the LORD began also, accompanied by trumpets and the instruments of David king of Israel. The whole assembly bowed in worship, while the musicians played and the trumpets sounded. All this continued until the sacrifice of the burnt offering was completed. (2 Chron. 29:25–28)

The occasion was a special one—Hezekiah's cleansing of the temple and restoration of offerings (2 Chron. 29:3–19)—and orchestrated *at the direction of prophets* "*in the way prescribed by David* and Gad the king's *seer* and Nathan the *prophet*" (v. 25, emphases added). The passage not only associates worship and prophetic direction, it makes a valuable contribution to understanding the relationship between the two. Direction for worship in this case came through prophets. In fact the phrase "in the way prescribed by David" is literally "according to the commandments of David" (במצות דויד, v. 25), using a term evocative of the Lord's commandments in the Mosaic covenant. The implication may well be that David's commands were also prophetic.[46]

There were also apparently occasions when worship led to prophetic utterance. That appears to be the point of a verse quoted above: "David, together with the commanders of the army, set apart some of the sons of Asaph, Heman, and Jeduthun for the ministry of prophesying, accompanied by harps, lyres and cymbals" (1 Chron. 25:1). One may offer as an

---

46 That would be consistent with David's claim that the Spirit gave him the plan and details for equipping the temple his son would build (1 Chron. 28:11–19) where, after all, the worship would take place. Cf. *ANETBT*, 91–92.

idea one cannot prove: the instruments could have been part of worship, and worship was answered by a stronger presence of the Holy Spirit, and, finally, the Spirit spoke through the prophet(s) in the "ministry of prophesying."

Evidence from Elisha's Ministry

We have suggested the Spirit came when David played the harp worshipfully before Saul, and the Spirit delivered the king. Elisha's request for a harp player in an encounter with three kings who sought guidance may provide a kindred example:

> Elisha said, "As surely as the LORD Almighty lives, whom I serve, if I did not have respect for the presence of Jehoshaphat king of Judah, I would not pay any attention to you. But now bring me a harpist." While the harpist was playing, the hand of the LORD came on Elisha and he said, "This is what the Lord says: I will fill this valley with pools of water. For this is what the LORD says: You will see neither wind nor rain, yet this valley will be filled with water, and you, your cattle and your other animals will drink. This is an easy thing in the eyes of the LORD; he will also deliver Moab into your hands. You will overthrow every fortified city and every major town. You will cut down every good tree, stop up all the springs, and ruin every good field with stones." (2 Kings 3:14–19)

Mesha, king of Moab, had rebelled against Israel to whom Moab had been a vassal state and to whom Mesha had rendered a regular tax/tribute of costly wool. Mesha rebelled when Ahab died and his son succeeded him to the throne. Such a scenario was not uncommon in the ancient Near East. Hittite emperors who ascended to the throne of their fathers recorded similar acts of rebellion. Suzerains in the ancient Near East imposed tax and tribute on their vassals and the impositions could be onerous. Assyrian emperors typically boasted that they had imposed the "heavy tribute of Ashur" on their vassals.[47] Under such circumstances, it was natural that a vassal could see the transition of power in the imperial capital as an opportunity to cast off the imperial yoke and be free of such a burden. Royal annals from those days record many campaigns not only to conquer new kingdoms and force them to become vassal states, but also to re-conquer vassals who had thrown off the imperial yoke, as Mesha had done.

---

47 Cf. *ANETBT*, 79–80.

When Mesha rebels, the king of Israel, Jehoshaphat king of Judah, and the king of Edom—a vassal state of Judah and thus also under compulsion to add military assistance to the king of Judah when such assistance was wanted—set out to re-subdue Mesha and restore Moab as a vassal state to Israel. The three kings lose their way, however, and that prompts Jehoshaphat to ask for a prophet of the Lord for guidance. Elisha is providentially close by, and the kings consult him with the result reported in the verses just quoted.

Elisha's address to Jehoram deserves comment. He speaks with the same boldness one saw when Elijah rebuffed Ahab, before that prophet's commanding performance on Mount Carmel (cf. 1 Kings 18:18–19). Such boldness probably comes from the Spirit who was working through him. Jehoram, by contrast, was no devoted Yahwist: "Joram son of Ahab became king of Israel in Samaria in the eighteenth year of Jehoshaphat king of Judah, and he reigned twelve years. He did evil in the eyes of the LORD, but not as his father and mother had done. He got rid of the sacred stone of Baal that his father had made. Nevertheless he clung to the sins of Jeroboam son of Nebat, which he had caused Israel to commit; he did not turn away from them" (2 Kings 3:1–3). The king continued an idolater and his bad example caused Israel to sin. His attitude when the three kings lose their way is the same attitude shown by Israel when they felt doomed in the wilderness: "'What!' exclaimed the king of Israel. 'Has the LORD called us three kings together only to deliver us into the hands of Moab?'" (2 Kings 3:10; cf. Moses' account of the people's rebelliousness: "You grumbled in your tents and said, 'The LORD hates us; so he brought us out of Egypt to deliver us into the hands of the Amorites to destroy us,'" Deut. 1:26–27). Jehoram's "read" of the situation is not one of faith, but one of fear—and fear has to do with judgment.

Despite Jehoram's unfaithfulness, Elisha asks for a harpist, and when the harpist plays, the "hand of the Lord" comes upon him and he prophesies (vv. 15–19). "Hand" is a metonymy for "power," and the power that comes upon Elisha is the Spirit of prophecy.[48] That is the source of the oracle Elisha gives the kings. The intriguing thing for the present discussion is the role of the harpist in the process. The verb used for his performance—he "played" (נגן)—is the same one used of David's ministry to Saul (נגן, 1 Sam. 16:17, 18, 23). The playing appears to be invocative of the Spirit's advent and work in Elisha's situation, as arguably was the

---

48 The Bible gives no evidence of such a thing as impersonal spiritual power.

case when David ministered to Saul. Consistent with the data surveyed, it is possible the playing in both cases involved worship, and not some quasi-magical way of invoking the Lord's presence, and that the Spirit responded similarly to both prophets.

Conclusions Regarding the Spirit and Worship

It seems, then, that music could be an accompaniment of both worship (2 Chron. 29:25–28) and prophecy (2 Kings 3:15–19; 1 Chron. 25:1). As 2 Kings 3:15–19 may suggest, worship could invite the Spirit for a work of prophecy. That would be consistent with Psalm 22:3 as we translated that verse. The data do not suggest that Old Testament prophecy occurred only in the context of worship; they do suggest that genuine worship could invoke the Spirit of prophecy. For the church also, one should not assume all prophecy occurs in the context of worship. On the other hand, genuine worship can still invoke the Spirit of prophecy.

THE PSALMS: LIFE UNDER THE DAVIDIC COVENANT

Although much could be written about life under the Davidic covenant, it is also true that a good deal of such life was actually and more importantly life under the Mosaic covenant, because it was obedience or lack of obedience to that covenant that served as the historian's standard by which he measured the goodness or badness of a king. In David's case, one aspect of life under the Davidic covenant deserves particular attention, and that aspect is the Psalms.

Psalms are poems composed by people who lived under the Mosaic covenant but also under the monarchy (excepting Pss. 90 [by Moses], 137 [exilic], and 126 [post-exilic]) and the messianic promises the Lord had made to David. So the Psalms are expressions that arose out of that life. Since it was the Mosaic covenant that actually governed or was meant to govern both people and kings, it is appropriate to view the Psalms as covenantal literature of a particular sort or sorts. It may also be possible to relate the various psalm types or *Gattungen* to respective elements of the covenant *Gattung* as poetic expressions of the way in which those covenantal elements or aspects impinged upon or found expression in and through the poet—as one who spoke for himself and for his people. Below is an outline of such correspondences arranged in terms of representative Psalms:

Psalm	Type	Covenantal Element	Covenantal Passage
29	Hymn	Title	[Deut. 1:1]
135	Salvation history	Historical prologue	Deut. 1–4
1	Torah	Stipulations	Deut. 5–26
	Blessing	Blessings	Deut. 28:1–14
	Curse	Curses	Deut. 28:15–68
2	Royal	Law of the king	Deut. 17:14–20
	Messianic	Promise of the prophet	Deut. 18:17–19

The array is only meant to be representative. Consequently not all Psalm types are included—for example, the laments (individual or corporate), the thanksgivings (individual or corporate), the vows, etc. With a nod to Gunkel, one understands that, although certain Psalms were "royal" in the first instance, they could also imply the future Messiah *par excellence* as in the case of Psalm 2.[49]

THE IMPRECATORY PSALMS

One type of Psalm not noted above—the so-called Imprecatory Psalms—is important because of the challenge those Psalms present to understanding and what they may show of the character of God and his psalmist.[50] They range from the psalmist's appeal to the Lord to do justice on his personal foes (cf. esp. Pss. 5:8–10; 17:6–14; 35:1–8, 26; 59:1, 12–13; 69:22–28; 70:2–3; 109:6–15, 19–20; 140:8, 10–11), to calls to God to break the power of evil men who oppress the poor (e.g., Pss. 10:12–15; 58:6–9), to calls for judgment on the foes of the Lord's people or of Zion (e.g., Pss. 79:6–7, 12; 83:9–18; 129:5–8), to calls for judgment on Babylon and her allies (e.g., Ps. 137:79). The ethos of these poems, which appears to be one of vengeance on the foe, seems contrary to the love of God. The

---

49 Of course Gunkel used the term "royal" precisely to avoid any such implications since he did not believe in predictive prophecy. Cf. Bernard Anderson, *Out of the Depths* (Louisville: Westminster John Knox, 2000)—a handy Gunkelian treatment of Psalm types.

50 The Imprecatory Psalms are Psalms 5, 10, 17, 35, 58, 59, 69, 70, 79, 83, 109, 129, 137, and 140. Note also the imprecatory call in Psalm 11, not noted in all lists of imprecatory Psalms (Ps. 11:5–6).

Conquest also seems contrary to the love of God, but we understand the Conquest was a judgment, and we know a far worse judgment awaits, and will be executed by that same Christ in whose face we see the love of God. Consequently God's judgment and his love are not contradictory. But what of the psalmist's cries for vengeance? It should be noted first that they are consistent with God's principle laid down in the Mosaic covenant: "It is mine to avenge; I will repay" (Deut. 32:35a). Moreover, the same principle is affirmed in the new covenant (Rom. 12:9; Heb. 10:30), and by Jesus himself (Matt. 5:43–48; cf. 1 Peter 2:23). The psalmist's cry for vengeance therefore is no mere cry of personal vindictiveness, but a cry for justice—for a just judgment—to the God who will judge all things and who does execute judgment even in the flow of history.[51] He calls for a judgment intrusion that adumbrates the final judgment—whether he knows it or not! But once again, the psalmist does not take it upon himself to execute judgment. He appeals to the Lord for that.

PENULTIMATE NOTE: THE ELOHISTIC PSALTER

Since eleven of the forty Elohistic Psalms are attributed to David (more than to any other author), and since he was apparently a major ground-layer of psalmic tradition in Israel, this seems an opportune place to comment on the curious collection known as the Elohistic Psalter. The category is not so much a matter of *Gattung* as it is of divine name usage. In this collection (Psalms 42–83), the name Elohim predominates, being used forty-two times (contrast the minimal use of Yahweh). One might try to explain this predominance of the name Elohim by proposing that the context for its use usually has to do with the nations. If that were so, it would parallel the uses of Elohim and Yahweh in, for example, Genesis, where as Cassuto noted, Elohim is used when the narrative has to do with pagan kings or with the world generally, and Yahweh is used when the Lord's covenant people are somehow the focus. This cannot be the case in the Elohistic Psalter, however, since in nineteen (virtually half) of the Elohistic Psalms the nations are not at all the focus, and nine of them (Pss. 42, 43, 51, 61, 62, 63, 64, 70, 73) do not mention the nations at all. In fact, eleven of them are poems of individual lament or trust by

---

51 This is true no matter how strong the Psalmist's feelings are when he calls out for God's judgment. Such a cry can be spiritually valid.

David.[52] Three Psalms are ambiguous in this regard, because they have to do either with corporate lament (in the context of the nations, Ps. 80) or with salvation history (with reflections on the international background or context, Pss. 78, 81)—two topics that naturally evoke other nations, and those topics also appear in "Yahwistic" Psalms.

In terms of provenance, the Elohistic psalter seems to be a thoughtfully organized and edited collection added to the larger collection of Psalms before that later collection was divided into the traditional five books (echoing no doubt the five books of Moses), since it spans books II and III of the Psalter. Laura Joffe has pointed to the number 42 as an important organizational principle in the Elohistic Psalter: it is the number of Psalms it includes, the number of times the divine name Elohim is used in it, and the number of its first Psalm. Burnett has further suggested that 42 was an important number in Egypt and Mesopotamia as it was the number of hymns claimed for the Sumerian royal daughter and high priestess Enheduanna (2285–2250 BC), although a connection between the Sumerian collection and the psalter—beyond the shared number 42—has not been demonstrated, and may not be possible to demonstrate.[53]

CONCLUSION

David is a hugely important figure in the Bible, as attest the 974 occurrences of his name—as compared with 22 for Adam, 56 for Noah, 57 for Abram/235 for Abraham, and 803 for Moses. The statistic alone shows how signal a figure he was, both in the life of Israel during his reign

---

52 That is, Psalms 51, 57–64, 69, and 70. Psalm 51 does mention Yahweh once (v. 15) and does not mention the nations at all. Eight of the other nine Psalms are either poems of personal lament (42, 43, 52, 54–56) or personal trust (71, 73). Psalm 50 has a broader focus but only because it calls on heaven and earth in covenant lawsuit against God's people.

53 Joel S. Burnett, "Forty-Two Songs for Elohim: An Ancient Near Eastern Organizing Principle in the Shaping of the Elohistic Psalter," *JSOT* 31, no. 1 (September 1, 2006): 81–101. Cf. earlier Laura Joffe, "The Elohistic Psalter: What, How, and Why?" *Scandinavian Journal of the Old Testament: An International Journal of Nordic Theology*, vol. 15, issue 1, 2001, 142–69. Enheduanna was the daughter of Sargon of Akkad and a high priestess and poetess. She composed personal poems devoted to the goddess Inanna and also a collection called "Sumerian Temple Hymns," as well as possibly other works; cf. William W. Hallo and J. J. A. Van Djk, *The Exaltation of Inanna* (New Haven, CT: Yale University Press, 1968), 3.

and as something of a standard subsequently, and also in his prophetic/ Christological role. Accordingly, a suitable conclusion to this chapter, and especially as the next volume takes up the new covenant, is a prophecy stated by Isaiah and quoted by Paul:

> The Root of Jesse will spring up,
>   one who will arise to rule over the nations;
>   in him the Gentiles will hope. (Rom. 15:2; cf. Isa. 11:10)

Bibliography

Ackerman, James S. "Joseph, Judah, and Jacob." In *Literary Interpretation of Biblical Narrative*, edited by Kenneth R. R. Gros Louis and James S. Ackerman, 2:85–114. Nashville: Abingdon, 1982.

Ackerman, S. "The Personal Is Political: Covenantal and Affectionate Love ('AHEB, 'AHABA) in the Hebrew Bible." *VT* 52, no. 4 (2002): 437–58.

Ahlström, G. W. "Der Prophet Nathan und der Tempelbau." *VT* 11, no. 2 (1961): 113–27.

Albert, Robert. *The Art of Biblical Narrative*. New York: Basic Books, 1981.

Albright, W. F. "Samuel and the Beginnings of the Prophetic Movement." In *Interpreting the Prophetic Tradition: The Goldenson Lectures, 1955–1966*, edited by H. M. Orlinsky, 149–76. New York: KTAV, 1969.

Alexander, P. S. "The Targumim and Early Exegesis of 'Sons of God' in Gen 6." *JJS* 23, no. 1 (1972): 60–71.

Alexander, T. Desmond. "Abraham Reassessed Theologically." In *He Swore an Oath: Biblical Themes from Genesis 12–50*, edited by R. S. Hess, G. J. Wenham, and P. E. Satterthwaite. Carlisle: Paternoster, 1994.

———. "From Adam to Judah: The Significance of the Family Tree in Genesis." *EQ* 61 (1989): 5–19.

———. "Genesis 22 and the Covenant of Circumcision." *JSOT* 25 (1983): 17–22.

Alighieri, Dante. *The Divine Comedy of Dante Alighieri*. Translated by Henry F. Cary. New York: F. Collier & Son, 1900.

Alter, R. *The Art of Biblical Narrative*. New York: Basic Books, 1981.

Andersen, Francis I. "Israelite Kinship Terminology and Social Structure." *BTrans* 20, no. 2 (1969): 29–39.

———. "Yahweh, the Kind and Sensitive God." In *God Who Is Rich in Mercy*, edited by Peter T. O'Brien and David G. Preston, 41–88. Homebush West: Lancer Books, 1986.

459

Andersen, Niels-Erik. *The Old Testament Sabbath*. Missoula, MT: Society of Biblical Literature, 1972.

Anderson, Bernard. *Out of the Depths: The Psalms Speak for Us Today*. Louisville: Westminster John Knox, 2000.

———. *Understanding the Old Testament*. 4th ed. Englewood Cliffs, NJ: Prentice-Hall, 1986.

Anderson, G. A. *Sacrifices and Offerings in Ancient Israel: Studies in Their Social and Political Importance*. Atlanta: Scholars Press, 1987.

Andrew, Maurice E. *The Ten Commandments in Recent Research*. Great Britain: SCM, 1962.

Archer, Gleason. *A Survey of Old Testament Introduction*. Chicago: Moody Press, 1964.

Arnold, W. R. *Ephod and Ark: A Study in the Records and Religion of the Ancient Hebrews*. Cambridge: Harvard University Press, 1917.

Bailey, L. R. "The Golden Calf." *HUCA* 42 (1971): 97–115.

Baker, Charles F. *A Dispensational Theology*. Grand Rapids: Grace Bible College, 1971.

Baltzer, K. *Das Bundesformular*. Neukirchen-Vluyn: Neukirchener Verlag, 1964.

———. *The Covenant Formulary in Old Testament, Jewish, and Early Christian Writings*. Philadelphia: Fortress, 1971.

Bar-Efrat, Shermon. *Narrative Art in the Bible*. Translated by Dorothea Shefer-Vanson. Sheffield: Sheffield Academic Press 1989.

Barnes, W. E. *The First Book of Kings* Cambridge: Cambridge University Press, 1911.

Barr, James. "Reflections on the Covenant with Noah." In *Covenant as Context: Essays in Honour of E. W. Nicholson*, edited by A. D. H. Mayes and R. B. Salters, 11–22. Oxford: Oxford University Press, 2003.

———. *Holy Scripture: Canon, Authority, Criticism*. Philadelphia: Westminster Press, 1983.

———. "Some Semantic Notes on Covenant." In *Beiträge zur Alttestamentlichen Theologie: Festschrift Für Walther Zimmerli Zum 70. Geburtstag*, edited by H. Donner, R. Hanhart, and R. Smend, 23–38. Göttingen: Vandenhoeck & Ruprecht, 1977.

Barth, Lewis M. "Introduction the Akedah: A Comparison of Two Midrashic Presentations." In *A Tribute to Geza Vermes: Essays on Jewish and Christian Literature*, edited by P. R. Davies and R. T. White, 125–38. Sheffield: JSOT Press, 1990.

Bartholomew, C. and M. W. Goheen. "Story and Biblical Theology." In *Out of Egypt: Biblical Theology and Biblical Interpretation*, edited by C. Bartholomew et al., 144–71. Grand Rapids: Zondervan, 2004.

Barton, George A. "National Israelitish Deities." Pages 86–115 in *Oriental Studies: A Selection of the Papers Read Before the Oriental Club of Philadelphia, 1888–1894*. Boston: Ginn & Co., 1894.

Barton, J. "Covenant in Old Testament Theology." In *Covenant as Context: Essays in Honour of E. W. Nicholson*, edited by A. D. H. Mayes and R. B. Salters, 23–38. Oxford: Oxford University Press, 2003.

Batto, B. F. *Slaying the Dragon: Myth Making in the Biblical Tradition*. Louisville: Westminster John Knox, 1992.

Bauckham, Richard. *Jesus and the God of Israel: God Crucified and Other Studies on the New Testament's Christology of Divine Identity*. Grand Rapids: Eerdmans, 2008.

Beale, G. K. *A New Testament Biblical Theology: The Unfolding of the Old Testament in the New*. Grand Rapids: Baker, 2011.

Beauchamp, P. "Propositions sur l'Alliance de l'Ancien Testament Comme Structure Centrale." *RSR* 58, no. 2 (1970): 161–93.

Becker, J. *Gottesfurcht im Alten Testament*. Rome: Pontifical Biblical Institute, 1965.

Beckwith, Roger T. "The Unity and Diversity of God's Covenants." *TB* 38 (1987): 93–118.

———. *The Old Testament Canon of the New Testament Church*. Grand Rapids: Eerdmans, 1985.

Beitzel, B. J. "The Right of the Firstborn (Pi Snayim) in the Old Testament." In *Essays in the Old Testament: A Tribute to Gleason Archer*, edited by W. C. Kaiser and R. F. Youngblood, 179–90. Chicago: Moody Press, 1986.

Bellefontaine, E. "The Curses of Deuteronomy 27." In *No Famine in the Land: Studies in Honor of John L. McKenzie*, edited by J. W. Flanigan and A. W. Robinson, 49–61. Missoula, MT: Scholars Press, 1975.

Benin, S. D. "The 'Cunning of God' and Divine Accommodation." *JHI* 45, no. 2 (1984): 179–91.

Benno, J. *Das Erste Buch der Tora Genesis*. Berlin: Schocken, 1934.

Bergen, R. D. "The Role of Genesis 22.1–19 in the Abraham Cycle: A Computer-Assisted Textual Interpretation." *CTR* 4 (1990): 322–24.

Berkhof, Louis. *Systematic Theology*. Grand Rapids: Eerdmans, 1941.

Bertholet, Alfred. *Das Buch Hesekiel*. Freiburg: Mohr Siebeck, 1897.

Bigalke, Ron J., Jr., ed. *Dispensationalism: An Analysis of the Movement and Defense of Traditional Dispensationalism*. Lanham, MD: University Press of America, 2005.

Blaising, Craig A., and Darrell B. Bock. *Progressive Dispensationalism*. Wheaton, IL: Victor Books, 1993.

———, eds. *Dispensationalism, Israel, and the Church: A Search for Definition.* Grand Rapids: Zondervan, 1992.

Blank, S. "The Curse, Blasphemy, the Spell, and the Oath." *HUCA* 23 (1950–51): 73–95.

Blenkinsopp, J. *A History of Prophecy in Israel: From the Settlement in the Land to the Hellenistic Period.* Philadelphia: Westminster Press, 1983.

———. *Prophecy and Canon: A Contribution to the Study of Jewish Origins.* Notre Dame: University of Notre Dame, 1977.

Blocher, Henri. *In the Beginning: The Opening Chapters of Genesis.* Translated by David G. Preston. Downers Grove, IL: InterVarsity Press, 1984.

Block, Daniel I. *The Book of Ezekiel, Chapters 1–24.* Grand Rapids: Eerdmans, 1997.

———. *Deuteronomy.* NIV Application Commentary. Grand Rapids: Zondervan, 2012.

———. *The Gospel according to Moses: Theological and Ethical Reflections on the Book of Deuteronomy.* Eugene, OR: Cascade, 2012.

———. "Israel's House: Reflections on the Use of BYT YSR'L in the Old Testament in the Light of its Ancient Near Eastern Environment." *JETS* 28, no. 3 (1985): 257–75.

———. "My Servant David: Ancient Israel's Vision of the Messiah." In *Israel's Messiah in the Bible and the Dead Sea Scrolls*, edited by R. S. Hess and M. D. Carroll R, 17–56. Grand Rapids: Baker, 2003.

———. "Preaching Old Testament Apocalyptic to a New Testament Church." *Calvin Theological Journal* 41/1 (2006): 17–52.

Blomberg, Craig L., and Sung Wook Chung, eds. *A Case for Historic Premillennialism: An Alternative to "Left Behind" Eschatology.* Grand Rapids: Baker, 2009.

Blumenthal, Yisroel C. "Fifth Response to Dalton Lifsey—Isaiah 9:5, 6 (6, 7)." *1000 Verses—A Project of Judaism Resources.* https://yourphariseefriend .wordpress.com/2012/02/08/fifth-response-to-dalton-lifsey-isaiah-956 -67/.

Boecker, H. "Anmerkungen zur Adoption im Alten Testament." *ZAW* 86, no. 1 (1974): 86–89.

———. *Law and the Administration of Justice in the Old Testament and Ancient East.* Minneapolis: Augsburg, 1980.

ten Boom, Corrie. *The Hiding Place.* Grand Rapids: Chosen, 1971.

Booji, T. "Psalm CX: 'Rule in the Midst of Your Foes.'" *VT* 41, no. 4 (1991): 396–406.

Bowker, J. W. "Psalm CX." *VT* 17, no. 1 (1967): 31–41.

Breitbart, S. "The Akedah: A Test of God." *Dor le Dor* 15 (1986–87): 19–28.

Brichto, H. C. "Kin, Cult, Land, and Afterlife: A Biblical Complex." *HUCA* 44 (1979): 1–54.

———. *The Names of God: Poetic Readings in Biblical Beginnings*. Oxford: Oxford University Press, 1998.

Bright, John. *Covenant and Promise: The Prophetic Understanding of the Future in Pre-Exilic Israel*. Philadelphia: Westminster Press, 1976.

———. "An Exercise in Hermeneutics: Jeremiah 31:31–34." *Int* 20, no. 2 (1966): 188–210.

———. *A History of Israel*. 3rd ed. Philadelphia: Westminster Press, 1982.

———. *The Kingdom of God*. Nashville: Abingdon, 1953.

Brodie, T. L. *Genesis as Dialogue: A Literary, Historical, and Theological Commentary*. Oxford: Oxford University Press, 2001.

Brokke, Harold J. *The Law Is Holy*. Minneapolis: Bethany, 1963.

Brown, Francis, S. R. Driver, and Charles A. Briggs, eds. *A Hebrew and English Lexicon of the Old Testament*. 1906. Reprint, Oxford: Clarendon Press, 1951.

Browne, Thomas. *Religio Medici*. New York: E. P. Dutton and Company, 1951.

Brueggemann, Dale A. "Brevard Childs' Canon Criticism: An Example of Post-Critical Naiveté." *JETS* 32, no. 3 (1989): 312.

Brueggemann, Walter. *Genesis*. Atlanta: John Knox, 1982.

———. *The Land: Place as Gift, Promise, and Challenge in Biblical Faith*. Philadelphia: Fortress, 1977.

Buber, M., and H. H. Rowley. "Priests and Levites in Deuteronomy." *VT* 12, no. 2 (1962): 129–38.

Burnett, Joel S. "Forty-Two Songs for Elohim: An Ancient Near Eastern Organizing Principle in the Shaping of the Elohistic Psalter." *JSOT* 31, no. 1 (September 2006): 81–101.

Buss, M. J. "The Covenant Theme in Historical Perspective." *VT* 16, no. 4 (1966): 503–504.

Butterfield, James R. "Yahweh's Refutation of the Baal Myth Through the Actions of Elijah and Elisha." In *Israel's Apostasy and Restoration*, edited by Abraham Gileadi, 19–38. Grand Rapids: Baker, 1988.

Calvin, John. *Commentary on the Book of Joshua* Grand Rapids: Eerdmans, 1949.

Carpenter, J. E., and G. Harford. *The Composition of the Hexateuch*. London: Longmans, Green & Co., 1902.

Carruth, William Herbert. *The Legends of Genesis*. Chicago: The Open Court Publishing Company, 1901.

Cassuto, Umberto. *Biblical and Oriental Studies*. 2 vols. Jerusalem: Magnes, 1973–75.

———. *A Commentary on the Book of Exodus*. Translated by I. Abrahams. Jerusalem: Magnes Press, 1967.

———. *A Commentary on the Book of Genesis*. 2 vols. Translated by I. Abrahams. Jerusalem: Magnes Press, 1978.

———. *The Documentary Hypothesis: Eight Lectures*. Translated by I. Abrahams. Jerusalem: Magnes Press, 1961.

Cazelles, H. "Biblical Messianism." In *Studia Biblia I*, edited by E. A. Livingstone, 49–58. Sheffield: JSOT Press, 1979.

———. "Les Structures Successives de la 'Berit' dans l'Ancien Testament." *Bulletin du Centre Protestant d'Etudes* 3 (1984): 33–46.

Childs, Brevard S. *Biblical Theology in Crisis*. Philadelphia: Westminster Press, 1970.

———. "The Canonical Shape of the Prophetic Literature." *Interpretation* 32 (1978): 54.

———. *Exodus: A Critical, Exegetical Commentary*. Old Testament Library. Philadelphia: Westminster Press, 1974.

———. *Introduction to the Old Testament as Scripture*. Philadelphia: Fortress, 1979.

———. *Myth and Reality in the Old Testament*. London: SCM, 1962.

———. *Old Testament Theology in a Canonical Context*. Philadelphia: Fortress, 1986.

Churchill, Winston. A House of Commons Speech. November 11, 1947.

Clark, W. M. "The Flood and the Structure of the Prepatriarchal History." *ZAW* 83, no. 2 (1971): 184–211.

———. "The Righteousness of Noah." *VT* 21, no. 3 (1971): 261–80.

Clements, Ronald E. *Old Testament Theology: A Fresh Approach*. Greenwood, SC: Attic, 1978.

Clines, David J. A., ed., *Dictionary of Classical Hebrew*. 9 vols. Sheffield: Sheffield Academic Press, 1993–2016.

Coats, G. W. "Abraham's Sacrifice of Faith: A Form-Critical Study of Genesis 22." *Int* 27, no. 4 (1973): 389–400.

Cogan, C. *Imperialism and Religion: Assyria, Judah, and Israel in the Eighth and Seventh Centuries BCE*. Missoula, MT: Scholars Press, 1974.

Coleran, J. E. "The Sacrifice of Melchisedech." *TS* 1, no. 1 (1940): 27–36.

Cooke, G. "The Sons of (the) God(s)." *ZAW* 76, no. 1 (1964): 22–47.

Cooper, A. M. "The Life and Times of King David according to the Book of Psalms." In *The Poet and the Historian*, edited by R. E. Friedman, 117–31. Chico, CA: Scholars Press, 1983.

Copeland, E. C. "The Covenant: The Key to Understanding the Bible." In

The Book of Books: Essays on the Scripture in Honor of Johannes G. Vos, edited by J. H. White, 29–37. Phillipsburg: Presbyterian & Reformed, 1978.

Cowper, William. *The Task*. Pages 197–98 in Book I of *The Poetical Works of William Cowper*. London: Macmillan, 1893.

Craigie, Peter C. *The Book of Deuteronomy*. NICOT. Grand Rapids: Eerdmans, 1976.

Cranfield, C. E. B. "'The Works of the Law' in the Epistle to the Romans." *JSNT* 43 (1991): 89–101.

Cross, Frank M. *Canaanite Myth and Hebrew Epic*. Cambridge: Harvard University Press, 1973.

———. *From Epic to Canon: History and Literature in Ancient Israel*. Baltimore: Johns Hopkins University Press, 1998.

———. "Studies in the Structure of Hebrew Verse: The Prosody of the Psalm of Jonah." Pages 159–67 in *The Quest for the Kingdom of God: Studies in Honor of George E. Mendenhall*, edited by H. B. Huffmon et al. Winona Lake, IN: Eisenbrauns, 1983.

Cross, Frank M., and David N. Freedman. *Studies in Ancient Yahwistic Poetry*. Missoula, MT: Scholars' Press, 1975.

Dahood, M. *Psalms I*. Anchor Yale Bible 16. Garden City: Doubleday, 1965.

Damrosch, D. *The Narrative Covenant*. San Francisco: Harper & Row, 1987.

Davidson, A. B. *The Book of the Prophet Ezekiel*. Cambridge: University Press, 1893.

———. *The Theology of the Old Testament*. Edinburgh: T&T Clark, 1952.

Davidson, Robert. "Covenant Ideology in Ancient Israel." In *The World of Ancient Israel*, edited by R. E. Clements, 323–47. Cambridge: Cambridge University Press, 1989.

Davies, Graham. "Covenant, Oath, and the Composition of the Pentateuch." In *Covenant as Context: Essays in Honour of E. W. Nicholson*, edited by A. D. H. Mayes and R. B. Salters, 71–90. Oxford: Oxford University Press, 2003.

Davies, G. H. "The Ark in the Psalms." In *Promise and Fulfillment*, edited by F. F. Bruce, 51–61. Edinburgh: T&T Clark, 1963.

Davis, John Jefferson. *Conquest and Crisis Studies in Joshua, Judges, and Ruth*. Grand Rapids: Baker, 1969.

———. *Moses and the Gods of Egypt*. 2d ed. Winona Lake, IN: BMH Books, 1998.

De Boer, P. A. H. "The Son of God in the Old Testament." *OTS* 18 (1973): 188–207.

De Fraine, J. *Adam and the Family of Man*. Staten Island, NY: Alba House, 1965.

De Quekker, L. "Noah and Israel: The Everlasting Divine Covenant with Mankind." In *Questions Disputees d'Ancien Testament*, edited by C. Brekelmans, 115–29. Louvain: University of Louvain Press, 1974.

Dean, David Andrew. "Covenant, Conditionality, and Consequence: New Terminology and a Case Study in the Abrahamic Covenant." *JETS* 57, no. 2 (2014): 298–301.

Dell, K. J. "Covenant and Creation in Relationship." In *Covenant as Context: Essays in Honour of E. W. Nicholson*, edited by A. D. H. Mayes and R. B. Salters, 111–34. Oxford: Oxford University Press, 2003.

Dennison, C. G. "Thoughts on the Covenant." In *Pressing Toward the Mark*, edited by C. G. Dennison and R. C. Gamble, 7–21. Philadelphia: Committee for the Historian of the Orthodox Presbyterian Church, 1986.

DeVries, Simon J. *1 Kings*. Word Biblical Commentary 12. Nashville: Thomas Nelson, 1985.

———. *Prophet against Prophet: The Role of the Micaiah Narrative (1 Kings 22) in the Development of Early Prophetic Tradition*. Grand Rapids: Eerdmans, 1978.

Dillard, R. G. "David's Census: Perspectives on II Samuel 24 and I Chronicles 21." In *Through Christ's World*, edited by W. R. Godfrey and J. L. Boyd, 94–107. Phillipsburg, NJ: Presbyterian & Reformed, 1985.

Dods, Marcus. *The Book of Genesis*. The Expositor's Bible 1, edited by W. Robertson Nicoll. Grand Rapids: Eerdmans, 1947.

Donaldson, M. E. "Kinship Theory in the Patriarchal Narratives." *JAAR* 49, no. 1 (1981): 77–87.

Donner, H. "Adoption oder Legitimation? Erwaungen zur Adoption im Alten Testament auf dem Hintergrund der Altorientalischen Rechte." *Oriens Antiquus* 8 (1969): 87–119.

Donner, H. u. W. Röllig. *Kanaanäische und Aramäische Inschriften*. 3 vols. Wiesbaden: Harrasowitz, 1971–76.

Driver, S. R. *Deuteronomy*. 3rd ed. Edinburgh: T&T Clark, 1901.

———. *Exodus*. Cambridge: Cambridge University Press, 1911.

Dumbrell, William J. *Covenant and Creation: A Theology of Old Testament Covenants*. Nashville: Thomas Nelson, 1984.

———. *Covenant and Creation: An Old Testament Covenant Theology*. 1984. Reprint, Exeter, UK: Paternoster, 2013.

———. "The Covenant with Noah." *RTR* 38, no. 1 (1979): 1–9.

———. "Creation, Covenant, and Work." *ERT* 13, no. 2 (1989): 137–56.

———. "The Davidic Covenant." *RTR* 39, no. 2 (1980): 40–47.

———. "The Prospect of Unconditionality in the Sinaitic Covenant." In *Israel's Apostasy and Restoration: Essays in Honor of Ronald K. Harrison*, edited by A. Gileadi, 141–55. Grand Rapids: Baker, 1988.

Dyrness, William. *Themes in Old Testament Theology*. Downers Grove, IL: InterVarsity Press, 1979.

Eichrodt, Walther. *Ezekiel*. Translated by Cosslett Quin. Philadelphia: Westminster Press, 1975.

———. *Theology of the Old Testament*. 2 vols. Philadelphia: Westminster Press, 1975.

———. *Theology in the Old Testament*. Translated by James Baker. Philadelphia: Westminster Press, 1967.

Eissfeldt, Otto. "The History of Israelite-Jewish Religion and Old Testament Theology." Pages 20–21 in *The Flowering of Old Testament Theology: A Reader in Twentieth Century Old Testament Theology, 1930–1990*, edited by Ben Charles Ollenberger et al. Winona Lake, IN: Eisenbrauns, 1992.

———. *The Old Testament: An Introduction*. Translated by Peter Ackroyd. Oxford: Blackwell, 1965.

Ellison, Henry L. *Genesis 1–11*. The New Layman's Bible Commentary. Grand Rapids: Zondervan, 1979.

Engnell, I. *Studies in Divine Kingship in the Ancient Near East*. 2nd ed. Oxford: Blackwell, 1967.

Epsztein, L. *Social Justice in the Ancient Near East and the People of the Bible*. London: SCM, 1986.

Faley, R. J. *Bonding with God: A Reflective Study of Biblical Covenant*. New York: Paulist, 1997.

Farris, T. V. *Mighty to Save: A Study in Old Testament Soteriology*. Nashville: Broadman, 1993.

Fensham, F. C. "Father and Son as Terminology for Treaty and Covenant." In *Near Eastern Studies in Honor of William Foxwell Albright*, edited by H. Goedicke, 121–35. Baltimore: Johns Hopkins University Press, 1971.

———. "Malediction and Benediction in Ancient Near Eastern Vassal-Treaties and the Old Testament." *ZAW* 74, no. 1 (1962): 1–9.

———. "The Covenant as Giving Expression on the Relationship between the Old and New Testament." *TB* 22 (1971): 82–94.

Ferguson, Sinclair. "How Does the Bible Look at Itself?" In *Inerrancy and Hermeneutics*, edited by Harvie M. Conn, 47–66. Grand Rapids: Baker, 1988.

Fesko, J. V. "On the Antiquity of Biblical Theology." In *Resurrection and Eschatology: Theology in Service of the Church*, edited by L. G. Tipton and J. C. Waddington, 443–77. Phillipsburg, NJ: P & R, 2008.

Fields, Weston W. *Unformed and Unfilled: A Critique of the Gap Theory*. Grand Rapids: Baker, 1976.

Finnegan, J. *Myth and Mystery: An Introduction to the Pagan Religions of the Biblical World*. Grand Rapids: Baker, 1989.

Fisch, H. "The Analogy of Nature: A Note on the Structure of Old Testament Imagery." *JTS* 6, no. 2 (1955): 161–73.

Flanagan, N. M. "The Covenant and How It Grew." *AER* 143 (1960): 145–56.

Fohrer, G. *Ezechiel*. Tübingen: Mohr Siebeck, 1955.

———. *Theologische Grundstrukturen des Alten Testaments*. New York: Walter de Gruyter, 1972.

Fokkelman, J. P. *Narrative Art and Poetry in the Books of Samuel: A Full Interpretation Based on Stylistic and Structural Analyses: Vol. III: Throne and City (II Sam. 2–8 & 21–24)*. Assen, Netherlands: Van Gorcum, 1990.

———. "On the Mount of the Lord There Is Vision." In *Signs and Wonders: Biblical Texts in Literary Focus*, edited by C. Exum, 41–57. Decatur, GA: Society of Biblical Literature, 1989.

———. "Time and the Structure of the Abraham Cycle." *VTSup* 25, 96–109. Leiden: Brill, 1989.

Fossum, J. E. *The Name of God and the Angel of the Lord*. Tübingen: J. C. B. Mohr, 1985.

Frankfort, H. *Kingship and the Gods*. Chicago: University of Chicago Press, 1948.

Freedman, David N. "Divine Commitment and Human Obligation: The Covenant Theme." *Int* 18, no. 4 (1964): 419–31.

Friedman, R. E. "The Hiding of the Face: An Essay on the Literary Unity of Biblical Narrative." In *Judaic Perspectives on Ancient Israel*, edited by J. Neusner et al., 207–22. Philadelphia: Fortress, 1987.

Gage, Warren Austin. *The Gospel of Genesis: Studies in Protology and Eschatology*. Winona Lake, IN: Carpenter, 1984.

Gager, J. G. *Curse Tablets and Biding Spells from the Ancient World*. New York: Oxford University Press, 1992.

Gakuru, G. *An Inner-Biblical Exegetical Study of the Davidic Covenant and the Dynastic Oracle*. Lewiston: Edwin Mellen, 2000.

Galloway, A. D. "Creation and Covenant." In *Creation, Christ, and Culture*, edited by R. McKinney, 108–18. Edinburgh: T&T Clark, 1976.

Gammie, J. G. *Holiness in Israel*. Minneapolis: Fortress, 1989.

Garcia-Treto, F. O. "Covenant in Recent Old Testament Studies." *Austin Seminary Bulletin* 96 (1981): 10–19.

Gaston, L. "Abraham and the Righteousness of God." *HBT* 2 (1980): 39–68.

Gehman, H. S. "The Covenant: The Old Testament Foundation of the Church." *Theology Today* 7, no. 1 (1950): 26–41.

———. "The Oath in the Old Testament: Its Vocabulary, Idiom, Syntax; Its Semantics and Theology in the Masoretic Text and the Septuagint." In *Grace upon Grace*, edited by J. I. Cook, 51–65. Grand Rapids: Eerdmans, 1975.

Gentry, Peter J., and Stephen J. Wellum. *Kingdom through Covenant: A Biblical-Theological Understanding of the Covenants*. Wheaton, IL: Crossway, 2012.

Gese, H. "Der Davidsbund und die Zionswerwahlung." In *Vom Sinai zum Zion*, edited by Harmut Gese, 113–29. Munich: Kaiser, 1974.

———. *Essays in Biblical Theology*. Minneapolis: Augsburg, 1981.

Gilchrist, Paul R. "Towards a Covenantal Definition of Torah." In *Interpretation and History*, edited by R. Laird Harris, Sevee Hwaquck, and Robert J. Vanjoy, 93–108. Singapore: Christian Life, 1956.

Gileadi, A. "The Davidic Covenant: A Theological Basis for Corporate Protection." In *Israel's Apostasy and Restoration: Essays in Honor of Roland K. Harrison*, edited by A. Gileadi, 157–63. Grand Rapids: Baker, 1988.

Gilkey, Langdon. *Maker of Heaven and Earth*. Garden City, NY: Doubleday, 1959.

Gissing, Anna Moseley. "Divine-Human Covenants: A Survey." Unpublished paper, South Hamilton, MA: Gordon-Conwell Theological Seminary, 2012.

Glueck, Nelson. *Hesed in the Bible*. Translated by A. Gottschalk. Cincinnati: Hebrew Union College, 1967.

Goldingay, John. *Theological Diversity and the Authority of the Old Testament*. Grand Rapids: Eerdmans, 1987.

———. *Approaches to Old Testament Interpretation*. Downers Grove, IL: InterVarsity Press, 1981.

Gordon, Cyrus H. *The Common Background of Greek and Hebrew Civilizations*. New York: Norton, 1965.

———. "Higher Critics and Forbidden Fruit." *CT* 4 (23 November 1959): 3–6.

Gower, Jeff, ed., "Revival Breaks Out Amidst Civil War: Colombia." *Everyhome Magazine* (June 2014): 10–12. Colorado Springs: EHC, 2014.

Graham, Billy. *Angels: God's Secret Agents*. Garden City, NY: Doubleday, 1975.

Grand, J. A., and A. I. Wilson, eds. *The God of Covenant: Biblical, Theological, and Contemporary Perspectives*. Leicester: Apollos, 2005.

Gray, G. B. *A Critical and Exegetical Commentary on Numbers*. Edinburgh: T&T Clark, 1903.

Grayson, A. Kirk. "A. O. 78.1." Vol. 1 in *Assyrian Rulers of the Early First Millennium BC*. Toronto: University of Toronto, 1991.

———. *Assyrian Royal Inscriptions*. 2 vols. Wiesbaden: O. Harrassowitz, 1972.

Gressmann, Hugo. *Mose und seine Zeit: Ein Kommentar zu den Mose-Sagen*. Göttingen: Vandenhoeck & Ruprecht, 1913.

———. *Der Ursprung der Israelitisch-Judischen Eschatologie*. Göttingen: Vandenhoeck & Ruprecht, 1905.

Grintz, J. M. "The Treaty of Joshua with the Gibeonites." *JAOS* 86 (1966): 113–26.

Gross, David. "Aristotle on Wit, and Conscience v. Law." *The Picket Line*. https://sniggle.net/TPL/index5.php?entry=10Oct09.

Grüneberg, K. N. *Abraham, Blessing, and the Nations: A Philological and*

Exegetical Study of Genesis 12:3 and Its Narrative Context. Berlin: Walter de Gruyter, 2003.

Guinan, M. D. *Covenant in the Old Testament.* Chicago: Franciscan Herald, 1975.

Gunkel, Hermann. *Genesis.* Translated by M. E. Biddle. Macon, GA: Mercer University Press, 1997.

Gunkel, Hermann and Heinrich Zimmern. *Schöpfung und Chaos in Urzeit und Endzeit: eine Religionsgeschichtliche Untersuchung über Gen 1 und Ap Joh 12.* Göttingen: Vendenhoeck und Ruprecht, 1895.

Gunn, D. M. *The Story of King David.* Sheffield: JSOT Press, 1978.

Ha, John. *Genesis 15: A Theological Compendium of Pentateuchal History.* Berlin: Walter de Gruyter, 1989.

Habel, N. C. *Yahweh versus Baal.* New York: Bookman, 1964.

Hafemann, Scott. *The God of Promise and the Life of Faith: Understanding the Heart of the Bible.* Wheaton, IL: Crossway, 2001.

Hafemann, Scott, and Paul H. House, eds. *Central Themes in Biblical Theology: Mapping Unity in Diversity.* Grand Rapids: Baker, 2007.

Hahn, S. W. "Covenant, Oath, and the Aqedah: Διαθήκη Galatians 3:15–18." *CBQ* 67, no. 1 (2005): 79–100.

———. *Kinship by Covenant: A Canonical Approach to the Fulfillment of God's Saving Promises.* New Haven: Yale University Press, 2009.

Hallo, William W., and J. J. A. van Dijk. *The Exaltation of Inanna.* New Haven, CT: Yale University Press, 1968.

Hamilton, James M., Jr. *God's Glory in Salvation through Judgment: A Biblical Theology.* Wheaton, IL: Crossway, 2010.

Hamilton, Victor. *Handbook on the Pentateuch.* Grand Rapids: Baker, 1982.

Hanson, Paul D. *The People Called: The Growth of Community in the Bible.* San Francisco: Harper & Row, 1986.

———. "The Song of Heshbon and David's NIR." *HTR* 61 no. 5 (1968): 297–320.

Haran, M. "The Berit 'Covenant': Its Nature and Ceremonial Background." In *Tehillah le-Moshe: Biblical and Judaic Studies in Honor of Moshe Greenberg,* edited by M. Cogan, B. L. Eichler, and J. H. Tigay, 203–19. Winona Lake, IN: Eisenbrauns, 1997.

———. *Temples and Temple Service in Ancient Israel.* Oxford: Clarendon Press, 1978.

Harless, H. *How Firm a Foundation: The Dispensations in the Light of Divine Covenants.* New York: Peter Lang, 2004.

Harrelson, W. *Interpreting the Old Testament.* New York: Holt, Rinehart, and Winston, 1964.

Harrison, R. K. *Introduction to the Old Testament.* Grand Rapids: Eerdmans, 1969.

Harris, R. Laird. "The Mist, the Canopy, and the Rivers of Eden." *JES* 11, no. 4 (1968): 177–79.

Harvey, J. "Le 'Rib-Pattern', Réquisitoire Prophétique sur la Rupture de l'Alliance." *Bib* 43, no. 2 (1962): 172–96.

Hasel, Gerhard. F. "The Meaning of the Animal Rite in Genesis 15." *JSOT* 19 (1981): 61–78.

———. "The Nature of Biblical Theology: Recent Trends and Issues." *Andrews University Seminary Studies* 32/3 (1994): 203–15.

———. *Old Testament Theology: Basic Issues in the Current Debate*. 4th ed. Grand Rapids: Eerdmans, 1991.

———. "Recent Translations of Gen 1:1: A Critical Look." *BTrans* 22, no. 4 (1971): 154–66.

Hayes, J. H. "The Tradition of Zion's Inviolability." *JBL* 82, no. 4 (1963): 419–26.

Heidel, Alexander. *The Babylonian Genesis*. Chicago: University of Chicago Press, 1950.

Henry, Matthew. *Isaiah to Malachi*. Vol. IV in *Commentary on the Whole Bible*. Grand Rapids: Christian Classics Ethereal Library, 2000. http://www.biblesnet.com/mhc4.pdf.

Henry, Thomas F. *Covenant and Kingdom: Or, A Right Relationship*. Unpublished thesis. St. Louis: Covenant Theological Seminary, 1989.

Hess, Richard S. "The Slaughter of the Animals in Genesis 15: Genesis 15:8–21 and Its Ancient Near Eastern Context." In *He Swore an Oath: Biblical Themes from Genesis 12–50*, edited by R. S. Hess, G. J. Wenham, and P. E. Satterwaite, 55–65. 2nd ed. Eugene, OR: Wipf and Stock, 2007.

Hesse, Hermann. *Siddhartha*. Frankfurt: Suhrkamp Verlag, 1969.

Hillers, Delbert R. *Covenant: The History of a Biblical Idea*. Baltimore: Johns Hopkins University Press, 1969.

———. "A Note on Some Treaty Terminology in the OT." *BASOR* 176 (1964): 46–47.

———. *Treaty-Curses and the Old Testament Prophets*. Rome: Pontifical Biblical Institute, 1964.

Hirsch, Samson R. *The Pentateuch*. Translated by Isaac Levy. New York: Judaic, 1971.

Hoffmeier, J. K. "The King as God's Son in Egypt and Israel." *JSSEA* 24 (1994): 28–38.

Holladay, J. S. "Assyrian Statecraft and the Prophet of Israel." *HTR* 63, no. 1 (1970): 29–52.

House, H. Wayne, ed. *Israel: The Land and the People*. Grand Rapids: Kregel, 1998.

House, Paul R. *Old Testament Theology*. Downers Grove, IL: InterVarsity Press, 1998.

Huffmon, H. B. "The Covenant Lawsuit in the Prophets." *JBL* 78, no. 4 (1959): 286–95.

Hugenberger, Gordon P. *Marriage as a Covenant: A Study of Biblical Law and Ethics Governing Marriage Developed from the Perspective of Malachi*. Leiden: Brill, 1994.

Hughes, Philip E. *Interpreting Prophecy*. Grand Rapids: Eerdmans, 1980.

Huntress, E. "'Sons of God' in Jewish Writings Prior to the Christian Era." *JBL* 54, no. 2 (1935): 117–23.

Hurowitz, V. *I Have Built You an Exalted House: Temple Building in the Bible in Light of Mesopotamian and Northwest Semitic Writings*. Sheffield: Sheffield Academic Press, 1992.

Hyer, Conrad. *The Meaning of Creation*. Atlanta: John Knox, 1984.

Ingram, L. Robert. "The Grace of Creation." *WTJ* 37, no. 2 (1975): 206–17.

Isaac, E. "Circumcision as Covenant Rite." *Anthropos* 59 (1964): 444–56.

Jacob, B. *The First Book of the Bible: Genesis*. New York: KTAV, 1974.

Jacob, Edmond. *Theology of the Old Testament*. Translated by Arthur W. Heathcote and Philip Alcock. New York: Harper, 1958.

Jacobsen, T. "The Eridu Genesis." *JBL* 100, no. 4 (1981): 513–29.

Janzen, J. G. *Genesis 12–50: Abraham and All the Families of the Earth*. International Theological Commentary. Grand Rapids: Eerdmans, 1993.

Jathanna, C. "The Covenant and Covenant Making in the Pentateuch." *BTF* 3 (1969–71): 27–54.

Jocz, Jacob. *The Covenant: A Theology of Human Destiny*. Grand Rapids: Eerdmans, 1968.

Joffe, Laura. "The Elohistic Psalter: What, How, and Why?" *Scandinavian Journal of the Old Testament: An International Journal of Nordic Theology* 15, no. 1 (2001): 142–69.

Johag, I. "TOB. Terminus Technicus in Vertragund Bündnisformularen des Alten Orients und des Alten Testaments." In *Bausteine Biblischer Theologie*, edited by H. J. Fabry, 3–23. Cologne-Bonn: Bonner Biblische Beiträge, 1977.

Johnson, A. R. *Sacral Kingship in Ancient Israel*. Cardiff: University of Wales Press, 1955.

Johnson, M. D. *The Purpose of Biblical Genealogies*. New York: Cambridge University Press, 1969.

Kaiser, Otto. *Introduction to the Old Testament*. Minneapolis: Augsburg, 1975.

Kaiser, Walter C., Jr. "The Blessing of David: The Charter for Humanity." In

The Law and the Prophets, edited by J. H. Skillen, 298–318. Nutley, NJ: Presbyterian & Reformed, 1974.

———. "Israel and Its Land in Biblical Perspective." In *The Old Testament in the Life of God's People: Essays in Honor of Elmer A. Martens*, edited by Jon Isaak, 245–56. Winona Lake, IN: Eisenbrauns, 2009.

———. *The Promise-Plan of God: A Biblical Theology of the Old and New Testaments*. Grand Rapids: Zondervan, 2008.

———. *Toward an Old Testament Theology*. Grand Rapids: Zondervan, 1978.

———. *Toward Rediscovering the Old Testament*. Grand Rapids: Zondervan, 1987.

———. "The Unfailing Kindness Promised to David: Isaiah 55:3." *JSOT* 45 (1989): 91–98.

Kalimi, Isaac. "The Land of Moriah, Mount Moriah, and the Site of Solomon's Temple in Biblical Hermeneutics." *HTR* 83, no. 4 (1990): 345–62.

Kalluveettil, Paul. *Declaration and Covenant*. Analecta Biblica 88. Rome: Biblical Institute Press, 1982.

———. "Covenant and Community: Insights into the Relational Aspect of Covenant." *Jeevadhara* 11 (1981): 94–104.

Kapelrud, A. S. "Temple Building: A Task for Gods and Kings." *Orientalia* 32 (1963): 56–62.

———. "The Prophets and the Covenant." In *In the Shelter of Elyon*, edited by W. B. Barrick and J. R. Spencer, 175–83. Sheffield: JSOT Press, 1984.

Karavites, P., and T. E. Wren. *Promise-Giving and Treaty-Making: Homer and the Near East*. Leiden: Brill, 1992.

Karlberg, Mark W. "Covenant and Common Grace." *WTJ* 50, no. 2 (1988): 323–337.

———. "Reformed Interpretation of the Mosaic Creation." *WTJ* 43, no. 1 (1980): 1–57.

Käsemann, E. *The Wandering People of God*. Minneapolis: Augsburg, 1984.

Kaufmann, Y. *The Religion of Israel*. Chicago: University of Chicago Press, 1969.

Keel, O. *The Symbolism of the Biblical World: Ancient Near Eastern Iconography and the Book of Psalms*. New York: Seabury, 1978.

Keil, Carl F., and Frans Delitzsch. *Biblical Commentary: The Pentateuch*. Translated by James Martin. Grand Rapids: Eerdmans, 1949.

———. *Ezekiel-Daniel*. Vol. 9 in *Commentary on the Old Testament*. Peabody, MA: Hendrickson, 1996.

———. *Psalms*. Vol. 5 in *Commentary on the Old Testament*. Peabody, MA: Hendrickson, 1996.

Keneally, Thomas. *Moses the Lawgiver*. New York: Harper & Row, 1975.

Kidner, Derek. *Genesis*. Downers Grove, IL: InterVarsity Press, 1967.

Kirkland, J. R. "The Incident at Salem: A Reexamination of Gen. 14: 18–20." *SBT* 7 (1977): 3–23.

Kitchen, Kenneth A. *Ancient Orient and Old Testament.* Chicago: InterVarsity Press, 1973.

———. "Ancient Orient, Deuteronomism and the Old Testament." In *New Perspectives on the Old Testament,* edited by J. Baron Payne, 1–24. Waco: Word Books, 1970.

———. *The Bible in Its World.* Downers Grove, IL: InterVarsity Press, 1978.

———. "Egypt, Ugarit, Qatna, and Covenant." *UF* 11 (1979): 453–64.

———. *On the Reliability of the Old Testament.* Grand Rapids: Eerdmans, 2003.

———. *Treaty, Law, and Covenant in the Ancient Near East.* Vols. 1–3. Wiesbaden: Harrassowitz, 2012.

Kline, Meredith G. "Abram's Amen." *WTJ* 31, no. 1 (1968): 1–11.

———. "Because It Had Not Rained" *WTJ* 20, no. 2 (1958): 146–57.

———. *By Oath Consigned.* Grand Rapids: Eerdmans, 1968.

———. "Divine Kingship and Gen. 6:1–4." *WTJ* 24, no. 2 (1963): 187–204.

———. "Double Trouble." *JETS* 32, no. 2 (1989): 171–79.

———. "Dynastic Covenant." *WTJ* 23, no. 1 (1960): 1–15.

———. *Glory in our Midst: A Biblical-Theological Reading of Zechariah's Night Visions.* Overland, KS: Two Age Press, 2001.

———. *Kingdom Prologue: Genesis Foundations for a Covenantal Worldview.* Overland Park, KS: Two Age Press, 2000.

———. "Oath and Ordeal Signs." *WTJ* 27, no. 2 (1965): 115–39.

———. *The Structure of Biblical Authorship.* Grand Rapids: Eerdmans, 1973.

———. *Treaty and the Great King: The Covenant Structure of Deuteronomy.* Grand Rapids: Eerdmans, 1963

Knoppers, Gary N. "Ancient Near Eastern Royal Grants and the Davidic Covenant." *JAOS* 116 (1996): 670–97.

Kofoed, Jens Bruun. Untitled book review of J. J. Niehaus' *Biblical Theology, Vol 1. RBL* (July 2015). Copenhagen, Denmark: Society of Biblical Literature. http://www.bookreviews.org/pdf/10029_11112.pdf.

Kohler, Lugwig. *Theologie des Alten Testament.* Tübingen: Mohr, 1966.

König, E. *Die Messianischen Weissagungen des Alten Testament.* Stuttgart: Belser, 1923.

Koroçec, V. *Hethitische Staatsverträge: Ein Beitrag zu ihrer juristischen Wertung.* Leipzig, Germany: Weicher, 1931.

Kraus, H. J. "David's Covenant." *VT* 35, no. 2 (1985): 139–64.

———. *Theology of the Psalms.* Minneapolis: Augsburg, 1986.

Kuenen, Abraham. *The Pentateuch and the Book of Joshua Critically Examined.*

Translated by J. W. Colenso. London: Longman, Green, Longman, Roberts & Green, 1865.

Kugel, James. *The Idea of Biblical Poetry: Parallelism and Its History*. New Haven, CT: Yale University Press, 1981.

Kutsch, E. *Verheissung und Gesetz: Untersuchungen zum Sogenannten Bund im Alten Testament*. New York: Walter de Gruyter, 1973.

Lagrange, M. J. "La Paternité de Dieu dans l'Ancien Testament." *RB* 5 (1908): 482–83.

Lamparter, Helmut. *Zum Wächter Bestellt: der Prophet Hesekiel*. Stuttgart: Calwer Verlag, 1968.

LaRondelle, Hans K. *The Israel of God in Prophecy*. Berrien Springs, MI: Andrews University Press, 1983.

Lawlor, J. I. "The Test of Abraham." *GTJ* 1 (1980): 19–35.

Leggett, Donald A. *The Leverite and Go'el Institutions in the Old Testament with Special Attention to the Book of Ruth*. Cherry Hill, NJ: Muck, 1974.

Lehmann, M. R. "Biblical Oaths." *ZAW* 81, no. 1 (1969): 74–92.

Lemche, N. P. *Early Israel: Anthropological and Historical Studies on the Israelite Society before the Monarchy*. Leiden: Brill, 1985.

Lemke, W. E. "Jeremiah 31:31–34." *Int* 37, no. 2 (1983): 183–87.

Leonard, J. *I Will Be Their God: Understanding the Covenant*. Chicago: Laudemont, 1992.

Letham, Robert. *The Westminster Assembly: Reading Its Theology in Historical Context*. Phillipsburg, NJ: Presbyterian & Reformed, 2009.

Levenson, Jon D. "The Davidic Covenant and Its Modern Interpretation." *CBQ* 41, no. 2 (1979): 205–19.

———. *Theology of the Restoration of Ezekiel 40–48*. Missoula, MT: Scholars Press, 1976.

Levine, B. A. *In the Presence of the Lord: A Study of Cult and Some Cultic Terms in Ancient Israel*. Leiden: Brill, 1974.

Lewis, Jack P. "The Days of Creation: An Historical Survey of Interpretation." *JETS* 32, no. 4 (1989): 433–55.

Lincoln, Abraham. "Annual Message to Congress." December 1, 1862.

———. "Second Inaugural Address." 1865.

Lind, Miller C. *Yahweh Is a Warrior: The Theology of Warfare in Ancient Israel*. Scottdale, PA: Herald Press, 1980.

Lints, Richard. *The Fabric of Theology: A Prolegomenon to Evangelical Theology*. Grand Rapids: Eerdmans, 1993.

Livingston, G. Herbert. *The Pentateuch in Its Cultural Environment*. Grand Rapids: Baker, 1987.

Lockyer, Herbert. *All the Women of the Bible*. Grand Rapids: Zondervan, 1967.

Loewenstamm, S. E. "The Divine Grants Land to the Patriarchs." *JAOS* 91, no. 4 (1971): 509–10.

Lohfink, N. "The Concept 'Covenant' in Biblical Theology." In *The God of Israel and the Nations: Studies in Isaiah and the Psalms*, edited by N. Lohfink and E. Zenger, 11–31. Collegeville, MN: Liturgical Press, 2000.

———. "Die Landverheissung als Eid, eine Studie zu Gn 15." *Stuttgarter Bibelstudien* 28. Stuttgart: Verlag Katholisches Bibelwerk, 1967.

———. *Great Themes from the Old Testament*. Edinburgh: T&T Clark, 1982.

———. *The Covenant Never Revoked*. New York: Paulist, 1991.

Lohfink, N. and E. Zenger. *The God of Israel and the Nations: Studies in Isaiah and the Psalms*. Collegeville, MN: Liturgical Press, 2000.

Long, B. M. "Notes on the Biblical Use of עד-עולם," *WTJ* 41, no. 2 (1978): 54–67.

Long, Burke O. "The Shunamite Woman in the Shadow of the Prophet." *BRev* 7, no. 2 (1991): 12–19, 42.

———. *1 Kings with an Introduction to Historical Literature*. Grand Rapids: Eerdmans, 1984.

———. *The Problem of Etiological Narrative in the Old Testament*. Berlin: Verlag Alfred Topelmann, 1968.

Longman III, Tremper. *Literary Approaches to Biblical Literature*. Grand Rapids: Zondervan, 1987.

Lowth, Robert. "Praelectio Vicesima Prima: Prophetarum Singulorum Proprii Characteres." Pages 281–85 in *De Sacra Poesi Hebraeorum*. 1753. Reprint, Whitefish, MT: Kessinger Publishing, 2009.

Lundquist, J. M. "Temple, Covenant, and Law in the Ancient Near East and in the Old Testament." In *Israel's Apostasy and Restoration: Essays in Honor of Ronald K. Harrison*, edited by A. Gileadi, 293–305. Grand Rapids: Baker, 1988.

———. "The Common Temple Ideology of the Ancient Near East." In *The Temple in Antiquity*, edited by T. G. Madsen, 53–76. Provo: Brigham Young University Press, 1984.

———. "What Is a Temple? A Preliminary Typology." In *The Quest for the Kingdom of God*, edited by H. B. Huffmon, F. A. Spina, and A. R. W. Green, 205–19. Winona Lake, IN: Eisenbrauns, 1983.

Lust, J. "A Gentle Breeze or a Roaring, Thunderous Sound?" *VT* 25, no. 1 (1975): 110–15.

Luther, Martin, *Commentary on Romans*. Translated by J. Theodore Meuller. Grand Rapids: Zondervan, 1954.

Mann, T. W. "'All the Families of the Earth': The Theological Unity of Genesis." *Int* 45, no. 4 (1991): 341–53.

———. *The Book of the Torah: The Narrative Integrity of the Pentateuch*. Atlanta: John Knox, 1988.

Martin, W. J. "'Dischronologized' Narrative in the Old Testament." *VTSup* 17, 179–86. Leiden: Brill, 1968.

Mason, S. D. *"Eternal Covenant" in the Pentateuch: The Contours of an Elusive Phrase*. New York: T&T Clark, 2008.

Mayes, A. D. H. *Deuteronomy*. London: Marshall, Morgan, & Scott, 1979.

Mayes, A. D. H., and R. B. Salters, eds. *Covenant as Context: Essays in Honour of E. W. Nicholson*. Oxford University Press, 2003.

Mazar, B. "The Historical Background of the Book of Genesis." In *The Early Biblical Period: Historical Studies*, edited by S. Ahituv and B. A. Levine, 49–62. Jerusalem: Israel Exploration Society, 1986.

McCarthy, Dennis J. "*Berit* in Old Testament History and Theology." *Bib* 53, no. 1 (1972): 110–21.

———. "Compact and Kingship: Stimuli for Hebrew Covenant Thinking." In *Studies in the Period of David and Solomon*, edited by T. Ishida, 75–92. Winona Lake, IN: Eisenbrauns, 1982.

———. "Covenant 'Good' and an Egyptian Text." *BASOR* 245 (1982): 63–64.

———. "Covenant in Narratives from Late OT Times." In *The Quest for the Kingdom of God*, edited by H. B. Huffmon et al., 77–94. Winona Lake, IN: Eisenbrauns, 1983.

———. "Covenant in the Old Testament: The Present State of Inquiry." *CBQ* 27, no. 3 (1965): 217–40.

———. "Covenant-Relationships." In *Questions Disputes d'Ancien Testament*, edited by C. Brekelmans, 91–103. Leuven: Leuven University Press, 1974.

———. "Further Notes on the Symbolism of Blood and Sacrifice." *JBL* 92, no. 2 (1973): 205–10.

———. " Israel: My First-Born Son." *The Way* 5 (1965): 183–91.

———. "Notes on the Love of God in Deuteronomy and the Father-Son Relationship between Yahweh and Israel." *CBQ* 27, no. 2 (1965): 144–47.

———. "Theology and Covenant in the Old Testament." *TBT* 26 (1964): 179–89.

———. "Twenty-five Years of Pentateuchal Study." In *The Biblical Heritage in Modern Catholic Scholarship*, edited by J. J. Collins and J. D. Crossan, 34–57. Wilmington, DE: Michael Glazier, 1986.

———. *Old Testament Covenant: A Survey of Current Opinions*. Richmond, VA: John Knox, 1972.

———. *Treaty and Covenant*. Analecta Biblica 21A. Rome: Pontifical Biblical Institute, 1978.

———. *Treaty and Covenant*. Rome: Pontifical Biblical Institute, 1963.

McComiskey, Thomas E. *The Covenants of Promise: A Theology of the Old Testament Covenants*. Grand Rapids: Baker, 1985.

McConville, J. G. "Abraham and Melchizedek: Horizons in Genesis 14." In *He Swore and Oath: Biblical Themes from Genesis 12–50*, edited by R. S. Hess et al., 93–118. Grand Rapids: Baker, 1994.

McCree, W. T. "The Covenant Meal in the Old Testament." *JBL* 45, no. 1–2 (1926): 120–28.

McEvenue, S. *The Narrative Style of the Priestly Writer*. Rome: Biblical Institute Press, 1971.

McKenzie, J. L. "The Divine Sonship of Israel and the Covenant." *CBQ* 8, no. 3 (1946): 320–31.

———. *A Theology of the Old Testament*. Garden City, NY: Doubleday, 1974.

McKenzie, Steven L. *Covenant*. St. Louis: Chalice Press, 2000.

McKenzie, Steven L., and H. N. Wallace. "Covenant Themes in Malachi." *CBQ* 45, no. 4 (1983): 549–63.

Meade, John D. "The Meaning of Circumcision in Israel: A Proposal for a Transfer of Rite from Egypt to Israel." *Adorare Mente* 1 (2008): 14–29.

Meir, Sternberg. *The Poetics of Biblical Narrative*. Bloomington, IN: Indiana University Press, 1985.

Mendelsohn, I. "On the Preferential Status of the Eldest Son." *BASOR* 56 (1959): 38–40.

Mendenhall, George E. *The Tenth Generation: The Origins of the Biblical Tradition*. Baltimore: Johns Hopkins University Press, 1973.

———. "Covenant." In *International Dictionary of the Bible*, edited by George A. Buttrick et al., 1:714–23. New York: Abingdon, 1962.

———. "Covenant Forms in Israelite Tradition." In *The Biblical Archaeology Reader: Volume 3*, edited by Edward F. Campbell and David N. Freedman. New York: Doubleday, 1970.

———. "The Monarchy." *Int* 29, no. 2 (1975): 155–70.

———. "The Nature and Purpose of the Abraham Narrative." In *Ancient Israel Religion*, edited by P. D. Miller et al., 337–56. Philadelphia: Fortress, 1987.

———. "The Suzerainty Treaty Structure: Thirty Years Later." In *Religion and law: Biblical-Judaic and Islamic Perspectives*, edited by E. B. Firmage, B. Weiss, and J. Welch, 85–100. Winona Lake, IN: Eisenbrauns, 1990.

Mendenhall, George E., and G. A. Herion. "Covenant." In *Anchor Bible Dictionary*, edited by D. N. Freedman, 1:1179–1202. New York: Doubleday, 1992.

Merkley, P. *The Greek and Hebrew Origins of Our Idea of History*. Lewiston: Edwin Mellen, 1987.

Merrill, Eugene H. "Covenant and Kingdom: Genesis 1–3 as Foundation for Biblical Theology." *TR* 1 (1987): 295–308.

———. "The Covenant with Abraham: The Keystone of Biblical Architecture." *Journal of Dispensational Theology* 12 (2008): 5–17.

Mettinger, Tryggvie N. D. "Abbild Oder Urbild? Imagio Dei in Traditionsgeschichtlicher Sicht." *ZAW* 86, no. 4 (1974): 403–24.

Meyers, C. "David as Temple Builder." In *Ancient Israelite Religion*, edited by P. D. Miller et al., 357–76. Philadelphia: Fortress, 1987.

Mickelsen, A. Berkeley. *Interpreting the Bible*. Grand Rapids: Zondervan, 1962.

Middleton, J. Richard. *The Liberating Image: The Imago Dei in Genesis 1*. Grand Rapids: Brazos, 2005.

Milgrom, J. B. *The Akedah: The Binding of Isaac*. Berkeley, CA: BIBAL, 1988.

———. *Leviticus 1–16: A New Translation with Introduction and Commentary*. The Anchor Bible 3. New York: Doubleday, 1991.

Millar, J. G. "Land." In *New Dictionary of Biblical Theology*, edited by T. D. Alexander et al., 623–27. Downers Grove, IL: InterVarsity Press, 2000.

Miller, J. W. *Biblical Faith and Fathering*. New York: Paulist, 1989.

Miller, Patrick D. *The Divine Warrior in Early Israel*. Cambridge: Harvard, 1973.

Miller, Patrick D., Paul D. Hanson, and Dean McBride, eds. *Ancient Israelite Religion*. Philadelphia: Fortress, 1987.

Miller, Stephen R. *Daniel*. New American Commentary 18. Nashville: Broadman & Holman, 1994.

Mitchell, C. W. *The Meaning of* BRK *"To Bless" in the Old Testament*. Atlanta: Scholars Press, 1987.

Milton, John. *Paradise Lost*. Vol. 1. Edited by Merrit Y. Hughes. New York: Odyssey Press, 1935.

Mitchell, J. J. "Abram's Understanding of Lord's Covenant." *WTJ* 32, no. 1 (1969): 24–48.

Moberly. R. W. L. "Abraham's Righteousness (Genesis XV 6)." *VTSup* 41, 103–30. Leiden: Brill, 1990.

Moltmann, J. *God in Creation*. San Francisco: HarperCollins, 1991.

Moran, W. L. "The Ancient Near Eastern Background of the Love of God in Deuteronomy." *CBQ* 25, no. 1 (1963): 77–87.

———. "The Kingdom of Priests." In *The Bible in Current Catholic Thought*. edited by John L. MacKenzie, 7–20. New York: Herder & Herder, 1962.

Mosca, P. G. "Child Sacrifice in Canaanite and Israelite Religion." PhD diss., Harvard University, 1975.

Motyer, J. Alec. *Isaiah: An Introduction and Commentary*. Tyndale Old Testament Commentaries. Downers Grove, IL: InterVarsity Press, 1999.

Motyer, S. "Israel (nation)." In *New Dictionary of Biblical Theology*, edited by T. D. Alexander et al., 581–87. Downers Grove, IL: InterVarsity Press, 2000.

Mowinckel, S. *Psalmenstudien III. Kultpropetie und Propetische Psalmen*. Oslo: J. Dybwad, 1923.

Moye, R. H. "In the Beginning: Myth and History in Genesis and Exodus." *JBL* 109, no. 4 (1990): 577–98.

Mueller, Wilhelm. "Rhetorical Criticism in Biblical Studies." *Jin Dao Journal of Bible and Religion* 4 (1995).

Muffs, Y. "Abraham the Noble Warrior: Patriarchal Politics and the Laws of War in Ancient Israel." *JJS* 33, no. 1–2 (1982): 81–108.

Muilenburg, J. "Abraham and the Nations: Blessings and World History." *Int* 19, no. 4 (1965): 387–98.

———. "The Form and Structure of the Covenantal Formulations." *VT* 9, no. 4 (1959): 347–65.

Mullen, E. T. "The Divine Witness and the Davidic Royal Grant: Ps. 89:37–38." *JBL* 102, no. 2 (1983): 207–18.

Murtonen, A. "The Use and Meaning of the Words *lebarek* and *berakhah* in the OT." *VT* 9, no. 2 (1959): 158–77.

Naylor, P. J. "The Language of Covenant: A Structural Analysis of the Semantic Field of ברית in Biblical Hebrew with Particular Reference to the Book of Genesis." D. Phil. diss. Oxford University, 1980.

Nel, P. "The Concept of 'Father' in the Wisdom Literature of the Ancient Near East." *JNES* 5 (1977): 53–67.

Newman, M. "The Prophetic Call of Samuel." In *Israel's Prophetic Heritage*, edited by B. W. Anderson and W. Harrelson, 86–97. New York: Harper, 1962.

Nicholson, Ernst W. "Covenant in a Century of Study since Wellhausen." *OTS* 24 (1985): 54–69.

———. *God and His People: Covenant and Theology in the Old Testament*. Oxford: Clarendon, 1986.

Niehaus, J. J. Amos. In *The Minor Prophets: An Exegetical and Expository Commentary: Hosea, Joel, and Amos*, edited by Thomas Edward McComiskey, 315–494. Grand Rapids: Baker, 1992.

———. "An Argument against Theologically Constructed Covenants." *JETS* 50, no. 2 (2007): 259–73.

———. *Ancient Near Eastern Themes in Biblical Theology*. Grand Rapids: Kregel, 2008.

———. *Biblical Theology, Volume 1: Common Grace Covenants*. Bellingham, WA: Lexham Press, 2018.

———. "The Central Sanctuary: Where and When?" *TB* 43, no. 1: 3–30.

———. "Covenant: An Idea in the Mind of God." *JETS* 52, no. 5 (2009): 225–55.

———. "Covenant and Narrative, God and Time." *JETS* 53, no. 3 (2010): 535–59.

———. *God at Sinai: Covenant and Theophany in the Bible and Ancient Near East.* Grand Rapids: Zondervan, 1995.

———. *God the Poet: Exploring the Origin and Nature of Poetry.* Bellingham, WA: Lexham Press, 2018.

———. "God's Covenant with Abraham," *JETS* 56, no. 2 (2013): 249–71.

———. "Joshua and Ancient Near Eastern Warfare." *JETS* 31, no. 1 (1988): 37–50.

———. "Paᶜam ehat and the Israelite Conquest." *VT* Vol. XXX, Fasc. 2 (April 1980): 236–39.

———. "The Warrior and His God: The Covenant Foundation of History and Historiography," in *Faith, Tradition and History: Old Testament Historiography in its Near Eastern Context*, ed. David Baker. Winona Lake, IN: Eisenbrauns 1994.

———. "When Did Eve Sin?" Forthcoming.

Noonan, Benjamin J. "Abraham, Blessing, and the Nations: A Reexamination of the Niphal and Hitpael of ברך in the Patriarchal Narratives." *Hebrew Studies* 51 (2010): 73–93.

Noth, Martin. *The Deuteronomistic History.* Translated by J. Doull. *JSOT Sup* 15. Sheffield: JSOT Press, 1981.

———. *A History of Pentateuchal Traditions.* Englewood Cliffs, NJ: Prentice-Hall, 1972.

———. *Überlieferungsgeschichtliche Studien I.* Tübingen: Max Niemeyer Verlag, 1942.

O'Connell, K. G. "Continuity and Change in Israel's Covenant with God." *BR* 1 (1985): 46–55.

Oden, Robert. "The Place of the Covenant in the Religion of Israel." *Ancient Israelite Religion*, edited by Patrick M. Miller, Paul D. Hansen, and S. Dean McBride, 429–48. Philadelphia: Fortress, 1987.

Ohler, A. *Studying the Old Testament from Tradition to Canon.* Edinburgh: T&T Clark, 1985.

Ortlund, Raymond C., Jr. *God's Unfaithful Wife: A Biblical Theology of Spiritual Adultery.* New Studies in Biblical Theology 2. Downers Grove, IL: InterVarsity Press, 2003.

Pao, D. W. *Acts and the Isaianic New Exodus.* Tübingen: Mohr Siebeck, 2000.

Parry, Jason. "Desolation of the Temple and Messianic Enthronement in Daniel 11:36–12:3." *JSOT* 54, no. 3 (2011): 485–526.

Patcas, H. "Akedah, The Binding of Isaac." *Dor le Dor* 14 (1985/86): 112–14.

Paul, S. M. "Adoption Formulae: A Study of Cuneiform and Biblical Legal Clauses." *Maarav* 2 (1979–1980): 173–85.

Payne, J. Barton. "The B'RITH of Yahweh." In *New Perspectives on the Old Testament*, edited by J. B. Payne, 240–64. Waco, TX: Word, 1970.

————. "Covenant (in the Old Testament)." In *The Zondervan Pictorial Encyclopedia of the Bible*, edited by Merrill C. Tenney et al., 1:1008. Grand
Rapids: Zondervan, 1975.

————. *Encyclopedia of Biblical Prophecy*. New York: Harper & Row, 1973.

————. *The Theology of the Older Testament*. Grand Rapids: Zondervan, 1962.

Peck, W. J. "Murder, Timing, and the Ram in the Sacrifice of Isaac." *ATR* 58,
no. 1 (1976): 23–43.

Pedersen, J. *Der Eid bei den Semiten*. Strassburg: Karl J. Trüner, 1914.

Perlitt, L. "Der Vater im Alten Testament." In *Das Vaterbild in Mythos und Ges-
chichte*, edited by H. Tellenbach, 50–101. Stuttgart: Kohlhammer, 1976.

————. *Bundestheologie im Alten Testament*. Neukirchen-Vluyn: Neukirchener
Verlag, 1969.

Petersen, D. L. "Covenant Ritual: A Traditio-Historical Perspective." *BR* 22
(1977): 7–18.

Ploeg, J. P. M. van der. "Slavery in the Old Testament." *VTSup* 22, 72–87. Leiden:
Brill, 1972.

Polzin, Robert. *Moses and the Deuteronomist*. New York: Seabury Press, 1980.

————. *Samuel and the Deuteronomist*. San Francisco: Harper & Row, 1989.

Pope, M. H. "Oath." In *International Dictionary of the Bible*, edited by George A.
Buttrick et al., 3:575–76. New York: Abingdon, 1962.

Porter, J. R. "The Succession of Joshua." In *Proclamation and Presence*, edited
by J. I. Durham and J. R. Porter, 102–34. Richmond: John Knox, 1970.

Porúbcan, S. *Sin in the Old Testament*. Rome: Herder, 1963.

Prentiss, J. J. "The Sacrifice of Isaac: A Comparative View." In *The Bible in the
Light of Cuneiform Literature: Scripture in Context III*, edited by W. W.
Hallow et al., 203–30. Lewiston: Edwin Mellen, 1990.

Preston, David G. *In the Beginning*. Downers Grove, IL: InterVarsity Press, 1984.

Prewitt, T. J. "Kinship Structures and the Genesis Genealogies." *JNES* 40 (1981):
87–98.

Price, I. M. "The Oath in Court Procedure in Early Babylonia and the Old Testament." *JAOS* 49 (1929): 22–29.

Pritchard, J. B. *Ancient Near Eastern Texts Relating to the Old Testament*. Princeton: Princeton University Press, 1955.

Pun, Pattle. *Evolution, Nature, and Scripture in Conflict*. Grand Rapids: Zondervan, 1982.

von Rad, Gerhard. *Deuteronomy*. Philadelphia: Westminster Press, 1966.

————. *Genesis: A Commentary*. Philadelphia: Westminster John Knox, 1972.

————. *Holy War in Ancient Israel*. Translated by Marva J. Dawn and John H.
Yoder. Grand Rapids: Eerdmans, 1991.

————. *Old Testament Theology*. 2 vols. New York: Harper & Row, 1965.

———. *The Problem of the Hexateuch and Other Essays*. Translated by E. W. Trueman Dicken. New York: McGraw-Hill, 1966.

Rae, Murray. "Texts in Context: Scripture in the Divine Economy." *JTI* 1, no. 1 (2007): 1–21.

Redford, Donald B. *Egypt, Canaan, and Israel*. Princeton, NJ: Princeton University Press, 1992.

Reisinger, John G. *Abraham's Four Seeds*. Fredrick, MD: New Covenant Media, 1998.

Rendsburg, G. A. *The Redaction of Genesis*. Winona Lake, IN: Eisenbrauns, 1986.

Rendtorf, Rolf. *Canon and Theology: Overtures to an Old Testament Theology*. Minneapolis: Fortress, 1993.

———. "Canonical Interpretation: A New Approach to Biblical Texts." *Pro Ecclesia* 3, no. 2 (1994): 141–51.

———. "Covenant as a Structuring Concept in Genesis and Exodus." *JBL* 108, no. 3 (1989): 385–93.

———. *The Covenant Formula: An Exegetical and Theological Investigation*. Translated by M. Kohl. Edinburgh: T&T Clark, 1998.

———. *Die Bundesformel*. Stuttgard: Katholisches Bibelwerk, 1995.

———. *The Old Testament: An Introduction*. Translated by J. Bowden. Philadelphia: Fortress, 1986.

Richardson, Alan. *Genesis 1–11*. London: SCM, 1953.

Ridderbos, Nico H. *Is There a Conflict Between Genesis 1 and Natural Science?* Grand Rapids: Eerdmans, 1957.

Robinson, R. B. "Literary Function of the Genealogies of Genesis." *CBQ* 48, no. 4 (1986): 595–608.

Rodd, C. S. "The Family in the Old Testament." *BTrans* 18, no. 1 (1967): 19–26.

Rogerson, J. W. *Anthropology and the Old Testament*. Atlanta: John Knox, 1979.

Rondelle, Hans K. *The Israel of God in Prophecy*. Berrien Springs, MI: Andrews University Press, 1983.

Ross, Allen P. "The Table of Nations in Genesis 10: Its Content." *BSac* 138 (1981): 22–34.

———. *Creation and Blessing: A Guide to the Study and Exposition of Genesis*. Grand Rapids: Baker, 1988.

Rost, Leonhard. *The Succession to the Throne of David*. Translated by Michael D. Rutter and David M. Gunn. Sheffield: Almond, 1982.

Rouiller, G. "The Interpretation of Genesis 22:1–9." In *Exegesis: Problems of Method and Exercises in Reading*, edited by R. Boven and G. Rouiller, 13–42; translated by D. G. Miller. Pittsburgh: Pickwick Press, 1978.

Rowley, H. H. *The Growth of the Old Testament*. London: Hutchinson's University Library, 1950.

Rushdoony, Rousas J. *The Institutes of Biblical Law*. Phillipsburg, NJ: Craig, 1973.

Safren, J. D. "Balaam and Abraham." *VT* 38, no. 1 (1988): 105–13.

Sailhammer, J. H. "The Mosaic Law and the Theology of the Pentateuch." *WTJ* 53, no. 2 (1991): 241–61.

———. *The Pentateuch as Narrative*. Grand Rapids: Zondervan, 1992.

Sakenfeld, Katherine D. *The Meaning of Hesed in the Hebrew Bible: A New Inquiry*. Missoula, MT: Scholars Press, 1978.

Sanders, James A. *Canon and Community*. Philadelphia: Fortress, 1984.

———. *Suffering as Divine Discipline in the Old Testament and Post Biblical Judaism*. Rochester: Colgate Rochester Divinity School Press, 1955.

———. *Torah and Canon*. Philadelphia: Fortress, 1972.

Santayana, George. *Life of Reason*. New York: Scribner's, 1905.

Saxe, Grace. *Studies in Biblical History*. Chicago: Moody Press, 1917.

Schaeffer, Francis A. *Joshua and the Flow of Biblical History*. Downers Grove, IL: InterVarsity Press, 1975.

Scharbert, J. "'Berît im Pentateuch." In *De la Tôrah au Messie*, edited by M. Carrez et al., 162–70. Paris: Desclee, 1981.

———. "Traditions und Redaktionsgeschichte von Gen. 6:1–4." *BZ* 11 (1967): 66–78.

Schlisske, W. *Gottessöhne und Gottessohn im Alten Testament*. Berlin: Kohlhammer, 1973.

Schmid, H. H. *Der Sogenannte Jahwist*. Zürich: Theologischer Verlag, 1976.

Schmidt, Werner H. *Die Schopfungsgeschichte*. Vluyn: Neukirchener, 1967.

———. *The Faith of the Old Testament*. Philadelphia: Westminster, 1983.

Schnabel, Eckhard J. "Scripture." In *New Dictionary of Biblical Theology*, edited by T. D. Alexander et al., 34–43. Downers Grove, IL: InterVarsity Press, 2000.

Schoonenburg, P. *Covenant and Creation*. London: Sheed and Ward, 1968.

Schreiner, S. *The King in His Beauty: A Biblical Theology of the Old and New Testaments*. Grand Rapids: Baker, 2013.

Schultz, Richard. "The King in the Book of Isaiah." In *The Lord's Anointed: Interpretation of Old Testament Messianic Texts*, edited by P. E. Satterthwaite, R. S. Hess, and G. J. Wenham, 141–65. Grand Rapids: Baker, 1995.

Schultz, Samuel. *Deuteronomy: The Gospel of Love*. Chicago: Moody Press, 1971.

Scofield, C. I., ed. *The New Scofield Reference Bible*. Oxford: Oxford University Press, 1970.

Selman, Martin J. "The Kingdom of God in the Old Testament." *TB* 40, no. 2 (1989): 161–83.

Shakespeare, William. *The Tragedy of Hamlet Prince of Denmark*, edited by

Tucker Brooke and Jack Randall Crawford. New Haven, CT: Yale University Press, 1952.

Shanks, Herschel, ed. *The Rise of Ancient Israel*. Washington, DC: Biblical Archaeological Society, 1992.

Simons, J. *Jerusalem in the Old Testament*. Leiden: Brill, 1952.

Skinner, John. *Genesis: A Critical and Exegetical Commentary*. New York: T&T Clark, 1910.

———. *Genesis: A Critical and Exegetical Commentary*. Rev. ed. Edinburgh: T&T Clark, 1930.

Smend, Rudolph. *Die Bundesformel*. Theologische Studien 68. Zürich: EVZ-Verlag, 1963.

Smith, R. L. "Covenant and law in Exodus." *SJT* 20, no. 1 (1977): 33–41.

Smith, S. "The Threshing Floor at the City Gate." *PEQ* 78 (1946): 5–14.

Snijders, L. A. "Genesis XV. The Covenant with Abraham." *OTS* 12 (1958): 261–79.

Soggin, J. A. *Introduction to the Old Testament*. 2nd ed. Philadelphia: Westminster Press, 1980.

Sohn, S. T. "'I Will Be Your God and You Will Be My People': The Origin and Background of the Covenant Formula." In *Ki Baruch Hu: Ancient Eastern, Biblical, and Judaic Studies in Honor of Baruch A. Levine*, edited by R. Chazen, W. W. Hallo, and L. H. Schiffman, 355–72. Winona Lake, IN: Eisenbrauns, 1999.

Speiser, E. A. *Genesis*. Garden City, NY: Doubleday, 1964.

Spriggs, D. S. *Two Old Testament Theologies*. London: SCM, 1974.

Stager, Lawrence E., and Samuel R. Wolff. "Child Sacrifice at Carthage: Religious Rite or Population Control? : Archaeological Evidence Provides Basis for a New Analysis." *BAR* (January 1984): 30–51.

Steinberg, N. "The Genealogical Framework of the Family Stories in Genesis." *Semeia* 46 (1989): 41–50.

Steinmetz, D. *From Father to Son: Kinship, Conflict and Continuity in Genesis*. Louisville: Westminster John Knox, 1991.

Stek, John. "Covenant Overload in Reformed Theology." *CTJ* 29, no. 1 (1994): 12–41.

Stuart, Douglas K. *Exodus*. New American Commentary. Nashville: B&H, 2006.

———. *Ezekiel*. The Communicator's Commentary. Dallas: Word, 1989.

———. *Studies in Early Hebrew Meter*. Harvard Semitic Monograph Series 13. Missoula, MT: Scholars' Press, 1976.

Tallqvist, Knut. *Akkadische Götter-epitheta*. Helsinki, Finland: Societas orientalis Fennica, 1938.

Talmon, S. "Amen as an Introductory Oath Formula." *Text* 7 (1969): 124–29.

Thompson, J. A. *The Ancient Near Eastern Treaties and the Old Testament*. London: Tyndale House, 1964.

———. *The Book of Jeremiah*. New International Commentary on the Old Testament. Grand Rapids: Eerdmans, 1980.

———. "The Significance of the Verb *Love* in the David-Jonathan Narratives in I Samuel." *VT* 24, no. 3 (1974): 334–45.

Thompson, R. J. "Moses and the Law in a Century of Criticism Since Graf." *VTSup* 19. Leiden: Brill, 1970.

Thundyil, P. *Covenant in Anglo-Saxon Thought*. Calcutta: Macmillian, 1972.

Tolkien, J. R. R. *The Lord of the Rings*. Boston: Houghton Mifflin, 1965.

Trible, P. *Genesis 22: The Sacrifice of Sarah*. Valparaiso: Valparaiso University Press, 1977.

Tucker, G. M. "Covenant Forms and Contract Forms." *VT* 15, no. 4 (1965): 487–503.

Unger, Merrill. "Rethinking the Genesis Creation Account." *BSac* 115 (1958): 27–35.

Van Gemeren, Willem. *Interpreting the Prophetic Word*. Grand Rapids: Zondervan, 1990.

———. "Israel as the Hermeneutical Crux in the Interpretation of Prophecy." *Westminster Theological Journal* 45/1 (1983): 132–44.

———. *The Progress of Redemption: The Story of Salvation from Creation to the New Jerusalem*. Grand Rapids: Zondervan, 1988.

———. "Systems of Continuity." In *Continuity and Discontinuity: Perspectives on the Relationship between the Old and the New Testaments*, 37–62. Wheaton, IL: Crossway, 1988.

Van Groningen, Gerard. *From Creation to Consummation*. Sioux Center, IA: Dordt College Press, 1996.

Van Selms, A. *Genesis*. Nijkerk: Callenbach, 1967.

Van Seters, J. *Abraham in History and Tradition*. New Haven, CT: Yale University Press, 1975.

Van Til, Cornelius. *Common Grace*. Philadelphia: Presbyterian & Reformed, 1947.

Van Till, Howard. *The Fourth Day*. Grand Rapids: Eerdmans, 1987.

Vasholz, Robert. *The Old Testament Canon in the Old Testament Church*. Lewiston, NY: Mellen, 1990.

Vattioni, F. "Recenti Studi Nell'alleanza Nella Bibbia E Nell, Antico Oriente." *AION* 17 (1967): 181–232.

de Vaux, Ronald. *Ancient Israel: Its Life and Institutions*. Translated by John McHugh. New York: McGraw-Hill, 1961.

———. *The Bible and the Ancient Near East*. Garden City, NY: Doubleday, 1971.

Vawter, B. *Genesis*. Garden City, NJ: Doubleday, 1977.

Vos, Geerhardus. *Biblical Theology: Old and New Testaments*. Grand Rapids: Eerdmans, 1948.

———. *The Idea of Biblical Theology as a Science and a Theological Discipline*. New York: A. D. F. Randolph, 1894.

Vriezen, Theo E. *An Outline of Old Testament Theology*. 2nd ed. Translated by S. Neuijen. Oxford: Blackwell, 1970.

Waltke, Bruce K. "The First Seven Days." *Christianity Today* 32, no. 11 (1988): 42–46.

———. *Genesis: A Commentary*. Grand Rapids: Zondervan, 2001.

———. "The Phenomenon of Continuity within Unconditional Covenants." Pages 123–29 in *Israel's Apostasy and Restoration: Essays in Honor of Ronald K. Harrison*, edited by A. Gileadi. Grand Rapids: Baker, 1988.

Waltke, Bruce K., with Cathi J. Fredricks. *Genesis: A Commentary*. Grand Rapids: Zondervan, 2001.

Waltke, Bruce K., with Charles Yu. *An Old Testament Theology*. Grand Rapids: Zondervan, 2006.

Walton, J. H. *Covenant: God's Purpose, God's Plan*. Grand Rapids: Zondervan, 1994.

———. *Genesis*. NIV Application Commentary. Grand Rapids: Zondervan, 2001.

———. *Genesis One as Ancient Cosmology*. Winona Lake, IN: Eisenbrauns, 2011.

———. *The Lost World of Genesis One: Ancient Cosmology and the Origins Debate*. Downers Grove, IL: InterVarsity Press, 2009.

Walvoord, John F. "Biblical Kingdoms Compared and Contrasted." In *Issues in Dispensationalism*, edited by Wesley R. Willis et al., 75–91. Chicago: Moody Press, 1994.

Warfield, B. B. *Biblical and Theological Studies*. Philadelphia: Presbyterian & Reformed, 1952.

Watts, R. E. "Exodus." In *New Dictionary of Biblical Theology*, edited by T. D. Alexander et al., 478–87. Downers Grove, IL: InterVarsity Press, 2000.

Weeks, Noel. *Admonition and Curse: The Ancient Near Eastern Treaty/Covenant Form as a Problem in Inter-Cultural Relationships*. Edinburgh: T&T Clark, 2004.

Weinfeld, Moshe. "בְּרִית berît." In *Theological Dictionary of the Old Testament*, edited by G. Johannes Botterweck et al., 2:253–79. Grand Rapids: Eerdmans, 2003.

———. "Berît- Covenant Versus Obligation." *Bib* 56, no 1 (1975): 120–28.

———. "The Common Heritage of Covenantal Traditions in the Ancient World." In *I Trattati nel Mondo Antico: Forma, Ideologia, Funzione*, edited by L. Canfora et al., 175–91. Rome: L'Erma di Bretschneider, 1990.

————. "The Covenant of Grant in the Old Testament and in the Ancient Near East." *JAOS* 90 (1970): 184–203.

————. "Covenant Terminology in the Ancient Near East and Its Influence on the West." *JAOS* 93 (1973): 190–99.

————. *Deuteronomy and the Deuteronomic School.* New York: Oxford University Press, 1972.

————. *The Promise of the Land: The Inheritance of the Land of Canaan by the Israelites.* Berkeley: University of California Press, 1993.

Welker, Michal. "Creation: Big Bang or the Work of Seven Days." *Theology Today* 52, no. 2 (1995): 173–87.

Well, P. "Covenant, Humanity, and Scripture: Some Theological Reflections." *WTJ* 48, no. 1 (1986): 17–45.

Wellhausen, Julius. *The Prolegomena to the History of Ancient Israel.* Edinburgh: A & C. Black, 1885. Reprint, New York: Meridian, 1957.

Wenham, Gordon J. *Exploring the Old Testament: A Guide to the Pentateuch.* Downers Grove, IL: InterVarsity Press, 2003.

————. *Genesis 1–15.* Word Biblical Commentary. Waco, TX: Word, 1987.

————. *Genesis 16–50.* Word Biblical Commentary. Waco, TX: Word, 1987.

————. *Leviticus.* New International Commentary on the Old Testament. Grand Rapids: Eerdmans, 1979.

————. *Numbers.* Tyndale Old Testament Commentary. Downers Grove, IL: InterVarsity Press, 1981.

————. "The Symbolism of the Animal Rite in Genesis 15: A Response to G. F. Hasel." *JSOT* 22 (1989): 134–37.

————. *Genesis 1–11: A Commentary.* Translated by John J. Scullion. Minneapolis: Augsburg, 1984.

Wette, W. M. L. *Dissertatio Critica qua Deuteronomium a prioribus Pentateuchi libris diversum alius cuiusdam recentioris opus esse monstratur.* Jena, Germany: University of Jena,1805.

Wette, W. M. L., and E. Schrader. *Lehrbuch der historisch–kritischen Einleitung in die kanonischen und apokryphischen Bücher des Alten Testaments.* Berlin: Georg Reimer, 1869.

Whedbee, J. W. "On Divine and Human Bonds: The Tragedy of the House of David." In *Canon, Theology, and Old Testament Interpretation*, edited by G. M. Tucker et al., 147–65. Philadelphia: Fortress, 1988.

White, Andrew A. "Abortion and the Ancient Practice of Child Sacrifice." *Journal of Biblical Ethics in Medicine* 1, no. 2 (1987): 27–42. http://bmei.org/jbem/volume1/num2/white_abortion_and_the_ancient_practice_of_child_sacrifice.pdf.

White, H. C. "The Divine Oath in Genesis." *JBL* 92 (1973): 165–79.

———. "The Initiation of Isaac." *ZAW* 91, no. 1 (1979): 1–30.

———. *Narration and Discourse in the Book of Genesis.* New York: Cambridge University Press, 1991.

Whitelam, K. W. *The Just King: Monarchical Justice Authority in Ancient Israel.* Sheffield: JSOT Press, 1979.

Whybray, R. N. *The Making of the Pentateuch.* Sheffield: JSOT Press, 1987.

Widengren, G. "King and Covenant." *JSS* 2, no.1 (1957): 1–32.

———. *Sakrales Königtum im Alten Testament und im Judentum.* Stuttgart: Kohlhammer, 1955.

Wilfong, M. W. "Genesis 22:1–18." *Int* 45, no. 4 (1991): 393–97.

Williamson, Paul R. *Abraham, Israel, and the Nations: The Patriarchal Promise and Its Covenantal Development in Genesis.* Sheffield: Sheffield Academic Press, 2000.

———. "Promise and Fulfillment: The Territorial Inheritance." In *The Land of Promise: Biblical, Theological, and Contemporary Perspective*, edited by Philip Johnston and Peter W. L. Walker, 15–34. Downers Grove, IL: InterVarsity Press, 2000.

———. *Sealed with an Oath: Covenant in God's Unfolding Purpose.* Downers Grove, IL: InterVarsity Press, 2007.

Wilson, R. R. "Enforcing the Covenant: The Mechanisms of Judicial Authority in Early Israel." In *The Quest for the Kingdom of God*, edited by H. B. Huffmon et al., 59–75. Winona Lake: Eisenbrauns, 1983.

———. *Genealogy and History in the Biblical World.* New Haven, CT: Yale University Press, 1977.

———. "The Old Testament Genealogies in Recent Research." *JBL* 94, no. 2 (1975): 169–89.

Wimsatt, William Kurtz. *The Verbal Icon.* Lexington: University of Press of Kentucky, 1954.

Winter, P. "Der Begriff 'Söhne Gottes' im Moselied Dtn 32, 1–43." *ZAW* 67, no. 1–2 (1955): 40–47.

Wolf, H. M. *Anthropology of the Old Testament.* Translated by M. Kohl. Philadelphia: Fortress, 1974.

———. "The Old Testament Genealogies in Recent Research." *JBL* 94, no. 2 (1975): 169–89.

———. "The Transcendent Nature of Covenant Curse Reversals." In *Israel's Apostasy and Restoration: Essays in Honor of Roland K. Harrison*, edited by A. Gileadi, 319–25. Grand Rapids: Baker, 1988.

Wood, Leon. *A Survey of Israel's History.* Grand Rapids: Zondervan, 1970.

Woudstra, Marten H. *The Book of Joshua.* Grand Rapids: Eerdmans, 1981.

———. "The Toledoth of the Book of Genesis and Their Redemptive Historical Significance." *CTJ* 5, no. 2 (1970): 184–89.

Wright, C. J. H. *God's People in God's Land: Family, Land, and Property in the Old Testament.* Grand Rapids: Eerdmans, 1990.

———. *Knowing Jesus Through the Old Testament.* London: Marshall Pickering, 1992.

Wright, David F., ed. *A Pathway into the Holy Scriptures.* Grand Rapids: Eerdmans, 1994.

Wright, G. Ernest . "The Lawsuit of God: A Form-Critical Study of Deuteronomy 32." In *Israel's Prophetic Heritage,* edited by B. W. Anderson and W. Harrelson, 26–67. New York: Harper, 1962.

———. *The Old Testament and Theology.* New York: Harper & Row, 1969.

Yadin, Y. *The Art of Warfare in Biblical Lands in the Light of Archaeological Studies.* 2 vols. New York: McGraw-Hill, 1963.

Young, Edward J. *An Introduction to the Old Testament.* Grand Rapids: Eerdmans, 1953.

———. *My Servants the Prophets.* Grand Rapids: Eerdmans, 1952.

———. *Studies in Genesis One.* Grand Rapids: Baker, 1964.

Youngblood, R. F. "The Abrahamic Covenant: Conditional of Unconditional?" Pages 31–46 in *The Living and Active World: Essays in Honor of Samuel J. Schultz,* edited by Morris Inch et al. Winona Lake, IN: Eisenbrauns, 1983.

Zerafa, P. "The Land of Moriah." *Angelicum* 44 (1967): 84–94.

Zevit, Z. "A Phoenician Inscription and Biblical Covenant Theology." *IEJ* 27, no. 2–3 (1977): 110–18.

Zimmerli, W. *Old Testament Theology in Outline.* Atlanta: John Knox, 1978.

———. *The Law and the Prophets.* New York: Harper & Row, 1965.

Ziony, Zevit. "Three Ways to Look at the Ten Plagues." *BRev* 6, no. 3 (1990): 16–23, 42.

Zlotowitz, M. and N. Scherman. *Bereishis = Genesis: A New Translation with a Commentary Anthologized from Talmudic, Midrashic, and Rabbinic Sources.* 2 volumes. New York: Mesorah, 1978.

Scripture Index

SUBJECT INDEX